ENEMY COMBATANTS, TERRORISM, AND ARMED CONFLICT LAW

ENEMY COMBATANTS, TERRORISM, AND ARMED CONFLICT LAW

A Guide to the Issues

Edited by David K. Linnan

PRAEGER SECURITY INTERNATIONAL
Westport, Connecticut · London

Library of Congress Cataloging-in-Publication Data

Enemy combatants, terrorism, and armed conflict law : a guide to the issues / edited by David K. Linnan.
    p. cm.
    Includes bibliographical references and index.
    ISBN–13: 978–0–275–99814–1 (alk. paper)
1. Terrorism—United States—Prevention. 2. War on Terrorism, 2001—Law and legislation—United States.
3. National security—Law and legislation—United States. 4. Civil rights—United States. 5. Detention of
persons—United States. 6. War on Terrorism, 2001—Law and legislation. 7. Combatants and noncombatants
(International law) 8. War (International law) I. Linnan, David K., 1953-
KF9430.E54   2008
343.73'01—dc22   2007040815

British Library Cataloguing in Publication Data is available.

Library of Congress Catalog Card Number: 2007040815
ISBN–13: 978–0–275–99814–1

First published in 2008

Praeger Security International, 88 Post Road West, Westport, CT 06881
An imprint of Greenwood Publishing Group, Inc.
www.praeger.com

Printed in the United States of America

The paper used in this book complies with the
Permanent Paper Standard issued by the National
Information Standards Organization (Z39.48–1984).

10 9 8 7 6 5 4 3 2 1

Contents

Introduction: Legitimacy, Religion, Ethics, and Armed Conflict Law in Context   1
  David K. Linnan

PART I: Media, Politics, and Religion   7

1 The Press, the Presidency, and Public Opinion since 9/11:   9
  Shaping U.S. Foreign Policy and Military Strategy
  Lowndes F. Stephens

2 Muslim Perspectives on the Invasion of Iraq: Informed Publics, Regime   37
  Leaders, and Islamic Jurists
  Shahrough Akhavi

3 Contested Morality in U.S. Foreign Policy   51
  Janice Love

PART II: Constitutional and Domestic Law: Structural and Institutional Emphasis   65

4 Paradigm Shifts, Executive Power, and the War on Terror   67
  Norman C. Bay

5 Promotion of Liberal Islam by the United States   85
  John H. Mansfield

6 The 9/11 Commission Report and Public Discourse Project   92
  Michael Hurley

PART III: Constitutional and Domestic Law: Individual Rights Emphasis   105

7 International Legal Limits on the Government's Power to Detain   107
  "Enemy Combatants"
  Geremy C. Kamens

8 Military Commissions: An Overview   121
  H. Wayne Elliott

9 War, Crime, or War Crime? Interrogating the Analogy Between War and Terror   145
   Miriam J. Aukerman

PART IV: Law of Armed Conflict: Religion and Armed Conflict   165

10 Legitimacy and Authority in Islamic Discussions of "Martyrdom Operations"/   167
    "Suicide Bombings"
    A. Kevin Reinhart

11 With a Mighty Hand: Judaic Ethics of Exercising Power in Extraordinary   184
    Warfare
    Jonathan K. Crane

12 Jesus and Mars: A Brief Introduction to the Christian Just War Tradition   207
    Michael Skerker

PART V: Law of Armed Conflict and International Law: Operational Law   221

13 Redefining Legitimacy: Legal Issues   223
    David K. Linnan

14 The Concept of Superior Responsibility under International Law as Applied   238
    in Indonesia
    Hikmahanto Juwana

15 The 2006 Conflict in Lebanon, or What Are the Armed Conflict Rules When   252
    Legal Principles Collide?
    George K. Walker

16 The Legal Way Ahead Between War and Peace   280
    Kevin H. Govern

PART VI: Legal Responsibility, Justice, and Reconciliation   305

17 Discerning Justice in the Trial and Execution of Saddam Hussein   307
    John D. Carlson

18 Individual Responsibility, Tribunals, and Truth and Reconciliation   327
    Commissions: Are We Asking the Wrong Questions?
    David K. Linnan

Appendix   341

Further Reading   381

Index   385

About the Editor and the Contributors   397

INTRODUCTION

Legitimacy, Religion, Ethics, and Armed Conflict Law in Context

The changing nature of war affects the law of armed conflict, at the same time as national security has now developed an internal as well as an external aspect. Traditional wars between nation states are no longer the rule. The nonstate actor as a threat has gained credence (popularly, terrorism and its claimed breeding ground in failed states), linked in practice to issues of intervention on the territory of states harboring such groups. In military circles, the idea of armed struggle between modern military forces and what were formerly called guerillas has now largely been replaced by the terminology of asymmetric warfare and the concept of intelligence and preventive action interchangeably within U.S. borders and overseas. And what are the nonmilitary issues overseas, given the accepted wisdom that problems in Iraq and Afghanistan are not accessible to purely military solutions?

The genesis of this book lies in an examination of legitimacy, in the broadest sense, in terms of religion, ethics, and law in conjunction with events in Iraq, Afghanistan, and the so-called War on Terror. The concerns should not be understood in terms of winning or losing, but rather what they tell us about ourselves. We cast the net broadly in looking at the issues from differing domestic and foreign perspectives, because, unusually for the United States, foreign events seemingly have forced their way into our domestic lives. With the dual perspective in mind, we initially focus on the domestic issues expressed in constitutional law terms, as well as support for U.S. foreign policy and public opinion, while subsequently addressing the international side from the armed conflict law and legal responsibility perspectives.

The ultimate question may lie in where to strike the balance in opposing national security to individual liberties and the rule of law, both internationally and domestically. We address the overlap between religion, ethics, armed conflict, and international law as well as constitutional law in the context of ongoing events. Broader issues are visible under domestic and international law in areas like intelligence, reconciliation of civil liberties, dealing with nonstate actor threats, and the permissible bounds of interrogation, treatment of prisoners, and armed conflict law developments generally.

We start our examination of the issues on the domestic side. In Part I covering media, politics, and religion, *Lowndes Stephens* commences with a review of how public opinion has changed since September 11, 2001. He looks at polling data on the public's changing view over time of the ongoing conflicts in Iraq and Afghanistan as well as the War on Terror, as it relates to the Bush administration's performance in the public eye. Not surprisingly, less than favorable developments in Iraq, including casualties, stand in an inverse relationship to the U.S. political leadership's performance ratings. Stephens focuses primarily on domestic public opinion, but crosses over also into foreign public opinion, particularly unfavorable within the Islamic world, through the lens of public diplomacy.

By contrast, *Shahrough Akhavi* then examines views within the Muslim world expressed chiefly in terms of general public opinion, but contrasts them also with the parallel views of Middle Eastern political and religious leadership. In that sense, he is looking at U.S. public diplomacy's challenges from the other end of the telescope. There is some understanding for U.S. actions in Afghanistan, but the invasion of Iraq is perceived negatively against the Middle East's historical experience of external intervention. According to Akhavi, whether perspectives improve in the longer run will depend on exit strategies, as well as the evolution of such regional issues as the Palestinian–Israeli conflict.

Janice Love looks finally at groups within the U.S. religious community, specifically at how the mainline Christian denominations versus evangelicals and televangelists have differed on the political level in their support for, and analysis under, various just war doctrines of the Bush administration's actions in conjunction with Iraq, Afghanistan, and the War on Terror. The Bush administration's support for nonsocial policy initiatives like Iraq, Afghanistan, and the War on Terror also has come from the religious right. Looking beyond politics, how much of this has to do with doctrinal, religious views? Beyond the just war tradition, Love examines as yet incomplete attempts among theologians to articulate doctrinal alternatives on the use of force in the modern world. All of this casts legitimacy in a different light domestically also, to the extent much of the U.S. Christian religious leadership, as moral leadership, have not actively supported U.S. military operations, in Iraq in particular, as "just war" in moral terms.

In Part II covering structural and institutional emphases in constitutional and domestic law, *Norman Bay* first explores the basic paradigm shift in terms of executive power, intelligence activities, and the War on Terror in particular. Beyond 9/11, communications and individual mobility have changed during the past dozen years in a fashion that rendered outdated older categories differentiating sharply between foreign and domestic surveillance. But civil liberties concerns remain a constant, and the problem is how to balance them in a changed world? Bay speaks as a law professor and former U.S. Attorney, offering a nuanced view of what would be lost if the rudder swings over too far toward pure law enforcement concerns.

John Mansfield then explores the issue that the U.S. government is trying to reach into the Islamic world in a fashion that might run afoul of the first amendment's religion clauses, by supporting liberal Islam against perceived religious extremism. This is important to the extent the War on Terror is seen as a longer exercise requiring engagement with the Islamic world. But are there constitutional constraints abroad if the U.S. government supports institutions like religious schools? Or do foreign affairs and national security concerns trump traditional American concern about any government involvement with religion?

Michael Hurley finally addresses, from the perspective of the 9/11 Commission and its successor 9/11 Commission Public Disclosure Project, the unfinished business of reforming intelligence oversight in the Congress. It is an intellectual companion piece to the *Bay* chapter because of the conviction that, as the legal authority of intelligence agencies increases as a result of post-9/11 reform legislation (particularly authorization of domestic activities), unified and more effective oversight would both preserve civil liberties, and longer term increase intelligence agencies' effectiveness and legitimacy. The problem is that simply expanding executive authority is an insufficient answer to the challenge of terrorism.

Part III has an individual rights emphasis in constitutional and domestic law. *Geremy Kamens* as lawyer for U.S. citizen Yaser Hamdi, whose case reached the Supreme Court, addresses initially the disputed scope of the executive branch's authority to detain individuals, depending upon whether they were taken into custody on the battlefield (e.g., Iraq or Afghanistan) or arrested in the U.S. typically as suspects in the War on Terror. There are technical questions about combatant status and detentions in U.S. facilities versus at Guantanamo Bay. But the underlying question may be the extent to which the terminology of a "war" on terror is mere rhetoric (compared to the real armed conflicts taking place in Iraq and Afghanistan) versus having legal effect. The Supreme Court has shown little sympathy thus far for the extremely broad view of executive power advanced by the Bush administration in the War on Terror.

H. Wayne Elliott then looks at military commissions and Geneva Convention status of prisoners, particularly those incarcerated at Guantanamo Bay, since one of the questions which has already reached the Supreme Court is the extent to which prisoners taken into custody overseas (sometimes on the battlefield, but sometimes also apprehended in third countries) have rights to a hearing to establish whether they are in fact combatants versus innocent bystanders. This is a problem of modern unconventional warfare where soldiers may no longer wear brightly colored uniforms as mark of distinction. But it represents equally the articulation of restraints on the executive.

Miriam Aukerman finally focuses on the "war" on terror weighing what are the implications of conceptualizing terrorism as a criminal or law enforcement problem, versus treating it as armed conflict problem under the traditional law of war. There are distinctive legal consequences associated with whatever choice is made, but, by deeming the War on Terror a war while denying the applicability of the Geneva Conventions, Aukerman sees the Bush administration as trying to have it both ways. On the one hand, the fight against terrorism is a war for purposes of justifying the indefinite detention of suspected terrorists without trial, but is not a war when it comes to protecting the rights of those who have been captured. On the other hand, in prosecuting alleged terrorists who have violated the law, but holding others indefinitely where criminal conduct cannot be proven, the Bush administration has invoked the criminal law selectively. Aukerman concludes that terrorism is better treated as criminal problem, while the analysis highlights the nature of the choices to be made.

Part IV moves the examination to the international side in addressing religion and armed conflict. Three scholars of religion were asked to opine on a series of hypothetical problems drawing on current armed conflict issues under the Islamic, Jewish, and Christian ethical traditions (e.g., permissibility of torture of a terrorist suspect with knowledge of a ticking time bomb, or targeted assassinations). Beyond that, they were left to address the underlying issue of religious ethics and armed conflict as they best saw fit under individual religion traditions. *A. Kevin Reinhart* addresses issues surrounding modern Islamic religious authority in the context of the discussions of "martyrdom operations"/"suicide bombings." The dual terminology reveals both the religious dimensions and differing cultural perspectives involved in an aspect of armed conflict in (non-Western) Iraq and Afghanistan rarely seen since the (non-Western) kamikazes at the end of World War II. Reinhart sees a significant development in the "Protestantization" of Islam, meaning that with the rise of the Internet and general education levels in Muslim majority countries, formal reliance on traditional Islamic scholarship has seemingly decreased as educated individuals are now willing to form individual ethical judgments on the requirements of their religions directly, with the result that modern "Islamic" discourse often is infused with nonreligious elements such as nationalism. Meanwhile, the traditional citadels of Islamic scholarship like Al Azhar University in Cairo face increasing competition for legitimacy from independently funded Islamic scholars on the Internet, perhaps comparable to the Christian televangelist phenomenon (remembering also from *Janice Love's* chapter that perhaps an analogous split is reflected in the differing reception of the Bush administration's actions in Iraq and Afghanistan by the mainline Christian denominations as opposed to evangelicals or televangelists).

Jonathan Crane addresses the Judaic ethics of exercising power in extraordinary warfare, which is shorthand for against terrorism. Like Islam, Judaism has a strong textual tradition and the issue that, much as Muslim majority states are rarely governed by *sharia* law in any meaningful sense, Israel as Jewish majority state is not governed by *halakhah* as Jewish law. Nonetheless, it is proper to speak of a Jewish tradition at the level of legitimacy and the ethics of armed conflict, which are implicated in Israeli responses to terrorism, of which Israel is a standing target. The tradition entails a rich array of laws and principles, some of which may be treated as jus cogens—laws unabrogable under any circumstances, yet most of which can be altered under limited conditions, as explored in addressing the hypotheticals.

Michael Skerker gives an overview of the Christian just war tradition. Beyond addressing the armed conflict hypotheticals, those familiar with the details of modern armed conflict law may be surprised to discover the medieval natural law roots of current legal concepts such as proportionality and the collateral damage problem under targeting law. In the religious sphere, Skerker goes beyond classical Catholic just war doctrine to review differences in Protestant development of the concepts based upon views of man's nature, including a more recent tendency among Protestant theologians to grant governments broader discretion to do what is necessary to restrain wickedness.

Part V addresses operational law and armed conflict, commencing with *David Linnan's* first chapter as an introduction to the modern law governing the use of armed force. Beyond introducing its concepts as background for the balance of the armed conflict law contributions, the focus is on legitimacy in terms of the extent to which the use of armed force in Iraq and Afghanistan is consistent with traditional American views of the law. The use of force in Afghanistan seems to fit within traditional views of the law, but conversely Iraq is not a comfortable fit. This distinction is important for purposes of legitimacy, because of the longer term problems likely to dog U.S. foreign policy, particularly in the Islamic world, as a result of the invasion of Iraq.

Hikmahanto Juwana then addresses the concept of superior responsibility under international law as applied in domestic (Indonesian) human rights trials concerning the responsibility of senior military commanders for events surrounding East Timor's secession from Indonesia. While the topic sounds technical, the analysis of analogous issues in a Muslim majority country carries over into the question of how high in the military hierarchy legal responsibility should go in Iraq for the Abu Gharib prison scandal. Again, this has a bearing on legitimacy both within the United States, where the issue is often understood as a metaphor for mistakes made in the prosecution of the Iraq armed conflict, and abroad. Abroad the issue is understood as a broader loss of U.S. legitimacy, often argued in conjunction with torture allegations, based upon questions concerning whether the orientation of the Bush administration towards terrorism as new kind of "war" have undercut the traditional U.S. reputation for rectitude also in armed conflict.

George Walker addresses technical issues of how to reconcile differing sources of legal obligations under armed conflict law. The problem in international humanitarian law now is that there are many different bodies of law with potential relevance for international armed conflict, so how should they relate to each other, and what is their individual priority? The analogous problem in noninternational armed conflict is the extent to which the mostly treaty-based rules of international armed conflict have now achieved customary law status applicable to noninternational armed conflict. Questions about the rules matter, as witnessed by the entire controversy behind arguments about combatant status and torture surrounding applicability of the Geneva Conventions to prisoners in U.S. custody. Again, adherence to a consistent vision of the law of armed conflict is a technical exercise, but also affects broader perceptions of legitimacy.

Kevin Govern addresses the work-a-day world of the U.S. military lawyer or judge advocate general in the current operational setting. The traditional law of armed force seemingly focuses on an image of high intensity, international armed conflict. Meanwhile, U.S. military operations are projected increasingly to be small wars or limited military operations, often noninternational in character, where military lawyers by virtue of their training may be actively involved in civil affairs and interface, particularly in the case of humanitarian operations, with NGOs, international organizations, and local governments. The concept is that the professional world of the practitioner of armed conflict law reflects general changes in U.S. military operations post–Cold War, but the package of new skills and legal areas covered is not generally recognized.

Part VI closes our examination in addressing justice and reconciliation. *John Carlson* addresses the topic of justice in the trial and execution of Saddam Hussein. Saddam Hussein's trial and execution were received differently around the world, and the practical problem is how to separate views on the invasion of Iraq more generally from those concerning Saddam Hussein's treatment. Carlson points to radically different views of justice, and tensions between the international community and Iraqi community, as affecting views of the trial's rectitude. Whereas the justice of Saddam Hussein's punishment is understood outside Iraq most commonly as a question of just desserts for a murderous dictator, within Iraq as transitional society the problem is that perhaps a broader view of justice was required in trying effectively to create a new Iraq based upon local values. Carlson characterizes the competing views as justice as rights (including the modern human rights view under international criminal law) as opposed to justice as right order (a broader relational view drawing upon classical sources).

David Linnan's second chapter addresses another aspect of transitional justice in distinguishing between competing approaches to post-conflict societies employing a truth and reconciliation commission approach versus an international tribunal approach to address wrongdoing. It is a companion piece to Carlson, arguing that truth and reconciliation commissions are premised on restorative justice, while international tribunals are premised upon retributive justice. The common wisdom is that we are moving into an extended period of armed conflicts mostly of noninternational character taking place outside the West. If so, the future may lie more with truth and reconciliation commissions than with international tribunals, notwithstanding extensive attention to, and investment of resources in, international criminal law tribunals since the early 1990s. Based upon state practice, the case can be made that the majority of developing countries in post-conflict situations are already voting with their feet in seeking more reconciliation via truth commissions than justice via tribunals. They are part of a wide-ranging complex of issues concerning how to reconstruct societies in the transitional justice phase, but raise broader issues implicitly looking at longer term outcomes particularly in Iraq.

This book also contains an appendix author panel and round table discussions from the April 8, 2005, Barnes Symposium held at the University of South Carolina School of Law (http://www.lfip.org/events/barnes05/video/video.htm). A substantial portion of the chapters in both volumes are under discussion in this free exchange, and the material is included because the authors engaged directly and commented upon how they saw the interrelationships between their individual topic areas. It ends with suggested further readings by topic areas to enable the interested reader to further pursue more deeply any area of particular interest.

What do seemingly theoretical concepts like legitimacy or competing views of justice have to do with the nuts and bolts of Iraq, Afghanistan, and the War on Terror? You could equally ask to what extent did so-called post-major armed combat choices in Iraq, such as disbanding the Iraqi army, extensive debaathification and Saddam Hussein's relatively quick trial and execution, represent mistakes now fanning the ongoing insurgency (with Iraq predicted to bedevil U.S. policy long after the Bush administration has leaves office)? It is now admitted that post-armed combat planning for Iraq was not informed by any theoretical insights and was largely visible by its absence. Beyond hindsight, the tantalizing question remains whether things could have been different in Iraq and Afghanistan in terms of lessons learned. The practical problem may be that it is hard to articulate even how all the pieces fit together under such circumstances, and our modest hope is that this book will set the reader on the road to such understanding by providing a framework within which to ask the questions.

PART I

Media, Politics, and Religion

CHAPTER 1

The Press, the Presidency, and Public Opinion since 9/11: Shaping U.S. Foreign Policy and Military Strategy

LOWNDES F. STEPHENS

This chapter focuses on international news (particularly the war on terrorism and the war in Iraq), sources of information we consult for our news as citizens, polling data on the war on terrorism and war with Iraq, and opinions about President George W. Bush's performance in handling these foreign policy concerns since September 11, 2001. Media bias against the Bush administration is often claimed, but domestic journalists have historically been "cheerleaders" in wartime and of foreign policy.[1] Media strategy is now part of international politics too. Thus, our treatment touches briefly also on "public diplomacy" as the term now used to describe attempted management of how American foreign policy is perceived in foreign media and public opinion.

Changing domestic and foreign perceptions post-9/11 reflect the reality that domestic versus foreign public opinion may cast legitimacy questions in a very different light. But even foreign public opinion is important in the longer term, as witnessed by concerns about the perceived failure of U.S. public diplomacy efforts. Finally, there is an issue whether political leadership consists of leading versus following public opinion on foreign affairs or national security. President Bush's expressed determination to "stay the course" has recently highlighted this issue as military operations in Iraq have increasingly lost domestic popular support.

RELEVANCE OF FOREIGN AFFAIRS/NATIONAL SECURITY ISSUES FOR DOMESTIC POLITICS

There is a tendency traditionally to view foreign affairs as a unitary category. However, this ignores the issue that foreign affairs in a post–Cold War world increasingly encompasses more than military affairs, or even national security as traditionally understood. For example, environmental concerns with significant economic overtones (think global warming) seemingly engage broad segments of the public, regardless of Bush administration positions.

A 2003 study by Anand and Krosnick concluded that citizens' evaluations of foreign policy goals had considerable influence on their candidate preferences in the

2000 presidential election.[2] The tendency for citizens to link candidate preferences to their evaluations of foreign policy goals was especially strong when (1) candidates took clear and distinct stands on the issues, (2) the foreign policy goals were related specifically to issues of personal importance to the citizen ("issue publics"), and (3) the citizens were especially attentive to public affairs.[3]

Anand and Krosnick concluded, based on extensive multivariate analysis of their data, that "large segments of the American public made considerable use of one or more foreign policy issues when evaluating the 2000 presidential contenders."[4] But the more interesting insight comes from the idea that the public was apparently almost as deeply engaged on

Table 1.1 Distribution of Attitudes Toward Foreign Policy Goals and Personal Importance of Foreign Policy Issues

Issues on Which Candidates Took Clear and Distinct Stands from One Another During 2000 Presidential Campaign	Values Indicating "Very Good" or "Somewhat Good" Thing for Federal Government to Do	Overall *n*	Values Indicating "Very Important" or "Extremely Important"	Overall *n*
Helping poor countries provide food, clothing, and housing for their people	71.3%	7,228	28.8%	7,210
Helping resolve disputes between two other countries	70.6%	7,221	31.9%	7,203
Preventing governments of other countries from hurting their own citizens	66.6%	7,209	29.1%	7,199
Preventing people in other countries from killing each other	54.9%	7,205	28.5%	7,194
Strengthening the militaries of countries that are friends of the United States	54.6%	7,214	25.9%	7,200
Building weapons to blow up missiles that have been or might be fired at the United States	87.5%	7,212	65.2%	7,186
Weakening the militaries of countries that might threaten the United States	66.4%	7,207	36.5%	7,188
Increasing military spending (response alternatives reported in far right column include percent indicating "a lot more" or "somewhat more")	45.0%	7,211	36.8%	7,214
Preventing other countries from polluting the environment	89.5%	7,214	59.4%	7,206
Making it easier for people from other countries to move to the United States (response alternatives reported in far right column include percent indicating "a lot easier" or "somewhat easier")	10.2%	7,221	44.1%	7,221

Source: Adapted from Sowmya Anand and Jon A. Krosnick, "The Impact of Attitudes Toward Foreign Policy Goals on Public Preferences Among Presidential Candidates: A Study of Issue Publics and the Attentive Public in the 2000 U.S. Presidential Election," *Presidential Studies Quarterly* 33, no. 1 (March 2003): 31–71.

environmental questions (preventing other countries from polluting the environment, respondent percentage indicating "very important," or "extremely important" 59.4 percent) as on direct military threat questions (building weapons to blow up missiles that have been or might be fired at the United States, comparable categories 65.2 percent). By contrast, as witnessed above, many other foreign policy areas did not engage the public to the same extent. The public appears to distinguish among aspects of foreign policy as differing in importance, but assumptions that traditional national security trumps all other areas are not entirely accurate. Along these lines, weakening the militaries of countries that might threaten the United States (respondent percentage indicating "very important" or "extremely important" 36.5 percent) and increasing military spending (comparable categories, respondent percentage indicating "very important" or "extremely important" 36.8 percent) receive almost identical scores, but preventing foreign environmental pollution scored considerably higher.

Arguably, the public makes careful distinctions concerning relative seriousness of a military threat even under the general rubric of national security. Traditional views of national security were certainly front-and-center in President Bush's State of the Union address on January 20, 2004. Shortly before, Toner and Elser summarized a *New York Times/CBS* poll (January 12–15, 2004, based on nationwide telephone interviews with a probability sample of 1,022 adults).[5] Despite the positive sentiments among the respondents in that poll concerning the President's policies regarding the war on terrorism (68 percent "approved" versus 28 percent who "disapproved"), only 48 percent approved of how he was "handling the situation in Iraq" (46 percent disapproved). The respondents were asked the following question, presumably as an indicator of their sentiments toward President Bush's preemptive strike doctrine: "Which comes closer to your opinion about what the U.S. policy should be after the war with Iraq? The United States should not attack another country unless the U.S. is attacked first, Or the U.S. should be able to attack any country it thinks might attack the United States?" Fifty-eight percent said the "U.S. *should not* attack," while only 32 percent said the "U.S. *should* attack."

Strong and divergent views on foreign affairs policy and performance were clearly on the public's mind, as was what might be considered degree of threat. The *New York Times/CBS* poll also included this question: "Which one issue would you most like to hear the candidate for President discuss during the 2004 presidential campaign?" An analysis of the dataset for this poll available at the *New York Times* Web site reveals that twenty-three different issues were specified—approximately 55 percent of the designated issues were distinctly "domestic" and 22 percent distinctly "foreign affairs" issues, with the balance mixed. It is difficult to weigh these categorically, but on a qualitative basis, foreign affairs were again of significant interest in the public's mind. This is despite the received wisdom that American media puts little emphasis on international news, precisely because they face a disinterested public.

Regarding foreign policy leadership, a 2001 study by Sobel examined the impact of public opinion on U.S. foreign policy in four case studies of U.S. intervention since the early 1950s.[6] He based his analysis on polls, public statements, memoirs, papers, and personal interviews with key policymakers. His conclusions were summarized as:

> that public opinion may constrain foreign policy making but also that policy leaders may rise above such restraints and, on occasion, lead the public. Drawing on the comments of participants, he argue[d] that policy makers see their primary task as making the best possible foreign policy or acting in the nation's best interest, not directly representing the views of the people. Policy makers are aware of and attentive to public opinion, but they are not slaves to it.[7]

Despite conventional wisdom that the American public is not engaged by international news and foreign affairs, the 9/11 attacks, war on terrorism, and military operations in Iraq and Afghanistan have undoubtedly heightened the public's interest in foreign affairs. Foreign policy issues seemingly influenced voters more than domestic issues in the November 2006 general elections, judging by both exit polls and political commentary. The latest public opinion polls reflect the view that the "War in Iraq" is by far the most important problem facing the country today. The *CBS/New York Times* nationwide random sample of 1,362 adults (margin of error±3.1 percent) was asked March 7–11, 2007, this open-ended question, "What do you think is the most important problem facing this country today?" Twenty-nine percent said the "War in Iraq." The second most frequently mentioned problems were the "economy/jobs" and "health care" each at 8 percent. In a similar *NBC News/The Wall Street Journal* poll, almost one in three respondents (30 percent) to a nationwide survey of 1,007 randomly selected adults (margin of error ±3.1 percent) March 2–5, 2007, specified the "War in Iraq" as the top priority issue for the federal government to address. The second most frequently mentioned priority was "health care" at 18 percent followed by "terrorism" (13 percent).

DOMESTIC AND INTERNATIONAL NEWS SOURCE PREFERENCES

The attentive public with high levels of political knowledge may continue to depend for their news on elite national newspapers/magazines as well as more thoughtful public affairs programs such as the *NewsHour With Jim Lehrer* on public television. However, most Americans depend on commercial television for their news. The Pew Research Center for the People and the Press ("Pew Center") released a media usage survey on January 11, 2004, focusing primarily on where Americans learn about the candidates and the 2004 presidential campaign.[8] Table 1.2 summarizes some of the Pew Center's findings.

Young adults are especially likely to turn to the Internet and the comedy shows (e.g., *Saturday Night Live* on NBC and Jon Stewart's *Daily Show* on Comedy Central) to learn about the candidates and the campaign.[9] Meanwhile, war remains famously a young man or woman's game.

The Pew Center's *2006 Media Consumption* survey contained a question about where citizens get their international news and some questions about particular stories.[10] Approximately, two in three Americans say that they get their international news from television. About 19 percent rely on newspapers for this kind of news, 15 percent on the Internet, and 4 percent from radio. There are, however, significant demographic differences in where people are getting this kind of news, as Table 1.3 illustrates.

On a statistically significant level, women, citizens with a high school education or less, lower income individuals, and citizens living in rural areas are especially likely to depend on television as a source for international news. Men, college graduates, higher income individuals, and citizens living in urban or suburban areas are somewhat more likely to rely on newspapers for international news. Dependence on the Internet for international news is especially pronounced among college graduates, among individuals under the age of 45, and among people with incomes of more than $100,000, but less than $150,000 a year. On an anecdotal (but not statistically significant) level, there is some evidence that citizens living in the South and Democrats are more likely to get their international news from television, while citizens living in the Northeast are more likely to get theirs from newspapers.

Table 1.2   Where Americans Learn About the Candidates and the Campaign (in 2004)

(...*regularly learn something from*...)					
	Overall		**By Age**		
Source	**Overall values**	**% Change Versus 2000 Survey**	**18–29**	**30–49**	**50+**
Local TV news	42%	-6	29%	42%	49%
Cable news networks	38%	+4	37%	37%	40%
Nightly network news	35%	-10	23%	32%	46%
Daily newspaper	31%	-9	23%	27%	40%
TV news magazines	25%	-4	26%	19%	30%
Morning TV shows	20%	+2	18%	18%	24%
Talk radio	17%	+2	16%	16%	18%
Cable political talk	14%	0	17%	15%	13%
National Public Radio	14%	+2	11%	15%	14%
Sunday political TV	13%	-2	10%	9%	19%
Internet	**13%**	**+4**	**20%**	**16%**	**7%**
Public TV shows	11%	-1	7%	10%	14%
Web sites of news organizations	11%	–	15%	13%	8%
News magazines	10%	-5	9%	9%	11%
News pages of ISPs (Internet service providers such as AOL and Yahoo)	10%	–	15%	13%	5%
Late night TV shows	9%	0	13%	7%	8%
C-SPAN	8%	-1	11%	7%	7%
Comedy TV shows	**8%**	**+2**	**21%**	**6%**	**3%**
Religious radio	5%	-2	3%	3%	9%
Online news magazines	2%	–	5%	2%	1%

Note: Princeton Survey Research Associates conducts the Pew Center surveys. This survey was based on telephone interviews among a nationwide sample of 1,506 adults, 18 years of age or older, during the period of December 19, 2003 to January 4, 2004. The overall sampling error (95 percent confidence) is±3%. In addition to sampling error, word-order effects and the practical difficulties in conducting surveys can introduce error or bias into the findings of opinion polls.

Pew found, in its 2006 biennial media consumption survey, that 45 percent of respondents were following "very closely" news "about the current situation in Iraq." More than one in three respondents also (35 percent) said they were following "very closely" news regarding "reports that the NSA had been collecting telephone records of millions of American citizens." Finally, 28 percent of respondents said they were following "very closely" news about "Iran's nuclear program." This 2006 dataset also reveals that about 18 percent of Americans follow news about international affairs very closely. My analysis of the original dataset shows that by comparison 41 percent of regular consumers of C-SPAN, 36 percent of regular consumers of the "Daily Show with Jon Stewart," and 33 percent of regular consumers of the "NewsHour With Jim Lehrer" follow news about international affairs "very closely." Despite conventional wisdom, there are significant groups of Americans following international news.

Table 1.3   Where Americans Get Most of Their International News

	Television	Newspapers	Internet	Radio	X^2 (Chi-square)	d.f.	P
Men	55%	21%	20%	4%	22.87	3	0.000
Women	68%	17%	11%	4%			
18–24	60%	16%	24%	–	67.79	15	0.000
25–34	60%	13%	23%	3%			
35–44	55%	16%	23%	6%			
45–54	60%	19%	15%	6%			
55–64	70%	18%	9%	2%			
65+	67%	27%	2%	4%			
White~Hispanic	61%	20%	14%	5%	9.14	9	0.425
Black~Hispanic	73%	13%	13%	2%			
Hispanic	66%	17%	15%	2%			
Other	55%	22%	19%	4%			
< HS	89%	8%	–	3%	53.31	9	0.000
HS Graduate	71%	15%	11%	3%			
Some College	60%	20%	16%	4%			
College +	51%	23%	20%	6%			
<$10K	78%	14%	8%	–	44.90	24	0.006
$10K to under $20K	71%	17%	7%	5%			
$20K to under $30K	72%	12%	11%	5%			
$30K to under $40K	65%	13%	17%	6%			
$40K to under $50K	63%	17%	17%	2%			
$50 to under $75K	57%	17%	20%	6%			
$75K to under $100K	48%	29%	19%	4%			
$100K to under $150K	47%	25%	24%	3%			
$150K or more	57%	22%	16%	5%			
[community type where you live] Rural	74%	13%	9%	4%	19.14	6	0.004
Suburban	59%	20%	17%	4%			
Urban	59%	21%	16%	4%			
[region of country where you live] Northeast	55%	23%	16%	6%	12.46	9	0.189
Midwest	63%	19%	14%	4%			
South	67%	16%	15%	3%			
West	58%	22%	16%	4%			
Republican	57%	21%	17%	5%	9.73	6	0.136
Democrat	66%	20%	11%	4%			

Independent	62%	17%	17%	3%		
Totals	**62%**	**19%**	**15%**	**4%**		
Totals (*n*)	**643**	**194**	**154**	**42**		

Source: The Pew Research Center 2006 Media Consumption Survey. The author downloaded the database and performed these calculations. Question 66dF2: (FIRST RESPONSE) "I'd like to ask where you get most of your news about some different subjects. First, [INSERT ITEM; RANDOMIZE]. Where do you mostly get INTERNATIONAL NEWS, or don't you follow this particularly closely?" The survey dataset is based on telephone interviews with a nationally representative sample of 3,204 adults living in continental U.S. telephone households. Princeton Survey Research International conducted the survey. The interviews were conducted in English from April 27 to May 22, 2006. Statistical results are weight to correct known demographic discrepancies. The margin of sampling error for the complete set of weighted data is±1.9%. In the above table, row totals may not add to 100 percent due to rounding. Base for percentages is the sum of respondents indicating one of the four sources designated in the table (*n* = 1,033). One-hundred and thirty respondents said they "don't follow" international news (about 11 percent of the 1,191 respondents answering this question). Eighteen respondents designated other sources.

Where citizens get their international news relates to their attitudes toward the media and to their knowledge of current events. The Pew Center 2003 media update dataset provides evidence regarding attitudes toward the media.[11] I examined how attitudes toward the media vary based on where people say they get most of their national and international news. People who rely mostly on television for national and international news, compared to people who say they rely primarily on newspapers, radio, or the Internet for this kind of news, are significantly more likely to believe that news organizations "stand up for America," that news organizations are not too "pro-American" in their coverage, and that "taking a strong pro-American point of view" is a "good thing" for news organizations to do. Citizens who rely primarily on radio and the Internet for national and international news, compared to people who say they rely primarily on television or newspapers for this kind of news, are significantly more likely to believe news organizations favor one side in presenting "news dealing with political and social issues," that news organizations are often influenced by "powerful people and organizations," and believe news organizations do not care about the "people they report on."[12] The 2003 Pew Center study also asked respondents who specified television as their first or second choice for news on national and international issues to identify particular sources. Most identified CNN cable news (22.7 percent), followed by the Fox News Channel (19.3 percent),[13] local news programming (13.5 percent), NBC network news (12.9 percent), ABC network news (10.8 percent), CBS network news (9.5 percent), MSNBC cable news (8.5 percent), and CNBC cable news (2.9 percent).

Concerning the media's role, many observers have been very critical of the news media's failure to play its "watchdog role" in covering the war on terrorism and the wars in Afghanistan and Iraq.[14] Some scholars have analyzed the strategic communication efforts of the Bush administration aimed at internal publics (American audiences) and concluded that these efforts were largely successful early on. Successful here refers to the period shortly after 9/11, when the President earned the highest approval ratings of any President since Gallup started polling during the 1930s, through Spring 2003 when the conventional wars in Afghanistan and Iraq seemed to be going well.[15] The *Washington Post* and the *New York Times,* for example, have been criticized for not being aggressive enough early on in challenging the Bush administration's claims that Saddam Hussein was hiding WMDs (weapons of mass destruction) in Iraq, as Secretary of State Colin Powell argued so persuasively, but apparently incorrectly, in his United Nation's speech on February 5, 2003.[16]

On the other hand, there are some examples of investigative, enterprise journalism in which the news media has played a "watch dog" role post-9/11. For example, the news media were aggressive in reporting apparent misbehavior of American soldiers in the Abu Ghraib prison abuse scandal in Iraq (April 30, 2004), domestic surveillance, and civil liberties issues, namely about the database of phone records (including calls being made by ordinary American citizens) maintained and used by the National Security Agency (May 11, 2006), and the treatment of war wounded including the dilapidated condition of Building 18 at the Walter Reed Army Medical Center (February 18, 2007).[17]

PUBLIC OPINION OBJECTIFIED: POLLING DATA CHANGING OVER TIME

Public opinion is captured in polling data, which is particularly striking in the Iraq conflict because it has changed over time, not unlike during the course of the Vietnam conflict 30+ years ago. This section looks first at changing responses over time to key domestic polling questions, then reviews scholarly interpretations of such data as they affect presidential approval ratings since 9/11, and finishes with a more limited review of public diplomacy's problems in terms of public opinion outside the United States.

Polling Data: Common Questions Over Time

PollingReport.com provides a roundup of national opinion polls on a variety of issues including the war on terrorism[18] and the war in Iraq.[19] These polls are based on nation-wide random probability samples of American adults, age 18 and above.[20] Expectations of the likelihood of further acts of terrorism on American soil are reflected in Figure 1.1 tracking opinions to a question in the *CNN/USA Today/Gallup* poll.

The proportion of respondents thinking the likelihood of more terrorist attacks on American soil was obviously high immediately after 9/11. The perceived likelihood varied considerably in subsequent tracking polls, reflecting various events from the beginning, and apparent victory of the "conventional" war with Iraq from the Spring 2003

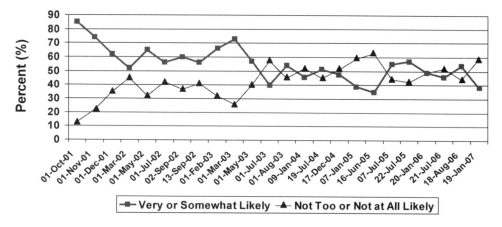

Figure 1.1   Likelihood of further terrorists acts in United States (CNN/USA Today Gallup/Opinion Research Corporation)

"How likely is it that there will be further acts of terrorism in the United States over the next several weeks?" Latest Poll: Jan 19–21, 2007, *n*=approximately 500 adults nationwide, sampling error (MoE±4.5%).

invasion to the capture of Saddam Hussein in December 2003. The chart reflects twenty-four polling periods from October 1, 2001 to January 19, 2007. The average proportion saying further acts of terrorism in the United States are "very or somewhat likely" during this tracking period is 55 percent. The period of most angst regarding this question was October 1, 2001, when 85 percent of respondents thought that further terrorist attacks in the United States were "very or somewhat likely." The lowest point in the line chart was June 16, 2005, when 35 percent of respondents thought further acts of terrorism in the United States were "very or somewhat likely."

Sentiments among Americans about who is "winning" the war on terrorism are reflected in the tracking poll results shown in Figure 1.2, again from the *CNN/USA Today/Gallup* poll.

This question has not been asked with the same frequency as the question about the likelihood of terrorist acts in the U.S. On average, during the eight times this question was asked from October 1, 2001 to January 19, 2007, 37 percent of the respondents have thought that the U.S. and its allies were winning the war on terrorism. This percent peaked May 1, 2003, when 56 percent of respondents thought the U.S. and its allies were winning the war on terror. Baghdad "fell" April 9, 2003, and President Bush delivered his "Mission Accomplished, Major Combat in Iraq is Over" speech on May 1, 2003. The low point in this series was January 19, 2007, when only 28 percent of respondents said the U.S. and its allies were winning the war on terrorism.

Two questions in the *ABC/Washington Post* tracking polls provide some insight into whether Americans believe the war with Iraq was worth fighting. The framework for each of these questions is consideration of costs and benefits. The results to the general question about whether the war was worth fighting are shown in Figure 1.3.

Any google search with the keywords "War on Terrorism Timeline" or "War in Iraq Timeline" will take the interested reader to various almanacs providing precise event dates, and these events undoubtedly have some influence on public opinion. This tracking poll question covers the aftermath of our conventional war in Iraq, including times proximate to the capture of Saddam Hussein on December 13, 2003 (as an example of an event possibly accounting for a temporary opinion surge). This series covers forty-five periods

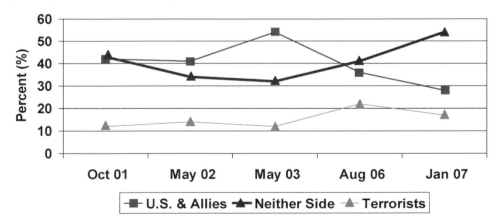

Figure 1.2 Winning the war on terrorism (CNN/USA Today/Gallup/Opinion Research Corporation)

"Why do you think is currently winning the war on terrorism : the United States and its allies , neither side or the terrorists?" Latest Poll: Jan 19–21, 2007, *n*= approximately 500 adults nationwide, sampling error (MoE±4.5%).

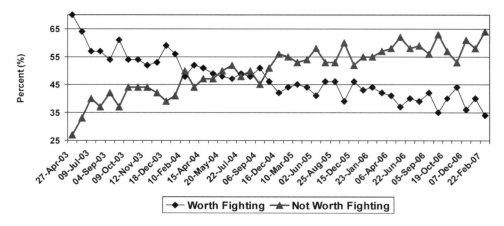

Figure 1.3   War in Iraq worth fighting? (ABC News/Washington post Poll)

"All in all, considering the costs to the United States versus the benefits to the United States, do you think the war with Iraq was worth fighting, or not?" Latest Poll: Feb 22–25, 2007, *n*=1,082 adults nationwide, sampling error (MoE± 3%).

from April 27, 2003 to February 22, 2007. On average during these periods, 47 percent of respondents have said the war with Iraq is worth fighting. That percent peaked on April 27, 2003, at 70 percent and reached a low of 34 percent on February 22, 2007.

The second question in this tracking poll focuses on the number of American military casualties but the question, asked very frequently in the first year of the War in Iraq by *ABC News/Washington Post,* apparently has not been retained in their tracking poll. The question was: "Again thinking about the goals versus the costs of the war, so far in your opinion has there been an acceptable or unacceptable number of U.S. military casualities in Iraq?" The high point was in April 9, 2003 (Baghdad had fallen), when two-thirds of respondents said the number was "acceptable." The low point in this series was in January 2004 when 33 percent said the number was "acceptable." The *Associated*

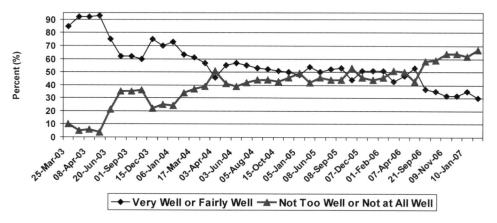

Figure 1.4   How Well Is Military Effort in Iraq Going? (Pew Research Center for the People and the Press)

"How well is the U.S. military effort in Iraq going? Latest Poll: Feb 7–11, 2007. *n*=1,509 adults nationwide. MoE ±3% (for all adults). RV, registered voters.

Press-Ipsos poll in February 12–15, 2007 (*n* = 1,002 randomly selected adults nationwide, margin of error±3.1%) asked: "Has there been an acceptable or unacceptable number of U.S. military casualties in Iraq? Fewer than one in five (19 percent) said "acceptable" and 77 percent said "unacceptable." Slightly fewer said in response to the same question with "Iraqi civilian casualties" as the frame of reference the number was "acceptable" (17 and 77 percent said "unacceptable"). American casualties in Iraq as of March 13, 2007, stood at 3,233 dead and 23,924 wounded.[21]

The Pew Research Center for the People and the Press has asked registered voters almost monthly since March 25, 2003: "How well is the U.S. military effort in Iraq going?" The results are shown in Figure 1.4. On average for the forty times the question has been asked, 56 percent of respondents have said "very well or fairly well." The peak response was April 10, 2003, when 93 percent of respondents said "very well or fairly well" and the low point was February 7, 2007, when 30 percent said "very well or fairly well." But the picture demonstrates far better than words that speaking of averages is misleading.

The *ABC News/Washington Post* poll has included a question since July 2003 about the trade-offs associated with keeping or withdrawing forces in/from Iraq. The trade-off involves the idea that staying in Iraq may lead to increasing American casualties, but premature withdrawal might mean that civil order would not be restored. These results are shown in Figure 1.5.

The question has been asked fifteen times and the results favored keeping forces in Iraq for most of this period, but positive and negative sentiment broke even in December 2006 (48 percent saying "keep" and 48 percent saying "withdraw"). In the latest poll, the split was 42 percent "keep" versus 56 percent "withdraw." Again, the mirror image and development of public opinion to favor withdrawal seem clear.

The Pew tracking poll of registered voters has also asked: "Do you think the U.S. made the right decision or the wrong decision in using military force against Iraq?" The results are shown in Figure 1.6.

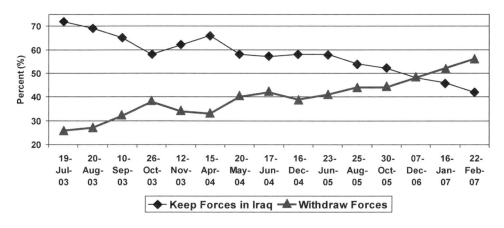

Figure 1.5   Keep Forces in Iraq? (ABC News/*Washington Post* Poll)

"Do you think the United States should keep its military forces in Iraq until civil order is restored there, even if that means continued U.S. military casualties; or do you think the United States should withdraw its military forces from Iraq in order to avoid further U.S. military casualties, even if that means civil order is not restored there?" Latest Poll: Feb 22–25, 2007. *n*=1,082 adults nationwide. MoE±3%. Fieldwork by TNS. RV, registered voters.

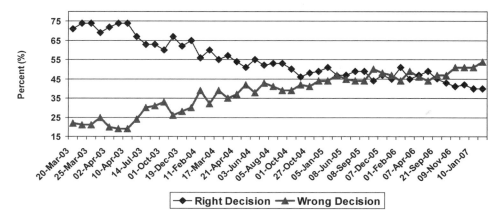

Figure 1.6   Use of Military Force in Iraq: Right or Wrong? (Pew Research Center for the People and the Press)

"Do you think the United States made the right decision or the wrong decision in using military force against Iraq?" Latest Poll: Feb 7–11, 2007. *n*=1,509 adults nationwide. MoE±3% (for all adults). RV, registered voters.

The question has been asked forty-six times from March 20, 2003 to February 7, 2007, and on average 55 percent of respondents have indicated the U.S. made the "right decision." Sentiment was most positive on March 25, 2003, (74 percent) and most negative on February 7, 2007 (40 percent). The pattern is similar to Figure 1.4, and as the public perception has grown that the military effort was not going particularly well, so too has the conclusion that it was wrong to use force in Iraq in the first place.

What has been the pattern over time in terms of public opinion of how well President Bush is performing his duties? The rest of this section focuses on his approval ratings. Figure 1.7 contains results for Gallup's tracking poll question: "Do you approve or disapprove of the way George W. Bush is *handling the situation in Iraq?"* (emphasis added). The question has been asked fifty-four times between October 2, 2002 and February 1, 2007, and on average 45 percent of respondents have said, "approve."

The sentiment was consistently positive until September 8, 2003, and it turned somewhat negative in the polling periods in October and November 2003, before turning modestly positive again in December 5, 2003 (before the capture of Saddam Hussein on December 14, 2003) and sharply positive in January 2, 2004, when the split was 61 vs. 36 (approve versus disapprove), the first polling point after Saddam's capture. The sentiment has been consistently negative since February 25, 2005, and the split at the last polling point on January 5, 2007, was 26 vs. 72 percent (approve versus disapprove).

Figure 1.8 tracks the approval ratings of President Bush's handling of terrorism.

The President gets better average approval ratings for his handling of terrorism than his handling of the situation in Iraq. The "handling of terrorism" question has been asked by USA/Gallup thirty-five times from January 31, 2003 to January 12, 2007 and on average 55 percent of respondents have "approved." Approval was highest January 31, 2003, at 71 percent and lowest January 5, 2007, when 44 percent "approved." In general terms, Figure 1.8 (President's handling of terrorism) looks more like Figure 1.6 (use of military force in Iraq, right or wrong?) than Figure 1.7 (approve President's handling of Iraq situation), perhaps reflecting different subgroups of respondents in the alternative who thought that military force would never work in Iraq, versus those who thought originally military

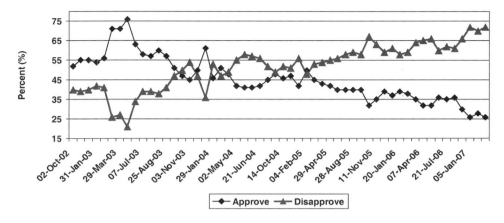

Figure 1.7 Approve President's Handling of Iraq Situation? (Gallup Poll)

"Do you approve or disapprove of the way George W. Bush is handling the situation in Iraq?" Latest Poll: Feb 1–4, 2007. *n*=1,007 adults nationwide. MoE±3%.

force might have worked, but subsequently concluded that the task has been bungled beyond redemption.

The President's overall job approval ratings as tracked by Gallup with 230 measures based on the same question asked from February 1–4, 2001 to March 2–4, 2007, are reported in Figure 1.9. The question is "Do you approve or disapprove of the way George W. Bush is handling his job as President?" Though the times are not shown in the chart, read left to right as from earliest to latest period. The sample size in these polls ranged from 800 to 2,014 and the average sample size was 1,013. The margin of sampling error is estimated to range from 2.2 to 3.5 percent.

The percent "approve" ranges from a high of 90 percent (as noted earlier a record high) September 21, 2001 to a low of 31 percent on May 5, 2006. The President's overall job approval rating was consistently positive until May 7, 2004 when it turned negative for

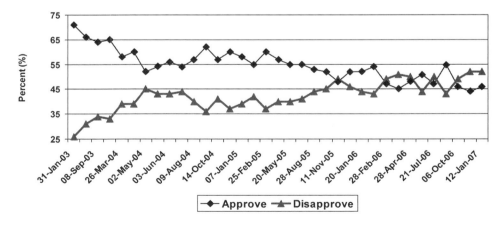

Figure 1.8 Approve President's Handling Terrorism? (USA/Gallup Poll)

"Do you approve or disapprove of the way George W. Bush is handling terrorism?" Adapted from USA Today/ Gallup Poll. Jan 12–14, 2007, *n*=1,003 adults nationwide. MoE±3%.

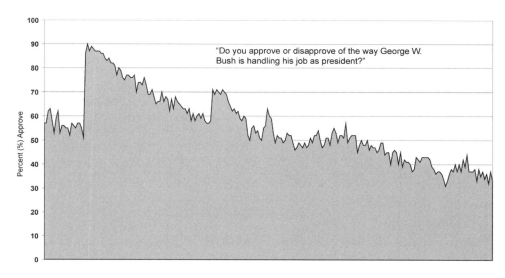

Figure 1.9   President Bush's Overall Job Approval Ratings (February 1–4, 2001 to March 2–4, 2007)

Adapted from Gallup/ CNN/ USA Today Tracking Poll (*n*=230).

the first time. Sentiment bounced from negative to positive from May 7, 2004 to July 25, 2005, and since that time, more people have "disapproved" than have "approved" of his overall job performance. Subject to a discount of approximately 15 percent for Iraq in particular, Figure 1.9's charting of the general development of President Bush's overall job approval rating largely parallels Figure 1.7's presentation of approval of his handling of the Iraq situation. This presumably represents the live by the sword-die by the sword aspect of the President's clear message that his was to be a Presidency focused on national security, linked with a judgment in the court of public opinion that the Iraq conflict as policy cornerstone was doubtful.

Nonetheless, the President's job approval rating has been better on balance than that of Congress based on the Gallup poll question: "Do you approve or disapprove of the way Congress is handling its job?" From February 2001 to February 2007, Gallup has asked this question seventy-eight times. The median percent approval level is forty-three and the median percent disapproval level is forty-eight. The highest approval level for Congress during this time was the first Gallup poll after 9/11 (October 11–14, 2001) when 84 percent of respondents approved of the job that the Congress was doing. The worst approval ratings for Congress during this period were 21 percent registered during the May and December 2006 Gallup polls. It is too early at this point to read much into the difference between Congress' and the President's approval ratings whether and how the clearly visible conflict between the new post-2006 Congressional election Democratic majority Congress and the President over Iraq policy will be received by American public opinion longer term.

Domestic Opinion: Factors Affecting Presidential Approval Ratings Since 9/11

Recent evidence in the literature is instructive in attempting to understand what accounts for variations in the President's approval ratings since 9/11. Gelpi, Feaver, and

Reifler recently examined public polling data and proprietary survey data on individual attitudes and perceptions toward the President's overall job approval, his handling of the situation in Iraq, measures of war success and support, and the effect of U.S. combat death in Iraq on these presidential approval ratings.[22] Gelpi et al. interpret the results from a series of national probability sample surveys to reflect a tendency for the public to be tolerant of increases in U.S. combat casualties so long as they also believe that the decision to use military force in Iraq was the right decision and that the probability of "success" is good. In other words, the public engages in cost-benefit analysis and is willing to accept increases in combat casualties so long as success is probable and the war is perceived as just. The authors examined weekly data on U.S. combat deaths from January 1, 2003, until November 1, 2004, and only polls that ask, "Do you approve or disapprove of the way George W. Bush is handling his job as President?" from March 2003 to November 2004. The polling firms that measure approval with that question are *Gallup/CNN/USA Today, ABC/Washington Post, CBS/New York Times,* and the Pew Research Center.

Gelpi et al. truncate the periods of analysis into three stages and do separate time-series calculations regressing presidential job approval ratings (dependent variable) on U.S. combat casualties in Iraq and other independent variables for each of these three phases of the war. The first phase of the war is defined as the "Major Combat" phase and starts from the invasion of Iraq on March 19, 2003 to May 10, 2003. During this phase, coalition forces toppled the Baath regime and positioned forces to occupy Iraq. The second phase of the war is defined as "Occupation." It covers the period from May 11, 2003 to June 28, 2004, when coalition forces occupied Iraq, until the end of June 2004 when Iraq formally regained its sovereignty in accordance with UN Security Council Resolution 1546. During this phase, insurgents begin to resist coalition forces. Finally, the third phase "Sovereignty" covers the period from end of June 2004 to the U.S. presidential election in November 2004.

Gelpi et al. find that U.S. combat casualties have a significant effect, a negative influence, on presidential job approval ratings during the "Occupation" phase of the war and a negative but insignificant effect during the "Sovereignty" phase. The relationship between casualties and approval during the initial phase, "Major combat" is positive and significant and reflects the fact that there were fewer casualties in this phase than the others and hence a possible calculus, at this stage of the war, in the public mind that the casualties are acceptable given the prospects of war success.

Gelpi et al. also used the Tyndall Report to track the amount of time the network news broadcasts spent on various issues each week during the study period. The volume of media coverage about Iraq just before the invasion and during the "Major Combat" stage of the war resulted in a positive rally effect on President Bush's job approval ratings, but the authors found media coverage during the "Occupation" or "Sovereignty" phases have had no significant impact on the President's job approval ratings. Media coverage of Democratic presidential candidates in the 2004 election reduced presidential approval significantly. Some events and rally effects also influenced approval ratings. The capture of Saddam Hussein in December 2003 boosted approval by nearly 4 percent points, while the release of the Kay report on the absence of WMD shrank approval by three points. Change in the Dow Jones Industrial Average equity stock market index was also significantly and positively related to the President's job approval ratings, so there remains the question to what extent any President's perceived success depends on domestic economic performance.

Eichenberg, Stoll, and Lebo recently used the same measure of overall job approval as the previous authors, but cover the period February 1, 2001 to the end of January 2006.[23]

They regress the average job approval ratings from these polls on five independent variables one of which is lagged values of President Bush's approval ratings to account for the
autoregressive nature of approval ratings (the tendency for current approval ratings to be
negatively correlated with prior approval ratings). Another independent variable is an
early term "honeymoon" effect (dummy measure of six for first month in office, five for
the second month, declining to zero for the seventh month, and all subsequent months the
President is in office). Another independent variable in their model is the state of the
economy as measured by changes in real disposable income per capita as reported by
the St. Louis Federal Reserve Bank and percentage change in consumer confidence over
the last 12 months as measured by the University of Michigan's Index of Consumer Sentiment. Another independent variable is a measure of American battle deaths in Iraq. Finally,
the authors include as independent variables political event dummy variables reflecting the
intensity and length of media coverage given several different rally or anti-rally events.

Their measure of the length and intensity of media coverage of certain events is how
they define rallies and anti-rallies. On the day after an event, they identified all individual
news stories that mentioned the event and tallied the total number of words that appeared
in these stories, using the *New York Times* online index. Seven days later, they repeat the
process and do so each week until the total number of words drops below 20 percent of the
highest word total that had appeared prior to that date. At this point, the authors assume
the rally is over. They then divided each weekly word total by the maximum weekly total.

They also calculate these time-series regression models for three periods: (1) the entire
period from February 2001 to January 2006, (2) the Prewar period from February 2001 to
March 18, 2003, and the (3) War period covering March 19, 2003 to the end of their time-
series, January 2006.[24]

There is a significant negative first-term honeymoon effect—perhaps the extreme close-
ness of the 2000 presidential election and the fact the U.S. Supreme Court was involved in
resolving the election's outcome (Florida) had a negative impact on President Bush's
early approval ratings. The President did get a small but significant and positive second-
term honeymoon effect on his presidential approval ratings. Both measures of the state
of the economy are significant and positive predictors of presidential approval for the
entire period and the prewar period, but none are significant (though they are positive)
predictors of approval during the war period.

Concerning Iraq's effect on the President, Eichenberg et al. tested a lagged measure of
battle deaths and a change measure of battle death. Only the lagged total battle deaths
measure is a significant—and negative—predictor of presidential approval. The authors
are confident that "American deaths in Iraq have had a negative impact on changes in
President Bush's approval."[25] The September 11, 2001, attacks and commencement of
the Iraq war are the only two events that are found to be significant predictors of the
President's job approval ratings, and the relationship is positive (all periods or weeks).
In the prewar period, while the September 11 attack is associated with a positive bounce
in approval ratings, there is no additional boost associated with the start of the war in
Afghanistan, possibly because it started October 7, 2001, less than a month after 9/11.
The only significant event is the capture of Saddam Hussein and it is associated with a
positive bounce in approval.[26]

Figure 1.10 is provided by Eichenberg et al. It plots changes in President Bush's approval ratings (left axis, line chart) and the word counts of articles in the online index of the
New York Times from the date of three crucial events (9/11 attacks, Iraq war's commencement, and Saddam's capture) until the word count dropped below 20 percent of the highest

word total that had appeared prior to that date (i.e., until the rally ended). The 9/11 attacks generated enormous media attention, and the President reached an historically high approval rating of 90 percent on September 22, 2001. The start of the Iraq war on March 19, 2003, results in a bounce in approval and significant media attention, but approval and media attention slide downward until the capture of Saddam Hussein December 14, 2003.

Similarly, Voeten and Brewer[27] analyzed a comprehensive set of tracking poll items to determine weekly changes in (1) public support for the war in Iraq, (2) perceptions of success of war in Iraq, (3) approval ratings of President Bush's management of the War in Iraq, and (4) overall job performance ratings for President Bush. They created a database of poll marginals to estimate trends in aggregate beliefs and attempt to adjust for item bias and other factors.[28] They found, among other things, that shifts in aggregate public support for the Iraq war have a greater impact on presidential approval ratings than do equivalent shifts in perceptions of war success, or approval of how well the President is handling the Iraq war. War casualties in particular negatively affect perceptions of "war success." Negative perceptions of war success in turn negatively affect the President's overall approval ratings. Moreover, they conjecture that discourse among elites is likely to have more influence on public support for the War in Iraq than "reality" indicators such as casualty reports and key events (e.g., in areas of operation).

A thread runs through the Gelpi et al., Eichenberg et al., and Voeten and Brewer studies in terms of major implications. The extent of combat casualties matters in terms of presidential approval ratings. The level of casualties and changes in casualties over time can influence perceptions about war success and, in turn, perceptions of war success can affect overall presidential approval ratings. These three studies ended their times series

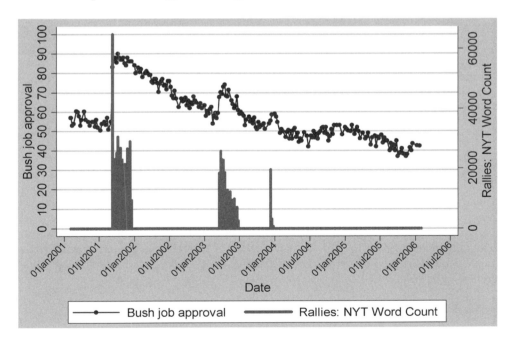

Figure 1.10   Bush Approval and 9/11, Iraq War, Saddam Capture Rallies

Source: "Figure 2: Bush Approval and 9/11, Iraq War, and Saddam Capture Rallies," p. 793 in Richard C. Eichenberg, Richard J. Stoll, and Matthew Lebo, "War President: The Approval Ratings of George W. Bush," Journal of Conflict Resolution 50, no. 6 (December 2006): 783–808.

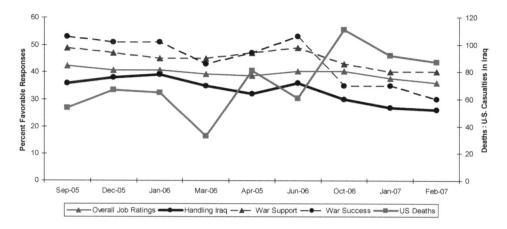

Figure 1.11   Presidential Approval, Iraq War Support and Success, and Casualties: Current Trends

Note: Overall job approval is average ratings from May 2005 to March 2007 based on 274 tracking poll questions from twenty-two polling organizations. Approval of President's handling of Iraq based on Gallup question (see Figure 7 in this chapter). Measure of war support based on Pew questions (see Figure 6 of this chapter). Measure of war success based on Pew question (see Figure 1.4 of this chapter). Casualties are U.S. combat deaths in Iraq as reported by GlobalSecurity.org.

at the latest in January 2006, and so we now pursue their issues to up to Spring 2007. For Figure 1.11, we identify comparable monthly polling points for the tracking poll measures of the President's handling of Iraq war (Figure 1.7), war support (Figure 1.6), and war success (Figure 1.4). Averages are calculated for measures with multiple polling points within the same month. There are measures for each of these variables for nine periods from May 2005 to March 2007. The President's overall approval rating is the least variable measure in the chart (coefficient of variation is 5 percent) and it averages 40 percent during this time (triangle, continuous line). The measure with the most variance is American combat deaths (coefficient of variation is 20 percent).

The highest monthly death figure is October 2006 with 111. In the prior period (June 2006), the death toll was sixty-one. The President's overall approval ratings in June 2006 averaged 40.2 and 40.3 percent in October 2006. War support averaged 49 percent in June 2006 and 43 percent in October 2006. On the other hand, the average proportion of favorable responses to the measure of perception of war success averaged 53 percent in June 2006 but only 35 percent in October 2006. I performed a separate statistical examination of the strength of relationships but not causality, using the Spearman rank-order correlation procedure, in which findings were consistent with all three studies previously reviewed. [29] As Eichenberg et al. noted, engineering public consent to strategies for winning the War in Iraq will require evidence that the strategies are actually working.[30] However, skepticism remains widespread concerning the outlook for success following newer tactics.[31]

Marketing Versus Policy: Public Diplomacy and International Opinion

Most of our study has been devoted to domestic American public opinion, but foreign government and foreign public opinion of American foreign policy is also part of international relations. However, the United States' public diplomacy efforts in conjunction with the Iraq conflict generally are conceded to have been a failure. Public diplomacy seems to be perceived almost as marketing rather than policy concern, which is, however, belied by the fact that the Iraq policy has also lost much support in domestic public opinion, as visible in our preceding review. How should this be understood?

Two recent "The Polls-Trends" features in *Public Opinion Quarterly* have attempted to synthesize the results of a number of tracking polls on public attitudes in the U.S. on the War in Iraq and war on terrorism. Everts and Isernia[32] review tracking poll results from major national firms beginning before the war in March 2003 through the end of December 2004. They concluded that both in the United States and Europe, the public believed it important and necessary for the United States (and its allies) to get support from the United Nations in order to legitimize the use of armed force in Iraq/Afghanistan and aggressive tactics in prosecuting the war on terrorism. Panagopoulos has analyzed post-9/11 polling data from the Roper Center's IPOLL database archive on American attitudes toward Arab and Muslim Americans and toward Islam.[33] He finds lingering resentment and reservations about Arab and Muslim Americans and low levels of awareness/knowledge about the basic elements of Islam. So the Iraq policy itself started with two distinct disadvantages in foreign eyes: (1) the concept of unilateral intervention in Iraq[34] was never generally accepted outside the United States, and (2) there was a basis for claiming bias within the American public against Moslems as a group, and perhaps against Islam itself as religion. The claimed bias against Moslems rendered it particularly difficult for the U.S. government's message to find any positive traction in the Islamic world.

What do we know about the perceptions of people in other countries about U.S. foreign policy? The most recent BBC World Service/PIPA (Program on International Policy Attitudes at the University of Maryland) polling initiatives in twenty-five countries (conducted by GlobeScan from November 3, 2006 through January 9, 2007, with more than 26,000 people) shows global attitudes toward the way the U.S. is handling the War in Iraq and war on terrorism going from "bad" to "worse" even as American public opinion has become more negative as well.

The PIPA World Public Opinion.org Web site in late February 2007 summarized some of the poll results:

> As the United States government prepares to send a further 21,500 troops to Iraq [the surge strategy], the survey reveals that three in four [foreign respondents] (73%) disapprove of how the US government has dealt with Iraq. The poll shows that in the 18 countries that were previously polled, the average percentage saying that the United States is having a mainly positive influence in the world has dropped seven points from a year ago—from 36 percent to 29 percent—after having already dropped four points the year before. Across all 25 countries polled, one citizen in two (49%) now says the US is playing a mainly negative role in the world. Over two-thirds (68%) believe the US military presence in the Middle East provokes more conflict than it prevents and only 17 percent believes US troops there are a stabilizing force…Interestingly the American public also seems to have serious doubts about US foreign policy. Majorities disapprove of how the US is handling the war in Iraq (57%)…A majority of 53 percent of Americans say that the US military presence in the Middle East "provokes more conflict than it prevents," with just 33 percent saying that it is a stabilizing force.[35]

The United States' efforts at public diplomacy, particularly improving impressions in the Islamic world, have failed. But the warning signs of failed public diplomacy have been evident for some time. The position of Undersecretary of State for Public Diplomacy and Public Affairs was created originally October 1, 1999, after the United States Information Agency was abolished by Congress in 1998 late in the Clinton administration. This occurred as part of a general reorganization of State Department functions for the post–Cold War world, alongside introduction of other concepts like economic diplomacy. Evelyn Lieberman, formerly director of the Voice of America, served as the first undersecretary from October 1, 1999 to January 19, 2001.

Charlotte Beers as the second undersecretary did not take office until October 2, 2001 (less than a month after 9/11). She served until March 28, 2003, or roughly until the commencement of military operations in Iraq. A branding expert from Madison Avenue, Beers was the architect behind the "Shared Values Initiative," the first-ever public diplomacy advertising campaign featuring television spots. The $15 million campaign, launched in October 2002 for dissemination abroad, included testimonials by Muslim Americans about how good their life was in America. The image campaign, which ran on a limited schedule through the Middle East and Asia through January 2003, included ordinary people like Hammuda, the baker in Toledo, and prominent people like Elias Zerhouni, director of the National Institutes of Health. Some scholars criticized the image campaign as blatant propaganda that may have been effective on internal audiences but not in the Arab world, but others have urged that the advertising war on terrorism, and this campaign in particular, be revitalized.[36]

Margaret Tutwiler as career diplomat served as the third undersecretary for only 6 months from December 16, 2003 until June 20, 2004. Tutwiler, a former ambassador to Morocco, had served as the assistant secretary of state for public affairs under President George H. W. Bush. Then Karen Hughes, a former television journalist and long-time advisor to President Bush, assumed the office of undersecretary on September 9, 2005. Hughes had worked as a television news reporter for 7 years prior to becoming director of communications for Bush when he was the Governor of Texas. She was counselor to the President with domestic responsibilities prior to her appointment as undersecretary, in which capacity she still serves. Hughes has the reputation of tightly controlling news flow from Washington also within American embassies abroad, so that it is probably accurate to characterize American public diplomacy as currently being a centralized rather than locally directed effort, particularly within the Islamic world.

Three years ago, the then-head of the State Department's public diplomacy efforts and the Advisory Group on Public Diplomacy sounded the alarm.[37] Margaret D. Tutwiler, former ambassador to Morocco and close associate of former Secretary of State James A. Baker III, had been recently appointed Undersecretary of State for Public Diplomacy, when she made her first public appearance in that role at a House appropriations subcommittee hearing on February 4, 2004. Her testimony was to the effect that America's standing abroad had deteriorated to such an extent that "it will take us many years of hard, focused work" to recover. Her conclusions were based in large measure on various recent reports of Ambassador Ed Djerejian's Advisory Group on Public Diplomacy (perceived as being close to Baker), the Council on Foreign Relations, the Heritage Foundation, and the Center for the Study of the Presidency. Ambassador Djerejian, a former ambassador to Israel and Syria, indicated that American prestige had dwindled, that much of its charity was overlooked and that its overall approach lacked strategic direction.[38]

James Glassman, at the time also a member of the State Department's Advisory Group on Public Diplomacy, writing in *The American Enterprise Online,* said the Congressionally mandated report of that group on how to fix the country's public diplomacy problems called for dramatic changes (mostly in management structure and resources). He noted:

> In Indonesia, the country with the largest Muslim population in the world and a reputation for embracing a moderate Islam, only 15 percent view the U.S. favorably, compared with 61 percent in early 2002. Similarly, in Turkey, a secular Muslim democracy that is a stalwart

member of NATO and a longtime supporter of America, favorable opinion toward the U.S. has dropped from 52 percent three years ago to 15 percent today. Shortly before the war against Saddam Hussein, by a greater than two-to-one margin, Muslims surveyed in Saudi Arabia, Qatar, and Jordan said that "the United States was a more serious threat than Iraq."[39]

Glassman also noted polling data in Spain, an ally in the War in Iraq, that only 3 percent of respondents had a very favorable view of the United States while 39 percent had a very unfavorable view. Polling data from the United Kingdom, he indicated, showed only 2 percent of Muslims there think that the United States supports democracy around the world, and large numbers of Muslims abroad thought that Americans actively discriminate against co-religionists here in the United States.

American national security elites believe the continuing problems are severe indeed. *Foreign Policy* and the Center for American Progress recently surveyed 100 leading national security policy elites, Republicans, and Democrats alike. The sample included former Secretaries of State, National Security Advisors, retired top military commanders, seasoned members of the intelligence community, distinguished academics, and journalists. Eighty-four percent of these elites opined that the United States is not winning the War on Terror. Respondents were sharply critical of our public diplomacy efforts, and they said the United States must use more tools that are nonmilitary in the War on Terror. Alarmingly, more than eight in ten of these elites expect an attack on the scale of 9/11 within a decade.[40] This informed group presumably reflects the conviction that military operations alone do not suffice to ensure national security in a changing world, even without regard to the fact that, as reviewed previously in this chapter, military operations in Iraq are not thus far perceived as having succeeded.

CONCLUSIONS

As opinion issue clusters, the "War on Terrorism" and the "Iraq/Afghanistan war" are interesting because the policy decisions about how to wage these "wars" have dramatic effects on domestic tranquility. Policy decisions growing out of 9/11 include the Patriot Act, the war in Afghanistan, intensified operations worldwide against al Qaeda/Bin Laden, and the war in Iraq. The Patriot Act contemplates trade-offs between the prospects of better security against terrorist threats and constraints on civil liberties. Work on general reformation of the U.S. intelligence apparatus continues following the widespread perception that 9/11 represented a massive intelligence failure. The war on terrorism and conventional military operations in Iraq and Afghanistan have led to large budget deficits at a time when the economic picture is uncertain. These wars have also resulted in unprecedented levels of mobilization of military reserve and National Guard troops, and to longer tours for all active forces. As a result, there are significant concerns that American military forces are overstretched, with the issue now being phrased in terms of longer term negative effects on military preparedness generally.

American news media coverage of the war on terrorism and the conventional wars in Afghanistan and Iraq might be characterized as mostly favorable, following the conventional wisdom that any press supports its government on foreign policy matters. However, news media also have focused considerable attention on the Bush administration's efforts to stabilize post–war Iraq following the self-declared end of major military operations in Spring 2003 (the now famous "Mission Accomplished" speech), the Iraqi insurgency (often claimed to represent a civil war), and on the President's dependence on faulty intelligence concerning the presence of WMDs in Iraq as the original rationale for invading Iraq.

What Americans think about the performance of the President and the legitimacy of our foreign and military policies and actions is reflected in public opinion polls. These polls are sponsored by a variety of special interest groups and by the news media. The mass media and new media can influence perceptions of legitimacy about U.S. foreign and military policy. While television, especially cable news channels, is the major source for national and international news, many young Americans and citizens who identify themselves as other than White, Black, or Hispanic, turn to the Internet for their news. And citizen opinions do appear to differ on the margin depending upon which traditional or newer media sources they consult.

The 2006 Congressional elections resulted in Democratic majorities in both the House and the Senate. Preelection polls and exit polls indicated that registered voters were not satisfied with the handling of the war in Iraq or the war on terrorism by the President and Congress. The interplay between domestic and foreign issues will likely have a major influence on the outcome of the 2008 presidential election. But by far, the most striking aspect of the turn in public opinion is the extent to which the increasingly unpopular Iraq conflict resembles the eventual turn in public opinion against the Vietnam war. The difference may lie in perceptions of the so-called War on Terror as opposed to conventional military operations in Iraq (or Afghanistan). Time will tell whether and how public opinion further differentiates between the two, recalling earlier arguments that the later was a detour in the war on terror, which issues may come alive again in the run up to the 2008 presidential election.

NOTES

1. Many observers bemoaned what they considered too much or too little pro-American bias in the reporting of the 2003 Iraq war. See, for example, Alessandra Stanley, "A Nation at War: The TV Watch, Lengthy Hours Magnify Strengths and Foibles," *New York Times,* March 26, 2003, Late Final Edition, Section B: 14; Harold Meyerson, "Fact-Free News," Opinion Column, *Washington Post,* October 15, 2003, Final Edition, Section A: A23; E.J. Dionne, Jr., "Slant of War News Depends on Who's Watching," Syndicated by the *Washington Post, The State* (Columbia, SC), October 27, 2003, A: Commentary: A9; Geoffrey Nunberg, "The Nation: It's Not Just the Media, These Days, Everybody's Biased," *New York Times,* November 9, 2003, National Edition, Section 4: Week in Review, The Nation: 4; Thomas Sowell, "The Mealy Mouthed Media: Incapable of Finding Truth," Viewpoint, *Investor's Business Daily,* January 7, 2004, National, Section A: Issues & Insights: A14; Andrew Stroehlein, "The Propagandists of War; Is There Space for Objective Reporting in Global Conflict?" *Online Journalism Review* April 2, 2002, University of Southern California's Annenberg School of Communication, February 6, 2004, http://ojr.org/ojr/ethics/1017781981.php; Andrew Stroehlein, "On the Frontline Online: Online Outlets in War Zones Suffer Challenges to Avoid Bias," *Online Journalism Review,* April 5, 2002, University of Southern California's Annenberg School of Communication, February 6, 2004, http://ojr.org/ojr/world_reports/p1017959968.php (last accessed August 13, 2004); Patrick Tyler, "BBC Faults Itself in Review of Furor on the Case for War," *New York Times,* January 22, 2004, National, A: International: A8; Jim Rutenberg and Robin Toner, "A Nation at War: The News Media, Critics of Iraq War Say Lack of Scrutiny Helped Administration to Press Its Case," *New York Times,* March 22, 2003, Section B: 10.

2. Sowmya Anand and Jon A. Krosnick, "The Impact of Attitudes Toward Foreign Policy Goals on Public Preferences Among Presidential Candidates: A Study of Issue Publics and the Attentive Public in the 2000 U.S. Presidential Election," *Presidential Studies Quarterly* 33, no. 1 (March 2003): 31.

3. Anand and Krosnick base their list of foreign policy goals paralleled in Table 1.1 above upon recommendations made by a panel of experts convened for that purpose at Ohio State University. They determined the candidates' positions on these goals by analyzing a sample of their stump speeches and interviews done with the candidates prior to the 2000 election. They also content analyzed newspaper reports on the candidates' speeches and the official platforms adopted by the Democratic and Republican Parties. The archives they depended on primarily were a CD prepared by Professor Shanto Iyengar of Stanford University, entitled "In Their Own Words: Sourcebook for the 2000 Presidential Election" and the Web site www.issues2002.org/2000 for newspaper reports. Ibid, 38–39. The sample of citizens was based on Internet sampling frames provided by Harris Poll Online (based on the Harris interactive method of selecting respondents) and Knowledge Networks (who provide respondents with a WebTV receiver to complete their surveys). Attempts were made to secure a sample representative of the population based on age, gender, and region of residence. The panel completion rate for the HPOL (Harris Poll Online) was 18 percent ($n = 2,306$ participated) and the panel completion rate for the Knowledge Networks sample was 70 percent ($n = 4,935$ participated). The combined sample of 7,216 citizens is better educated and had higher incomes than the population as a whole based on census data (same cohorts, 2000 Current Population Survey March Supplement, $n = 51,016$).

4. Sowmya Anand and Jon A. Krosnick, "The Impact of Attitudes Toward Foreign Policy Goals on Public Preferences Among Presidential Candidates: A Study of Issue Publics and the Attentive Public in the 2000 U.S. Presidential Election," *Presidential Studies Quarterly* 33, no. 1 (March 2003): 67.

5. Robin Toner and Janet Elser, "Poll Bolsters Bush on Terrorism But Finds Doubts on Economy," *New York Times,* January 18, 2004, Final Late Edition, Section 1: 1.

6. Richard Sobel, *The Impact of Public Opinion on U.S. Foreign Policy* (New York: Oxford University Press, 2001).

7. Linda Andrade, *Presidential Studies Quarterly,* 32, no. 4 (December 2002): 826, 827.

8. See "Cable and Internet Loom Large in Fragmented Political News Universe, Perceptions of Partisan Bias Sees as Growing, Especially Among Democrats," The Pew Research Center for the People and the Press, January 11, 2004, http://peoplepress.org/reports/display.php3?ReportID=200.

9. See Peter Johnson, "Lifeline: Cable, Internet Gain on Campaign Trail," *USA Today,* January 12, 2004, Final, D: Life: 1D.

10. I downloaded the dataset named "Biennial Media Consumption 2006" from Pew's Web site at http://people-press.org/dataarchive/#2006. The results in Table 1.3 of this chapter are based on my analysis of that dataset.

11. The 2001 Henry J. Kaiser Family Foundation/*Public Perspective* Polling and Democracy Survey is a comprehensive study that helps explain why the public and policymakers often resent the media. The project included telephone interviews with a national probability sample of 1,206 adults. Parallel surveys were done of policy leaders and journalists. The policy leader sample included 300 senior executive branch officials, senior congressional staff members, think tank scholars, lobbyists, trade association executives, and two members of Congress. The 301 journalists included media professionals at the top 50 circulation daily newspapers, major television networks' news divisions, major radio networks' news divisions, major news services, and major news magazines. Mollyann Brodie and others, "Polling and Democracy: The Will of the People," Special Issue on Polling and Democracy, *Public Perspective* (The Roper Center for Public Opinion Research, University of Connecticut, Storrs, CT 06269-1164), July/August 2001, 10–14.

Thomas B. Edsall, who covers national politics for *Washington Post,* writes about the Kaiser/*Public Perspective* Polling and Democracy Survey that "[t]he new Kaiser/*Public Perspective* survey on polling and democracy clearly suggests that journalists, especially those who make use of polling data, face substantial and potentially dangerous credibility issues. Such issues center on the public perception that the press, in terms of beliefs, ideas, and political values, stands apart from the rest of the citizenry." Thomas B. Edsall, "The People and the Press: Whose Views Shape the News?" Special Issue on Polling and Democracy, *Public Perspective* (Storrs, CT: The Roper Center for Public Opinion Research, University of Connecticut, July/August 2001), 29.

Edsall continues, ibid., 29–30: (1) according to the survey, journalists and others in the field tend generally to be more confident of the accuracy of poll data than either policy leaders or the public at large; (2) journalists are substantially more cynical about the motives of politicians than either the public or the policy elites; (3) and perhaps most significantly, the media diverge from both the public and from the policymaking community in terms of partisanship and ideology (only a tiny fraction of the media identifies itself as either Republican (4 percent), or conservative (6 percent); this is in direct contrast to the public, which identifies itself as 28 percent Republican and 35 percent conservative, and to policy leaders, who describe themselves as 24 percent Republican and 18 percent conservative); and (4) *these areas of divergence between the public and the press lend themselves to conflict, both with the consumers and the makers of news, and threaten to diminish the legitimacy of American journalism.* (emphasis added)

12. See "Strong Opposition to Media Cross-Ownership Emerges; Public Wants Neutrality and Pro-American Point of View," The Pew Research Center for the People and the Press, July 13, 2003 (http://people-press.org/reports/display.php3?ReportID=188) and the original dataset available at http://people-press.org/dataarchive/. The cross tabulations based on sample weighting show 70.4 percent of viewers primarily dependent on television say "stand up for America" versus 66.7 percent of all respondents who express this sentiment (as opposed to "too critical of America"). The other breakdowns (primarily television-dependent viewers first) are 77.9 percent versus 72.8 percent "not too pro-American;" 76.9 percent versus 73.7 percent "taking a strong pro-American point of view is a good thing." Similarly, 79.3 percent of primarily radio-dependent viewers and 84.2 percent of primarily Internet-dependent viewers versus 72.1 percent of all respondents believe "news organizations tend to favor one side in news dealing with political and social issues." The other breakdowns (radio-then Internet-dependent viewers, followed by all respondents) are 82.9 percent and 83.1 percent versus 75.5 percent "news organizations are often influenced by powerful people and organizations;" 65.8 percent and 64.1 percent versus 58.1 percent "news organizations generally do not care about the people they report on."

13. Parsing attitudes toward the press based on the "first mentioned" source for news on national and international issues reveals some interesting differences. Viewers relying primarily on the Fox News Cable Channel are more critical of the press than other viewers are. They are much more inclined to believe that (based on sample weighting): that press criticism keeps political leaders from doing their job [(viewers who rely primarily on local news programming are also likely to hold this sentiment); 44.6 percent of viewers primarily dependent on Fox News and 47.3 percent of viewers primarily dependent on local news, versus 37.3 percent of all respondents]; press criticism of the military weakens defense [(a sentiment also shared by viewers of CNBC cable news); 64.9 percent of viewers primarily dependent on Fox and 74.7 percent of viewers primarily dependent on CNBC, versus 50.6 percent of all respondents]; news organizations produce stories and reports that are often inaccurate (68.1 percent of viewers primarily dependent on Fox News, versus 60.8 percent of all respondents); news about political and social issues tend to favor one side (84.9 percent of viewers primarily dependent on Fox News, versus 71.7 percent of all respondents); news organizations try to cover up their mistakes (a view shared by CBS viewers); 84.3 percent of viewers primarily dependent on Fox News and 83.1 percent of viewers primarily dependent on MSNBC, versus 74.7 percent of all respondents]; news organizations are becoming too critical of America (79.1 percent of viewers primarily dependent on Fox News, versus 51.7 percent of all respondents); news organizations are too critical of the Bush administration (47.3 percent of viewers primarily dependent on Fox News, versus 26.5 percent of all respondents); and a pro-American point of view in the press would be/is a "good thing" (83.2 percent of viewers primarily dependent on Fox News, versus 76.6 percent of all respondents).

A columnist for the *Washington Post* summarized some of the findings of a series of polls done from May to September 2003 by the PIPA (Program on International Policy Attitudes). He says that these polls indicate that while many Americans have misconceptions about what is fact and what is not regarding the war with Iraq, Fox News Cable Channel viewers were much more likely to get the facts wrong (i.e., falsely believing the United States had evidence establishing a close working relationship between Saddam Hussein and al Qaeda; that the United States had found WMD (weapons of mass destruction) in Iraq; and that most people in other countries had backed the U.S. war against Saddam Hussein. See Meyerson, "Fact-Free News," Opinion Column, *Washington Post,* October 15, 2003, Final Edition, Section A: A23. Absent a systematic content analysis of the Fox News Channel's coverage of the Iraq war and its aftermath, I am not ready to conclude that Fox was more or less balanced in its coverage than other television news outlets. It is worth noting that the director of the Joan Shorenstein Center on the Press, Politics and Public Policy at Harvard University wrote a piece in *New York Times* in December 2002 arguing that many observers, including the president of the Council on Foreign Relations, find Fox to be the most balanced and comprehensive source of international news. See Alex S. Jones, "Fox News Moves from the Margins to the Mainstream," *New York Times,* December 1, 2002, The Nation: WK4.

14. See, for example, Michael Ryan, "Mainstream News Media, an Objective Approach, and the March to War in Iraq," *Journal of Mass Media Ethics* 21, no. 1 (2006): 4–29; Philip Seib, *Beyond the Front Lines: How the News Media Cover a World Shaped by War* (New York: Palgrave Macmillan, 2004), and Norman Solomon, *War Made Easy: How Presidents and Pundits Keep Spinning Us to Death* (Hoboken, NH: Wiley, 2006); and Mark Danner and Frank Rich, *The Secret Way to War: The Downing Street Memo and the Iraq War's Buried History* (New York: New York Review of Books, 2006). Other scholars have examined the decision by the Department of Defense in 2002 to implement an embedded journalist program as a means of managing news coverage of the invasion of Iraq that ensued in March 2003. Zeide argued that despite the risk of news accounts by embedded reporters having a pro-military tone and the restrictions placed on embedded reporters mobility that the embedded journalists program was the best alternative for protecting First Amendment principles (Elana J. Zeide, "In Bed with the Military: First Amendment Implications of Embedded Journalism," *New York University Law Review* 80, no. 4 (October 2005): 1309–43). Fox and Park analyzed *CNN* coverage of the "Shock and Awe" air campaign from March 22–25, 2003, and found that even though embedded reporters tended to use first-person singular pronouns in its various forms in their coverage that these journalists were nevertheless able to remain impartial in their news reporting (Julia R. Fox and Byungho Park, "The 'I' of Embedded Reporting: An Analysis of CNN Coverage of the 'Shock an Awe' Campaign," *Journal of Broadcasting & Electronic Media* 50, no. 1 (March 2006): 36–51). Finally, Pfau and a group of graduate students who are active duty military officers found in their content analysis of television news coverage of the invasion and occupation of Iraq that news stories filed by embedded journalists were more favorable in overall tone toward the military than news stories by nonembedded journalists (Michael Pfau et al., "Embedded Reporting During the Invasion and Occupation of Iraq: How the Embedding of Journalists Affects Television News Reports," *Journal of Broadcasting & Electronic Media* 49, no. 4 (2005): 468–87).

15. See Michael Ryan, "Framing the War Against Terrorism: US Newspaper Editorials and Military Action in Afghanistan," *Gazette* 66, no. 5 (October 2004): 363, Ray Eldon Hiebert, "Public Relations and Propaganda in Framing the Iraq War: A Preliminary Review," *Public Relations Review* 29, no. 3 (September 2003): 243–55, and Richard C. Eichenberg, Richard J. Stoll, and Matthew Lebo, "War President: The Approval Ratings of George W. Bush," *Journal of Conflict Resolution* 50, no. 6 (December 2006): 787.

16. See Edward Helmore, "Media: Media Matters: Never Trust a Spy (or a Journalist)," *The Observer* (New York), October 23, 2005, Business: 8; David Jackson, "Iraq Leak Helped Make Case for War; Bush Role Alleged on WMD, But Not CIA Officer's Name," *USA Today,* April 7, 2006, Final, A: 1A; and Neil A. Lewis, "Libby, Ex-Cheney Aide, Guilty of Lying in C.I.A. Leak Case," *New York Times,* March 7, 2007, National, A: A1, A17.

17. See Michael Schudson, "For a Few Dollars More Never Mind Morality, Objectivity or Contextuality—the Truth is That Sometimes Journalists in Pursuit of Their Least Noble Instincts Produce Their Most Noble Work," *Financial Times,* July 31, 2004, Weekend Magazine—The Media Department: 10; Leslie Cauley, "NSA Has Massive Database of Americans' Phone Calls; 3 Telecoms Help Government Collect Billions of Domestic Records," *USA Today,* May 11, 2006, Final, A: 1A; and Dana Priest and Anne Hull, "Soldiers Face Neglect, Frustration at Army's Top Medical Facility," *Washington Post,* February 18, 2007, Final, A: A01.

18. See http://www.pollingreport.com/terror.htm.

19. See http://www.pollingreport.com/iraq.htm.

20. PollingReport.com discloses much of the information that the AAPOR (American Association for Public Opinion Research) recommends should be provided to the media and other consumers. For example, the actual questions, dates of data collection, sponsoring organization, and margin of sampling error are provided. It is important to be wary of how these polls are interpreted by the sponsors who provide news on them or by policymakers, interest groups or journalists that interpret them (see Walter Pincus, "Data Reveal Inaccuracies in Portrayal of Iraqis," *Washington Post,* September 29, 2003, Final Edition, Section A: A14 and Krisztina Marton and Lowndes F. Stephens, "The New York Times' Conformity to AAPOR Standards of Disclosure for the Reporting of Public Opinion Polls," *Journalism & Mass Communication Quarterly* 78, no. 3 (Autumn 2001): 484–503). The best approach is to go directly to the Web sites for the actual datasets.

21. See http://www.globalsecurity.org/military/ops/iraq_casualties.htm for running casualty counts. The number of American military dead in Iraq reached 1,000 in September 2004, 2,000 in November 2005, and 3,000 in January 2007. The Iraq conflict has also been the deadliest of modern times for journalists, according to the Committee to Protect Journalists, which reports that ninety-seven journalists and thirty-seven media support workers have been killed in Iraq as of March 13, 2007; reported on CPJ homepage at http://www.cpj.org/.

22. Christopher Gelpi, Peter D. Feaver, and Jason Reifler, "Success Matters: Casualty Sensitivity and the War in Iraq," *International Security* 30, no. 3 (Winter 2005–2006): 7–46.

23. Eichenberg et al., "War President: The Approval Ratings of George W. Bush," 783–808.

24. Eichenberg et al. conclude that since one of the assumptions of time-series regression is not met (that the dependent and independent variables of interest are stationary or they are jointly stationary in the long-run; neither presidential approval nor the indicator of American battle deaths are stationary), they must use a correction-model based regression procedure, (Cochrane–Orcutt estimator). While they also report the results of OLS (ordinary least squares) regression, this author will base his synthesis of findings on the Cochrane–Orcutt estimator results because it was methodologically wrong to give OLS results given that an assumption of time-series regression was not met.

25. Eichenberg et al., "War President: The Approval Ratings of George W. Bush," 801.

26. Because the OLS regression results and the Cochrane–Orcutt results are inconsistent, Eichenberg et al. conclude that none of the event variables in the war phase is a significant predictor of presidential approval. However, their use of the OLS results is methodologically incorrect for reasons previously mentioned, so that we follow only the Cochrane–Orcutt results as indicator.

27. Erik Voeten and Paul R. Brewer, "Public Opinion, the War in Iraq, and Presidential Accountability," *Journal of Conflict Resolution* 50, no. 5 (October 2006): 809–32. The archived survey items (Table 1, p. 815) used in the analysis include twenty-five items measuring war support (such as "Do you think the situation in Iraq is/was worth going to war over, or not?" Measures of war support generated 420 observations over 187 weeks, starting August 6, 2002, and going through May 2006. Eighteen items (such as "In general, how would you say things are going for the U.S. in Iraq; very well, moderately well, moderately badly, or very badly?") measured perceptions of war success. These measures of war success generated 183 observations over 154 weeks starting March 25, 2003, and going through May 2006. Ten items measured the President's approval on handling the situation in Iraq (such as "Do you approve or disapprove of the way George W. Bush is handling the situation with Iraq?"). These measures generated 246 observations over 164 weeks starting January 16, 2003, and ending May 2006. Finally, seven items were measures of Bush's overall approval (such as "Do you approve or disapprove of the way George W. Bush is handling his job as President?" These measures generated 482 observations over 187 weeks starting August 7, 2002 and ending May 2006. Their analytics are comparable to Eichenberg et al.—for example, they use error correction models and time-series regression; measures of political events as rally and anti-rally points; changes in casualties and lagged cumulative causalities; lagged values of the dependent variables. The dependent variables, on the other hand, not only include changes in the President's overall approval rating but changes in his approval ratings on handling the situation in Iraq, changes in measures of perception of war success and changes in measures of perception of war support.

They do use different measures of the state of the economy—ABC/*Money* magazine's Consumer Comfort Index and weekly changes in that index.

28. For example, extent to which question items are directly relevant to concepts of interest, variance from baseline measures on same issue cluster, etc.

29. The Spearman rank-order correlations (r_{sp}) of war deaths with time is 0.68 ($p = .04$)—deaths increase over time and the correlation is significant. The r_{sp} of war deaths with overall job approval ratings is −0.43 ($p = .24$)—relationship is inverse as would be expected but the relationship is not significant. The r_{sp} of war deaths with perceptions of the President's handling of Iraq is −0.63 ($p = .07$)—inverse relationship as expected but relationship is not significant. The r_{sp} of war deaths with perceptions of war support is −0.66 ($p = .05$)—inverse relationship and modestly significant. Finally, the r_{sp} of war deaths with perceptions of war success is −0.68 ($p = .04$)—inverse relationship as expected and relationship is significant. The President's overall job approval ratings, including domestic as well as foreign affairs, are significantly correlated with perceptions of the President's handling of Iraq ($r_{sp} = 0.82$, $p = .01$) and perceptions of war success ($r_{sp} = 0.73$, $p = .02$).

30. Eichenberg et al., "War President: The Approval Ratings of George W. Bush," 802.

31. That is, the "surge" strategy.

32. Philip Everts and Pierangelo Isernia, "The Polls—Trends: The War in Iraq," *Public Opinion Quarterly* 69, no. 2 (Summer 2005): 264–323.

33. Costas Panagopoulos, "The Polls—Trends: Arab and Muslim Americans and Islam in the Aftermath of 9/11," *Public Opinion Quarterly* 70, no. 4 (Winter 2006): 608–24.

34. That is, not working through the UN Security Council.

35. See http://www.worldpublicopinion.org/pipa/articles/international_security_bt/306.php? nid=&id=&pnt=306.

36. For an ethical audit/evaluation of the campaign see Patrick Lee Plaisance, "The Propaganda War on Terrorism: An Analysis of the United States' 'Shared Values' Public-Diplomacy Campaign After September 11, 2001," *Journal of Mass Media Ethics* 20, no. 4 (2005): 250–68. Two advertising professors at Southern Methodist University (Karen Hughes' alma mater) determined, based on a series of experiments involving use of the "Shared Values" advertising spots, that the campaign was effective, and should have been continued. See Jami A. Fullerton and Alice Kendrick, *Advertising's War on Terrorism: The Story of the U.S. State Department's Shared Values Initiative* (Spokane, WA: Marquette Books, 2006).

37. The Advisory Group on Public Diplomacy's 2003 report on how to fix the country's image abroad opined the $600 million currently being spent on public diplomacy by the State Department was too meager and that the portion of that going to the Arab and Muslim world (about $150 million) to be so inadequate as to be characterized as "absurd and dangerous." While the group was asked to focus specifically on the Arab and Muslim world, its report, released October 1, 2003, concluded that the inadequacy of American public diplomacy is a broader problem. The report advised that strategic direction for public diplomacy be moved from the State Department to the White House. That may have been accomplished through personnel rather than organizational change when Karen Hughes as close advisor to President Bush assumed the undersecretary position. Hughes gets good marks from some observers for engaging the business community to help with public diplomacy efforts, for increasing spending on public diplomacy in the Middle East and in South Asia, 25 and 40 percent, respectively, from 2004 to 2006, and for creating the "Global Cultural Initiative" in 2006. See Joshua Kurlantzick, "Karen Hughes Isn't Such a Bad Public Diplomat. The Medium is the Message," *The New Republic Online,* March 8, 2007, The New Republic.

38. Direct and indirect quotes from Tutwiler and Djerejian are from Christopher Marquis, "U.S. Image Abroad Will Take Years to Repair, Official Testifies," *New York Times,* February 5, 2004, National, A5. For a copy of her testimony see Margaret B. Tutwiler, "Prepared Testimony of Margaret B. Tutwiler Under Secretary for Public Affairs Before The House Appropriations Committee Subcommittee On Commerce, Justice, State and the Judiciary: Subject—Public Diplomacy: Reaching Beyond Traditional Audiences," Transcript by Federal News Service, *LexisNexis Congressional* (Washington, DC), February 4, 2004. For a copy of Djerejian's statement,

see Edward Djerejian, "Statement of Ambassador Edward Djerejian Chairman, Advisory Group on Public Diplomacy, Committee on House Appropriations Subcommittee on Commerce, Justice, State and the Judiciary, February 4, 2004," Transcript by Federal Document Clearinghouse Congressional Testimony, *LexisNexis Congressional* (Washington, DC), February 4, 2004.

39. James K. Glassman, "The U.S. Needs More Effort on P.R.," *The American Enterprise Institute Online* December 2003, Published in The View from Abroad December 2003, January 28, 2004.

40. "The Terrorism Index," *Foreign Policy,* July/August 2006, 49–52.

CHAPTER 2

Muslim Perspectives on the Invasion of Iraq: Informed Publics, Regime Leaders, and Islamic Jurists

SHAHROUGH AKHAVI

There is a tendency to discuss America's poor reputation in the Islamic world in terms of a failure of its public diplomacy. However, this assumes that the only problem U.S. diplomacy suffers is a failure of marketing, as opposed to the idea of policy differences. This chapter focuses on common perceptions within the Islamic world concerning the invasion of Iraq, which, unlike the invasion of Afghanistan following 9/11, was not viewed as justified. This is an exercise in understanding others' point of view, because the invasion of Iraq should be understood against the Middle East's historical experience of external intervention. This is a cautionary tale, all the more so as policy mistakes may have long echoes, judging by Middle East examples like current strained relations between the United States and Iran, which many trace back ultimately to 1950s intervention. It seems probable that Muslim perspectives of the invasion will continue to be extremely negative into the foreseeable future. Thereafter, whether perspectives improve in the longer run will depend a great deal on exit strategies and conduct of occupation forces, as well as the evolution of such regional issues as the Palestinian–Israel conflict.

LAW, MORALITY, AND LEGITIMACY IN ISLAM

In Islam, preeminence is given to law over all the other disciplines. The only exception to this principle is the sufis or Muslim mystics, for whom gnosis and theology trump the law because of their conviction that it is possible to know God and even to merge with the Supreme being in an inward journey of the soul. For mainstream (Sunni) Islam and also the Shi'i variant, however, it is essentially unprofitable to seek direct knowledge of God's nature, attributes, and divine essence, since these are beyond the ability of human beings to grasp. However, God's commands are accessible and knowable, and it is to their systematization and rationalization that the learned doctors of jurisprudence (*ulama*) have given their sustained attention. Of course, this does not mean that the religious scholars eschew theology, and, indeed, that science is an important one in the seminaries. But those scholars regard themselves as jurists first, and then specialists in theology, theosophy, scriptural exegesis, prophetic traditions, or any of the other branches of learning available in those educational institutions.

Once the believer commits to the commands of God, His law, in its turn, considers that anything which harms the Muslim's life or property is to be avoided and censured. Morality, thus, consists in carrying out the divine commands and protecting the lives and interests of the believers. Such moral ends can only be achieved, according to the teachings of Islam, through the creation of a community of believers. Once established, moreover, the integrity of this community must be defended and its interests promoted, for the welfare of the community is the only assurance that God's commands are being carried out.

Involvement of this community in war is strictly forbidden by Islamic law unless this war is for the sake of materializing God's commands. In the early experiences of the community, war was legitimate only for this purpose. The Prophet did encounter hostility on the part of certain tribes that not only refused to accept the new faith but also attacked its proponents. Thus, the tradition was established that those abiding in the realm or abode of the new religion (*dar al-islam*) would have to fight those abiding in the realm of dissidence (*dar al-harb*—literally, abode of war). Exerting efforts for the sake of God (*jihad*) was thus established as a principle and seemingly became the basis for a Muslim theory of international relations. But care must be taken not to overdetermine this relationship between Muslims, on the one hand, and Jews and Christians, on the other.

The founders of the four Sunni schools of law did hold that, technically speaking, a state of war existed between the Muslims against the Jews and Christians. But it was mainly al-Shafi'i (d. 820) who insisted that such a war not only existed in a technical sense, but also that it amounted to a permanent state of conflict. Abu Hanifa (d. 767) and Malik ibn Anas (d. 795), two other founders of Sunni schools, refrained from holding that the Muslims had to fight the Jews and the Christians just because they did not accept Islam. The founder of the fourth school, ibn Hanbal (d. 855) seems not to have addressed this issue explicitly, but his most famous disciple, ibn Taymiyyah (d. 1328) adopted the same position as Abu Hanifa and Malik ibn Anas. For all of them, rather, *jihad* was mandated against Jews and Christians only if they attacked the Abode of Islam. These jurists noted that Jews and Christians were the protected people because they accepted God, and their scriptures were not only respected by Muslims, but also those writings comprised a goodly portion of the Qur'an itself.[1]

IRAQ AND MUSLIM PERSPECTIVES ON THE AMERICAN INVASION

The preceding discussion has already suggested that Muslim legists have adopted varying positions on issues and that, therefore, there is no such thing as a *single* Muslim perspective on policy matters, including the American-led invasion of Iraq in March 2003. Accordingly, this chapter is entitled *Muslim Perspectives on the Invasion of Iraq*. To clarify matters, I will examine three different constituencies of Muslims and examine how they have looked at this topic. These three groups are informed publics, regime leaders, and religious scholars. Although in all three cases, the perspectives are critical of American actions, the reasons for the negative attitudes vary. The following three caveats need to be kept in mind, as well: (1) among the informed publics, one finds at least some support for the removal of Saddam Hussein and his regime, even if the overwhelming reaction is nonetheless on the negative side; (2) among the regime leaders, their negative perspective is tempered by some satisfaction at the fact that the unpredictable leader, Saddam Hussein, has fallen from power; (3) the Muslim perspectives surveyed in this chapter are those adopted by Muslims in the Middle East, though it is my strong conviction that similar attitudes have been shared by their fellow Muslims in Africa, South Asia, Southeast Asia, Europe, Latin America, and North America.

Informed Publics

"Informed publics" refers to sectors of the population who participate in political discourse. Usually, the people in this category have secondary and often tertiary education, but this is not a strict requisite, as political activists can include those who only acquired a primary school education, but nevertheless keep themselves informed of current issues of the day. Broadly speaking, informed publics include professionals, such as lawyers, physicians, educators, journalists, scientists, labor leaders, businessmen, financiers, students, and the like. They could also include workers and cultivators, though this group would be less well represented. Members of the "petite bourgeoisie" (self-employed, small shopkeepers, and retail merchants in the domestic economy) may also be included.

The few polls conducted inside Iraq since the American-led invasion in March 2003 and the initial end of organized fighting in early April showed that Iraq is generally expect improvements in conditions in Iraq and in their own lives.[2] One such poll was carried out by Zogby International (located in Washington, DC) on behalf of the conservative think tank, American Enterprise Institute. It showed that almost 70 percent expected either significant (31.7 percent) or slight (38 percent) improvements in the country's prospects in the future. These figures appear to hold up across age, ethnic, and religious groups. Christians and those who had lost relatives in the war were optimistic at higher than average levels (77.8 and 77.4 percent respectively). Even Sunni Iraqis felt generally optimistic for the country's future (67.6 percent—but no breakdown is available for determining the degree of optimism, whether significant or slight). All groups polled expressed the desire for rapid termination of the occupation, with 31.6 percent demanding an end within 6 months, 34 percent within 1 year, and 25 percent within 2 years. Most of the Christians (77.8 percent) hoped the occupation would last more than 2 years, while most of those above the age of 65 (more than 50 percent) wanted the occupation to end within 6 months.[3]

In August–September 2003, the Gallup Poll released findings that only 35 percent of Baghdadis felt that the United States would permit Iraqis to establish their own political system free of interference by Washington. A plurality of respondents (39 percent) stated their preference for a "multiparty democracy," followed by 29 percent who prefer a political system based on the concept of consultation (*shura*), a concept found in the Qur'an. A smaller number (10 percent) favored an Iranian-style system, followed by almost as many (8 percent) preferring a constitutional monarchy.[4]

Two other polls, this time administered by the ICRSS (Iraq Center for Research and Strategic Studies), in August–September 2003 and September–October 2003, also provided some interesting data. In the earlier poll, ICRSS found that one-third of the respondents favored an "Islamic system," though what that actually means is unclear. Thirty percent favored "democracy" (again, not clearly defined), while 24 percent favored a blend of the two. A majority (61 percent) declared that they did not trust any Iraqi political leader. In the later poll, covering seven cities and undertaken on behalf of the U.S. State Department, regional variations emerge in regard to whether an "Islamic" or a "democratic" political system is preferable. In Irbil and Sulaymaniya (Kurdish towns), between 50 and 75 percent favored a "democratic" system; in Basra (in the Shi'i south) a plurality held out for "democracy;" in Baghdad, the response was even between "democracy" and an "Islamic" system; in Fallujah and Ramadi, cities in Central Iraq, a plurality (Fallujah) and a majority (Ramadi) favored an "Islamic" state; while in Najaf (dominated by the Shi'ah), the population by far preferred an "Islamic" state.[5]

In late winter 2004, the findings of an extensive poll conducted in Iraq among a random and representative sample that included 2,737 Iraqis from February 9 through February 28, 2004 were released. This is the most detailed poll yet. It showed that 48 percent believed that it was right for the United States and its partners to attack Iraq, while 39 percent believed that it was wrong, while 13 percent expressed no opinion. As the report states, these numbers represent "hardly the unreserved welcome some U.S. policymakers had anticipated." These numbers change dramatically, however, when those polled are broken down into Arab and Kurdish Iraqis. Among the Arab population of the country, 46 percent maintained that the invasion was wrong, while 40 percent held that it was right. The corresponding figures for Kurdish Iraqis were 87 percent stating that it was right, while only 9 percent declared themselves against the invasion.[6]

Unfortunately, the poll did not distinguish between Sunni Arabs and Shi'iah Arabs. Because of this, it is only possible to refer to the results for all Arabs. With this in mind, note that only 33 percent of the Arab population of Iraq believed the consequence of the invasion was to liberate the country, while 48 percent maintained that the invasion humiliated its people. Among the Kurds, however, those arguing the invasion liberated Iraq included 82 percent of all Kurds polled, while only 11 percent believed that it humiliated the country. Only 30 percent of all Arabs supported the continued presence of coalition forces, while 60 percent opposed this. Among the Kurds, the numbers were 82 percent in favor and 12 percent opposed, respectively .

A majority of all communities worried about the lack of jobs and about the lack of security that has existed throughout the land. On the positive side, 70 percent of all those questioned believed things were "good" at the time of the poll, while only 29 percent believed they were "bad." However, when asked to compare the situation at the time of the poll with the prewar situation in Iraq, 56 percent declared the situation to be better now, while 23 percent reported that it was about the same, and 19 percent felt it was worse. When asked to project into the future 1 year from the time of the poll (i.e., to February 2005), 71 percent predicted the situation would be better, 9 percent that it would be the same, and 7 percent that it would be worse. In rating specific local conditions, 72 percent declared that the situation of schools was "good," while 26 percent said it was "bad." But when asked to compare the situation of these schools with the prewar period, the numbers change dramatically, with 47 percent responding that the situation is better now, 9 percent declaring it is worse, and 41 percent saying it is about the same. In regard to crime protection, 53 percent declared that the situation was "good," while 44 percent declared it was "bad." For clean water, the corresponding numbers were 50 percent "good," but 48 percent "bad."

Polls have shown that the reaction of non-Iraqi Arabs to the American invasion and occupation of Iraq is overwhelmingly negative. While some in the region (as well as expatriates living outside the region, but with continuing ties and connections to it) are happy to see the end of the regime of Saddam Hussein, even they have expressed a sense of humiliation that it required external intervention to bring this about. They also see that Iraq is under American-led military occupation, note that many Iraqis continue to lack electricity, that abductions and criminality in Iraq are mounting, and that health care and education in the country have either sharply declined or have stagnated. Polls have shown that Muslim perceptions on the invasion of Iraq have turned far more negative lately than in the year immediately following the invasion.

Although many Arabs condemn the bomb explosions in Iraq that have killed Iraqi civilians,

> most Arabs would also have some sympathy for those fighting to end what they see as the US occupation of Iraq. The observers also say that public animosity in Arab and Muslim countries toward US foreign policy is so great now, that it is difficult to publicly show any sympathy at all for the US effort in Iraq.[7]

Firstly, the general sentiment among informed publics in the Middle East is that Iraq did not pose a threat to the national security of the United States. They do not believe it to be credible that a small country such as Iraq could constitute such a threat. Even if it had turned out to be true that the Ba'thist regime had possessed WMDs (weapons of mass destruction) and would have been able to operationalize such weapons within 45 minutes, the informed Muslim publics do not believe that such capability would have amounted to a threat to the national security of the vastly powerful United States.

Secondly, informed publics have reacted with profound cynicism to the rhetoric of the administration in Washington that it sought to bring democracy to Iraq and then, by extension, the Arab world. Given the record of American foreign policy in the region, these publics believe that the United States is not the agent one could rely upon to transmit democracy. Although the record of the United States in the mid-1940s was generally a good one in the mind of these publics, matters began to change with the Anglo-American Committee of Inquiry (1946), which was formed to assess how the British Mandate over Palestine ought to be terminated. Although President Truman promised the British government in advance that his administration would adhere faithfully to all the recommendations that were to be made in the report of this Commission of Inquiry, he abandoned all of the recommendations except the one that called for immediate authorization to permit 100,000 Jews to migrate to Palestine. He unilaterally abrogated provisions that called for a binational state with parity for both Jewish and Palestinian communities, gave the Palestinian side a veto over future Jewish immigration to Palestine beyond the 100,000 additional immigrants, and recommended the opening up of Western borders to accommodate Jewish immigration to Western countries. These policies, including American support for the creation of the state of Israel, was considered by Muslim informed publics to be the abandonment of Wilsonian principles of self-determination and thus a betrayal of America's own democratic legacy.

Later, the United States supported the overthrow of the democratically elected government of Prime Minister Muhammad Musaddiq in Iran in August 1953 and tried several times to achieve the same purpose against the populist regime of President Gamal Abdel Nasser in Egypt after 1956. The United States also backed the repressive Iraqi monarchy prior to 1958, endorsed the authoritarian rule of King Hussein in Jordan, of King Hasan in Morocco, and of the various dynasts in Saudi Arabia after the death of the founder of that Kingdom, ibn Abd al-Aziz, in 1953. The United States intervened on behalf of the Falangist Maronites in the Lebanese Civil War of 1975–1991, supported Saddam Hussein throughout the period of the Iran–Iraq War (1980–1988), and endorsed the Algerian army's coup in January 1992 that prevented democratic elections in that country. Finally, the United States routinely vetoed resolutions in the United Nations that these mass publics believed represented just censorship of Israel for its policies in the occupied Palestinian territories of the West Bank and Gaza Strip. Middle Eastern informed publics were keenly aware that at the time when the international media were focusing their attention on Baghdad's use of poison gas against the Iranians during the

Iran–Iraq War, the State Department tried its utmost to divert attention from this by suggesting that it was actually the Iranians who were resorting to poison gas. The administration in Washington knew very well that the Iranians were not resorting to poison gas attacks, but still attempted to shift the blame to the Iranians, since it was embarrassing to be seen to support a government, Iraq, that was actually doing so. These publics also know about the American betrayal of the Iraqi Kurds in 1975, when Henry Kissinger arranged a deal that led to the abandonment of the Kurds to the tender mercies of the Ba'thist government of Iraq of the time. Washington also tried to prevent the over-throw of their client, the Shah of Iran, in the fateful days of 1978–1979, when the Iranian revolution was underway.

Informed publics in the Middle East also reject the accusations made by Vice President Richard Cheney, Defense Secretary Donald Rumsfeld (and his deputies, especially Paul Wolfowitz and Douglas Feith), National Security Advisor Condoleeza Rice, and certain other appointees of the administration that Saddam Hussein's government was cooperat-ing with the leadership of al Qaeda in a campaign of international terrorism whose main target was the United States. The President himself espoused such views until it became untenable, and he finally had to admit that no evidence existed of any such connection between Saddam Hussein's government and Osama bin Laden. Since imminent use of WMDs and Iraqi support for international terrorism were the two strongest arguments that the Bush administration advanced to justify its invasion, and since both of these have been shown to be false, informed Middle East publics believe themselves vindicated in their refusal to believe the version advanced by the Bush administration.

Beyond this, they note that the doctrine of *preemptive attack* that the administration has newly adopted would, if consistently applied, provide justification for the government of any nation-state in the world to attack its rivals on grounds that unless it did so, the rival could at some point represent a mortal threat to it. This line of thinking distills, in the thinking of Muslim informed publics in the Middle East, to a license to ignore international law and to act unilaterally in a coercive manner in pursuit of national inter-ests. This not only undermines international law, but also the major institutional guardian of that law, the United Nations. As far as Middle Eastern informed publics are concerned, the fact that the Security Council of the United Nations refused explicitly to authorize the use of military force in the months and weeks leading up to the war, but Washington proceeded with the invasion nevertheless, starkly shows imperialist behavior on the part of the world's only superpower.

Middle East informed publics note that the only governments in the region that supported America's armed attack on Iraq were Kuwait and Israel. If most regimes in the region did not see themselves so threatened by Saddam Hussein's government as to warrant an invasion of Iraq, what was it then that led the United States, some 6,000 miles away, to feel so threatened?

The thinking among these publics is that the United States wanted to open the Iraqi economy to participation by American corporations and remembered former Secretary of State James Baker's famous comment to the press at the time of the first Gulf War (1990–1991) that "this war is about jobs, jobs, jobs." In other words, economic motives were then, as well as again in 2003, driving American behavior in a major way. It has been suggested in some quarters that the United States had nothing material to gain by attacking Iraq, and it did so for noble purposes. But this view is dismissed by the informed publics in the Middle East. They retort that it is not necessary for the United States to take direct control over the Iraqi oil industry for Washington to be able to have its way in regard to oil prices economically favorable to it. A regime in Baghdad friendly to the United States would, on this argument, do its best to protect the American interest by keeping oil prices at levels most helpful to the U.S. economy. Iraq's oil reserves are second only to Saudi Arabia's, and some authorities consider that it is the world's leading state, surpassing even Saudi reserves. Middle Eastern informed publics cannot believe that U.S. purposes were merely to end the rule of an oppressive ruler, and not to establish a dominant voice over the operation of the Iraqi oil industry.

Meanwhile, of course, oil is not the only sector of the economy in Iraq. Informed Muslim publics believe the opportunity for American corporations to participate in the full range of sectors of the Iraqi economy was a powerful incentive leading the Bush administration to war and then to offer recovery through contracts granted to such companies as Bechtel, Haliburton, and the like. They believe that in the reconstruction process as well as in the period after reconstruction, a chief objective of the U.S. foreign policy was to squeeze out the commercial activities of business interests from other advanced states.

On the issue of wanting to encourage democratization in Iraq, Middle East informed publics note that democracy is not a monolithic model of representing interests. While the Anglo-Saxon tradition of democracy stresses individual liberty, the continental European tradition stresses equality. These two themes may well conflict with one another. Although Bush administration spokespersons routinely declare that they do not have a blueprint of democracy that they want to impose on the Iraqi people, it is evident that "one person one vote" is not what they have in mind. When this is proposed, for example, by the grand mujtahid, Ayatollah Ali Sistani, the response in Washington is that this is not what the United States wants because of fears that the minority Kurds and Sunnis will be disadvantaged. The problem is that American historical traditions, rooted in Madisonian fears of the "tyranny of the majority" are alien to Middle Eastern institutions and processes in general and Iraqi ones in particular.

Because support for the American-led action has drastically dropped among the American people themselves, it is hardly surprising that the negatives in the Muslim perceptions have increased in intensity. This opinion is mindful of the symbolism of foreign occupation. Although colonial invasions and occupation have a longer history in other parts of the world, Carl Brown is correct when he insisted that the Middle East "is the most penetrated international relations subsystem in today's world."

> The entire world has been shaken and shaped by the West in modern times, but nowhere has the political dimension of that fateful confrontation been more thorough and more consistent than in the Middle East....The idea of a penetrated political system...is not simply a measure of the intensity of outside political or economic domination. Many countries and regions, for example, have experienced a longer, more violent, or more disruptive period of outside domination than the Middle East [the Muslim territories of Central Asia in the Soviet period, for instance]. In other areas the outside impact was at one time more intensive than what the Middle East endured, but such confrontation was not sustained....A penetrated political system is one that is neither effectively absorbed by the outside challenger nor later released from the outsider's smothering embrace. A penetrated system exists in continuous confrontation with a dominant outside political system.[8]

In a broadcast aired in late 2003 by the VOA (Voice of America), which is a division of the United States Information Agency, located in the executive branch of government, interviews with a number of intellectuals in the Arab world about the United States' actions in Iraq were summarized. Here are some of the major points that emerged from these interviews, as identified by VOA broadcaster, James Martone: (1) the Iraqi resistance to the U.S. presence in Iraq, deemed an occupation, was perceived as justifiable, in the implicit context of the colonial legacy; (2) the targeting of innocent civilians by elements of this resistance, though perceived as unacceptable by the respondents, was nevertheless downplayed because of the greater importance to these respondents of resisting foreign occupation; (3) a double standard was perceived in the American countenancing of Israel's occupation of the West Bank and Gaza Strip and justifying its own invasion of Iraq by reference to a desire for democracy. If the United States were really opposed to occupation, on this argument, why did it not encourage this as well for the Palestinians, who were eager to enjoy its fruits but could not under occupation?[9]

Polling of Muslim public opinion is becoming increasingly reliable, led, perhaps, by Zogby International and the Pew Research Center for People and the Press. Although the Middle East is not equivalent to the Muslim world, one cannot ignore the results of recent polls that show how deep the resentments of the United States have become. Compare the figures for public opinion about the U.S. Government's policies for four Arab states in two different years (Tables 2.1 and 2.2), the first prior to the U.S. invasion of Iraq and the second following that event.

Table 2.1 Public Opinion About the U.S. Government's Policies for Four Arab States in Two Different Years

Country	April 2002 Percent Unfavorable	July 2004 Percent Unfavorable
Egypt	76	98
Saudi Arabia	87	94
Morocco	61	88
Jordan	61	78

Source: Data from "Freedom and Democracy American Style," *Labour and Trade Union Review,* February 2005, http://www.david-morrison.org.uk/iraq/freedom-american-style.htm.

Table 2.2 Changes in Perceptions About the United States in Various Arab States Over the Course of the Year From 2004 to 2005

Change	Egypt	Jordan	Lebanon	Morocco	Saudi Arabia	UAE
Better	5%	13%	21%	6%	8%	8%
Worse	84%	62%	49%	72%	82%	58%
Same	11%	18%	27%	21%	9%	31%

Factor	Egypt	Jordan	Lebanon	Morocco	Saudi Arabia	UAE
War in Iraq	57%	48%	34%	45%	49%	31%
Bush's promotion of democracy and reform	4%	6%	16%	2%	9%	9%
Developments in the Arab–Israeli front	8%	13%	19%	8%	8%	7%
American treatment of Arabs and Muslims	28%	28%	22%	40%	32%	41%
Other	0	3%	4%	2%	0	5%

Source: James Zogby, *Attitudes of Arabs, 2005* (Washington, DC: Arab American Institute/Zogby International/ Young Arab Leaders, 2005), 12.

Indeed, even according to the U.S. Defense Department's Defense Science Board Task Force on Strategic Communication of September 2004, "*in the eyes of Muslims,* American occupation of Afghanistan and Iraq has not led to democracy there but only to more chaos and suffering. U.S. actions appear in contrast to be motivated by ulterior motives and deliberately controlled to best serve American interests at the expense of truly Muslim self-determination."[10]

In a study issued by James Zogby in 2005, figures are provided on changes in perceptions about the United States in various Arab states over the course of the year from 2004 to 2005. The information is revealing, particularly when juxtaposed to information provided by Zogby in regard to the most important factor determining people's changes of attitude, which was the war in Iraq.

Muslim Regime Perspectives

In gauging the reaction of Muslim regimes, I will focus upon those in the Middle East, though I feel that these can be generalized to non-Middle Eastern cases. The reaction has been mixed, depending to some extent upon which audience these regimes are addressing. Objections to the American-led invasion of Iraq by regime leaders may be divided into three categories. In the first place, many of these regimes are narrowly based and lack broad popular legitimacy. The masses in the countries headed by these regimes have been, as we have seen, keenly opposed to the invasion of Iraq. Radicalizing these masses by giving them the impression that the regimes, because they pursue pro-American policies, endorse the war on Iraq is a serious problem that they face. The last thing they need is to give their people additional reasons beyond the ones they already have for being angry at them. This is a major reason why such leaders as President Husni Mubarak of Egypt and Crown Prince Abdallah of Saudi Arabia tried to avert the war.

A second reason why these regimes opposed the American-led war on Iraq is that some of them may have believed that this precedent would make it easier for the United States to seek their own overthrow if Washington perceived them to be obstacles hindering the American project in the region. No doubt the leaders in Syria and Iran have been disturbed at the implications of the war against Iraq for their own ability to hold on to power. It might be argued that the United States would be hard put to succeed in any military intervention in either of these two countries, but the regime leaders in Tehran and Damascus, among others, apparently believe the rhetoric from Washington, DC that they may be in the line of fire.

A third reason for Muslim regimes to oppose the invasion of Iraq relates to memories of colonialism and a strong sense of the injustices associated with the colonial era in the Middle East. On this argument, regime leaders are no different from the populations that they govern: both they and their people have collective memories, if not personally, then certainly as crystallized in the social mythos of their nation-state experience, of the humiliation of foreign invasion and occupation. Although the policymakers of the states that invaded Iraq have proclaimed that their enterprise is not a colonial one, Muslim regime leaders are not so different from their informed publics in remaining unpersuaded that motives of gain and advantage in international politics and global economic markets have had no role to play in this affair.

Be this as it may, the overthrow of the Saddam Hussein regime was also a positive development for a number of the leaders of the region, though, with the exception of Kuwait, they could not afford to be seen or heard saying so openly. This is certainly true of the Iranian government and almost as certainly true for the Syrians. Indeed, none of

Iraq's neighboring governments lamented the removal of the Baghdad regime, with the possible exception of Turkey.

The explanation there is that Turkey's leaders have long been fearful that a regime collapse in Iraq will signal the rise to prominence of the Kurdish issue and, at the very least, the creation of an autonomous Kurdish region within a weakened Iraq. Turkey's leaders, needless to say, had objected to the instability in that region generated by unpredictable Iraqi behavior under Saddam Hussein. Accordingly, they may not have been unhappy to see the end of his rule. But on the other hand, the risk that Iraqi Kurds might succeed in staking their claim to an independent Kurdish state, thereby stimulating pressures among Turkish Kurds to secede, has been too strong to allow Ankara to look upon developments in Iraq with any equanimity. From this perspective, better a troublemaking Saddam Hussein still in power than a scenario in which Iraq implodes. Similar concerns apply in the case of Iran, but because of the long Iran–Iraq War (1980–1988), the Iranians have been more willing then the Turks to see the end of the Hussein government. As for Jordan's leaders, because of the integration of the Jordanian and Iraqi economies, the government in Amman also tried to discourage an American invasion of Iraq. This was not out of support for Saddam Hussein's policies, obviously, but rather due to Jordanian desires for stability in the markets of both countries.

Muslim Jurists' Perspectives

When speaking about the perspectives of the Muslim jurists regarding the invasion of Iraq, it is apposite to distinguish between Sunni and Shi'i interpretations. This is not the place for a detailed discussion of such distinctions. Suffice it to say that a corpus of Sunni and Shi'i law has developed over the centuries whereby the jurists of each side have refrained from drawing precedents for their interpretations of the law from the legal traditions of the other party. Historically, the differences between Sunnis and Shi'i have to do with a political dispute over the succession to the Prophet and also a doctrinal dispute pertaining to the role of religious leaders.

Because of the persecution of the Shi'ah—a minority in the Islamic world consisting of about 10 percent of all Muslims, but a majority in Iran and Iraq—by the Ba'thist regime of Saddam Hussein and his predecessors, the reaction of Shi'i jurists to the American invasion has been nuanced. However, even those Shi'i jurists who have celebrated the removal of their tormentor, Saddam Hussein, and his government, have couched their approval in pragmatic, not doctrinal or legal terms. Muslim jurists have always condemned as reprehensible wars fought between the Muslims themselves, so it need hardly be stressed that wars commenced by non-Muslims against Muslims would be considered anathema by the jurists of Islamic law.

As pointed out earlier in this chapter, the protection of the interests of the believers, as servants of God, is a categorical imperative that cannot be derogated except in the direst of situations. Thus, for example, if the enemy of the believers is advancing on the camp of the believers and the enemy has captured some believers and is using them as human shields in their advance, is it lawful for the defenders of the camp to fire on the enemy, knowing that the captives would be in the line of fire. This classic example in the seminaries of Muslim jurisprudence sheds light on the supreme value attributed to protecting the life and interests of the Muslim in Islamic law, given that the Muslim has the task of carrying out God's commands. The answer is that it is lawful to fire, even if the captives are killed, on the argument that if the defenders do not defend the community, then not only a few Muslims would be killed, but the entire Muslim community would be destroyed.

Extrapolating, jurists maintain that anything which harms the interests of the believer (provided that the believer is sincere and is in all good conscience seeking to carry out God's commands, of course) is to be avoided. This being the case, it is almost impossible for a jurist, whether Sunni or Shi'i, to endorse an invasion of a Muslim country by non-Muslim foreign attackers.[11] For such an invasion inevitably puts at risk the lives not merely of a few Muslims but thousands of them. Given that the Muslim community of Iraq, though its leaders were treated harshly by the Saddam Hussein regime, was never in danger of extermination, then what could be the doctrinal or legal justification for a Muslim jurist finding in favor of the foreign attackers?

On the historical record, one hardly finds a single case in Islamic law and Islamic history in which Muslim jurists generally endorsed an attack on a Muslim country by non-Muslim forces. This includes Shi'i jurists. For example, when the British invaded Iraq and forced their Mandate over that country after World War I, a massive uprising occurred, with especially heavy resistance in the regions south of Baghdad (historically, the region where Shi'ah were and still are concentrated in the country). This uprising occurred despite the fact that the Ottoman empire, which was ruled by Sunni leaders and controlled Iraq prior to 1918, had pursued policies in the Shi'i regions that had been resented by the Shi'ah.

An interesting situation developed in neighboring Afghanistan in the aftermath of the attacks on the World Trade Center in New York City and the Pentagon in Washington, DC on September 11, 2001. Here, the question arose as to the legality of U.S. forces invading Afghanistan, a Muslim society whose state was under the control of the Taliban. That regime was believed to be knowingly shielding the suspected planner of those attacks, Osama bin Laden, a Saudi expatriate construction engineer who had moved to Afghanistan. In this case, Muslim jurists were divided, with some arguing that the Unites States had no right to attack because it would inevitably threaten the lives of innocent civilians. But others, including influential jurists such as the Shaykh al-Azhar, Sunni Islam's most important mosque and university outside the Grand Mosque in Mecca and the Prophet's mosque in Medina, maintained that the attacks in New York and Washington were violations of Islamic law on the sanctity of human life, including the lives of nonbelievers.

One jurist, Yusuf al-Qaradawi, an Egyptian expatriate living in the United Arab Emirates, issued an authoritative opinion (*fatwa*) in response to questions posed to him by Muslims in the U.S. armed forces. This came in the immediate aftermath of the attacks on September 11. The questions dealt with whether or not it was licit for them to participate in the attack on Afghanistan, a Muslim country. Qaradawi's response was that it was legal for them to fight the Taliban if that regime did not agree to expel bin Laden, whom he labeled an unbeliever (*kafir*) from Afghanistan or to deliver him into the custody of the United States. The reasoning upon which Qaradawi based his ruling was public interest (*maslahah*).[12] He acknowledged that innocent Afghan civilians might be killed but held that the greater interest of defending the reputation of Islamic law supervened concerns over the loss of individual Muslim lives. Collaterally, he ruled that other Muslim states should not participate in the attack on Afghanistan.

However, such an opinion begs the question. Legal defense of an attack on the Pentagon and even the World Trade Center (a financial, rather than a military target) might be given under Islamic law, especially the school of al-Shafi'i, if it could be shown that American military and financial resources constituted a dire threat to Islam. Osama bin Laden himself was persuaded that not only was Islam under threat from Western capitalism and military power but even from the transmittal of what he considers to be uniform Western cultural values through the movies, television, books, and other forms of transmission. Though not trained and hence not qualified to issue legal opinions, bin Laden did not hesitate to issue *fatawa* authorizing attacks on America and Americans. By contrast, most responsible Muslim jurists hold that such an extreme interpretation of what constitutes a threat to the interests of the Muslims could not be derived from the writings of the classical schools of jurisprudence.

At any rate, in Muslim eyes, the situation in Iraq differs from that in Afghanistan. In the case of Iraq, the American and British governments maintained that they had to attack Iraq because the Iraqi government constituted a "grave and immediate threat" to them. No evidence has arisen to justify this claim in the eyes of the American and British people themselves, much less to Muslims. And, indeed, the justification for the American actions that are now emanating from official quarters in Washington and London are much reduced and amount to the argument that the Iraqi people are better off without Saddam Hussein and that, somehow, the world is a "safer place" now that he is gone. Muslim jurists reject such arguments as tantamount to a license to remove leaders in the Muslim world whenever the great powers feel that those leaders should be removed. This, maintain the jurists, is an open invitation to permit attacks, which threaten the lives of Muslims, whenever non-Muslims believe such attacks advance their interests.

Shi'i jurists, such as Ali al-Sistani and Muhammad Baqir al-Hakim have privately maintained that it is a good thing that Saddam Hussein was overthrown, but they have rued the fact that it took the military forces of non-Muslim governments to accomplish this. Meanwhile, they are urging a rapid transfer of authority to the Iraqis and will look very closely at the drafts of the constitution that the occupation authorities favor; the contracts that have been and will be awarded by agencies appointed by the occupation authorities to Western, and especially American, companies for the reconstruction and development of Iraq's economy and resources; and the electoral law that the occupation authorities favor. In each of these three domains, Shi'i jurists are suspicious that the intent is to restrict the power of the Shi'i community, even though that community represents approximately 60 percent of the country's population. Heightening their suspicions was the explicit statement by the former U.S. Civil Administrator in Iraq, Paul Bremer, that the United States will not permit a constitution for the country that is based on the *shari'ah,* or Islamic law.[13] From their perspective, this is a matter that outsiders cannot decide but must be determined by the Iraqi people themselves.

CONCLUSIONS

While the U.S.-led attack on Iraq in March 2003 proved popular in the United States and remained so for sometime, eventually public opinion has evolved to the point that almost a year later close to half the population believed that the war should not have been launched and by 2006 60+ percent believed that it had been a mistake to invade Iraq. In the Muslim world, the overwhelming sentiment among informed publics and Muslim jurists has been that the war was unjust. Among regime leaders, unhappiness over the implications of the war for their own rule and for Muslim solidarity has been tempered by relief that the war was short and that Saddam Hussein was overthrown, however, the costs have been high. Thus, estimates of Iraqi civilian casualties that ran into the neighborhood of 10,000 about 1 year into the war[14] and 4 years into the war above 60,000,[15] cannot be welcomed by the leaders of the mainly narrowly based governments in the Islamic world, especially when compared to the numbers of U.S. and British soldiers killed in the war and afterwards (about 550–600 in the first year but, in late 2006 estimated at significantly more than 3,000).

While no one can state with assurance how the occupation will continue to operate or what its consequences for Iraq and the region will be in the short and long terms, it is certain that the war has created a new situation on the ground. Whether an independent Kurdish state might emerge that could prove a powerful magnet for Kurds living in Turkey, Iran, Syria, and the Caucasus is unclear, but it can neither be ruled out nor can it be maintained that a Shi'i-dominated Iraq might emerge from the aftermath of the invasion that could resemble the Islamic Republic of Iran. Neither of these developments would, most likely, meet with the approval of the governments of the United States or the United Kingdom. The considered opinion seems to be that Muslim perspectives of the invasion will continue to be extremely negative into the foreseeable future. Whether they improve in the longer run will depend a great deal on the exit strategies and conduct of the occupation forces in the coming months, as well as the evolution of such regional issues as the Palestinian–Israel conflict.

NOTES

1. The best treatment on *jihad* in English is Rudolph Peters, *Islam and Colonialism: The Doctrine of Jihad in Islamic History* (The Hague: Mouton, 1979); see also Peters, trans. and annotator, Jihad in Medieval and Modern Islam: The Chapter on Jihad from Averroes' legal handbook, Bidayat al-Mujtahid and the Treatise on the Koran and Fighting by the Late Shaykh al-Azhar, Mahmud Shaltut (Leiden: E.J. Brill, 1977).

2. This was effectively the high point, since public opinion within Iraq has greatly deteriorated over time as the insurgency and violence has reached levels compared with civil war. See Voices from Iraq 2007: Ebbing Hope in a Landscape of Loss: National Survey of Iraq, abc news, March 19, 2007, http://abcnews.go.com/us/story?id=2954716&page=1.

3. Abdel-Moneim Said, "From Pulse to Poll," *al-Ahram Weekly,* October 30–November 5, 2003, http://weekly.ahram.org.eg/2003/662/op40.htm.

4. Carnegie Endowment for International Peace, Arab Reform Bulletin, I: November 5, 2003, http://www.ceip.org/files/Publications/ARB-11-15.asp?from=pubtype#polls. The ARB is a publication of the Carnegie Endowment, and this particular number was a Special Issue on Iraq.

5. Ibid.

6. The findings were released on line on March 15, 2004. The poll was cosponsored by ABC, the German Broadcasting Network ARD, the BBC and the NHK in Japan, with sampling and field work by Oxford Research International, Oxford, UK. http://abcnews.go.com/images/pdf/949a1 Iraqpoll.pdf.

7. James Maritone, "US Foreign Policy Creates Animosity Toward Americans in Muslim World," Voice of America, October 27, 2003.

8. L. Carl Brown, *The International Relations of the Middle East* (Princeton, NJ: Princeton University Press, 1984), 4–5.

9. Martone, "US Foreign Policy Creates Animosity Toward Americans in the Muslim World," Voice of America, Cairo, October 27, 2003, 17:52 UTC (Coordinated Universal Time).

10. United States Department of Defense, Office of the Undersecretary of Defense for Acquisition, Technology and Logistics, Defense Science Board, *Report of the Defense Science Board Task Force on Strategic Communication,* Washington, DC, September 2004, 40.

11. On the other hand, a Muslim state could depend upon the support of a non-Muslim state in the face of a determined anti-Muslim enemy. Thus, the Ottoman Empire, in the Crimean War (1853–1856) willingly accepted British, and later, French support to fight the Russians, who were seeking to project their power in Ottoman domains by demanding the open-ended right to protect the interests of certain Greek Orthodox Christians. Accepting support from nonbelievers, provided

the nonbelievers offering that support were true in that support, certainly has precedents under Islamic views of foreign relations and international law.

12. *Maslahah* had been a lapsed concept in Islamic law for many centuries between 1100 and 1900. It is usually translated as "interest" or "public interest." Qaradawi's argument was that the attacks on the WTC and Pentagon had harmed the interests of the Muslims and thus of Islam because they violated long-standing norms in Islamic law of "do no harm" if others are not directly attacking you. The issue reverts to the discussion earlier in this paper about interpretations of *jihad* according to the jurists of the four schools of Islamic law.

13. Edith M. Lederer, "Iraq Council May Miss Deadline," Associated Press, February 24, 2004.

14. See www.iraqbodycount.net for an estimate ranging from a minimum of 8,249 to a maximum of 10,093. These estimates are generated by a private group located in London whose Web site address is www.iraqbodycount.org. It describes itself as "a human security project to Iraq resulting from military actions by the USA and its allies in 2003."

15. Ibid., this may be regarded as a conservative estimate. In late 2006, at the high end, there was an estimate of circa 600,000 by an American–Iraqi report published by the British medical journal, *Lancet,* The *New York Times,* October 11, 2006.

CHAPTER 3

Contested Morality in U.S. Foreign Policy

JANICE LOVE

This chapter addresses the debate among U.S. Christian leaders over the morality of the United States' March 2003 invasion of Iraq in the context of two larger scholarly foreign policy discussions. The first involves the nature and understanding of American power in the world. The second involves contending perspectives on where the current U.S. government's war against terrorism fits into the long-term path of American foreign policy. This assessment should contribute substantially to understanding contentious arguments over the legitimacy, or lack thereof, of the U.S. government's actions in Iraq, and the war on terrorism more generally.

Our ultimate conclusion is that, in international relations theory terms, the Iraq conflict represents the U.S. government's apparent choice for hard over soft power. When governments choose to use hard power as the primary means of exercising influence, they strive to harness a sufficient stock of soft power, too, so that their actions will be widely perceived as legitimate. Religion is an important dimension of soft power, and governments often seek the blessings of religious leaders to help legitimize the use of hard power.

In the case of this war, however, there is a split within the U.S. Christian community. The vast majority of church leaders representing historic, mainline Protestant and Catholic traditions, claim that the U.S. government's choice to go to war and its prosecution of the war fail to meet the criteria of a just war contained in the just war doctrine. These U.S. leaders have overwhelming support from their denominational affiliates abroad, including the late Pope John Paul II. In contrast, Christian leaders from the Southern Baptist Church and prominent U.S. televangelists set aside the multidimensional and more complex historic just war doctrine in favor of applying one particular criterion adapted from the just war theory. They argue that the U.S. government, a legitimate political authority blessed by God to exercise Christian leadership in world affairs, chose a just course of action in prosecuting the Iraq war. These leaders' endorsement of the war added soft power to the government's exercise of hard power.

THE HARD VERSUS SOFT POWER DEBATE IN INTERNATIONAL RELATIONS THEORY

Since World War II, the concept of power has been at the center of the study of international relations. In general, most scholars would agree that power is the ability of political actors to achieve their goals. Packed into this assertion is a distinction between the two aspects of power: *capabilities,* the resources an actor directly controls; and *influence,* the actor's ability to change the values or behavior of another political player. More conservative analysts, the *Realists,* usually presume that capability causes influence, and consequently consider that little meaningful differentiation can be made between the two. More liberal scholars, the *Pluralists,* argue that interactions among political players can affect the conversion of capabilities into influence. Therefore, the distinction potentially makes a big difference.[1]

Building on Pluralist assumptions, Joseph Nye[2] revises and relabels these distinctions to analyze U.S. foreign policy. In his terms, capability becomes a sophisticated notion of *hard power,* while a multidimensional concept of *soft power* builds on and embellishes the idea of influence. As for definitions, hard power on the whole rests "on inducements (carrots) or threats (sticks)." This is a more material base.[3] The United States has a large arsenal of both carrots and sticks. In contrasts to this notion, soft power "co-opts people rather than coerces them," and thereby gets them to do what you want.[4] Therefore, the basis for soft power rests more in ideas than on material incentives, either of positive or negative kinds.

Building on Machiavelli's view of power as a mixture of coercion and consent, Gramsci wrote extensively about the moral, political, and cultural values of a dominant group becoming so widely dispersed that less powerful or even subordinate groups incorporate them as unquestioned common sense.[5] In distinguishing soft power from the older notion of influence, Nye argues that soft power is only one form of influence, and that it is "more than persuasion...It is the ability to entice and attract. And attraction often leads to acquiescence or imitation." Soft power inspires "the dreams and desires of others..."[6]

Typical instruments of soft power include popular culture embodied, for example, in telecommunications such as film or television, as well as in education and cultural exchange. As with hard power, governments do not control all these instruments, but in contrast to governments' considerable command of a large amount and wide array of instruments of hard power, nonstate actors often have greater access to soft power. Furthermore, in the second half of the twentieth century, nongovernmental organizations and transnational social movements have become remarkably adept at using soft power to their advantage. Again, following Nye, in an information age, countries increasing their soft power are likely to be those with a culture closer to prevailing global norms; access to multiple channels of communication in which they can frame the issues; and credibility based on their domestic and international performance.[7] As with capability and influence, the close relationships between hard and soft power can be significant, and they often reinforce each other. Both can be central to achieving an actor's goals. "But," warns Nye, "soft power is not simply the reflection of hard power."[8]

Nye uses the concepts of hard and soft power to analyze the larger frameworks of foreign policy choices facing the U.S. government and society. His terms will be used in this chapter more narrowly to examine contentious claims about the morality of the Iraq War. This examination, however, needs to be set in the wider context of two contemporary and contending views of the history of U.S. foreign policy.

CONTENDING PERSPECTIVES ON U.S. FOREIGN POLICY: BENEVOLENT DOMINATION VERSUS IMPERIALISM

Since the end of the Cold War, analysts have sought to define the next challenge to America's physical security and basic social, political, and economic values in grand, overarching perspectives. Samuel Huntington's (1996) famous assertion of a "clash of civilizations" provided one possibility of "the West against the Rest," whereas Robert Kaplan suggested that the crucial test would be massive chaos, i.e., an anarchic world with disintegrating nation-states, warring ethnic groups, overpopulation, and struggles over increasingly scarce resources.[9]

The 9/11 attacks jolted everyone, and for those searching for a way to characterize security problems in a post–Cold War world, a new clarity emerged. In the wake of the 9/11 attacks, *New York Times* columnist Thomas Friedman popularized a particular version of the history of large-scale challenges to the United States and its allies in the twentieth and twenty-first centuries. Fascism arose in the first half of the twentieth century and was defeated by nations that embraced freedom and democracy. Then communism reared up menacingly in the second half of the century, only to implode at century's end due to its inability to compete effectively with national systems of democracy and capitalism backed by large, credible military arsenals. The events of 9/11, Friedman argues, demonstrated that terrorism, under girded by religious extremism, constitutes the new mega-threat to freedom and democracy in the new era.[10]

From this point of view, even if not all analysts would agree with Friedman's particular telling of the big trends of history, the United States had an *obligation* to invade Iraq. This duty arose not primarily from the need to protect the physical security of our homeland, but rather in the long term to exercise "the revolutionary side of U.S. power," to instill a model of freedom and democracy in a region that has little experience of such. This makes the Iraq war, in Friedman's language, a war of choice, not necessity; a war "to unleash a process of reform in the Arab-Muslim region that will help it embrace modernity and make it less angry and more at ease with the world...." Our job, he says, "is to build a regime in Iraq that won't produce any more battered human skulls."[11] This grand mission, a war without end carried out by a "benign U.S. hegemon," may not be finished in his lifetime, he reports, or even that of his children. It is a "war for what America stands for."[12]

This grand perspective finds no fault in characterizing the United States as imperial or hegemonic in its post–Cold War domination of world affairs. American domination is a good thing for infusing other nations and cultures with the values of democracy and religious liberty. The second grand perspective, however, orients its understanding of U.S. foreign policy in the twentieth and twenty-first centuries as part of a larger project of imperial aspirations that began in the nineteenth century.[13]

Inspired in part by the British and other European empires, U.S. political leaders actively began pursuing a substantial American presence in Asia and Latin America in the late nineteenth century. This vision has been well documented by prominent historians and students of foreign policy.[14] One of the early emblematic and specific policy manifestations was "supple and highly innovative." For example, the United States demanded an open door policy with China in 1899. The United States would honor China's territorial integrity if allowed the same privileges granted to European powers and Japan, i.e., a foothold from which to access Chinese markets. American policymakers' expectations were that U.S. companies and others would "reap more than their fair share of the benefits. An ostensibly level playing field actually tilted in favor of American enterprise.

In short, the policy of the open door was 'a classic strategy of non-colonial imperial expansion.'"[15] And it applied remarkably well to other regions of the world, too.[16]

From this perspective, World War I became a "crusade to graft American values onto the entire world and to thwart all others—such as Lenin—who fancied themselves engaged in an analogous undertaking," with any notion of isolationism being only a "legend."[17] Meanwhile, also in the early decades of the century, U.S. military incursions repeatedly propped up authoritarian dictators in Latin America and the Caribbean.

After World War II, the United States continued to pursue open doors, leading the Western world and the global economy by default, a state of affairs that many labeled "Pax Americana." By the 1970s, West European and Japanese economic prowess, built on the foundation of their American-assisted post–war recovery, gave rise to the need for U.S. leadership in a coordinated, more multilateral approach to global affairs that exercised open door policies through international financial institutions like the International Monetary Fund, the World Bank, and the Paris Club. Moreover, the United States' military guarantee of West European and Japanese security against the possible threat of Soviet aggression provided all these big economic and political players strong incentives to work together under U.S. leadership. Yet, a number of U.S.-backed coups d'etat in support of "third world" dictators as well as the Vietnam War demonstrated a readiness to use military force to preserve global influence, especially in competition with another large imperial presence in the world, the USSR.

By 1991, the dissolution of the USSR and the disintegration of its military might brought an end to the Cold War. Russia as well as most of its former satellites became open for American commercial influence, too. And as indicated by Nye, the United States began to enjoy a very rare position in world history. No other nation comes close currently to exercising this country's military, economic, political, and cultural power.

Many American policymakers and citizens hold fast to the belief that the United States is a reluctant imperial power and that the nation's hegemonic reign is benign. Analysts who view the U.S. imperial impulse as stretching back more than a century would disagree, however, as do many people in various parts of the world subjected to the blunt instruments of U.S. military or economic might. In this context, from this perspective, the March 2003 invasion of Iraq appears to be one more imperial attempt at opening doors to further U.S. economic, military, political, and cultural interests, rather than the grand experiment of a benevolent hegemon undertaking democratic nation building. The imperial perspective on American foreign policy notes that among the scores of U.S. overt and covert military invasions or interventions, only two resulted in the implementation of democratic capitalism: Germany and Japan. The outcome in Iraq, if anything other than chaos, they claim, is more likely to resemble Cuba in 1898 or 1906, Nicaragua beginning in 1909, Haiti beginning in 1914, Guatemala or Iran in 1954, the Congo in 1960, Vietnam in the early 1960s, Chile in 1973, or other such instances where the consequences of U.S. military involvement undercut or crushed the possibility of budding democratic impulses.

U.S. CHRISTIAN LEADERS AND THEIR FOREIGN POLICY PERSPECTIVES

Although not entirely divorced from hard power, religion, moral philosophy, and ideology feature soft power—as does law. These potent societal sources of influence often provide important foundations for national or wider cultures, and thus can implicitly or explicitly enhance or undermine a government's exercise of power. Governments often recognize the significance of such sources of soft power by seeking assistance and public blessings from religious leaders or others with moral or ideological legitimacy.

The missionary expansion of Christianity that anticipated and accompanied imperial conquest by European powers and the United States has its own history about which much is written. Christian missions often played the paradoxical role of providing soft power for sanctioning the expansion of empires while at the same time humanizing them. A famous African adage, for example, states: "When the missionaries came, Whites had the bible and we had the land. Now we have the bible and the Whites have the land."

When the colonies of Africa, Asia, and Latin America sought their independence, most Protestant missions also pursued freedom from ecclesial colonialism, that is, separated their governance from their parent churches in the West. Thus Anglicans, Methodist, Presbyterians, Baptists, Lutherans, etc. in these various continents became churches in their own right, no longer controlled, for example, by the English Anglicans, the German Lutherans, or the U.S. Methodists, Presbyterians, or Baptists. These newly independent leaders often spoke with different interests in and understandings of world affairs. Among Catholics, Vatican II, convened by Pope John XXIII, called on the faithful worldwide to use their convictions to address the problems of the world. Furthermore, the rise of liberation theologies out of Latin America, Asia, and Africa in the 1960s and 1970s challenged both Protestant and Catholic Christians in rich countries to examine their previous support for or complicity in systems of colonial and neocolonial domination, the racism embedded explicitly or implicitly in their doctrines, and their use of resources in a world of extreme poverty. Theologians from the so-called third world also began to offer new insights in the interpretation of sacred scripture, the articulation of doctrine, and practices of the faith. Moreover, these changes across the world unfolded at the same time that the civil rights movement challenged racially divided Christian churches at home.[18]

The two broad and contending historical perspectives on the history of U.S. foreign policy, together with shifts globally within Christendom and in secular world affairs, had a profound influence on U.S. church leaders. In the first half of the twentieth century, most readily (but not uncritically) believed the United States to be a benevolent hegemon. Many believed that American military, economic, and political international engagement made the world safer for democracy and human well-being. In the second half of the century, however, the challenges articulated by theologians from the so-called third world, combined with deep domestic unrest over the Vietnam War and other military interventions, brought new insights and understandings for church leaders. They now had to function in worldwide Christian arenas where many church leaders from other parts of the globe criticized the United States as an oppressive imperial power. Whether or not American church leaders agreed with this perspective, they could not ignore it.

Vietnam provided the watershed to shift many U.S. church leaders' perspective. Most began to take official stands against the Vietnam War reluctantly and fairly late. For example, the U.S. Conference of Catholic Bishops issued a 1966 statement concluding that the United States' prosecution of the war was reasonable. By 1968, their enthusiasm had officially waned, but only by 1971 did they explicitly call for an immediate halt to U.S. military engagement in Southeast Asia. Nevertheless, Vietnam was a major turning point in their understanding of the United States and world affairs. Thereafter most leaders of the Catholic and mainline Protestant churches have called fairly consistently for restraint in the use of American military force to address international problems, giving strong preference to conciliation and negotiation.[19] Yet, with often carefully considered nuance, many continued to embrace nonmilitary U.S. foreign policies that promoted causes such as human rights, debt relief, and economic development. If judged by their public pronouncements below, most can be characterized as multilateralists rather than unilateralists. Nevertheless, their relative reticence in recent decades to deploy their soft power to bless the use of force is noteworthy.

By contrast, the NCR (New Christian Right), which arose in force in the 1970s, on the whole endorses the use of military might to achieve U.S. foreign policy goals. The NCR consists of organizations headed by televangelists like Pat Robertson, Jerry Falwell, Bob Jones II, and Franklin Graham who find unity in their commitment to change laws and government structures in light of their understanding of the biblical ideal. For much of the twentieth century, these conservative evangelical and fundamentalist Protestants on the whole shunned political engagement. Rapid social changes during the 1960s, mainline religious opposition to the Vietnam War, and the perceived threat of secular humanism transformed them into activists. As Charles Kimball notes "(t)he literature and rhetoric of groups in the New Religious Right reveal nostalgia for an ideal time that has been lost—usually connected somehow with the founders of the country—and warnings about the danger awaiting this nation if it continues to turn its back on God."[20]

These leaders' largest political mobilizations began in the 1980s and continued through the early 1990s. They articulated a clear theological position: God ordained the United States to be a Christian nation, a city on the hill, a light to the nations. Often labeled Dominion or Reconstruction Theology,[21] this understanding of the faith asserts "that Christianity must reassert the dominion of God over all things, including secular politics and society."[22] Followers seek "to remove the political and institutional barriers to God's law in order to impose the rule of God's law."[23] As Karen Armstrong describes it "God gave Adam and later Noah the task of subduing the world. Christians have inherited this mandate and they have the responsibility of imposing Jesus' rule on earth before the Second Coming of Christ."[24]

This theology obviously embraces the perspective that the U.S. domination in world affairs as well as the government's foreign policy decisions are benevolent, but followers push further. America has an obligation to, and blessings from God to spread U.S. influence and that of the Christian faith worldwide. For example, this perspective most steadfastly condemned any attempts at rapprochement with the USSR during the Cold War. Leaders of this persuasion have been invited to the White House regularly under the Nixon, Reagan, and second Bush administrations. Interestingly, the primary spiritual adviser to President George H.W. Bush was Archbishop Edmond Browning, the presiding bishop of the Episcopal Church. During the 1991 Gulf War, in keeping with similar expressions by other mainline religious leaders, Archbishop Browning regularly, both in private and in public, challenged the President's decision to mobilize the military because he and others believed that all other options had not yet been exhausted (one of the criteria for a just war).

In sum, as mainline Catholic and Protestant church leaders in the late twentieth century became more critical of U.S. foreign policy, particularly as exercised through military means, they became less welcome to provide counsel to the executive branch. Moreover, they became increasingly reluctant to lend their considerable stock of soft power to the military campaigns and foreign policy decisions that lacked moral legitimacy from their perspective. Therefore, since the 1970s, Presidents and their administrations, with some exceptions, have relied more on the religious right not only for counsel, but also for blessing their decisions to go to war or to intervene militarily in other nations. Thus, in recent decades, the U.S. government's hard power has been increasingly augmented with religiously legitimizing soft power from the religious right.

These overall trends of contending perspectives on U.S. foreign policy as well as in church leaders' reactions to them provide the backdrop against which to understand divergent Christian positions on the morality of the Iraq war. Prior to discussing the specifics of this debate, however, we review the spectrum of traditional Christian ethical positions on war.

CHRISTIAN PERSPECTIVES ON WAR

Three traditions, with some noteworthy variations, dominate Christian ethical perspectives on war. These are the *pacifist, crusade,* and *just war* traditions. The oldest is the pacifist.

Most scholars agree that in the whole Christ's teaching and example reinforce a message that violence and war are wrong. For the first three to four centuries, the early church adhered to pacifism, which meant opposition to all killing, military service, and warfare. In addition to being true to Jesus' own witness, a range of reasons explains this stance. They included generally the nonpolitical orientation of church life within the Roman Empire and an expectation of a near-term apocalypse. This perspective declined with the Constantinian establishment of Christianity in the fourth century, but it survived nonetheless to be embraced by a number of prominent Christian leaders including Francis of Assisi, Erasmus of Rotterdam (fifteenth and sixteenth centuries), and in the twentieth century, Martin Luther King, Jr. The historic peace churches, including the Mennonites, the Church of the Brethren, and the Society of Friends (Quakers) continue to adhere to pacifism.

Early in the fourth century, Constantine adopted Christianity and linked it to the state. Drawing on Plato and Cicero, Augustine (fourth and fifth centuries) outlined the beginnings of the just war theory, which evolved across the medieval and modern periods, and is explored more fully in a parallel chapter. A distinction is usually made between the just resort to war (*jus ad bellum*) and just conduct in war (*jus in bello*). The six most common principles of *jus ad bellum* are: (1) just cause (in response to an aggressive attack or serious threat of evil), (2) just intent (not to devastate another nation totally or seek self-aggrandizement, but to restore peace with justice), (3) limited objectives (with the values preserved through force being proportionate to those sacrificed through force), (4) last resort (exhausting all possibilities of peaceful settlement prior to pursuing war), (5) legitimate authority (a properly constituted government), and (6) reasonable hope of success. The two main principles of *jus in bello* are: (1) discrimination (respecting and protecting the lives of noncombatants, and committing no atrocities, reprisals, looting, or wanton violence) and (2) proportionality (inflicting damage that is strictly proportionate to the ends sought, i.e., the war's harm must not exceed the war's good).[25]

In the 1960s and 1970s, liberation theology attempted to transform this tradition into one that would support *just* revolutions. This variation essentially challenged the criterion of legitimate authority. Since so many brutal and authoritarian governments in so many places had no popular legitimacy, any use of force against regime opponents could not be judged to appropriately within the standard. In contrast, however, if insurgents had broad and deep support, they could be considered a legitimate authority allowed to consider exercising the use of military force.

Nonetheless, just war teachings, including most variations on this tradition, and pacifism seek to prevent war. They presume that peace is better than war. If war cannot be avoided, however, a just war ethic seeks to restrict and reduce its horrors. Although begun by the Greeks and refined by Christian theologians, principles similar to those from the just war doctrine can be found in many religions. They now have also become partially embodied in secular international humanitarian law.

A third tradition within Christianity is that of the crusade where Christians wield the sword as a matter of faith. The violent savagery of the early crusades beginning in 1095 has modern echoes among religious extremists today, but virtually all churches and prominent religious leaders reject this option.[26]

The Roman Catholic Church formalized and continues to adhere to the just war tradition. In its thirty-six member churches, the NCCCUSA (National Council of Churches of Christ in the USA) gathers under one ecumenical umbrella most mainline Protestant, Anglican, and Orthodox member denominations in the country. Although differences exist among them, most members of the NCCCUSA also adhere to some variation of just war teachings, as do most Christians around the world. Thus, most churches adhere to the belief that under very limited, rigorously, and prayerfully considered conditions, Christians might use violence. A few NCCCUSA members, however, like their counterparts in other countries, come from the historic peace church tradition that continues to uphold pacifism as a faithful witness.

As noted earlier, when commenting on or giving advice to the U.S. government in its exercise of foreign policy, these mainline denominations, the Roman Catholic Church, and the NCCCUSA have, on the whole, called for restraint in the use of military force, especially since the Vietnam era. Church leaders regularly draw attention to the intimate connection between means and ends, a principal tenet of both just war teachings and of pacifism. Achieving just and peaceful ends becomes increasingly difficult to accomplish through the use of violent means. Furthermore, church leaders often lift up the need for systems of common security that safeguard the well-being of all people everywhere. They assert that the safety and success of the United States can only be achieved and sustained through relationships of reciprocity that secure justice and freedom for all peoples and nations.

CHURCHES' RESPONSES TO THE 2003 INVASION OF IRAQ

In the months leading up to the March 2003 U.S. invasion of Iraq, most of the NCCCUSA member churches called on the U.S. government to continue to seek alternatives to war. They repeatedly expressed the judgment that U.S. decision-makers had not yet exhausted all policy options short of declaring war. The NCCCUSA itself issued statements and drew together leaders of other faith traditions to give a united witness for peace both from within the mainline Christian community and across religions. The U.S. Conference of Catholic Bishops carefully compared the government's rationale for the Iraq war to the criteria enunciated by the just war doctrine. They concluded that this war did not meet these standards and called on world leaders to step back from the brink to "work for a peace that is just and enduring."[27] All churches called for prayers for American leaders, world leaders, and all the people standing in harm's way. The WCCs (World Council of Churches), a fellowship of about 340 Protestant, Anglican, and Orthodox churches from more than 100 countries, made similar statements, as did the Pope John Paul II on behalf of the Roman Catholic Church worldwide. Rarely have Christian churches the world over been so united in their call for the pursuit of a more peaceful and just alternative to a particular war.[28]

Yet, some prominent Christian leaders in the United States disagreed. Officials of the Southern Baptist Convention, for example, like the prominent televangelists (Pat Robertson, Jerry Fallwell, and Bob Jones II), argued that a legitimate political authority was pursuing a just cause, using war as a last resort. This particular adaptation of just war theory emphasizes the criterion of legitimate authority. It trumps all the others due its grounding in Paul's admonition in Romans 13:1. "Let every person be subject to the governing authorities; for there is no authority except from God, and those authorities that exist have been instituted by God." According to NCR leaders' application of just war principles and their proclivity to understand God to be blessing American hegemony in world affairs, the war against Iraq became an unpleasant but necessary duty of a Christian nation.[29]

Others, like Jean Bethke Elshtain, argued in favor of the war against Iraq on similar but somewhat different grounds. Elshtain and a number of other Christians have for more than a decade expressed the need to forge a twenty-first century standard for humanitarian intervention. When should governments violate the sovereignty of a particular nation and intervene militarily to save lives in places plagued by massive injustice, gross violations of human rights, or campaigns of ethnic cleansing? Many people of good will the world over believe that situations like Bosnia, Kosovo, and Rwanda demonstrated the need to intervene with military force when helpless populations face dire peril. Arguing that America, as the world's sole superpower bears an awesome but necessary burden in a violent world, Elshtain supported the U.S. government's invasion to remove the oppressive regime of Saddam Hussein. The implicit comparison was to how the U.S. military under the Clinton administration had bombed Serbia when its government threatened ethnic cleansing in Kosovo. Furthermore, she attacked mainline Christian leaders for opposing the Iraq war by accusing them of wearing ideological blinders inherited from their earlier, youthful resistance to the Vietnam War. Her analysis seemed to rule out any possibility of a genuine conviction that this particular war fell far short of the classical criteria of a just war.[30]

The WCCs also took up the question of ethical standards for humanitarian intervention. Like Elshtain, this global ecumenical organization expressed the need for guidance on when and how the community of nations should intervene to respond to ominous circumstances within particular countries. Although still in the process of studying the issue, the WCC has repeatedly emphasized the need to uphold the principles of international law. In order to be legitimate and legal, and thereby undergirded with soft power, any intervention for the protection of peace, security, and human rights must be decided and implemented multilaterally, not by individual governments working unilaterally. From the WCC's point of view, the world's common security is best upheld, and the full implementation of human rights everywhere is best secured, through use of mutually agreed, longstanding multilateral processes of pursuing peace with justice for all nations, not just one or a few. If one or more governments, like the United States, find multilateral institutions like the United Nations to be less than perfect instruments for pursuing security and human rights, work to reform them rather than to sideline or undermine them, the WCC urges.[31]

To address these kinds of complex issues and the question of how to create peace and justice in the long term, in 1999, the NCCCUSA adopted a policy statement, "Pillars of Peace for the 21st Century." Rather than repeating the criteria for resorting to violence, this statement approaches the dilemma more positively and proactively by examining comprehensively the conditions that make for security and attainment of human rights. The document provides an important framework within which to ponder America's role in the world.[32] The statement reads, in part:

> Peace rooted in justice requires increased political collaboration and accountability within the United Nations system, among regional bodies, governments, local authorities, peoples' organizations, and global economic structures to seek the common good and equality for all. . .

Peace rooted in justice requires the participation of vulnerable and marginalized groups, seeking to promote justice and peace, in those mechanisms capable of redressing the causes and consequences of injustice and oppression.

Peace rooted in justice requires the nurturing of a culture of peace in homes, communities, religious institutions, nations and across the world; the use of non-violent means of resolving conflict; appropriate systems of common security; and the end of the unrestrained production, sale and use of weapons worldwide.

Peace rooted in justice requires respect for the inherent dignity of all persons and the recognition, protection and implementation of the principles of the International Bill of Human Rights, so that communities and individuals may claim and enjoy their universal, indivisible and inalienable rights...

Others also have sought to provide an alternative to just war theory and pacifism. One group of theologians and conflict resolution specialists came up with a list of ten key guidelines for pursuing peace with justice:

1. Support nonviolent direct action. 2. Take independent initiatives to reduce threat. 3. Use cooperative conflict resolution. 4. Acknowledge responsibility for conflict and injustice and seek repentance and forgiveness. 5. Advance democracy, human rights, and religious liberty. 6. Foster just and sustainable economic development. 7. Work with emerging cooperative forces in the international system. 8. Strengthen the United Nations and international efforts for cooperation and human rights. 9. Reduce offensive weapons and weapon trade. 10. Encourage grassroots peacemaking groups and voluntary associations.[33]

Attempts at moving away from debates over just and unjust wars in favor of charting ethical principles in order to undercut violence are still a work in progress. They do not yet pervade Christian doctrines and teachings. It remains to be seen whether they will come to be convincing standards or guidance among church leaders and the Christian community. Only then might they have any impact on larger policy discussions, whenever purveyors of soft power lobby those with access to large arsenals of hard power. At present, however, there is more agreement on the validity if not detailed application of just war theory approaches, even while the active search continues for a broader Christian framework more oriented toward conflict resolution or avoidance than the use of force as such in our globally interrelated community.

CONCLUSIONS

The U.S. invasion of Iraq constitutes one of its more controversial foreign policy decisions in recent history. Many allied governments objected, as did their populations. Many adversaries also objected, as did their populations. International organizations such as the United Nations were bypassed when they sought to slow the rush to war. In the face of such substantial opposition, the U.S. government risked much of its stockpile of soft power at the same time that it was mobilizing one of the strongest applications of hard power the world has witnessed in recent decades.

If judged by Nye's indicators of how to increase soft power, the Iraq war may squander the U.S. government's credibility and undercut future attempts to communicate its support for prevailing global norms of liberalism, pluralism, and autonomy through a benevolent hegemony. Many across the world who already believed the United States to be a self-serving and sometimes ruthless imperial power will see the war as confirming their point of view that America had little soft power to spare.

By contrast, the virtually unprecedented display of unity against the war among mainline U.S. Protestant churches, the U.S. Catholic church, national and world ecumenical institutions, and the Vatican more closely fits Nye's indicators of how to build a political actor's reserve of soft power. However, the deep disputes between the NCR and its tele-vangelists on the one hand, with the mainline Christian leaders on the other, display a continuing divide over how America's Christians view the United States' role in the world. This spawns in turn significant differences over when and how to support or undercut a government's exercise of hard power with religious institutions' soft power. The questions stand on the border of religion and politics, religious doctrine, and international relations theory.

NOTES

1. See, more generally, John Baylis and Steve Smith, *The Globalization of World Politics: An Introduction to International Relations* (New York, NY: Oxford University Press, 2001), 378; Charles W. Kegley, Jr. and Eugene R. Wittkopf, *World Politics: Trend and Transformation* (Boston, MA: Bedford/St Martin's, 2001), 457–62.

2. Joseph Nye, *The Paradox of American Power: Why the World's Only Superpower Can't Go It Alone* (New York, NY: Oxford University Press, 2002), 35–36.

3. "In military power, we are the only country with both nuclear weapons and conventional forces with global reach. Our military expenditures are greater than those of the next eight countries combined, and we lead in the information-based 'revolution in military affairs.' Economically, we have a 27 percent share of world product which...was equal to that of the next three countries combined (Japan, Germany, France). We are the home of fifty-nine of the hundred largest companies in the world by market value (compared to thirty-one for Europe and seven for Japan.) Of the *Financial Times'* listing of the 500 largest global companies, 219 were American, 158 European, and 77 Japanese. In direct foreign investment, we invested and received nearly twice as much as the next ranking country (Britain) and accounted for half of the top ten investment banks. American e-commerce was three times that of Europe, and we are the home of the seven of the top ten software vendors. Forty two of the top seventy-five brands were American, as well as nine of the top ten business schools." (ibid., 8).

4. Ibid., 8.

5. Far from being a Marxist, Nye nonetheless asserts that "*Soft power* rests on the ability to set the political agenda in a way that shapes the preferences of others. The ability to establish preferences tends to be associated with intangible power resources such as an attractive culture, ideology, and institutions. Soft power arises in large part from our values expressed in our culture, in the policies we follow inside our country, and in the way we handle ourselves internationally. Like love, [soft power] is hard to measure and to handle, and does not touch everyone, but that does not diminish its importance" (ibid., 9).

6. Ibid., 9.

7. Ibid., 69.

8. For instance, "[t]he Vatican did not lose its soft power when it lost the Papal States in Italy in the nineteenth century. Conversely, the Soviet Union lost much of its soft power after it invaded Hungary and Czechoslovakia..." (ibid., 10).

9. Robert D. Kaplan, *Balkan Ghosts: A Journey Through History* (New York, NY: St. Martin's Press, 1993); Robert D. Kaplan, *The Coming Anarchy: Shattering the Dreams of the Post Cold War* (New York, NY: Random House, 2000); Robert D. Kaplan, *The Ends of the Earth: A Journey to the Frontiers of Anarchy* (New York, NY: Vintage Books, 1996).

10. Thomas Friedman, "The Middle East: An Update on Changing Events" (The Solomon-Tenenbaum Lecture in Jewish Studies, University of South Carolina, Columbia, SC, 2003).

11. Thomas Friedman, "The Meaning of a Skull," *New York Times,* April 27, 2003 and "The War Over the War," *New York Times,* August 3, 2003.

12. Thomas Friedman, "Come the Revolution," *New York Times,* April 2, 2003.

13. Andrew J. Bacevich, *American Empire: The Realities and Consequences of U.S. Diplomacy* (Cambridge, MA: Harvard University Press, 2002); Michael Ignatieff, "Why Are We in Iraq?"

New York Times Magazine, September 7, 2003; Johnson Chalmers, *Blowback: The Costs and Consequences of American Empire* (New York, NY: Henry Holt, 2000); Arundhati Roy, "Confronting Empire" (speech, Porto Alegre, Brazil, January 28, 2003).

14. For an excellent account of the argument, see, for example, Bacevich, *American Empire,* 26 ss. Beginning in the nineteenth century "the weltanschauung guiding American politics was a simple one: 'problems are solved by growth or further expansion'. . . 'a charming but ruthless faith in infinite progress fueled by endless growth' became central to the American way of life. But the closing of the frontier by the 1890s and the onset of severe economic crisis in the same decade obliged Americans to look farther afield. But the United States pursued expansion abroad in a way that reflected particular American interests and values. After a brief, unsatisfactory experiment with old-fashioned empire in the wake of the Spanish-American War, American leaders abandoned efforts to assemble an array of distant possessions as the preferred means of sustaining economic growth. Given the costs of pacification, administration, and defense, colonies offered a poor return on the dollar. In addition, the nation's own revolutionary heritage and its traditional anti-imperial sympathies were at odds with the notion of U.S. soldiers subduing alien populations. The challenge confronting American leaders was to formulate policies that provided the benefits of empire without its burdens. In that regard, what mattered was not ownership or even administrative control but commercial access."

15. Bacevich, *American Empire,* 26.

16. "America's own commitment to openness testifies to its own benign intentions—and therefore justified American exertions on behalf of an open world. . . 'Most imperialists believed that an American empire would be humanitarian, and most humanitarians believed that doing good would be good for business.' The dogma of openness became a component of American ideology, the principle upon which the world should be organized, the basis for a broad national consensus on foreign policy, and a rationale for mustering and employing American power. In essence. . . the open-door policy legitimated 'the endless expansion of the American frontier in the name of self-determination, progress, and peace.'" (Ibid., 26).

17. Ibid., 27.

18. Kenneth D. Wald, *Religion and Politics in the United States,* 5th ed. (Washington, DC: Congressional Quarterly Press, 1997).

19. Ibid., 272–77.

20. Charles Kimball, *When Religion Becomes Evil: Five Warning Signs* (San Francisco, CA: Harper San Francisco, 2002).

21. Some scholars claim Reconstruction Theology to be an extreme form of Dominion Theology. This distinction does not make a substantial difference for the analysis here.

22. Mark Juergensmeyer, *Terror in the Mind of God: The Global Rise of Religious Violence,* 3rd ed. (Berkeley, CA: University of California Press, 2003).

23. Ibid., 118.

24. Karen Armstrong, *The Battle for God* (New York, NY: Ballentine, 2000), 361.

25. Mark R. Amstutz, *International Ethics: Concepts, Theories, and Cases in Global Politics* (Lanham: Rowman & Littlefield, 1999); Terry Nardin and David R. Mapel, eds., *Traditions of International Ethics* (New York, NY: Cambridge University Press, 1992).

26. Juergensmeyer, *Terror in the Mind of God.*

27. See the National Conference of Catholic Bishops' Web site for the full text (usccb.org/bishops/iraq.htm; last accessed December 5, 2004). See also the NCCCUSA Web site for a series of statements made by its governing bodies and interfaith gatherings, as well as program initiatives that promote peace with justice and liturgical resources (ncccusa.org). See also the Web site of your own denomination to discover how it currently and historically has approached the issues of peace and justice.

28. For more information, consult the Web sites for the World Council of Churches (wcc-coe.org) and the Roman Catholic Church (vatican.va/phome_en.htm; last accessed August 28, 2007); see also, Jim Wallis, "Dangerous Religion: George W. Bush's Theology of Empire," *Sojourners Magazine,* September–October 2003.

29. See Art Toalston and Dwayne Hastings, "Land: Military Action Again Iraq Meets Ethical Standards for War," September 9, 2002 (bpnews.net); and Jason Hall, "Fighting a Just War in Iraq," April 2003 (sbclife.net).

30. See different works by Jean Bethke Elshtain, "Thinking about War and Justice," The Religion and Culture Web Forum, May 2003.

31. WCC Central Committee, "The Responsibility to Protect: Ethical and theological Reflections," 2003.

32. See the NCCCUSA Web site for the complete text (ncccusa.org).

33. Quoted in Kimball, *When Religion Becomes Evil,* 184.

PART II

Constitutional and Domestic Law: Structural and Institutional Emphasis

CHAPTER 4

Paradigm Shifts, Executive Power, and the War on Terror

NORMAN C. BAY

The war on terror raises the question of how to balance liberty interests against national security concerns. This is more than just a question of individual rights, for government action may also raise structural issues regarding the horizontal distribution of power among the three branches of federal government, and the vertical distribution of power between the federal government and the states. In examining the war on terror, several themes emerge. First, courts have difficulty in deciding cases that involve national security. For reasons grounded in separation of powers and institutional competency, courts tend to be overly deferential to the President and Congress in times of war.

Second, the war on terror has resulted in an expansion of executive authority. In particular, two paradigm shifts have occurred. The first shift has been the militarization of our response to terrorism. In general, prior to 9/11, the government responded to terrorism through the criminal justice system. Post-9/11, the government viewed terrorism as a military issue, not a law enforcement problem. The second shift has been the centralization of intelligence functions within the executive branch. Two recent Acts of Congress are of particular importance. The Intelligence and Terrorism Prevention Act of 2005 has created a powerful DNI (Director of National Intelligence) who has authority over the entire intelligence community, including both civilian and military agencies.[1] The Patriot Act concurrently lowers the wall between foreign intelligence and domestic law enforcement.[2]

ROLE OF THE COURTS

Since *Marbury v. Madison*,[3] it has been well established that federal courts have the power of judicial review. "It is emphatically the province and duty of the judicial department to say what the law is," Chief Justice Marshall famously declared.[4] Courts can serve as an important check on the other branches of government during the time of war. It is, however, difficult for them to do so. For reasons grounded in separation of powers, courts often have difficulty in deciding cases that involve national security. First, courts will often be deferential to the President in recognition of his constitutional authority in the area of foreign policy and military matters. Second, courts have very real institutional limits that caution restraint when reviewing the actions of the political branches of government. Principles of justiciability, including the political question doctrine, give expression to separation of power concerns. Finally, courts are not immune to the pressure and perceived exigencies of the day.

Courts recognize, as they must, the formidable powers of the President in the area of foreign affairs and national security. Under Article II of the Constitution, the executive power of the United States is vested in the President, who has the duty to "take Care that the Laws be faithfully executed"[5] and to "preserve, protect, and defend the Constitution."[6] The President is the Commander in Chief of the armed forces, receives and appoints ambassadors, and makes treaties with the advice and consent of the Senate. "In this vast external realm, with its important, complicated, delicate, and manifold problems, the President alone has the power to speak or listen as a representative of the nation."[7] As a constitutional matter, respect for and recognition of the President's power counsels judicial restraint in reviewing the legality of executive action in matters involving foreign affairs and national security.

Institutional limits also constrain the courts when reviewing executive action in national security or foreign policy matters. Courts are not well situated to assess threats to national security. Nor may they properly second-guess policy judgments rendered by the political branches. Judges may lack the experience to handle such issues as well as the information that would allow them to make reasoned judgments. The Supreme Court has long recognized its lack of institutional competence to review executive action that relates to foreign affairs:

> The President, both as Commander-in-Chief and as the Nation's organ for foreign affairs, has available intelligence services whose reports neither are not and ought not to be published to the world. It would be intolerable that courts, without the relevant information, should review and perhaps nullify actions of the Executive taken on information properly held secret. Nor can courts sit in camera in order to be taken into executive confidences. But even if courts could require full disclosure, the very nature of executive decisions as to foreign policy is political, not judicial. Such decisions are wholly confided by our Constitution to the political departments of the government, Executive and Legislative. They are delicate, complex, and involve large elements of prophecy. They are and should be undertaken only by those directly responsible to the people whose welfare they advance or imperil. They are decisions of a kind for which the Judiciary has neither aptitude, facilities nor responsibility and have long been held to belong in the domain of political power not subject to judicial intrusion or inquiry.[8]

Concerns grounded in separation of powers and institutional competence are reflected in principles of justiciability, in particular the political question doctrine. In *Marbury v. Madison,* Marshall noted that "[b]y the constitution of the United States, the President is invested with certain important political powers, in the exercise of which he is to use his own discretion, and is accountable only to his country in his political character, and to his own conscience."[9] Thus, courts will decline to hear cases that raise political questions. This often occurs in cases involving foreign affairs, including deciding whether a war has begun or ended or whether the President's use of war power is constitutional.[10]

In *Baker v. Carr,*[11] the Supreme Court articulated six factors to be considered in determining whether an issue is justiciable or barred by the political question doctrine: (1) "a textually demonstrable commitment of the issue to a coordinate political department"; (2) "a lack of judicially discoverable and manageable standards for resolving [the issue]"; (3) "the impossibility of deciding without an initial policy determination of a kind clearly for nonjudicial discretion"; (4) "the impossibility of a court's undertaking independent resolution without expressing lack of the respect due coordinate branches of government"; (5) "an unusual need for unquestioning adherence to a political decision already made"; and (6) "the potentiality of embarrassment for multifarious pronouncements by various departments on one question."[12]

Each of those factors may be implicated in national security cases. The executive branch will often be able to argue that there is a textually demonstrable constitutional commitment of the issue to the political branches. The political branches, not the courts, make foreign policy. The executive branch may be able to assert that there is a lack of judicially discoverable and manageable standards for resolving the issue. How is a court to decide if national security requires the government to take a certain action? Similarly, the matter may be impossible to decide without an initial policy decision of a kind clearly for nonjudicial discretion. Judicial involvement in foreign affairs may express a lack of respect for the executive, undercut a political decision already made, or lead to varying pronouncements from different branches of government on the same question.

Nor are courts immune to the exigencies of the day. Chief Justice Rehnquist noted that "there is...the reluctance of courts to decide a case against the government on an issue of national security during a war."[13] As a result, the timing of when a court hears the case may be critical to its outcome. "A court may also decide an issue in favor of the government during a war, when it would not have done so had the decision come after the war was over."[14]

Cases amply illustrate the importance of timing. In *Ex parte Milligan,*[15] the petitioner, a civilian, was charged with treason during the Civil War, tried by a military tribunal, and sentenced to death. The Supreme Court ultimately granted Milligan's habeas petition. One can almost hear Justice Davis breathe a sigh of relief that he is deciding the case after the Civil War has ended:

> During the late wicked rebellion, the temper of the times did not allow that calmness in deliberation and discussion so necessary to a correct conclusion of a purely judicial question. Then, considerations of safety were mingled with the exercise of power; and feelings and interests prevailed which are happily terminated. Now that the public safety is assured, this question, as well as all others, can be discussed and decided without passion or the admixture of any element not required to form a legal judgment.[16]

By way of contrast, *Korematsu v. United States,*[17] widely regarded as one of the worst decisions in the history of the Supreme Court,[18] upheld the military order that excluded Japanese Americans from the west coast during World War II. More than 110,000 individuals—including children, women, and the elderly—were forced from their homes and confined to detention camps without any individualized showing of guilt. *Korematsu,* unlike *Milligan,* was decided while the conflict that gave rise to the legal challenge, still continued.

In *Woods v. Cloyd W. Miller Co.,*[19] Justice Jackson called the war power "the most dangerous one to free government in the whole catalogue of powers."[20] Justice Jackson noted that "[i]t usually is invoked in haste and excitement when calm legislative consideration of constitutional limitation is difficult. It is executed in a time of patriotic fervor that makes moderation unpopular. And, worst of all, it is interpreted by judges under the influence of the same passions and pressures."[21] In such circumstances, the government is "[a]lways...urg[ing] hasty decision to forestall some emergency or serve some purpose and pleads that paralysis will result if its claims to power are denied or their confirmation delayed."[22]

TWO PARADIGM SHIFTS

In his celebrated condemnation of the internment of Japanese Americans during World War II, Eugene Rostow observed that "[t]he relationship of civil to military authorities... is one of the two or three most essential elements in the legal structure of a democratic society."[23] A modern-day revision of that list might well add another element: the democratic control of the intelligence agencies of the executive branch, with sufficient legal constraints placed on their conduct to ensure that the liberties of citizens are respected. Together, the combined might of the military and intelligence community is formidable. Each has power enough to subvert democracy.

Two paradigm shifts have occurred in the war on terror that involve both the military and the intelligence apparatus of the United States. The first shift involves a military response to terrorism. In general, prior to 9/11, the government dealt with terrorism through the criminal justice system.[24] The United States indicted the alleged perpetrators. This occurred, for example, after the first World Trade Center bombing in February 1993,[25] the bombing of Khobar Towers in Al-Khobar, Saudi Arabia in June 1996,[26] the August 1998 embassy bombings in Kenya and Tanzania,[27] the foiled January 1, 2000, millennium bomb plot,[28] and the October 2000 attack on the USS *Cole* in Aden, Yemen.[29]

Post-9/11, the Bush administration shifted from the criminal justice system to a military response to terrorism. This response included the indefinite detention of suspected terrorists by the military as enemy combatants.[30] The government claimed the prerogative to detain indefinitely suspected terrorists—citizens and noncitizens alike—without any judicial oversight. It was, perhaps, the boldest assertion of executive power since Truman's seizure of the steel mills half a century earlier.

As an analytical matter, four different categories of combatant-detainees have emerged: (1) a citizen captured on a battlefield in Afghanistan; (2) a citizen captured in the United States; (3) a noncitizen captured overseas, whether Afghanistan or elsewhere; and (4) a noncitizen captured in the United States. The Supreme Court has only spoken on the first category in *Hamdi v. Rumsfeld.*[31] We now have some guidance in this area. The other three categories involve cases that are wending their way through federal court in habeas litigation that challenges the government's detention power.

Citizen Captured Overseas

In *Hamdi,* the Supreme Court decided two issues: (1) whether the executive has the authority to detain citizens who are enemy combatants; and (2) if so, how much process is due a citizen who disputes his enemy-combatant status.[32] On the first issue, the plurality of Justices O'Connor, Rehnquist, Kennedy, and Breyer, plus the dissenting Justice Thomas, concluded that the President had the authority to detain Hamdi as an enemy combatant because Congress had authorized Hamdi's detention through the AUMF (Authorization for Use of Military Force).[33] This resolution, passed 1 week after September 11, 2001, enabled the President to "use all necessary and appropriate force against those nations, organizations, or persons he determines planned, authorized, committed, or aided the terrorist attacks" or "harbored such organizations or persons, in order to prevent any future acts of international terrorism against the United States."[34] The plurality reasoned that "[b]ecause detention to prevent a combatant's return to the battlefield is a fundamental incident of waging war, in permitting the use of 'necessary and appropriate force,' Congress has clearly and unmistakably authorized detention in the narrow circumstances considered here."[35]

On the second issue, the Court applied *Mathews v. Eldridge*[36] to rule that a citizen-detainee must receive notice of the factual basis for his classification as an enemy combatant and a fair opportunity to rebut the government's factual assertions before a neutral decision-maker.[37] The government's proposed standard—that "some evidence" was adequate—failed to satisfy the requirements of due process.[38] To alleviate the burden upon the government in a time of war, however, the Court allowed the use of hearsay evidence and a rebuttable presumption in favor of the government's evidence,[39] and acknowledged that a properly constituted military tribunal might suffice.[40] Separation of powers principles did not mandate "a heavily circumscribed role" for the courts.[41] "We have long since made clear that a state of war is not a blank check for the President when it comes to the rights of the Nation's citizens."[42]

In practical terms, with the exception of Justice Thomas, eight of the nine Justices rejected the broadest claim of executive power—that is, that the President has the all but unreviewable discretion to detain a citizen indefinitely as an enemy combatant. Four Justices (Souter, Ginsburg, Scalia, and Stephens) said that the President lacks such authority. Another four Justices (the plurality) concluded that Hamdi could be detained but that he was entitled to a certain amount of process—more than the government had been willing to provide—to challenge his enemy combatant designation. Absent a suspension of the writ of habeas corpus, the courts do have a say in reviewing the detention of citizens.

But *Hamdi* is hardly a sweeping vindication of civil rights.[43] On its facts, it applies only to citizens detained within the territorial jurisdiction of a U.S. court.[44] In his dissent, Justice Scalia asserted that the constitutional requirements may differ for a citizen who is captured abroad and held outside the United States,[45] and *Hamdi* did not address that issue. Moreover, in important respects, *Hamdi* represents a victory for the executive branch. The Supreme Court accepted the President's authority to detain a citizen combatant captured on a foreign battlefield. The detention could be indefinite without a criminal trial, subject only to the principle that detention last no longer than active hostilities.[46] A citizen who wished to challenge his designation as an enemy combatant was given basic but limited process, and there was fairly deferential judicial review of that designation.[47]

Citizen Captured in the United States

The case of Jose Padilla raises issues similar to those of *Hamdi*, with the critical distinction that Padilla, unlike Hamdi, was not captured on a distant battlefield, but on U.S. soil as he stepped off an airplane. Much like *Hamdi*, the government has made broad claims of executive power to detain even citizens as enemy combatants. And much like *Hamdi*, the courts have struggled to resolve the issues. The district court denied Padilla's habeas petition and accepted the government's claim that the President has the authority to detain citizens captured on U.S. soil as enemy combatants in a time of war;[48] the Second Circuit reversed.[49] The Supreme Court reversed the Second Circuit on jurisdictional grounds, holding that under the habeas statute, the case was improperly filed against the Secretary of Defense in the Southern District of New York.[50] Padilla's claim was dismissed without prejudice.[51]

Padilla then filed his habeas petition in the District of South Carolina. A district court there granted the petition. First, the court held that the AUMF did not authorize Padilla's detention and that detention was contrary to the requirements of the Non-Detention Act, which "forbids *any* kind of detention of an U.S. citizen, except that which is specifically allowed by Congress."[52] The critical distinction between this case and *Hamdi* was that Padilla was not captured on a distant battlefield, but in the United States.[53] No language

in the AUMF empowered the President to hold Padilla as an enemy combatant or overcame the terms of the Non-Detention Act.

Second, the court rejected the assertion that the President had the inherent authority to
detain Padilla as an enemy combatant. Citing *Youngstown Sheet & Tube Co. v. Sawyer,*[54]
the court held that the President had taken steps inconsistent with the will of Congress.
Thus, the President's authority was at its lowest ebb. "'Congress, not the Executive,
should control utilization of the war power as an instrument of domestic policy.'"[55] To
accept the President's claim of inherent authority "would not only offend the rule of law
and violate this country's constitutional tradition, but it would also be a betrayal of this
Nation's commitment to the separation of powers that safeguards our democratic values
and individual liberties."[56]

A theme throughout the district court's opinion was its concern that the executive have
the power to order the indefinite and unreviewable detention by the military of a citizen
arrested on U.S. soil. In the absence of, and indeed contrary to, congressional authorization, the President was handling through military means a situation that could be handled
through the courts. "Simply stated, this is a law enforcement matter, not a military
matter."[57] Criminal laws also allowed for the prosecution and punishment of terrorists.
Unlike the President's claim of inherent authority, however, the criminal process allowed
for accountability and helped to prevent arbitrary government action.[58]

On appeal, however, the Fourth Circuit reversed the district court.[59] The Fourth Circuit
held that just as the AUMF authorized Hamdi's detention, it authorized Padilla's detention
as well. There was "no difference in principle between Hamdi and Padilla."[60] The locus of
capture was irrelevant, as was the availability of criminal prosecution.[61] According to the
Fourth Circuit, the district court had been insufficiently deferential to the President's
determination that detention was necessary and appropriate in the interest of national
security.[62]

Noncitizen Captured Overseas

At present, it is unclear if noncitizens detained as enemy combatants are entitled to the
same due process rights as citizens, even if held within the territorial jurisdiction of a
federal court. In *Rasul v. Bush,*[63] decided the same day as *Hamdi,* the Supreme Court held
that noncitizens detainees at Guantanamo Bay, Cuba, are entitled to file habeas claims in
federal court. The Court stressed the special status of Guantanamo Bay; it was "territory
over which the United States exercises exclusive jurisdiction and control."[64] In the
District of Columbia, the court litigated the question of whether noncitizen detainees at
Guantanamo Bay are protected by the Due Process Clause of the Fifth Amendment. [65]

Noncitizen Captured in the United States

Al-Marri v. Hanft raises the issue of whether a noncitizen may be detained as an enemy
combatant, when he is captured on U.S. soil.[66] Al-Marri was initially arrested in Peoria,
Illinois, and charged with various federal crimes. A month before his scheduled trial date,
the government designated him an enemy combatant and transferred him to military
custody.[67] The district court in South Carolina that had granted Padilla's habeas petition
heard Al-Marri's claim as well. In this case, unlike *Padilla,* the court denied the habeas
petition and upheld Al-Marri's detention as an enemy combatant.[68] According to the
court, as a noncitizen, Al-Marri is not accorded the same constitutional protections as a
citizen and the terms of the Non-Detention Act apply only to citizens.[69]

It is possible that the Supreme Court will eventually hear *Padilla, Al-Marri,* and the litigation involving noncitizens detained in Guantanamo Bay. Each case raises difficult questions regarding the limits of executive prerogative, as well as the interplay between the AUMF, Non-Detention Act, and the President's Article II power. Although *Hamdi* rejected the broadest assertion of unreviewable executive power to detain a citizen, the upshot of the litigation may be to expand, not contract, the parameters of executive power. From this perspective, the President asked for a yard, and ended up with a foot or two. More than that, however, the President shifted the parameters of the debate so that there is no longer any question that, as long as the AUMF applies, the President can detain a citizen captured abroad as an enemy combatant.[70] The government may also be able to proceed against the citizen detainee in a properly constituted military tribunal, where it may rely upon hearsay evidence and a rebuttable presumption in favor of its evidence.

Beyond a shift from the criminal justice system to a military response to terrorism, a second paradigm shift has occurred as well: the centralization of intelligence functions, both civilian and military, within a single bureaucratic structure in the executive branch. This unprecedented centralization has occurred through the IRTPA (Intelligence Reform and Terrorism Prevention Act of 2004).[71] The Patriot Act furthers this centralization by dismantling the wall that traditionally separated foreign intelligence activities from domestic law enforcement.[72] Together, IRTPA and the Patriot Act have enhanced the power of the national security apparatus and blurred the historical line that separated external security or foreign intelligence from internal security or domestic law enforcement.

Director of National Intelligence

The framers of the National Security Act of 1947 intentionally diffused power between different intelligence agencies. They created a wall between foreign intelligence collection and domestic law enforcement. The Act specifically provided that the CIA "shall have no police, subpoena, or law enforcement powers or internal security functions."[73] The CIA, in other words, was intended to focus on external security: to combat the foreign enemies of the United States, not its domestic wrongdoers.[74] The FBI, in contrast, had statutory police powers and an internal security function, even with respect to counterespionage investigations.

The framers of the National Security Act sought to avoid giving the CIA too much power. The CIA was not to become a centralized national security apparatus with control over both foreign and domestic intelligence functions.[75] Truman emphasized that "this country wanted no Gestapo under any guise or for any reason."[76] Stuart Baker, former General Counsel to the National Security Agency, has explained that "American intelligence agencies were shaped by individuals who understood the mechanics of totalitarianism and wanted none of it here. They knew that the Gestapo and Soviet KGB had in common a sweeping authority to conduct internal and external security and intelligence gathering."[77]

The separation between external security or foreign intelligence and internal security or law enforcement was essentially maintained for more than half a century after the CIA's creation.[78] Pre-9/11 the intelligence community remained decentralized. The DCI (Director of Central Intelligence) was the Director of the CIA as well as the titular head of the U.S. intelligence community. Nevertheless, the DCI had limited authority over the intelligence community. The DCI stated the community's priorities and coordinated development of its budget, but lacked line authority over the heads of other agencies, as well as the power to shift or allocate resources within the community.[79]

To remedy the failure to "connect the dots" that led to 9/11, the 9/11 Commission recommended the creation of a powerful DNI who would oversee and coordinate the efforts of the intelligence community, both foreign and domestic.[80] Based on that recommendation, Congress enacted the IRTPA.[81] Among its most important features, IRTPA creates a Senate-confirmed DNI, popularly known as the "intelligence czar," who is the head of the intelligence community and principal adviser to the President on intelligence matters related to national security.[82] The DNI has budgetary authority over the intelligence community,[83] as well as authority over the hiring of key officials in the intelligence community, including the Director of the CIA and the Director of the NSA.[84]

More changes, however, were to follow that consolidated the DNI's authority over the FBI. On March 31, 2005, the Commission on the Intelligence Capabilities of the United States Regarding WMDs (Weapons of Mass Destruction Commission) issued its report.[85] The WMD Commission issued seventy-four recommendations to strengthen U.S. intelligence capabilities. Among other things, the Commission noted that the DNI's authority over the FBI was "troublingly vague."[86] In response to the WMD Commission's recommendations, on June 29, 2005, President Bush clarified and centralized the DNI's authority over the FBI's intelligence program.[87] The President ordered the creation of a National Security Service within the FBI that combines the FBI's counterterrorism, counterintelligence, and intelligence elements. The DNI has authority to approve the hiring of the head of the National Security Service, who will report to both the Director of the FBI and to the DNI.[88] Moreover, the DNI was given authority over the FBI's three billion dollar intelligence budget.[89]

Patriot Act and Foreign Intelligence

In addition to IRTPA's centralization of intelligence functions under the DNI, the Patriot Act lowers the wall between foreign intelligence and domestic law enforcement. Most importantly, the Act amends the FISA (Foreign Intelligence Surveillance Act). FISA governs the collection of foreign intelligence and, in general, does not require a showing that comports with the traditional criminal standard of probable cause.[90] Prior to the Patriot Act, to avoid the misuse of FISA surveillance, FISA required that "the purpose" of the order be to obtain foreign intelligence information.[91] Courts, in turn, construed "the purpose" test to require the government to establish that "the primary purpose" was to obtain foreign intelligence information, and not to further a domestic criminal investigation.[92] This issue arose in criminal cases in which the government sought to introduce evidence at trial that had been collected pursuant to a FISA order.

The Patriot Act relaxed the rules separating foreign intelligence investigations from criminal investigations, based on concern that the rules had become overly restrictive. One amendment to FISA, for example, provides that the collection of foreign intelligence need only be "a significant" purpose, and not "the purpose" of the investigation.[93] As a result, the "primary purpose" test has been legislatively set aside.[94] The "significant purpose" test is not difficult to meet. The Foreign Intelligence Surveillance Court of Review has concluded that the government's "sole objective" cannot be to gather evidence for prosecution purposes.[95] Thus, the government may use FISA surveillance when its primary, but not exclusive, purpose is to gather evidence to prosecute a foreign intelligence crime or ordinary crime "inextricably intertwined" with foreign intelligence crime, "[s]o long as...[it] retains a realistic option of dealing with the agent other than through criminal prosecution."[96]

Similarly, the Patriot Act facilitates the two-way flow of information between the intelligence and law enforcement communities. The Act makes clear that "[n]otwithstanding any other provision of law...foreign or counterintelligence...information obtained as part of a criminal investigation...[may] be disclosed to any Federal law enforcement, intelligence, protective, immigration, national defense, or national security official in order to assist the official receiving that information in the performance of his official duties."[97] Grand jury information, which ordinarily must be kept confidential, may be shared by criminal investigators with other government officials for counterterrorism purposes.[98] Information gathered under Title III may also be shared "to the extent that such contents include foreign intelligence or counterintelligence."[99] Similarly, officials who collect foreign intelligence information are allowed "to consult with Federal law enforcement officers to coordinate efforts to investigate or protect against...sabotage or international terrorism by a foreign power or an agent of a foreign power."[100]

In tandem, the two paradigm shifts have blurred the line between the military and domestic law enforcement on the one hand, and between domestic law enforcement and foreign intelligence on the other. Yet those traditional lines were drawn to prevent the accumulation of excessive power in the executive branch. We have set aside those concerns in pursuit of the war on terror. The shifts may help prevent terrorism; that certainly was the intent. Perhaps they are necessary measures; we live in troubled times. Acts of terrorism seem to occur around the world with tragic and depressing regularity. But it is important to recognize that there could be significant costs to the paradigm shifts that have occurred as a result of the war on terror.

First, the shifts enhance the power of the executive branch. The executive has far more discretion when he acts as the Commander in Chief than when he acts as a prosecutor. Characterizing terrorism as a military issue, not a law enforcement problem, has the inexorable consequence of expanding the scope of executive discretion. In a criminal proceeding, the judiciary checks the power of the executive; the executive must establish guilt beyond a reasonable doubt and the full panoply of constitutional rights protects the accused. When a matter is viewed as military in nature, however, courts are more deferential to the executive for reasons grounded in separation of powers and institutional competency.

The centralization of intelligence functions also enhances executive power. IRTPA creates a powerful, new DNI who has authority over the entire intelligence community, including the military, CIA, and FBI. The intentional diffusion of power established by National Security Act of 1947 has been set aside. The executive has greater discretion to share information between the intelligence and law enforcement communities. Under FISA's "significant purpose" test, the executive also has greater latitude to use foreign intelligence methods regulated under FISA for domestic law enforcement purposes.

This enhancement of executive authority must be viewed in its historical context. It is widely accepted that power has accumulated in the executive branch since the founding. The modern President is not only the head of government but also the head of a political party as well. Justice Jackson explained that the "rise of the party system has made a significant extraconstitutional supplement to real executive power."[101] The modern President also commands center stage in American political life. Technology, including the radio and television, has only advanced the President's ability to dominate public debate.[102]

Moreover, "[v]ast accretions of federal power, eroded from that reserved by the States, have magnified the scope of presidential activity."[103] Modern American history has witnessed the rise of the regulatory state and administrative agencies with delegated lawmaking powers.[104] Many of these agencies are executive in nature. The President appoints their heads and establishes their policies as well. Similarly, executive power has increased through the profusion of federal laws, especially criminal laws, that the President is charged with enforcing.[105]

Of course, the United States' response to the Cold War also increased executive power. In the aftermath of World War II, the government founded a permanent and powerful military establishment to which a substantial portion of the nation's resources was directed.[106] The United States also created standing agencies devoted to the collection and analysis of intelligence.[107] The President is both the Commander in Chief of the military and directs the intelligence agencies. Technological advances have magnified the ability of agencies to monitor the lives of citizens.[108] In addition, the President has the classification power. Once classified, information cannot be made publicly available, and it can be a laborious process to seek declassification of that information.[109]

Not only is increased executive power in the war on terror part of a larger historical trend, but also that power is unlikely to diminish in the near future. The government has stated that the war on terror could last several generations and that the conflict will be of unprecedented length.[110] Indeed, it will be hard to know when it does end, as there is unlikely to be a formal ceasefire. Moreover, two independent commissions have concluded that al Qaeda has tried to obtain WMD for the past decade.[111] The threat of WMDs, much like WMDs themselves, is unlikely ever to disappear. We are likely, then, to find ourselves on a permanent wartime footing. Hamilton once warned that "[t]he violent destruction of life and property incident to war, the continual effort and alarm attendant on a state of continued danger, will compel nations the most attached to liberty, to resort for repose and security to institutions which have a tendency to destroy their civil and political rights."[112]

The paradigm shifts may also increase the risk of civil rights abuses. In *Bissonette v. Haig*,[113] the Eighth Circuit explained:

> Civilian rule is basic to our system of government. The use of military forces to seize civilians can expose civilian government to the threat of military rule and the suspension of constitutional liberties. On a lesser scale, military enforcement of the civil law leaves the protection of vital Fourth and Fifth Amendment rights in the hands of persons who are not trained to uphold these rights. It may also chill the exercise of fundamental rights, such as the rights to speak freely and to vote, and create an atmosphere of fear and hostility which exists in territories occupied by enemy forces.[114]

Military methods in time of war differ from those used by civilians in time of peace. The battlefield has little use for due process. Military culture differs from civilian culture. As an example of this proposition, FBI agents who witnessed interrogations of detainees at Guantanamo Bay objected to the harsh methods being used.[115]

As the military plays an ever expanding role in the war on terror and in homeland defense, difficult line-drawing issues are likely to arise on the limits of executive prerogative. Yet another question is whether "mission creep" will result, so that the military become adjuncts of civilian officials in any number of areas.[116] If so, it is likely that the executive will argue that, as a matter of separation of powers and institutional competency, a court should review military action under a more deferential standard than might otherwise be applied.

Similar concerns arise out of the centralization of the intelligence apparatus. First, centralization creates a greater risk that intelligence will be politicized to suit a President's agenda.[117] The decentralized system that existed prior to IRTPA made it more difficult for the President to pressure or manipulate the entire intelligence community; the voice of the

CIA Director, for example, was one among many. Whatever its faults, decentralization encouraged a diversity of views, competition in the gathering and analysis of intelligence, and independent thinking.[118] As an institutional matter, this may be particularly important for agencies largely shielded from public scrutiny that serve top officials in the executive branch. Even without centralization, "[n]o other part of the government has so narrow an audience—or responds so enthusiastically to guidance from above."[119] Centralization and the creation of a DNI who oversees the intelligence community means that "the President will have only one mind in the intelligence community to bend to his will."[120]

Second, lowering the wall between foreign and domestic intelligence creates the risk that foreign intelligence and methods used to acquire foreign intelligence will be used for domestic law enforcement purposes in an effort to circumvent legal safeguards that would otherwise apply, even in cases unrelated to international terrorism. Baker observes that "[i]ntelligence gathering tolerates a degree of intrusiveness, harshness, and deceit that Americans do not want applied against themselves."[121] Very different legal regimes apply to government action with respect to external or internal security, and the constitutional standards may differ. As a matter of constitutional criminal procedure, for example, the Fourth Amendment does not apply to extraterritorial searches of nonresident aliens absent a substantial connection between the alien and the United States.[122] Nor are aliens entitled to Fifth Amendment due process rights outside the sovereign territory of the United States.[123]

Similarly, different statutory regimes govern the collection of information depending on whether it is being used for external or internal security. FISA applies to foreign intelligence collection; Title III regulates domestic law enforcement. Prior to the Patriot Act, agents may have been tempted to use a FISA order or information derived from a FISA order when they were unable to meet the requirements of Title III. That temptation, however, was checked by the "primary purpose" test then in place under FISA. The new test—one that requires only "a significant purpose"—will have the opposite effect. It creates an incentive to seek a FISA order instead of one under the more onerous requirements of Title III. The information sharing provisions of the Patriot Act create a similar risk that an agent will be able to access information otherwise inaccessible under the laws that constrain domestic law enforcement activity.

Third, there are important cultural differences between the worlds of cops and spies, and they approach their work differently. According to Admiral Stansfield Turner, a former Director of the CIA, "The FBI agent's first reaction when given a job is, 'How do I do this within the law?' The CIA agent's first reaction when given a job is, 'How do I do this regardless of the law of the country in which I am operating?'"[124] Similarly, Stewart Baker has noted that "[c]ombining domestic and foreign intelligence functions creates the possibility that domestic law enforcement will be infected by the secrecy, deception, and ruthlessness that international espionage requires."[125] Or, as Richard Posner adds, "The idea that the CIA would engage in domestic intelligence gives even conservatives the creeps; yet the Intelligence Reform Act takes a step in that direction by placing the DNI over both the CIA and the domestic intelligence activity of the FBI."[126]

An interesting and important question is what the cumulative impact of the two paradigm shifts will be. Any one shift would be significant in and of itself. Now, however, there are two, each of which complements the other. Will the effects of each shift converge in ways that are difficult to predict? No doubt there will be a temptation for the military to be involved in domestic surveillance, especially since the United States is viewed part of the battleground in the war on terror.[127] The executive branch will also coordinate its law enforcement and military efforts. Indeed, it already is in determining whether to detain an individual as an enemy combatant.[128] Difficult legal questions may also arise. If the government tries an individual in federal district court and the individual is acquitted, could the government then detain the individual militarily as an enemy combatant? The Double Jeopardy Clause is generally viewed as barring successive prosecutions by the same sovereign for the same criminal offense.[129] The government with no doubt would argue that military detention based on an enemy-combatant designation is an adjudication of status, not a criminal prosecution. Under such a theory, the Double Jeopardy Clause would be inapplicable.[130]

CONCLUSIONS

The war on terror has raised a number of structural constitutional issues. From a separation of powers perspective, courts have difficulty with cases involving claims of executive prerogative in matters involving foreign affairs and national security. More than that, the war on terror has enlarged executive authority. Two paradigm shifts have occurred. First, there has been a militarized response to terrorism. Until 9/11, in general, terrorism was viewed as a law enforcement problem. Post-9/11, the executive branch has claimed the prerogative to detain even citizens, whether captured on a foreign battlefield or in the United States, as enemy combatants. Second, the government has centralized its intelligence functions by creating a DNI and has lowered the historical wall that separated external security or foreign intelligence from internal security or domestic law enforcement. An interesting and important question is what the cumulative effect of these two paradigm shifts will be, as the line blurs between law enforcement and the military on the one hand, and between foreign intelligence or external security and law enforcement or internal security on the other. While both paradigm shifts may be thought necessary to ensure national security, there may be costs as well. Not the least of those costs may be an increased risk of abuses of civil liberty.

NOTES

1. *Intelligence Reform and Terrorism Prevention Act of 2004,* Public Law 108-458, § 1011, *U.S. Statutes at Large* 118 (2004): 638.

2. *Uniting and Strengthening America by Providing Appropriate Tools Required to Intercept and Obstruct Terrorism (PATRIOT Act) Act of 2001,* Public Law 107–56, *U.S. Statutes at Large* 115 (2001): 272.

3. 5 U.S. (1 Cranch) 137 (1803).

4. *Marbury v. Madison,* 5 U.S. (1 Cranch) 137, 177 (1803).

5. U.S. Const. art. II, § 1, cl. 1.

6. U.S. Const. art. II, § 1, cl. 8.

7. *United States v. Curtiss-Wright Export Co.,* 299 U.S. 304, 319 (1936).

8. *Chicago & Southern Air Lines, Inc. v. Waterman S.S. Corp.,* 333 U.S. 103, 111 (1948) (Jackson, J.). See also *Harisiades v. Shaughnessy,* 342 U.S. 580, 589 (1952) ("policies in regard to the conduct of foreign relations [and] the war power...are so exclusively entrusted to the political branches of government as to be largely immune from judicial inquiry or interference").

9. *Marbury,* 5 U.S. at 165–66.

10. See generally Erwin Chemerinsky, *Constitutional Law: Principles and Policies,* 2nd ed. (New York: Aspen, 2002), 138–41.

11. 369 U.S. 186 (1962).

12. Ibid., 217.

13. William Rehnquist, *All the Laws But One: Civil Liberties in War Time* (New York: Alfred A. Knopf, 1998), 221.

14. Ibid., 222. See also Laurence H. Tribe, *American Constitutional Law,* vol. 1, 3rd ed. (New York: Foundation Press, 2000), 670 (noting that two decisions limiting the President's power to declare and enforce martial law were decided after hostilities had ended; "one may doubt that the Court would have been so courageous had war still been underway").

15. 71 U.S. (4 Wall.) 2 (1866).

16. Ibid., 109.

17. 323 U.S. 214 (1944).

18. For a contemporaneous condemnation of the treatment of Japanese Americans, see Eugene V. Rostow, "The Japanese American Cases—a Disaster," *Yale Law Journal* 54 (1945): 489 (henceforth cited as "The Japanese American Cases"). Seldom in legal scholarship will one find an article as passionate, eloquent, and unsparing in its criticism of the government, including the Supreme Court.

19. 333 U.S. 138 (1948).

20. Ibid., 146 (Jackson, J., concurring).

21. Ibid.

22. Ibid.

23. Rostow, "The Japanese American Cases," 491.

24. National Commission on Terrorist Attacks Upon the United States, *The 9/11 Commission Report,* 2004, 73 (hereinafter cited as *9/11 Commission Report*) ("Legal processes were the primary method for responding to these early manifestations of a new type of terrorism."); Steve Coll, *Ghost Wars: The Secret History of the CIA, Afghanistan, and Bin Ladin from the Soviet Invasion to September 10, 2001* (New York: The Penguin Press, 2004), 254 ("Americans were still much more likely to die from bee stings than from terrorist strikes during the early 1990s. In that respect it made more sense to treat terrorism as a law enforcement problem.... By the time the Clinton administration settled into office, this legalist approach to terrorism was well established within the American bureaucracy."); Ronald J. Sievert, "War on Terror or Global Law Enforcement Operation?" *Notre Dame Law Review* 78 (2003): 307, 312 ("[W]ith rare exception, before September 11, 2001, we had developed the habit of classifying all attacks, regardless of target, as criminal acts of terrorism to be dealt with by civilian courts under U.S. criminal law."); Note, "Responding to Terrorism: Crime, Punishment, and War," *Harvard Law Review* 115 (2002): 1217, 1224 ("[T]he United States has traditionally treated terrorism as a crime.").
    There were a few notable exceptions. After the bombing of a German nightclub in 1986 that killed and wounded several U.S. soldiers, President Reagan sent planes to bomb targets in Libya. See Barry E. Carter, Phillip R. Trimble, and Curtis A. Bradley, *International Law* (New York: Aspen, 2003), 1016. In 1993, President Clinton launched a limited strike on Baghdad after learning of an Iraqi plot to kill former President Bush. Ibid., 997. In 1998, in response to the al Qaeda bombings of U.S. embassies in Kenya and Tanzania, the United States launched cruise missiles against targets in the Sudan and Afghanistan and sought indictments as well. Ibid., 1022.

25. *9/11 Commission Report,* at 71–73; *United States v. Salameh,* 152 F.3d 88 (2nd Cir. 1998) (per curiam), *cert. denied,* 525 U.S. 1112 (2000); *United States v. Yousef,* 327 F.3d 56 (2nd Cir.), *cert. denied,* 540 U.S. 933 (2003).

26. *9/11 Commission Report,* at 60. A federal grand jury in the Eastern District of Virginia returned a 46-count indictment that charged fourteen individuals for the bombing. David Johnston, "14 Indicted by U.S. in '96 Saudi Blast; Iran Link Cited," *New York Times,* June 22, 2001.

27. *9/11 Commission Report,* at 68–70. Although more than a dozen individuals including Osama bin Laden were charged for the bombings, only a few have stood trial to date. Benjamin Weiser, "A Nation Challenged: The Courts; 4 are Sentenced to Life in Prison in 1998 U.S. Embassy Bombings," *New York Times,* October 19, 2001.

28. *9/11 Commission Report,* at 174–80. Ahmed Ressam, who planned to bomb Los Angeles International Airport, was convicted at trial. Eli Sanders, "Judge Delays Terrorist's Sentencing Hoping for Cooperation," *New York Times,* April 28, 2005.

29. *9/11 Commission Report,* at 190–97. An indictment was returned against two Yemeni men in May 2003. Eric Lichtblau, "After Effects: The Cole Bombing; U.S. Indicts 2 Men for Attack on American Ship in Yemen," *New York Times,* May 16, 2003.

30. Of course, there were exceptions. The government prosecuted John Walker Lindh, a citizen captured while fighting with the Taliban, see Neil A. Lewis, "Traces of Terror: The Captive; Admitting He Fought in Taliban, American Agrees to 20-Year Term," *New York Times,* July 16, 2002, Zacariah Moussaoui, a conspirator in the 9/11 plot, see Neil A. Lewis, "Moussaoui Tells Court He's Guilty of a Terror Plot," *New York Times,* April 23, 2005, and Richard Reid, the shoe-bomber, in federal court on criminal charges, see Pam Belluck, "Threats and Responses: The Bomb Plot; Unrepentant Shoe Bomber Is Given a Life Sentence for Trying to Blow Up Jet," *New York Times,* January 31, 2003.

31. 542 U.S. 507 (2004).

32. For a clear and concise analysis of *Hamdi,* see Erwin Chemerinsky, "Enemy Combatants and Separation of Powers," *Journal of National Security Law and Policy* 1 (2005): 73, 76 (hereinafter cited as "Enemy Combatants").

33. *Hamdi,* 542 U.S. at 587.

34. Ibid., 510 (quoting *U.S. Statutes at Large* 115: 224).

35. Ibid., 519. Thus, under Justice Jackson's analytical framework in *Youngstown Sheet & Tube Co. v. Sawyer,* 343 U.S. 579, 635 (1952) (Jackson, J., concurring), the President's authority was coupled with that of Congress. Under such circumstances, "his authority is at its maximum, for it includes all that he possesses in his own right plus all that Congress can delegate." Ibid., 636.

36. *Hamdi,* 542 U.S. at 529 (citing *Mathews v. Eldridge,* 424 U.S. 319 (1976)).

37. Ibid., 532–33.

38. *Hamdi,* 542 U.S. at 537.

39. Ibid., 533–34.

40. Ibid., 538.

41. Ibid., 535.

42. Ibid.

43. For critical commentary of *Hamdi,* see Chemerinsky, "Enemy Combatants," 73 and 80 (noting that the in *Hamdi* "the Supreme Court emphatically upheld the rule of law and the right of those being detained as part of the war on terrorism to have access to the courts" but that the government also scored a "significant victor[y]"); Rosa Ehrenreich Brooks, "War Everywhere: Rights, National Security Law, and the Law of Armed Conflict in the Age of Terror," *University of Pennsylvania Law Review* 153 (2004): 675, 701 (Supreme Court has left open the possibility that "Hamdi might be entitled only to a sort of 'due process lite'").

44. *Hamdi,* 542 U.S. at 577 (Scalia, J., dissenting).

45. Ibid.

46. Ibid., 519–20.

47. See David B. Rivkin, Jr. and Lee A. Casey, "Bush's Good Day in Court," *Washington Post,* August 4, 2004 (arguing that *Hamdi* was a victory for the government); Chemerinksy, "Enemy Combatants," at 80 (calling *Hamdi* "significant" victory for the government).

48. *Padilla v. Rumsfeld,* 233 F. Supp. 2d 564 (S.D.N.Y. 2002).

49. *Padilla v. Rumsfeld,* 352 F.3d 695 (2nd Cir. 2003).

50. *Padilla v. Rumsfeld,* 542 U.S. 426 (2004).

51. Ibid., 450.

52. *Padilla v. Hanft,* 385 F. Supp. 2d 678, 688 (D.S.C. 2005).

53. Ibid.

54. 343 U.S. 579, 634 (1952) (Jackson, J., concurring).

55. *Padilla,* 385 F. Supp. 2d at 690 (citing Youngstown, 343 U.S. at 644 (Jackson, J. concurring)).

56. Ibid., 690.

57. Ibid.

58. Ibid., 691.

59. *Padilla v. Hanft,* 423 F.3d 386 (4th Cir. 2005).

60. Ibid., 391.

61. Ibid., 393–95.

62. Ibid., 395.

63. 542 U.S. 466 (2004).

64. Ibid., 467.

65. See *In re Guantanamo Detainee Cases,* 355 F. Supp. 2d 443 (D.D.C. 2005), *reconsideration denied by Odah v. U.S.,* 355 F. Supp. 2d 482 (D.D.C. Feb 7, 2005) *and reconsideration denied by In re Guantanamo Detainee Cases,* 355 F. Supp. 2d 482 (D.D.C. Feb 8, 2005); *Khalid v. Bush,* 355 F. Supp. 2d 311 (D.D.C. 2005), *appeal vacated by Boumediene v. Bush,* 476 F.3d 981 (D.C. Cir. Feb 20, 2007); *certiorari denied by Boumediene v. Bush,* 127 S.Ct. 1478 (2007).

66. 378 F. Supp. 2d 673 (D.S.C. 2005).

67. Ibid., 674.

68. Ibid., 682.

69. Ibid., 677–80.

70. See Chemerinsky, "Enemy Combatants," at 80 ("The Court ruled in *Hamdi* that American citizens apprehended in foreign countries can be detained as enemy combatants.").

71. *Intelligence Reform and Terrorism Prevention Act of 2004,* Public Law 108-458, § 1011, *U.S. Statutes at Large* 118 (2004): 638.

72. For purposes of this article, "the wall" is used in a broad sense to refer to more than the restrictions on sharing information gathered under the Foreign Surveillance Intelligence Act, but to the historical separation of the CIA and FBI, and their respective functions. See generally *9/11 Commission Report,* at 78–80.

73. 50 U.S.C. § 403-3(d)(1).

74. Stewart A. Baker, "Should Spies Be Cops?" *Foreign Policy* 97 (1994): 36–37 (hereinafter cited as "Should Spies Be Cops).

75. Select Committee to Study Governmental Operations with Respect to Intelligence Activities, *Report on Intelligence Activities and Rights of Americans,* 94th Congress, 1976, Book I, 136, n. 31 (hereinafter cited as *Intelligence Activities and Rights*) (during the floor debates in the House of Representatives, "[i]t was frequently remarked that the [Central Intelligence] Agency was not to be permitted to act as a domestic police or 'Gestapo'"); Coll, *Ghost Wars,* at 254 ("[I]n the aftermath of a catastrophic war against Nazism, Congress also sought to protect the American people from the rise of anything like Hitler's Gestapo, a secret force that combined spying and police methods.").

76. Harry S. Truman, *Memoirs,* vol. 1 (Garden City, NY: Doubleday, 1955), 117. Truman repeats that he was "very much against building up a Gestapo." Ibid., 253. For Truman's recollections on the intelligence reorganization following World War II, see Harry S. Truman, *Memoirs,* vol. 2 (Garden City, NY: Doubleday, 1955), 73–79.

77. Baker, "Should Spies Be Cops," at 36. Baker most recently served as General Counsel to the WMD Commission.

78. Ibid., 37; Department of Defense, *Strategy for Homeland Defense and Civil Support,* 2005, 23 (hereinafter cited as *Strategy for Homeland Defense*).

79. *9/11 Commission Report,* at 86, 410.

80. Ibid., 407–19.

81. *Intelligence Reform and Terrorism Prevention Act of 2004,* Public Law 108-458, § 1011, *U.S. Statutes at Large* 118 (2004): 638. See generally Senate Commission on Governmental Affairs, *Summary of Intelligence Reform and Terrorism Prevention Act of 2004,* December 6, 2004, available at http://www.senate.gov/~govt-aff/_files/ConferenceReportSummary.doc; Richard A. Posner, *Preventing Surprise Attacks: Intelligence Reform in the Wake of 9/11* (Lanham, MD: Rowman & Littlefield, 2005), 62–69 (hereinafter cited as *Preventing Surprise Attacks*).

82. *Intelligence Reform and Terrorism Prevention Act of 2004* § 1011(a), *U.S. Statutes at Large* 118 (2004): 3643–44 (codified at *U.S. Code* 50 (2005): § 403).

83. Ibid., § 1011(c) and (d), *U.S. Statutes at Large* 118 (2004): 3644–47 (codified at *U.S. Code* 50 (2005): § 403-1(c) and (d)).

84. Ibid., § 1014, *U.S. Statutes at Large* 118 (2004): 3663–64 (codified at *U.S. Code* 50 (2005): § 403-6).

85. Commission on the Intelligence Capabilities of the U.S. Regarding Weapons of Mass Destruction, *Report to the President of the United States,* 2005 (hereinafter cited as *WMD Commission Report*).

86. Ibid., 457.

87. George W. Bush, *Memorandum to Vice President, Secretary of State, Secretary of Defense, Attorney General, Secretary of Homeland Security, Director of OMB, Director of National Intelligence, Assistant to the President for National Security Affairs, Assistant to the President for Homeland Security and Counterterrorism,* June 29, 2005, available at http://www.whitehouse.gov/news/releases/2005/06/print/20050629-1.html (hereinafter cited as *Memorandum*). See also Dan Eggen and Walter Pincus, "Bush Approves Spy Agency Changes," *Washington Post,* June 30, 2005; Douglas Jehl, "Bush to Create New Unit in F.B.I. for Intelligence," *New York Times,* June 30, 2005.

88. Bush, *Memorandum,* at 1–2.

89. Ibid., at 1; Eggen and Pincus, "Bush Approves Spy Agency Changes."

90. See *In re Sealed Case,* 310 F.3d 717, 741 (Foreign Int. Surv. Ct. Rev. 2002) ("[W]hile Title III contains some protections that are not in FISA, in many significant respects the two statutes are equivalent, and in some, FISA contains additional protections. Still, to the extent the two statutes diverge in constitutionally relevant areas—in particular, their probable cause and particularity showings—a FISA order may not be a 'warrant' contemplated by the Fourth Amendment."); Baker, "Should Spies Be Cops?" at 42 (noting that FISA surveillance "saves...[law enforcement officials] much of the hassle of meeting Title III standards for the wiretap"); Stephen J. Schulhofer, "No Checks, No Balances: Discarding Bedrock Constitutional Principles," in *The War on Our Freedoms: Civil Liberties in an Age of Terrorism,* ed. Richard C. Leone and Greg Anrig, Jr. (New York: The Century Foundation , 2003), 79 ("FISA surveillance is permitted after showing only a diluted form of suspicion not equivalent to the traditional criminal standard of probable cause.").

91. *In re Sealed Case,* 310 F.3d at 723.

92. Ibid., 725–27 (describing origin of "primary purpose" test).

93. *PATRIOT Act* § 218, *U.S. Statutes at Large* 115 (2003): 291 (codified at *U.S. Code* 50 (2003): §§ 1804(a)(7)(B) and 1823(a)(7)(B)).

94. *In Re Sealed Case,* 310 F.3d. at 736.

95. Ibid., 735.

96. Ibid., 735, 736.

97. *PATRIOT Act* § 203(d)(1), *U.S. Statutes at Large* 115 (2003): 281 (codified at *U.S. Code* 50 (2003): §403-5d). The Homeland Security Act broadened the disclosures to state, local, and foreign government officials. *Homeland Security Act* of 2002 § 897 (codified at *U.S. Code* 50 (2003): § 403-5d).

98. Ibid., § 203(a)(1), *U.S. Statutes at Large* 115 (2005): 278–79 (codified at *U.S. Code* 18 (2005): Appendix, Federal Rules of Criminal Procedure 6(e)(3)). The Intelligence Reform and Terrorism Prevention Act of 2004 also allows federal authorities to share grand jury information about terrorist threats with state, local, tribal, and foreign government officials. *Intelligence Reform and Terrorism Prevention Act of 2004* § 6501, *U.S. Statutes at Large* 118 (2005): 3760 (codified at *U.S. Code* 18 (2005): Appendix Federal Rules of Criminal Procedure 6(e)(3)(A), (D) and (E)).

99. *PATRIOT Act* § 203(b)(1), *U.S. Statutes at Large* 115 (2005): 280 (codified at U.S. Code 18 (2005): § 2517).

100. Ibid., § 504, *U.S. Statutes at Large* 115 (2003): 364–65 (codified at *U.S. Code* 50 (2003): § 1806).

101. *Youngstown,* 343 U.S. at 653 (Jackson, J., concurring).

102. Ibid.

103. Ibid., 654.

104. Richard H. Fallon, Jr., *The Dynamic Constitution: An Introduction to American Constitutional Law* (Cambridge: Cambridge University Press, 2004), 178–79.

105. ABA Task Force on Federalization of Criminal Law, *The Federalization of Criminal Law,* 1998, 7 ("of all federal crimes enacted since 1865, over forty percent [were] created since 1970").

106. See Michael J. Hogan, *A Cross of Iron: Harry S. Truman and the Origins of the National Security State 1945–1954* (Cambridge: Cambridge University Press, 1998), 264 ("[By 1950,] [t]he

nation had established a permanent peacetime military establishment for the first time in its history and the armed forces enjoyed an unparalleled degree of autonomy.").

107. *Intelligence Activities and Rights,* 9–10.

108. Ibid., 10.

109. See generally Leslie Gielow Jacobs, "A Troubling Equation in Contracts for Government Scientific Research: 'Sensitive But Unclassified' = Secret But Unconstitutional," *National Security Law and Policy* 1 (2005): 113, 118–23.

110. See *In re Guantanamo Detainee Cases,* 355 F. Supp. 2d at 465; *Strategy for Homeland Defense,* at 1.

111. *WMD Commission Report,* at 267–76; *9/11 Commission Report,* at 380.

112. Alexander Hamilton, "Federalist Number 8," in *The Federalist Papers* (New York: Penguin Putnam, 1961).

113. 776 F.2d 1384 (8th Cir. 1985), *aff'd,* 800 F.2d 812 (8th Cir. 1986) (en banc), *aff'd,* 485 U.S. 264 (1988).

114. Ibid., 1387.

115. David Johnston, "More of F.B.I. Memo Criticizing Guantanamo Methods Is Released," *New York Times,* March 22, 2005; Eric Lichtblau, "Justice Dept. Opens Inquiry into Abuse of U.S. Detainees," *New York Times,* January 14, 2005.

116. Richard H. Kohn, "Using the Military at Home: Yesterday, Today, and Tomorrow," *Chicago Journal of International Law* 4 (2003): 165, 188 ("The greatest worry is the gradual transformation of military forces into adjuncts of the law enforcement, domestic intelligence, and prosecutorial functions that have heretofore been strictly civilian. This has happened before–during almost every war since the mid-nineteenth century, with harm to American civil liberties and to the relationship between the armed forces and the American people.").

117. Posner, *Preventing Surprise Attacks,* at 116.

118. Ibid., 7, 43, 84, 99–162.

119. Baker, "Should Spies Be Cops?" at 40.

120. Posner, *Preventing Surprise Attacks,* at 116.

121. Baker, "Should Spies Be Cops?" at 40.

122. *United States v. Verdugo-Urquidez,* 494 U.S. 259, 274–75 (1990). See generally Fallon, *The Dynamic Constitution,* at 249 (*"The Constitution affords few if any rights that extend outside the territory of the United States to citizens of other countries."*) (italics in original).

123. *Verdugo-Urquidez,* 494 U.S. at 269 (citing *Johnson v. Eisenstrager,* 339 U.S. 763, 784 (1950)).

124. Benjamin Wittes, "Blurring the Line Between Cops and Spies," *Legal Times,* September 9, 1996.

125. Baker, "Should Spies Be Cops?" at 36–37.

126. Posner, *Preventing Surprise Attacks,* at 57.

127. *Strategy for Homeland Defense,* at 1 ("Our adversaries consider US territory an integral part of a global theater of combat.").

128. Alberto R. Gonzales, "Remarks at the Meeting of the American Bar Association Standing Committee on Law and National Security" (speech, February 24, 2004), 13, available at http://www.fas.org/irp/news/2004/02/gonzales.pdf.

129. *United States v. Blockburger,* 284 U.S. 299, 304 (1932).

130. An enlarged executive branch not only will affect the horizontal distribution of power among the three branches of government, but may also affect the vertical distribution of power between the federal government and the states in ways that are difficult to predict. At one level, the federal government may seek to tap state resources, including law enforcement personnel. An example of this followed 9/11, when Attorney General John Ashcroft asked local police to assist the FBI in interviewing 5000 young Middle Eastern men nationwide. See Fox Butterfield, "A Nation Challenged: The Interviews; A Police Force Rebuffs F.B.I. on Querying Mideast Men," *New York Times,* November 21, 2001. Based on racial profiling concerns, the police in several Oregon cities, including Portland, refused to do so. Similarly, the REAL ID Act of 2005 establishes uniform

standards for state driver's licenses and requires states to verify that a license applicant is lawfully present in the United States. See *REAL ID Act of 2005, Public Law* 109–13, § 202, *U.S. Statutes at Large* 119 (2005): 311, 312–15. The nation's governors have predicted that the law will impose an enormous burden on the states. See Michael Janofsky, "Governors Warn of High Costs Arising from New ID Law," *New York Times,* July 19, 2005.

At another level, it also possible that the war on terror will raise federalism issues that involve a conflict between competing constitutional values, including those of state sovereignty and the President's foreign affairs power. On the one hand, under current Tenth Amendment law, the federal government cannot commandeer state governments. *Printz v. United States,* 521 U.S. 898, 935 (1997). On the other hand, the federal government's treaty power has generally been viewed as sufficient to overcome state sovereignty concerns. *Missouri v. Holland,* 252 U.S. 416, 433 (1920). What happens, however, if the anticommandeering principles of the Tenth Amendment collide with the President's foreign affairs or national security powers? This scenario could arise if a treaty or executive agreement obligates the United States to do certain things that are viewed as infringing upon matters traditionally left to the states.

CHAPTER 5

Promotion of Liberal Islam by the United States

JOHN H. MANSFIELD

Erastianism is the name usually given in Western accounts to the promotion of a particular religious belief by the state, sometimes for the sake of souls, but more often for this-world effects. Erastianism may be what the United States is presently engaged in various parts of the world by its efforts to promote a particular version of Islam—a liberal version as opposed to a fundamentalist version—in order to reduce the risk of terrorist attacks.[1] Such an approach if employed in the United States clearly would violate the Establishment Clause of the First Amendment of the Constitution. Erastianism was a policy that continued to be embraced by a number of American states even after the American Revolution. It was outlawed so far as the federal government is concerned by the First Amendment, through its prohibition against any law "respecting an establishment of religion, or prohibiting the free exercise thereof. . . ." At a later date, these prohibitions became applicable to the states as well. The question we have to deal with today is whether what is prohibited within the United States is constitutional when engaged in abroad.

In Indonesia, to mention only one country, the United States appears to have in place a number of programs through which it attempts to promote a liberal version of Islam.[2] It funds educational programs in Islamic *pesantren* schools. It brings moderate Muslim leaders to the United States. It pays for American speakers to go to Indonesia. It produces TV programs and books that encourage a particular understanding of Islam. An example found on a State Department Web site is a grant made to "support leaders who have sought to build a synthesis between Islam and democracy. . . ."[3]

Since I first wrote on the topic of the applicability of the Religion Clauses to U.S. government activity abroad, nearly 20 years ago,[4] the Supreme Court has made important changes in Establishment Clause doctrine so far as domestic cases are concerned. Thus, whereas before under the regime of decisions handed down by the Court from the 1950s through the mid-1980s, there could be no aid to "pervasively sectarian schools"—which Indonesian *pesantren schools* certainly are—even though the aid was designed to promote secular education and was available to a wide range of educational institutions, both secular and religious, today the limitations on grants to institutions are greatly relaxed, and in a program of sufficient breadth, the government may even pay for an individual to go to a seminary.[5] Both the "purpose" and "primary effect" tests set forth in the earlier decisions—that the purpose must not be to aid religion, nor may that be its primary effect —have been so transformed by the Court as to eliminate barriers that these tests were clearly originally intended to erect. However, this change in the jurisprudence of the Establishment Clause has not eliminated the constitutional prohibition against promoting belief as against unbelief, much less the prohibition against promoting a particular religious belief.

There have been equally drastic changes in the Supreme Court's understanding of the Free Exercise Clause. If earlier an individual believer might be constitutionally exempt from a generally applicable requirement on account of his or her conscientious religious objection, unless there was a compelling governmental reason to override it, this exemption was swept away by a Supreme Court decision in 1990.[6] However, the Court's revolution in Free Exercise doctrine did not touch those situations in which religion is "targeted" by government, or a particular religion is targeted, either for the imposition of a disadvantage or the conferral of a benefit.[7] Thus, if in the United States the government provides money for the preaching of a particular interpretation of Islam, this almost certainly will violate the Free Exercise rights of Muslims who adhere to other interpretations, at least if they can show that they are significantly disadvantaged by the subsidy. Could the adverse effects on the disfavored versions of Islam be justified by a compelling state interest, for example, to prevent terrorist attacks? If they could, perhaps not only may the favored version of Islam be funded, but also the mosques of the disfavored versions closed down. But even if these actions would not violate the Free Exercise Clause because of a compelling state interest, there would still remain the barrier of the Establishment Clause. To import into the Establishment Clause a "compelling state interest" exception,[8] arguably would run counter to the history that led to that Clause's adoption. Those who wanted to maintain the Anglican establishment in Virginia in the late eighteenth century and those who favored continuing the Protestant establishment in Massachusetts in the early nineteenth century, certainly believed that there were compelling reasons for doing so. They thought that organized society would collapse without government financial support for particular religions. But the idea that state support for religion was not necessary for the maintenance of social order, and indeed corrupted religion itself, prevailed and found expression in the constitutional prohibition against Congress passing any law "respecting an establishment of religion."

One can imagine a non-Erastian government program, one whose aim is not to promote religion, much less a particular religion, but to promote a secular interest, an interest claimed to stand independently of any religious teaching. Here we confront the perennially challenging question of the distinction the Constitution itself draws between religion and the secular, and the question of whether there is such a thing as ethics apart from religion. American governments are all the time and on a large scale, promoting a morality claimed to be secular. This is done not only through the public school system, but also by various programs directed to the adult population as well. Perhaps government support for the teaching of tolerance—one facet of the U.S. government's program in Indonesia— may be seen in such a light, so long as it is not suggested that tolerance is to be embraced because all religions are equally true. A case in 1988 suggests this approach.[9] In that case, the Supreme Court held that a program using tax money to fund sex education for young people, which permitted the participation of religious organizations, did not violate the

Establishment Clause, so long as teaching under the program did not give religious reasons for behaving in a particular way. In addition, it should be noted, it may not violate the Establishment Clause for the United States to urge other countries to adopt the American constitutional model of the relationship between government and religion, even though one of the reasons this model found its way into our Bill of Rights was itself the profoundly religious belief that government involvement with religion was especially displeasing to God. It may be possible to propound sufficient secular reasons for other nations to adopt our model.[10]

Another way around objection under the Establishment Clause would be a program that does not involve a government purpose to promote religion, or a particular religion, but simply to provide an opportunity for individuals or groups to pursue their own interests, whether they are religious or nonreligious. For such a program to survive Establishment Clause scrutiny, the criteria for entitlement to participate must be broad indeed. In the case referred to earlier, in which tax money was allowed to be used to attend a seminary, this was the rationale employed: the student had a wide range of options to choose among, religious and secular, and, as it happened, he or she chose a religious one.

The issue of the Religion Clauses abroad has in our day been caught up in a highly charged atmosphere with wide-ranging questions about whether other provisions of the Constitution are applicable to U.S. government activity abroad.[11] Decisions regarding these other provisions are likely to influence the application of the Religion Clauses themselves. Fears and passions will lap over from one area of constitutional law to another. Among the other constitutional provisions involved are the Due Process Clause of the Fifth Amendment, the privilege against self-incrimination, the prohibition against unreasonable searches and seizures, the war and emergency powers of Congress and the President, the President's designation in the Constitution as Commander in Chief of the Armed Forces, and the authority of the political branches of the government to conduct foreign relations. In respect to all of these topics, the question of immediate interest is the significance of extraterritoriality. Although the Religion Clauses have their own history and independent force, the Constitution must be taken as a whole and the interpretation of one part harmonized with that of others.

When the United States acts within the territory over which it is sovereign, it acts within a legal framework entirely its own, except in regard to restrictions imposed by international law. But when it acts outside the United States, the laws and cultures of other nations must be considered. When the United States acts in another country, a distinction can be drawn between those situations in which it simply supports a policy chosen by the government of the other country and situations in which it makes its own choice of the policy it wishes to pursue and the methods it wishes to employ, either with or without the consent of the other government. In the first situation, it can be argued that a foreign policy interest in supporting the aims of another government justifies departure from a restriction that would be applicable in a purely domestic situation.[12] For example, it probably is constitutional for the United States to provide funds to a foreign government to strengthen that government's judicial system with the aim of promoting the "rule of law," even though such a judicial system would not be constitutional within the United States as a component of any American government. On the same rationale, it might be permissible for the United States to provide funds to Islamic schools in a foreign country if it is the policy of the government of that country to support such schools. In the second situation, on the other hand, when the United States has made the policy choice and independently pursues its own objectives, justification for the program cannot be deference to the wishes of a foreign government or respect for another culture. Instead, the argument must be that the Constitution permits being done outside the United States what may not be done within it, simply because it is outside the United States. In other words, that limitations in the Constitution were intended to apply only to actions performed within a certain territory and not simply to any exercise of power under the Constitution. Thus a detention center erected outside the United States would not be subject to the restraints of the Due Process Clause.[13] The Guantanamo Center, of course, because of the peculiar character of the lease under which it is held and the fact that the United States exercises complete control over it, is a special case.[14]

The distinction between inside and outside the United States is not so easy to apply. For example, in *United States v. Verdugo-Urquidez,*[15] a 1990 Supreme Court decision involving the applicability of the Fourth Amendment to the search of a house in Mexico owned by a Mexican, the search possibly being in violation of Mexican law, the federal officials who authorized the search were in Washington when they authorized it, and the evidence obtained by the search was sought to be used to convict the owner of the house in a trial in California. So also, so far as the Establishment Clause is concerned, assistance to a religious group abroad, even if there are no direct effects on the followers of that religion in the United States, nevertheless may relieve them of the burden of supporting their coreligionists abroad and enhance the prestige of the denomination as a whole, including within the United States.[16]

In the *Verdugo-Urquidez* case, it seemed important to the Supreme Court that the man whose house was searched in Mexico was not an American citizen. If he had been, the Court suggested, the result might have been different. The Bush administration's different treatment of citizens and noncitizens detained on suspicion of being enemy combatants or terrorists, also attaches importance to the distinction. The only connection the defendant in *Verdugo-Urquidez* had with the United States was that he was kidnapped in Mexico and brought to the United States against his will, and put on trial for violations of U.S. laws by acts committed in Mexico. Aliens, of course, have many rights under the U.S. Constitution, including protection against unreasonable searches and seizures in the United States. Even if they have nothing to do with the United States except that they own property here, their property is protected against expropriation without just compensation. Whether aliens having absolutely no connection with the United States except that they are injured by it in a foreign country have any rights under the Constitution—other than the Fourth Amendment right the Court in *Verdugo-Urquidez* determined that they do not have—is the topic of the day.[17] So also it was about 100 years ago during an earlier period of extension of American power abroad after the Spanish-American War. That period gave rise to a series of Supreme Court decisions known as *The Insular Cases,* which involved the applicability of various provisions of the Constitution in the former Spanish colonies.[18] More recently, a federal court of appeals has held that a citizen and resident of Colombia, who had a bank account in Switzerland that allegedly was interfered with by officials of the United States, might have standing to present claims under the Fourth and Fifth Amendments.[19] If the United States prolongs its occupation of Iraq and its presence in Afghanistan and continues to detain people in these countries without charges or any sort of process, will they acquire rights under the Constitution along with rights they already have under international law? Could U.S. promotion of a particular interpretation of Islam in Iraq or Indonesia violate rights under the Free Exercise Clause of Muslims who adhere to different interpretations, but who are not U.S. citizens?[20]

Citizens and perhaps permanent residents and other persons having some substantial connection with the United States have at least some constitutional protections against United States' actions abroad that affect them. As mentioned above, the Court suggested in *Verdugo-Urquidez* that it might have made a difference if the house searched in Mexico had belonged to a U.S. citizen. In 1957, the Supreme Court held that the United States could not court-martial a civilian U.S. citizen who had accompanied U.S. Armed Forces abroad: she was entitled to trial by jury, at least in a capital case, under the Sixth Amendment.[21] If U.S. support of a particular interpretation of Islam in a foreign country adversely affects the religious practice of an American citizen abroad, perhaps himself or herself a Muslim, might there be a violation of the citizen's rights under the Free Exercise Clause?

In the Court's opinion in *Verdugo-Urquidez,* there are passages suggesting that extraterritorial applicability of the Constitution may vary with the particular right invoked. If there was any violation of the Fourth Amendment, the Court said, it only occurred in Mexico. This seems a strained argument if one bears in mind that the chain of causation that led to the search began in Washington. The Court contrasted the Fourth Amendment with the Fifth Amendment privilege against self-incrimination, and said that the latter is violated only when evidence obtained by compulsion is used against a person in a trial. Thus, if there was compulsion in Mexico that led to the use of evidence in California, the privilege might prevent its introduction.[22] If U.S. officials in Washington authorize the assassination of a religious figure in Indonesia, possibly an American citizen, because he or she is expounding a "fundamentalist" version of Islam, would an invasion of the interest intended to be protected by the Free Exercise Clause take place solely in Indonesia?

In 1991 in *Lamont v. Woods,*[23] the Court of Appeals for the Second Circuit held that using tax money to fund religious schools abroad violated the Establishment Clause. Congress had authorized grants to American schools that served as examples of American educational ideas and practices. The money was not to be used to train people for religious pursuits or to construct buildings that would be used for religious worship or instruction, and recipient schools were not allowed to discriminate in admissions. Included among the schools entitled to receive grants, but not limited to them, were religiously affiliated schools. In spite of the restrictions contained in the authorizing statute, the court held that grants to "pervasively sectarian" schools—the test it found applicable at the time to domestic schools—violated the Establishment Clause, and that the extraterritorial location of the grantee institutions made no difference. In regard to the particular program before it, the court could not see that any serious foreign policy or national security interests were implicated. But the court suggested that under some set of circumstances, there might be a compelling reason for setting aside the ordinary rule against aid to pervasively sectarian schools, though it doubted that such an exemption would ever extend to the outright promotion of religious doctrine.

The court in *Lamont* discussed *Verdugo-Urquidez* and its teaching that the violation of the Fourth Amendment occurred solely in Mexico. But in the case of the Establishment Clause, as the court conceived, the constitutional violation occurred when the law authorizing the grants was enacted, or at least when a government administrator in the United States made the grants to the American sponsors of the overseas schools, and did not await the actual transfer of funds abroad. Furthermore, the effect on federal taxpayers of increased taxes was notably domestic. The Establishment Clause, unlike the Fourth Amendment, the court said, was a basic limitation on the power of Congress. Still, the very language that introduces the Establishment Clause—"Congress shall make no law"—also introduces the Free Exercise Clause, but would it be argued that there is a violation of that clause also simply by the enactment of a law, even though no adverse effects follow to the free exercise of anyone's religion?

More persuasive perhaps than the phrasing of particular provisions of the Constitution is the suggestion that there is a hierarchy of rights in the Bill of Rights and that this has significance for their applicability abroad and for their ability to resist competing claims from other parts of the Constitution, such as the war power, the power to direct foreign relations, and the President's designation as Commander in Chief of the Armed Forces.[24]

The Free Exercise Clause, insofar as it prohibits active persecution on grounds of religion, may embody so fundamental a value that it is proof against all rival considerations, whether they are put forward as a matter of the United States' own policy or that of a foreign government, just as may the Due Process Clause's prohibition against official conduct that "shocks the conscience." The Establishment Clause, on the other hand, could be viewed as the product of a special history, linked no doubt to an idea of what is authentic in religion and to religious freedom, but not necessarily to be insisted upon, at least not through a particular understanding, in all places and under all circumstances. It bears noticing that when Congress enacted the Indian Civil Rights Act in 1968,[25] it imposed upon the Indian tribes in the United States, which are viewed as quasi-sovereign nations, a requirement that they respect the free exercise of religion, but it did not impose upon them the restriction of the Establishment Clause. In Anglo-American history, the idea that there should be legal protection of free exercise long preceded the notion that establishments should be prohibited. Thus, in regard to the present programs of the United States that are designed to promote a particular interpretation of Islam, it may make a difference whether they are claimed to violate the Free Exercise Clause or the Establishment Clause and whether the United States has initiated these programs as a matter of its own policy or at the behest of a foreign government.

NOTES

1. See, e.g., reports of projects in Indonesia of the State Department's Human Rights and Democracy Fund, U.S. State Department, "HRDF Project Highlights," U.S. State Department, www.state.gov/r/pa/prs/ps/2002/13615.htm (accessed February 11, 2005); Bureau of Democracy, Human Rights, and Labor, "FY 2001–2002 Human Rights and Democracy Fund Projects," U.S. State Department, June 1, 2004, www.state.gov/g/drl/rls/32959.htm (accessed February 14, 2005).

2. Ibid.

3. Bureau of Democracy, Human Rights, and Labor, "Human Rights and Democracy Fund."

4. John H. Mansfield, "The Religion Clauses of the First Amendment and Foreign Relations," *DePaul Law Review* 36 (1986): 1.

5. *Witters v. Washington Dept. of Services for the Blind,* 474 U.S. 481 (1986).

6. *Employment Division v. Smith,* 494 U.S. 872 (1990) (involving the use of peyote in religious ceremonies).

7. See *Church of the Lukumi Babalu Aye v. City of Hialeah,* 508 U.S. 520 (1993).

8. Which the court in *Lamont v. Woods,* 948 F.2d 825, 842 (2d Cir. 1991), suggests as a possibility.

9. *Bowen v. Kendrick,* 487 U.S. 589 (1988).

10. See *DKT Memorial Fund Ltd. v. Agency for Int'l Development,* 887 F.2d 275, 290 (D.C. Cir. 1989) (noting that the government may promote the right of freedom of opinion and expression).

11. See the Supreme Court's decisions in *Hamdi v. Rumsfeld,* 542 U.S. 507 (2004); *Rasul v. Bush,* 542 U.S. 466 (2004); *Rumsfeld v. Padilla,* 542 U.S. 426 (2004); *Hamdan v. Rumsfeld,* 126 S. Ct. 2749 (2006).

12. See *DKT Memorial Fund v. Agency for Int'l Development,* 887 F.2d 275, 291 (D.C. Cir. 1989) (justifying on grounds of "recognition of the sovereignty and self-determination rights of other states" different treatment of foreign governments and foreign NGOs so far as concerns subsidizing entities that promote abortion).

13. See Gerald L. Neuman, "Closing the Guantanamo Loophole," *Loyola Law Review* 50 (2004): 1, 44, 51 (expressing concern with extraterritorial prisons).

14. See *Rasul,* 542 U.S. 466.

15. *United States v. Verdugo-Urquidez,* 494 U.S. 259 (1990).

16. See *Lamont v. Woods,* 948 F.2d 825, 834–35 (2d Cir. 1991) (suggesting that funding of Catholic schools in the Philippines may strengthen the Catholic Church worldwide, including in the United States).

17. In *Verdugo-Urquidez,* the Court suggested, in dictum, that Fifth Amendment rights were not available to nonresident aliens who had no substantial connection with the United States. *Verdugo-Urquidez,* 494 U.S. at 269. See also *Harbury v. Deutch,* 233 F.3d 596 (D.C. Cir. 2000), reversed on other grounds, 536 U.S. 403 (2002), and judgment vacated, 44 Fed. Appx 522 (D.C. Cir. 2002) (Guatemalan tortured in Guatemala by CIA "assets" not deprived of any rights under the Due Process Clause even though officials in the United States directed it). But the court in *In re Guantanamo Detainees Cases,* 355 F. Supp. 2d 443 (D.D.C. 2005), petition for interlocutory appeal granted, 2005 U.S. App. LEXIS 4651, suggests that the Court's dictum in *Verdugo-Urquidez* has been weakened by its subsequent opinion in *Rasul v. Bush,* 542 U.S. 466 (2004).

18. For example, *Dorr v. United States,* 195 U.S. 138 (1904) (jury trial in the Philippines).

19. *Cardenas v. Smith,* 733 F.2d 909 (D.C. Cir. 1984).

20. See *DKT Memorial Fund,* 887 F.2d at 284 (holding that foreign NGOs have no standing to raise claims of violation of constitutional rights of free speech and association).

21. *Reid v. Covert,* 354 U.S. 1 (1957).

22. See Mark A. Godsey, "The New Frontier of Constitutional Confession Law," *Georgetown Law Journal* 91 (2003): 851 (suggesting that the Due Process rule against involuntary confessions is not available to an alien coerced abroad if the confession is sought to be used in a trial in the United States, but that the privilege against self-incrimination is, because the former is a "freestanding civil liberty," whereas the latter is a "trial right").

23. *Lamont,* 948 F.2d 825.

24. See *In re Guantanamo Detainees Cases,* 355 F. Supp. 2d 443 petition for interlocutory appeal granted, 2005 U.S. App. LEXIS 4651, discussing the notion of "fundamental rights" that emerged in the *Insular Cases;* Neuman, "Closing the Guantanamo Loophole," 51 (suggesting freedom of conscience is a fundamental right).

25. *Indian Civil Rights Act, U.S. Code* 25 (2005): §§ 1301–41.

CHAPTER 6

The 9/11 Commission Report and Public Discourse Project

MICHAEL HURLEY

The 2004 publication of the 9/11 Commission Report marked the official conclusion of the investigation of the *National Commission on Terrorist Attacks Upon the United States* (9/11 Commission) into the events of September 11, 2001. The Report itself was designed to be a starting point, to the extent it sought to determine the shortcomings which had permitted the attacks, perceived generally to reflect a gross failure of intelligence (but with a view to fixing problems rather than assigning blame). For a year following the Report's publication, the 9/11 Commission members and some of its former senior staff, including the author of this chapter as Senior Director of Policy, were actively engaged in publicizing the Report's recommendations, including issuing "report cards" on progress in adopting them, under the 9/11 PDP (9/11 Public Discourse Project).[1]

The Report laid the groundwork for a thorough restructuring of both the executive branch, including related agencies, and the legislative branch in matters concerning intelligence and security, in the first instance under the IRTPA (Intelligence Reform and Terrorism Prevention Act of 2004). As witnessed by the 9/11 PDP report cards, however, the American people are still not as safe as they should be and the Commission's agenda is unfinished as a practical matter. The purpose of this chapter is to review again the Report's recommendations as work in progress from the 9/11 PDP perspective, to the extent they provide the background to understanding changes in intelligence gathering and approaches since September 11, 2001, but also potential future changes. The concern is that, the further the events of 9/11 recede from public consciousness, the more attenuated the reform impulse becomes, hence the problem of unfinished business from the perspective of the Report's recommendations.[2]

The Commission issued forty-one recommendations aimed at improving the work of government in general and the intelligence community in particular to fulfil a mandate of guarding against future attacks.[3] The recommendations laid out in the 9/11 Report were divided into three areas: (1) homeland security, emergency preparedness, and response; (2) reforming the institutions of government; and (3) foreign policy, public diplomacy, and nonproliferation. The following focuses chiefly on only one of the three areas covered in the Report, namely the reform of government institutions as they affect the intelligence function. In the final series of 9/11 PDP events, it was recognized that reforming the intelligence structure within the executive branch was far more successful than reforming the Congressional (committee) oversight function,[4] and that even within the executive branch problems remained,[5] despite the Commission's convictions concerning its importance.

The articulated basis for the Commission's concerns with the uncompleted reworking of Congressional oversight was threefold. First, that because of the secret nature of intelligence work, Congressional oversight was particularly necessary because third parties such as the media could not effectively exercise a watchdog function as would be the case for normal governmental activities. Second, that those portions of the Commission's recommendations concerning restructuring intelligence on the executive branch side which had already been accepted had so increased the authority and potential intrusions of intelligence agencies into citizens' lives so that a more powerful intelligence community required an equally powerful oversight body to prevent abuses (particularly given the reality that traditional divisions such as foreign versus domestic intelligence were no longer perceived as valid). And third, that oversight was required to advise and use the budgetary power where necessary to move the intelligence functions in new directions in a challenging world, if there were a perception that the intelligence community were again not succeeding in its appointed tasks. The main thrust of this chapter is to present the 9/11 Commission and PDP conclusions that the restructuring of the intelligence community without a similar restructuring of Congressional committees and attendant oversight should be seen as implementing only one half of interdependent measures. In chiefly reforming the structure of the intelligence community on the executive side, Congress left much unfinished business.

To argue this point, I first review Congress's structural role in the intelligence area and ultimately its (and the executive's) shortcomings in preventing the 9/11 attacks. I then lay out the Commission's recommendations concerning Congressional oversight and the restructuring of Congressional committees, including the full implementation of a Privacy and Civil Liberties Oversight Board. The remainder of the chapter will follow the question of why these reforms matter and should not be delayed. Lastly, I will address the hurdles that Congress has to overcome in order to comply with the bulk of the 9/11 Commission's unfulfilled recommendations, and the role of the public in reaching that goal.

Congress has, in the past, exercised considerable oversight over the intelligence community through the use of various committees, all of whom have jurisdiction over some portion of the intelligence process. The problem with this oversight through many differing bodies is that it has been scattershot and unconnected. The 9/11 Commission found that there was a failure to connect the dots from disparate sources leading up to the terrorist attacks as a result of both misguided oversight and failure to share information among different agencies concerned.

Where was this failure to connect the dots most evident? The events of September 11, 2001, should not be perceived as isolated instances. A previous attack on the World Trade Center occurred in 1993, and numerous other al Qaeda plots were uncovered and prevented by the intelligence services during the 1990s. In 1993, the same year as the first attack on the World Trade Center, a plot to blow up the Lincoln and Holland Tunnels in New York City was discovered. The Somali tribesman responsible for shooting down an American Blackhawk helicopter, which we now know as "Black Hawk Down" were trained in al Qaeda camps. In 1995, a plot to blow up twelve 747s over the Pacific Ocean was disrupted. In 1998, Osama Bin Laden declared that it was Allah's will that all Muslims can kill any American, military or civilian, anywhere in the world, at any time.

In August 1998, al Qaeda carried out simultaneous truck bombings targeting U.S. Embassies in East Africa. In December 1999, an al Qaeda operative was caught at the United States/Canadian border, trying to enter the United States. He was on his way to bomb Los Angeles International Airport. And on October 12, 2000, operatives of al Qaeda successfully attacked the USS *Cole* while it was in port in Yemen. It is believed that the attack on the *Cole* was the second attempt to strike a United States ship. An earlier plot to bomb the USS *The Sullivans,* on January 3, 2000, failed when the overloaded boat carrying the explosives sank.

Similarly to the structure of the intelligence community, corresponding Congressional oversight remained unchanged following the end of the Cold War. Throughout the described developments, the shift of threat from nation states to (nonstate actor) terrorists was not debated in the Congress. The very modest number of hearings held in relation to terrorist threats reflect that "terrorism was a second- or third-order priority within the committees of Congress responsible for national security."[6] Instead, the committees responsible for the FAA (Federal Aviation Administration) and air travel were focusing on airport congestion and a Passenger Bill of Rights. The committees responsible for immigration issues focused on the U.S. border with Mexico, with little or no attention paid to the Canadian border. Very few hearings were held focusing on the growing terrorist threat.

The 9/11 Commission found that, due to the decentralized nature of the executive branch, no single person was responsible for the conduct of national intelligence prior to 9/11. Congress took steps to remedy this by creating the DNI (Director of National Intelligence, a recommendation of the 9/11 commission in terms of intelligence reform), but then failed to create effective oversight for this new position. Congressional oversight largely still mirrors the intelligence function's organization within the executive branch prior to 9/11, notwithstanding creation of the Department of Homeland Security. It provides so much (fragmented) oversight that it is only marginally effective. Currently, eighty-eight different committees or subcommittees have jurisdiction over the Department of Homeland Security. Some 412 members of Congress and all 100 senators sit on one or more of these committees. With so many people having some say, no one has ultimate responsibility.

While both the House and Senate have Select Committees on Intelligence, they have limited authority. Neither committee has exclusive jurisdiction over intelligence agencies. Appropriations for the intelligence community are determined by the Appropriations Committee and channelled through the defense appropriations process. The Armed Services Committees have jurisdiction over the intelligence services within the DOD (Department of Defense, DIA, NRO, NGA, and the intelligence sections of the respective branches). The problem is therefore not only one of determining ultimate responsibility, but also of knowledge. None of these bodies have full knowledge of the performance of the intelligence community, preventing effective oversight.

Furthermore, tenure on these select committees was limited by the rules of both Houses. Members traditionally could only serve on each committee for a limited period of time. Many members believe these restrictions prevent committee members from developing needed expertize which is required for effective oversight.

Finally, while secrecy is necessary in intelligence work, it can also harm effective oversight. The overall budget of the intelligence community remains classified, as are most of its activities. Members of the Select Committees cannot rely on public disclosure and investigative journalism or watchdog organizations to spur them to action like other committees can, nor can they even rely on the public's general sense whether it is getting its money's worth based on the magnitude of investment. This prevents the people's representatives from raising public awareness to legitimize their function and give them leverage in their oversight task as it stands.

In order to remedy these problems, the 9/11 Commission came up with several recommendations to improve Congressional oversight. They were designed to help make Congress a full partner in the business of collecting, analyzing, and acting on intelligence information developed by the U.S. intelligence community. It was understood that Congressional oversight could be accomplished in different ways, but what was the preferred solution? First, Congress should create two Permanent Standing Committees, one for Intelligence and one for Homeland Security, in both the House of Representatives and the Senate. These committees should have sole jurisdiction over all intelligence activities and the Department of Homeland Security. The intelligence committees in particular should have control over both the authorization and appropriation of funds. They should be smaller than the standard committees, perhaps limited to seven or nine members. This would have two effects. First, it would make each member feel individually more responsible for the work of the committee. Second, it would limit the number of people who have access to classified information, and thus reduce the potential for leaks (a practical problem, but also limiting access to information does limit oversight). The committees should have a nonpartisan staff, which works for the committee as a whole, rather than for individual members. Additionally, the majority party's representation on these committees should never exceed the minority's representation by more than one.

One of the first tasks of the standing committees would be to conduct continuing studies of the activities of the intelligence agencies and to report problems relating to the collection and use of intelligence information to all members of the House and Senate. Second, additionally to receiving budgetary control, the topline number for the entire intelligence budget should be made public permanently, and the national intelligence program should be appropriated to the sole jurisdiction of the National Director of Intelligence, and not the Secretary of Defense. Moreover, the intelligence committee should have a subcommittee whose sole purpose would be oversight of the intelligence community, without any responsibility for working on the consuming process of working on the budget.

In order to ensure that the Intelligence Committees are fully informed on all issues relating to intelligence, four of the members on each committee should also serve on Armed Services Committee, the Judiciary Committee, the Foreign Affairs Committee, and the Defense Appropriations subcommittee. This would ensure that important interests related to intelligence are represented and integrated with the work of the new committees.

Perhaps the most important change is that tenure on these Permanent Standing Committees should not be limited to any specific term of years. It is the constant turnover on the current committees that has led to a general lack of experience with intelligence matters among those who are responsible for oversight. One cannot give effective oversight to an issue if one is unfamiliar with the ins and outs of the subject matter. Unfortunately, the current set-up of the Intelligence Committees ensures that this familiarity can never be achieved.

The Department of Homeland Security itself currently answers to eighty-eight committees or subcommittees. This is unheard of in any other executive agency. The House created a Select Committee on Homeland Security, but the Senate did not follow suit. Furthermore, the House Committee may soon be eliminated. Creating a single body responsible for the oversight of the Department of Homeland Security will provide a single, clear authority of the type currently overseeing the Departments of Justice and Defense.

To remedy these issues and to begin to address the morass that is the current oversight of DHS, the Commission recommended the creation of a single, principal point of oversight, and review for homeland security to which intelligence relates. The Commission left it up to Congress to determine which committee(s) should have jurisdiction and its duties. But it recommends that there be one committee in the House and one in the Senate, that the committee(s) should be permanent standing committee(s), and that it have a nonpartisan staff, much like the Intelligence Committees recommended above.

If congressional leaders choose not to vest authorization and appropriations authority in one intelligence committee in the House and in the Senate, another meritorious approach is to create separate appropriations subcommittees to deal with all appropriations for the intelligence community (taking the intelligence budget out of the defense budget). The House and Senate already have homeland security appropriations subcommittees; there should also be, under this model, intelligence appropriations committees, with exclusive control over the appropriations of the Cabinet agencies under their jurisdiction. This will help ensure that the intelligence community as well as the Department of Homeland Security are funded at acceptable levels and that the funding for these agencies will not depend on the rise and fall in popularity of the funding of the DOD, which is the current practice.

In issuing their recommendations regarding Congressional oversight, the 9/11 Commission had two specific goals in mind. Firstly, effective oversight must be created to set the balance between civil rights and liberties on one hand and security on the other. Secondly, but equally important, a check on whether the system is working must be provided. That includes controlling the setting of priorities, the formation of adequate responses to new developments in threats and the rate of success in measures taken by the intelligence community.

In order to provide adequate oversight and in order to accomplish these two goals, the structure of Congressional oversight of the intelligence community must adapt in the same manner the intelligence community had to adapt to a new threat. It has to be condensed and centralized in order to provide the counterpart for the intelligence community. In short, the Congressional committee structure and thus oversight structure should correspond to the new structure of the intelligence community. Committee tasks must reflect the changes and challenges the modified intelligence community presents. The first of these goals, the balancing of civil liberties and security, must respond to the potential threat to privacy and civil liberties which the diffusion between domestic and foreign intelligence collection poses.

This diffusion was implemented intentionally with the passage of the IRTPA. It incorporates the major changes that Congress enacted following the terrorist attacks on New York and Washington, DC, creating the NCTC (National Counterterrorism Center) and the position of DNI. It also represents the biggest change in the structuring of the intelligence community since the passage of the National Security Act of 1947. The intelligence community had grown as a response to the Cold War and—until the passage of the IRTPA—had remained essentially unchanged even after the collapse of the Soviet Union in 1991. The strict division between domestic and foreign intelligence collection, mainly allocated to the FBI and CIA, respectively, made sense during the Cold War, but proved to be useless and fatal in the prevention of terrorist attacks involving nonstate actors. The creation of the DNI was designed to fill that gap. This office, currently held by John Michael McConnell, is charged with overseeing all sixteen agencies that are responsible for intelligence.[7] Thus, information flow between the different agencies can be directed and comes together in the office of the DNI.

As the intelligence community has concentrated much power in the office of the DNI, an equally powerful watchdog is needed. Traditionally, this oversight role has been performed by Congress, principally through committees that corresponded to the structure of the intelligence community. The restructuring of the latter without a reform of Congressional oversight leads to a lack of accountability. Who assesses the work of the DNI? Who ensures that the newly empowered intelligence agencies do not abuse their power, overstepping the line between civil liberties and security? And, most importantly, who will decide where this line is to be drawn?

As the debate regarding the Patriot Act[8] has shown, the blurring of boundaries that strictly separated intelligence collection within and outside American borders may provide for more security. However, it may also curtail the protection of civil rights and liberties of U.S. citizens. The protection of privacy and civil liberties of a person under surveillance traditionally did not matter as long as that person was not an American citizen and the surveillance took place outside the United States. However, as the enemy in the fight against terrorism cannot be identified by citizenship and cannot be determined geographically, domestic surveillance has become more important. That also implies an increase in the possibility of violating American citizen's privacy and civil liberties. As the wall between domestic and foreign intelligence collection is lowered and new mandates emerge calling for coordination of both, two steps now have to be followed by Congress. It has to ensure that privacy and civil liberties are still protected, and it has to measure effectiveness and evaluate the work of the Department of Homeland Security, the DNI, and the intelligence agencies it oversees.

In order to ensure that the proper balance between security and civil liberties was struck, the 9/11 Commission recommended the creation of a Privacy and Civil Liberties Oversight Board. Both Senate and the executive have been slow in its implementation. The President's nominations for Chair and Vice Chair were not submitted until late 2005. It took another half year for Senate to approve them. The board held its first meetings in 2006, and submitted its first annual report in March 2007. The board is a unit within the Executive Office of the President, and it remains unclear yet what role Congress will play in conjunction with the board as the effective ombudsman within the executive branch for civil liberties touched upon by intelligence gathering activities.

There is a false sense on occasion that the intelligence community itself is a reluctant subject of oversight. However, the intelligence community has no vested interest in limiting Congressional oversight. On the contrary, functional, concentrated, and centralized Congressional oversight is in the intelligence community's best interest. It is not only in the citizen's but also in the intelligence community's interest that the government takes its role in oversight seriously. The first priority of the intelligence community must be and remain the security of the country. To place the responsibility of guarding civil liberties on the same shoulders that are responsible for providing security, in its most obvious sense completely forgoes checks that must be made by opposing interests. It is improbable that the intelligence community on its own would provide satisfactory self-restraint according to the public's wishes. Such a double responsibility would furthermore constrain the intelligence community from acting to the best of its ability. It cannot work effectively if it constantly must weigh the comparative merits of one or both of neglecting security versus not protecting civil liberties. Instead, control should rest with the elected representatives of the people.

Similarly, the second goal, general oversight of the intelligence community, can most expeditiously be provided by Congress in simply following the recommendations made by the 9/11 Commission. However, the simple truth is that the restructuring of Congress according to the recommendations is a difficult matter because it would redistribute power within the Congress. The real problem is not a battle between the executive and legislative branches, but between competing Congressional committees and individual member interests. Though the need for reform is universally acknowledged within Congress, the question of which form these reforms should take delays progress. Though two committees, one each in House and Senate, have been created to oversee the Department of Homeland Security, their powers remain limited, and many other committees claim jurisdiction. The 9/11 Commission recommendations to reform the structure of intelligence oversight have not been implemented.

What stands in the way of oversight reform is the decentralized nature of power in the Congress and the reluctance of current committees charged with important oversight functions to give up their powers. Ironically, the failure to implement these recommendations has the same roots as the problem they are supposed to solve. The lack of a central authority in a structure that distributes power to several groups renders it unresponsive. Members of Congress agree that intelligence oversight must be reformed; just as the need for reform of the intelligence community after the end of the Cold War was generally accepted.

In the case of reforming the intelligence community, the solution to the dilemma was supposed to be Congress. The significance of Congressional oversight becomes clearer in this regard when looking at the post–Cold War, pre-9/11 intelligence community. Having built up a system of expertize in areas that were no longer supposed to be a priority, individual agencies within the intelligence community faced the problem of justifying their continued existence and budget. This was supposed to be addressed by the DNI reprogramming and redirecting resources within the intelligence community, but that ran afoul bureaucratically of separation of intelligence from defense activities (because of tensions whether intelligence activities should be focused primarily at the strategic level, versus at the operational level of war-fighters in places like Iraq and Afghanistan). There is also an inherent inflexibility pertaining to any decentralized bureaucratic apparatus, making centralized reform difficult. Adding to these structural problems, the make up of the intelligence community traditionally reflected a relatively homogeneous personnel not including key groups fitting in within the Muslim and Arab worlds. It seems only natural that reform, which would have included loss of power and jobs, could not be expected to occur from within. Without an overreaching restructuring plan for the entire community, every agency's first priority then had to be to work best as they could with the resources and assets already in hand.

The homogeneity of its members made a shift in any direction difficult. It reduced the amount of dissent, necessary for responding to any external change. This kind of "groupthink" constrained the sphere in which changes could occur, limiting it to a smaller area of expertise. In trying to cope with the changed world, officers were assigned to fields in which they had little expertise. The training of new personnel with expertise in the Arabic language and culture was further complicated by the concern for penetration of the agencies by "moles." Considering that the study of Arabic languages at colleges and universities in the United States was and still is rare, this only adds to the problem as does the considerable amount of time that has to be invested in any new hire before he or she can be sent into the field.

It should also be recalled at this point, that the enemy had not only shifted "geographi-cally." The intelligence community was not dealing solely with nation states anymore. Instead, it now had to understand the motivations and tactics of nonstate actors such as al Qaeda as opposed to leaders, agencies, or spies that acted under the umbrella of a nation state. This was certainly not an easy task to the extent the intelligence community was perceived moving only slowly away from Cold War priorities, while new threats posed by radically different nonstate actors were proliferating rapidly.

In bringing these facts to light, the 9/11 Commission Report essentially addressed two failures. First, the failure of the intelligence community in foreseeing or preventing the attacks. Second, the root of the former—the failure in not having adapted quickly enough to a new, post–Cold War threat. The 9/11 Commission's task was not primarily to place the blame, but basically to finally do what should have been done in the 1990s: to analyze how security concerns correspond to the measures in place—only now there existed a concrete example, and everybody was listening.

Congress, executive agencies, and senior political officials failed to connect the dots leading to 9/11. In light of these failures, the main normative question became who should be responsible for the performance of the intelligence community which itself became more important in shaping recommendations for reform. A look at the past showed that Congressional oversight had never been very strong when it came to the intelligence com-munity. The agencies have traditionally been responsive to the executive. Intelligence failures such as the Bay of Pigs invasion or the plots to assassinate Castro have presented a fiasco for the intelligence community more than for the executive, whose involvement or spearheading of such projects has often found refuge behind the veil of secrecy so readily accepted in matters of intelligence. At the same time, Congress's oversight function has diminished over time. With committees overseeing only parts of the intelligence process and the lack of expertise of its members due to the high turnover and classification of material, Congress had neglected the "traditional review of the administration of programs and the implementation of law."[9] It oftentimes relied on "fire-alarm" oversight, waiting for interest groups, individuals, or the media to point out wrongful implementations of their policies. In the case of the intelligence community, such a tactic is not possible since most of the intelligence community's activities are rightfully classified.

That is a scenario to be avoided, not lastly in the interest of the intelligence community itself. Though at first glance it might seem desirable for the intelligence community to avoid effective Congressional oversight, in reality that only weakens it. It allows the exec-utive to place the responsibility for any failed operations on the intelligence community and thus damages the legitimacy of the latter's actions. Furthermore, as the practices of the intelligence community between 1991 and 2001 have shown, they are—ironically—ill-equipped independently to react to a change of priorities. Congressional oversight can thus be seen as a partner to the intelligence community. They complement each other, each being responsible for different tasks, which combined validate both Congress and the intelligence community in their raison d'être.

If the legitimacy of the intelligence community rests in the hands of functioning Congressional oversight, the legitimacy of the proposed Congressional committees rests in the hands of the electorate. That, in turn, requires transparency. If terrorism was a second- or third-order priority within the committees of Congress responsible for national security, it took an even lower priority in the minds of most American citizens. However, the public did not have access to the information possessed by Congress and the executive. Again, security issues involve a certain amount of secrecy, but information about the extent of terrorism threats and the importance of making antiterrorism work a number one priority is not classified. Had the public been more focused on the threat terrorism constantly posed during the 1990s, had it understood that more than just a nuisance, it was rapidly becoming a first order threat—especially after the USS *Cole* attack—it could have exerted pressure on the executive and Congress to act accordingly. The same mistake should not be made again.

The recommendations of the 9/11 Commission stress the importance of declassifying the topline intelligence budget to bring more transparency for the public. Despite some criticism that transparency may interfere with the intelligence function, the sometime classification of the topline budget serves little purpose. An aggregate number for intelligence spending does not reveal the sensitive workings of the intelligence community. The numbers for military intelligence are already provided by the executive, therefore part of the budget is known and that fact has not led to criticisms arguing that enemies have thus gained insight into American intelligence capabilities.

As long as parts of the budget remain classified, no separate annual appropriations bill for the intelligence community is possible. This also means that a centralized Congressional committee, as recommended by the 9/11 Commission, cannot gain control of the budget. As has been stressed earlier, the recommendations of the 9/11 Commission work as a package. A centralized and more compact committee providing oversight can solve the problem of communication and improve the dedication of each member to its oversight task. Unlimited tenure addresses the problem of expertise and understanding the committees must have in order to fulfil their tasks. The bipartisan element avoids the influence of partisan politics to a certain degree, whereas including members of other intelligence-related committees such as the Armed Services, Foreign Affairs, Judiciary, and Appropriations Committee address both the issues of transparency and communication as well as expertise.

Control of the budget is essential to ensure that any committee's oversight efforts are acted upon by the executive. The question of budget control and allocation of committee jurisdiction is certainly one of the difficult questions that have to be resolved by Congress in order to implement the 9/11 Commission's recommendation regarding Congressional oversight of the intelligent community.

Congress most recently took action under the Implementing Recommendations of the 9/11 Commission Act of 2007. Public law 110-53 (August 3, 2007) addresses several of the shortcomings mentioned in this chapter, especially in bolstering the authorities of the Privacy and Civil Liberties Oversight Board, and declassifying the top line of the intelligence budget (subject to presidential waiver). However, the new law does not alter the structures of congressional oversight for intelligence and homeland security. The new law only expresses the sense of the Senate that the Senate Homeland Security and Intelligence Committees should report by December 2007 on their recommendations to improve oversight in response to the 9/11 Commission Report.

It is important that the public and interest groups continue to monitor Congress and apply pressure to ensure the continued improvement in securing the country against terrorist threats while protecting civil rights and liberties. The longer the Congress waits to reform its committee structure, the less likely it becomes that the recommendations of the 9/11 Commission and the reforms of the executive branch will be implemented as needed. The moment needs to be seized. The more time passes, after the attacks, the less attention is given to this issue, as new priorities emerge and public pressure wanes.

The attacks of 9/11 uncovered a problem of communication and chain of command that is not restricted to one part of government, but to government's handling of security as a whole. As such, the implementation of only part of the recommendations presents a problematic development. First, the 9/11 Commission Report has clearly pointed to the necessity of implementing all changes, since they do not present independent, but interdependent parts of a national security issue. Second, the implementation of some of the recommendations might lead to a false sense of security, forgoing the remainder of the necessary reforms to adjust to a changing world containing changing threats.

The work of the 9/11 Public Discourse Project concentrated on educating the public about both the findings published in the 9/11 Commission Report and the progress made in following up on its recommendations. Though the 9/11 PDP limited its work to sixteen months, interest groups, in particular the families of the 9/11 victims, continue to watch the progress in the implementation of the recommendations. Ultimately, the recommended structure is a democratic response to the security concern. It is built upon the notion that a legitimate model based on checks and balances is in the best interest of all involved and also the best response to a possibly changing dynamic of priorities. Most importantly, it will provide a measure of success for the actions taken by and policies regarding the intelligence community.

I would recommend heartily that all citizens read the 9/11 Commission Report. By reading it, citizens will understand the role they can play in improving security after 9/11. They provide the ultimate check on the performance of government—including the intelligence community. The gap between the intelligence community and Congressional oversight severs the intelligence community from the public. Strengthening Congressional oversight is the best precaution to ensure that the intelligence community is ultimately working in the best interest of the public.

The implementations of the 9/11 Commission's recommendations do not provide complete security from future attacks, and the 9/11 Commission rightly admitted that hindsight is more accurate than foresight. Intelligence pointing to the attack on Pearl Harbor in 1941 was also available, but analysis of the available intelligence—and this after all is the main and most difficult task of the intelligence community—did not consider it particularly noteworthy. Out of the masses of information that are gathered by the numerous agencies, threats are certain to be collected every day.

However, the recommendations of the 9/11 Commission are not built on foresight. They address present concerns. Foresight, as can be seen in the case of 9/11, can be nothing more than ensuring that the intelligence community acts on what after the end of the Cold War had become common perception: a change of threat. Congress has an important role to play ensuring that the priorities of the intelligence community match the threat we face. By doing so, the Congress will give the intelligence community exactly what it wants and needs to be its best: legitimacy.

In the areas of foreign policy, public diplomacy, and nonproliferation, progress has been similarly diffused. Bilateral and multilateral efforts in combating terrorism in the Middle East have been made but there still is much to be worked on, including assistance to Pakistan and Saudi Arabia in their efforts to combat terrorism and establishing a permanent contact group of leading governments to coordinate a unified counterterrorism strategy. The U.S. has also failed to engage in a common coalition approach for detention and prosecution standards concerning captured terrorists. Criticism of U.S. detention and prosecution of terrorist suspects will furthermore make it harder to build alliances which are necessary for a successful strategy against terrorism. In a similar vein, securing

WMD (weapons of mass destruction) is still not the top national security priority of either Congress or the President, though WMDs in the hands of terrorists has been declared to be the biggest threat to our country.

NOTES

1. The 9/11 PDP Web site is still accessible at http://www.9-11pdp.org (last accessed June 26, 2007), including much of its work product.

2. Institutional reformation of the intelligence community has been a long-running theme in Washington, see Richard A. Best, Jr., "Proposals for Intelligence Reorganization," 1949–2004 (July 29, 2004), *CRS Report for Congress Order Code RL32500.* The attacks on New York and Washington as well as mistakes concerning alleged weapons of mass destruction in Iraq were also not the first generally acknowledged intelligence failures, with examples regularly cited including the surprise that Sputnik represented as well as the Bay of Pigs fiasco.

3. "Final Report on 9/11 Commission Recommendations," December 5, 2005, http://www.9-11 pdp.org/press/2005-12-05_report.pdf (accessed last on June 26, 2007). An update to their findings is available in Thomas H. Kean and others, *9/11 Commission Report* (New York: Barnes & Noble, 2006). In the first area, some progress has been made to remedy the faults uncovered in 9/11 and the aftermath of Katrina, including securing a radio spectrum for responders, setting a deadline for compliance with the unified Incident Command System, implementing a biometric entry–exit screening system and in standardizing secure identifications. Unresolved issues concern the allocation of funds more as a matter of pork-barrel spending rather than as a function of risk and, not unrelated to that, assessing risks and vulnerabilities. Still uncompleted also are the improvement of passenger prescreening, the screening of bags and cargo and international collaboration in border and document security.

4. *The 9/11 Commission Report: The Unfinished Agenda, Session 5: Congressional Reform,* http://www.9-11pdp.org/ua/2005-07-11_transcript.pdf (last accessed June 27, 2007; discussion featuring Sen. Slade Gordon and Rep. Tim Roemer as former 9/11 Commission members, Sen. Pat Roberts as Chair of the Senate Select Committee on Intelligence, and Ambassador Thomas Foley as former Speaker of the House of Representatives).

5. Progress in reforming the FBI in particular was viewed as unfinished, see *The 9/11 Commission Report: The Unfinished Agenda, Session 1: CIA and FBI Reform,* http://www.9-11pdp.org/ua/ 2005-06-06_transcript.pdf (last accessed June 26, 2007; discussion featuring Jamie Gorelick as former 9/11 Commission member, former Attorney General Richard Thornburgh, former National Intelligence Council Chair John Gannon, and journalist Chitra Ragavan), but also questions remain(ed) regarding implementation of the entire revamped intelligence structure under the newly created office of the Director of National Intelligence including what amounted to cultural changes under a new structure modeled on the Goldwater-Nichols joint services approach as opposed to the structure largely put into place under the National Security Act of 1947 to fight the Cold War, see *The 9/11 Commission Report: The Unfinished Agenda, Session 2: Challenges Facing the Director of National Intelligence,* http://www.9-11pdp.org/ua/2005-06-13.htm (last accessed June 26, 2007; discussion featuring John F. Lehman as former 9/11 Commission member, Rep. Jane Harmon as HPSCI ranking member, Admiral William O. Studeman as former Deputy Director of Central Intelligence, and Siobhan Gorman as journalist).

6. *The 9/11 Commission Report* (Washington, DC: US Government Printing Office, 2002), 107. Also available online at http://www.gpoaccess.gov/911/pdf/fullreport.pdf (accessed last on June 26, 2007).

7. The sixteen agencies include the Central Intelligence Agency (CIA), the National Security Agency (NSA), the National Reconnaissance Office (NRO), the National Geospatial-Intelligence Agency (NGA), the Defense Intelligence Agency (DIA), the Bureau of Intelligence and Research (INR) in the State Department, the Office of Intelligence and Counterterrorism and Counterintelligence Divisions of the Federal Bureau of Investigation (FBI), the intelligence agencies of the four

military branches (Army, Navy, Air Force, and Marines), the Department of Homeland Security (DHS), the Coast Guard, now part of DHS, the Energy Department's Office of Intelligence, the Department of the Treasury's Office of Terrorism and Finance Intelligence, and the Drug Enforcement Administration (DEA).

8. Officially named the Uniting and Strengthening America by Providing Appropriate Tools Required to Intercept and Obstruct Terrorism Act of 2001 (USA PATRIOT Act).

9. *The 9/11 Commission Report* (Washington, DC: US Government Printing Office, 2002), 105. Also available online at http://www.gpoaccess.gov/911/pdf/fullreport.pdf (accessed last on June 26, 2007).

PART III

Constitutional and Domestic Law: Individual Rights Emphasis

CHAPTER 7

International Legal Limits on the Government's Power to Detain "Enemy Combatants"

GEREMY C. KAMENS

Revelations of abuse and even torture of detainees by American soldiers have steadily emerged since April 28, 2004, the day the Supreme Court heard oral argument in the case of *Hamdi v. Rumsfeld*. That evening, photos of naked Iraqi detainees stacked in a pyramid, hooded with arms outstretched, crumpled on a cement floor and tied by a leash, and cowering before attack dogs burst onto television screens around the world. Those images are the consequence of the Bush administration's about-face from codified standards of basic human treatment—standards that, ironically, arose from and trace their development to America's most divisive conflict.

Although legal principles requiring humanitarian treatment of enemy belligerents predate the establishment of the United States, it was only in the latter half of the nineteenth century that such principles became codified. During the Civil War, a professor at Columbia College, Dr. Francis Lieber, championed the promulgation of codified rules governing the conduct of soldiers in the field, including the proper treatment of captured enemy soldiers. Dr. Lieber's efforts resulted in a compendium of rules issued by the War Department in 1863 that was the first of its kind in the world. The Lieber Code, as it became known, was subsequently adopted by the governments of France, Great Britain, and Prussia (not to mention the Confederate States of America), and is considered the precursor to the Hague Conventions of 1899 and 1907 as well as the Geneva Conventions of 1949. Accordingly, as President Ronald Reagan once accurately informed the Senate, "the United States has traditionally been in the forefront of efforts to codify and improve the international rules of humanitarian law in armed conflict."

That is, until now. As disclosed in recently revealed internal government documents, the Bush administration has devised and implemented a strategy to insulate the treatment of detainees held at Guantanamo Bay, Cuba, and elsewhere from judicial review, avoid application of the Geneva Conventions, and evade liability under domestic and international laws proscribing torture and war crimes. Moreover, legislation passed in the wake of the Supreme Court's decision in *Hamdan v. Rumsfeld* striking down the

President's ad hoc military commissions, the Military Commissions Act of 2006, explicitly provides that "[no] person may invoke the Geneva Conventions or any protocols thereto in any habeas corpus or other civil action or proceeding to which the United States, or a current or former officer, employee, member of the Armed Forces, or other agent of the United States is a party as a source of rights in any court of the United States or its States or territories."[1]

The government's abandonment of international standards of treatment for detainees raises the following question: do the international humanitarian principles set forth in the Geneva Conventions constitute a limitation on the Executive's power to detain enemy combatants? Most commentary on this question has centered on the question of whether the Geneva Conventions are "self-executing" and thereby provide cognizable rights capable of judicial enforcement. If, as a number of courts have held, the Geneva Conventions are "nonself-executing" and thus cannot be enforced by individuals in the absence of implementing legislation, the Guantanamo Bay detainees arguably have no way to vindicate alleged violations of the Geneva Conventions aside from seeking diplomatic enforcement through their home countries.

The Supreme Court case of *Hamdi v. Rumsfeld,* however, suggests an alternate, and far simpler, view of how the Geneva Conventions have become incorporated as part of our domestic law: the Congress has not authorized the President to violate clearly established principles of international humanitarian law contained in the Geneva Conventions. To explain this argument, this chapter will (1) broadly outline the obligations imposed by the Geneva Conventions in the context of the administration's policies toward detainees; (2) discuss the source of the President's power to detain enemy belligerents and contend that it must derive from Congress; and (3) consider the case of *Hamdi v. Rumsfeld* in the context of the use of international law as a tool of statutory construction.

PROBLEM OF EXECUTIVE AUTHORITY UNCHECKED BY INTERNATIONAL HUMANITARIAN LAW

The 1949 Geneva Conventions are comprised of four international treaties that govern the treatment of persons captured during warfare: those wounded and sick on land, and those wounded and sick at sea, prisoners of war, and civilians. As a general matter, the Conventions prohibit torture, violence, and intimidation, and instead require humane treatment of detainees. The treaties also provide detailed rules regarding communication rights as well as procedural and substantive protections in the event of disciplinary or criminal prosecution of detainees. Importantly, the Geneva Convention Relative to the Treatment of Prisoners of War (POW Convention) contains a provision requiring that a detainee "shall enjoy the protection of the present Convention until such time as their status has been determined by a competent tribunal" "should any doubt arise" as to whether the detainee is entitled to prisoner of war status. Finally, the treaties guarantee repatriation at the conclusion of hostilities.

The United States is a party to each of the four Geneva treaties. Even if the United States was not a party, however, the Geneva Conventions constitute customary international law.[2] In other words, the basic provisions of the Geneva Conventions reflect state practice and are widely accepted as binding on the international community.

Moreover, regulations governing the armed forces explicitly require that "[a]ll persons taken into custody by U.S. forces will be provided with the protections of the [POW Convention] until some other legal status is determined by competent legal authority."

In sum, the United States is bound by virtue of its ratification of the Conventions as well as by its own regulations to afford detainees the protections of the Geneva Conventions.

In recent years, however, the Bush administration has steadfastly opposed the application of the Geneva Conventions to detainees seized during the conflict in Afghanistan and has fought against any judicial oversight of its detention of citizens and noncitizens alike. Indeed, the very decision to house detainees in Guantanamo Bay, Cuba, was driven by the conclusion that locating detainees there would help to shield the detention and treatment of such detainees from judicial review. In late 2001, Bush administration lawyers concluded that "a federal district court could not properly exercise habeas jurisdiction over an alien detained at" Guantanamo Bay, Cuba. From very early on, then, the Bush administration endeavored to avoid judicial scrutiny of its detention policies.

In early 2002, former White House counsel and then Attorney General Alberto Gonzales, urged the President to conclude that the POW Convention did "not apply to al Qaeda and the Taliban." Mr. Bush accepted this recommendation, and on February 2, 2002, issued an order stating that "none of the provisions of Geneva apply to our conflict with al Qaeda in Afghanistan or elsewhere throughout the world." Moreover, the presidential order unilaterally determined that "the Taliban detainees are unlawful combatants and, therefore, do not qualify as prisoners of war under Article 4 of Geneva." These determinations mean that, from the administration's point of view, the POW Convention affords no protection to detainees allegedly connected to al Qaeda or the Taliban.

By August 2002, former Assistant Attorney General Jay S. Bybee—now a judge on the Court of Appeals for the Ninth Circuit—asserted that domestic and international laws proscribing "torture" applied only to pain "associated with serious physical injury so severe that death, organ failure, or permanent damage resulting in a loss of significant body function will likely result." Pain of a lesser sort inflicted upon a detainee, Bybee contended, was not unlawful.

The administration's resistance to international and domestic standards of acceptable treatment of detainees inevitably led to the expansion of interrogation techniques applied to detainees held at Guantanamo Bay. An October 2002 memorandum, for example, seeks approval for the use of hoods during interrogation of detainees, 28-hour interrogations, removal of clothing, and the use of "detainee-individual phobias (such as fear of dogs) to induce stress."

These aggressive interrogation techniques also migrated to Iraq. In fact, the former warden of the Abu Ghraib prison in Iraq, the scene of the prisoner abuse photos, has noted that he attended a meeting in September 2003 in which the commander of the Guantanamo Bay detention center extolled the effectiveness of dogs used to intimidate prisoners.

With respect to the detainees held at Guantanamo Bay, such treatment has bolstered the claims by human rights groups that the U.S. government is violating the Geneva Conventions. Additionally, such groups as well as lawyers representing detainees held in Guantanamo maintain that the administration has violated the Geneva Conventions through the classification procedures it has employed to establish amenability to prosecution as well as its unilateral and categorical determination that the Geneva Conventions are inapplicable.

As for further judicial review of the Bush administration's detention policies in the context of the Geneva Conventions, the prospects at present are dim. In December 2005, Congress enacted the Detainee Treatment Act, which on the one hand proscribed the "cruel, inhuman, or degrading treatment or punishment" of detainees, while on the other purported to drastically limit habeas corpus review by Guantanamo detainees.[3]

More recently, the Military Commissions Act of 2006 (MCA) severely circumscribes the availability of habeas corpus for any "alien detained by the United States who has been determined by the United States to have been properly detained as an enemy combatant or is awaiting such a determination."[4] In particular, the MCA also states that "[n]o person may invoke the Geneva Conventions or any protocols thereto in any habeas corpus or other civil action or proceeding to which the United States...is a party as a source of rights in any court in any court of the United States or its States or territories."[5]

Nonetheless, consideration of domestic enforcement of the Geneva Conventions should not ignore a principle of statutory construction at the heart of the Supreme Court plurality's opinion in *Hamdi:* that Congress's authorization for the use of military force is limited by clearly established principles of the law of war. And few principles are more clearly established elements of the law of war than the core protections embodied in the Geneva Conventions. Under this view, the Geneva Conventions serve not as a source of individual rights, but rather as a limitation on the scope of congressional authorization for the Executive's treatment of detainees.

IMPACT OF THE SUPREME COURT'S DECISIONS ON THE ADMINISTRATION'S TREATMENT OF DETAINEES

Whether President Bush remains free to ignore the Geneva Conventions is a matter of significant doubt. A trio of Supreme Court cases issued in the Summer of 2004—*Hamdi v. Rumsfeld,*[6] *Rumsfeld v. Padilla,*[7] and *Rasul v. Bush*[8]—represent the Court's first substantial response to the government's detention of citizens and noncitizens arising out of the so-called "War on Terror." The Court's holdings in *Hamdi* and *Rasul* were widely construed to have rejected the broadest claims of executive authority asserted by the Bush administration. Furthermore, the *Padilla* opinion, although decided on procedural grounds, is significant because the four dissenting Justices coupled with Justice Scalia's dissent in *Hamdi* strongly imply that five Justices would reject the claim that the executive branch has the power to detain an American citizen found in the United States as an "enemy combatant."

Nonetheless, the precise import of these decisions with respect to the limitations imposed on the Executive's authority to detain individuals as "enemy combatants" remains a matter of much dispute. For example, in the ongoing litigation involving the detention of Ali Saleh Kahlah Al-Marri—the Qatari citizen and legal resident arrested by the FBI in Peoria, Illinois, and detained by the military without criminal charge for over 3 years—the government has maintained that it holds the power to designate aliens seized inside the United States as "enemy combatants" and thereby detain them indefinitely in military custody without criminal charge. Meanwhile, in the ongoing litigation involving the detention of noncitizens at the U.S. military base in Guantanamo Bay, Cuba, the government argues that the detainees cannot assert any judicially enforceable claims drawn from treaty obligations imposed by the Geneva Conventions.

The executive branch's objection to even modest limitations on its power to detain so-called "enemy combatants" is predictable. After all, it faces the substantial prospect of public blame in the event of another terrorist attack. On the other hand, expanding executive authority to detain individuals as "enemy combatants" at the expense of judicial review poses a distinct danger that the government could wield uncheckable power against entirely innocent citizens or even its political enemies. The Court's recent opinions, however, unambiguously rejected the prospect of unreviewable executive authority to detain.

The plurality opinion in Hamdi also suggests another limitation on the government's power to detain: legislative constraints on the source of executive authority to detain combatants. In particular, the Court's plurality opinion analyzed international law as an interpretive limitation on the scope of Congress's authorization to use force. Put differently, the Court in *Hamdi* reasserted the significance of international law as a limit on the scope of congressional authorization for the use of military force.

Given the Hamdi plurality's acknowledgment that Congress's authorization for the use of force in Afghanistan should be read consistent with recognized international humanitarian principles, it is therefore plain that Congress did not authorize the Executive to violate the guarantee of basic human treatment contained in the Geneva Conventions. Regardless of whether the Geneva Conventions have otherwise been incorporated into U.S. law, therefore, detainees in Guantanamo Bay and elsewhere should be permitted to assert that the Executive branch has exceeded the authority derived from Congress when the detention violates basic provisions of the Geneva Conventions.

The Source of the Authority to Detain

The executive branch of government possesses power solely by virtue of the Constitution and the Congress. The starting point for understanding the limitations imposed on the power to detain "enemy combatants," therefore, is an understanding of the source of that power. Does the executive branch, by virtue of Article II of the Constitution, possess an independent power to detain individuals seized during wartime for the duration of the conflict, or does the authority to detain "enemy combatants" derive from Congress? If the executive branch possesses a broad independent power drawn from the Constitution, neither the Courts nor Congress could do much to restrain that power, other than limit funding to the military or impeach the President.

Does Article II Give the Executive Power to Detain "Enemy Combatants"?

The cornerstone of the administration's argument that it possesses broad power to detain citizens and noncitizens seized incident to the "War on Terror" is that this power derives from Article II, Section 2 of the Constitution, wherein the President is designated as the Commander in Chief of the armed forces. The precise scope of the Executive's "war powers" remains a matter of much dispute. Nonetheless, the executive branch's traditional authority in the area of foreign diplomacy and military affairs arguably supports the idea that it possesses a unique extrastatutory authority to detain enemy soldiers during the course of armed conflict. The administration therefore maintains that the power to detain "enemy combatants" is of a piece with the executive power to wage armed conflict.

Historically, however, the Commander in Chief Clause has not been so broadly interpreted. In one of the few Supreme Court cases to discuss that Clause in detail, *Fleming v. Page,* the Court noted that the "power [is] purely military." And in the words of Alexander Hamilton—the Founder most closely associated with the defense of broad executive authority—the Commander in Chief power "amounts to nothing more than the supreme command and direction of the military and naval forces."[9] Given this narrow compass, the Clause itself would hardly authorize the executive branch to detain individuals outside the areas of armed conflict. Indeed, that is the import of the Supreme Court's celebrated decision in the Civil War case of *Ex parte Milligan,* in which the Court held that military rule is "confined to the locality of actual war," and "can never exist where the courts are open."

Moreover, the Court has intimated several times that deprivations of liberty can only be effected pursuant to an act of Congress. In *Valentine v. United States,*[10] for example, the Court stated that "the Constitution creates no executive prerogative to dispose off the liberty of the individual. Proceedings against him must be authorized by law." Similarly, the Court has stated that if constitutionally protected liberty "is to be regulated, it must be pursuant to the law-making functions of the Congress."[11] And both the Supreme Court and lower courts have repeatedly expressed reluctance to sanction military authority over nonsoldiers outside of areas of armed conflict. In particular, courts during the War of 1812 repeatedly refused to sanction military prosecution of citizens suspected of spying on behalf of the British. Likewise, the Supreme Court has refused to sanction the prosecution by court martial of civilians, such as the wives of servicemen, who have committed crimes after accompanying a spouse overseas.

Finally, the earliest practice of the Congress suggests that the detention of enemy soldiers required an act of Congress. During the undeclared war with France, for example, Congress enacted statutes authorizing the detention and exchange of French sailors. Congress also authorized the Executive to detain prisoners of war during the War of 1812, one of the few wars in which Congress issued a formal declaration of war. During that war, Congress also passed a statute regulating the capture of prisoners found on ships seized as prizes. As Chief Justice John Marshall wrote in an 1814 decision for the Court, these statutes "afford[] a strong implication that [the President] did not possess those powers by virtue of [a] declaration of war,"[12] and thus suggest that the detention of enemy aliens and prisoners of war in the United States requires statutory authorization. Put differently, if the President already possessed an extrastatutory power to detain prisoners of war, why did the earliest incarnations of the Congress enact statutes designed to authorize those very same detentions?

The significance of congressional authorization in determining the extent of the President's power to detain enemy belligerents was evident in the four separate opinions issued by the Justices in *Hamdi*. Notwithstanding the administration's claim that it enjoyed inherent authority to detain Mr. Hamdi by virtue of the Commander in Chief Clause in Article II of the Constitution, only Justice Thomas appeared inclined to agree with the argument. Justices Scalia and Stevens rejected it outright, while Justices Souter and Ginsburg were content to "note the weakness" of the administration's claim given that the plurality opinion avoided the question altogether. All of the Justices instead focused upon the question of Congressional authorization as central to the determination of the scope of the President's authority to detain enemy belligerents.

The question of executive power to detain an American citizen alleged to be an "enemy combatant" was squarely before the Court in the case of *Hamdi v. Rumsfeld*. Although the four published opinions failed to issue a definitive answer with respect to persons seized outside of the battlefield, the Court supplied a degree of guidance as to the limitations imposed on the government's authority to detain prisoners seized in armed conflict.

Hamdi v. Rumsfeld and the Power to Detain Enemy Combatants

Background

The *Hamdi* case arose from a habeas corpus petition filed on behalf of a 21-year old man, Yaser Esam Hamdi, born in Baton Rouge, Louisiana. Hamdi was seized by the U.S. military in Afghanistan in late 2001, and then detained in solitary confinement at several Navy brigs in the United States. Two basic issues were before the Court: (1) what authority exists to detain an American citizen as an "enemy combatant;" and (2) was Hamdi entitled to challenge the factual basis for his detention? In the decision under review, the Fourth Circuit had determined that the Constitution vests the President with the authority to detain individuals captured in armed conflict overseas and that judicial inquiry into the factual basis for such detentions would violate the separation of powers.

With respect to the first question, the administration argued not only that it enjoyed inherent power to detain Hamdi but also that Congress, by virtue of a law passed 1 week after the September 11, 2001, attacks, had authorized the President to detain enemy combatants seized in Afghanistan. That law is known as the AUMF (Authorization for the Use of Military Force). The AUMF authorized the President to:

> Use all necessary and appropriate force against those nations, organizations, or persons he determines planned, authorized, committed, or aided the terrorist attacks that occurred on September 11, 2001, or harbored such organizations or persons, in order to prevent any future acts of international terrorism against the United States by such nations, organizations, or persons.

A plurality of the Court, in an opinion authored by Justice O'Connor and joined by Chief Justice Rehnquist, Justice Kennedy, and Justice Breyer, concluded that (1) Congress had authorized the detention of persons who were "part of or supporting forces hostile to the United States or coalition partners" and "engaged in an armed conflict against the United States" in Afghanistan, but that (2) a citizen detainee is entitled to notice of the allegations underlying the detention, access to counsel, and a fair hearing before a neutral tribunal. The plurality emphasized that Congress's authorization to detain was not a "blank check," and was subject to both judicial review and procedural due process.

With respect to the authority to detain an American citizen as an "enemy combatant," Justice O'Connor reasoned that Congress's authorization of military force following the September 11, 2001, attacks necessarily gave the President power to detain persons seized in the armed conflict in Afghanistan. Specifically, the plurality opinion concluded that the extent of congressional authorization is shaped by the laws and customs of armed conflict. A general authorization of military force, Justice O'Connor found, permits the detention of captured combatants—including American citizens—as a necessary part of battlefield operations. At the same time, detention practices that are inconsistent with "a clearly established principle of the law of war" fall outside the scope of such a resolution. Consequently, in accordance with the POW Convention, the Hague Conventions, and the 1929 Geneva Convention, Congress's authorization under the AUMF for the detention of prisoners extends only "for the duration of the relevant conflict."

The citizenship status of the detainee, according to the plurality, made no difference. Indeed, a purported American citizen was tried along with German soldiers for violations of the law of war during World War II, and the plurality reasoned that both citizens and noncitizens presented an identical threat from release if they fought on behalf of America's enemies.

As noted earlier, the plurality declined to address the question of the President's inherent authority to detain citizens. Nonetheless, the plurality made an important distinction between the process due after the military's initial capture of a detainee on a battlefield. Specifically, the Court noted that "when the determination is made to *continue* to hold those who have been seized," the detainee is entitled to notice of the factual basis for their detention and a fair opportunity to rebut the government's assertions before a neutral decisionmaker. This conclusion is not only practical but also consistent with the idea that the length of detention affects the degree of process that is required.[13]

In no uncertain terms, the plurality also rejected the Fourth Circuit's separation of powers holding. Circumscribing judicial review of the Executive's enemy combatant determinations "cannot be mandated by any reasonable view of separation of powers, as this approach serves only to *condense* power into a single branch of government." Had the Court upheld the view that judicial review infringed upon the separation of powers, the decision would have opened the door to unchecked and uncheckable authority by the government to detain both citizens and noncitizens without recourse to the courts.

Justice Souter, in a concurring opinion joined by Justice Ginsburg, rejected the plurality's conclusion that Congress had authorized the noncriminal detention of citizens seized by the military in the absence of a clear and explicit expression permitting such detentions. Nonetheless, Justice Souter agreed that a citizen detained as an enemy combatant would be entitled to challenge the factual basis for the detention.

Justice Scalia, in a dissenting opinion joined by Justice Stevens, argued that the Constitution prohibited the government from detaining, without criminal charge, a citizen seized in armed conflict. Finally, Justice Thomas dissented on the ground that the judiciary has no role to play in determining whether a detainee is in fact an "enemy combatant."

Implications of Hamdi v. Rumsfeld for Citizens

The *Hamdi* plurality rejected the argument that citizenship was relevant to whether Congress had authorized the detention of an individual seized on the battlefield, a conclusion arguably at odds with precedent. For example, in *Johnson v. Eisentrager,* a case arising out of claims made by German prisoners in World War II, the Court took pains to make a distinction between executive authority over citizens and noncitizens in the context of armed conflict.[14] Furthermore, in another case arising out of the internment of Japanese-Americans, the Court appeared to require Congress to enact explicit language permitting the detention of citizens before it would find that Congress had authorized such detentions:

> We must assume that the Chief Executive and members of Congress, as well as the courts, are sensitive to and respectful of the liberties of the citizen. In interpreting a wartime measure we must assume that their purpose was to allow for the greatest possible accommodation between those liberties and the exigencies of war. We must assume, when asked to find implied powers in a grant of legislative or executive authority, that the law makers intended to place no greater restraint on the citizen than was clearly and unmistakably indicated by the language they used.[15]

More recently, the Court has observed that "[t]he status of citizenship was meant to have significance in the structure of our government.... [It] denotes an association with the polity which, in a democratic republic, exercises the powers of governance."[16] Accordingly, an executive power to detain American citizens arguably presents greater ramifications for the character of our government than does the detention of enemy aliens. Nonetheless, in the specific context of a citizen seized by the military "in a foreign combat zone," the plurality saw no need for specific language by Congress authorizing the detention of a citizen alleged to be fighting against U.S. forces.

As for the process due such detained citizens, the flexible procedural mechanics outlined by the plurality in the event the government designates an American citizen as an "enemy combatant" may turn out to be rarely invoked. For one thing, the seizure of an American citizen alleged to be fighting alongside enemy forces abroad is a rare event that has occurred only a handful of times over the past century, and only twice in the context of the conflict in Afghanistan.[17] For another, the definition of "enemy combatant" recognized by the plurality remains very limited—a citizen "would need to be 'part of or supporting forces hostile to the United States or coalition partners' and 'engaged in an armed conflict against the United States' to justify...detention in the United States for the duration of the relevant conflict."[18] In other words, the citizen must actually bear arms against the United States to fall within the definition of an "enemy combatant."

Furthermore, the criminal process is available in every case involving a citizen seized under such circumstances. As Justice Scalia noted in his dissenting opinion in *Hamdi,* a wide assortment of criminal statutes are designed to apply to the very conduct alleged by the government in the *Hamdi* case. In fact, criminal proceedings may provide a surer means of obtaining intelligence through plea negotiations given the plurality's statement that "indefinite detention for the purpose of interrogation is not authorized."[19]

Finally, significant disadvantages may follow, from the government's point of view, from designation of a citizen as an enemy combatant. First, the detainee must be released at the conclusion of hostilities.[20] Second, significant hurdles may prevent criminal prosecution of those detained as enemy combatants.[21] Third, if the government uses the enemy combatant designation only in cases in which substantial incriminating evidence is unavailable, courts may be more likely to insist upon rigorous procedural requirements. Fourth, designation of additional American citizens as "enemy combatants" likely would invite a great deal of criticism that is just as easily avoided. For these reasons, faced with the choice of prosecuting a citizen for bearing arms against the United States or simply detaining that citizen as an "enemy combatant," the government may have significant incentives to choose the former.

Hamdi and International Legal Rights Afforded to Noncitizens Detained as "Enemy Combatants" by the United States

The *Hamdi* case may have greater import in the context of how courts address international law, and specifically the Geneva Conventions, in the context of noncitizen detainees held in Guantanamo Bay, Cuba, and elsewhere. In particular, the *Hamdi* plurality opinion provides an answer to the Government's claim that the Geneva Conventions afford no judicially enforceable rights to detainees alleging violations of the laws of war.

At the same time that Yaser Hamdi was asserting his right to challenge the factual basis for his detention in federal court, noncitizen detainees seized by the United States in Afghanistan and held in Guantanamo Bay, Cuba, sought to vindicate their rights merely to get in the courthouse door. Relying on the case of *Johnson v. Eisentrager,* the Court of Appeals for the District of Columbia had ruled against the detainees, holding that the habeas statute did not permit noncitizens outside the United States to challenge their detention by the military.[22]

The Supreme Court reversed.[23] In an opinion authored by Justice Stevens, the Court held that the habeas statute, 28 U.S.C. § 2241, required only jurisdiction over the custodian of the petitioner to establish proper jurisdiction.[24] *Eisentrager,* the Court found, was decided at a time when the habeas statute was viewed as requiring the presence of the petitioner within the territorial jurisdiction of the lower court. That limited view of the statutory reach of the habeas statute, the Court noted, had been subsequently overruled.[25] Accordingly, the Court remanded the cases to the district court for further proceedings.

On remand, many of the detainees claim that the military has failed to comply with the POW convention.[26] In particular, article 5 of the POW Convention requires that a detainee's status be "determined by a competent tribunal" if any doubt arises whether the detainee is entitled to prisoner of war status.[27] In the absence of such a tribunal, the detainee cannot be treated as an unlawful combatant and must be afforded the protections of the POW Convention.

For its part, the government has repeatedly argued that the POW Convention is not self-executing.[28] Accordingly, the government claims that the detainees have no basis upon which to assert claims drawn from the terms of that treaty—an argument that has received approval in the Fourth and D.C. Circuit Courts of Appeals.[29]

In *Hamdi,* however, the plurality used the POW Convention and the international law of war to define the scope of Congress' authorization for the President to use force. The AUMF, as noted earlier, authorized the Executive to "use all necessary and appropriate force against those nations, organizations, or persons he determines planned, authorized, committed, or aided the terrorist attacks" against the United States on September 11, 2001. According to the plurality opinion, Congress authorized the detention of enemy combatants, citizens, and noncitizens, because the detention of prisoners "is so fundamental and accepted an incident to war as to be an exercise of the 'necessary and appropriate force' Congress has authorized the President to use."[30] On the other hand, the *Hamdi* plurality also noted that such authorization was limited to the duration of the relevant conflict "based on long-standing law-of-war principles."[31] The plurality therefore looked to the customs and principles of the LOAC (law of armed conflict) to identify the scope of congressional authorization for the use of force.

Incidentally, the plurality's analysis appears directly at odds with the Court's reasoning in *Brown v. United States,* a case that addressed an almost identical question and that went unmentioned by the plurality.[32] The question before the Court in *Brown* was whether the United States could seize timber originally carried by a British ship during the War of 1812 without authorization from Congress. The government's principal argument to support its seizure of the timber was that Congress had declared war and "authorized [the President] to use the whole land and naval force of the United States," thereby authorizing the Executive to seize enemy property.

In an opinion authored by Chief Justice Marshall, the Court rejected this argument. The Court noted that "[w]ar gives an equal right over persons and property," and the existence of statutes relating to the detention of prisoners of war and enemy aliens found within the United States indicated that a declaration of war by itself did not authorize the President to seize property or anything else.[33] In addition, the Court explained that parts of the Constitution, such as Congress's power to make rules concerning captures on land and water, would be superfluous if a declaration of war acted in itself to authorize seizures.[34]

In reasoning not dissimilar from that used by the *Hamdi* plurality, Justice Story argued in dissent that the declaration of war was enacted in "very general terms" and therefore permitted the executive branch to capture enemy property in accordance with the LOAC:[35]

> [W]hen the legislative authority, to whom the right to declare war is confided, has declared war in its most unlimited manner, the executive authority, to whom the execution of war is confided, is bound to carry it into effect. He has a discretion vested in him, as to the manner and extent; but he cannot lawfully transcend the rules of warfare established among civilized nations. He cannot lawfully exercise powers or authorize proceedings which the civilized world repudiates and disclaims.[36]

Like the plurality opinion in *Hamdi,* Justice Story found the Executive's authority to seize enemy property within a general authorization to use force, but also looked to international law to describe the scope of the Executive's authority incident to congressional authorization.

International law has developed a great deal since Justice Story penned his dissent in *Brown*. In particular, the core provisions of the POW Convention are almost universally considered to reflect the most basic tenets of international law related to armed conflict. Consequently, the POW Convention undoubtedly constitutes a restraint on congressional authorization to the extent that international law otherwise defines the scope of congressional authorization to use force.

A potential counter argument, however, is that while the AUMF provides authorization to the President to use force, it contains no countervailing *prohibition* against violations of international law. At most, the argument goes, the AUMF is merely silent on the issue of international law and simply contains no affirmative authorization for the President to violate international law. This characterization of the AUMF is potentially an important one because it relates to Justice Jackson's tripartite analysis of presidential power outlined in the famous Steel Seizure case.[37] Under Justice Jackson's rubric articulated in his concurring opinion, presidential powers fluctuate depending upon whether the President acts in accordance with express or implied congressional authorization, whether the President acts in the absence of a congressional say in the matter, or whether the President acts contrary to the expressed or implied will of the Congress. As long as Congress does not affirmatively prohibit the President from violating international law, his actions fall within an area of potentially concurrent authority and likely will be upheld as necessary in the absence of congressional action.

This argument is flawed in a number of respects. First, it presupposes the existence of an inherent executive power to detain—the very question the *Hamdi* plurality declined to answer. In other words, if executive authority to detain requires congressional authorization in order for the detention to be lawful, then the characterization of the AUMF as *failing to authorize* violations of the law of war instead of *prohibiting* such violations is irrelevant. Put differently, because the existence of congressional authorization of executive detention is—as every member of the Supreme Court apparently agrees— critical to an evaluation of its lawfulness, the absence of congressional authorization is the same as an express congressional prohibition. Second, given that Congress has criminalized, at Title 18 U.S. Code section 2441, war crimes—which it defines as a grave breach of the Geneva Conventions, conduct prohibited by certain articles of the 1907 Hague Convention, or violations of Common Article 3 of the Geneva Conventions—it is exceedingly hard to say that Congress is indifferent to violations of basic international humanitarian norms. Third, this argument is directly contrary to the plurality's reasoning in Hamdi, in which Justice O'Connor wrote that the AUMF did in fact contain implicit limitations derived from "clearly established principle[s] of the law of war."

That statutes should be construed in accordance with international law breaks no new ground. Early in this country's history, the Supreme Court articulated a principle of statutory construction designed to avoid conflict between domestic statutes and international law. Specifically, in *Murray v. The Schooner Charming Betsy*,[38] Chief Justice Marshall wrote that "an act of congress ought never to be construed to violate the law of nations if any other possible construction remains...." The Charming Betsy was a schooner alleged to have been used to conduct trade with France, and thus subject to seizure under the Nonintercourse Act of 1800. The owner of the Charming Betsy, however, argued that he was a Danish citizen and that application of the Nonintercourse Act to him would violate international law. In construing the Nonintercourse Act, the Court concluded that it did not apply to the ship owner.

The rule of construction drawn from that case has become known as the *Charming Betsy* principle. In construing the scope of the AUMF, the *Hamdi* plurality has, without saying so, applied the *Charming Betsy* principle to require the alignment of Executive uses of force with the international LOAC. The fact that international law, and specifically the Geneva Conventions, limits Congress's authorization to the Executive branch is significant because it suggests that—regardless of whether the POW Convention is self-executing—the Executive branch exceeds its authority derived from Congress to the extent it does not comply with the terms of that authorization.

In this context, recognition of the right of detainees to challenge their treatment as inconsistent with the law of war is little different from the well-worn principle that "judicial relief is available to one who has been injured by an act of a government official which is in excess of his express or implied powers."[39] In fact, the Supreme Court has long permitted claimants to challenge conduct by the Executive branch on the ground that a federal officer acted beyond the reach of statutory or constitutional authority. The famous Steel Seizure case is a prime example of this sort of "nonstatutory review." In that case, steel companies brought a personal action against the Secretary of Commerce who had carried out the order of President Truman to seize the companies. The basis of their claim was simply that the President had exceeded the authority granted to him under the Constitution and by the Congress. More recently, Judge Silberman of the D.C. Circuit noted that "when an executive acts *ultra vires,* courts are normally available to reestablish the limits on his authority." Likewise, executive officers who act beyond the power granted to them by Congress in the AUMF should be subject to judicial enforcement of the limits of their authority.

Few courts in recent times have been willing to find that customary and treaty-based international law imposes judicially cognizable limitations on domestic government actors. Moreover, the passage of the Detainee Treatment Act of 2005 and the Military Commissions Act of 2006 may pose significant obstacles to the meaningful judicial review of the executive branch's detention of detainees both within and outside the United States.

At the same time, we should keep in mind Justice O'Connor's admonition in *Hamdi* that "[i]t is during our most challenging and uncertain moments that our nation's commitment to due process is most severely tested; and it is in those times that we must preserve our commitment at home to the principles for which we fight abroad." The *Hamdi* plurality's explicit use of the international law of war to limit the scope of Congress's authorization to the executive branch suggests a different means by which the POW Convention has become part of U.S. law. If legal principles that regulate the conduct of war drawn from international law are construed to limit the scope of authorization to use force provided by Congress, such principles unquestionably constrain and confine executive conduct. We should not abandon our tradition of respect for the international rules of humanitarian law in armed conflict, and should enforce such limitations on the conduct of the executive branch of government.

NOTES

1. *Military Commissions Act of 2006* § 5(a), Public Law 109-366, *U.S. Statutes at Large* 120 (2006): 2631 (amending 28 U.S.C. § 2241).

2. See *Hamdan v. Rumsfeld,* 126 S.Ct. 2749, 2794 (2006) ("[R]egardless of the nature of the rights conferred on Hamdan, [the Geneva Conventions] are, as the Government does not dispute, part of the law of war.") (citations omitted).

3. *Detainee Treatment Act of 2005,* Public Law 109-48, *U.S. Statutes at Large* 119 (2005): 2739.

4. *Military Commissions Act of 2006* § 7(a), Public Law 109-366, *U.S. Statutes at Large* 120 (2006): 2631 (amending 28 U.S.C. § 2241).

5. Ibid. § 5(a). In seeking to eliminate the Geneva Conventions as a basis for judicial decision-making, Congress may well have violated the separation of powers. In *United States v. Klein,* 80 U.S. (13 Wall.) 128, 145–47 (1871), the Supreme Court rebuffed an arguably similar effort by Congress to influence the decision and jurisdiction of federal courts with respect to property claims made in the aftermath of the Civil War. Striking down legislation which precluded consideration of whether the claimant had received a presidential pardon, and thus was eligible to recover property seized by the government, the Court held that Congress had "passed the limit which separates the legislative from the judicial power." Ibid., 147. Having provided jurisdiction for federal courts to consider such claims in the first place, Congress could not "prescribe rules of decision to the Judicial department of the government." Ibid., 146. Similarly, to the extent that federal courts have jurisdiction to address habeas corpus petitions filed by detainees at all, it should be up to federal courts to decide whether the Geneva Conventions constitute a "source of rights" or are otherwise enforceable against the government.

6. 542 U.S. 507 (2004).

7. 542 U.S. 426 (2004).

8. 542 U.S. 466 (2004).

9. Alexander Hamilton, "The Federalist No. 69," in *The Federalist Papers* (New York: Penguin Putnam, 1961); accord *Youngstown Sheet & Tube Co. v. Sawyer,* 343 U.S. 579, 646 (1952) (Jackson, J., concurring) (noting that President's power as commander in chief "is not a military prerogative, without support of law, to seize persons or property because they are important or even essential for the military and naval establishment.").

10. 299 U.S. 5, 9 (1936).

11. *Kent v. Dulles,* 357 U.S. 116, 128 (1958).

12. *Brown v. United States,* 12 U.S. (8 Cranch) 110, 126 (1814).

13. See, e.g., *Moyer v. Peabody,* 212 U.S. 78, 85 (1909) (noting that case involving extended detention may "raise a different question" then temporary detention with respect to process due under the Due Process Clause).

14. 339 U.S. 763, 774 (1950).

15. *Ex parte Endo,* 323 U.S. 283, 300 (1944). In fact, the Court has on several occasions reacted skeptically toward statutes cited to support congressional authorization of the exercise of military control over citizens. See *Duncan v. Kahanamoku,* 327 U.S. 304, 324 (1946) (holding that Congress did not intend to supplant civilian court system when it authorized martial law in territory of Hawaii); *Raymond v. Thomas,* 91 U.S. 712, 716 (1875) (holding that military order annulling judicial order unauthorized by Congress and therefore void); *Ex parte Milligan,* 71 U.S. (4 Wall.) 2, 135 (Chase, C.J., concurring) (noting that Congress had not authorized Milligan's seizure).

16. *Ambach v. Norwick,* 441 U.S. 68, 75 (1979).

17. See *United States v. Lindh,* 227 F. Supp. 2d 565, 567–69 (E.D. Va. 2002).

18. *Hamdi,* 542 U.S. at 526.

19. Ibid., 521.

20. Ibid.

21. See 18 U.S.C. § 3161 et seq. (*Speedy Trial Act*); Richard B. Schmitt, "U.S. May Still Charge 'Enemy Combatant,' Gonzales Says," *L.A. Times,* March 8, 2005 (noting that Attorney General Gonzales conceded that government may not be able to charge Padilla).

22. *Al Odah v. United States,* 321 F.3d 1134, 1144 (D.C. Cir. 2003).

23. *Rasul,* 542 U.S. 466.

24. Ibid., 468.

25. Ibid., 478.

26. "Geneva Convention Relative to the Treatment of Prisoners of War," August 12, 1949, *United States Treaties and Other International Agreements,* 6, pt. 3 (1956): 3316.

27. Ibid., Art. 5, 6: 3324.

28. See *In re Guantanamo Detainee Cases,* 355 F. Supp. 2d 443, 478 (D.D.C. 2005); *Hamdan v. Rumsfeld,* 344 F. Supp. 2d 152, 164 (D.D.C. 2004).

29. *Tel-Oren v. Libyan Arab Repub.* 726 F.2d 774, 809 (D.C. Cir. 1984) (Bork, J., concurring); *Hamdi v. Rumsfeld,* 316 F.3d 450, 468 (4th Cir. 2003), *reversed on other grounds by* 542 U.S. 507 (2004).

30. *Hamdi,* 542 U.S. at 518.

31. Ibid., 521.

32. 12 U.S. (8 Cranch) 110 (1814).

33. Ibid., 126.

34. Ibid.

35. Ibid., 145 (Story, J., dissenting).

36. Ibid., 154–55.

37. *Youngstown Sheet & Tube Co.* 343 U.S. 579.

38. 6 U.S. (2 Cranch) 64, 117–18 (1804); see also *Weinberger v. Rossi,* 456 U.S. 25, 32 (1982); *Clark v. Allen,* 331 U.S. 503, 508–11 (1947); *Cook v. United States,* 288 U.S. 102, 118–20 (1933).

39. *Harmon v. Brucker,* 355 U.S. 579, 581–82 (1958).

CHAPTER 8

Military Commissions: An Overview

H. WAYNE ELLIOTT

Military commissions are at issue post-9/11 particularly for al Qaeda prisoners held at Guantanamo. They implement a policy of trying detainees for alleged war crimes, but raise peculiar issues because the detainees themselves are seemingly agents of nonstate actors in what may be viewed technically as internal armed conflicts despite the War on Terror's international reach. However, this chapter does not address the complications of detainee status as prisoners of war (POWs) or unlawful combatants (combatant status review), and disputes concerning their interrogation and general treatment (prohibition on cruel, inhuman, or degrading treatment).[1] Instead, we look to the American history of military commissions for the light it sheds on their prospective constitutionality, now that Congress has passed the 2006 Military Commission Act[2] in response to the Supreme Court's *Hamdan v. Rumsfeld* decision declaring unconstitutional military commissions initially constituted under executive order.[3]

Military tribunals stand at two intellectual intersections. Under one stream, military commissions are viewed constitutionally in opposition to regular U.S. military courts-martial or military courts, and implicitly beyond that to regular courts. Here courts-martial draw chiefly domestic procedural interest with a jurisdictional flavor, with the traditional focus on issues like whether American civilians accompanying the U.S. military overseas should be subject to courts-martial jurisdiction (as opposed to being entitled to civilian jury trial). Under the other intellectual stream, military tribunals generically are also the traditional forum for war crimes trials. Here courts-martial have drawn chiefly international jurisdictional interest since World War II, with the dual issues whether war crimes trials belong in international tribunals (e.g., the Rome Treaty discussion) and whether courts-martial have jurisdiction not only over domestic and foreign military personnel, but also over foreign civilians. The later is really an international (armed conflict) law discussion conducted also partially in terms of trial process standards, with links into treaty law in the form of Common Articles 2 and 3 of the 1949 Geneva Conventions (namely the Third Geneva Convention relative to the Treatment of Prisoners of War[4] or "POW Convention" and the Fourth Geneva Convention relative to the Protection of Civilian Persons in Time of War[5] or "Civilian Convention").

BACKGROUND

On September 11, 2001, the United States was attacked. The perpetrators of the attacks were members of an international terrorist band known as al Qaeda, a nonstate actor bent on destroying the United States and killing Americans. The leadership of al Qaeda was based openly in Afghanistan. Diplomatic demands were made on Afghanistan for the surrender of those responsible, but the demands were ignored. The President under Congressional authorization responded militarily.[6] Major combat ended very quickly with the collapse of the Afghan (Taliban) government and the capture of many people who, at least initially, appeared to have some connection with al Qaeda. Some of these captives were taken on the battlefield, others in post-combat Afghanistan, and some were found in other parts of the globe. The captives were eventually brought to Guantanamo Bay, Cuba and held there awaiting decisions as to their status, their future, and, for some, their criminal liability. The President initially determined that trials would be held before military commissions[7] prior to the President's Order, a trial forum not seriously studied since World War II.[8]

On July 9, 2004, one suspected member of al Qaeda, Salim Ahmed Hamdan, was formally charged with conspiracy as war crime and was to be tried before a military commission.[9] On November 8, 2004, the U.S. District Court for the District of Columbia ruled (1) that Hamdan's trial could not proceed as planned unless it were determined that Hamdan was not a prisoner of war, and (2) that, because the planned procedures permitted the exclusion of the defendant from the courtroom (contemplating the problem of classified evidence), the planned trial would be inconsistent with the requirements of the Constitution, Uniform Code of Military Justice (UCMJ), and international law.[10] The Appeals Court for the District of Columbia reversed, but on certiorari, the Supreme Court rejected the government's arguments that relied heavily upon claims of broad executive power and special exigencies in the war on terror.

Chief Justice Roberts did not participate in the 5 to 3 decision, while a plurality of four Justices held that the military commission to try Hamdan lacked the power to proceed because its "structure and procedures" violated the UCMJ and the 1949 Geneva Conventions. Meanwhile, Justice Kennedy as fifth vote concurred in the result, but seemingly did not go so far in embracing Geneva Convention issues, stressing more the absence of presidential authority (given conflicting Congressional action, under a standard *Youngstown Sheet & Tube Co. v. Sawyer* analysis) to create military commissions as institutions seemingly in violation UMCJ procedural and evidentiary mandates.[11] Questions exist whether military commissions now authorized under the Military Commission Act of 2006 as subsequent Congressional enactment articulated with an eye to *Hamdan* will be upheld, but it is generally assumed that the Supreme Court eventually will take up another Guantanamo-related case to revisit these issues. Hence we look to the history of military commissions in anticipation of the next Supreme Court opinion.

WAR CRIMES TRIAL FORA

Historically, military tribunals have served as the forum of choice for war crimes trials. Military tribunals include a formal court-martial and the traditional war court—the military commission.

General Courts-Martial

U.S. military courts are courts of limited jurisdiction.[12] For a U.S. military court to exercise jurisdiction, the defendant[13] and the offense[14] must be subject to military jurisdiction. Additionally, the defendant must have been subject to the UCMJ at the time of the offense and at the time of trial.[15] Those persons who are normally subject to the jurisdiction of a court-martial are set out in Article 2 of the UCMJ. Prisoners of war are specifically listed in Article 2 as persons subject to the Code.[16] However, it would be a very rare set of circumstances in which a prisoner of war could commit a war crime while being held as a POW. In most cases, the war crime alleged will have occurred before capture and hence the usual military jurisdiction requirements cannot be met.[17] The normal requirement that court-martial jurisdiction over the defendant exist both at the time of the offense and at the time of trial could make a prisoner of war's trial by court-martial, even for a war crime, legally suspect if the court's in personam jurisdiction is derived solely from Article 2 of the UCMJ.

Article 18 of the UCMJ sets out the subject matter jurisdiction of general courts-martial. With regard to war crimes, the article provides that general courts-martial have jurisdiction to "try any person who by the law of war is subject to trial by a military tribunal...." The phrase "any person" is a clear statement that nonmilitary persons (i.e., persons other than those listed in Article 2 of the UCMJ as being subject to its provisions) are subject to trial by general court-martial for particular offenses. However, note that the actual grant of jurisdiction is limited to the individual defendant *"who by the law of war is subject to trial by a military tribunal."* In effect, this chapter incorporates by reference the prior practice of military commanders in dealing with persons who violate the law of war or who violate occupation decrees. Article 18 is a stand-alone grant of jurisdiction to military tribunals when the defendant is charged with a very limited category of criminal activity—a violation of the law of war. The jurisdictional grant incorporates all the provisions of the law of war, including the substantive rules on the conduct of warfare, whether treaty-based or under customary law.

The *1969 Manual for Courts-Martial* explained this grant of general court-martial jurisdiction as follows:

> In addition, they [General Courts-Martial] have power to try any person who by the law of war is subject to trial by military tribunal for any crimes or offenses against the law of war and for any offense against the law of territory occupied as an incident of war or belligerency whenever the local civilian authority is superseded in whole or in part by the military authority of the occupying power.[18]

The *1984 Manual for Courts-Martial* again addressed the law of war jurisdiction of general courts-martial:

> General Courts-Martial may try any person who by the law of war is subject to trial by military tribunal for any crime or offense against:
>
> (a) The law of war; or
> (b) The law of the territory occupied as an incident of war or belligerency whenever the local civil authority is superseded in whole or in part by the military authority of the occupying power. The law of the occupied territory includes the local criminal law as adopted or modified by competent authority, and the proclamations, ordinances, regulations, or orders promulgated by the competent authority of the occupying power.[19]

The 1984 language was repeated in the *2002 Manual for Courts-Martial*,[20] so there is no doubt concerning the jurisdictional competence of a general court-martial in war crimes cases.

In the post–World War II case of *Aikens and Seevers,* the Army Board of Review discussed the war crimes jurisdiction of a general court-martial. The two defendants, both

American citizens, were charged with several offenses, including the murder of a Japanese national in occupied Japan, and were sentenced to death. The defendants claimed that they were not subject to court-martial because their term of service had expired and they had been discharged from active duty. The Board rejected their argument, but then went on to point out that even if they had actually been discharged from the Army, they would remain subject to military jurisdiction under either of two theories. First, the crime occurred in occupied Japan and the courts of the occupying power had jurisdiction over everyone in the occupied territory. Second, the murder of an enemy civilian by members of the occupying force would be a violation of the law of war, and Article of War 12 (now Article 18, UCMJ) grants general courts-martial jurisdiction over anyone who violates the law of war.[21]

The Board of Review pointed out that the defendants *might* have been tried by military commission for violations of the law of war. And, as the jurisdiction of a military commission is concurrent with that of a general court-martial then "[i]t follows, ipso facto, that if a military commission would have jurisdiction over the offenses and the accused, so also would a general court-martial."[22] Of course, this idea could be looked at from the other side—it follows, ipso facto, that if a general court-martial has jurisdiction over the offenses and the accused, then so also would a military commission, at least where the charged offense is a violation of the law of war.

In spite of Article 18's jurisdictional grant, a war crimes trial by general court-martial would not be without practical and legal problems. A trial by general court-martial would have to meet all the requirements of U.S. law, satisfy all the Constitutional safeguards available to U.S. military personnel accused of a crime, and meet the requirements of the law of war. Compliance with these requirements could make successful prosecution in a general court-martial for a precapture offense virtually impossible. The evidentiary difficulties might be insurmountable. Strict application of the rules of evidence could work to the disadvantage of both the prosecution and the defense. War crimes trials often demand a procedural flexibility which is unavailable in a court-martial.

The Military Commission

History

Congress provided the necessary procedural and evidentiary flexibility by retaining the historic forum most suitable for war crimes trials—the military commission.[23] The *2002 Manual for Courts-Martial* reaffirmed the concurrent jurisdiction of military commissions and general courts-martial.[24]

Military commissions are common law war courts and historically operated without specific statutory authorization. In fact, even the criminal offenses tried by commissions were similar to those found at common law. There was no legislature to formally declare an act to be a crime so that military commanders promulgated their own list of offenses and created the necessary tribunals for the trial and punishment of offenders. The tribunals in which the cases were tried were collectively known as "war courts." Military commissions were just another disciplinary tool in the field commander's arsenal. The power to conduct trials by military commission was considered to be an inherent part of command.

During the 1847 Mexican War, American General Winfield Scott made extensive use of military commissions in order to maintain law and order among the soldiers of his command and the civilian population in Mexico. In a General Order, Scott provided a list of prohibited acts and set out the rationale for military jurisdiction. The order provided that there is an "unwritten" military code, in addition to the *written* military code, prescribed by Congress in the rules and articles of war, and which unwritten codes, all armies, in hostile countries, are forced to adopt—not only for their own safety, but also for the protection of unoffending inhabitants and their property about the theatres of military operations, against injuries on the part of the army, contrary to the laws of war.[25]

The criminal offenses listed in General Scott's order, including violations of the law of war, were subject to trial before a military commission. The offenses were essentially the common crimes committed in Mexico by American soldiers and Mexican civilians which normally would have been tried in a court-martial or a Mexican court. However, at that time, the jurisdiction of a court-martial was not considered to be extraterritorial, and there were no functioning Mexican courts. Responsibility for law and order fell to the commander of the occupying forces. With that came the need to establish a forum in which to hear criminal cases. Thus, because a court-martial had no express statutory authority to act outside the territory of the United States and the civil courts in the United States had no extraterritorial jurisdiction,[26] the only forum in which an American soldier could have been tried for any crime was the military commission. Additionally, because the Mexican courts were not operating in the parts of Mexico occupied by the American forces, the only forum in which Mexicans could be tried was also the military commission.

Criminal acts which were violations of the law of war were tried before a special military commission called a "Council of War." There was no difference between the Council and the commission, other than the type of case heard. By the Civil War, the two forums had merged and all war-related offenses committed by civilians, including violations of the law of war, were tried before "military commissions."[27] At the same time, soldiers who violated the law of war could be tried in either a court-martial or a military commission.

Courts-martial unquestionably have extraterritorial jurisdiction and military commissions are specifically authorized by Article 21 of the UCMJ. Still, the procedure and authority for military commissions is derived from historical practice and armed conflict law. General courts-martial are "convened" by designated general officers. Military commissions have historically been "appointed" by commanders in the field. Under the procedures initially promulgated under presidential order for the conduct of the post-9/11 military commissions and later under the Military Commission Act of 2006, the SecDef (Secretary of Defense) or his or her designee may issue orders from time to time appointing one or more military commissions to try specified individuals on war crimes charges. Practically, though, there is no difference in the process of creating a tribunal to hear a war crimes case from any other military case. For most precapture offenses, a military commission will still be the forum of choice.

In the World War II German saboteur case, *Ex Parte Quirin,* the Supreme Court addressed the constitutional basis for military commissions. The defendants in the case were eight German soldiers who had been delivered to the east coast of the United States by submarine for the purpose of conducting sabotage.[28] They were captured quickly after coming ashore and were brought before a military commission for trial. One of the charges alleged a violation of the law of war by crossing the military lines of the United States while out of uniform and remaining in the guise of civilians. This act made them unlawful belligerents under the law of war, and they were also charged with espionage, sabotage, and conspiracy to commit these crimes. They appealed their eventual convictions to the Supreme Court, challenging the jurisdiction of the military commission. The Court rejected their appeal, stating:

> Congress, in addition to making rules for the government of our Armed Forces, has thus exercised its authority to define and punish offenses against the law of nations by sanctioning,

within constitutional limitations, the jurisdiction of military commissions to try persons and offenses which, according to the rules and precepts of the law of nations, and more particularly the law of war, are cognizable by such tribunals.[29]

In essence, the Court said that Congress had recognized the historical jurisdiction of military commissions and had deferred to military commanders (in this case the President, as Commander in Chief, had ordered the trial by military commission) to determine the exact offenses triable by military commissions. The Court's view of the military commission's jurisdiction was affirmed in the next major war crimes case to come before the Court.

Prisoners of War

The Supreme Court again reviewed the authority of military commissions in the post–World War II case of General Tomoyuki Yamashita, former Japanese commander in the Philippines. Yamashita was tried for war crimes by a military commission convened in the Philippines. The Yamashita military commission permitted the introduction of evidence which clearly would have been excluded in a court-martial, including depositions, affidavits, and hearsay. Yamashita was convicted and sentenced to death. On appeal to the Supreme Court, his attorneys argued that Article 63 of the 1929 Geneva Prisoner of War Convention required that he be tried by the same forum, using the same procedures and evidentiary rules, as would have be used for the trial of an American soldier.[30] The Court, noting that the Convention referred to "prisoners of war," opined that Article 63 only applied to postcapture offenses and that POWs, even though subject to the Articles of War (today the UCMJ), were entitled to trial by court-martial only for postcapture offenses. Trials for precapture offenses were simply not covered by Article 63. On the jurisdiction of military commissions, the Court said:

> By thus recognizing military commissions in order to preserve their traditional jurisdiction over enemy combatants unimpaired by the Articles [of War], Congress gave sanction, as we held in Ex Parte Quirin, to any use of the military commission contemplated by the common law of war. But it did not thereby make subject to the Articles of War persons other than those defined by Article 2 as being subject to the Articles, nor did it confer the benefits of the Articles of War upon such persons.[31]

In short, the Court decided that a person who is subject to the jurisdiction of a military commission for a violation of the law of war is not, thereby, automatically brought within the class of people who are subject to the Articles of War by virtue of Article 2. And, if the defendant was not included within one of the classes set out in Article 2, then all the procedural safeguards set out in the rest of the Articles of War (now the UCMJ) did not apply.

The 1949 Geneva Prisoner of War Convention deliberately changed the rule in the 1929 Convention. Today, the POW Convention in Article 102 recognizes the right to prosecute a POW for precapture offenses, but provides that the defendant POW retains the benefits of the Convention throughout the trial.[32]

POW Status and the District Court *Hamdan* Opinion

The Memorandum Opinion of the lower court in *Hamdan*[33] discussed the issue of POW status and its impact on any war crimes trials by military commission. Judge Robertson essentially accepted that because Hamdan *claimed* to be a POW, he was entitled to be treated as such until a formal tribunal (called an Article 5 Tribunal under the 1949 Geneva Conventions) was convened to address his status. The opinion states:

If Hamdan is entitled to the protections accorded to prisoners of war under the Third Geneva Convention [Prisoners of War], one need look no further than Article 102 for the rule that requires his habeas petition to be granted:

"A prisoner of war can be validly sentenced only if the sentence has been pronounced by the same courts according to the same procedure as in the case of members of the armed forces of the Detaining Power, and, if furthermore, the provisions of the present Chapter have been observed."

The Military Commission is not such a court. Its procedures are not such procedures.[34]

Judge Robertson read the Geneva POW Convention provision as one which "unmistakably mandates trial of POWs only by general court-martial...."[35] But does it?

The court determined that "[u]ntil or unless such a tribunal decides otherwise, Hamdan has, and must be accorded, the full protections of a prisoner of war."[36] Accepting for the moment that Hamdan is a prisoner of war, then what effect does that status have on his trial for war crimes? And, what exactly are the "full protections of a prisoner of war" when it comes to trials for violations of the law of war? Article 102, Geneva Convention on Prisoners of War, says "A prisoner of war can be validly sentenced only if the sentence has been pronounced by the same courts according to the same procedure as in the case of members of the armed forces of the detaining power...." Hence, one benefit is the right to be tried in the same courts, using the same procedures, as would be used to try "members of the armed forces" of the detaining power.[37] But who are "members of the armed forces" for POW Convention purposes? The POW Convention provides some guidance.

Its Article 4 sets out the categories of persons entitled to be treated as prisoners of war. The very first category listed is "members of the armed forces of a Party to the conflict as well as members of militias or volunteer corps forming a part of such armed forces."[38] The treaty requires that members of such a militia be "commanded by a person responsible for his subordinates." The Commentary gives some further guidance on this: "His [the commander's] competence must be considered in the same way as that of a military commander. Respect for this rule is moreover in itself a guarantee of the discipline which must prevail in the volunteer corps...." Hence a key element of being entitled to the POW Convention protections because of membership in an armed force is that of being subject to some sort of military discipline. Should not the same POW Convention definition be applied to the "members of the armed forces" of the detaining power?

So who is a member of the armed forces of the detaining power–in this case the United States–and how does that status relate to court-martial jurisdiction? A key component of service in the U.S. armed forces is that the service member is subject to military discipline (which, for example, is not the case for so-called military contractors, of which there are many in current armed conflict zones such as Iraq). Discipline in the U.S. armed forces is exercised through the UCMJ.[39] The Manual for Courts-Martial provides that a person becomes "subject to court-martial jurisdiction upon enlistment in or induction into the armed forces."[40] However, as previously noted, for there to be court-martial jurisdiction the defendant must be subject to the Code at both the time of the offense and at the time of the trial. There can be no ordinary, Article 2 jurisdiction over a preenlistment offense because the defendant was not a member of the "armed forces" at the time of the offense. Applying the same reasoning, then a prisoner of war should also not be subject to Article 2 court-martial jurisdiction for a precapture offense. To grant the POW a right to trial by general court-martial, while denying that same right to a member of the U.S. armed forces, would be a derogation from Article 102's requirement that the same courts and same procedures as are used in the trial of members of the armed forces of the detaining power also be used in the trial of any POW.

If an American soldier is to be tried for a preenlistment offense against the law of war, then we have to look outside of Article 2, UCMJ, for jurisdiction. Even though the soldier may not be a "member of the armed forces" for war crimes *court-martial* purposes, he would certainly fall within the "any person who by the law of war is subject to trial by a military tribunal" language of Article 18, UCMJ. Thus, the U.S. soldier could be tried by General Court-martial for a preenlistment war crime because of Article 18's "any person" language. And, therefore, a prisoner of war could be tried for a precapture offense because he too would be "any person." Because Article 21, UCMJ makes the jurisdiction of a military commission concurrent with that of a General Court-martial in cases of offenders or offenses against the law of war, the prisoner of war might also be tried before an military commission of an offense against the law of war, i.e., a war crime. In short, if an American soldier can be tried before a military commission for a war crime, so too can a prisoner of war. The jurisdictional issue then becomes: could an American soldier be tried by a military commission today? The real question Judge Robertson should have considered was not whether a POW could be tried only by court-martial, but rather could an American soldier be tried by military commission? The answer to that question is "yes." The issue was addressed in a review of the *1951 Manual for Court-Martial*. The review provided: "[a]s stated before they [General Courts-Martial] have concurrent jurisdiction with military tribunals to try any person who by the law of war is subject to trial by military tribunals . . . . Under this clause, there is no question that members of our armed forces may be tried for violations of the law of war, either by military tribunals or general courts-martial."[41]

So an American soldier *could be tried* by a military commission, though he would normally be tried by court-martial. Therefore, a prisoner of war held by the United States and accused of a war crime *could also be tried* either by general court-martial or by military commission.[42] No absolute immunity from trial before a military commission can be found in Article 102 of the Prisoner of War Convention. While detainees might be properly afforded the "full protections of a prisoner of war" as a matter of policy, immunity from trial before a military commission is not one of them.

Procedural Issues

The 1949 Prisoner of War Convention provides that prisoners of war "shall" be tried in military courts unless the civil courts of the detaining power are permitted to try members of the detaining power's own forces for a similar offense.[43] The use of the word "shall" clearly indicates a preference for trial in military courts. The courts in which the prisoner of war is tried must employ the same procedures and evidentiary rules as would be used in the trial of members of the detaining power's forces.[44]

Although the Manual for Courts-Martial requires military commissions to follow the same procedures as courts-martial,[45] traditionally the President could direct that other procedures be used. This position was rejected by Justice Kennedy in his *Hamdan* concurrence on the basis of analyzing executive authority under a standard *Youngstown Sheet & Tube Co. v. Sawyer* analysis as narrowed by prior Congressional action; and now the Military Commissions Act of 2006 largely mandates following courts-martial procedure. However, it also recognizes under 10 U.S.C. Chapter 47, Section 949a that all

> [P]retrial, trial and post-trial procedures, including elements and modes of proof. . .may be prescribed by the Secretary of Defense, in consultation with the Attorney General. Such procedures shall, so far as the Secretary considers *practicable or consistent with military or*

intelligence activities, apply the principles of law and rules of evidence in trial by general courts-martial. [Emphasis added]

President Roosevelt, in his Executive Order appointing the military commission which tried the World War II German saboteurs addressed the commission's procedures. "The Commission shall have the power to and shall, as occasion requires, make such rules for the conduct of the proceeding, consistent with the powers of military commissions under the Articles of War, as it shall deem necessary for a full and fair trial of the matters before it." The order also provided that "Such evidence shall be admitted as would, in the opinion of the President of the Commission, have probative value to a reasonable man."[46] Thus, the procedural and evidentiary rules which would normally be employed by a court-martial could be altered under Roosevelt's presidential order to enable a full and fair trial.

The Confrontation Concern

As previously noted, because of Article 21, UCMJ, the trial of a POW charged with a war crime is not limited to a general court-martial. Nor must a military commission follow, in every respect, the procedures for a court-martial. There is one aspect of proposed trials now pending under the Military Commission Act of 2006 which merits careful scrutiny. The problem involves dealing with evidence or testimony incorporating classified information and its substitution or denial of access to defendants under a national security privilege (now 10 U.S.C. Chapter 47, Section 949d (f)). The problem is that, by the very nature of these proceedings, it is reasonably foreseeable that liberal use may be made of this exception with consequent confrontation problems for the defendant. This provision raises issues on both the international and the national level. The trial judge in Hamdan found the possibility of a defendant's exclusion from the proceedings on account of classified information to be "troubling" and to be "obvious beyond any need for citation for such a dramatic deviation from the confrontation clause could not be countenanced in any American court."[47] However, the matter deserves closer examination.

In *Quirin* the Supreme Court found that the Constitutional protections of the Fifth and Sixth Amendments do not extend to trials before military courts. The Court said, "We conclude that the Fifth and Sixth Amendments did not restrict whatever authority was conferred by the Constitution to try offenses against the law of war by military commission, and that petitioners, charged with such an offense not required to be tried by jury at common law, were lawfully placed on trial by the commission without a jury."[48] If, as the Supreme Court said, there is no right to be tried before a jury in a military commission case, is there a right for the defendant to be present at all? The Sixth Amendment also provides that "in all criminal prosecutions, the accused shall enjoy the right to...be confronted with the witnesses against him."[49]

Does this Constitutional right to be present extend to trials before military commissions of defendants accused of violating international law? The UCMJ, Article 39, does address the right of an accused to be present at every stage of the trial—*where the trial is one by court-martial.* (Emphasis added)[50] Would the same requirement apply in a trial before a military commission? That question has now been answered, from a Congressional perspective, under the Military Commission Act of 2006's provisions now at 10 U.S.C. Chapter 47, Sections 949a and 949d addressing classified information and the national security privilege.

In fact, the Congress recognized the right of the President to prescribe procedures for trials in "courts-martial, military commissions, and other military tribunals" in UCMJ

Article 36.[51] The enumeration and recognition of both war crimes forums in one Article is the evidence that the Congress understood that the President needed the legislative authority to make the rules and regulations for courts-martial and for military commissions distinct. Meanwhile, Congress directed under the UMCJ that the President "so far as he considers practicable, apply the principles of law and the rules of evidence generally recognized in the trial of criminal cases in the United States District courts,"[52] but as recited above now leaves under the Military Commission Act of 2006 a similar determination to the SecDef, in consultation with the Attorney General, as resolution for military commissions, but only subject to a national security privilege covering classified materials. This then raises the issue of just how much leeway the SecDef in consultation with the Attorney General (acting ultimately for the President) have in determining what is "practicable" in a trial before a military commission. Invoking the national security privilege now places the onus on a military judge as head of the military commission in terms of attempting to minimize the problem, but if revealing the classified evidence to the defendant would endanger the success of the continuing war effort, then it is hardly "practicable" to comply with all the procedural rules which would apply to a trial in a general court-martial or provide full access to classified information.

Accepting for the moment that the Sixth Amendment requirement does, or should, apply to trials in U.S. military commissions, just how absolute is its requirement for confrontation? The Supreme Court in *Maryland v. Craig*[53] may have provided some guidance. While it involved a child's testimony in a sexual abuse case, the Court opined that there is a "preference for face-to-face confrontation at trial." But the Court also recognized that the preference "must occasionally give way to considerations of public policy and the necessities of the case." The "necessities of the case" may well require the redaction of classified information as well as that documentary evidence and hearsay be introduced in any war crimes trial in lieu of live testimony. Indeed, in war crimes cases, such evidence may well be the rule and not the exception. The "necessities of the case" might also require that nothing occur during the trial which would threaten the war effort. It is also important to keep in mind that trials for war crimes are instruments of war. It is difficult to imagine a greater "public policy" than one whose aim is to protect the public from the criminal actions of those who would indiscriminately kill and destroy that very public. As the Supreme Court has said, "no governmental interest is more compelling than the security of the nation."[54]

As war crimes trials find their *raison d'etre* in international law, is there some guidance in that body of law? Article 12 of the Nuremberg Rules permitted the exclusion of the defendant. The Rule provided that the "Tribunal shall have the right to take proceedings against a person charged with crimes...in his absence,...if the Tribunal, for any reason, finds it necessary, in the interests of justice, to conduct the hearing in his absence."[55] It should be noted that the Nuremberg Rules were adopted in August 1945–after the cessation of military action against Germany, a time when, presumably, there would have been less need for excluding the defendants for any reason, including national security. Yet, the power to exclude was specifically recognized in the Nuremberg Rules. Can the power be any less important where the enemy still exists and while the war continues?

As the defendant in a war crimes trial will in many, if not most, cases be treated as a prisoner of war, the Geneva POW Convention may provide a clue as to the limits of the right of the defendant to be present in a trial. Article 99 sets out the "Essential Rules" for defense. This Article does require that the defendant POW be given "an opportunity to present his defense...." The Commentary to the Article explains the right of defense.

The defendant must be given the right to "question or to have questions put to witnesses for the prosecution in the presence of the accused and to question witnesses for the defense, in the same way as witnesses for the prosecution are questioned and in accordance with the normal rules of procedure (accusatorial or inquisitorial)."[56] Thus, again, the right of the defendant to be present does not seem to be absolute. While the Commentary finds the right to be present as "necessary for the accused," the treaty language actually only mandates that the defendant be given an "opportunity to present his defense and the assistance of a qualified defense counsel."

There is another aspect of the Geneva POW Convention which might help shed some light on the presence requirement and the need for security. Article 105 addresses trial procedure. The POW Convention provides for the appointment of Protecting Powers to monitor the imprisonment of POWs, including criminal trials of POWs. But, that article also provides that the Protecting Power has the right to "attend the trial of the case, unless, this is held in camera, in the *interest of State Security*." If the Protecting Power, a neutral State with a function akin to that of diplomatic protection, can be lawfully excluded "in the interest of State Security," then it is not beyond the pale to suggest that an enemy combatant, even if he is the defendant in a criminal trial, might also be denied access to evidence in the "interest of State Security."

Some critics of trials by military commission find support in the International Covenant on Civil and Political Rights.[57] Article 14 of the Covenant does provide that the accused must "be tried in his presence." [58] However, the same document provides that states may derogate from their obligations under the Covenant "[i]n time of public emergency which threatens the life of the nation and the existence of which is officially proclaimed."[59] President Bush proclaimed a national emergency on September 14, 2001, 3 days after the terrorist attacks directed against the United States. Of note is the fact that derogation from the Covenant is not permitted from some articles of the Covenant even in times of "public emergency." However, Article 14 is not one of the articles from which no derogation is possible. Thus, the right of a defendant to confront witnesses against him and be present during the confrontation may not be absolute as a matter of international law.

Finally, we must not lose sight of the fact that any war crime proceeding will always be measured against a standard of fundamental fairness. The procedural and evidentiary advantages for the government (and possibly the defense) of trial by military commission would mean little if the results are tainted by chicanery or unfairness, whether real or perceived. In *Johnson v. Eisentrager,* another postwar case, the Supreme Court responded to the petitioner's argument that, by virtue of his status as a prisoner of war and the Geneva Convention's requirement that trials of prisoners of war be in the same forum using the same procedures as would be used for the trial of an American soldier, he should have been given the benefits of a trial by court-martial. The Supreme Court said, "[i]t may be noted that no prejudicial disparity is pointed out as between the Commission that tried prisoners and those that would try an offending soldier of the American forces of like rank."[60] Had there been some procedural prejudice, the implication is that the Supreme Court might have decided the case differently.

Those who criticize trials by military commission as being somehow fundamentally unfair because of the less formal rules for their conduct should consider the following commentary is a helpful guide when considering fundamental fairness. After reviewing the post–World War II military commission trials, one commentator opined that:

[A] most remarkable work was performed by these bodies. The offenses committed were widespread. Many persons were involved in their commission. In many cases all, or nearly all, of the victims were dead. In the aftermath of war, witnesses were scattered and documents lost or destroyed. . . . It is an astounding commentary that in not a single instance was there a claim of completely mistaken identity. . . . Equally remarkable is the fact that these tribunals, composed of officers who had been at war with the nations of those accused only a short time before, or who were judges of occupied countries which had suffered at the hands of the enemy, were able to rule fairly upon the law and evidence, and even acquit many of those whose guilt seemed clear, but which they did not deem had been established beyond a reasonable doubt. . . . When nations have attorneys, military officers, and judges imbued with this passion for fairness, the doctrine of justice will prevail in postwar trials, as well as in courts of the United States.[61]

Hopefully, that sentiment will follow any trials of suspected al Qaeda war criminals.

Civilians

Suppose Hamdan were not legally a POW, would the jurisdictional situation be different when the defendant is a civilian detainee? Some argue that a civilian could not be tried by military authorities because the Supreme Court, in a series of cases some 35 years ago,[62] ruled that civilians are not subject to court-martial (the problem of American civilians accompanying the U.S. military overseas).[63] The Court declared Article 2(11) of the UCMJ, which subjected certain civilians to courts-martial, to be unconstitutional. However, the Court based its rulings in those cases on the constitutional power of Congress to make rules and regulations for the armed forces.[64] The Court decided that civilians were not members of the armed forces and, therefore, were not subject to military discipline, at least in peacetime. It is important to note, however, that the Court was not addressing military jurisdiction over civilians accused of war crimes.[65]

The 1969 revision of the *Manual for Courts-Martial* took the Supreme Court's opinion on jurisdiction over civilians into account and provided "[n]otwithstanding the provisions of Article 2(11), persons serving with, employed by, or accompanying the armed forces cannot be tried by courts-martial under that article in peacetime."[66] In discussing the revision, the DOD (Department of Defense) said "[t]he target of the sentence was carefully limited to Article 2(11); and it does not relate to the extent of jurisdiction over civilians relative to the law of war under Article 18."[67]

The jurisdictional issue turns, of course, on the right to grand jury indictment and the availability of all the trial safeguards guaranteed by the Constitution. The Constitution, however, exempts "cases arising in the land and naval forces" from the requirement for grand jury indictment and, impliedly, from some of the other trial safeguards. Does the phrase "in the. . .forces" refer to cases or persons? In spite of the specific reference to cases, some have argued that the word *in* simply refers to persons in the military and that persons not in the military can not be tried by the military. On the issue, one commentator concluded:

> But, even if the foregoing interpretation of the Constitution were upheld [that "in" refers to persons, not cases], it would not follow that there could be no trials of civilians before military commissions. In the *Quirin* case, the opinion held that in no event can a defendant demand as a constitutional right, trials by jury, unless the offense with which he is charged was triable by a jury at common law and at the time of the adoption of our Constitution. Hence, where a civilian is charged with an offense against the law of war, the *Quirin* case settles the rule that such a person can be tried by military commission without reference to the fact of whether the case is one 'arising out of [*sic*] the land or naval forces,' or whether the offense was committed in the theater of operations, for jury trials in cases against the

law of war were unknown to the common law, or American jurisprudence at the time of adoption of the Constitution.[68]

U.S. Citizens

The Military Commission Act of 2006 specifies that only foreign unlawful enemy combatants may be subject to military commission proceedings. It specifically excludes coverage of U.S. citizens as unlawful enemy combatants (e.g., Jose Padilla), but there is precedent that the exclusion is not constitutionally required. In the World War II case *Colepaugh v. Looney,*[69] the defendant, William Curtis Colepaugh, was charged with passing through U.S. lines in civilian clothes for the purpose of committing espionage and sabotage. Colepaugh and a German, named Gimpel, had been dropped off on the coast of Maine by a German submarine. Colepaugh turned himself in and aided in the FBI's capture of Gimpel. Colepaugh, an American citizen, was tried by a military commission, convicted, and sentenced to death. The sentence was later commuted to life in prison. On appeal to the 10th Circuit, he argued that the military commission had no jurisdiction and that the trial should have been in the civil courts where "his claimed constitutional rights to a jury trial and assistance of counsel would be vouchsafed."[70] The appellate court said:

> [T]here can be no doubt of the constitutional and legislative power of the president, as Commander in Chief of the armed forces, to invoke the law of war by appropriate proclamation; to define within constitutional limitations the various offenses against the law of war, and to establish military commissions with jurisdiction to try all persons charged with defined violations.[71]

The court found that, in accordance with the law of war, an unlawful combatant (which Colepaugh was because he was not in the uniform of the German forces) is not only subject to capture and detention, but also subject to trial. The court summarized the law on a military commission's jurisdiction:

> Judged by this concept of common law military justice, the charges and specifications before us clearly state an offense of unlawful belligerency, contrary to the established and judicially recognized law of war—an offense within the jurisdiction of the duly constituted Military Commission with power to try, decide, and condemn. And, the petitioner's citizenship in the United States does not divest the Commission of jurisdiction over him, or confer upon him any constitutional rights not accorded any other belligerent under the laws of war.[72]

The military commission is "simply an instrumentality for the more efficient execution of the war power vested in Congress and the power vested in the President as Commander in Chief of the armed forces."[73] It would seem undeniable that if a military commission is "an instrumentality for the more efficient exercise of the war power, then there is no reason to deny war crimes jurisdiction to the military commission. Providing a forum in which claimed violations of the law of war can be fairly and efficiently tried is an integral part of a nation's war effort.

The Last Military Commission Trial

There is a general impression that the last trials by military commission pre-9/11 were directly related to the crimes of World War II. But a more recent case addresses the relationship between the usual criminal law and procedures applicable in U.S. courts and the special rules which apply in war crimes trials. The limits of the war power were at the heart of the legal issue in the case of *United States v. Tiede,*[74] a case which arose in occupied Berlin. In 1977, defendant Tiede hijacked a Polish airliner to the American sector of West Berlin and, in due course, was charged with the offense of hijacking by the American occupation authorities. Tiede was not an American citizen. The trial was to be before the U.S. Court for Berlin, a Court which had never before sat. A U.S. District Court judge was sent to Berlin to hear the case. The defense argued that because the trial was to take place in a U.S. court the defendant was entitled to trial by jury. The prosecution responded, essentially, that the court was a creature of the legal status conferred on the Americans by the fact of occupation and that the occupation authorities could lawfully restrict the right to trial by jury. In other words, this court was actually a military commission entitled to exercise jurisdiction over crimes and criminals within occupied territory.

The judge agreed with the defense and ordered an American style jury trial (something unknown in German law) with Germans as members of the jury. The judge's ruling was based on the peculiar status of the occupation of Berlin. In his view, the occupation of Berlin in 1977 was an accident of postwar politics, not the result of military action. What is relevant for our purposes is what the judge did not hold. The court stated:

> [T]his court does not hold that jury trials must be afforded in occupation courts *everywhere* and under *all* circumstances; the Court holds only that if the United States convenes a United States court in Berlin, under present circumstances, and charges civilians with nonmilitary offenses, the United States must provide the defendants with the same constitutional safeguards that it must provide to civilian defendants in any other United States court.[75] (Italics in the original)

The judge noted that the case "does not involve...a violation of the law of war."[76] Thus, the court recognized that where the offense charged is a violation of the law of war, the Constitution's protections, at least as relates to trial by jury, do not apply. If there is no constitutional right to trial by jury in a war crimes case tried before a military commission, a strong argument can be made that the constitutional requirement of confrontation also must yield to the demands of the war effort.

Given the history of military commissions, one can reasonably conclude that "the United States is presently in a position to conduct trials, and adequately punish all war criminals including U.S. civilians, through the use of the military commission."[77] One writer goes even further, "if any U.S. tribunal presently has jurisdiction to try [civilians] for violations of the law of war, it must be the military commission."[78]

The Impact of the 1949 Geneva Conventions

Given the relative paucity of U.S. war crimes cases, the actual jurisdictional limits of possible U.S. forums are somewhat conjectural. However, it will be recalled that a party to the 1949 Geneva Conventions is obligated to enact penal legislation to implement the grave breach provisions of the Conventions. In reviewing the 1949 Conventions as part of the ratification process, the Justice Department stated that there was no need for implementing legislation.[79] In 1967, the United States reported to the Secretary General of the United Nations that:

> The Uniform Code of Military Justice provides, in article 18 that "General courts-martial shall also have jurisdiction to try any person who by the law of war is subject to trial by military tribunal and may adjudge any punishment permitted by the law of war." Thus, the law of war is incorporated into United States military law. The law of war includes the provisions of the Geneva Convention which became part of United States law upon its adherence.[80]

The U.S. report to the United Nations is explicit recognition that U.S. military tribunals are proper forums for war crimes trials and that the substantive offenses in the law of war are captured by the existing law and practice of the United States.[81] This is not to say, of course, that a proposal to try an American, or perhaps a foreign, civilian before a U.S. military tribunal, even for a war crime, would be without criticism. It is unfortunate, but inevitable, that a decision to conduct a war crimes trial would involve major political questions. Yet, any decision concerning the prosecution of war crimes is, or at least should be, initially based on the requirements of the law.[82] The political situation may dominate the legal situation.[83]

TRIAL SAFEGUARDS IN INTERNATIONAL LAW

An American, whether a soldier or a civilian, tried for a war crime in a U.S. court is entitled to be tried in accordance with the usual requirements of U.S. criminal law. The posture of the Supreme Court's *Hamdan* decision, however, leaves open the issue of the exact scope of Geneva Convention Common Article 3 protections applicable to military commissions. Where a defendant is a person protected by the Conventions, then mere compliance with domestic law in the conduct of the trial would be inadequate. The forum trying the case would also have to meet all the standards and requirements set out in the Conventions. As will be seen, these may be more than the usual criminal defendant might receive.

To examine the international standards for a war crimes trial, we might assume that the defendant is granted (even if not entitled to) the protections of the POW Convention because, practically, the United States would provide the utmost legal protection to the defendant, and for Geneva treaty purposes that level of protection is found in the POW Convention. Further, the defendant would probably demand prisoner of war treatment because the protections afforded by the Geneva Conventions to prisoners of war are greater than those afforded civilians (the difference between Common Articles 2 and 3). For the defense to argue that the defendant is not covered by the POW Convention, but is instead a civilian, might open him up to an added charge of being an unlawful combatant.

The requirements for the trial of a prisoner of war are set out in articles 99 through 108 of the POW Convention. Exactly what are those requirements? The POW Convention makes it a grave breach to willfully deprive a prisoner of a "fair and regular trial."[84] The standards for a fair and regular trial must, therefore, be those set out in the Geneva Convention.[85] The POW Convention forbids the trial of a prisoner of war by any court which fails to offer "essential guarantees of independence and impartiality as generally recognized...."[86] Rather than to leave open the issue of exactly what guarantees are "generally recognized," the drafters of the Convention set out a list of the minimal requirements in Article 105. The article serves as a "Bill of Rights" for prisoners of war pending criminal trial.

No physical or moral coercion can be used to force the defendant to make incriminating statements.[87] The defendant must be given the opportunity to present evidence on his behalf and choose his own counsel. If the defendant cannot secure counsel, the Protecting Power[88] must attempt to find suitable counsel. If no appropriate counsel is found by the Protecting Power, the Detaining Power must appoint one. Counsel must be given at least 2 weeks to prepare the defense. The defense counsel may meet privately with the defendant and interview witnesses. The charges must be in a language that the defendant understands. An interpreter must be provided if needed, and representatives of the Protecting Power may attend the trial unless security concerns prevent their presence.[89] The Geneva

POW Convention also guarantees the defendant the right to present a defense. But, the Convention does not address how that defense is to be presented. Must the defendant testify only under oath or is he permitted to make an unsworn statement? The practice at Nuremberg was to permit both. Today, a court trying a prisoner of war for a war crime would be well advised to permit the defendant to make the decision.

Practically speaking, the same international law requirements would apply to trials of enemy war criminals who, for some reason, are not technically prisoners of war. If a person protected by the Civilians Convention is charged with a war crime, similar safeguards apply.[90] The DOD regulations require that enemy civilians in territory occupied by the Army be tried only by a general court-martial sitting in the occupied territory.[91] However, where a war crime is alleged, the trial might be held before a military commission because of its statutorily mandated concurrent jurisdiction with a general court-martial. Enemy POWs could be tried in any level U.S. court-martial for a postcapture offense, but only in a general court-martial or military commission for a precapture war crime.

All war crimes are, in principle, punishable by death.[92] However, the punishment should fit the crime.[93] The Conventions also place some restrictions on when the death penalty can actually be imposed.[94] It is also possible to impose fines or direct the forfeiture of property as part of the punishment.[95]

Article 106 of the Prisoner of War Convention requires that the defendant be granted the right to appeal any conviction and sentence to the same extent as a member of the Detaining Power's forces might appeal. The appeal could be to a higher judicial body or a higher military commander, or both. The procedures for appeals must be explained to the defendant. On appeal, the defendant can request that the sentence be revised or quashed or that the trial be reopened on the merits. Reopening a case is an especially important appellate right in a war crimes case. Where the war crime occurred before capture (the most likely scenario) and the trial takes place during captivity, it would probably be very difficult for the defense to produce witnesses or procure other exculpatory evidence.[96] This provision permits the defendant to ask for a trial de novo at the conclusion of hostilities.

The International Red Cross Commentary broadly describes the special grounds for appeal derived from the conventions:

> Apart from the obligations incumbent on the Detaining Power to apply the same rules to prisoners of war as in the case of members of its own armed forces, attention should be drawn to the following Articles [of the Prisoner of War Convention] which, if not respected, would give grounds for appeal or petition:
> Article 86, "non bis in idem;"[97]
> Article 99, paragraph 2 prohibition of coercion;
> Article 99, paragraph 3 rights of defence;
> Article 100, paragraphs 2 and 3 [the death penalty];
> Article 101, delay in execution of the death penalty;
> Article 103, paragraph 2 [pretrial confinement];
> Article 104, paragraph 4 [notification of proceedings];
> Article 105, rights of defence.

This list is not exhaustive, but merely indicates the most important provisions of the Convention. In addition to the cases quoted above, any failure on the part of the Detaining Power to comply with its own law concerning appellate rights applicable to members of its armed forces would also constitute grounds for an appeal or a petition for clemency.[98]

Finally, and perhaps most importantly, the trial must actually be perceived by neutral observers as having been fairly conducted. Technical compliance with the letter of the

Conventions will count for little if the outcome of the trial is a foregone conclusion. In the post–World War II subsequent proceedings case of *United States v. Flick,* the court described the necessity for fairness:

> Facing this Tribunal are private citizens of a conquered state being tried for alleged international crimes. Their judges are citizens of the victor states selected by its war department. There may be misgivings as to the fairness of such a trial. These considerations have made the judges of the Tribunal keenly aware of their grave responsibility and of the danger to the cause of justice if the conduct of the trial and the conclusions reached should even seem to justify these misgivings. To err is human, but if error must occur it is right that the error must not be prejudicial to the defendants. That we think is the spirit of the law of civilized nations. It finds expression in the following principles well known to students of Anglo-American criminal law:
>
>   1. There can be no conviction without proof of personal guilt.
>   2. Such guilt must be proved beyond a reasonable doubt.
>   3. The presumption of innocence follows each defendant throughout the trial.
>   4. The burden of proof is at all times on the prosecution.
>   5. If from credible evidence two reasonable inferences may be drawn, one of guilt and the other of innocence, the latter must be taken.[99]

Any war crimes trial which satisfies these precepts would be above reproach.

CONCLUSIONS

The war on terror is different from other wars in many respects. The enemy knows no bounds and respects no rules. Al Qaeda as nonstate actor functions without the open sanction of a state. Determining exactly when the conflict is at an end will be problematic. Yet, in one respect, this war is just like all other wars. Those who violate the laws of war must be tried and, if found guilty, punished. Punishment of war criminals serves the usual purposes of criminal law—deterrence of others and punishment of the wrongdoer. Those who violate the law of war must not expect immunity. But the legality of the trial process must be judged by standards different from those which apply in peacetime. Trials by military commission for those who violate the law of war have long been seen as an important and necessary part of any war effort. As we approach questions that arise with regard to this war, the historical context of military law, war tribunals, and traditional criminal law provide guidance to new questions.

NOTES

1. *Detainee Treatment Act of 2005,* Public Law 109-148 (December 30, 2005), div. A, title X, *U.S. Statutes at Large* 119 (2005): 2739 (to be codified at *U.S. Code* 42 (2005): Sections 2000dd to 2000dd-1 and other provisions of the U.S. Code). See also Knut Dormann, "The Legal Situation of "Unlawful"/Unprivileged Combatants," *International Review of the Red Cross* 849 (2003): 85; George Aldrich, "The Taliban, Al Qaeda and the Determination of Illegal Combatants," *American Journal of International Law* 96 (2002): 893.

2. *Military Commission Act of 2006,* Public Law 109-366 (October 17, 2006), *U.S. Statutes at Large* 120 (2006): 2600. See also Douglas Hass, "Crafting Military Commissions Post-Hamdan: The Military Commissions Act of 2006," *Indiana Law Journal* 82 (Spring 2007).

3. *Hamdan v. Rumsfeld,* 126 S.Ct. 2749, 2759 (2006).

4. "Third Geneva Convention Relative to the Treatment of Prisoners of War," August 12, 1949, *United States Treaties and Other International Agreements* 6: 3316 ("POW Convention").

5. "Fourth Geneva Convention Relative to the Protection of Civilian Persons in Time of War," August 12, 1949, *United States Treaties and Other International Agreements* 6: 3516 ("Civilian Convention").

6. *Authorization for Use of Military Force,* Public Law 107-40, §§1–2, *U.S. Statutes at Large* 115 (September 18, 2001): 224 ("AUMF").

7. *Military Order, Detention, Treatment, and Trial of Certain Non-citizens in the War Against Terrorism, Federal Register* 66 (2001): 57,833; 57,834 ("Military Order No. 1").

8. See, for example, Robinson O. Everett and Scott L. Silliman, "Forums for Punishing Offenses Against the Law of Nations," *Wake Forest Law Review* 29 (1994): 509, 519. "Very little attention has been paid in recent years to the possibility of using American military tribunals to enforce the law of war. Such a use, however, appears to be a permissible option supported by precedent." Note this piece was written seven years before the 9/11 attacks. The best explanations for the apparent lack of interest are probably one of both of the international push to create a standing war crimes tribunal under the Rome Treaty and U.S. views concerning unlawful combatants. The two practical difficulties are that the United States has been strongly opposed to the Rome Treaty since at least 2000, plus did not enter into the 1977 Additional Protocols (which much of the rest of the world now regards as customary law) because of disagreements about their apparent treatment of unlawful combatants. Under current circumstances, the likeliest circumstances of a U.S. general court-martial enforcing the laws of war against persons other than American soldiers might be against so-called military contractors, some of whom have been involved in armed clashes incidental to the security protection roles.

9. Department of Defense, "Military Commission List of Charges for Salim Ahmed Hamdan," Department of Defense http://www.defenselink.mil/news/Jul2004/d20040714hcc.pdf.

10. *Hamdan v. Rumsfeld,* 344 F. Supp. 2d 152 (D.D.C. 2004). On July 15, 2005, the Court of Appeals for the District of Columbia reversed the District Court's opinion. That opinion is available at 415 F.3d 33 (D.C. Cir. 2005).

11. *Hamdan,* 126 S.Ct. at 2759.

12. "Military and Civil Defense" in *American Jurisprudence Proof of Facts,* vol. 53, 2nd ser. §225 (Eagen, MN: Thompson West, 1970).

13. "RCM (Rule for Court-Martial) 201(b)(4)," in *Manual for Courts-Martial, United States* (Washington, DC: U.S. GPO, 2002) ("MCM").

14. Ibid., 201 b(5).

15. "To be valid, a court-martial must have personal jurisdiction over the accused: The accused must have been subject to the U.C.M.J. both at the time of the offense and at the time of trial..." David A. Schlueter, *Military Criminal Justice: Practice and Procedure* (Charlottesville, VA: Michie Co., 1999), 155.

16. *Uniform Code of Military Justice,* Article 2(9), U.S. Code 10 (2005) § 802(a)(9).

17. The POW Convention specifically provides for the trial of prisoners of war for precapture offenses. Even after conviction the prisoner retains the protections of the Convention. Art. 85.

18. MCM 1969, ¶ 14a.

19. MCM 1984, RCM 201(f)(1)(B)(I).

20. MCM 2002, RCM 201 (f)(1)(B).

21. *United States v. Aikens and Seevers,* 5 B.R.(J.C.) 331, 348–361 (1949).

22. Ibid., 361.

23. Military commissions have been used throughout American history. A military commission, though called a Board of Officers, tried John Andre during the Revolutionary War. Benedict Arnold betrayed his command at West Point to Andre, the Chief of British Intelligence. Andre was captured shortly after leaving West Point. He was tried and sentenced to death for spying by a seven member tribunal. He was executed by hanging. Robert Lecklie, *George Washington's War: The Saga of the American Revolution* (New York: HarperCollins, 1992), 576–81.

24. "The provisions of the code and this Manual conferring jurisdiction upon courts-martial do not deprive military commissions, provost courts, or other military tribunals of concurrent jurisdiction with respect to offenders or offenses that by statute or by the law of war may be tried by military commission, provost courts, or other military tribunals." MCM 2002, RCM 201(g).

25. "G.O. 267, HQ Army (Mexico) Sep. 17, 1847," reprinted in H.A. Smith, *Military Government* (Ft. Leavenworth, KS: The General Staff School, 1920), 109, 110. See also, Elbridge Colby, "Courts-Martial and the Law of War," *American Journal of International Law* 17 (1923): 109, 112. ("Since the days of General Scott, not only have courts-martial gained the power of trying soldiers in instances where the commander in Mexico found himself powerless until he made the law himself, they can try civilians now also.").

26. "When [Zachary] Taylor resorted to sending the worse offenders in chains to New Orleans, they were rapidly released on writs of habeas corpus." Joseph B. Chance, "South of the Border," *American History* (May/June 1996), 48, 51.

27. Harold L. Kaplan, "Constitutional Limitations on Trials by Military Commission (Part 1)," *University of Pennsylvania Law Review* 92 (1943): 119, 122.

28. The training in Germany included instruction on the use of explosives and their employment at weak spots in the United States such as factories, railroads, bridges, and canals. The Director of the School also "advised the men to plant bombs in major American railroad stations. . . as well as prominent Jewish-owned department stores such as Macy's, Gimbels, and Abraham and Straus." Alex Abella and Scott Gordon, *Shadow Enemies: Hitler's Secret Terrorist Plot Against the United States* (Guilford, CT: Lyons Press, 2002), 22. The authors refer to the German training as having been conducted at "terrorist training camps." Ibid., 20. The information released so far on the conduct of the pre-9/11 al Qaeda terrorists indicates that they too were trained in terrorist training camps to seek out and destroy civilian objects and civilians in the United States. "Al Qaeda's central function is to train militant Islamic terrorists at its headquarter camps in Afghanistan." Jaime Jackson, "Trial of Accused Taliban and al Qaeda Operatives Captured in Afghanistan and Detained on a U.S. Military Base in Cuba," *Cumberland Law Review* 34 (2004): 195, 202. This formal training for the commission of violations of the law of war provides yet another similarity between the 1942 Nazis tried by military commission and the current members of al Qaeda who also face trial by military commission.

29. *Ex Parte Quirin,* 317 U.S. 1, 28 (1942).

30. Interestingly, the United States had taken the same position against Japan during the war. The Japanese government tried and executed several captured American flyers for allegedly bombing nonmilitary targets in Japan. The United States protested the convictions citing the Geneva Conventions. *Department of State Bulletin,* vol. 8 (1943), 337.

31. *In re Yamashita,* 327 U.S. 1, 20 (1945); see also *Johnson v. Eisentrager,* 339 U.S. 763, 790 (1950).

32. "Prisoners of war prosecuted under the laws of the Detaining Power for acts committed prior to capture shall retain, even if convicted, the benefits of the present convention." Art. 85, POW Convention. All communist countries made a reservation to this Article, essentially providing that after conviction the POW loses the protections of the Convention.

33. *Hamdan,* 344 F. Supp. 2d 152.

34. Ibid., 14.

35. Ibid., 26.

36. Ibid., 18–19.

37. "A prisoner of war can be validly sentenced only if the sentence has been pronounced by the same courts according to the same procedure as in the case of members of the armed forces of the Detaining Power, and, if, furthermore, the provisions of the present Chapter have been observed." Art. 102, POW Convention.

38. Note that there are two categories here, members of the armed forces and members of militias or volunteer corps who form a part of the armed forces. The Commentary to the POW Convention sets out four tests for such militias and volunteer corps to gain POW treatment:

1. That of being commanded by a person responsible for his subordinates;
2. That of having a fixed distinctive sign recognizable at a distance;
3. That of carrying arms openly;
4. That of conducting their operations in accordance with the law of laws and customs of war.

Jean Pictet, *Commentary on the Geneva Conventions of 12 August, 1949* (Geneva: International Committee of the Red Cross, 1960), 47–48 (hereinafter cited as *Commentary*). While not required by the Convention, any regular armed force should meet these four tests.

39. "The 2nd Article of War [now the UCMJ]…defines those who are subject to military law, i.e., those who are subject to the disciplinary jurisdiction of the Articles of War as administered by the army and trial by army court-martial." *McCune v. Kilpatrick,* 53 F. Supp. 80, 86 (E.D. Va. 1943).

40. MCM, RCM 202 (a), Discussion (2).

41. Department of Defense, *Legal and Legislative Basis,* in MCM 1951 (1958): 17. Available in the library of The Judge Advocate General's School.

42. "The military commission might have been used to try the major war criminals, and, had it been used, the trials of such criminals might have been more expeditious and conducted more in accord with established military and legal procedure." A. Wigfall Green, "The Military Commission," *American Journal of International Law* 42 (1948): 832. In spite of the tone of the quote, Green does not criticize the International Tribunal but simply describes the history and legal authority of American military commissions.

43. Art. 84, "GPW" Article 84, *United States Treaties and Other International Materials* 6: 3316. The Red Cross Commentary for this Article recognizes the preference for military trials and adds that the reference to trials in civilian courts was put in because "[i]n some countries, in particular the United Kingdom, civil tribunals alone are competent to deal with certain offenses, whether or not committed by members of the armed forces to whom prisoners of war are assimilated." *Commentary,* 412. It is important to note then that this provision anticipates postcapture offenses because an enemy soldier could hardly be assimilated to the forces of the detaining power before capture.

44. "A prisoner of war can be validly sentenced only if the sentence has been pronounced by the same courts according to the same procedure as in the case of members of the armed forces of the Detaining Power, and if, furthermore, the provisions of the present Chapter have been observed." Art. 102, POW Convention. Where the prisoner of war is tried by court-martial the "same procedure" would include all the pretrial Constitutional and statutory safeguards as well as the usual trial safeguards. The pretrial issue was considered in a World War II case in which three Italian prisoners of war were accused of theft in violation of Article 93 of the Articles of War. They were tried and convicted in a U.S. courts-martial. The three had confessed after an interpreter told them "if they told everything they knew about the case, why things would be much easier for them." In reversing the trial court, the Army Board of Review cited the language of article 63 of the 1929 Prisoner of War Convention (now article 102) and concluded that the prisoners "had the same right, therefore, as our own soldiers, to expect that they would be dealt with truthfully and that their trust and confidence in the word of an American official would not be abused." *U.S. v. Peshiera,* 55 B.R. 409, 412 (1945). Note, though, that this case involved a postcapture offense and not a violation of the law of war.

45. MCM (2002), ¶ 2(b)(2).

46. *Federal Register* 7 (July 7, 1942): 1503. The German saboteurs challenged the procedural provisions of the Order.

As to the procedure, petitioners contended that if they were to be tried by military commission, they were entitled to the protection of the procedure set forth by Congress in the Articles of War; the President's Order prescribing the procedure for their trial was contrary to the Articles of War, and hence unlawful. The Court ruled against the petitioners on this too, stating that while they had no occasion to inquire whether the Congress could restrict the President in dealing with enemy belligerents they were unanimously of the opinion that the Articles of War provided no basis for the writ [of Habeas Corpus]. It was mentioned, however, that a majority of the court could not agree upon a proper reason for such ruling. Some of the Justices felt that the Articles of War were not intended to apply to Presidential military commissions convened to try enemy belligerents; the remaining Justices were also of the opinion that even though the trial was subject to the provisions of the Articles of War which relate to military commissions, the procedure prescribed by the President and employed by the Commission was not prohibited or foreclosed by those Articles, in a trial of offenses against the law of war. . . .

Kaplan, "Constitutional Limitations," 140 (footnotes omitted). But see, Charles F. Barber, "Trial of Enemy Belligerents," *Cornell Law Quarterly* 29 (1943): 53, 85 (1943) ("The flexibility and uncertainty of procedure which now characterizes the common law of war military commission is capable of serious abuse.").

47. *Hamdan,* 344 F. Supp. 2d at 168.

48. *Ex Parte Quirin,* 317 U.S. at 32.

49. US Constitution, Amend. VI. "One of the most basic of the rights guaranteed by the Confrontation Clause is the accused's right to be present in the courtroom at every stage of the trial." *Illinois v. Allen,* 397 U.S. 337, 338 (1970) (citing *Lewis v. U.S.,* 146 U.S. 370 (1892)).

50. *UCMJ,* Art. 39(a).

51. *UCMJ,* Art. 36.

52. Ibid., Art. 36(a).

53. *Maryland v. Craig,* 497 U.S. 836, 850 (1990).

54. *Haig v. Agee,* 433 U.S. 280, 307 (1981).

55. Reprinted in Telford Taylor, *The Anatomy of the Nuremberg Trials* (New York: Knopf, 1992), 649.

56. Pictet, *GPW Commentary,* 472.

57. See, e.g., Jordan J. Paust, "Legal Responses to Terrorism: Security, Prosecution, and Rights," *American Society of International Law Proceedings* 97 (2003): 13, 16.

58. "International Covenant on Civil and Political Rights" (December 16, 1966), *United Nations Treaty Service* 999: 171.

59. Ibid., Article 4.

60. 339 U.S. 763, 790 (1950).

61. John A. Appleman, *Military Tribunals and International Crimes* (Westport, CT: Greenwood Press, 1954), 344–45.

62. Even where the civilian is a former soldier charged with an offense committed while on active duty, the Court found no military jurisdiction. *United States ex rel. Toth v. Quarles,* 350 U.S. 234 (1955). The primary case, concerning dependents of military personnel, is *Reid v. Covert,* 354 U.S. 1 (1957). See also, *McElroy v. Guagliardo,* 361 U.S. 281 (1960) (civilian employees of the military departments).

63. For a discussion of the practical problems caused by the Court's decision, see, e.g., Gregory A. McClelland, "The Problem of Jurisdiction over Civilians Accompanying the Forces Overseas— Still with Us," *Military Law Review* 117 (1987): 153.

64. US Constitution art. I, §8, cl. 14.

65. The exercise of military jurisdiction over civilians accused of war crimes has a stronger historical basis than that which extended jurisdiction over civilians who accompany the force and which was declared to be unconstitutional. Albert J. Esgain and Waldemar A. Solf, "The 1949 Geneva Convention Relative to Prisoners of War: Its Principles, Innovations, and Deficiencies," *North Carolina Law Review* 41: 537 reprinted in *Military Law Review* Bicentennial Issue (1976): 303.

66. MCM (1969), ¶ 9. Congress has not yet changed the UCMJ to reflect the Supreme Court's decisions. Article 2(11) still lists certain civilians as subject to the Code.

67. Department of the Army, "Pamphlet 27-2, Analysis of Contents, Manual for Court-Martial," United States, 1969, Revised edition, (July 1970), 4-1. RCM 202a(4).

68. Harold L. Kaplan, "Constitutional Limitations on Trials by Military Commission (Part 2)," *University of Pennsylvania Law Review* 92 (1944): 272.

69. 235 F.2d 429 (10th Cir. 1956). Note that Colepaugh was apparently still in prison ten years after the end of hostilities.

70. Ibid., 432.

71. Ibid.

72. Ibid.

73. Donald L. Shaneyfelt, "War Crimes and the Jurisdictional Maze," *International Law* 4 (1970): 924, 929.

74. 86 F.R.D. 227 (1979).

75. Ibid., 260.

76. Ibid., 245.

77. Shaneyfelt, "War Crimes," 931.

78. "Note, Jurisdictional Problems Related to the Prosecution of Former Servicemen for Violations of the Law of War," *Virginia Law Review* 56 (1970): 947, 953. The statement quoted in the text could be challenged as too limiting. If a military commission has jurisdiction to try a war criminal, then so does a general court-martial. See also, Robinson O. Everett and Scott L. Silliman, "Forums for Punishing Offenses Against the Law of Nations," *Wake Forest Law Review* 29 (1994): 509, 519 ("[T]he rationale of *Madsen v. Kinsella* might suggest that a military commission could try a service member for any violation of the law of war.").

79. The Department stated:

> A review of existing legislation reveals no need to enact further legislation to provide effective penal sanctions for those violations of the Geneva Conventions which are designated as grave breaches.

Hearing Before the Committee on Foreign Relations on the Geneva Conventions for the Protection of War Victims, U.S. Senate, 84th Cong., 1st Sess., June 3, 1955, at 58.

80. Quoted in Jordan J. Paust, "My Lai and Vietnam: Norms, Myths and Leader Responsibility," *Military Law Review* 57 (1971): 99, 124.

81. Nonetheless it might be desirable for Congress to clarify the jurisdiction with regard to civilians or former members of the armed forces. See, e.g., Howard Levie, "Penal Sanctions for the Maltreatment of Prisoners of War," *American Journal of International Law* 56 (1962): 433, 454–57.

82. The following exchange, which occurred in a House Committee hearing on the former Yugoslavia, is indicative of the political implications of even alleging the commission of war crimes. Assistant Secretary of State Thomas Niles was testifying on U.S. initiatives in the war torn country. Representative Peter Kostmayer was pushing Niles to declare the leaders of Serbia war criminals. Niles was reluctant to do so. Neither seemed to fully understand that war crimes are governed by law. Whether war crimes have been committed is a question of fact. A trial for war crimes involves questions of jurisdiction and individual responsibility.

> *Mr. Kostmayer.*   But you don't respond to the Chairman's inquiry about why not calling Milosevic up as an international war criminal, which he clearly is. That's a simple thing to do.
>
> *Mr. Niles.*   This is a legal issue, Congressman, and I am simply not—
>
> *Mr. Kostmayer.*   Oh, legal schmegal.
>
> *Mr. Niles.*   Well—
>
> *Mr. Kostmayer.*   Oh, baloney.
>
> *Mr. Niles.*   Well, sometimes these nuances are of some importance.
>
> *Mr. Kostmayer.*   Oh, baloney.
>
>   . . .
>
> *Mr. Niles.*   I see the point you are trying to make. I am simply saying that I am not sure if there is jurisdiction in this case.
>
> *Mr. Kostmayer.*   Why not?
>
> *Mr. Niles.*   Well, they are all—

Mr. Kostmayer.   Oh, baloney. Jurisdiction.

"Developments in Yugoslavia and Europe—August 1992 Hearing Before the Subcomm. on Europe and the Middle East of the House Comm. on Foreign Affairs," 102 Cong., 2nd Sess., August 4, 1992 at 52.

83. After the My Lai incident there were proposals to try several former soldiers for their part in the massacre. Legal scholars were divided over whether a military forum could be used for the trials. The *Washington Post* wrote that "legal experts" had concluded that "the issue is 'too hot' politically now." No discharged soldier was tried, though the issue may well have become moot because they had been given grants of immunity for their testimony against Lieutenant Calley. Jordan J. Paust, "After My Lai: The Case for War Crimes Jurisdiction over Civilians in Federal District Courts," *Texas Law Review* 50 (1971): 6.

84. POW Convention, Art. 130.

85. There is, however, a preference for disciplinary punishment rather than judicial punishment. POW Convention, Art. 83.

86. POW Convention, Art. 84

87. POW Convention, Art. 99.

88. The Protecting Power concept is set out in articles found in each Geneva Convention. See, for example, POW Convention, Art. 8. The Protecting Power is a "State instructed by another State (known as the Power of Origin) to safeguard its interests and those of its nationals in relation to a third Power (known as the Detaining Power)." *Commentary* at 93.

89. POW Convention, Art. 105.

90. The penal procedure in the Civilian Convention is based on that in the GPW. The procedures apply not only in occupied territory but in the territory of the parties to the conflict. See, Pictet (GC) 353. Arts. 71–78, GC.

91. ¶. 6-13a(4), Army Reg. 190-8/OPNAVINST 341.6/AFJI 31-304/MCO 3461.157, *Enemy Prisoners of War, Retained Personnel, Civilian Internees, and Other Detained Personnel,* October 1, 1997.

92. The death sentence cannot be pronounced on a prisoner of war unless the court has been reminded that the defendant is not a national of the sentencing state and owed it no allegiance. POW Convention, Art. 100. A similar requirement is found in the Civilian Convention. Art. 68, GC. It would seem that this provision was intended for the case where a POW kills someone while attempting to escape or the civilian in occupied territory kills a member of the occupying force. Only then would allegiance and duty to the defendant's country be a mitigating factor. Yet, the Convention does not exempt war crimes trials from the article's requirements. The proposed international tribunal for the trial of war criminals in the conflict in the former Yugoslavia would not be empowered to impose the death penalty. The maximum sentence would be life imprisonment. Art. 24, ¶. 1, S.C. Res. 827, U.N. SCOR, 48th Sess., 3217 Mtg., U.N. Doc. S/RES/827 (1993), reprinted in 32 International Legal Materials 1203 (1993).

93. FM 27-10, ¶. 508.

94. No person protected by the Civilians Convention may be executed who was under eighteen at the time of the offense. Art. 68, GC. In both the POW and the Civilians Conventions the Protecting Power must be notified that a death sentence has been pronounced. The death sentence cannot be carried out for a period of six months after the receipt of the notice by the Protecting Power. Art. 101, POW Convention; Art. 75, GC.

95. See, e.g., Greiser, *Law Report of Trials of War Criminals* 104 (1949): 13. The defendant was sentenced to death, the loss of civil and political rights, and forfeiture of all his property.

96. The Red Cross Commentary takes a strong position against trials during hostilities:

Proceedings in respect of war crimes may not be brought against prisoners of war in conditions and at a time when any normal defense of the prisoners' interests is impossible. As long as hostilities continue, a prisoner of war accused of such offenses will usually be unable to adduce the proof or evidence which might absolve him of responsibility or reduce that responsibility. It seems necessary that, except in special cases, prisoners of war accused of war crimes should not be tried until after the end of hostilities, that is to say when communications have been re-established between the belligerent countries and the prisoner is in a position to procure the necessary documents for his defense and to call witnesses.

If prisoners of war were nevertheless tried while hostilities were still in progress, in conditions which would not afford them a proper defense, they would in fact be deprived of the regular trial to which they are entitled under Article 99. A trial conducted in such circumstances would then constitute a grave breach of the Convention, as covered in Article 130.

Commentary at 422.

97. "No prisoner of war may be punished more than once for the same act or on the same charge." POW Convention, Art. 86.

98. *Commentary* at 494–495.

99. *Trials of War Criminals before the Nuremberg Military Tribunals under Council Law No. 10,* vol. 6 (Washington, DC: U.S. Government Printing Office, 1949–53): 1189.

CHAPTER 9

War, Crime, or War Crime?: Interrogating the Analogy Between War and Terror

MIRIAM J. AUKERMAN

The War on Terror, which the United States has been fighting since the 9/11 attacks is, according to the Bush administration and many of its supporters, a real—not just metaphorical—war. Yet framing terrorism as war reflects a deliberate choice which not only shapes our thinking, but also deviates from the historical treatment of terrorism as a criminal matter.[1] The administration has applied the war framework inconsistently, treating some enemy combatants as prisoners of war who can be held without trial until the war on terror is over, while treating other alleged terrorists as criminal defendants, subject to prosecution and punishment through the regular criminal justice system, even when their crimes would not be illegal under the laws of war.[2]

In defining America's struggle with terrorism as war, and simultaneously denying that enemy combatants captured in this war are entitled to prisoner of war status or other protections of the Geneva Conventions,[3] the Bush administration has sought to have it both ways: the fight against terrorism is a war for the purposes of justifying the indefinite detention of suspected terrorists without trial, but is not a war when it comes to protecting the rights of those who have been captured.[4] Similarly, in prosecuting alleged terrorists who have violated the law, but holding others indefinitely where criminal conduct cannot be proven, the administration has invoked the criminal law selectively: alleged terrorists are criminals in cases where there is enough evidence to prosecute them, but they are enemy combatants in cases where such evidence is lacking. By choosing when to frame terrorism as a military issue and when to frame it as a criminal justice matter, the administration has largely succeeded in evading both the limitations imposed by the laws of war and the due process protections required in criminal proceedings.

This chapter first explores the implications of conceptualizing terrorism as war as opposed to conceptualizing terrorism as crime. It argues that the war framework and the crime framework reflect fundamentally different approaches to the use of force; in the context of war, violence is considered legitimate, whereas in the context of crime it is not. Second, this chapter addresses the logical conclusions that stem from equating terror with war instead of conceptualizing it as crime. Third, it discusses the distinction between legitimate and illegitimate war-time violence, and analyzes whether Taliban and al Qaeda fighters should be categorized as lawful versus unlawful combatants. Fourth, this work assesses to what extent the competing frameworks of war and crime contribute to achieving the goals of retribution against terrorists, prevention of further terrorist attacks, and public condemnation of terrorist violence. Finally, these arguments are summarized to support the conclusion that terrorism is better understood as crime than as war.

CRIME AND WAR: ILLEGITIMATE VERSUS LEGITIMATE VIOLENCE

One function of the law is to distinguish between illegitimate and legitimate violence. Domestically, most acts of violence are considered crimes, subject to prosecution and punishment. Because, in general, only the state may lawfully use violence, individual acts of violence are rarely permissible, regardless of how understandable the offender's motivation may be. Thus, a person who kills his child's killer is himself guilty of murder. While the sentence imposed may reflect compassion for the parent's anguish, that anguish does not excuse the parent's violent act. Intentionally causing the death of another is still murder. There are, of course, a few situations where individuals may lawfully commit violence. For example, the law recognizes the right to self-defense in situations where the state is unable to protect an individual from attack. This right is not unique to American law; it has also been acknowledged by other legal systems and traditions. However, such cases are still exceptions, and not the rule. In the domestic context, individual violence is almost always illegitimate and, therefore, punished.

The fact that violent acts by individuals are almost always crimes reflects the state's virtual monopoly on violence. Although individual violence is illegitimate, law enforcement violence—or as it is more delicately called, the *use of force*—is legitimate because it is undertaken to further governmental purposes, not individual ones. In using force, the state must act through individual law enforcement personnel. However, those individuals are acting on behalf of the state, not for themselves. Thus, they are immune from criminal liability. Acts which would be criminal if committed by ordinary citizens are lawful when undertaken by law enforcement officers. However, law enforcement must comply with the ROE (rules of engagement). Police may neither shoot a fleeing suspect in the back nor beat a confession out of a defendant. Law enforcement officers can be prosecuted and punished for such unauthorized violent acts. Even if they can resort to the use of force, they may only employ it within certain boundaries.

In war, like in law enforcement, violence is considered legitimate because it is undertaken to further governmental purposes, not individual ones. Again, the state must act through individuals, in this case, soldiers. However, those individuals are immune from criminal liability because they are acting for the state, not for themselves. Soldiers, like police officers, are entitled to use force on the state's behalf. In fact, many actions which would be criminal under domestic law—such as killing, assault, and damage to property —are essential elements of warfare. Consequently, we do not usually prosecute soldiers for killing or assaulting enemy soldiers, or for destroying enemy property. The idea that soldiers can, with impunity, commit acts that, in the domestic context would be considered heinous crimes, is called the *combatant's privilege*.

Related to the concept of the combatant's privilege is the requirement that captured soldiers be held as prisoners of war. Because they are entitled to the combatant's privilege, captured enemies cannot be prosecuted or punished for taking up arms. However, the capturing forces also cannot be expected to let enemy soldiers return to the battlefield. Thus, captured enemy soldiers can be held as prisoners of war until the "cessation of active hostilities" (POW Convention, art. 118). Once the war is over, however, the enemy soldiers must be released. They have done nothing wrong and, given the lack of danger that they will return to the battlefield, there is no justification for holding them.

There are three primary limitations on the combatant's privilege. First, in committing violent acts, soldiers must be acting on the state's behalf. While a combatant cannot be prosecuted for killing an enemy soldier, a combatant can be prosecuted for killing his wife. The soldier's immunity depends not on his status as a soldier, but rather on the fact that he is acting on behalf of the government.

Second, soldiers are not entitled to immunity for war crimes, even if those crimes are authorized by the chain of command or serve governmental purposes. Soldiers who intentionally target civilians, who execute unarmed prisoners of war, or who commit similar atrocities can be tried for these crimes. Such guilt is individual, not collective. An individual combatant who obeys the laws of war is entitled to immunity, even if other troops or the military leadership are responsible for atrocities.

Third, only persons who are in fact *combatants* are entitled to claim the combatant's privilege. While a soldier who kills enemy soldiers cannot be prosecuted, a noncombatant who does the same thing can be tried for murder. The rationale is that one must be able to distinguish between civilians and combatants. If combatants are indistinguishable from civilians, then soldiers will be tempted to disregard the laws of war which prohibit the targeting of civilians. Accordingly, only combatants may engage in combat.

The restrictions on the combatant's privilege, like the laws of war generally, reflect both an acknowledgment that horrible violence is inherent in warfare and a desire to minimize the resulting pain as much as possible by limiting those who are authorized to use force, and by defining those who are legitimately its targets. Thus, to distinguish between permissible and impermissible acts of death and destruction during war, we must be able to distinguish between civilians and combatants. Moreover, because violence is not justified if there is not a war, we must be able to distinguish between war and conflicts that are not war.

The laws of war governing the conduct of military personnel are the international equivalent of the legal ROE for domestic law enforcement officers. Both seek to limit the use of force, while accepting that the use of force is necessary. However, the restrictions on soldiers are much more permissive than those on law enforcement. For instance, while a police officer may not kill an individual who does not pose a threat, a war-time sniper can kill an enemy soldier, whether or not that enemy soldier presents any risk to the sniper or the sniper's unit. Nevertheless, even in the context of war, certain conduct goes too far. A sniper cannot target a civilian. Thus, while in general, soldiers are not criminally responsible for their violent acts, soldiers who violate the laws of war, like police officers who use excessive force, may be prosecuted and punished.

Significantly, none of the aforesaid limitations on the combatant's privilege concern the legitimacy of the state for which a soldier fights. Soldiers are covered by the combatant's privilege regardless of whose side they are on. The political merits of their cause are irrelevant, since in a war, violent acts by soldiers on either side are considered acceptable. Soldiers fighting for righteous democracies or brutal dictatorships are equally entitled to the combatant's privilege and, if captured, to prisoner of war status. Although soldiers are criminally liable for any atrocities they personally commit, they are not liable simply for killing enemy soldiers on behalf of an unjust regime.[5]

Why is violence seen as legitimate for soldiers, even if undertaken on behalf of a brutal government, while violence is seen as illegitimate for ordinary citizens, even if undertaken for completely understandable reasons? It might at first glance seem that the difference lies in the political nature of military violence. However, the distinction between legitimate military violence and illegitimate criminal violence does not turn on the presence or absence of a political purpose. After all, some violent political acts, such as the assassination of a government official, are crimes. Another explanation could be that soldiers follow orders, whereas ordinary citizens act on their own. However, citizens who act on orders, such as "foot soldiers" in an organized criminal conspiracy, are individually culpable. Violence is not legitimate simply because an individual is carrying out orders from above. It matters if those orders come from a general or a drug lord.

A more plausible answer is that the legitimacy of violence depends on whether violent acts are the acts of individuals, or whether they are state-sanctioned. Because soldiers pick up weapons at the command of their government, they are not personally responsible for the righteousness of that government's foreign policy. Because law enforcement officers are executing a governmental crime control strategy, they are not personally responsible for arresting the wrong person under a legitimate warrant. By contrast, individuals who commit crimes are acting without governmental sanction, and therefore their violence is illegitimate.

A primary justification for treating cogs in a military organization differently from cogs in a criminal organization has to do with individual choice. Because wars are typically between states, and states typically have tremendous control over the destinies of individuals, we do not punish individuals simply because they fight for unjust regimes. A German conscript, whether sent to the front or assigned to be Hitler's driver, may have had little choice in the matter (although he may also have signed on enthusiastically). By contrast, participation in a criminal enterprise is typically understood to be voluntary, and therefore it is appropriate to prosecute and punish those who provide even low-level support.

To summarize, the fundamental difference between war and crime lies in the underlying assumptions about the legitimacy of violence. By criminalizing individuals' acts of violence, we define them as illegitimate. By contrast, acts of violence are legitimate in war, regardless of which side one is on. Although violent acts which infringe the laws of war are illegitimate, the use of violence in pursuit of the state's political aims is not wrong per se.[6]

TERROR AS WAR VERSUS TERROR AS CRIME

While historically terrorism has been viewed as a criminal matter, the Bush administration now insists that we are in a war on terror. If war involves the legitimate use of violence by combatants, and crime involves illegitimate violence, what are the implications of equating terror with war instead of equating terror with crime?

Is Terrorist Violence Legitimate Under a War Paradigm?

If we adopt a war paradigm, then we need to accept that the use of force by our opponents is legitimate, so long as our opponents abide by the laws of war. War is a sanctioned form of political violence. Therefore, individual *soldiers* cannot be condemned for committing violent acts, regardless of how reprehensible the policies for which they fight are. Under a war framework, al Qaeda fighters, like Nazi ones, would be entitled to act violently; so long as they complied with the laws of war.

The utter preposterousness of suggesting that al Qaeda violence is legitimate indicates that it is mistaken to consider al Qaeda as an opposing army in a "war on terror." Usually, terrorists are depicted as criminals and murderers, not as soldiers. If this is the case, why is the fight against terrorism depicted as a war? Criminals do not fight wars. Soldiers do. By defining the struggle against terrorism as a war, we also define combatants on both sides as soldiers who are entitled to commit violent acts. In other words, we conceive of the violence of the other side as legitimate, as long as it complies with the *jus in bello*. However, as a matter of principle, terrorists, unlike soldiers, cannot legitimately pursue political goals through violence. Moreover, we do not believe that the al Qaeda rank and file should be immunized because foot soldiers are not responsible for the evil aims or horrible atrocities of their leaders during war. In conclusion, a parallelism between terrorists and soldiers cannot be established.

The argument could be made that, even though al Qaeda violence occurs during a war, it is still illegitimate because al Qaeda violates the laws of war. Al Qaeda members, the argument goes, are criminals because they target civilians and commit other violent acts that are impermissible even in war. Under this theory, it is possible to distinguish illegitimate terrorist violence which occurs during a war from legitimate military violence which occurs during a war by looking at who the casualties are.

This argument is intuitively appealing. After all, most terrorist violence is illegally aimed at civilians. However, this argument is problematic. The sole fact that al Qaeda targets civilians cannot justify the administration's claim that we are at war, just that al Qaeda's affiliates are never entitled to use force against civilians. Moreover, as a preliminary matter, it should be recognized that many civilians are killed by soldiers in conventional wars. Certainly, there is a moral difference between targeting civilians and causing incidental civilian deaths in a campaign against military targets. Nevertheless, the fact that we expect nonmilitary deaths in war and sometimes even adopt strategies that we know will cause massive civilian casualties, such as the bombing of Dresden or the dropping of atomic bombs over Hiroshima and Nagasaki, suggests that there is not a bright-line distinction between war-time violence that legitimately versus illegitimately causes civilian deaths. What some denounce as the killing of innocents, others may justify as military necessity.

More importantly, the belief that terrorism is illegitimate violence does not in fact depend on who the targets are. We do not think that the 9/11 hijackers acted legitimately by flying into the Pentagon, but went too far when they hit the Twin Towers. We see both as reprehensible acts. We do not accept the bombing of the USS *Cole* as a legitimate act of warfare. Yet the target there was a purely military one. Moreover, the administration has refused to treat combatants captured in Afghanistan as enemy soldiers, who must be granted the status of prisoners of war. Yet those combatants were not targeting civilians, but rather were fighting U.S. military forces. If this is war, then enemy soldiers can legitimately target our country's military headquarters, attack our military vessels, or fight our troops.

The United States is not alone in refusing to recognize the legitimacy of terrorist violence that is directed at military rather than civilian targets. When Palestinian suicide bombers or Irish Republic Army fanatics detonate their explosives at military checkpoints, rather than crowded markets, their use of force is still considered unjustified. If captured, such terrorists are treated not as prisoners of war, who are immune from liability, but rather as criminals who are subject to prosecution and punishment. In other words, terrorists are not seen as acting legitimately when they attack military targets. Terrorist violence is illegitimate per se, regardless of who or what the targets are. This conclusion seems correct at the level of gut instinct. However, if al Qaeda, and other terrorists more generally are not entitled to use force against military targets, then logically the analogy to war starts to fall apart.

Finally, it could be argued that al Qaeda's violence, unlike other military violence, is illegitimate because al Qaeda is not a state.[7] The difficulty for the argument that we are at war but that al Qaeda's violence is unjustifiable because al Qaeda is not a state, is that the state/nonstate distinction undercuts the very notion that we are at war. The Geneva Conventions effectively apply only to the "High Contracting Parties,"[8] and thus also effectively limit the concept of war to interstate violence, or at most proto-interstate conflict.[9] Al Qaeda is clearly not a state, and also does not qualify as a proto-state, since it does not control a defined territory. If the administration is correct that al Qaeda's lack of statehood means al Qaeda fighters are not prisoners of war, then this also means that there is no war. In other words, if the legitimacy of war-time violence turns on whether or not such violence is at the behest of a state, this suggests that nonstate violence cannot be considered war at all.

Are Supporters of Terrorism Immune from Liability under a War Paradigm?

A second logical conclusion of treating the fight against terrorism as a war is that individuals on the other side cannot be prosecuted simply for being on the other side. Wars are between political entities, not between individuals. Individuals are not culpable just for being affiliated with our opponents. Their soldiers have just as much right to fight our soldiers as our soldiers have to fight theirs. Their civilians have just as much right to support the war effort as ours do. Of course, soldiers and civilians on both sides are culpable for acts violating the laws of war. But they are not criminally responsible just for being on the wrong side.

The fact that soldiers can be prosecuted for war crimes is very important if we understand our conflict with al Qaeda as a war. As noted above much, though not all, terrorist violence violates the laws of war, since much, though not all, terrorist violence targets civilians. Indeed, some terrorist attacks, such at those on the World Trade Center, are intended to cause massive civilian casualties. If one understands terrorism as war, enemy "soldiers" who attack civilians are not immune from liability, but can be prosecuted and punished for committing war crimes.

At the same time, it is critical to recognize that if we are engaged in a war on terror, then our opponents—be they Taliban soldiers or al Qaeda fighters—are not criminally responsible so long as they do not violate the laws of war. They cannot be punished simply for supporting the efforts of their side or for being soldiers. While the horrific acts we associate with terrorism are almost all war crimes, there also appear to be many enemy foot soldiers who are not personally responsible for those atrocities, and whose actions are entirely legal under the laws of war.

The Bush administration insists that we are fighting a war on terror, and more specifically, a war on al Qaeda. Yet the administration has refused to accept the logical result of adopting a war framework, which is that individuals who merely support or associate with al Qaeda have done nothing illegal. The administration has prosecuted not just terrorist acts (which typically violate both domestic law and the laws of war), but also material contributions to or affiliation with al Qaeda (which may violate domestic law, but are not war crimes). Under a crime framework, support for terrorism can be criminalized. There is a long tradition of punishing accessories to crime under the criminal law. But under a war framework, mere support for enemy forces—at least so long as it does not rise to the level of support for specific war crimes—is not itself criminal.[10]

Some examples may help to clarify the point. Neither Germans nor Americans who bought war bonds during World War II could be prosecuted or punished for supporting their own side in the war. Similarly, a German arms dealer would not have been liable for selling bombs to the German government, nor an American one for selling bombs to the U.S. government. Thus, under a war paradigm, providing financial or material support to one's own side in a military conflict is not illegal. By contrast, under a crime paradigm, providing financial or material support to a criminal conspiracy can be criminalized. Laundering money for or selling weapons to a known drug cartel are criminal acts.

Another example of the differences between adopting a war framework or a crime framework can be found in the treatment of low-level functionaries, whether civilians or soldiers. Under a war paradigm, an individual who is merely a driver or secretary for an opposing leader cannot be punished for this work. It was not a war crime to chauffeur Hitler or to type his letters, even though Hitler himself was responsible for horrendous atrocities. By contrast, a driver or secretary for an organized crime ring is criminally responsible. Thus, a driver or secretary for Osama bin Laden would be exempt from punishment under a war paradigm, but would be culpable under a crime paradigm.

In fact, the United States captured and attempted to try Salim Hamdan, an alleged driver for Osama bin Laden, before a military tribunal, an approach that was ultimately rejected by the U.S. Supreme Court (*Hamdan v. Rumsfeld,* 2006). The government alleged that Hamdan served as bin Laden's personal driver and bodyguard, delivered weapons to al Qaeda members, drove bin Laden to al Qaeda training camps and safe havens in Afghanistan, and trained at an al Qaeda-sponsored camp. Soldiers who drive, provide personal security, deliver weapons, or receive military training are not committing war crimes, and it is inconsistent with the war paradigm to prosecute them as violating the laws of war.[11] By contrast, individuals who provide such support to criminal enterprises are committing crimes and can be prosecuted.

Another example can be found in the case of Yaser Hamdi, an American citizen who was held as an enemy combatant, and was accused of being "affiliated with a Taliban military unit and receiv[ing] weapons training" (*Hamdi v. Rumsfeld,* 2004).[12] Under the war paradigm, there is nothing inherently wrong with belonging to an opposing military force or receiving military training.[13] That is what soldiers do. Conversely, under a crime paradigm, Hamdi could be tried and punished. However, unlike in Hamdan's case, the administration decided not to prosecute Hamdi, but instead argued that it could hold Hamdi as an enemy combatant.

It is true that under a war framework, trained military personnel affiliated with enemy units can be held as prisoners of war. However, prisoners of war are entitled to the protections of the Geneva Conventions, which include the right to a determination whether or not the individual is in fact a combatant.[14] The administration contended that Hamdi had no right to challenge the administration's designation of him as an enemy combatant. After the Supreme Court rejected that argument, Hamdi was released.[15]

The *Hamdan* and *Hamdi* cases highlight the differences between a war paradigm and a crime paradigm. They also suggest that the administration's approach—which characterizes the struggle with terrorism as a war, but criminalizes the activities of low-level functionaries who have not committed war crimes—is internally inconsistent.

Post-Hostility Release of Prisoners under a War Paradigm

A third significant result of treating the struggle against terrorism as a war is that, under a war framework, when the hostilities are over, those captured must be released. Since the purpose of detaining opposing forces is not to punish them, but to prevent them from returning to the battlefield, once there is no longer a battlefield to return to, there is no longer a justification for holding them.

Unlike in a traditional war, it is unclear when or whether the war on terror will ever end. The problem does not lie so much in the lack of a specific end-date. After all, in conventional wars too, it is impossible to know at the outset exactly how long the war will last. Rather, the problem lies in the inability to know whether the war will ever end. Furthermore, if the war does end, how will we know it is over? Who would announce the cessation of hostilities or sign a peace treaty? If in fact terrorist cells are loosely organized, is it even possible for terrorist leaders to reign in their followers? Moreover, if it is possible to completely eliminate al Qaeda (which itself seems unlikely, given that younger recruits are likely to replace those leaders who are killed or captured), how do we know that other groups with other grievances will not turn to terrorism? In other words, even if the United States could win the war on al Qaeda, could it win the "War on Terror"?

The uncomfortable but probable truth is that terrorism will always exist. This suggests that the framework of a war on terror is fundamentally misguided. Wars are something you win or lose. Wars are discrete events, with a starting point and an ending point. There is some fluidity, of course. After all, U.S. forces continue to fight in Iraq long after President Bush declared that the mission had been accomplished. Nevertheless, the point is that the Iraq war, like all wars, has or will have an endpoint, whether one defines that as the toppling of the Hussein regime or the withdrawal of U.S. forces. There is no similar endpoint in the more general "War on Terror."

Proclaiming a war on terror is a bit like proclaiming a war on murder. Terror is a strategy, not an entity. It is possible to catch particular terrorists and particular murderers. But winning a war on terror is as unfeasible as winning a war on murder. If we acknowledge that terrorism is an ugly, but probably permanent feature of modern life, then it seems more apt to understand terrorism as a criminal rather than a military problem. After all, crime will always exist. It is impossible to eliminate crime completely. Thus, instead of trying to end crime, the goal is to keep crime rates low. Hence, the real objective in combating terrorism is not to eliminate it, but rather to keep the rate of terrorist attacks as low as possible.

ILLEGITIMATE USE OF FORCE IN WAR: LAWFUL VERSUS UNLAWFUL COMBATANTS

The Bush administration contends that, because we are at war, the Guantanamo detainees are combatants, not criminals, and therefore they can be held indefinitely without trial like prisoners of war. At the same time, the administration argues that the detainees' actions, though undertaken in war, were illegitimate, and that the detainees therefore lack the rights accorded to prisoners of war and can be prosecuted for mere participation in hostilities or for the sheer support of our enemies. The administration and its supporters attempt to reconcile these contradictory claims by asserting that the detainees are neither criminal defendants nor prisoners of war, but *unlawful combatants*.[16]

To understand this argument, we must look more closely at the distinctions between illegitimate and legitimate uses of force during war-time. As noted above, war legitimizes the violence of both sides, and therefore it is generally incompatible with the war paradigm to claim both that we are at war and that our opponents are not entitled to use force against us. However, certain uses of force are illegal even in war. These fall into two basic categories. First, the laws of war prohibit certain acts, regardless of who commits them. One cannot target civilians, commit genocide, or execute prisoners of war. The second major way in which the laws of war limit violence is by restricting the use of force to certain actors, namely soldiers. Here, the question is not whether the act per se is unlawful, but rather whether the person committing it has the right to do so. Soldiers may kill. Civilians may not. Thus, war-time acts that are perfectly legal if done by soldiers are illegal if undertaken by those who are not lawful combatants.

If the United States is fighting a war on terror, then the violence of our enemies is legitimate unless it falls into one of these two categories. Strikingly, the Bush administration has not really focused on the fact that terrorist attacks on civilians violate the laws of war. Perhaps this is because, if one highlights the unlawfulness of al Qaeda attacks on civilians, one would have to admit that, under a war framework, attacks on military targets are permissible. As discussed above, neither the Bush administration nor most Americans believe that al Qaeda violence is ever justified, even if al Qaeda is targeting U.S. military forces.

The Bush administration, in trying to argue both that we are at war and that al Qaeda violence is illegitimate, has thus emphasized the second category of prohibited war-time violence. In other words, the Bush administration has claimed that our opponents are unlawful combatants, not soldiers. By defining the detainees in this way, it is possible to hold them for the duration of hostilities (since they are combatants), to deny them prisoner of war status (since only lawful combatants receive it), and to prosecute them not just for war crimes, but for ordinary military actions (since they are not entitled to the combatant's privilege).

Article 4A of the Geneva POW Convention spells out which combatants are entitled to prisoner of war status and the combatant's privilege. Those fighters who do not fall within these categories are unlawful combatants.[17] By claiming that the detainees held at Guantanamo and elsewhere are not entitled to prisoner of war status, the administration and its supporters have argued that the detainees do not meet the criteria set out in the aforementioned article, and are therefore unlawful combatants. The great majority of these detainees have been associated with either al Qaeda or the former Taliban regime in Afghanistan.

The wholesale designation of Taliban fighters as unlawful combatants is incorrect. Afghanistan is a state and a contracting party to the Convention. Taliban fighters thus fall into either subsection (1) of article 4A, as "members of armed forces of a Party to the conflict," or into subsection (3), as "members of regular armed forces who profess allegiance to a government of an authority not recognized by the Detaining Power." While there has been some debate about whether Taliban fighters meet the criteria set in subsection (2), such as having a fixed distinctive sign, those parameters do not apply to soldiers falling into categories (1) or (3). Nothing in the text suggests that these criteria should be imported into the other two subsections.[18] Therefore, Taliban soldiers are lawful combatants entitled to the combatant's privilege and prisoner of war status.

By contrast to the Taliban detainees, al Qaeda fighters do not qualify as unlawful combatants if the conflict with al Qaeda is understood as war. As noted above, Article 4(A) only applies to conflicts between "High Contracting Parties," that is states. As mentioned earlier, al Qaeda is neither a state nor a contracting party. Moreover, al Qaeda operatives generally do not comply with the requirements established in subsection (2), that is, they do not have a fixed sign, they do not carry arms openly, and they do not conduct their operations in accordance with the laws and customs of war.

However, the fact that al Qaeda fighters are not lawful combatants should not end the inquiry. First, the Geneva Conventions enshrine a presumption that captured combatants are prisoners of war, and require them to be treated as such unless a competent tribunal determines they are not prisoners of war. The administration's initial blanket decision that the Guantanamo detainees were unlawful combatants not only failed to meet the requirement of the Geneva Conventions for individualized status determinations, but also resulted in great injustice. After all, whether or not someone is an unlawful combatant—indeed whether someone is a combatant at all—will depend on the circumstances of the case. For example, an alleged al Qaeda operative captured in Afghanistan might in fact actually be an ordinary Afghan soldier (who would be entitled to prisoner of war status) or a civilian swept up in the conflict. Without an individualized status determination, it is impossible to tell.

Second, while the Geneva POW Convention applies only to those who meet the criteria for lawful combatants, this does not mean that if the alleged al Qaeda detainees are unlawful combatants, they are unprotected under the Geneva Conventions and other international agreements. As the Commentary to the Geneva Conventions of the International Committee of the Red Cross notes, "nobody in enemy hands can fall outside the law."[19] Unlawful combatants, like other persons not entitled to prisoner of war status, are protected under a variety of treaties, including the Geneva Civilian Convention. While this treaty does not contain some of the protections of the former, it ensures certain basic rights such as due process rights (including the right to a fair trial if criminally prosecuted), the right to humane treatment, freedom from coercive interrogation, freedom from discrimination, and the right to repatriation. Thus, international law accords civilians, including unlawful combatants, most of the same rights as prisoners of war, with the exception of combatant immunity and the right to be treated under military law like the detaining power would treat its own soldiers.[20]

Third and most importantly, the fact that someone is not a lawful combatant does not automatically mean that the individual is an unlawful combatant. The individual might not be a combatant at all. Determining that an individual is outside the scope of Article 4(A), and hence is not a lawful combatant, does not answer the question of whether the individual is an unlawful combatant or a civilian. To be an unlawful combatant, the individual must engage in combatant activities. For example, the little old lady tending her garden in the middle of a war zone is neither a lawful combatant nor an unlawful combatant: she is a civilian.

If we cannot classify in a simple manner anyone who is not a lawful combatant as an unlawful combatant, then the question becomes: how do we distinguish between unlawful combatants and civilians? In other words, how do we know if the person has engaged in combat? At the ends of the spectrum, the distinctions are clear. The little old lady in her garden is a civilian. A nonsoldier planting bombs during a declared war is an unlawful combatant. But there is a large gray area in the middle. What if the little old lady buys war bonds? We typically do not tend to think of such financial transactions as combat. Can we, then, characterize an individual who provides financial support to al Qaeda as an unlawful combatant? What about a civilian who acts as a chauffeur for enemy leaders? We typically do not think of driving as combat. Can we, then, characterize an al Qaeda driver as an unlawful combatant?

The importance of determining whether an act is combat highlights a fourth and final point. In order for there to be combatants—whether lawful or unlawful ones—there has to be a war. In the absence of war, those who commit unlawful acts are criminals, not unlawful combatants. Criminal defendants cannot be held without trial and, when tried, must be prosecuted through the regular criminal justice system. At the same time, criminals can be prosecuted and punished for all sorts of conduct that do not obviously deserve the label "combat". For example, while providing financial support for al Qaeda is not clearly a type of combat, it is definitely a crime.

Thus, the question of whether the Guantanamo detainees are unlawful combatants or whether they are civilians who may have committed criminal acts takes us back, in a somewhat circular fashion, to the question of whether we are at war. The Geneva Conventions apply to "all cases of declared war or any other armed conflict" that arise between states that are parties to the Conventions (Geneva POW Convention, art. 2). The war with Afghanistan falls within that definition, since it was an international conflict between two states. By contrast, the war with al Qaeda is not an international armed conflict.[21] Al Qaeda lacks an international legal personality. It is not a state, and it is not a party to the Geneva Conventions.

The administration and its supporters have used the inapplicability of the Geneva Conventions to deny alleged al Qaeda detainees the rights accorded to prisoners of war. But if alleged al Qaeda detainees are not entitled to prisoner of war status because the conflict with al Qaeda does not meet the legal definition of war, as spelled out in the Geneva Conventions, then this must mean that we are not at war with them. And if we are not at war, then the detainees are neither lawful nor unlawful combatants. They are not combatants at all.

RESPONDING TO TERROR: RETRIBUTION, PREVENTION, AND COMMUNICATION

To further tease out the implications of using a war paradigm versus a criminal justice paradigm, we have to bear in mind the primary goals we have in responding to terror: we want to punish those responsible for committing atrocities; we want to prevent further violence; and finally, we want to communicate our outrage. How does framing terrorism as war versus framing it as crime affect our ability to meet these goals?

Retribution

In the wake of terrorist attacks, there is a strong demand for retribution. Terrorist attacks bring horrible suffering. Because such violence is typically indiscriminate and unpredictable, it is especially terrifying. In the aftermath, politicians and the public inevitably and understandably vow to hunt down and punish those responsible. This demand for vengeance is a retributive response.

Retribution involves punishing the offender because the offender deserves it. The demand for retribution is, at its core, a demand that people who commit crimes should pay. Thus, for retributivists, there is a Kantian categorical imperative to punish, regardless of whether punishment will prevent future crimes.

Nevertheless, retribution is an inappropriate justification for war. After all, retribution is about individual culpability, and requires that punishment be restricted to those who committed offenses. Conversely war, by its nature, involves a collective punishment. And collective punishment is morally problematic: one should not inflict suffering on people because of the faults of their leaders. The concept of war, then, does not fit comfortably with our desire to punish terrorists individually without unduly affecting the lives of many people who did not take part of their enterprise.

Notably, at least some courts have recognized that retribution cannot be used to justify indefinite war-time detention. For example, the United States declined to prosecute Jose

Padilla, a U.S. citizen arrested in the Chicago airport, and instead claimed that he was an enemy combatant who could therefore can be held indefinitely. The district court rejected arguments that such indefinite military detention was unconstitutional, noting that the administration did not have a retributive purpose in holding Padilla.[22] That court thus recognized that detention for retributive purposes is incompatible with a military framework. By contrast, a criminal justice framework—whether through civilian or military courts—allows for a retributive response to terrorist violence. Trials determine individual culpability, which is a prerequisite for retribution. In the criminal process, those found responsible for terrorist acts are punished.

Even in a criminal justice framework, however, retribution can be elusive. Once a suicide bomber has blown him or herself up, it is impossible to punish that person further. It is hard to get even with those who are already dead. Still, not all terrorists are suicide bombers. Retributive justice is possible against those who plot out suicidal crimes or undertake nonsuicidal ones. But if we want retribution, we must use a criminal justice paradigm, not a military one.

Prevention

The primary goal of antiterrorism efforts, we are repeatedly told, is to protect the public from future terrorist attacks. This may well be true, but it does not tell us what prevention strategy we should adopt. As Jeremy Bentham has explained, there are three principal ways to prevent crime: take away the physical power to violate the law, take away the desire to offend, or make the individual afraid of offending. "In the first case," Bentham explains,

> . . .(T)he individual can no more commit the offense; in the second, he no longer desires to commit it, in the third, he may still wish to commit it, but no longer dares to do it. In the first case, there is physical incapacity; in the second, a moral reformation; in the third there is intimidation or terror of the law.[23]

Each of these three approaches—incapacitation, rehabilitation, and deterrence—suggests different ways of dealing with terrorism.

Incapacitation

The goal of incapacitation is to make it physically impossible to commit offenses. The concept of incapacitation fits under both a war framework and a crime framework. War can be understood as an attempt to incapacitate our enemy: by destroying enemy forces, toppling an enemy regime, or occupying an enemy country, we seek to eliminate the opportunity for that enemy to take actions which might harm us. In addition to, or in the course of incapacitating enemy forces or enemy states, we may also incapacitate individual enemy soldiers by detaining them so that they cannot return to the battlefield. Since enemy soldiers are entitled to the combatant's privilege (assuming they do not violate the laws of war), there is no retributive justification for detaining enemy soldiers. Therefore, such detention is only justifiable on preventive grounds. Prisoners of wars are not being punished; they are simply being held until they can safely be released once the hostilities are over.

In the context of crime, we incapacitate offenders in order to prevent them from committing further crimes. Here, preventive goals may be intertwined with retributive ones. Thus, we may incarcerate an individual even though that individual is unlikely to reoffend because we want to ensure the individual is punished. For example, a person convicted of negligent homicide may be unlikely to commit further offenses, but may still be given a long sentence because that person caused the death of another. Alternately, a likely recidivist may end up with a light sentence because the offense is a minor one, and lengthy punishment is considered inappropriate. Thus, while a drug addict convicted of possession may be likely to use drugs again, he or she will probably be released (if incarcerated at all) long before the danger of recidivism has passed.

An important distinction between detention under a war framework and detention under a criminal justice framework is that, in the first case, the length of incapacitation is determined by an external event (the end of the war), while in the second the duration of incapacitation reflects an individualized assessment of dangerousness (the likelihood of recidivism), among other factors. In a war, individual soldiers are not entitled to release simply because they would not actually return to the battlefield and therefore pose no further threat. A detaining state can hold a paraplegic soldier until the war is over, even if there is no chance that the soldier will ever take up arms again. Though the justification for incapacitation in war is purely preventive, determinations are made in gross, resulting in the detention of some individuals who are not a threat to the detaining power.[24]

By contrast, in criminal cases, the length of incapacitation depends greatly on the perceived dangerousness of the individual offender. At least in theory, more dangerous offenders receive longer sentences than less dangerous ones, and parole hearings are used to assess whether a prospective parolee would be dangerous if released. As noted above, because incapacitation in the criminal justice system is not focused exclusively on prevention, but serves other goals, most notably retributive ones, the length of incarceration reflects not just an assessment of likely recidivism, but also an assessment of the seriousness of the underlying crime. Thus, some individuals who are not a threat will remain incarcerated, while some individuals who are likely to reoffend will be released.

Incapacitation has been central to the United States approach to terrorism, and in particular to the administration's justification for the indefinite detention of those held at Guantanamo and elsewhere. It is certainly true that if we lock people up, we make it difficult or impossible for them to commit terrorist acts. But that does not tell us whether such incapacitation is being justified under a war framework or a criminal framework, since either allows for incapacitation.

In practice, the administration's approach reflects elements of both a military and a criminal law paradigm. On the one hand, the administration has argued that it has the power to hold detainees until the war on terror is over—whenever that might be—so that they cannot return to the battlefield.[25] It has insisted that the detainees are not entitled to individual adjudications of guilt, but may be held simply because of their association with the enemy. These assertions reflect military thinking. On the other hand, the administration has quietly released a considerable number of detainees after determining that they never posed or no longer pose a threat to the United States, effectively conceding that it should only hold those who are dangerous. Such releases reflect a criminal justice rather than a military approach. After all, the war on terror is not over, and under a war framework enemy soldiers are not entitled to release until the conflict ends.

These releases also reflect an implicit acknowledgment that if there is no retributive justification for holding someone (since the person committed no crime), then it is deeply disturbing to justify that person's detention as incapacitation, if in fact the individual is not dangerous. In war, we do not expect individualized assessments of dangerousness, because once the war is over, everyone gets to go home. But such a broad-brush approach to individual liberty is deeply troubling if the war is unlikely ever to end. The fact that the administration has been quietly releasing those it deems not dangerous—even though such individuals could be held under a war framework—suggest that concepts of dangerousness rather than analogies to war are controlling here.

If our real focus is dangerousness, then there are three possible justifications for incapacitation. First, incapacitation can be justified during war as a temporary immobilization of opposing forces. In war-time detention, though individuals are entitled under the Geneva Conventions to a determination of combatant status, they can be held for the duration of hostilities regardless of whether they personally are dangerous. Therefore, no individualized assessment of dangerousness is required. As suggested above, in a war without end, detention that is not based on an individualized assessment of dangerousness presents a grave threat to individual liberty. If we justify incapacitation as a way to prevent a return to the battlefield during ongoing, and never-ending, hostilities, and if such incapacitation, being military in nature, does not require an individualized assessment of dangerousness, then framing terrorism as war allows for the indefinite detention of people who have committed no crime and are not dangerous. This is morally unacceptable.

A second possibility is to justify incapacitation based on prior criminal activity, whether ordinary crimes or war crimes. In such cases, allegedly dangerous individuals are entitled to due process under either domestic criminal law or military/international law, can be held pending trial, and can be imprisoned if found guilty of past crimes. A finding of past criminal acts supports incapacitation, and the ongoing dangerousness of convicted terrorist can be considered in determining appropriate sentences.

However, the fear of those who prefer a war framework is that, under such a criminal justice approach, the government would have to prove that an individual committed a prior criminal/terrorist act in order to incapacitate that individual. A war framework, they argue, allows for preventive detention, which is something they need to combat terrorism. Hence, their argument is that if we treat terrorism as crime, we would be hamstrung because we could not proactively hold those who have not yet committed crimes, but are likely to do so. In other words, we might know that someone is a dangerous terrorist, even though we cannot prove that he or she committed a criminal act.

This argument is clearly flawed. It is true that a person can be dangerous without having previously committed crimes. But an assessment that someone is dangerous must rest on some sort of predicate acts, in other words, on factual allegations about the individual which may or may not be true. People are not dangerous in the abstract, or because of their race or creed. Rather, we suspect that people are dangerous because of things they have done in the past: predictions about future conduct rest on assessments of past conduct.

This last point brings about the third justification for incapacitation. Even absent the prior commission of a crime or the existence of a state of war, domestic law allows—under very limited circumstances—for detentions based on present dangerousness. For example, the U.S. Supreme Court has upheld the involuntary civil commitment of sexually violent offenders.[26] However, in such cases, the Court has required strict procedural safeguards, upholding "preventive detention based on dangerousness only when limited to specially dangerous individuals and subject to strong procedural protections," including access to counsel. Moreover, since a dangerous person may stop being dangerous, individuals who are detained on this basis are entitled to periodic reviews to assess whether they continue to be a threat.

Supporters of the administration argue that some detainees are too dangerous to be released, even if it cannot be proven that they committed crimes. The inability to prove a crime, however, is no excuse for an unwillingness to prove dangerousness. If the justification for detaining alleged al Qaeda members is present dangerousness, then the administration must prove dangerousness. By insisting that the detainees are "enemy combatants" who can be held for the duration of the never-ending war on terror, the administration is not only trying to avoid the necessity of proving criminal guilt, but also trying to avoid the necessity of proving that each individual detainee is in fact presently dangerous, as the administration claims. While preventive detention is itself morally problematic, if that is the administration's justification for holding the detainees, then at a minimum the administration must prove that the detainees are in fact a threat.

Rehabilitation

Rehabilitation, like incapacitation, focuses on preventing crime. While incapacitation makes it physically impossible for the potential offender to act, rehabilitative approaches seek to change attitudes so that potential offenders will not desire to commit crimes in the future. In the context of terrorism, then, rehabilitation means eliminating the potential terrorist's desire to commit terrorist acts.

Hence, rehabilitation refers not simply to efforts to change the values and actions of particular offenders, but also to structural approaches that seek to shape public life and values. In dealing with ordinary crime, it is possible to seek to rehabilitate individual offenders. Alternately, or in addition, it is also possible to provide education, economic opportunity, substance abuse programs, and mental health treatment as a way to reduce the likelihood that people will want to commit crimes. Similarly, in the context of terrorism, rehabilitation should be understood not only in terms of convincing former terrorists of the error of their ways, but also in terms of changing societal conditions that give rise to terrorist violence.

Although there has been much rhetoric about preventing terrorism, little attention has been paid to rehabilitation as a preventive strategy. Some lip service has been given to the notion of winning the hearts and minds of the people in those societies from which terrorists most frequently spring. However, little money has followed the rhetoric. Instead, the primary preventive tactic has been incapacitation.

In theory, it should be possible to pursue incapacitation and rehabilitation simultaneously. In practice, the methods used to incapacitate have undermined the efforts to convince potential terrorists not to engage in terrorism. While holding suspected terrorists indefinitely in Guantanamo may successfully incapacitate them, it also fans the sort of hatred towards the United States that breeds further terrorism. Abuse of detainees is particularly damaging. In determining the overall preventive effect of detentions, then, the benefits of incapacitation, but also the costs to our rehabilitative goals.

Deterrence

The theory of deterrence assumes that potential offenders desire to commit crimes, but are too afraid to do so because the risk of getting caught is too great or the consequences of getting caught are too severe. In other words, potential offenders undertake a two-part calculation, weighing the gravity of the consequences, and the likelihood of getting caught. Thus, deterrence only works against individuals who care about the likelihood and consequences of getting caught.

Preventing terrorism is cumbersome, particularly if the consequences of succeeding in one's terrorist act are more severe than the consequences of being apprehended. The threat of life imprisonment, or even the death penalty, is unlikely to be a significant constraint when a terrorist is already planning to commit suicide. Of course some potential terrorists may be scared off by the threat of sanctions. But where potential terrorists are willing to die for their cause, there are few sanctions that one can attach to terrorist acts which could be effective deterrents.

Of course deterrence is based not just on the consequences of getting caught, but also on the likelihood of capture. Increasing the risk of apprehension may have some deterrent value since terrorists, though they may not care about the consequences of getting caught, presumably do care about successfully executing their plots. For example, punishing airplane bombings with the death penalty will presumably matter little to the suicide bomber who intends to go down with the plane. However, beefing up security at airports might be a deterrent, since prospective bombers are more likely to be captured before they can bring down an aircraft, and may therefore abandon their plans. After all, suicide bombers likely act with a view to a glorious martyrdom, not to dishonorable failure and anonymous imprisonment. Measures designed to increase the risk of apprehension, and hence the rate of deterrence, can also be understood as a form of incapacitation. By screening passengers, inspecting cargo, and monitoring the internet we seek to make it more difficult for potential terrorists successfully to complete their plots.

The problem with strategies that focus on increasing the risk of apprehension is that it is not possible to ensure that every terrorist will get caught or every plot will be foiled. In the context of ordinary crime, we can make it more difficult to commit crime, but we cannot make it impossible to commit crime. It is possible to catch some criminals, but we cannot catch all of them. We should recognize that the same is true of terror.

Communication

Finally, an important goal in responding to terrorism is to communicate that such conduct is utterly wrong. Terrorism violates our fundamental moral code and, unless addressed, will weaken that code. We need a way to express our shared moral outrage, and thereby strengthen and reaffirm the norms of social life. Both a war framework, in which terrorists are enemies, and a crime framework, in which terrorists are criminals, allow us to express outrage. However, the paradigm we choose fundamentally shapes our own thinking, as well as the message that we communicate to others.

By criminalizing terrorist conduct, we communicate how very wrong we think it is. There is no safe harbor for those who would strike at military targets or those who merely provide support, but are not directly involved in attacks. Treating terrorism as crime also focuses our attention on the individual, and reminds us that punishment is only appropriate after an individualized determination of guilt. And if we want to determine individual culpability, we have to provide due process.

By contrast, the analogy of terrorism to war shifts our focus away from the individual, towards the idea of societies in struggle. That concept, in turn, suggests a cultural war, and encourages us to demonize the religion and people that have become associated with terrorism in the public mind. Moreover, if our paradigm does not focus on the individual, it is easier to argue that the individual does not deserve a real trial, and is merely a nameless enemy combatant who can be detained until the war is over, whenever that might be. The analogy to war suggests that the measures taken are extraordinary ones, and they will be abandoned when the war is over. But the fight against terrorism is not like a traditional battle where you fight, win, and go home.

The framework of war also suggests that terrorism involves attacks by outsiders, by a foreign enemy. As the case of Timothy McVeigh shows, however, the use of terrorist methods to make political points is not limited to foreigners, much less to al Qaeda. Despite the similarities between domestic and foreign terrorism, we treat the two completely differently. Alleged domestic terrorists are criminal defendants who receive due process. Alleged foreign terrorists are enemy combatants who do not. Treating natives and nonnatives differently contradicts a prime criminal law principle, which is that all persons deserve the same basic set of procedural rights, regardless of citizenship. Once we shift to a war paradigm, how much due process a suspect receives depends not on the person's acts, but on the person's country of origin.

This distinction between foreign and native terrorists is breaking down, however, because some of our alleged enemies, like Yaser Hamdi and Jose Padilla, are U.S. citizens. The Bush administration has contended that even they can be denied the protections of the criminal law in the war on terrorism. This means that how much due process an alleged terrorist gets depends neither on the person's acts, nor on the person's citizenship, but rather on the person's beliefs. An individual, who blows up buildings because he or she is a white supremacist, gets the protections of the criminal law. An individual, who blows up buildings because he or she is an al Qaeda sympathizer, does not.

CONCLUSIONS

Although the Bush administration insisted that we are at war, the administration has not applied the military paradigm consistently. The very notion of war is that it is a form of legitimate violence in pursuit of political goals. If our opponents' violence is never legitimate and if there are no lawful combatants on the other side, how can we be at war? There is something disingenuous not only about claiming that we are at war, but also asserting that all of our opponents are unlawful combatants because they are not fighting in a war, as defined under the Geneva Conventions.

Certain international conflicts related to terrorism—such as the war in Afghanistan—can legitimately be described as war. After all, the fighting in Afghanistan was a state-on-state conflict. However, just because criminal justice concerns motivate us to go to war, that does not mean that those criminal justice concerns themselves transmogrify into a war. For example, if the United States went to war with a country for harboring the ring leaders of a drug cartel, that would not turn all of those involved in the war on drugs into enemy combatants subject to indefinite detention until we win the never-ending war on drugs. Similarly, the fact that the administration fought a war in Afghanistan because the Taliban was giving sanctuary to a criminal organization, namely al Qaeda, does not turn the conflict with al Qaeda itself into a war. One should not elide the conflict in Afghanistan, which was a war, with the struggle against terrorism, which is not.

Once we understand terrorism as crime, we can adopt the lessons we have learned from the war on crime. With terrorism, as with ordinary crime, there is a balance to be struck between public safety and other values. There would be less ordinary crime if we installed government cameras in every home or if we gave every criminal suspect a life sentence without trial. But we recognize that preventing crime is the only one value in a free society, and that we must balance that goal both against the rights of law-abiding citizens and against the rights of suspects. In the context of terrorism, we have to strike a similar balance. Preventing terrorism, like preventing other crimes, is the only one value in a free society, and therefore we must balance that goal, both against the rights of law-abiding citizens and against the rights of alleged terrorists.

The analogy between war and terror shifts our attention away from this balancing act towards the goal of winning. This effort to win is then used as a consequentialist paradigm, to justify actions that are completely unacceptable under a criminal justice framework, such as indefinite detention of unlawful combatants, which is effectively a life sentence without trial. Instead of trying to win a nonwinnable war at all costs—a strategy which erodes the very democracy we seek to protect—we should jettison the war framework. We should recognize terrorism for what it is: a particularly dangerous and complex form of crime. And we should respond to this threat accordingly, with the tools that the well-developed criminal justice framework provides.

NOTES

1. A wide range of terrorist activities are criminalized under US law. See, e.g., 18 U.S.C. §2381 (2000) (treason); 18 U.S.C. §32 (2000) (destruction of aircraft or aircraft facilities); 18 U.S.C. §2332 (a) (2000) (use of weapons of mass destruction); 18 U.S.C. §2332(b) (2000) (acts of terrorism transcending national boundaries); 18 U.S.C. §2339A (2000) (providing materials support to terrorists); 18 U.S.C. §2339B (2000) (providing material support to certain terrorist organizations); 18 U.S.C. §2382 (2000) (misprision of treason); 18 U.S.C. §2383 (2000) (rebellion or insurrection); 18 U.S.C. §2384 (2000) (seditious conspiracy); 18 U.S.C. §2390 (2000) (enlistment to serve in armed hostility against the United States); 50 U.S.C. §1705(b) (2000) (prohibiting, under 31 C.F.R. §595.204 (2000), the "making or receiving of any contribution of funds, goods, or services" to terrorists.)

2. Human rights activists and scholars have expressed their concern about the doubtful legality of the *illegal combatant* status, accorded to alleged terrorists in Guantanamo Bay and other detention facilities during the war on terror. The detentions have allegedly been based on the individuals' dangerousness, rather than on an interim or definitive determination of their responsibility for wrongdoings. See Christopher Wilke, "War vs. Justice: Terrorism Cases, Enemy Combatants, and Political Justice in U.S. Courts," *Politics and Society* 33, no. 4 (December 2005): 637–70.

3. See the "Third Geneva Convention Relative to the Treatment of Prisoners of War," August 12, 1949, *United States Treaties and Other International Agreements* 6, 3316 ("POW Convention"); and the "Fourth Geneva Convention Relative to the Protection of Civilian Persons in Time of War," August 12, 1949, *United States Treaties and Other International Agreements* 6, 3516 ("Civilian Convention").

4. The Bush administration has taken advantage of the difficulty of interpreting the aforementioned conventions. For a discussion in this respect, see Derek Jinks, "The Declining Significance of POW Status," *Harvard International Law Journal* 45 (2004): 367 (hereinafter cited as Jinks); Neil McDonald and Scott Sullivan, Note, "Rational Interpretation in Irrational Times: The Third Geneva Convention and the War on Terror," *Harvard International Law Journal* 44 (2003): 301.

5. For example, during the Second World War, individual soldiers—unless they committed atrocities or otherwise violated the laws of war—were combatants entitled to use violence against opposing forces and were entitled to prisoner of war status if captured. While Nazi leaders were tried at Nuremberg for the atrocities committed by the German regime, ordinary German soldiers were not. Captured German soldiers were just as much prisoners of war as captured American ones.

6. For a discussion of the theoretical justifications for the combatant's privilege, see Christopher Kutz, "The Difference Uniforms Make: Collective Violence in Criminal Law and War," *Philosophy & Public Affairs* 33, no. 2 (2005): 148.

7. This is plausible, but nonetheless questionable. After all, the notion that German conscripts in World War II could not be held criminally accountable for fighting on behalf of an evil regime while al Qaeda soldiers can, reflects in part the fact that al Qaeda members actively choose to join the battle to achieve the political goals of a nonstate entity, while German soldiers simply participated, whether willingly or unwillingly, in a war on behalf of the country to which they belonged. While the question of individual choice suggests that al Qaeda members are more like criminals than soldiers, it also suggests that Taliban affiliates are more like soldiers than criminals.

8. Common Article 2 of the Geneva Conventions provides: "In addition to the provisions which shall be implemented in peace time, the present Convention shall apply to all cases of declared war or of any other armed conflict which may arise between two or more of the High Contracting Parties, even if the state of war is not recognized by one of them. The Convention shall also apply to all cases of partial or total occupation of the territory of a High Contracting Party, even if the said occupation meets with no armed resistance. Although one of the Powers in conflict may not be a party to the present Convention, the Powers who are parties thereto shall remain bound by it in their mutual relations. They shall furthermore be bound by the Convention in relation to the said Power, if the latter accepts and applies the provisions thereof," "Geneva Conventions," 1949, common art. 2.

9. Nathaniel Berman discusses efforts to extend the concepts of *war* and *armed conflict* beyond traditional state-on-state conflicts, noting that the combatant's privilege remains largely restricted to interstate, or, at most, proto-interstate conflict. See Nathaniel Berman, "Privileging Combat? Contemporary Conflict and the Legal Construction of War," *Columbia Journal of Transnational Law* 43 (2004): 1 ("Berman"). In fact, although the Geneva Conventions also have some applicability to intrastate conflict, the conflict with al Qaeda is not a civil war.

10. Of course, U.S. citizens who support enemy forces might still be guilty of treason under domestic law.

11. As Justice Stevens pointed out in rejecting the administration's contention that Hamdi could be tried before a military commission, "[a]t a minimum the Government must wake a substantial showing that the crime for which it seeks to try a defendant by military commission is acknowledged to be an offense against the law of war" *Hamdan v. Rumsfeld*.

12. Quoting a declaration of Michael Mobbs, which was the sole evidence provided by the government as a basis for Hamdi's detention (See "Declaration of Michael Mobbs," in *Hamdi v. Rumsfeld*, 542 U.S. 507 (2004) (hereinafter cited as *Hamdi*)).

13. Hamdi, of course, was a U.S. citizen, which would make support of a foreign military organization potentially treasonous. But there are presumably many noncitizens held at Guantanamo who, like Hamdi, did little more than affiliate with the Taliban and receive weapons training.

14. The Geneva POW Convention states: "Should any doubt arise as to whether persons, having committed a belligerent act and having fallen into the hands of the enemy, belong to any of the categories enumerated in Article 4, such persons shall enjoy the protection of the present Convention until such time as their status has been determined by a competent tribunal." "POW Convention," art. 5. In addition, Paragraph 2 of Article 45 of Protocol 1 to the treaty, states: "If a person who has fallen into the power of an adverse Party is not held as a prisoner of war and is to be tried by that party for an offence arising out of the hostilities, he shall have the right to assert his entitlement to prisoner-of-war status before a judicial tribunal and to have that question adjudicated." "Protocol Additional the Geneva Conventions of 12 August 1949, and Relating to the Protection of Victims of International Armed Conflicts," *United Nations Treaties Series* 1125, 3.

15. This development raises doubts about whether the administration had adequate proof that Hamdi was even a Taliban soldier—something Hamdi had denied.

16. See Office of the Press Secretary, *White House Fact Sheet: Status of Detainees at Guantanamo,* February 7, 2002, stating that neither al Qaeda detainees nor Taliban detainees are entitled to prisoner of war status; see also Lt. Col. Joseph Bialke, "Al-Qaeda and Taliban Unlawful Combatant Detainees, Unlawful Belligerency, and the International Laws of Armed Conflict," *Air Force Law Review* 55 (2004): 1, arguing that the Guantanamo detainees are unlawful combatants.

17. Specifically, Article 4(A) of the Geneva POW Convention provides that those entitled to prisoner of war status include: (1) Members of the armed forces of a Party to the conflict as well as members of militias or volunteer corps forming part of such armed forces; (2) Members of other militias and members of other volunteer corps, including those of organized resistance movements, belonging to a Party to the conflict and operating in or outside their own territory, even if this territory is occupied, provided that such militias or volunteer corps, including such organized resistance movements, fulfill the following conditions: (a) that of being commanded by a person responsible for his subordinates; (b) that of having a fixed distinctive sign recognizable at a distance; (c) that of carrying arms openly; (d) that of conducting their operations in accordance with the laws and customs

of war; (3) Members of regular armed forces who profess allegiance to a government or an authority not recognized by the Detaining Power, POW Convention, art. 4(A).

18. The majority of international lawyers believe that the subsection (2) requirements do not apply to the other sections, although some scholars and the Bush administration disagree. See Berman. Even if those requirements did apply, Taliban soldiers might well qualify. They carried arms openly and, according to at least some sources, wore distinctive black turbans. See Lawyers Commission for Human Rights, *Assessing the New Normal: Liberty and Security for the Post-September 11 United States,* 2003, 54.

19. International Committee of the Red Cross, *Commentary: IV Geneva Convention Relative to the Protection of Civilian Persons in Time of War,* 1958, 51.

20. See Jinks, "Declining Significance of POW Status," 367–68.

21. Nor is the conflict with al Qaeda an internal armed conflict, such as a civil war, which would also fall under the Geneva Conventions.

22. *Padilla v. Bush,* 233 F. Supp. 2d 564, 591 (S.D.N.Y. 2002), affirmed in part and reversed in part by *Padilla v. Rumsfeld,* 352 F.3d 695 (2d Cir., 2003), reversed on other grounds, *Rumsfeld v. Padilla,* 542 U.S. 426 (2004).

23. Jeremy Bentham, "Punishment and Deterrence," in *Principled Sentencing: Readings on Theory and Policy,* eds. Andrew von Hirsch and Andrew Ashworth (Oxford: Hart Publishing, 1998), 53–4.

24. Note that while individuals detained during war are entitled to an individualized determination of whether they are combatants who can claim prisoner of war status, they are not entitled to an individualized determination of whether they are dangerous, or whether they would return to the battlefield if released.

25. See, e.g., *Kansas v. Hendricks,* 521 U.S. 346 (1997).

26. *Zadvydas v. Davis,* 533 U.S. 678, 691 (2001).

PART IV

Law of Armed Conflict: Religion and Armed Conflict

CHAPTER 10

Legitimacy and Authority in Islamic Discussions of "Martyrdom Operations"/ "Suicide Bombings"

A. KEVIN REINHART

The American invasion of Iraq and related Iraqi resistance offer an occasion to reflect on the forms of Islam triggered in part as response. Among the most demoralizing practices in Iraq have been the "martyrdom operations"/"suicide bombings." But the Iraqi resistance only took over these preexisting practices from Palestinian, Lebanese, and Singhalese dissident movements. Intra-Muslim discussions of this and other issues give us a point from which to understand not only the epistemology of traditional Islamic law, but also the novel debates regarding the justification of these practices. This kind of discourse arises as Muslims try to determine what authority and which forms of argument are morally and religiously persuasive in the contemporary world.

In the late twentieth and early twenty-first (Christian) centuries, Muslims refer to the *idea* of traditional authority but a kind of Protestantization of Islam has in fact taken place that gives individual Muslims the belief that they are competent to decide complicated issues of conscience and practice. We will illustrate the nature of Islamic law and its contemporary changes by viewing these through the lens of debates about the legitimacy of "suicide bombings"/"martyrdom operations." Particularly in the work of al-Qaradāwī, it becomes clear that the motivations to suicide attacks are more nationalist than religious.

HYPOTHETICALS

As background, three scholars of religious studies, specialists in the Christian, Jewish, and Islamic traditions, were provided with a set of hypotheticals and asked how "their tradition" would respond to them. I want to use the issues raised by the posing of this problem to examine important issues of authority and legitimation in contemporary Islam.

To determine "the Islamic position" on these hypotheticals, I turned, as both Muslim and non-Muslim scholars do, first to a set of secondary works, mostly products of what I would call the "Muslim academy," that is, a set of Muslim scholars who have written articles within the body of the Western academic literature following the form of normal academic scholarship. I also examined non-Muslim academic discussions of these issues in the scholarly literature. And, like both of the sorts of scholars described above, I turned to the premodern works of Islamic law (*fiqh*) to determine what had been the legal consensus of the great scholars of the past who continue to influence Muslim thought today. This is the standard procedure when attempting to determine "what Muslims think" about some particular issue.[1] Here is then a brief response to the hypotheticals.

(A) Consider the problem of permissible interrogation and the border with torture (the classic problem is whether torture is permissible for a terrorist who knows where the ticking time bomb is located; and does generally proscribed torture goes beyond the physical infliction of pain).

Though one might get to permission to torture under the heading of public weal (*maslaḥah*), or under the principle of "removal of harm," torture is strongly condemned in *fiqh* jurisprudence, first as an act of cruelty, but secondly as a form of coercion (*ikrāhah*).[2] All judicial acts, including confession, made under coercive duress are invalid.[3] Moreover, unless there was absolute certainty that the person under interrogation had the knowledge sought, the judicial officer would risk a severe retribution in this world and the next if he were inflicting harm wrongly.[4] Tort action would, in theory, be the right of the wrongly tortured person.

(B) The conflict inherent in protected facilities under the law of war, like mosques, which are sought out in Iraq for fighting positions by insurgents both for public relations effects and because of genuine religious feelings.

In the nature of things, Islamic law does not apply to enemy forces, and most agree that it does not even address non-Muslims.[5] Moreover, the mosque is not a "sacred place" in Islamic law. Instead, it is a place whose ritual purity is guaranteed. So, theoretically, using a mosque as a staging area is no worse than using a house.[6] But the sentiments of Muslims may differ from the rules expressed in law. Using a mosque might be perceived as derogation or insult, and insulting the religion is perceived as an actionable offense.

(C) The civil liberties quandary of arresting 3000 innocent Arab-Americans willy-nilly to maybe catch perhaps thirty truly dangerous "terrorists."

Is this hostage-taking, kidnapping, collective punishment, preventative detention, or simply the indifference of the state of the plight of other humans? There is considerable debate on "preventative detention."[7] Some jurists ban it altogether, some approve it reluctantly, some allow certain classes of people to be detained when there is evidence that leads to suspicion of them, but they require more evidence for confining their betters.[8] Insofar as it is a kind of punishment of those not adjudged guilty, it violates the presumption of innocence (*barā'at al-dhimmiyyah*) that is one of the basic principles (*qawā'id*) of Islamic jurisprudence.[9] To judge this case, a much fuller picture of the circumstances would be needed.

(D) The apparent practice of detaining noncombatant family members to procure the surrender of insurgents (argued to be a denial of support but appears as if it is hostage taking).

This would seem to fall under the last portion of the paragraph above. Unless the family is involved in a wrongful act directly, they are presumed innocent of blame and any sort of punishment is wrongful (a tort in legal terminology).

(E) The problem of destruction of houses and livelihoods, such as fruit groves, beyond the bounds of military necessity (which looks like a reprisal in traditional legal terms).

The Islamic legal tradition pulls in two directions on this question. On the one hand, it affirms the absolute ownership by the Muslim ruler (on behalf of Muslims) of the property of those conquered by force. As such, the ruler may dispose of the property he holds as he sees fit. That would include destroying it.[10]

On the other hand, what we might call the empathetic or pragmatic side of Islamic juris-prudence condemns wanton destruction of palm trees, for example, as an act of profligacy and cruelty. So, according to some jurists, destruction of fruit-bearing trees and cattle, and even the destruction of buildings is explicitly prohibited unless there is need to deprive the enemy of support.[11] Here is a clear case where the "what does Islam say about X" question is inappropriate. Moreover, even a jurist who belonged to a school that adhered to one position or another would have to know about particular circumstances before he could rule.

(F) Proportionality of force problems (targeting law and asymmetry in legal terms, collateral damage, etc.).

One might find reference to this problem under the general problem of defense against assault. One defends with the least force possible *(al-ashal)*. In other words, "if you know that he is repelled by shouting he may not strike him."[12]

(G) A "civilian" suicide bomber attacking noncombatants or soldiers.

The entire question of "suicide bombers"/"self-sacrificing martyrs" has aroused consid-erable discussion. There is no doubt that traditional sources condemn suicide unequivo-cally. Moreover, a reckless or hopeless act of war is similarly condemned by many of the premodern sources.[13] Many contemporary apologists for the bombers/martyrs (some of them quite authoritative) have recast the argument in such a way as to permit suicidal attacks.[14] We will present this discussion much more extensively below. We should note, however, that as many Muslims of many different ideological convictions argue that suicide bombing and all forms of terrorism are "incompatible with Islam." It is my argument that their declaration is an important Islamic datum that we must take seriously.

(H) General questions of harms resulting from war as they affect noncombatants versus combatants.

John Kelsay has made the argument that there is no real Islamic theory of noncombatant protection in the sources he uses.[15] The most often-cited proof text in this context is the *hadīth* "They are from them," referring to dependents of those Arabs who were enemies of the early Islamic community. It is clear that unintentional killing of noncombatants is acceptable in a siege. And insofar as the women and children of enemy combatants in classical law are property, that property becomes the property of Muslims and may be destroyed. This dehumanizing tendency in the law is believed to be subordinated to a command not to execute captives.[16]

THE TRADITION

In Islamic terms, when we consider information of the sort cited above in conjunction with the hypotheticals, what do we actually have? The answer is: nothing very significant. To understand why, we need to consider something of the legal and moral epistemology that constitutes what we call Islamic law. It should be obvious that for the academic study of Islam it is impossible to define "the" Islamic position on anything. No tradition that is 1400 years old, and is more truly a global religion than any other, could be anything other than diverse. Hence, sentences that begin with "Islam says," "Islam requires," and the like are dubious unless the enterprise is explicitly theological.

For political and religious elites, the aspiration to arrive at definitive Islamic positions has been embodied in the commitment to a scriptural corpus of Arabic books: the *Qur'ān*, and an enormous collection—also in Arabic—of anecdotes recording the prophet Muḥammad's sayings, deeds, and observances—the *ḥadith*. The body of (humanly

determined) normative action derived from these two sources—understood to be episte-
mologically probable, but not certain—is what is referred to as Islamic law (*fiqh*).[17] It is
obvious that Islamic law will be diverse and far from monolithic. This is particularly the
case because Islamic legal reasoning is casuistic in the strict sense of the word. Islamic
legal scholars reason from cases to cases, using diverse and often conflicting sources such
that each source of moral knowledge is invoked proportionally against the others. Legal
judgment is not just the determination of facts, but the assessment of legal and moral
resources for judgment, and the application of them in the appropriate manner.[18]

Most importantly, the scholar asks about the circumstances of the act under consideration—who, what, where, why, when, by what means, how much, are asked. In strict practice, legal scholars cannot discuss the question of, say, abortion, or torture, except in the
most vague and unhelpful way—as a preliminary sorting tool perhaps, or to help establish
a pattern as an exercise to train the jurist or the individual conscience. Real '*ulamā*' cannot
move directly from a position on "torture" to a consideration of American interrogation
techniques without asking about these particulars and without factoring them into the
answer. The Islamic law books that academics and others consult to determine "the
Islamic ruling" on some issue are just a kind of exercise—they are real cases stripped of
their particulars—but it is only the particular case with all their variants and differences
that matters.[19] In the end, the Sunnī Muslim casuist offers certainty only that his method
is correct—the result of his reasoning is only probable. This epistemological humility is
signified—even in the most assertive works of someone like Ibn Taymiyyah—in a
concluding formula to a *fatwá* (that is, an authoritative legal finding), with a phrase such
as "And God knows better," or "we rely upon God."

ISLAM AS A FIELD OF DISCOURSE

In fact, a serious response to the question "what is Islam's position, Judaism's position,
the Christian position on something" is not so much a definitive answer to the question as
it is proof that there are many contested answers to the question. A case in point is the
issue of (the nomenclature is contested) "suicide bombing" or "martyrdom operations,"
or "self-sacrificing operations." As we shall see, there are many different answers to the
question of whether such acts are permitted. But more instructive than the answers to these
questions are the media through which they are answered. The diverse answers, sources
for answers, and above all the diversity of those who believe themselves qualified to
answer, tell us a number of important things about the present moment in Islam's history,
in particular the contested state of authority and legitimacy within the tradition.

Suicide bombings and other means of warfare are a particularly good lens through
which to examine these questions because violence in particular seems to require legitimation. It is not enough that the actor be convinced that his/her act is legitimate. People
realize that violent acts done with only individual sanction are indistinguishable from
either crime or madness. Suicide bombing, with its particular intensity—wherein the actor
destroys himself in the act of executing others—seems in particular to provoke discussion
and to require some sort of public sanction.[20]

The arena of legitimation for these self-killings is not solely Islamic, but by far, the
most important discourse comes from within various Islamic traditions. This is partly the
fruit of a campaign against liberalism in Islamdom that persuaded many Muslims that the
liberal tradition—whether Smith and Ricardo, or Kant and Hume, was alien to Muslims.[21]
It is also the fruit of the recognition that in many respects the thought of Western

philosophers is grounded—more than they acknowledge—in particular cultural values and procedures whose roots often enough are clearly Christian. Nationalism might seem to be a competitor with "Islam" as a source of values but it is fair to say that, since 1967, nationalism per se has largely been discredited, though it remains a force underestimated and perhaps under-articulated, in places like Iran, Palestine, Egypt, Pakistan, or Bangladesh. As Hourani said "Nationalism is not a system of thought; it is a single idea which does not suffice by itself to order the whole life of society. But it is a potent idea, one of those which serves as centers of attraction to others."[22] Nationalism is not an ethic but a sentiment like honor or revenge. So, in a way that is not the case for most Christians and I would guess, most Jews, the religious tradition is the only game in town for Muslims.

An American soldier going to war is constrained by the Military Code of Conduct and his or her training in the various Conventions which—at least until recently—the United States followed. He does not consider, say, Thomas Aquinas on the definition of a "just war," so, why would any discussion of the classical Islamic sources be relevant to an understanding of Muslim insurgents' behavior?

First, it has to be said that, in an important way, it is not. Muslim fighters are for the most part no more able to read al-Sarakhsī or Ibn Rushd, than an American solider is able to read *Summa Contra Gentiles* in the original Latin. It is much too readily assumed that the use of terms like *jihād* means that Muslims are acting from timeless Muslim urges governed by ancient law books.[23] Yet no actor and no state, including Iran, and Saudi Arabia, moves directly from the *fiqh* book to state practice—and there is a sense in which the endeavor to find classical legal explanations for the acts of contemporary Muslims is antiquarian, if not Orientalist, in both the descriptive and pejorative sense of the word.

Nonetheless, the combination of the social and the violent nature of war seems to require legitimacy and legitimation from a source outside the merely legal. While some in America have contented themselves with simple pieties and references to good and evil, others have inquired both formally and informally into the ways in which, for example, the American–Afghan War, or the Iraq war might be justified. Both the formal and the informal American justifications appealed not only to religious texts—Biblical or other theological works— but also to a tradition of moral reasoning that is either complementary or alternative—Kantian, Utilitarian, and so forth.[24]

Similarly in Islamdom, the populace has in questions of war and violence sought to determine the legitimacy of some particular path of resistance or attack, retaliation, or expansion. Indeed, Robert Pape has argued that suicide bombing, in particular, requires legitimation, and that religion can be particularly effective at it.[25] While many Muslim intellectuals, particularly outside the Arab world, are familiar with and are engaged with the world of European philosophy—Habermas and Marx, even Dilthey and Austin—and such works are found relatively easily in Turkey or Iran, for instance, there nonetheless seems to be a popular conviction that the answer to moral questions must somehow be grounded in the rhetoric of Islam. This is partly simply a question of popularly perceived authenticity: the Persian Ibn Sina is "ours" to Arabs in a way that Camus—a native of Algeria—is not. The adjective "European" or "French," or "American" increasingly alienates the Muslim public from a discourse that is popularly linked to the domination of colonialism and neocolonialism. In addition, the discourse of European philosophy is far more European and Christian than its practitioners recognize or admit. Hence, particularly in the last two decades, the public discourse of legitimation and justification—whether in the realm of personal morality or political action—has appealed to the Islamic tradition or some understanding of it.

It is not that hoi polloi are diving into arcane *fiqh* works. As we will see, the appeal to *fiqh,* theology and the commentarial literature is largely delegated to experts or appeals to sentiments believed to be derived from the classics of Islamic religious literature. The appearance of the Internet has facilitated the influence of official *muftīs* like Shaykh 'Abdal'azīz al-Shaykh in Arabia, al-Ṭanṭāwī of the Azhar in Egypt. However, it is inescapable that Muslims are appealing to "Islam" as a source of knowledge and guidance in domains where Islam would not have been evoked 50 years ago.

NEW DEVELOPMENTS IN MUSLIM MORAL DISCOURSE

It might be argued that "Islam" has resumed the role it had before colonialism as the primary discourse through which Muslims understood themselves and their society. It would be a mistake, however, not to recognize the novelty of contemporary Muslims' appeal to their tradition, because it is for the most part very untraditional in form as well as in content. To begin with, the actors opining about "what Islam requires" are very much different from what was the case in the nineteenth century. Then it was state-recognized scholars, for the most part, speaking from state-recognized positions in *madrasahs,* or from within the state bureaucracy: a *shaykh al-Islam,* or a chief *muftī,* perhaps. Yet now there are at least three sets of actors producing Muslim opinion on, for example, suicide bombing.

The Muslim Academy

The first of these actors is a newly developed "Muslim academy." These are university scholars and other teachers who master at least some of the premodern sources, but who are also in dialog in one way or another with the global academy and concepts common to it: the prisoner's dilemma, human rights concepts, and concepts of law that are standard in most Islamic countries' jurisprudence and that are shared with Continental Law or Anglo-American common law.[26] They write books, publish sets of collected articles, and are employed in universities, think-tanks and even at newspapers and journals. Their qualification to speak is usually an academic credential combined with a commitment that comes to be recognized as expertise. The sources cited above in the discussion of the conference's legal hypotheticals are mostly from members of this Muslim academy.

Islamic "Protestantism"

The second actor creating Muslim opinion is the involved Muslim laity. The inclusion of the laity here points to a notable development that we might call the Protestantization of *fatwá-culture.*[27] In this aspect of Islamic discourse, we see various Muslims—doctors, businesspeople, and even a civil engineer last seen in Tora Bora—opine on matters of Islamic law and conduct. These actors cite mostly Muslim Scriptures—*hadīth* of the Prophet (often in translation) and Qur'an (often translated as well) or the works of Ibn Taymiyyah, Mawdudi, and Qutb. Often, there are references to what might be called "deductive Islamic principles" such as "the spirit of Islam," "Islam is a religion of peace," "Islam treats all believers equally," or "Islam is a religion of liberation," for example.

As an instance of this Protestantization of Islam, consider the following news-group exchange from soc.religion.islam which I quote at length to capture the flavor of the newer Islamic discourse:

(1) From: J.G. Moore
Date: Thurs, Jun 7 2001 8:14 am
Groups: soc.religion.islam

Apologies for posting before a suitable period of reading, but I have a relatively simple question. As I understand it, Islam teaches that soldiers killed in battle go immediately to a special sort of Paradise. Is this also applicable to suicides who believe they are participating in some sort of righteous battle? What is the Islamic position on suicide in general? Thank you for your attention.

(2) From: HJ—
Date: Sat, Jun 9 2001 3:29 pm
Groups: soc.religion.islam

J.G. Moore wrote [the question is quoted]

Suicide is categorically forbidden in Islam, but a self-sacrificing soldier is not considered a suicide. The basic difference is intention and, in Islam, actions are only judged according to intentions.

Hajj Gibril

(3) From: ziphyre—
Date: Sat, Jun 9 2001 3:47 pm
Groups: soc.religion.islam

First of all, please do excuse my English...Suicide is one of the most important sins in Islam like any other religion. Any kind of suicide is unacceptable. Islam teaches that soldiers killed in battle go immediately to a special sort of Paradise. Most people do not understand that there is no strict rules like this, the most important thing is God knows everything, and He is the only one who will judge...

(4) From: Fred—
Date: Wed, Jun 13 2001 10:50 am
Groups: soc.religion.islam

Hi all, Regarding suicide I have here two examples: (1) The person who bombed himself two weeks ago in Israel killing more than 20 young people. (2) A person who suffer a cureless disease who kill himself just to stop the pain and suffer. Is it fair to consider the first person as a great man or a hero while considering the second one as a coward or damned person? Is Allah going to reward the first person for killing other people? Is Allah going to punish the second one because he just didn't afford the pain?

(5) From: HA—
Date: Wed, Jun 13 2001 11:09 pm Email: [deleted]

Hi there, Before I say anything, I'd like to point out that everyone is individually judged by Allah for their actions. 1—You'd need to look at the intentions of the suicide bomber. Seeing as he specifically targeted civilians, I get the feeling that his intentions of deliberate murder will be punished rather than his suicide, which he would have believed was in the cause of Islam. 2—It is not our right to end our lives without just cause. Pain can be [borne], unless of course you're in a Russian concentration camp.

And a later exchange:

(6) From: vminai—
Date: Thurs, Jun 7 2001 7:23 am

Anjum" wrote: In the Name of Allah, The Beneficent, The Merciful AsSalaamu 'alaikum Wa Alaykum AsSalam. Can you tell me if these suicide bombings to kill CIVILIANS is Islamic?

Yes and no. Should we advocate and support them? I doubt it very much. Should we apologize for them? I don't think...

(If you have time, you should also read an article titled "banAo aur bigAR" by Maududidi).

Quran repeatedly asserts that Allah(SWT) Abhors fasAd (corruption), and mufsideen. Apparently there is a very good reason for it. Namely that it creates even more violence and fasAd, and before long the situation gets out of hand.

Allah(SWT) Knows Best, but it seems that such is His Law. Like water, if heated will eventually boil.]

VA

(7) From: ibn ul-filibbeeni—
Date: Fri, Jun 8 2001 1:49 am
Can you tell me if these suicide bombings to kill CIVILIANS is Islamic?
the following fataawaa can be found @ http://www.fatwa-online.com in the worship category, under jihaad. they were made by some of the top scholars
From amongst the hiyaat kibaar al-'ulamaa of our era.
1) Attacking the enemy by blowing oneself up
Question: There are those who tie a magazine of explosives around their waist, then they enter a government or residential building or a gathering of people either kuffaar or other than them, then they blow themselves up, so what is the ruling regarding this? And is something like this act considered an aspect of jihaad, and is the one doing so considered a shaheed (martyr) or one who has committed suicide (muntahir)?...

(8) From: HJ—
Date: Wed, Jun 13 2001 11:00 am
As-Salamu 'alaykum:
Some or most of the fatwas quoted by ibn ul-filibbeeni fail to define to satisfaction the act of suicide as the intent to end one's life without further motive, while the suicidal act of war is primarily an attack against the enemy aiming at devastation in the latter's ranks and morale, in "accidental" (philosophically speaking) consequence of which one is certain to end one's physical life. Since, in Islam, actions count only according to intentions, it is inexcusable to overlook the distinction. What is more, there are specific and explicit precedents in the Sunna, while the Qur'ānic verses and hadīths quoted by the objectors are out of place because they only address wanton self-endangerment and self-destruction. This is why Shaykh Yusuf al-Qaradāwī brushed aside all the specious objections of certain Egyptian and Saudi muftis and said that in most cases Muslims' suicidal bombings are martyrdom or rather "the soul of martyrdom" ('ayn al-shahada) and Allah knows best. [sic]

Hajj Gibril...

(9) From: Surayya—
Date: Sun, Jun 17 2001 9:11 am Assalam'alaikum,
... The point was that, suicide aside, there are other prerequisites in the shariah that must be satisfied as to the strategy militarily, the avoidance of civilian targets, and by whom gives the order.

Which nobody has bothered to address. The last poster gave the impression that as long as my intentions are for martyrdom, I can blow up who I like claiming it to be 'aiming at devastation in the latter's ranks and morale'. And so any idiot can do what they like, blowing themselves up when they like and at who they like, all claiming the role of martyrs. No that is NOT Islam, but Arab culture and middle-east politics.

And all this comes from those who have no military training or background, which only some muslims in certain areas of the muslim world have retained those muslim military traditions. The Arabs are well known to have lost those traditions completely and utterly.

In London we know first hand the mentality of those who plant bombs, whether its in cars or on themselves, it makes no difference, claiming to be striking a blow against the British government. The overwhelming public opinion is that they are murderous maniacs with no regard for life, no-one buys their cowardly pathetic excuses.

Wa salam
sister Surayya

(10) From: ABE—

Date: Sun, Jun 17 2001 11:47 pm

Groups: soc.religion.islam

Surayya wrote: In London we know first hand the mentality of those who plant bombs, whether it is in cars or on themselves, it makes no difference, claiming to be striking a blow against the British government. The over-whelming public opinion is that they are murderous maniacs with no regard for life, no-one buys their cowardly pathetic excuses.

Military jihad, like all other Muslim activities, is a carefully organized and orderly activity. Modern Muslims have many more options in warfare than their ancestors had. Certainly, they would have been amazed and appalled by tear gas, grenades, bombs, nuclear weapons, biological warfare, missiles, etc., all assisted by remote-controlled, electronic technology. Nevertheless, the teachings of the Prophet Muhammad (God's grace and peace be on him) show us that we are forbidden to use most of that terrible arsenal.

It is the consensus of the early scholars and most modern ones that "jihad must be waged according to the same principles of justice and humanitarian concern that were observed by the Prophet. He ordered Muslims to refrain from killing civilians, inflicting unnecessary injury, creating unnecessary destruction, and killing by the use of fire.... In the modern world, jihad continues to be a just struggle that does not countenance wanton murder and destruction."

The quoted passage in the preceding paragraph is from _Islamic Jihad: An Historical Perspective_ by Jamilah Kolocotronis, American Trust Publications, 1990, ISBN 0-89259-086-6...

In 1985, terrorists claiming to be Muslims hijacked a TWA Boeing 727. They demanded the release of Arab prisoners being held by Israel. Before a settlement was reached with the help of Syria, the terrorists killed one of the passengers and brutalized the others, whom they held prisoner on board the airplane for 16 days. At the very beginning of the incident, in an editorial entitled "These Cowardly Acts", the following comments appeared, in the _Arab News_, 17 June 1985, Vol. X, No. 202, p.8: "In fact, this kind of violence, in which the world media are witness to the brutalities of individuals purporting to act in the name of Palestinians and Arabs...is the most artful way of maligning the noble objectives for which the Palestinian people are struggling."

—Peace to all who seek God's face.

ABE

. . .

(11) From: DS—

Date: Thurs, Jun 21 2001 6:59 pm

Groups: soc.religion.islam

[But it is strange that they do it at civilian targets, like streets or buses, that display no military strategy, except for killing civilians and annoying the enemy government into further oppression and violence on civilian muslims.]

That's not true sis! The majority of the martyrdom operations are carried out against military targets. Few were carried out against settlers whom are either army reserves or army personnel on their day off, read the facts and don't just rely on TV pics. The prophet (pbuh) used to order his army not cut a tree down, not to kill women, not to kill elderly people, not to kill those who surrender their weapons. In the Israeli case, Israeli civilians (especially the settlers) are heavily armed and pose danger to Palestinian civilians. People keep talking about Israeli civilians and forget about the Palestinian civilians whom, for the past 50 years, endured the worst living under a very atrocious military occupier.... I would expect more sympathy from you for civilian Palestinians and not Israeli civilians....

(12) From: ABE—

Date: Sat, Jun 23 2001 1:25 am

Groups: soc.religion.islam

[The majority of the martyrdom operations are carried out against military targets].

The question of suicide bombings does not turn on the identity of the victims nor the legitimate claims and aspirations of the perpetrators.

There are only two possible contexts in which these actions are carried out:

1. As a part of jihaad fii sabiil allah (righteous struggle in God's way) or

2. As part of a non-Islamic political struggle over the ownership and hegemony over the so-called "occupied territories".

If the actions are part of a jihaad, they are wrong and contrary to the plain teachings and practices of the Prophet Muhammad (God's grace and peace be on him) and the Prophet's Companions (God be pleased with them). The use of fire as a weapon of war or punishment of evil is reserved exclusively to Allah Most Mighty.

If the actions are part of a geopolitical war, then suicide bombings violate Allah's prohibition of suicide. And when such bombings are carried out in buses and against targets where the identity of the victims cannot be reasonably known in advance or where the risk of "collateral victims" is high, then those actions violate the general prohibition against murder and gratuitous violence. In the sight of Allah Most Kind Most Merciful, the wrongful homicide of a non-Muslim is just as sinful as the murder of a Muslim. In the Qur'an, God says that if you kill one person it is as if you had killed all humanity and if you save the life of one person it is as if you saved all humanity.

There is no difference in the sight of Allah between Israeli civilians and Palestinian civilians or between Christian or Jewish or Muslim civilians. The only basis for distinction, God says in the Qur'an, is the degree of piety of a person.

. . .

ABE

(13) From: Surayya—
Date: Sun, Jun 24 2001 2:23 am
Groups: soc.religion.islam

Assalam'alaikum,

[DS writes: That's not true sis! The majority of the martyrdom operations are carried out against military targets. Few were carried out against settlers whom are either army reserves or army personnel on their day off, read the facts and don't just rely on TV pics. [sic]]

You cannot target army personnel on public streets or buses, where civilians are present. What started off as military targets, is increasingly turning into indiscriminant targeting of civilians.

Your excuses are nothing, it does not justify anything, even if they have a good track record of targeting military personnel, how does that justify targeting a crowd of civilians just to kill a couple of ordinary military personnel?. . .

Wa salam
sister Surayya

(14) From: DS—
Date: Mon, Jun 25 2001 11:09
Groups: soc.religion.islam

[Surayya wrote: You cannot target army personnel on public streets or buses, where civilians are present. . . .

The muslims have still not addressed the shariah on this matter: 'there are other pre-requisites in the shariah that must be satisfied as to the strategy militarily, the avoidance of civilian targets, and by whom gives the order.' Otherwise anyone may target who they like, when they like, and blow themselves up.]

You're WRONG!!! Fatwas, one after another, have been published in the middle east and the latest by Sheik Qardawy who confirms that the struggle in the land of Palestine is pure Jihad without exceptions. . . . I tell you, you need to quit watching CNN..

(15) From: DS—
Date: Mon, Jun 25 2001 11:09 am
Groups: soc.religion.islam

[ABE wrote: The question of suicide bombings does not turn on the identity of the victims nor the legitimate claims and aspirations of the perpetrators.]

Excuse me sir but they are called "martyrdom operations" thank you very much! Both Sheik Yusuf Qardawy and previously, Sheik Kishk gave fatwa in this regard. With all do respect, you are not the Qardawy nor sheik Kishk. So, for you to utter such words would only give me the reason not to respond to your response....

(16) From: Surayya—

Date: Tues, Jul 3 2001 11:53 am

Groups: soc.religion.islam

[Assalam'alaikum,

DS writes

[Invaders]; are invaders! I don't care what they wear!]

Well that's the problem, its all about what you CARE, and not shariah. That is not Islam, and we are discussing Islam and shariah.

Refer to shariah, not your personal whims or cares!...

[The muslims have still not addressed the shariah on this matter:

You're WRONG!!!. Fatwas, one after another, have been published in the middle east and the latest by Sheik Qardawy who confirms that the struggle in the land of Palestine is pure Jihad without exceptions...I tell you, you need to quit watching CNN.]

Produce a fatwa that allows anyone to blow themselves up according to what I wrote, and what you now claim that there are fatwas one after another that allow the opposite of this:

['there are other prerequisites in the shariah that must be satisfied as to the strategy militarily, the avoidance of civilian targets, and by whom gives the order.' Otherwise anyone may target who they like, when they like, and blow themselves up.]

Produce a fatwa.

Afghanistan won its freedom, but they cleansed themselves of their own murdering monsters, and they won their freedom quicker than your kind. They may have sunk to that level of the enemy, but they did not stay at that level or remain content with being at that level, despite being occupied and having suffered worse atrocities.

Learn from those who know better, and who have been there and done it.

Wa salam
sister Surayya

Each of the Muslims involved in this exchange believes himself or, notably, herself, entitled to her opinion. There is no hand-off of the decision to some officially constituted authority. When authority is invoked, it is invoked in the manner of casuistry. Various authorities are weighed against each other with none categorically privileged (though some assert the priority of one source or another). In (6), V directs the reader to an article by the Pakistani Islamist Maududi, "if you have time;" in (7) Ibn al-Filibbeeni directs the reader to a set of *fatwas*. Yet, Hajj Gibril in (8) brushes these *fatwas* aside and alludes to a *fatwa* from another scholar—probably the *fatwa* of al-Qaradāwī translated below—and to one (less likely) from Shaykh Kishk.[28] In (10), ABE refers to a product of the Muslim academy—a work published in Indiana and to a newspaper article. Several refer or allude to *sharī'ah* as a general set of guidelines, rather than to a detailed set of prescriptions; the *sharī'ah* is understood as an injunction to avoid civilian targets (9); as requiring deference to a military authority; as a proscription of fire as a weapon of war (10 and 12); as a general prohibition of murder and gratuitous violence (13); as establishing the equivalence of Muslim and non-Muslim lives (12); and the obligation not to sink to "the level of the enemy" (10). Finally, these *sharī'ah* rules blend into a set of ethical principles: suicide is forbidden (2), actions are judged by intentions (2 and 5), God is the sole judge (3), and corruption should be avoided because it causes more corruption (6).

This kind of public argument constitutes a profound shift in Muslims' ethical episte-mology. The use of diverse sources and the disinclination to quote from the Scriptural sources is notable. What is most radical however is the self-confident way in which these Muslims feel free to opine about matters about which a century ago they had no right to an opinion whatsoever. In these exchanges, several Muslims justify their position by refer-ence to recognized Islamic experts. But, for the most part, they seem content that they are equipped to recognize or define what "Islam requires" regarding the question of martyrdom/suicide operations. The popularization, Protestantization, or even democrati-zation of Islamic judgment is perhaps the single most significant change in contemporary Islamic intellectual life.[29]

The Independent Magisterium

Despite the self-confidence of some Muslims, other Muslims in this exchange display a yearning for an authority that can construct unity and certainty amidst the bewildering number of opinions on any particular topic. This longing for intellectual order, together with the discrediting of state-sanctioned religious establishments, has created an indepen-dent magisterium whose authority comes from the learning of individual scholars and his —and sometimes even her—reputation for probity and independence. These independent *'ulamā'* propagate their messages from what might be thought of as think tanks (funded by devoted donors) through a cascade of books and pamphlets and, increasingly, across the Internet.

Among the foremost of these Sunnī scholars is Yūsuf al-Qaradāwī, an Egyptian scholar whose many books and pamphlets are found throughout Islamdom. He also has a very active Web site and a popular program on the al-Jazeera television network. His *fatwá* on "suicide-bombing" is much cited (including in the Internet discussions quoted above). It is worth translating and analyzing because it is seen by many Muslims as both authori-tative and persuasive; therefore, it is a good source with which to conclude our reflection on authority and legitimacy in contemporary Islam.

We would expect a *fatwá* justifying the so-called Islamic suicide bombing to show the hallmarks of the "Islamicness" of these acts. The usual tropes in journalistic accounts of the suicide bombing culture include the *houris* that reward the martyrs, the "green birds" in which their souls are transported immediately to heaven, and so forth. Yet this *fatwá*, clearly directed against Muslim critics, justifies "self-martyrdom" in ways quite unex-pected and so is worth a closer look.

Translation: al-Qaradāwī on "Martyrdom Acts"

After the recent bomb attacks (*tafjīrāt*) that have taken place in Jerusalem, Tel Aviv, and Ascalon, and the killing of the Zionists [in these attacks] as a result of martyrdom operations that youth of the Islamic resistance movement Hamās have undertaken, many have asked about the [moral] status of these operations that are called "suicide" [bombings]. Are they considered "*jihād* in the path of God" or terrorism? Are these youth who slaughter[30] them-selves in these operations considered martyrs, or terrorists, because they kill themselves with their own hands [through their own agency]? Are the deeds of these considered to belong to the category of "cast by their own hands to ruin" of which the Qur'ān speaks when God says, "Do not cast [yourself] by your own hands to ruin."[31]

I want to say here [the following]: These operations are considered among the mightiest (*a'zam*) kinds of "*jihād* in the path of God." It is the kind of permitted terror to which the Qur'ān points when God says "make ready for them all you can of force and tethered horses that thereby you may terrify the enemy of God and your enemy."[32]

[7] To call these acts "suicide" is a mistake, an error—these are acts of heroic self-sacrifice (*'amaliyāt fidā'iyyah*) by means of "seeking martyrdom" (*istishhād*).[33] These are as far as can be from suicide, and one who undertakes it is as far as can be from the psyche of a suicide.

A suicide kills himself for himself whereas the *mustashhid* privileges sacrifice (or "victim-hood") (*al-ḍaḥiyah*) on behalf of his religion and his nation (*ummah*) over himself. A suicide is a person who gives up all hope for himself and the spirit of God (*ruhu llāh*) [that is in him.] The warrior for the faith (*mujāhid*) is a person who has perfect hope in the spirit of God and His mercy. The suicide rids [himself] of himself and his concerns by killing himself; the warrior for God attacks the enemies of God and his enemies with [this] novel weapon whose power has been placed in the hands of the oppressed/down-trodden by which [he can] resist the tyranny of the arrogant and the powerful (*jabrūt al-aqwiyā' al-mustakbirīn*). The warrior for God becomes a human bomb that explodes in a particular place at a particular time among the enemies of God and the homeland (*waṭan*) who stand powerless before this heroic martyr who ransoms himself (*bā' nafsahu*) for God and puts his trust in Him, seeking to bear witness [be a martyr] in the way of God.

These youth who defend their land—the land of Islam—and their religion and their honor (*'irḍahum*) and their religious community (*ummatahum*) are not suicides: they are the farthest thing possible from a suicide. They are true martyrs, exerting their spirits willingly (*raḍūn*) in the way of God. So long as their intention is toward God, and as long as they [8] are compelled to this course by the terrorism (*ar'āt*) of the enemies of God who persist in their enmity and who are deluded by their power and the support of the Great Power that they have.

The matter is as the poet [al-Kumayt] said:

If there is nothing but the points of spears to be ridden, then there is nothing to do but ride them. [If only weapons remain then one is forced to battle]. [34]

They are not suicides; they are not terrorists; they are the resistance; it is the legitimate [or licit or moral] resistance to those who have occupied their land and made them and their families homeless and usurped what was theirs and confiscated their future and still practice their enmity toward them. Their religion makes it is a duty on them to defend themselves and does not permit them voluntarily to give up their homes which are part of the Abode of Islam.

The action of these heroes is not considered "[those who] cast [themselves] by their own hand to ruin" as some simple-minded people conceive it. It is rather a dangerous, moral, praiseworthy act of *jihād* by which one intends to harm the enemy, to kill some of them, to put fear in the hearts of the rest of them, and to encourage the Muslims against them.

Zionist society is a military society; its men and women are soldiers in the army; they may be called up at any moment. If one kills a child or an old man [9] in this operation, it is unintentional; it is a mistake, and has the status of compulsion of war [collateral damage?] or a necessity that allows something otherwise forbidden.

Perhaps it would not be amiss if I quote here what other scholars have said in this regard and what commentators have said about the verse "[those who] cast [themselves] by their own hand to ruin."[35]

[Here he quotes the Hanafī al-Jaṣṣāṣ (d. 981); the Mālikī al-Qurṭubī (d. 1272); the Shāfi'ī al-Rāzī (d. 1210), Ibn Kathīr (d.1373), al-Ṭabarī (d. 923) the Ḥanbalī Ibn Taymiyyah (d. 1328), al-Shawkānī (d. 1839) and Rashīd Riḍā' (d. 1935).]

[21] What is to be understood [from these passages] is that the calculated licit danger by which one hopes to terrify the enemy of God and our enemy and by which one seeks to aid the Truth rather than to follow his passion is not "casting [themselves] by their own hand to ruin"

I believe that the truth [of the matter] has been made as clear as day and that these [Qur'ānic] phrases of condemnation refer entirely to the pretentious ones who attack these youth—who have faith in their Lord Who has given them great guidance, who redeem themselves for God and are killed in His way—[asserting] that they are suicides and "cast [themselves] by their own hand to ruin".

They, if God wills, are of the rank of martyrs [now] with God; they are the vital element, an expression of the vitality of the community (*ummah*), and its perseverance in resistance; they are alive and deathless, and abiding without cease.

[22] All that we seek here is that these martyrdom-seeking acts take place after study and a weighing of the positives and negatives. They ought to take place through collective reflection by the trustworthy[36] Muslims. If they find good in proceeding, let them proceed and rely upon God. And who relies upon God—God is Mighty and Wise.[37]

Trying to understand the logic of "martyrdom operations," observers have "fetishized" the Islamic component. It is clear that the majority of suicide attacks—at least before the American invasion of Iraq—were not done by Muslims. The best study of the phenomenon concludes that religion can be a language of motivation but the goals of suicide bombers are not religious but, are instead *national*—the recovery of land perceived as occupied from a country that has an elected form of government.[38] Al-Qaradāwī's *fatwá* confirms this finding, and a careful reading of it can help us both to understand the phenomenon itself and the role of Islamic rhetoric in mobilizing and justifying contemporary political action.

Al-Qaradāwī begins with a title that is usefully ambiguous: *shar'iyyah* is the ordinary term for "legitimate" or "legal." It draws on the word for revelational morality (*al-shar'*) yet it is also a standard bureaucratic term that indicates licitness or state-sanctioned behavior.

The problematic issue of the essay would seem to be a religious one—are these people martyrs? Is their activity properly called *jihād*? Yet the term *shahīd* is much broader than a person killed in a religious struggle. The term's use, even in Scriptural sources, is so broad as to leave one scholar wondering uncomprehendingly who is not a martyr?[39] That is the point. The word has a scope much broader than the technically religious, so that it is akin to the way the American press uses the word "hero" to describe every man or woman serving in the armed forces, or the unfortunate men and woman who had the bad luck to be aboard the hijacked planes or in the World Trade Center on September 11, 2001. The term "victim" is not used to refer only, or mainly, to someone offered in a meaningful religious sacrifice, but for any misfortunate person who dies. Essays like the one translated here might be seen as an effort to recapture the term for the religious-minded, but the effect is to ratify the nonspecific use of the term.

The first turn of the essay is to define the appropriate term for this activity as "seeking martyrdom," rather than "suicide" or "terrorism." Suicide is defined as killing oneself from selfishness; self-martyrdom as killing oneself from *selflessness*. Everyone agrees that suicide is a sin; al-Qaradāwī asserts that the internal disposition and overt goal, the public and political nature of the act, redefines the locus of meaning from killing the self to dying in battle.

The second task of this *fatwa* is an explicitly Islamic one—to determine whether those who are "martyrdom seekers" are subsumed under the category of "those who cast [themselves] by their own hand to ruin" an act explicitly prohibited by the Qur'ān and a concept used by the religious critics of those acts.

Al-Qaradāwī's defense against this argument is strikingly nonreligious. It is that these are soldiers who have found a novel weapon. It is a weapon that is equivocal in its value —al-Qaradāwī must establish that its use is justified. He does so with a set of arguments that make no reference to texts or overtly religious values, but to terms that draw their contemporary meanings from the emotive language of nationalism. The martyr is defending the homeland, the land, honor, and community. They are down-trodden and oppressed, and have no other recourse against an enemy who is arrogant and supported by great powers. They are the Resistance responding to occupation. Al-Qaradāwī accepts the distinction between civilians and soldiers but argues that it does not apply in the universal-call-up society of Israel. And if some true civilians are killed, that is simply collateral damage, a cost that certainly the United States and Israel recognize as acceptable in war.

This is not to deny that al-Qaradāwī uses religious language—the closing passage that begins on page 21 of the Arabic text is full of affective religious phrases and images. Revealingly, the notion that drives his argument is a nationalist outrage at occupation and humiliation—not an evocation of *houris* and Qur'ānic commands to flight the believer.

One other notable point: it is striking that when al-Qaradāwī comes to support his case that the would-be martyr is not "one who casts [him or herself] by their own hand to ruin" he cites a set of authorities that are overwhelmingly medieval—with the sole exception of M. Rashīd Riḍā'. This confirms the point that Islamic scholars have a limited amount of authority in disputed matters. Al-Qaradāwī cites no one alive in the past 70 years and he mostly cites sources that could be described as ancient or early medieval. Fakhraddīn al-Rāzī and al-Qurṭubī are still names to conjure with; Shaltūt, Hudaybī, or Ibn Badīs are not.

CONCLUSIONS

The point of this discussion is that the authority of the classical tradition and its representatives is much more problematic than in the past. While official *muftīs* and jurists have the coercive power of the state behind them, they are often perceived to have little or no legitimacy. Those who have legitimacy for one group may not have it for another group of Muslims. And some Muslims feel authorized to decide for themselves what Islam requires. In all cases, however, assumptions and terminologies of Islamic discourse have been saturated by non-Islamic concepts; the only authoritative rhetoric is Islamic— whether it is constructed by the use of proof texts, or references to what are believed to be incontestably Islamic principles. Public opinion now has a saliency that cannot be ignored and global notions of, say, "sacred space," shape Muslim responses to images of American troops in mosques. Though there was initially resistance to suicide bombing, the critical—mostly establishment—voices were soon drowned out by public approval and scholars were compelled to follow suit.

What is striking is that, while recognizably Islamic discourse remains the medium for ethical discussion and reflection, the cultural phenomenon we call Islam is changing rapidly. Scholars are regaining their autonomy from the state, while there is also a popular Islamic discourse that is more and more confident. For both these reasons, Islamic ethical thought is becoming—as Muslims themselves are becoming—more and more part of the shared global discourse. Al-Qaradāwī cites the right of the occupied to resist and uses nationalist rhetoric. The laity cite scripture, legal texts, academics, activists, and their own insights. Some support, some oppose martyrdom operations. If these debates prove the continued importance of Islam and Islamic discourse, they also establish its diversity and plurality.

NOTES

1. Jonathan E. Brockopp, ed. "Islamic Ethics of Killing and Saving Life." Special Issue, *The Muslim World* 89, no. 2 (1999).

2. Ibn al-Naqib, Ahmad ibn Lu'lu'. *The Reliance of the Traveller: A Classic Manual of Islamic Sacred Law,* Trans. Noah H.M. Keller (Evanston, IL: Sunna Books, 1991) 685.

3. Ibn 'Abdalrafi', Ibrāhīm ibn Ḥasan. *Mu' īn al-hukkām 'alá al-qaḍāyā wa-al-aḥkām.* Ed. Muḥammad ibn Qāsim ibn 'Ayyad (Beirut: Dār al-Gharb al-Islāmī, 1989) 2: 883.

4. Kemal Güran, "İşkence," *Türkiye Diyanet Vakfı Islâm ansiklopedisi* (Istanbul: Türkiye Diyanet Vakfı, 1988).

5. This is the problem in the *uṣūl* sources of whether the 'rejector is addressed by the Revelational moral knowledge (*hal kāna al-kuffār mukhātabūna bi-l-shar'*).

6. H. A. R. Gibb and others, "Masjid" *The Encyclopaedia of Islam,* 2nd ed. 11+ supplement vols (Leiden: E. J. Brill, 1960).

7. Cherif Bassiouni, ed. *The Islamic Criminal Justice System, International Association of Penal Law. Arab Organization for Social Defense Against Crime.* (London: Oceana Publications, 1982).

8. M. A. Abdel Haleem, Adel Omar Sherif, and Kate Daniels, *Criminal Justice in Islam: Judicial Procedure in the Shari'a* (New York, NY: I. B. Tauris, 2003; in the United States of America and Canada distributed by Palgrave Macmillan).

9. Gibb and others, "Barā'a" *Encyclopaedia of Islam.*

10. al-Naqib 1991.

11. Ibid.

12. Ibid.

13. Bernard K. Freamon, "Martyrdom, Suicide, and the Islamic Law of War: A Short Legal History," *Fordham International Law Journal* 27, no. 1 (2003): 299–369.

14. Freamon, "Martyrdom, Suicide, and the Islamic Law of War"; Robert Anthony Pape, *Dying to Win: The Strategic Logic of Suicide Terrorism,* 1st ed. (New York: Random House, 2005).

15. John Kelsay, *Islam and War: A Study in Comparative Ethics,* 1st ed. (Louisville, KY: Westminster/John Knox Press, 1993).

16. Averroës, [Ibn Rushd]. *The Distinguished Jurist's Primer: A Translation of Bidāyat al-mujtahid,* trans. I. A. K. Nyazee and R. B. M. A. Rauf, 1st ed. (Reading, UK: Centre for Muslim Contribution to Civilization: Garnet Pub, 1994).

17. *Fiqh* is the understanding derived from the sources. This understanding is, it is hoped, consonant with God's stipulation of normative action, the *sharī'ah.* Often these two are conflated but in Islamic theory, they are quite distinct.

18. Albert R. Jonsen and Stephen Toulmin, *The Abuse of Casuistry: A History of Moral Reasoning* (Berkeley: University of California Press, 1988).

19. Wael B. Hallaq, "From Fatwás to Furū': Growth and Change in Islamic Substantive Law," *Islamic Law and Society* 1, no. 1 (1993): 29–65.

20. Robert Pape, *Dying to Win: The Strategic Logic of Suicide Terrorism,* 1st ed. (New York: Random House, 2005).

21. Albert Habib Hourani, *Arabic Thought in the Liberal Age, 1798–1939* (Cambridge: Cambridge University Press, 1983).

22. Ibid.

23. David Cook, "Suicide Attacks or 'Martyrdom Operations' in Contemporary Jihad" *Nova Religio* 6, no. 1 (2002): 7–44.

24. G. Weigel, "Iraq: Then & Now," *First Things* (April #162, 2006), 34–42.

25. Ibid.

26. Haleem, Sherif, and Daniels, *Criminal Justice in Islam;* Bassiouni, ed., *The Islamic Criminal Justice System;* Sohail H. Hashmi, ed. *Islamic Political Ethics: Civil Society, Pluralism, and Conflict,* Ethikon Series in Comparative Ethics (Princeton, NJ: Princeton University Press, 2002); Hashmi and Steven Lee, eds. *Ethics and Weapons of Mass Destruction: Religious and Secular Perspectives,* The Ethikon Series in Comparative Ethics (Cambridge: Cambridge University Press, 2004).

27. Olivier Roy, *Globalized Islam: The Search for a New Ummah* (New York: Columbia University Press, 2004).

28. Shaykh Abdalḥamīd Kishk died in 1996.

29. Dale Eickelman and Jon Anderson, *New Media in the Muslim World: The Emerging Public Sphere,* 2nd ed. (Bloomington, IN: Indiana University Press, 2003); Gary Bunt, *Islam in the Digital Age: e-jihad, Online Fatwas and Cyber Islamic Environments* (London: Pluto Press, 2003).

30. The word *yadhūna* "slaughter" is evocative: it is the same word used of a sacrificed lamb on the festival of sacrifice, *ʿīd al-adḥa*.

31. Q2:195.

32. Q8:60.

33. The 10th form of the root *sh-h-d* would mean to seek, to consider something as "witnessing," the literal meaning of *shahīd*.

34. Al-Kumayt b. Zayd al-Asadi, *Dīwān al-Kumayt ibn Zayd al-Asadī*, ed. M.N. Tarīfī (Beirut: Dār al-Ṣādir, 2000). Thanks for assistance with this passage to Sinan Antoun and Everett Rowson.

35. Q2:195.

36. *Muslimīn thiqāt* likely meaning here "religious scholars."

37. Q8:49.

38. Pape, *Dying to Win.*

39. Cook, "Suicide Attacks or 'Martyrdom Operations'."

CHAPTER 11

With a Mighty Hand: Judaic Ethics of Exercising Power in Extraordinary Warfare

JONATHAN K. CRANE

The *Haggadah* Jews read at Passover retells the liberation of the Israeli people from Pharaoh's enslavement. The repeated refrain *"with a mighty hand, an outstretched arm and awesome might, signs and wonders"*[1] refers to God's intervening power during this struggle. The *Haggadah* links this phrase to the ten plagues that were intended to spark terror in the hearts of Egyptians in general, and Pharaoh in particular. This was a threat purported to generate a change in national policy: to release the people of Israel from the horrid conditions of slavery.[2]

However successful the liberation movement for the people of Israel may have been, the deliberate and supposedly legitimate use of violence over the Egyptians raises a formidable question. For this chapter's purposes, we conceive *"terrorism"* as *"the intentional use of, or threat to use violence, against civilians or against civilian targets, in order to attain political aims;"*[3] should we infer that Passover celebrates terrorism? But this assumption is not accurate, because it was *God* who enacted the plagues, and not *humans*. Hence, *if* any terror is to be inflicted, is it to be done *only* by divine hands, and *not* by human hands?

This would contrast sharply with what the broad history of humanity attests and recent years witness, because humans *do* bloody their hands in terror-inducing activity. Moreover, on the one hand, terrorism may have at one time been relegated to the murky edges of conflicts in today's world, but terrorism has become a central strategy and an essential tactical maneuver for some parties. On the other hand, just as the shape, scope, and damage of terrorism has changed through centuries of human warfare, so too have defenses against terrorism been adjusted to better protect certain populations. Therefore, studying terrorism from a Judaic perspective is particularly challenging, not only because assessing the Hebraic tradition is a complicated task, but also because "terrorism" potentially encompasses different activities, which is intertwined within the broader question of justifiable warfare. The aim of this chapter is to provide a clearer vision of these controversial issues by examining different angles of terrorism from a Judaic standpoint.

This chapter reviews Judaism's rich and variegated textual traditions in search of methodological approaches to this sensitive issue. It then turns to practices (hypotheticals) drawing loosely on contemporary events in the Middle East in an attempt to render Jewish principles relevant in addressing modern concerns regarding legal constraints in armed conflict.

MODERN JEWISH THOUGHT ON VIOLENCE AND WAR

Our method of analysis sidesteps two practices found in the vast majority of modern Jewish thought on violence and war in general. The first is the invocation of certain principles, and the second is the exploration of the categories of war.

In regards to the first practice, we attempt to avoid wrestling with Judaism's nuanced and sometimes contradictory legal and ethical positions on modern armed conflict. Modern authors often invoke general principles in support of one position or another, following an eclectic approach, which enables them to elide textual difficulties.[4] We argue that this practice of using principles to constrain or expand religiously sanctioned forms of exercising military power in defense against terrorism silences vast swaths of the textual tradition. A more sophisticated approach is needed to make sense of problematic texts and to argue how and why these positions do not, or ought not, shape national defense policies. Otherwise, the positions publicly advocated represent only a slim and biased portion of the Judaic tradition.

The second practice often found in modern Jewish scholarship on these topics is a full analysis of the traditional categories of war. Though it is a fascinating discussion and worthy of further exposition, it is not our central concern here. It may be helpful, however, to be familiar with the basic rubrics of Jewish thinking about warfare. The textual tradition explicitly mentions three categories of war: (1) *Milchemet reshut* are discretionary wars deployed for the aggrandizement of political leaders' reputation or geographic expansion of a polity; (2) *Milchemet mitzvah* are commanded wars like defensive warfare; (3) *Milchemet chovah* are obligatory wars and are also defensive in nature.[5] We also suggest that there is a fourth category of war which is not explicit in the texts: (4) *milchemet asur*—forbidden warfare, which ought not be fought. For this chapter's purposes, our discussion is of 'defensive warfare' tactics, which uniformly fall under the rubric of commanded wars (*milchemet mitzvah*).

Hence, this chapter probes texts, both legal and ethical in orientation, in search of a Judaic perspective on how best to defend against contemporary terrorism. After glancing at the paradigmatic biblical case of terrorism, we explore other methodological challenges in speaking about terrorism from within the Judaic tradition. We then contextualize the rest of the discussion in what is called extraordinary warfare, meaning the military struggle to defend against opponents employing illegitimate means such as terrorist tactics. The bulk of this chapter surveys two levels of defense in extraordinary war: strategic and tactical. Of the former, attention is given to proportionality, privileged spaces, and privacy. Of the latter, two levels (collective and individual) of punishment subdivide into permitted and prohibited tactics. After briefly highlighting shared themes with other religious traditions, the conclusion emphasizes Judaic ethical difficulties in thinking about and exercising power when defending against modern terrorism.

THE CONCEPT OF TERRORISM IN THE JUDAIC TRADITION

Let us first describe a Judaic perspective of events which closely resemble today's concept of terrorism, that is, deliberate human attacks against civilians. A biblical example—the story of Amalek and its attack on Israelites—will allow us to understand that there are important moral and spiritual components to be considered in conjunction with the physical and legal aspects of surviving terrorist attacks.

In the wilderness at Rephidim, the tribe of Amalek launched a surprise and unprovoked lethal attack against straggling and defenseless Israelites trudging through the desert.[6] The text does not express why Amalek attacked the Israelites, but we can surmise that it was done to assert political and military dominance by means of intimidation. Centuries later, the prophet Samuel enjoined King Saul to exact a penalty against the tribe of Amalek for this assault: *"Now go, attack Amalek, and proscribe all that belongs to [that people]. Spare no one, but kill alike men and women, infants and sucklings, oxen and sheep, camels and asses!"*[7] When Saul did not fully carry out the command, Samuel rebuked him. Samuel reminded Saul that as sovereign over Israel and on a mission enjoined by God, Saul's obedience to God took precedent over petty political concerns like people wanting war spoils.[8]

A superficial reading of these accounts suggests that Amalek conducted a terrorist attack. The Israelite response can be rightly understood as proper defense. But a lengthier look at the case is necessary, for it raises serious issues about terrorism and the conditions according to which it should be counteracted. A more elaborated argument would entail a discussion about the applicability of statutes of limitations, the rightful authority to exact punishment, the strategic and tactical extent of that punishment against people and nonhumans, the balancing of countervailing (political) interests, and the issue of accountability.

More important than those caveats are the *theological* implications of this case. Whereas Amalek attacks without cause and ought to be militarily defeated, the key point is that such defense is neither solely in human hands, nor is it done exclusively for human purposes. Though the Israelites do the actual battling against Amalek, their fight is part of God's war throughout the ages as it is God who will blot out the memory of Amalek from under heaven.[9] It is God's eternal task to eradicate humanity of Amalek (e.g., terrorism), just as it is humanity's responsibility to secure themselves against terrorists.[10]

METHODOLOGICAL ISSUES

The example cited above clearly shows that a comprehensive approach to terrorism from a Judaic perspective requires a combination of laws and ethical principles, all couched in a theological paradigm. There are difficulties in reading the Jewish textual traditions in light of today's armed conflicts and, as we have seen, superficial readings render misleading conclusions. Therefore, it is necessary to address some methodological concerns before attempting to examine practical hypotheticals of modern day conflicts from a Judaic perspective. In this chapter, we draw attention to four specific methodological challenges: (1) the general geopolitical and historic context, (2) Israel's existence, (3) internal extension, and (4) external extension. The meaning and boundaries of each of these issues is discussed as follows:

General Geopolitical Context

Contemporary Jewish scholars must contend with the fact that the bulk of Judaic literature comprising normative laws and ethical principles, especially on warfare, emerged in geopolitical worlds radically different from today.

For example, the notion of sovereignty is particularly troublesome. Though some materials originated in (or speak of) a Jewish monarchy sovereign in a circumscribed location, the majority of the texts were written in, to and for situations when Jews were not burdened with political sovereignty.[11] In regard to military conflict itself, Jewish governmental monopoly on violence as a form of conflict mediation was confined to periods of Jewish geopolitical dominance. Those periods, however, were quite a long time ago, ending with the Roman conquest of the Hasmonean Kingdom in 37 BCE. The strategies, tactics, technologies, and materials of warfare during those periods differ radically from our contemporary circumstances and, consequently, do not comport to modern legal instruments or sensibilities.

Although it would be easy to dismiss these texts for their ancientness and outmoded character, this would silence the Judaic tradition that has nonetheless survived innumerable conflicts and has much to say about conflict mediation generally. So, despite these historical differences between the texts' times and today, reading ancient texts *as if* they and we exist in the same geopolitical context helps to produce a longitudinal and cohesive conversation in which we can participate.

Israel's Existence

On the other hand, importing ancient legal and ethical texts as unimpeachable rulings for modern warfare begs the question especially in regard to Israel. Some modern scholars equate modern Israeli popularly elected leadership to the ancient divinely appointed kings or to the *Sanhedrin,* a court of rabbis elected by their peers. In so doing, they render modern Israeli governments accountable to ancient *halakhah*—Jewish law. [12] Others apply *halakhah* directly to Israel generally without questioning if this comports with Israel's legal self-conception.[13]

Israel makes our conversation problematic to the extent that it influences Jewish self-perception. This, because some Jews (and gentiles as well) think that the state's exercise of power is synonymous with the exercise of Judaism. This fallacy, however, ignores the fact that Israel does not see itself bound to the Judaic tradition. In fact, it functions as most other nation-states and should be understood as such, and not as a Jewish polity incomparable to others.[14] What Israel does or does not do militarily in defense against terrorism, be it from Jews or gentiles, has little bearing on or reflection of Judaic textual traditions or normative Judaic sensibilities.[15]

Because the government, judiciary, military, and even nongovernmental organizations all understand Israel to function independent of *halakhah,* we cannot conclude that Israeli governmental policy or military behavior is tantamount to Judaism. So, as to avoid ambivalence, apologetics, or criticism of official IDF (Israeli Defense Force) policies and practices, and because this chapter seeks a *Judaic* perspective on terrorism, we bracket them out here so as to focus on the Judaic tradition.

Internal Extension of *Halakhah*

A third methodological concern is internal to *halakhah* itself. Is it reasonable to elaborate internal analogies in order to apply the Judaic tradition to today's issues? To what extent can laws explicitly discussing actions in one arena be applied to actions in another? More specifically, are *all* rules pertaining to an individual automatically applicable to the collective (and vice versa)?[16] As a matter of principle, a sophisticated analysis of Judaic laws and ethics goes to great length to discuss them according to their arenas without extending them to others. There are, however, exceptional cases in which concepts, laws, and procedures can be instructive by analogy. In these instances, a sophisticated approach applies such analogies only to comparable arenas in which they are found.

External Extension of *Halakhah*

How does *halakhah,* a mandatory legal system enjoined upon Jews, apply to gentiles? Certainly, many laws on armed conflict speak of Jews warring against gentiles. But what of laws about Jews in conflict with fellow Jews—can these be applied to gentiles? Conversely, to what degree is it reasonable to ask or require a gentile to comport with Jewish law?

A possible solution is that Jewish perspectives about warring with gentiles should be confined only to those laws explicitly mentioning gentiles. Such an approach unnecessarily curtails the breadth and depth of Jewish legal and ethical thinking about war and terrorism. On the other hand, inasmuch as *halakhah* and corollary ethical principles enable human beings to be ever more holy as God is holy, perhaps it is reasonable to extend Jewish law and ethics to gentiles. This theological argument, however, can be easily undermined by claims of paternalism and colonialism, particularly because gentiles are not expected to uphold the entirety of the *halakhic* system.[17] This concern comes to the fore especially on issues of personal status (i.e., birth, conversion, marriage, and burial).

However, on issues of war and peace, and to the degree that the Judaic tradition conceives all humanity—Jews and gentiles alike—obliged to uphold at least general moral standards, the issue of external extension does not require curtailing our study only to those texts explicitly mentioning gentiles. Instead, because terrorism is a mode of conflict *prosecution* that any group or individual, Jewish or gentile, can employ, this external challenge is put aside so as to consider the broadest scope of Jewish thinking on these issues. Hence, although we acknowledge there is a great amount of disagreement on the applicability of *halakhah* to gentiles, this chapter is based on the assumption that the Jewish tradition knows no general boundaries in this respect on this issue.

All the arguments expressed above make clear that this is a theoretical exercise. It is *hypothetical,* inasmuch Jewish law is not currently binding upon any military in the world today. What would a military force do in the face of terrorism *if* indeed it were bound by Jewish textual traditions? It is to this question we now turn.

CONCEPT OF EXTRAORDINARY WARFARE FROM A JUDAIC VIEWPOINT

For all intents and purposes, the following discussion assumes *hora'at sha'ah*—a state of emergency—like war. In regard to warfare generally, the Jewish textual tradition offers a broad array of material discussing *jus ad bellum* as well as *jus in bello* issues. In other words, the tradition constructs standards that must be met *prior* to engaging in war with rightful opponents, and certain strategies and tactics are proscribed and others permitted *during* the execution of different categories of war. An important restriction exists here. This chapter's concern is not *normal* warfare but *extraordinary* warfare. Extraordinary warfare is for our purposes the military struggle to defend against opponents employing illegitimate means such as terrorist tactics.

This premise has critical theoretical and practical consequences. Major assumptions fall by the wayside in extraordinary warfare. For instance, *who* combatants are is blurred. In earlier eras, differentiating military personnel from noncombatants could be done with a quick glance at an individual's garb. Today, even invasive scans cannot pinpoint precisely who considers him- or herself militarily involved in a conflict. Similarly, *how* people fight has also changed. Prior rules and guidelines for strategies and tactics no longer adequately describe or predict contemporary violent conflict behavior. Moreover, though the reasons *why* people take on certain risks, especially lethal ones, are not all new, the prevalence of certain rationales, like religious fundamentalisms and hyper-nationalisms, marks a different tenor in modern warfare than found previously.

Altogether, these novelties challenge whether traditional Jewish legal and ethical texts on warfare can and should be applied, by analogy or by extension, to contemporary warfare. How does the Judaic tradition contend with *extraordinary* warfare? The Book of Maccabees tells us. When Mattathias and his friends learn that coreligionists are being slaughtered by gentiles because they refuse to fight on the Sabbath, they cry: *"If we all do as our kindred have done and refuse to fight with the gentiles for our lives and for our ordinances, they will quickly destroy us from the earth."* The group quickly concludes: *"Let us fight against anyone who comes to attack us on the Sabbath day; let us not die as our kindred died in their hiding places."*[18] Whereas the bible describes the community making this policy decision, Josephus, the early historian of Jews, shifts the emphasis onto the figure of Mattathias himself.[19]

Prior to this attack, the rule was that no Jew could carry a weapon on the Sabbath, which obviously rendered the Jewish community militarily vulnerable at least one day a week. This policy reflects early rabbinic opinion that one's business travels and a community's military campaign (also requiring travel) must be planned so as to protect the Sabbath.[20] Like boats at sea, wars already begun need not stop for Shabbat; yet normal wars cannot begin on Shabbat.

The significance, therefore, of the Macabbees narrative lies on the textual acknowledgment of the alteration of the old rules of warfare. The narrative highlights conflicting critical values: the rule of (old) law on the one side and the needs of an immediate emergency situation on the other. What we learn is that the Judaic tradition has considered the case that *in certain circumstances even the rules of warfare may be bent or abandoned so as to preserve the public body.*[21]

Not only can the rules of war be changed, those very innovations emerge from a deliberative and inclusive process instead of dictatorial authority. In those times, people could consider their options and discuss them with each other. But the nature of extraordinary national emergencies, ancient and modern alike, may preclude meaningful and inclusive deliberation. Hence, Jewish sages throughout the centuries declare that defensive wars are *milchemet mitzvah* (commanded wars), and that Jewish leaders have the prerogative to make unilateral decisions on behalf of the community.[22]

Now we know that laws of warfare *may* be bent in order to best defend the community from belligerent opponents. But, who is a *legitimate* military opponent? The use of lethal force is not sufficient to constitute a combatant.[23] A distinction should be made between legal and illegal combatants. A *legal combatant* is one who rightfully employs lethal or injurious force, like in a normal war setting. An *illegal combatant* is one who unrightfully uses lethal or injurious force regardless of context. This definition differentiates someone using force in legitimate self-defense from a suicide bomber, i.e., a terrorist. Though the Judaic tradition grants some flexibility when dealing with illegal attackers *in principle,* there are also *real* boundaries of what is and is not acceptable defense.

STRATEGIC PRINCIPLES

The strategic level addresses general guiding principles that shape the motive, nature, and scope of specific actions. The principles assist leaders in making decisions to the degree principles demarcate boundaries of appropriate behavior outside of which actions are considered illegal or immoral or both. Regarding extraordinary warfare, the Judaic tradition raises three general principles of concern: *proportionality, privileged spaces,* and *privacy.* Each of these principles hones the development of specific tactics that will be discussed below.

Proportionality

Judaism acknowledges the principle of proportionality, at least in the realm of self-defense.[24] The central tenet of the principle of proportionality is inevitability. An unintended result from a particular maneuver, *davar she'eino mitkaven,* is permitted as long as that result is *not* inevitable.[25] If, however, that double-effect will necessarily ensue, and if that double-effect is itself a forbidden act, then the initiating maneuver itself is prohibited.[26] This principle is important and has many potential applications.[27]

Related to proportionality is the rationale of vengeance or retribution, that is, reactive defense. The vast majority of Jewish scholars acknowledge that defensive wars are by definition commanded wars (*milchemet mitzvah*), and that commanded warfare is the only operable legal category of warfare today.[28] This is generally so today inasmuch as the Nuremburg judgments consider aggressive war to violate international law and defensive war does not. The Jewish tradition explicitly addresses the question of permissible defense, though it provides different—even contradictory—ways with respect to the level of harm that can be inflicted.[29]

A last comment should be made about preemptive defensive wars. Not all defensive wars are technically reactive to an initial attack. The Jewish tradition does permit anticipating an attack and preemptively disarming an imminent threat.[30] Once again, the proportionality principle is relevant. Anticipatory defensive attacks *must be only as intrusive as is necessary* to defuse an imminent threat. Excessive force is prohibited even in the face of extraordinary situations.[31] Disproportionate defense, whether reactive or proactive, is overwhelmingly discouraged within the textual tradition.

Privileged Spaces

Turning to the battlefield itself, the Torah recognizes that warfare occurs in both rural and urban settings. But, are there privileged spaces within these combat zones? Are there locations in which fighting must not happen? In this respect, the tradition provides important insights with respect to the immunity of criminal prosecution and punishment in religious shrines, and the invulnerability of criminals in shelter cities.

Are religious shrines protected places? The trajectory of biblical and rabbinic thinking on this matter arcs from the affirmative to the negative. From as early as the revelation at Mount Sinai, altars offer asylum for anyone but willful criminals.[32] Someone who inadvertently killed another could ostensibly exit the jurisdiction of the profane world by entering an altar and touching it.[33] Finding sanctuary in an altar, known as 'grasping the horns of the altar' (*yechazek b'karnot hamizbeach*), was a protection upheld as late as King David. His son, Solomon, however, recognized this institution's potential threat to civil authority, and shifted the jurisdiction of the profane world to reach even to the altar to pursue criminals as well as political dissidents.[34] When Solomon built the Temple, he ruled that only priests could enter the innermost shrines. Laymen, especially criminals of any sort, could not find sanctuary there.[35] By the Second Temple period, the idea of the shrine offering asylum no longer appeals because it renders any refugee subject to the death penalty.[36] A third century *halakhic midrash* reiterates the biblical rule that willful criminals can find no sanctuary at the altar.[37] And the Talmud a few centuries later asserts that even priests guilty of crimes cannot find protection within the Temple.[38] It follows from this historical arc that religious institutions today do not offer special protection for people, whether priest or layperson, legal combatant, or terrorist.

Yet the idea of protected locations was generally not obliterated. The Torah commands the establishment of cities of refuge (*'arei miklat*—asylum cities) to which certain classes of criminals can flee and be protected from punishment.[39] Blood redeemers, those permitted by law to avenge a wrongful death, are not allowed into these cities to pursue guilty criminals. Instead, criminals can live freely within the confines of these cities; moreover, they should be provided means of livelihood while there.[40] If criminals exit these cities within a particular time period they are no longer protected and can be avenged by blood redeemers.[41] Not every criminal is afforded enduring protection within these cities. Only those who *inadvertently* killed someone may obtain such asylum.[42]

Historically, the institutionalization of asylum cities was well entrenched by the First Temple period. Later biblical texts about Israel's restoration (like Ezekiel), however, do not mention cities of refuge, possibly because the institution of blood redeemers was by then virtually eliminated and made asylum itself obsolete. Though the *idea* of privileged location persists within the Judaic textual tradition, the historical *practice* of this institution faded.[43] Whereas shrines in particular and cities in general no longer afford protection during wartime, the only space possibly endowed now with *sancta contagion* is a hospital, although this may also be debatable.

Privacy

Another dimension related to privileged spaces is privileged information. The Jewish tradition frames this topic in the form of personal privacy. The idea of personal privacy and the attitude that privacy ought to be protected are, at least biblically, ancient, and universally applicable. This is well symbolized in the story of Noah's nakedness and his reaction to the disrespectful attitude shown by his son Ham.[44] Just as information regarding the body is privileged information, so too are the happenings in a private home.[45] Privacy of home life enjoys *a priori* protection and can be compromised only by the consent of the individuals whose privacy would be affected. In regard to information outside the bounds of a home, letters may not be read without permission, and even accidentally opening letters is considered criminal.[46]

In brief, private information is privileged information and is not available for public scrutiny, unless and only if the persons involved give their consent. Extrapolating from these texts, it is possible to say that public policies circumscribing civil liberties of privacy (like wire-tapping) are possible only to the degree they are explicitly endorsed by the affected public themselves.

A final caveat is necessary. These strategic principles of proportionality, privileged spaces and privacy, offer guidance for mediating violent conflicts. They do not, however, address the legality or morality of specific actions. Their purpose is to provide an overarching moral and legal framework within which political and military leaders can assess which maneuvers best reflect Judaic values. Given these guidelines, it is therefore incumbent upon modern leaders to choose the most efficacious tactics appropriate for particular conflicts. It is to these particulars we now turn.

PRACTICAL HYPOTHETICALS: COLLECTIVE AND INDIVIDUAL PUNISHMENTS

Two levels of tactical responses to contemporary armed conflict are considered here. On the level of *collective punishment,* the general issue relates to holding responsible a community as a whole for individual terrorists' actions. Such tactics deliberately involve people who are not terrorists, and property that does not belong to the wrongdoers themselves. In this respect, several questions become relevant: what can Judaism say about detaining family members of terrorists, destroying property associated with terrorists, and destroying livelihoods of communities surrounding terrorists? Next, at the level of *individual punishment,* the focus is on the terrorist: what can Judaism say about interrogation, torture, and the value of information gathered thereby?

Collective Punishment: Individual Versus Collective Responsibility

Is it possible to hold a community responsible for some individual's—terrorist—crime? Some contemporary scholars endorse this notion,[47] relying on interpretations of the story of Simeon and Levi killing inhabitants of Shechem in retribution for the rape of their sister Dinah.[48] Perhaps they reach this conclusion from a premodern assumption that the acts of an individual can be attributed to the whole community or nation.[49] On the other hand, a different interpretation emphasizes pursuing communal honor after someone has been shamed.[50]

Both approaches nonetheless impose the guilt of an individual criminal upon the collective. Though both rationales emerge from *aggadic,* or literary, material and not *halakhic* or legal material and we may be tempted to disregard their legal merit altogether, we cannot completely ignore the fact that they are employed by contemporary scholars to justify *intentional* collateral damage. The issue at hand is less the material these arguments depend on, and more the legal principle of punishing people for a crime they did not commit.[51] To illustrate, idolatry is a biblically based capital crime for which a whole community and its environs may be punished.[52] Some sages say that collective punishment is justified because *some* people enticed *others* to idolatry, while others wonder whether this truly means *every* person in the suspect town deserves such punishment.[53] Either way, it would be difficult to argue that the Judaic textual tradition prohibits collective punishment for an individual's crimes.

Contrast this with a countervailing biblical principle that each person individually accrues legal and ethical culpability regardless of what others in a community or family have done. For example, Abraham challenges God's plan to destroy Sodom by holding God accountable to the standards of justice God seeks in humanity.[54] Whereas here the tradition acknowledges the *theoretical* principle of collective punishment with the assumption that God is the only one who may enact it, its *practical* application may be applied only upon a collection of guilty persons. Even God must preserve the innocent from amongst the guilty. This principle of individualized punishment is clearly established in the tradition.[55] From this, it is unreasonable to punish lethally family members for the crimes of one member.

On the other hand, the tradition finds it reasonable to consider the family accountable for the moral upbringing of that wayward member.[56] This punishment, however, is to be nonlethal so as to teach a lesson to the erring individual, to the criminal's family members, as well as to surrounding neighbors. Obviously this does not mean that arbitrary or punitive detention or punishment is obligatory; it merely establishes permission for this particular tactical maneuver. Rigorous calculation may show that nonlethal collective punishment is neither the most effective nor efficient response to deterring or defending against terrorists.

As is obvious, the tradition is divided in respect to holding a community accountable for an individual's offense. Disparate interpretations preclude a unified view on this point, giving space for competing possibilities. A noncontroversial conclusion, nonetheless, is plausible: holding a family morally responsible for an individual's action, albeit a restricted yet potentially useful tactic, is morally and legally reasonable.

Collective Punishment: Destroying Property

A different tactic of collective punishment—destroying the homes and property of terrorists—may prove less effective against extant terrorists than for deterring others from choosing to become terrorists themselves. Once again, there is no explicit provision in regard to this tactic. Hence, in order to answer whether it is valid to destroy someone's property from the Judaic perspective, it is necessary to rely on analogies that leave considerable room for disagreement.

For instance, as we have discussed above, it is reasonable to destroy belongings of a whole family of an idolater regardless whether the family supported the idolater in any meaningful way. Idolatry is identified and evaluated from the assumption of God's monopoly to determine what proper or improper worship is. Nevertheless, this line of argumentation is problematic because it assumes that a terrorist is tantamount to an idolater, which is not necessarily true.

On the other hand, there is also great difficulty with the fact that terrorism can be conceived of as a version of conflict *prosecution,* alongside those modes that have developed and been accepted by the vast majority of the geopolitical world as 'normal' versions of warfare. Because there is no monopoly on how to fight conflicts, labeling one form of conflict prosecution, or another as a perversion does little to mediate the conflict itself; instead, it adds emotional and moral fuel to the fire.

To avoid this troublesome argument, a more useful analogy for modern terrorists is the *rodef*—a criminal with lethal intent actively pursuing an intended victim. The trajectory of the textual tradition asserts that Jews are not merely permitted but legally obliged to intervene and prevent a *rodef* from lethally attacking an intended victim.[57] In this sense, there are several ways to conceive the destruction of the terrorist's property as a legitimate action. For instance, if oneself is being pursued, one is permitted to destroy the pursuer's property but not others' so as to prevent the impending lethal attack.[58] Greater leniency is provided for an intervener attempting to save the pursued.[59] What matters is that interveners should not be too concerned about property when their primary motive is to save an intended victim's life—this is the principle of *pikuach nefesh.*[60]

Nevertheless, though the category of *rodef* correlates better to contemporary terrorists than idolaters, it is not a perfect fit. One weakness is that the discussion of personally defending against or of intervening to prevent *rodfim* from actualizing their lethal attack on intended victims exists primarily in the realm of *personal* self-defense and *personal* intervention. It may be unreasonable, therefore, to extend this analogy to undergird *national* defense policies. On the other hand, at the national level, a sovereign has the right to confiscate and destroy private property during wartime.[61] The sovereign is granted dispensation not to abide by the general principle of not destroying someone else's property to save one's own or another's life. Just as this applies to confiscating Jewish property, all the more so is it reasonable to conclude that the sovereign's entitlement to destroy an opponent's property during wartime is indisputable.[62]

Collective Punishment: Destroying Means of Livelihood

This leads directly to a third form of collective punishment, the destruction of livelihood. The general principle here is the prohibition known as *bal tashchit*—the proscription of wanton destruction.[63] Whoever does engage in such tactics transgresses the command not to destroy.[64] For Maimonides, at least, destroying either homes *or* property necessary for sustenance is prohibited. However, he submits that the punishment from biblically sanctioned lashings should be left to the discretion of a rabbinic court. This shift suggests that, while religiously damned before the fact (*l'hatchilah*), this transgression may be politically palatable afterwards (*b'diyavad*) in the eyes of a human court. We can derive from this teaching that there is an overall prohibition of denying civilians, even those in an opponent's camp, access to sustenance and sustaining livelihoods. This prohibition holds only as long as the opponents agree to *all* the conditions offered.[65]

This tactic is problematic. It appears to be a method to prevent possible future attacks upon one's own citizenry, a special type of anticipatory defense against *possible* danger. This is *preventive* defense, as distinct from *preemptive* defense against *probable* and impending danger. This particular tactic is not a legitimate form of defense against attacks already suffered because it functions as a form of retributive defense that is itself prohibited. As Dorff[66] observes, this permission countenances the possibility of not distinguishing between combatants and noncombatants which is also stridently condemned.

To complicate the situation, the above cases of collective punishment assume terrorists act as emissaries for one family, group, community, or nation. In *halakhah,* the sending out of an emissary as one's representatives called *shelichut.* According to the Talmudic principle *ein shaliach l'davar aveirah,* a Jewish emissary is culpable for the crime committed whereas a principal agent (the one who sent that person) is not.[67] Extending this principle to our case, however, assumes that "a gentile (unlike a Jew) can serve as a proxy for evildoing."[68] And it also assumes that the principals supporting a criminal emissary are culpable as well for that individual's crime. These statements are hotly contested among contemporary scholars, for a gentile emissary may not have the legal status of *shelichut* at all and therefore acts as a free agent, and hence no one else should be held accountable for a terrorist's actions.

Individual Punishment: Interrogation

In regard to individual punishment, apprehending an individual terrorist may not adequately defend a population from other terrorists' activity. Yet, a captured individual may be a fount of information about imminent and future attacks by others. Accessing this information provokes three questions: (1) what can Judaism say about interrogation of criminals generally, (2) to what degree are torture techniques permitted, and (3) what is the value of the intelligence once it is divulged?

The Talmud delineates specific rules about what constitutes credible information in a court case and how to go about acquiring that information from witnesses.[69] Extracting confessions for normal court procedures may be done by using mild physical discomfort such as binding and stocks.[70]

These normal juridical procedures may not be sufficiently timely or efficient for cases of terrorism. If we use the analogous category of *mosrim*—informers bent on endangering Jews—we may find *halakhic* precedence more suitable for our case of a captured terrorist.

As a side note, we should be aware that *mosrim* refers to *Jews* informing on fellow Jews to gentiles, and not about *gentiles* informing against Jews or fellow gentiles. Medieval emergency courts of selectmen (*berurei averot*) developed special procedures to gather evidence and testimony regarding *mosrim*.[71] Nonlethal methods were preferred to dismantle the threat posed by a *moser*, like denunciation or banishment, general bans, and tattoos.[72] These nontraditional investigative measures could be employed only as long as these courts seek the truth and prevent damage.[73]

However, not all medieval sages support these nonlethal and noninjurious methods of protecting Jews against informants. For instance, Maimonides understands killing a *moser* before that person informs to be a religious obligation.[74] This religious duty and merit devolve onto *individuals,* not courts or militaries. He hereby condones the practice of individual Jews taking the law into their own hands. Moreover, if a *moser* is captured after already divulging potentially damaging information against Jews to others, it is, in Maimonides' opinion, prohibited to lethally injure that individual unless and until it is proven *in court* that that person indeed informed. Also, Maimonides records that some Jewish communities had the practice of extraditing their informants to gentile courts for punishments.[75]

In addition to these nonlethal physical interrogatory methods, courts also employed deception to extract information.[76] Deceitful interrogation, however, risks transgressing the biblical prohibition of putting a stumbling block before the blind.[77] Deception may also lead to "stealing the good sense" of another (*genevat da'at*), which is also prohibited.[78] On the other hand, it may be necessary to be "crafty with the crafty" and engage in deceitful tactics so as to protect Jews. For example, if one draws legal implications from the narrative of the Book of Esther, it is possible to say that national survival warrants desperate measures of deception.[79] Legally, it is permissible to use deceit entrap someone suspected of engaging in or enticing others to engage in illegal and/or immoral activity (like idolatry).[80]

Entrapment, for Maimonides, might be too late: like with *mosrim,* he would rather have people use lethal intervention preemptively to stop a *mesit* (an enticer to idolatry) from urging others toward transgressive behavior.[81] But he does not render such lethal preemptive intervention a religious obligation (*mitzvah*); he merely says this tactic is legally permissible—for courts and not for individuals. Nor does he say that such tactics are the most effective or efficient means of protecting a society.

Individual Punishment: Torture

Though some nonlethal and deceptive methods of extracting information from dangerous people are permitted, the question of employing torture (deliberately injurious tactics) is more problematic.[82]

Torture techniques to extract intelligence might be justified by the concept of *rodef,* the pursuer with lethal intent, introduced earlier. It is legally permissible to prevent a pursuer from engaging in unlawful behavior by using lethal force to stop him.[83] Maimonides renders this preemptive intervention obligatory.[84] The significance of this teaching is that Jews do not need to wait for courts to intervene to save someone's life. Individual agency is paramount for protecting someone else's life. Moreover, one who *can* intervene and does not, transgresses the biblical command not to stand idly on the blood of your neighbor.[85]

We should note, however, that not every person has the capacity to intervene. There may be some who are exempt from this responsibility because they lack the skills necessary to intervene successfully. Hence, Maimonides stops short of saying that *all* Israelites are absolutely religiously obliged to preemptively kill *rodfim in every case* when other tactics may be (more) effective and efficient.[86]

Maimonides permits both (a) deliberately (and significant) injurious intervention to save a life from a *rodef already* on the attack and (b) deliberately injurious intervention *prior* to a criminal actualizing a lethal attack.[87] Even though an individual's criminal thoughts are sufficient grounds to justify deliberately injurious intervention, Maimonides nonetheless distances himself from saying that any and every mode of deliberately injurious intervention is justifiable. That is, saving a victim from a criminal's intention is justified in principle, but one must be careful that one's own intervention is not egregious or sloppy.

Consonant with the strategic principle of proportionality discussed above, unnecessarily brutal intervention is not merely damnable, according to Maimonides, but is itself a capital crime according to the Talmud.[88] Differentiating unreasonably injurious intervention from reasonably injurious intervention is critical, as it distinguishes between those who uphold the law and those who transgress it. A sixteenth century law code concludes: should less-injurious methods suffice to prevent a *rodef* from actualizing intended harm, not only are those methods preferred but also anyone using more force is culpable for unnecessary aggression.[89]

Returning to the issue of torture itself, we must ask the question if the category of *din rodef*—laws of intervention to protect against a lethal attack—justifies imposing deliberately injurious interrogatory techniques on modern terrorists. Though answering in the affirmative may be tempting given the above discussion, this conclusion is not tenable for several reasons. A *rodef* is one person pursuing another, and that victim is identifiable and thus known. Modern terrorists, though, rarely intend to attack just one individual, and, because of terrorists' clandestine strategies, hardly ever are the intended victims identifiable either prior to or even during an attack. More importantly, the laws of intervention speak in terms of single citizens acting extrajudiciously—of "taking the law into their own hands" outside the court system, military tribunal, or police investigation. Though the principle of employing deliberately injurious intervention is permissible for *individuals* in limited circumstances, these laws do not permit *governments* (or their instrumentalities) to use these same tactics. (Unless, that is, one thinks it reasonable to extend laws pertaining to individuals to also shape national policies—a step that is legally, philosophically, and ethically questionable.)

But surely defending a population from criminal activity is the duty and prerogative of a government and its instrumentalities. It appears, therefore, the Judaic tradition can countenance the use of deception and mild physical pressure to extract information from an individual terrorist.[90] Whether the police, military, or judicial court, governmental instruments are permitted or enjoined to use such nonlethal methods, they are to do so with great humility and discretion.[91] Even (gentile) criminals are due basic respect; deliberately inflicting them undue suffering compromises not only their basic humanness, but also undermines the reputation of the Judaic tradition generally.[92] Hence, speaking on behalf of modern Jewry, contemporary rabbinic associations across the spectrum of Judaism condemn deliberately injurious interrogation—or torture.[93]

Individual Punishment: Worth of Intelligence from Torture

Even if someone or a court obtains information from a terrorist in captivity, what is the value of that data? In capital cases like terrorism, self-incrimination, even when given voluntarily, is forbidden and must be disregarded. This is based on the biblical injunction *"not to join hands with the guilty to act as a malicious witness."*[94] The sages of the

Talmud made this a principle. If one admits to acceding to an act deserving the death penalty, one is considered wicked (*rasha*) and thus disqualified as acting as a witness. Furthermore, because each person is considered a relative to oneself, no one can engage in self-incrimination.[95] Therefore, whatever information a terrorist divulges cannot be used against that same individual.[96]

But what of that individual's information generally—is *any* of it credible, even if it does not implicate that very person? Maimonides delineates ten classes of people who are not legally competent to offer testimony, one of which is the wicked (*harasha'im*).[97] The wicked are those who willfully engage in transgressive behaviors like criminal activity.[98] That terrorists and their collaborators willfully engage in transgressive behavior disqualifies whatever testimony they might provide: their information is legally vacuous. For those who may be coerced into terrorist activity, their information does contain legal merit. Despite the nonlegal status of such data, information extracted from willful terrorists may be the only source available to curtail or prevent life-endangering attacks and therefore should be taken seriously—albeit with a grain of salt.

CONCLUDING THOUGHTS AND RELIGIOUS PARALLELS

This survey of methodological, strategic, and tactical issues in the Judaic tradition resonates with other religious (Christian and Islamic) traditions' approaches to dealing with modern terrorism. For example, the principle of discrimination appears common. Militaries are obliged to differentiate true combatants from civilians. The latter's protection is to be zealously guarded. Unnecessarily harming civilians incurs religious disdain or damnation as well as legal punishment. Another commonality is proportionality. Tactics employed to defend a polity from external aggression are to be reasonably measured so as only to dismantle the threat. Because excessive response is prohibited— a position clearly articulated in the Judaic tradition—cathartic retribution is therefore proscribed. Should vengeance be appropriate, it is only God's to manifest, not humanity's.[99] The traditions also share the principle that the only kind of warfare potentially religiously justifiable in the modern world is a defensive war. Aggressive warfare for personal or geopolitical gain is prohibited, at least according to the trajectory of the Judaic tradition. Anticipatory defense is permitted only in certain circumstances.

There remain, of course, issues and themes needing greater clarity. For example, deciding which tactics constitute preventive detention is complex. Certainly the argument to preventively detain proven criminals is reasonable, as precedent is found both in the detention of the mentally insane who endanger themselves and/or others and in the detention of recidivist sexual offenders. In a related fashion, is quarantining a famously bellicose population to a village, geological area, or in a prison, all considered the same according to religious traditions? If it is politically or practically impossible to extract people with criminal intent from a larger population, what are the limits of permissible collective detention?

Timing is another critical issue. The Jewish legal tradition often speaks in terms of *l'hatchilah*—before the fact, and *b'diyavad*—after the fact, when discussing limits to behavior. As an illustration, the tradition delineates what, from the outset, are the limits of interrogation. If an individual (already convicted of having intent to murder) dies during interrogation, the tradition says that, though that person's death is morally damnable, those causing that person's death are not punishable by a judiciary. This does *not* mean that killing proven criminals is condoned by the Judaic tradition. On the contrary, it means that the tradition abhors unnecessary physical force in defense of a community's welfare. (Moreover, the textual tradition has all but made capital punishment a null option; no Jewish court, including Israeli courts, may put someone to death.) Clarifying *jus in bello* prior restraints and subsequent consequences of breaches of those laws may manifest greater conformity to the ROE (rules of engagement) endorsed by law-promoting and law-abiding governments and their militaries.

A third area deserving further attention is prevention. Terrorists, like all other human beings, respond to stimuli. There may be a matrix of stimuli that, in varying degrees and circumstances, constitute sufficient cause for some people to choose terrorist behavior to mediate perceived and real conflicts instead of other (less violent) methods. Some sample causes include socioeconomic grievances, geopolitical impotence, religious fervor, and ultranationalism. Identifying the causes for the terrorism, a community suffers may help governments devise policies that prevent people from practising terrorist tactics. For example, investing in communities economically and politically may assuage grievances and dissuade people from pursuing terrorist behavior. Attending to the causes of terrorism in a preventive manner may relieve a government of resorting primarily to military defense mechanisms, mechanisms that have proven to be economically, physically, morally, and emotionally costly. Preventive diplomatic defense, as is biblically enjoined, may be the most effective means of eradicating terrorism from the outset and in the end.

As indicated earlier, it is possible to avoid these texts and issues altogether by invoking certain general principles that undergird one's position in favor of or against particular strategies or tactics. But this practice unnecessarily silences the rich Judaic textual tradition that reflects upon the real struggles and conflicts Jews have faced throughout their history. In order to honor the past and its textual legacy, it is necessary for us to engage these texts, however much we may find them upsetting to our modern sensibilities in this regard.

It is possible, however, to use the textual tradition and its principles in ways that are malignant. Often, Jews bent on using the textual tradition for lethal personal or political purposes invoke principles as dogma. Two cases in the 1990s are particularly telling illustrations of how dogmatic readings of the textual tradition endanger innocents. In 1994, Baruch Goldstein, a physician by training, gunned down twenty-nine Muslims praying in a mosque in Hebron before he was killed by Muslim interveners. Despite general and overwhelming condemnation from Jews around the world about this unprovoked attack on unarmed civilians, a few rabbis and lay leaders in Israel and North America praised Goldstein's murderous action and death as an act of martyrdom (*kiddush hashem*). The second, feeding off the virulent tenor of the first, was the assassination of then Israeli Prime Minister Yitzhak Rabin by Yigal Amir in 1995. In his defense hearings, Amir admitted that he was merely following *din rodef*—of the obligation to intervene on behalf of an intended victim being pursued by a criminal with lethal intent. That is, Amir considered Rabin a *rodef*—a position publicly proffered by rabbis during the Oslo negotiations —and his was a religiously mandated duty to intervene lethally.[100] What Amir failed to do was consider the overwhelming breadth and depth of the tradition's positions regarding those perceived as *rodfim:* *if* intervention is truly necessary, *nonlethal* intervention is the first and laudable course of action (and a broad range of nonlethal actions are put forward); only as an absolute *last resort* should lethal intervention be considered. That Goldstein and Amir "took the law into their own hands" highlights the danger of both relying upon and permitting civilian extrajudicial conflict resolution. Obviously, and it need not be expanded upon: such myopic abuse of the textual tradition is not exclusive to the Jewish tradition; extremists and literalists imposing their blinkered readings of religious texts are found in virtually every community.

For these reasons, wrestling with the broad Judaic textual tradition is especially important when exercising (military) power. With mighty hands comes great(er) responsibility to understand one's own legal and moral foundations. For Jews, the Jewish textual tradition offers a solid and yet complex grounding, particularly in regard to warfare. The tradition entails a rich array of laws and principles, some of which can be treated as *jus cogens*—laws unabrogable under any circumstances, yet most of which function in the realm of realism and can be altered only under limited conditions. It is incumbent upon Jews and Jewish polities to appreciate that permission to employ a particular tactic does not automatically render it obligatory, effective or efficient. If anything this survey has shown, it is that the Judaic tradition expresses anxiety about exercising military power. On the whole, the tradition is loath to advocate or require action compromising the dignity of an agent, victim, bystander, and God. Because the overall thrust of the Judaic tradition is toward preserving life, should an emergency arise, bending the ROE in extraordinary warfare is permissible as long as it is within the bounds of maintaining the dignity of all—including enemy combatants. Such limits to human agency are critical reminders that humans are not, and ought not act like, God. The tradition is clear: when forced to defend, do so only in a manner that is appropriate for mighty *human* hands.

NOTES

BT, Babylonian Talmud; CCAR, Central Conference of American Rabbis (Reform); ISC, Israeli Supreme Court; MT, Mishneh Torah, by Maimonides; SA, Shulkhan Arukh, by Karo; RA, Rabbinical Assembly (Conservative); RCA, Rabbinical Council of America (Orthodox); RHR, Rabbis for Human Rights; RRA, Reconstructionists Rabbinical Association; YT, Jerusalem Talmud.

1. Deuteronomy 26:8.
2. Exodus 3:19–20; see Rashi, Ramban, and Ralbag, ad loc.
3. Boaz Ganor, "Defining Terrorism: Is One Man's Terrorist Another Man's Freedom Fighter?" 2004 (accessed at http://www.ict.org.il/articles/define.htm, June 30, 2005).
4. This relativistic practice, demonstrated here by contemporary rabbinic association resolutions, facilitates avoiding positions found in the normative textual tradition that may be considered morally, intellectually, or politically questionable or dangerous in today's milieu. For example, there are some principles which obviously hinder the use of some forms of violence: The principle *betzelem elohim*, that all are created in the image of God, is invoked to render (many forms of) violence morally reprehensible and thus to be avoided—like torture (CCAR 2005; RHR 2005; RRA 2005); The principle to love one's neighbor (*ahavtah l're'echa camochah*) can also be invoked to limit violence (RCA 2005); and the value of preserving self-esteem (*marchivin da'ato*) can hold sway against arguments supporting collective punishment like home demolitions (CCAR 2004). Conversely, other principles can be deployed to justify *expanding* military options. The principle of *pikuach nefesh*—the imperative to save human life—usually permits that which is otherwise prohibited or undesirable—even in times of war. E.g., Yanki Tauber, "Land for Peace?" 2004; CCAR 1999.
5. There is disagreement about the requirements of these last two categories; for example, whether everyone in a community is obliged to engage in military battle, or only those who are physically capable should fight. Another dispute is about the classification of anticipatory defense. Depending on the nature of the threat, some sages consider anticipatory attacks within the realm of commanded wars, others view them as optional. This distinction is important because a significant difference between the last two categories and the first is that the latter two do not require a political sovereign to attain approval from other leadership institutions; discretionary wars can *only* be instigated after this consent has been obtained. Because these other (religious) leadership

institutions no longer exist and thus cannot grant approval, the category of discretionary war no longer exists in reality. Hence, if anticipatory warfare is merely discretionary, then it is not a legally viable option for a national military strategy.

6. Exodus 17:8–17; Deuteronomy 25:17–19.

7. I Samuel 15:3.

8. Ibid., 15:4–35.

9. Exodus 17:14–16.

10. Cf., Deuteronomy 25:19; Numbers 24:20; *Targum Onkelos* at Numbers 24:20; Rashi at Numbers 24:20; Ibn Ezra at Deuteronomy 25:19.

11. Nonetheless, throughout their history Jews were often obliged by host cultures to engage in self-policing and taxation, and to provide for their own social welfare services—issues about which the rabbis spilled a great deal of ink. These texts present *ideal* governing practices; and because these texts do not tell what was *actually* practiced by the people their historicity or veracity is questionable.

12. For example, Reuven Kimelman, "War," in *Frontiers of Jewish Thought,* ed. S.T. Katz, (Washington, DC: B'nai B'rith Books, 1992), 309–32.

13. Such methods ignore the fact that Israel's founding documents do not bind the country to *halakhah.* This is particularly true in regard to issues of armed conflict, as Israeli governments determine what the Israel Defense Forces (IDF) should do considering taking *halakhah* in their deliberations. Even the Israeli Supreme Court only occasionally invokes *halakhah* to adjudicate the legal boundaries of IDF action (e.g., ISC 1999, on torture techniques during interrogation); only when no precedent in Israeli law suffices may the court resort to *halakhah,* British common law and general notions of justice, to reach a final ruling, e.g., A. Soloveichick, "Wagging War on Shabbath," *Tradition.* 20/3: 179–87 (1982).

14. A case in point is Alan Dershowitz's *The Case for Israel* (Hoboken: Wiley, 2003), in which he argues against the apparent international double-standard applied to Israel generally and Israeli military maneuvers in particular. Though Dershowitz succeeds in making a strong modern and secular legal argument, he fails to offer any thoroughgoing analysis of traditional Jewish texts or sensibilities on these issues. See also Alan Dershowitz, *Why Terrorism Works* (New Haven: Yale University Press, 2002); Alan Dershowitz, "Tortured Reasoning," in *Torture: A Collection,* S. Levinson, ed. (New York: Oxford University Press, 2004).

15. For example, *B'tzelem,* an Israeli human rights organization, critically addresses Israeli interrogatory tactics without invoking the Judaic tradition in its argumentation.

16. Self-defense illustrates this internal extension challenge. Some scholars think it appropriate to extend *halakhot* about personal self-defense to other arenas like communal and national defense. See Jonathan Crane, "Command Self-Defense: An Ethical Puzzle," (paper presented 2003 at the Society for Jewish Ethics), note 10. They justify this move either by literary comparison or by an appeal to reason. However, there are cases where analogies become more problematic. For instance, it would be unreasonable to ask a community to uphold laws of humility enjoined upon individuals. The converse is similarly challenging, because the community has the right to levy taxes but individuals therein do not (see Walter Wurzburger, Ethics of Responsibility: Pluralistic approaches to covenantal ethics (Philadelphia: Jewish Publication Society, 1994), 93; David Novak, *Covenantal Rights: A Study in Jewish Political Theory,* (Princeton: Princeton University Press, 2000), 209–11).

17. The great medieval sages Maimonides and Nahmanides disagree precisely on this issue of external extension. Though both concur that gentiles are bound to moral laws (generally called the *mitzvot b'nei noach*—the Noahide laws or commandments), they diverge on who is responsible for holding gentiles accountable to these moral laws. Maimonides argues that when Jews have political sovereignty over gentiles, Jews should enforce even the Noahide laws upon gentiles. Nahmanides sees gentiles as more independent than that: gentile moral agency does not need Jews (see discussion in David Novak, *Jewish Social Ethics* (New York: Oxford University Press, 1992), 187ff.

18. I Maccabees 2:39–41.

19. "There were about a thousand [who were slaughtered by the military of King Antiochus], with their wives and children, who were smothered and died in these caves; but many of those that

escaped joined themselves to Mattathias, and appointed him to be their ruler, who taught them that unless they would [fight on Shabbat], they would become their own enemies, by observing the law [so rigorously], while their adversaries would still assault them on this day, and they would not then defend themselves; and that nothing could then hinder [their attackers] but they [the Jews] must all perish without fighting. This speech persuaded them; and this rule continues among us to this day, that if there be a necessity, we may fight on Sabbath days." *Antiquities of the Jews,* 12.6.2/275–76.

20. Disagreement, of course, exists on this point. Our Rabbis taught: One may not set out in a ship less than three days before the Sabbath. This was said only [if it is] for a voluntary purpose, but [if] for a *mitzvah* [a religious obligation], it is well; and [the Jew] stipulates with [the gentile owner of the ship] that it is on condition that he will rest [on the Sabbath], yet he does not rest: this is Rabbi's view. R. Simeon b. Gamaliel said: It is unnecessary. But from Tyre to Sidon it is permitted even on the eve of Sabbath. Our Rabbis taught: Gentile cities must not be besieged less than three days before the Sabbath, yet once they commence they need not leave off. And thus did Shammai say: until it falls, even on the Sabbath. (BT *Shabbat*19a).

21. Yet neither the Books of Macabbees nor Josephus are canonized in normative Jewish textual collections like the *Tanakh,* Talmud or *midrashim.* Though it may be logical to dismiss these texts because of their extracanonical status, they are nonetheless embraced by the Jewish tradition, historically and in scholarship, and their lessons, especially this one, deserve inclusion here.

22. For example, MT *Melachim U'Milchamoteihem,* chap. 5, 6.

23. Though Jews are commanded not to murder (Exodus 20:13; Deuteronomy 5:17), killing, albeit a criminal offense, is permitted in certain circumstances like self-defense (BT *Sanhedrin* 72a).

24. BT *Sanhedrin* 72a; Rashi ad loc.; Asher b. Yehiel. *Piskei HaRosh* on BT *Baba Kama* 3:13; R. Israel Isserlein, *Pesakim U'Ketuvim,* 208. Some scholars assert that this principle pertaining to individuals ought to constrain legislative policies for the community writ large (e.g., Cohn 1977) —a question-begging argument, as stated earlier.

25. BT *Beitzah* 23b.

26. *Tosafot,* cited by *Hiddushei HaRan,* BT *Sanhedrin* 84b. A modern scholar therefore concludes, "military action which of necessity will result in civilian casualties cannot be justified on the contention that the killing of innocent victims is unintended, since the loss of those lives is the inescapable result of such action." J. David Bleich, "Nuclear War Through the Prism of Jewish Law: The Nature of Man and War." In *Confronting Omnicide,* ed. D. Landes (Northvale: Jason Aronson, 1991), 218. Conversely, only unforeseen, unintended and not-illicit collateral damage may be permitted, though it certainly is discouraged and is morally liable. Such *accidental* collateral damage may be suffered upon a population during and only during the pursuit of a legitimate target.

27. To illustrate this principle, let us imagine an attack on a vehicle full of people. Should that vehicle be full of military personnel only, it is permissible to attack them with lethal intention and effect (unless there are nonlethal ways of securing their capitulation). If, however, half of the people riding in the vehicle are military personnel and the other half civilians, then this principle would forbid a lethal attack on that vehicle as a whole. This is because the death of innocent civilians would be the *inevitable* outcome of an attack on the whole vehicle, regardless if those civilians' deaths were unintended. If it were possible to use great precision and to attack (lethally) *only* the military personnel in that vehicle, then such an attack would be permitted. If by chance civilians were unintentionally hurt (even mortally) in this precision attack, those casualties would be permissible because they were not inevitable. Obviously an attack on a vehicle full of civilians is prohibited and morally condemned by the Judaic tradition.

28. For example, YT *Sotah* 8.10/23a; MT *Melachim U'Milchamoteihem* 5.1.

29. Consider the case of the destruction of an enemy's city as a vengeful strategy. The command by the prophet Elisha to the kings of Israel and Judah to *"smite every fortified [Moabite] city and every choice city, and you shall fell every good tree and stop up all wells of water, and every fertile field you shall ruin with stones"* seems to counter the Deuteronomic command *against* wanton destruction of a city and environs when laying siege against a city (II Kings 3:19; Deuteronomy 20:19). The nineteenth century Rabbi Meir Leibush Malbim argues that these texts can be reconciled according to the *intention* of the military. "Battling against it to capture it"

(Deuteronomy 20:19)—this is added because siege may be made against the city in order to destroy it and make it uninhabitable as a city. Therefore, the explanation is that the intention should only be to capture the city to inhabit it, but this consideration is eliminated if they want to destroy the city as in the case of Moab. [II Kings 3:19] (*Sefer HaTorah VeHaMitzvah* (Jerusalem 1957). Found in David Novak, "Nuclear War and the Prohibition of Wanton Destruction," in Violence and Defense in the Jewish Experience, 100–20, ed. S.W. Baron and G.S. Wise (Philadelphia: Jewish Publication Society, 1991), 104. That is, *if* one *intends* to destroy a city altogether then the prohibition against wanton destruction or retribution for the sake of inflicting harm does not apply. On the other hand, vengeful strategies are proscribed should one desire to capture a city and keep it standing. A further condition, opined by the fifteenth century Rabbi Elijah Mizrahi, is whether the siege is undertaken as a maneuver in a defensive or offensive war. If the latter, then the city may never be demolished *en toto;* in a defensive war the city is to be razed (*Sefer Otzar Ha-Paryushim Al Ha-Torah: Mizrahi* (New York, 1965). Found in Novak 1991, 104). Hence, in theory, only when a Jewish polity *already* suffers unwarranted attacks may it destroy completely a city it is besieging in a defensive campaign. This permission, however, is not an obligation.

30. Kehati *Mishnah Sotah* 8.7; R. Abraham Isaiah Karelitz, *Hazon Ish, Orach Chayyim-Mo'ed,* 114: 2; R. Israel Lipschutz, *Tiferet Israel, Mishnah Sotah* 8.7; David Frankel, *Shiyure Korban,* addenda to *Korban Ha-Edah* on YT *Sotah* 8.10; CCAR *Responsa* 5762.8 "Preventive War."

31. See Bleich, "Preemptive War in Jewish Tradition." Tradition 21, no. 1 (Spring 1983): 3–41.

32. *He who fatally strikes a man shall be put to death. If he did not do it by design, but it came about by an act of God, I will assign to you a place* (makom) *to which he can flee. When a man schemes against another and kills him treacherously, you shall take him from My very altar* (mizb'chi) *to be put to death* Exodus 21:12–14.

33. cf., Rashi ad loc.

34. *Adonijah, in fear of Solomon, went at once [to the Tent of Adonai] and grasped the horns of the altar. It was reported to Solomon: "Adonijah is in fear of King Solomon and has grasped the horns of the altar, saying, 'Let King Solomon first swear to me that he will not put his servant to the sword.'" Solomon said, "If he behaves worthily, not a hair of his head shall fall to the ground; but if he is caught in any offense, he shall die." So King Solomon sent and had him taken down from the altar. He came and bowed before King Solomon, and Solomon said to him, "Go home"* (I Kings 1:50–53). *When the news reached Joab, he fled to the Tent of the Adonai and grasped the horns of the altar—for Joab had sided with Adonijah, though he had not sided with Absalom. King Solomon was told that Joab had fled to the Tent of Adonai and that he was there by the altar; so Solomon sent Benaiah son of Jehoiada, saying, "Go and strike him down." Benaiah went to the Tent of Adonai and said to him, "Thus said the king: Come out!" "No!" he replied; "I will die here." Benaiah reported back to the king that Joab had answered thus and thus, and the king said, "Do just as he said; strike him down and bury him, and remove guilt from me and my father's house for the blood of the innocent that Joab has shed...So Benaiah son of Johaiada went up and struck him down. And he was buried at his home in the wilderness* I Kings 2:28–31, 34.

35. The formula *kol hanoge'a yikdash* (any*thing* [but not any*one*] that touches...becomes sanctified") teaches that the contagion of sancta does not apply to persons; therefore, the altar itself does not extend sanctuary for asylum seekers. See Exodus 29:37, 30:26–29; Leviticus 6:11, 20; Excurses 75 in Milgrom's *JPS Torah Commentary: Numbers* (Philadelphia: JPS), 505.

36. Nehemiah, 6:10–11; Numbers 4:15, 17:27.

37. Michilta, *Mishpatim,* 21:14.

38. BT *Yoma* 85a.

39. Numbers 35:9–32; Deuteronomy 19; Joshua 21.

40. Deuteronomy 4:42; BT *Makkot* 10a; YT *Makkot* 6.

41. MT *Nezikin* 5.11, 6.8.

42. Maimonides in the twelfth century acknowledges that though at one time willful killers also sought asylum in cities of refuge, now the practice is to extradite them for trial and possible capital punishment. "Originally, a manslayer with intent or without intent would flee immediately to one of the cities of refuge. The court (bet din) of the city in which the killing took place sends and fetches

him from there and try him…If he is condemned to death they will execute him…If he is exonerated they will set him free…If he is condemned to exile, he is sent back to his place" MT *Rotzeach U'shmirat Nefesh* 5.7.

43. For example, Ephraim Urbach, "Jewish Doctrines and Practises in Halakhia and Aggadic Literature," in *Violence and Defenses in the Jewish Experience,* 87–112, ed. S.W. Baron and G.S. Wise (Philadelphia: Jewish Publication Society, 1977); Emanuel Rackman, "Talmudic Insights on Human Rights," *Judaism* 1/2 (April 1977) 158–63.

44. Genesis 9:20–26.

45. Rules about building houses next to each other stipulate that windows should be situated in such a way to prevent voyeurism into adjoining homes because seeing is considered an injurious action (BT *Baba Batra* 22a–b; Tur, *Choshen Mishpat,* 154:17). On the other hand, a neighboring homeowner may permit such an opportune window (SA, *Choshen Mishpat* 154:17).

46. *Sefer Kolbo* 116; Rav Chayyim Shabbetai, *Sefer Torat Chayyim* 3:47.

47. For example, Meir Batiste, "Collective Punishment," in *Crossroads: Halakhah and the Modern World,* vol. 5 (Jerusalem: Zomet Institute, 1999), 233–50; Ya'acov Blidstein, "The Treatment of Hostile Civilian Populations: The Contemporary Halakhic Discussion in Israel," *Israel Studies* 1, no. 2 (September 30, 1996): 27–45; Ehud Luz, "'Jewish Ethics' as an argument in the public debate over the Israeli reaction to Palestinian terror," *Israel Studies* 7, no. 3 (Fall 2002): 134–57.

48. Genesis 34.

49. A fifteenth century explanation: [The children of Jacob and the people of Shechem] are considered as two nations, therefore they were allowed to make war, like the law of a nation which comes to make war against another nation, which the Torah allowed…even though only one [individual] of them did [the act]…and thus it is in all wars…even though there are many who did not do [anything], this makes no difference. As they belong to the same nation which did them harm, they are allowed to wage war against them (Rabbi Judah Loew of Prague (Maharal). *Gur Aryeh* to Genesis 34:14).

50. The modern arguments also invoke a version of this story from the nineteenth century in which Dinah's brothers are imagined to speak to each other: "Since we are few in number and strangers in the land, and they have begun to lash out at us, as in this act of treating our sister as a whore, if we keep silent they will do with us as they wish, so we must show them that we are capable of revenge against whoever harms us" (Malbim, *HaTorah VehaMitzvah* to Genesis 34:31).

51. Writing specifically about this case of Shechem, Batiste asserts, "*Halakhists* [strict legal scholars] fundamentally reject punishing a person for a sin he himself did not commit. Therefore they were forced to attribute the killing of the people of Shechem to some wrongdoing on the part of the Shechemites themselves." See "Collective Punishment," 237. Later sages, desiring to justify *on halakhic grounds* Simeon's and Levi's attack on Shechem, had to construct a crime the Shechemites could be construed as doing—a crime worthy of being put to death—and to read that crime *into* the biblical text so as to provide scriptural foundation for apparent collective punishment.

52. Deuteronomy 13:13–17.

53. Maimonides, for example, rules that children and wives of idolaters are to be killed as ancillaries to the crime of idolatry (MT *Avodah Zarah* 7.4, 7.6; *Moreh Nevukim* 1:54). This differs from earlier texts that posit that if women are to be killed they should be killed for their own crimes; or that children are to be saved no matter what; or that neither wives nor children of idolaters should be harmed and only property is eligible for destruction (e.g., *Tosefta, Sanhedrin* 14.1; *Mishnah Sanhedrin* 10.2). It is possible Maimonides bases his opinion on another text which asserts that, irrespective of whether family members were ancillaries to the crime, they are to be destroyed: their innocence or guilt is irrelevant (*Sifrei Deuteronomy* 94). Moreover, Maimonides thinks that the culpability of certain sins or crimes bleeds onto children and property alike: "There are sins for which the punishment is inflicted on the sinner in this world, on his person or on his property or on his young children, since a man's young children, who have no mind of their own and have not reached the age of responsibility for observing the commandments, are like his property; the verse

"*[a] person shall be put to death only for his own crime*" (Deuteronomy 24:16) applies only when the child becomes a man. MT *Teshuvah* 6.1.

54. Genesis 18:25. Similarly, when Korah unrightfully challenges Moses' leadership and God threatens to annihilate the whole community, Aaron and Moses plead, "*O God, Source of the breath of all flesh! When one man sins, will You be wrathful with the whole community?*" Numbers 16:22.

55. In regard to idolatry, only that individual who engages in it or entices others to idolatry is to be killed (Deuteronomy 13:7–12). Moses summarizes the principle of individualized punishment for an individual's guilt: "*Parents shall not be put to death for [the crimes of their] children, nor children be put to death for [the crimes of their] parents: a person shall be put to death only for his own crime*" (Deuteronomy 24:16). Ezekiel echoes this sentiment and augments it with the contrapositive—an individual's goodness remains with that person: "*The soul that sins shall die; the son shall not bear the iniquity of the father with him, neither shall the father bear the iniquity of the son with him; the righteousness of the righteous shall be upon him, and the wickedness of the wicked shall be upon him*" (Ezekiel 18:20). That is, guilt (or righteousness) cannot be transmitted (at least through the generations).

56. BT *Sukkah* 56b.

57. For example, BT *Sanhedrin* 73a; MT *Rotzeach U'Shmirat Nefesh* 1:6.

58. MT *Chovel U'Mazik* 8.13; but see also BT *Baba Kama* 60b.

59. If one chases after a *rodef* to rescue the intended victim, and one breaks property of the *rodef* or of anyone else, he is exempt. This matter is not strict law but is an enactment so that one will not refrain from rescuing [intended victims] or lose time through being too careful when chasing a *rodef*. MT *Chovel U'Mazik* 8.14.

60. It should be noted, however, that permission to destroy property of a *rodef* is granted only *during* the chase; destroying property at any other time is a criminal offense.

61. BT *Sanhedrin* 20b; Rashi ad loc. [The king] may burst through [the fences surrounding private fields or vineyards] to make a road and no one may take issue with him. There is no limit [in breadth] to the road the king [may make]. Rather, it may be [as wide] as necessary. He need not make his road crooked because of an individual's vineyard or field. Rather, he may proceed on a straight path and carry on his war. MT *Melachim U'Milchamoteihem* 5.3.

62. BT *Baba Kama* 60b.

63. According to the *locus classicus* biblical text on warfare, trees surrounding a city under siege may not be destroyed; only nonfruit-bearing trees may be cut for military purposes (Deuteronomy 20:19–20). On the other hand, no matter how gruesome a war becomes, no permission is granted for burnt earth tactics, as attested by ancient Jewish historians. See Josephus' *Against Apion,* II:30/211–13; Philo's *The Special Laws,* IV:224–27.

64. The sentiments of *bal tashchit* are also found in a *midrash* on the biblical injunction to engage in diplomacy before besieging a city: *When you draw close to a city*—scripture speaks here of a discretionary war—*unto a city*—not a metropolis nor a village—*to fight against it*—not to reduce it through lack of food or water nor to slay its inhabitants through disease—*then proclaim peace unto it*—great is peace for even the dead require peace. *Sifre,* Deuteronomy 20:10.

65. *And if [the city] will not make peace* [i.e., accept all the terms] *with you, but will make war against you*—scripture informs you that if it will not make peace with you, it will eventually (*l'sof*) make war against you—*then you shall besiege it*—even by reducing it through lack of food or water or by slaying its inhabitants through disease. *Sifre,* Deuteronomy 20:12.

66. Dorff, "Bishops, Rabbis, and Bombs," in *Confronting Omnicide: Jewish Reflections on Weapons of Mass Destruction,* ed. D. Landes (Northvale: Jason Aronson, 1991), 176.

67. BT *Kiddushin* 43a.

68. Batiste, "Collective Punishment," 248.

69. For example, BT *Sanhedrin* 40a.

70. BT *Baba Metzia* 24a; BT *Baba Batra* 167a; *Responsa* of Simon b. Tzemah Duran, 3:168, cp. n. 1; see also Passamaneck, *Police Ethics and the Jewish Tradition* (Springfield: Charles C. Thomas Publishers, 2003), 126, 155.

71. *Responsa Ribash* #234–239, 373, 376.

72. Rosh, *Responsa* 17:8; Maharam of Rothenburg, *Responsa,* Ed. Prague #485; Moses b. Israel Isserles, *Choshen Mishpat* 388:10; BT *Baba Kama* 117a; Simeon b. Tzemah Duran, *Tashbetz* 3:158; *Takkanot Va'ad Arba Aratzot,* in Assaf, *Ha-Onshin Acharei Hatimat Ha-Talmud;* Baer, Spain 2 (1961):130, 264ff.

73. See *Responsa Rashba* 3:393.

74. Maimonides claims that a *moser* may be killed anywhere, even at the present time when we do not try cases of capital punishment, and it is permissible to kill him before he has informed: As soon as one says he is to inform against someone's person or property, even if it were a trivial amount of property, he surrenders himself to death [to be killed]. He must be warned and told, "Do not inform," and if he is stubborn and replies, "No! I will inform against this person," it is a religious duty (*mitzvah*) to kill him, and he who hastens to kill him acquires merit. MT *Chovel U'Mazik* 8:10.

75. If any [*moser*] oppresses a community and troubles them, it is permissible to send him to gentile authorities to be beaten, imprisoned and fined. But, if [a *moser*] troubles only an individual, he must not be handed over. Although it is permissible to physically punish a *moser,* it is forbidden to destroy his property, for it belongs to his heirs. (MT *Chovel U'Mazik* 8:12). What matters for Maimonides is that a particular *moser* must pose a substantial threat to a plurality in a community before that informer is exposed to gentile punishment (this, because gentile courts were responsible for meting out punishments for civil crimes; Jewish courts primarily handled issues of personal status and religious transgressions). A particular criminal may not pose a sufficiently substantial threat to warrant extradition or any of these kinds of punishments.

76. For example, BT *Sanhedrin* 43b; JT *Sanhedrin* 23b; *Bamidbar Rabbah* 23:5.

77. Leviticus 19:14; BT *Pesachim* 22b; BT *Avodah Zarah* 6a.

78. SA *Choshen Mishpat,* 227–40.

79. See Passamaneck, *Police Ethics and the Jewish Tradition,* 133–54.

80. A *mesit* is a [seducing] layman, and the one seduced is also a layman. [The *mesit*] says, "There is an idol in a particular place; it eats this, it drinks this, it does so much good and so much harm." For all whom the Torah condemns to death no witnesses are hidden to entrap them, except for this one. If he incites two [to idolatry], they themselves are witnesses against him, and they bring him to a court and stone him. But if he enticed one, and that one responds "I have friends who desire [to engage in idolatry, so tell them too]." If he was cunning and declined to speak before them, witnesses are hidden behind a partition, while he who was incited says to him, "Make your proposal to me now in private." When the *mesit* does so, the other replies, "How shall we forsake our God in Heaven to go and serve wood and stones?" Should he retract, it is well and good. But if he answers, "It is our duty [to worship idols], and it is good for us," then the witnesses stationed behind the partition take him to court and have him stoned. If he says, "I will worship it," or [other phrases suggesting idolatry, guilt is incurred] *Mishnah,* at BT *Sanhedrin* 67a; see also MT *Avodah Zarah* 5:2.

81. MT *Sanhedrin* 11.5.

82. See Talal Asad, *Formations of the Secular: Christianity, Islam, Modernity* (Stanford: Stanford University Press, 2003), chap. 3.

83. Mishnah, *Sanhedrin* 8:7 at BT *Sanhedrin* 73a.

84. Regarding the *rodef* pursuing a fellow with lethal intent, even if that *rodef* is a minor, every Israelite is commanded (*mitzuvin*) to save the pursued from the *rodef* even at the expense of the *rodef*'s life. MT *Rotzeach U'Shmirat Nefesh* 1:6.

85. Leviticus 19:16. Any person who can save a person's life (*kol ha'yachol l'hatzil*) but fails to do so, he transgresses [the negative commandment] "do not stand [idly] on your neighbor's blood." Likewise, anyone who sees a colleague drowning at sea or being attacked by robbers or by a wild beast and could save that person or could hire others to save that person [but does not, is equally in transgression]. Likewise, anyone who hears gentiles or informers (*mosrim*) conspiring to harm a colleague or planning a snare for him, and does not inform him or notify him [of the danger, is equally in transgression]. Likewise, anyone who hears of a gentile or a man of force [who has a complaint] against a colleague, and he could appease [the aggressor] on behalf of his colleague, but he

fails to do so [is equally in transgression]. Likewise in all analogous instances, the one who [fails to] act transgresses "do not stand [idly] on your neighbor's blood." MT *Rotzeach U'Shmirat Nefesh* 1:14, 1:15; SA *Choshen Mishpat* 426:1.

86. MT *Rotzeach U'Shmirat Nefesh* 1:7; see also SA *Choshen Mishpat* 425:1.

87. The intent of the verse ["you must cut off her hand, you may not show pity" (Deuteronomy 25:12)] is, whenever a person intends to strike a colleague (*hachoshev l'hacot chavero*) with a blow that could kill him, the pursued should be saved by "[cutting off the] hand" of the *rodef*. If this cannot be done, [the victim] should be saved by taking the *rodef*'s life, as the verse continues, "you may not show pity." MT *Rotzeach U'Shmirat Nefesh* 1:8.

88. Regarding the intervener pursuing a *rodef* who himself is trying to kill another, should it be possible to save [the intended victim] by [injuring] one of the attacker's limbs but [the intervener] does not save [the victim] in this manner, the intervener should be killed on this account (*neharag 'alav*). BT *Sanhedrin* 74a.

89. SA, *Choshen Mishpat* 421:13.

90. In his thoroughgoing analysis of Judaic approaches to police ethics, Passamaneck makes the following observation about interrogation practices: "Severe bodily torture was simply not part of any traditional [Jewish] interrogatory process, or any other legal process, though some degree of duress was clearly acceptable." *Police Ethics and the Jewish Tradition*. (Springfield: Charles C. Thomas Publishers, 2003), 126. He concludes: "The [Jewish] tradition recognizes, without any particular negative comment, the practice of confinement and some sort of physical pressure, though not severe bodily torture, to extract confession in some pecuniary matters. A system that would permit this approach surely would not refrain from the use of lies or other modes of deception against persons whose conduct has rendered them suspect.... But there are many forms of deception that are licit and these the tradition need not reject when properly used. The tradition would thus appear to endorse the 'crime control' view of deception in law enforcement so long as deception is indeed targeted toward those who in fact are highly suspect in some criminal enterprise or who in fact do engage in criminal activity. The tradition draws a very bright line between the law abiding and the nonlaw abiding, much as police officers do in the modern world, and the non-law abiding, now as then, are, or should be, identified by their actual behavior." Ibid., 155–56.

91. MT *Sanhedrin* 25:1.

92. Ibid., 24:10.

93. CCAR 2005; RHR 2005; RRA 2005; compare RA 2005. See note 4 above.

94. Exodus 23:1.

95. BT *Sanhedrin* 9b.

96. MT *Sanhedrin* 18:6; Rackman, "Talmudic Insights on Human Rights," *Judaism* 1, no. 2 (April 1952): 158–63; Susser 1980; Arnold Enker, "Duress as a Defense to Murder," in *Rabbi Joseph H. Lookstein Memorial Volume*, ed. L. Landman (New York: Ktav, 1980), 111–17; Fletcher 1991; Steven H. Resnicoff, "Criminal Confessions in Jewish Law," *Jewish Law Commentary: Examining Halachah, Jewish Issues and Secular Law*, 2004; CCAR 1989.

97. MT *Edut* 9:1.

98. Ibid., 10:2–4.

99. For example, Ezekiel, chap. 25; Romans 12:19; compare to *Surah* 8 about fighting fairly.

100. Allan Brownfield, "Mirror-Image Jewish and Islamic Religious Extremists Threaten Israel's Movement Toward Peace," in *Washington Report on Middle East Affairs*, 1999; Milton Viorst, *What Shall I Do with This People? Jews and the Fractious Politics of Judaism* (New York: The Free Press, 2005).

CHAPTER 12

Jesus and Mars: A Brief Introduction to the Christian Just War Tradition

MICHAEL SKERKER

The first part of this chapter offers a historical survey of the Christian tradition on *just war*. The presentation follows some of the basic arguments that thinkers have developed with respect to the justice of going to war (*jus ad bellum*), and the moral criteria that governs the actual fighting *(jus in bello)*. We will discuss the evolution of the different doctrines, explain their similarities and differences, and highlight the tensions between the more restrictive classical doctrines and their more permissive modern incarnations.

The second part of this chapter applies just war criteria to dilemmas encountered in the *War on Terror*. We will consider whether dragnet arrests and preemptive detention for "suspect" populations are just; whether a civilian who becomes a suicide bomber should be treated as a combatant; whether targeting holy places used for storing military materials is permissible; whether the destruction of civilian infrastructure is just; whether military attacks targeting civilians are permissible; and, lastly, whether the use of interrogatory torture can ever be justified.

EARLY CHRISTIANITY

Early Christian theologians who wished to develop a "Christian position" on war were hard pressed to find a consistent message in Scripture. The Old Testament portrays God as sometimes ordering the Israelites into genocidal wars with other nations while the New Testament relays Jesus' strange instruction that hatred should be repaid with love. Further, Jesus counsels Peter to sheathe his sword in the garden of Gethsemane; instructs his followers to turn the other cheek if the first one is struck; and promises that those who live by the sword will perish at its edge. Beyond the question of military service, Jesus' *Sermon on the Mount* and St. Paul's *Letter to the Romans* seem to counsel complete disengagement from the political realm, perhaps because the coercive roles of soldier, jailer, lawyer, tax collector, and judge are inconsistent with the radical demands of emulating a God who responds to sin with love, and who allows the sun to shine equally on the heads of the wicked and the good.

Following Jesus' teachings literally, early Christians endeavored to create separate, self-sufficient communities in which all were brothers and sisters in faith. The only direct form of coercion in these communities was social isolation. Participation in the soldiering life was seen as unacceptable as it required behaviors apparently in direct contradiction to Jesus' message. Further, soldiering would have included loyalty oaths to the Roman emperor, obeisance to Roman gods, and exposed Christians to the general moral depravity associated with the legions. Subsequent Christian attitudes toward the state's use of force would be oriented around the understandings reached about the separation from conventional society and pacifism counseled in various ways in the New Testament. Whether the separation is a matter of the flesh or the spirit would depend on the interpretation of Christ's role. Did Christ mean to lead the kingdom of God on earth, or to herald its future realization in heaven?

Such debates took on an increased importance with the official Christianizing of the empire in 313 CE. This event forced Church leaders to confront a new set of political responsibilities the early Christian communes could afford to refuse. In addition to their now being responsible for all the coercive functions of the state, there was also a developing theological conviction among fourth century Christians that the social stasis St. Paul recommended in his epistles could no longer be justified by the imminence of Christ's return. Instead, it appeared that the current Christian era—awaiting Christ's return—would last indefinitely.[1] If the world of political coercion could easily be seen as "other" when the Roman state was persecuting the early Church, even by the late second century, the perseverance of the Church forced its thinkers to recognize that the Church prospered in part because of its support by and integration with the Roman world. For all of Rome's crimes, the *Pax Romana* provided a stable environment for the exercise and spread of Christianity.

THE AUGUSTINIAN CONCEPTION OF JUST WAR

In the early fifth century, St. Augustine (354–430) addressed the question of Christian separation by determining that members of God's kingdom, or city, share the physical realm with those reprobate humans destined for hell. Both the elect and the condemned benefit from earthly peace. For Augustine and subsequent theologians justifying Christian participation in the state's use of force, the separation from the world Christianity demands is spiritual rather than physical. This is because all sin is consequent to a will which perversely loves material and changeable things over God. A properly ordered will leads one to use, rather than enjoy the things of this world. A good Christian appreciates that power and wealth are mere means to sustain one's physical life until called to God, rather than sources of inherent value. A given profession may pose dangers in its opportunities for irregular passions, but Augustine observes that two men may occupy the same position, one dispassionately acquitting his duty, while the other glories in the power associated with it.[2] Thus, it is purposeless to restrict Christians from certain professions, because any opportunity can be misused and any object or person improperly loved.

Augustine argues Christians ought to do what they can to maintain social peace and order during their earthly sojourn. If they are rulers, this obligation extends to the power to make war for these purposes, as it is the natural role of a political ruler to care for his citizens. This obligation is put into the context of a theological history by Augustine, but is derived from the natural order of the world, accessible to reason, and so to pagans as well as to Christians.

Thus, Augustine could approve of the Roman conception of, and criteria for just war (e.g., as articulated by Cicero in *De Officiis*). These include *right authority*—only the duly appointed political ruler has the right to declare war. Also, wars may only be fought for a *just cause,* for example, defense, redress of wrongs, restitution of stolen property, or (Augustine would add, in deference to the Old Testament examples) execution of divine decree. Further, war must be publicly proclaimed after demands for reparations are issued, and then only waged as a *last resort.* Lastly, wars must have the *aim of peace,* and the damage done in the contemplated war must be worth the good expected.[3]

It is important to note that Augustine is not offering positive prescriptions for the attainment of social or spiritual goods with these criteria. Force per se is alien to the ethics of the kingdom of God. Augustine refers to *"justum bellum"* as a conventional concept taken from a secular vocabulary; it is a feature of the material world that Christians are to use in the appropriate way (as they are to use all worldly things). The just use of force is a concession to a world far from God's kingdom, one in which other people are seen as competitors or means to ends instead of siblings in faith. Thus, it is with an air of resignation that Augustine concedes that a good king will have to make just wars.[4]

The importance of the distinction between prescribing action and granting license for action is made clearer by Augustine's discussion of Rome's martial history in *City of God.* One could not describe as good, some of the pointless and wasting wars in Rome's history—despite their possible adherence to the formal criteria of justice. These wars seem to evince a pure lust for violence, glory, and domination; it is these things rather than the death and destruction which are the true evils of war (because every material thing dies or decays anyway).[5] Augustine observes a shallowness in Roman just war thinking which ignores the status of leaders' and soldiers' wills in favor of an objective categorization of the justice of a campaign. This categorization is indexed to the interests of states, rather than men. Yet a war with a just cause could be fought by soldiers glorying in the opportunity to conquer and destroy, or to honor a state they idolatrously claim to deserve global domination. These factors would seem to evacuate the war's moral content.

The criteria are also only formal evaluations, and so blind to other kinds of evil. The justice of a cause and the point of last resort are relative to a nation's contingent material situation, and this situation may have been brought about through immoral actions. For example, Rome was constantly under attack, or threat of attack at its peripheries, but this was because it had unjustly conquered and subjugated other peoples.[6] Further, the leader with the right authority to declare wars could just as easily be a warmongering tyrant as a benevolent ruler. And while all wars are fought for the sake of peace, Rome's were fought for a peace of Roman domination, not one of mutual consent.[7]

Just the same, Augustine learned from his mentor St. Ambrose that the use of force could be understood as fulfilling the Christian requirement to love one's neighbor.[8] That one must use force to do so is indicative of the fallen state of the world, but nonetheless, force can be used to protect the innocent and lovingly correct the wicked. The moral difference between a violent act meant to aggrandize the self, and one meant to restrain wickedness or protect the innocent is provided by the actor's *intention.*

The Christian soldier or king may use force to fulfill his vocational goals, just as a pagan should, but must empty his heart of vengefulness, pride, and self-interest in order to perform them in a Christian way. Purity of motive is so important on Augustine's view that he prohibits private citizens defending themselves with force—a position most of his theological heirs do not endorse—because doing so evinces a disordered love of one's physical body (which one temporarily occupies anyway) over the objectively more valuable soul of the attacker. (If the attacker is killed in the midst of his unjust attack, he will die in a state of mortal sin, unreconciled with God.) Using force is morally "safer" for soldiers, executioners, and interrogators than for private citizens, because the state agents act, or can act out of obedience rather than personal animus. The force a soldier wields is in service of social order, the just punishment of aggressors, and the protection of the innocent, instead of self-love. The individual soldier is not culpable for the overall justice of the war, which he did not elect to start, nor need he inquire about the justice of a campaign before participating. Rather, he fulfills his duty simply by obeying his rulers.[9] In battle, he is still free to love his neighbor; to hope that his enemies realize the folly of their aggressive invasion and repent of it before death; and to pray that God have mercy on their souls. Ironically, the egolessness enforced by obedience actually helps protect soldiers from some of the passions that might assail private citizens in similarly threatening situations.

On Augustine's understanding, God meant for all human beings to be at peace with one another. Hence, the standard for *right intention* has to be the restoration of a just peace of harmonious relations between neighboring states or peoples. True peace is possible only when the same love for God relativizes the importance of any particular holding of territory or treasure. *Caritas,* or charity—the particularly Christian self-giving, other-oriented love present in friendship and typified by Christ—can perfect the (retributive) justice that a king seeks, for example, when he defends his territory. Retributive justice can be perfected by being put in the service of an ordered peace in which the human family is returned to comity. The goal of a harmonious order (which is only possible if all people love the same inexhaustible resource, God) that a good Christian king intends eliminates the material incentive of empire; such an incentive could spur greed and vainglory if he is not careful. By seeking this universal harmony important to God (and which, in a sense, could only be important to an entity invested in every single human being), the king effectively removes his ego from the equation and acts as a simple instrument of God's will.

In sum, *right intention* is Augustine's signal contribution to the just war tradition, a substantive standard that embeds the theological and teleological virtue of charity into the formal criteria of *jus ad bellum.* Charity answers the question begged by the Roman list of just war criteria: in service of what, ultimately, is this war, this peace? The teleological element draws the analysis of a contemplated war beyond the immediate provocations and state interests to a horizon which the theological aspect puts beyond complete human conceptualization. This infinite horizon refuses any pat human calculation of justice, a calculation which might limit other-regarding activity, e.g., at the minimal level when one's duty is fulfilled, or when due diligence is paid.

Further, the theological element treats the human being, created by God, rather than the state, created by man, as the basic unit of moral analysis. The Roman criteria are responsive to the needs and dimensions of states (e.g., seizures of land are "assaults" against states); the groans of the human beings caught in the conflict are not relevant to the moral calculus. From a divine perspective, all human cries are heard and all human lives are of equal value. Practically, this teleological and theological horizon would direct warfighters to see their enemies as equals, and so to minimize their harm and suffering; to attempt every avenue of peaceful conciliation before resorting to war; to treat the defeated mercifully; and to help repair the damage done once the war has concluded.

ST. THOMAS AQUINAS: THE NATURAL LAW PERSPECTIVE

St. Thomas Aquinas (1225–1274) received Augustine's comments about war in epigrammatic form from Gratian. Aquinas's terse presentation of a three part *jus ad bellum* formula (right authority, just cause, and right intention) in turn becomes the standard reference for his scholastic heirs.[10]

With Augustine, Aquinas locates the concept of just war in the order of charity. He understands upright martial activity to be oriented toward universal concord, rather than mere retributive justice. He also endorses Augustine's contention that the moral character of an action is different if committed in one's public role as opposed to his private capacity. For example, concealing strategy from enemies and conducting ambushes do not constitute deception, because of their utilization in the service of peace.[11] Similarly, soldiers' and executioners' acts of homicide do not constitute murder. These state agents do not choose to kill out of personal animus, but as part of their public role, sundering miscreants from society the way a surgeon does an infected limb.[12] Normally, human beings deserve to be treated in a way that respects their rational dignity unless, in electing unjustly to use force against others, they themselves have compromised that dignity by acting in a bestial manner. In such instances, public authorities may treat them in a less deferential manner, asking what utility their lives play for the larger society. Aquinas applies this justification of the political coercion of criminals to the confrontation of external enemies as well.

The complex natural law schematic Aquinas uses for adjudicating moral dilemmas serves as a model for subsequent Roman Catholic and some Protestant ethicists. The moral character of actions is constituted by the actor's aim in acting, the circumstances in which the action is done, and the moral object of the action, meaning the moral species under which the act is objectively categorized (e.g., murder, defensive homicide, execution, etc.). Importantly for just war thinking, acts with a good moral object—those conducive to natural goods such as life, health, peace, knowledge, friendship, and procreation—can be deformed by a malicious aim, or by circumstances disproportionate to the desired end. Thus, a permissible action like using force to defend oneself from unjust attack becomes sinful if one acts out of vengeance, or with bigoted rage; so too is the act deformed if one uses more force than necessary.[13] Acts, the objects of which are evil (directly in opposition to natural goods), are *malum in se,* evil unto themselves, and cannot be made good with noble aims or prudent measures. Later just war thinkers mention murder (e.g., the intentional killing of a civilian), torture, and rape as examples of such actions.

Aquinas uses this moral schematic to articulate what would become known as the *Doctrine of Double Effect,* which is often utilized in just war thinking to assess actions that have simultaneous good and bad effects.[14] An action with simultaneous and inseparable good and bad effects can be elected if the good effect alone is intended; the bad effect is not a means to the good; the good accomplished is proportionate to the bad effect; and the actor has no less damaging option available to him.[15]

"JUST WAR" AFTER AQUINAS: ERASMUS, VITORIA, SUAREZ, AND GROTIUS

Erasmus (1466–1536) expresses the generally dubious Christian view of war in less technical terms than the scholastics. The legalistic and technical nature of the criteria can be mistaken as implicitly prescribing, rather than granting permission for wars (i.e., when criteria are met, we must go to war). Erasmus's ground-level depiction of the effects of war can be read as an implicit critique of the legalistic style of just war thinking, or at least a critique of a mentality which limits its moral evaluation of war to a dry perusal of a checklist. He emphasizes in *The Education of a Christian Prince*[16] that wars should be undertaken as a last resort; that few wars are just (many instead motivated by greed); that most wars lead to more war; and that even in a just war, commoners with no stake in the war usually pay the heaviest price. He points to the absurdity of Christian princes both invoking the justice of their cause in battling one another, as if Jesus could bless both sides. Erasmus reminds his reader that God denied the great warrior-king David the privilege of building the Great Temple, because of the blood on his hands.[17]

In the early modern period, thinkers such as Vitoria, Suarez, and Grotius would incorporate *jus in bello* (justice in war) restrictions into the tradition based on the medieval codes of chivalry.[18] The codes prohibited intentionally killing noncombatants, because there was no honor for a knight to kill a person other than another knight. Such honor was extended to fellow brothers in arms that it was thought wrong to kill more combatants than necessary to achieve one's objective or to kill when capturing was possible. These vocational standards were appropriated by moralists in the form of three main principles of *jus in bello:* (1) *discrimination,* which prohibits the intentional targeting of noncombatants; (2) *proportionality,* which demands that the damage done in an action be proportionally justified by the good accomplished; and (3) a specification of proportionality, a *prohibition on weapons* causing more suffering than necessary in incapacitating combatants. Further *jus ad bellum* criteria were added or reemphasized during this time as well including the necessity of there being a reasonable probability of the war's success; that the war be the last resort to mediating interstate conflict; and that the good sought in the war be worth the damage anticipated to both sides.[19]

Franciscus de Vitoria (1483–1546) makes an important contribution relevant to contemporary conflicts with nonstate actors who do not observe the Western laws of war. Addressing Spain's wars with the indigenous populations of South America, Vitoria argues that the Indians are due the same *jus in bello* protections as European combatants, irrespective of their race, religion, and even the justice of their cause; they are due these protections simply because they are human beings.[20] In fact, Vitoria writes, it is often the case that both sides in a war believe themselves to have a just cause—and in some respects, it is possible for both sides to have just causes—and therefore it is all the more important that combatants fight in a just manner, in case the ends do not actually justify the means.[21]

Vitoria takes the natural law tradition into an international setting, charting the outlines of our modern system of international law along with his near contemporaries Francisco Suarez and Hugo Grotius (a Dutch Protestant). These Christian jurists contribute a mixed legacy to just war theory by taking a theological construal of natural law outside its sectarian frame. To their credit, they helped to advance the notion that law could govern the external behavior of nation-states—so rapacious states, for example, could be held to account. In its mature incarnation in the twentieth century's Hague and Geneva conventions, the international law of war prohibits waging aggressive war, directly targeting civilians and civilian infrastructure, using certain particularly loathsome weapons, employing child soldiers, and mistreating prisoners of war and wounded combatants. The secularization of natural law has enabled its internationalization in a patchwork of multilateral conventions indexed to the claims of *humanity* rather than a sectarian construal of divine will.

This secularization came with a price though. Internationalization and secularization occurred at the expense of the teleological elements of natural law oriented to the fulfillment of friendship between men loving one another in emulation of a God who loves all in excess of their deserts. By contrast, the duties corresponding to just behavior are relatively minimal, requiring deference to the other side commensurate with the deference it in turn has paid. In practice, the evacuation of teleological elements from just war thinking has entailed an identification of what is permissible in warfare with what is not unjust—or not illegal—rather than what is morally good.[22]

Also, the procedural and reciprocal basis of the norms means they vary relative to the behavior and material circumstances of the belligerents. For example, tactics that do not intentionally target civilians and do not cause civilian deaths disproportionate to the military value of the target are considered just. Yet there is no absolute ceiling on the number of deaths or substantive standard for how much discriminatory effort is required. The bias against violence and for peace implicit in Aquinas's chapter title for his discussion of just war is lost when the just war criteria are used to ask *which* wars are just, rather than ask, with Aquinas, *"[i]s war always sinful?"* Rather, the presupposition in secularized just war theory is that war and war-making per se are legitimate, with the criteria merely for determining which campaigns and tactics are exempted from this legitimacy. The risk then is that rather than the ideal of universal comity, the material conditions of well-armed nations will form the practical context for just war theorizing. For example, a formally just cause may be an aggressive enemy action which the defending nation's foreign policy provoked in the first place. Also, the tactics which are discriminate in a particular situation depend on the technical means available to the agent (development and procurement of which may have been driven by political rather than moral considerations), and the tactics which are proportionate are dependent on the agent's particular war aims.

By contrast, theological just war theory assumes peace as normative, and then asks if there are situations in which war is the least bad option available to political leaders.[23] It is instructive that Augustine and Aquinas do not ask if there are "good wars," but rather, if there are *any* wars in which a Christian can participate without endangering his soul.[24] The practical import to this distinction is this: within a theological framework, the constant teleological pressure of the ideal of charity should press war-fighters to always elect the least damaging, efficacious option available, and to constantly seek more discriminate and proportionate tactics and weapons.[25]

PROTESTANT REFORMERS' VIEWS

Contrary to the Roman Catholic view which assumes peace as normative, early Protestant reformers like Luther and Calvin endorsed political coercion as a necessity in a world that was fractured by sin. Martin Luther (1483–1546) writes that God authorizes political coercion to restrain wickedness and preserve peace. Like Aquinas, Luther justifies interstate violence via a comparison to the state's responsibility to restrain domestic criminals.[26] War unto itself is terrible but, like an amputation, good to the extent it restores the health of the community. Princes do God's will in waging just wars, and soldiers, their duty in obeying, but these are civic rather than uniquely Christian duties. Therefore, these duties are equally incumbent on both Christians and non-Christians.

Luther understands war-fighting in this way, because in his view, no human action has currency in the economy of salvation. God has seen to the administration of the material world by creating the social structures, or estates, of government, church, and family. Christians do God's will in this world by doing their duty in each estate. Every person is called by God to a specific vocation within these estates so the particular, end-oriented imperatives of the estates (e.g., victory, in the military) should be diligently sought.

Since the inherent (i.e., God-given) purpose of political rule is to maintain peace, a prince ought to do what is necessary to preserve peace, only resorting to war if it is necessary. Princes ought to proceed cautiously when considering war. Luther seems to feel that struggling with evil involves substantial risks of moral corruption; with Augustine, Luther is aware that violence can offer its own illicit pleasure.[27] However, since actions do not merit salvation, Luther does not work out *jus in bello* restrictions in detail. Luther even calls on soldiers to fight as ferociously as possible (though limiting their violence to other soldiers) in order to end the war sooner.

As mentioned above, Luther does endorse the Augustinian view that political coercion is part of the natural order in a fallen world, rather than a specifically Christian office. He also understands the scriptural admonitions against vengefulness and hatred to regard a soldier's or prince's affective state, rather than his outward bodily behavior. The state of the combatant's conscience is largely related to his motivation for war-making. A prince should only go to war only to preserve peace, and a soldier should only fight out of obedience to his prince. Neither should go to war out of greed, vainglory, pride, or love of violence.[28] Luther also agrees with Augustine that sin brings its own temporal punishments, though he pegs the ill consequences directly to Providence rather than the created structure of the world.[29]

Like Luther and Aquinas, Jean Calvin (1509–1564) understands the magistrate's use of the sword to be different in kind from the private citizen's. The magistrate's power is given him by God in order to restrain and punish the wicked. Challenging those who advocate imitating Jesus' nonviolence, Calvin emphasizes the impious folly of pacifism in the face of evil. It would be an abdication of their duty for magistrates to "...sheathe the sword, and keep their hands from shedding blood, while the swords of desperadoes are drenched in murders."[30]

Calvin also applies the justification of the domestic use of force to interstate conflict. With Augustine, he counsels against wanton cruelty and allowing vengeful passions to guide political and martial policy. Given the Protestant emphasis on Scripture, Calvin must address critics who point out that the New Testament has no analogue to the Old Testament's divinely sanctioned wars, nor any explicit endorsement of the military life. Calvin argues that the former can be explained by the historical setting of the New Testament, and on the latter point, defers to Augustine's interpretation of a scene from the New Testament involving John the Baptist. The military profession is implicitly endorsed by John, Augustine argues, because when asked by soldiers what is required for their salvation, he counsels only that they are to be content with their pay. Jesus' pacifist sayings, Calvin says, ought to be understood to refer to the spiritual kingdom of God, to be enjoyed in heaven.

Some contemporary mainline Protestant theologians have endorsed the just war criteria articulated in the main by Roman Catholic thinkers, referring to Protestants' and Catholics' common Augustinian and biblical heritage. They tend to employ the criteria with less systematic rigor than the Catholics, and tend to root the criteria in the command to love (and so to care for) the neighbor rather than in the concept of justice. Compared especially to medieval and post–World War II Catholic thinkers, there is a tendency amongst the Protestant theologians who have addressed these issues to grant governments broader discretion to do what is necessary to restrain wickedness, particularly among those theologians with a dim view of human potential. The inevitability of sin functions in two ways to give states license to use force. First, as Niebuhr puts it, in *Why the Christian Church is Not Pacifist,*[31] universal egoism (a function of Original Sin) makes universal cooperation among men impossible, necessitating government coercion. Second, since all men are sinners, including those in government, coercion will only result in a relative amount of justice.[32]

Thus, the optimism implicit in the Catholic penchant to work out moral requirements in precise detail is largely absent in Protestant just war thinking. Neither is the fallen human mind capable of articulating, nor the errant human will capable of achieving full justice in the world. In any case, the divine standard of love exceeds all rational calculations of fairness. As with Roman Catholics and the early Protestant reformers, twentieth century Protestant theologians like Niebuhr, Ramsey, and Childress endorse a separation between a soldier's inward charitable disposition toward his enemies and his outward coercive behavior toward them. In Protestantism, no bodily action per se wins or loses salvation, but since God granted governments dominion over the bodies and property of men, performing one's professional duty in governmental roles is generally in keeping with God's will. Given the decentralization of Protestantism, particular congregations in some mainline denominations are also free to endorse pacifism.

During the Reformation, some radical Protestant reformers felt Luther did not go far enough in conforming doctrine to Scripture, and committed their new churches to the pacifism and complete separation from earthly government that Jesus seems to demand in the Sermon on the Mount. These were the antecedents of some of the historic "peace churches" including the Amish, Mennonites, and Quakers. There is a range of pacifisms among these churches, ranging from complete refusal to participate in martial or political activities, to allowance of passive resistance to attack and nonviolent participation in the war effort (e.g., serving as medics).[33]

MODERN CATHOLIC VIEWS

The papacy dedicated new attention to the subject of war in the twentieth century. If the latitude to wage war reached its most permissive phase with Suarez (who, for instance, includes insults to a prince's honor as a possible just cause), two global wars and the nuclear arms race have led popes to demand increasingly strict definitions of just cause, such that defense is now considered the only acceptable just cause. The new mood is well summed up by Pope Pius XII's 1942 Christmas broadcast. "The calamity of a World War, with the economic and social ruin and the moral excesses and dissolution that accompany it, must not on any account be permitted to engulf the human race for a third time."[34]

Arguably, war was viewed more as an existential condition than a simple political event in the Church's early centuries, emblematic of a world governed by principles alien to the kingdom of God. War was demystified in the late medieval and early modern periods. The same metrics for analyzing other political activities were marshaled for discussions of war. Yet in the second half of the twentieth century, at least on the rhetorical level, war once again is seen as tied up in the mystery of evil, imperiling the human race as a whole.

Hence, as Pope John Paul II said on a visit to Hiroshima: "From now on it is only through a conscious choice and through a deliberate policy that humanity can survive."[35] John Paul II in particular focuses on the immense tragedy of war, whether justified or not, viewing it as a symptom of human sinfulness hostile or indifferent to life in all its phases;

it is a disposition too willing to mediate difficulties with solutions that arrogate human control over what is properly the divine realm of life and death. In the Catholic conception, the basic morphology of Original Sin sees human beings attempting to assume God's authority and improve on God's design, to ill effect. Nuclear weapons, with their power to literally undo creation, have been presented as a singular mark of this disposition, and have been especially condemned by the popes and bishops, with John XXIII calling for their abolition.[36]

Amidst the development of just war thinking in the Roman Catholic Church, the early understanding of Jesus' teachings to refer literally to *outward* actions rather than inward dispositions remained an acceptable doctrine for Catholics, such that Catholics could endorse nonviolence and refuse military service. While an inward disposition of nonmaleficence is required of all, it is understood that some are specially graced with the fortitude to imitate Jesus in outward pacific behavior. Catholics choosing pacifism are still obliged to help their fellow human being when they are able, and to take positive steps to contribute to the peace and order of their immediate and broader communities. States however, are not allowed to adopt nonviolence exclusively and must use force when the safety of its inhabitants can in no other way be protected.

BRIEF ANALYSIS OF HYPOTHETICALS

Preliminary answers follow to a series of concrete questions related to the "War on Terror." These short discussions will allow us to frame provocative queries within the disparate theoretical frameworks of the Christian *Just War* tradition. Exhaustive treatment of each issue is beyond the introductory purposes of the present work. However, the following discussion reflects the subtle doctrinal differences addressed in historical discussion above.

(1) Are Dragnet Arrests and Preventative Detention for "Suspicious" Populations Just?

Dragnet arrests violate the peaceful order of society and the due process guarantees characterizing such order. Catholic just war thinking is based on the state's imperative to uphold justice and create friendship amongst men. Protestant just war thinking is based on the state's imperative to care for the innocent (an extension of Christian's duty to love the neighbor). Starting from either basis—charity or protection—one can see that arbitrary arrest is unjust and does not defer to the innocent.

(2) Is a Civilian who Becomes a Suicide Bomber to be Treated as a Combatant?

The generic justification for coercion can be articulated with Thomistic language. Rational creatures properly use language and reason to change other's actions. Using force to assert one's will in the first instance is characteristic of nonhuman animals. Humans may licitly control nonhuman animals. Illicitly using force reduces a person to that bestial level where he is liable to be prudentially manipulated by others. Thus, one may use force to restrain or incapacitate a person who is unlawfully violent, in order to restore the peace the violator disturbed.

This duty first applies to state authorities, but devolves to private citizens if no state agent is present. Attacking enemy soldiers, identifiable by their uniforms, are always legitimate targets for domestic soldiers. On the other hand, civilians (no uniforms) cannot be treated prudentially (i.e., as animals or objects to be controlled by force) until they commit or are about to commit an act of violence. Strapping on a suicide belt qualifies for this treatment, just as would wielding a gun. The difficulty with confronting suicide-bombers of course is that they typically look like civilians, making it hard to identify them before they attack.

(3) Can Holy Places Used to Store Military Materiel be Treated as Military Targets?

By similar reasoning, holy places become military targets if used as firing platforms or to store military materiel. However, given the prima facie duty not to attack nonmilitary targets, particularly those of special value like places of worship, a force would need to consider if the attack was utterly vital. Extraordinary restraint is indicated in such cases.

There is also a prudential (and practical) consideration which urges avoidance of these technically licit targets, if possible. The enemy is deliberately taking advantage of the rules of war protecting holy places in order to forestall attack, or failing that, to use images of damaged holy sites for propagandistic effect.[37] The other side may wish to frustrate this tactic by taking alternate measures, if possible.

(4) Can Agricultural Areas be Destroyed in the Course of Anti-Insurgent or Counter-Terrorist Campaigns?

The just war tradition dictates that noncombatants cannot be directly targeted. It therefore follows that the resources which make their life possible cannot be deliberately targeted. Moreover, force is justified against individual aggressors, not the common life of a polity, so infrastructure and institutions making daily civilian life possible should not be attacked.[38] The question is more difficult to answer if foodstuffs, food plants, and other elements of infrastructure serve both the military and the civilian population.

There are both theorists who allow and who do not allow attacks on such dual-use sites. The argument for allowing such attacks is based on the Doctrine of Double Effect, which permits actions that will have foreseeable, simultaneous, and inseparable good and bad effects. Intentionally destroying dual-use food sources would be allowed by the doctrine if the intention was to deprive the military of provisions; there was no other way to limit the military's supplies; doing so was militarily necessary; and the associated civilian suffering was proportionate to the damage done to the military. (For instance, if one side suspected enemy soldiers had additional stockpiles of foods on military bases, but also availed themselves of fields used by civilians, an attack on the fields would not be warranted because without serious military effect, yet devastating to civilians.) Destroying groves or orchards simply to punish civilians is not acceptable and has been shown historically to actually bolster civilian support for the war effort.

Further, all theories of just war are indexed to the restoration of peace, and so counsel against actions that would make normal life postbellum impossible, e.g., destroying orchards, salting the earth, contaminating the environment. Particularly from a Christian perspective, such tactics can be seen as devoid of charity, as they envision a permanent state of enmity between the people. Christian just war thinkers ought to be especially sensitive to the destruction of agricultural lands as there are specific biblical injunctions against destroying vineyards and groves.[39]

(5) Can Military Attacks go Forward with the Knowledge that Civilians will also Suffer?

As already mentioned, civilians cannot be intentionally targeted. Military targets can be attacked however, with the knowledge that civilians will be killed as a simultaneous side effect of the action, provided that there are no less damaging options and the good achieved in destroying the military target is judged proportionate to the civilian damage.

This proportionality judgment is perhaps the most controversial part of just war thinking. How is one civilian's life weighed relative to the value of one artillery piece in the context of the overall war effort? Renick points out that on a Christian construal of double effect, charity compels war fighters to exceed the minimal requirements of justice (e.g., no intentional targeting of civilians) to seek tactics incurring the least amount of damage possible consistent with legitimate military aims. Theologians remind military leaders that Christ died for all humans, even those people currently identified as enemies.[40] So charity compels one to not rest satisfied with a mere proportionality judgment, say, that fifty civilian casualties are proportionate to one killed Baathist leader (this was the calculation made by the United States in over twenty air strikes at "high value targets" in the opening days of the Iraq war), but instead, to use the most discriminating weapons in one's arsenal and to push for the development of more precise weapons in order to reduce civilian deaths.[41] A further implication of this argument would be that a force must use the most discriminating weapons it has (e.g., smart bombs), even if more expensive than less accurate ones.[42]

(6) Can Interrogatory Torture of Terror Suspects be Justified?

First, it is worth pointing out that contrary to public perception, the conventional wisdom amongst professional interrogators is that torture mostly fails as an interrogation tool. Physical coercion usually either brutalizes the detainee into an insensible and apathetic state, or it produces unreliable information. The torture victim will say anything to make the torture stop. By contrast, noncoercive methods of interrogation, familiar to viewers of police dramas, are largely successful. The efficacy of a morally questionable action is relevant to (at least) Catholic ethics because actions with simultaneous good and bad effects are licit if the good effects outweigh the bad and only the good actions are intended. An ineffective measure is one with no good effects, only bad ones. To knowingly elect it then is evil.

The Church's own history with interrogatory torture is complicated and speaks to the tensions in adopting the coercive tools of the state. Pope Innocent IV authorized the use of interrogatory torture in 1252, its use in the Inquisition peaking in the late sixteenth century before the Inquisition formerly ended in 1834. Current Roman Catholic theology has simple answers to the question of whether any form of physical coercion is allowed in interrogation and the question of what constitutes torture. Any form of mental or physical coercion meant to break the will is a gross offence against human dignity and natural law. It is not a certain level of pain which defines torture, but the end toward which that pain is geared: the disintegration of the victim's will. Human dignity is inviolable because indexed to the divine image. The nature of this will distinguishes God, angels, and humans from all other entities. This core of human nature is prior to any national, political, or religious allegiance; any attempt to violate it is evil.

CONCLUSIONS

A teaching common to the various branches of Christianity is that expediency and morality do not always coincide.[43] A fixture of Original Sin is the disposition to seek the easiest route in every situation, regardless of its moral fittingness. The fact that an immoral act, be it torture, the launching of an unjust war, the punitive destruction of civilian infrastructure, or the cavalier use of relatively inaccurate air power, may seem necessary in a given situation is a reflection of the structures and history of sin leading up that situation. So often, for instance, the "messiness" of unconventional wars against insurgents or terrorists is occasioned by years of immoral government policies, oppression, greed, and neglect. Catholics believe in a world in which immoral action is never necessary. It may be that the relevant moral act is more difficult, more expensive, or less immediately satisfying than an immoral act, but it is ultimately blasphemous to believe that one has no option but to sin. The Church's stringent teachings serve then as a constant call to look closer and try harder in order to do the right thing.

On some Protestant views, genuinely tragic decisions are sometimes necessary because of the pervasiveness of sin. Or at least, some Protestant thinkers reject the Catholic notion that moral prescriptions can be worked out with precision. In the tradition, there is more of a sense that military actions are a microcosm of all human actions, characterized by their distance from a divine standard. Yet at the same time, this distance also provides an opportunity to renew the bond of faith characterized on one end by an inexplicably persistent divine love. This love is seen as a model for overcoming even the most seeming intractable and bitter divisions in the human family, even while there is disagreement among Protestant denominations as to whether it can happen in this world or the next.

With respect to the hypothetical questions, I argued that dragnet arrests are at odds with Christian principles of just war; that a civilian who becomes a suicide bomber is not innocuous and, therefore, can legitimately be treated as a combatant; that holy places which store military materiel can become military targets, but that it is more advisable to find alternatives to their destruction; that destroying means of livelihood should not be done to punish civilians; that every military action where civilians will bear the consequences requires a difficult, but compulsory, proportionality judgment; and, finally, that torture is an unacceptable and mostly useless method to conduct interrogations, no matter the setting. Each of these questions requires, for sure, more extended treatment. However, it is expected that the discussion above had provided the tools to start discussing such topics in reference to the Christian Just War tradition.

NOTES

1. James T. Johnson, "Historical Roots and Sources of the Just War Tradition in Western Culture," in *Just War and Jihad,* eds. J. Kelsay and James Turner Johnson (New York: Greenwood, 1991), 9.

2. Augustine, *Reply to Faustus the Manichean 22. The Nicene and Post-Nicene Fathers* (1st series). trans. R. Stothert, ed. Philip Schaff (Grand Rapids: W.R. Eerdmans Pub., 1956), 4, §78.

3. Cicero, *De Officiis 1. War and Christian Ethics,* trans. W. Miller, ed. Arthur F. Holmes, 29.

4. This tragic necessity goes along with that of upright judges who will have to sometimes torture and execute the innocent because unsure of their innocence. Even parents will have to beat their children to keep them from becoming completely wicked. Augustine writes, a fitting prayer one in authority might offer is *"deliver me from my necessities."* City of God (New York: Penguin, 1972), XIX.6.

5. Augustine, *Faustus,* §74.

6. Augustine, *City of God,* trans. Henry Bettenson (New York: Penguin, 1972), XIX.7.

7. Ibid.

8. Johnson, "Historical Roots," 9.

9. Providence makes use of even unjust violence to punish the wicked and test the righteous. Augustine, *Faustus,* §75.

10. Thomas Aquinas, *Summa Theologica,* II–II, Q 40.1.

11. Ibid., Q 40.3.

12. Ibid., Q 64.3, 7.

13. Ibid., Q 64.7.

14. Ibid., Q 64.7.

15. This predates the clean separation of modern law's focus on *jus ad bellum* and *jus in bello,* but prefigures modern law's concepts like proportionality. Aquinas introduces the notion in a discussion of self-defense, but it is later used by Vitoria to justify the civilian deaths that are foreseen but not intended by the bombardment of a city—the context in which the doctrine is most frequently invoked today in the guise of targeting law.

16. Erasmus, *The Education of a Christian Prince,* ed. Arthur F. Holmes, 180.

17. Ibid., 182.

18. Johnson, "Historical Roots," 11.

19. Contemporary thinkers disagree as to whether some or all the criteria need be met in order for a war to be justified, whether there is a serial or lexical order to them, or whether they are rules of thumb rather than hard and fast criteria. See James Childress, "Just War Criteria," in *War in the 20th Century,* ed. Richard Miller (Lousiville: Westminster, 1992), 364.

20. Franciscus de Vitoria, *De Indiis et de Iure Belli Relectiones,* trans. J.P. Bate, ed. Arthur F. Holmes, 122–25.

21. Ibid., 135.

22. Timothy Renick, "Charity Lost: The Secularization of the Principle of Double Effect in the Just War Theory," *The Thomist* 58 (1994): 455.

23. U.S. Conference of Catholic Bishops, 2005.

24. Aquinas, *Summa Theologica,* II-II, Q 64.7.

25. Renick, "Charity Lost," 456. I agree with Renick's assessment of the practical latitude the secularization of just war thinking has afforded warfighters. I am less sure that this is an inherent effect of secularizing just war thinking. It strikes me that just war thinking and particularly the doctrine of double effect mediate two contradictory demands placed on the warfighter, to defer to the rights of all civilians, foreign and domestic, and to protect his homeland. The latter requires him to engage in behavior that may have an ill effect on foreign civilians. Innocent people have an absolute right not to be attacked with violence, because they have done nothing to justify coercion. The absolute nature of that right puts constant pressure on the warfighter to fully defer to it, even while also meeting his protective obligation. Such constant pressure ought to lead to constant attempts to find tactics and weapons enabling ever more discriminatory and prudential operation.

26. Martin Luther, "Whether Soldiers, Too, Can Be Saved," trans. C.M. Jacobs, rev. R.C. Schultz, ed. Arthur F. Holmes, 143.

27. Ibid., 152.

28. Ibid., 150, 153, 161.

29. "God restrains such (warmongering) princes by giving fists to other people too." "Whether Soldiers," trans. C.M. Jacobs, rev. R.C. Schultz, ed. Arthur F. Holmes, 153.

30. Jean Calvin, *The Institutes of the Christian Religion. War and Christian Ethics,* trans. J. Allen, ed. Arthur F. Holmes (Grand Rapids: Baker, 1975), 167.

31. Reinhold Niebuhr, "Why the Christian Church Is Not Pacifist?" in *War in the Twentieth Century; Sources in Theological Ethics,* ed. Richard Miller (Kentucky: Westminster/John Knox Press, 1992).

32. Ibid., 35.

33. See Richard B. Miller, *Interpretations of Conflict* (Chicago: University Press, 1991), for an excellent discussion of this variety.

34. Pope Pius XII, Broadcast message, Christmas 1941, AAS 34 (1942) 17.

35. U.S. Conference of Catholic Bishops, 2005.

36. Pope John XXIII, *Pacem in Terris (Peace of Earth)* (Washington, DC: United States Conference of Catholic Bishops Publishing Office, 2003), §112.

37. Michael Skerker, "Just War Criteria and the New Face of War," *The Journal of Military Ethics* 3, no. 1 (2004).

38. Miller, *Interpretations of Conflict,* 26.

39. Dt. 20:19–20

40. Renick, "Charity Lost," 455.

41. Douglas Jehl and Eric Schmitt, "Errors Are Seen in Early Attacks on Iraq's Leaders," *The New York Times* (June 13, 2004), A1, 16.

42. Skerker, "The Moral Case for Improved Technology, Training, and Intelligence," U.S. Air Force Academy, May 29, 2005.

43. This chapter has not explored the third branch of Christianity, Eastern Orthodoxy. There are few texts about this tradition and war available in English translation. My understanding is that Eastern Orthodox theologians who address war tend to utilize natural law categories.

PART V

Law of Armed Conflict and International Law: Operational Law

CHAPTER 13

Redefining Legitimacy: Legal Issues

DAVID K. LINNAN

The purpose of this chapter is twofold. First, to provide an overview of modern use of force law to enable the nonspecialist better to understand the more technical legal essays on the law of armed conflict that follow. Second, to relate arguments worldwide about the legality of American use of force in Iraq and Afghanistan to nonlegal arguments about legitimacy. International law is peculiar not the least because it lies on a fault line between politics and law, to the that extent states typically justify their actions in terms of legality while their actions themselves may make law in a technical sense. These concerns are visible in the domestic and international debates surrounding Iraq, Afghanistan and the so-called GWOT (global war on terror).

We can, however, take some suspense out of the legal analysis already in terms of ultimate conclusions. In international law terms, the use of armed force in Afghanistan falls within most international lawyers' zone of comfort. However, the same cannot be said in unequivocal terms about the use of armed force in Iraq even under traditional U.S. views. Arguments about legality then directly influence perceptions of legitimacy.

ARMED CONFLICT LAW AND LEGITIMACY

Traditional armed conflict law addresses "international armed conflicts," understood as wars between states, but consensus is more fleeting concerning "noninternational armed conflicts" (e.g., civil wars) and the proper treatment of nonstate actors (whether as participants in a civil war, or as "free agents" in the manner of individuals or movements carrying out cross-border violence). Nonstate actors and terrorism are not new problems, as witnessed by nineteenth and early twentieth century anarchists and ethnic nationalists, remembering how World War I started. However, the legal problem is that nonstate actors do not exist in a vacuum so that problems typically spill over into relations between states. Issues arise both in terms of the legality of using force against or on the territory of another state (traditionally, *jus ad bellum* or the law of going to war, now understood as restraining the use of force) and the treatment of combatants (traditionally, *jus in bello* or the law of how war should be conducted; basically whether combatants associated with nonstate actors should enjoy the full treaty or customary law protections which have grown up around international armed conflict).

The former *jus ad bellum*-type issue is typically joined when one state desires to use armed force on the territory of another against nonstate actors. How to reconcile the two states' competing interests in a political and legal sense? Concretely, that was the problem in Afghanistan post-September 11, 2001, with the Taliban government of Afghanistan willingly sheltering al Qaeda as nonstate actor on its territory following its attacks on the United States. The problem is allegedly repeating itself again now in the Pakistani border areas, where al Qaeda may be sheltering, while the Pakistani government remains unable or unwilling for domestic political reasons to take action.

Separately *jus in bello*-type issues have haunted military operations in Iraq and Afghanistan as well as the so-called GWOT, in terms of treatment of combatants and alleged terrorists. The concerns involve questions about methods of interrogation (the torture question) and theoretically indefinite incarceration. These issues have arisen domestically in cases like *Hamdi* and *Hamdan* addressed in parallel chapters, as well as internationally in conjunction with Abu Gharib, Guantanamo, rendition and claimed secret prisons reported on by the European Parliament. They are particularly complex to the extent domestic constitutional law (power of the executive versus the courts or legislative branch in national security matters) often overlaps with international law issues (content of the Geneva Conventions). But, particularly for an American audience, it is necessary to understand the (foreign) legal views behind the fact that military operations in Iraq and Afghanistan generally have been received poorly outside the United States. This impacts legitimacy directly, to the extent questions about the legality of the initial use of force lead to a hypercritical examination of the conduct of armed conflict.

Speaking as a lawyer, the striking thing about the use of armed force in Iraq is that, while it might have been possible to make a colorable case to fit it within traditional use of force categories (e.g., anticipatory self-defense), for whatever reason the U.S. government choose not to try to cloak its policy decision to use armed force in traditional legal terms. Instead, it apparently intended to establish as a matter of principle the claim of a new concept to justify the use of armed force (so-called preventive war, premised on what appear now to be faulty assumptions about weapons of mass destruction [WMD] in Iraq). Thus, without the cover of a Chapter VII UN Security Council Resolution or traditional self-defense law, the United States invaded Iraq. Had WMD or concrete evidence of military relationships between the state of Iraq and al Qaeda terrorists been found, claims about preventive war probably would have been regarded as overblown political rhetoric overlaid over traditional legal categories like self-defense. The supposed special character of WMDs presents scant comfort, because there is a tradition reaching back to the 1960s of treating them under anticipatory self-defense doctrine (first strike problems).

The aggressive assertion of "preventive war" in the absence of formal justification now looks problematic, however, since there is no mistake or similar doctrine in international law justifying the unilateral use of armed force on the basis of mistaken assumptions concerning WMDs in Iraq. The subsequent fallback position in legal terms, that humanitarian intervention could also justify the use of armed force in Iraq, is unconvincing as judged by its not even lukewarm reception by most states and publicists. Ultimately, the so-called "preventive war" approach simply appears to be a bridge too far in legal terms. Others may assess its legitimacy and the effects of its failure under those circumstances, assuming it to be a good faith mistake, albeit one not acknowledged by the law.

POST-9/11 FACTUAL AND POLICY BACKGROUND

The background for the current use of armed force in Iraq and Afghanistan reaches separately back to early 1990s problems involving what are now judged to be al Qaeda operations against U.S. interests, such as the original 1993 bombing of the World Trade Center, the 1998 bombing of the American Embassies in Kenya and Tanzania, and the 2000 attack on the USS *Cole*. In this light, the September 11, 2001, airplane attacks on the World Trade Center represent the culmination of an ongoing process rather than an isolated event. For these purposes, it suffices to note that al Qaeda, commonly referred to as a terrorist organization, in legal terms does not appear to have been affiliated with a state or government in carrying out its attacks on U.S. interests (i.e., in ordinary English, there has been no convincing proof offered of a link between any state and al Qaeda despite sometimes loose assertions concerning share interests between al Qaeda and the so-called "Axis of Evil" states, particularly Iraq and Iran). In legal terms al Qaeda was and still appears to be a "nonstate actor," and "terrorism" for these purposes describes an approach to the calculated use of unlawful violence with more political than legal content (once a determination is made that the violence is unlawful, lawyers largely do not care about motivation).

Whether or not a state were involved, international lawyers noted that U.S. political and military doctrine began to consider asymmetric threats such as terrorist attacks already during the Clinton administration under policy statements (military "white papers") culminating in the September 2002 Bush administration's NSS (National Security Strategy).[1] The NSS, issued post-9/11, and related reports contemplate a world in which military-style threats are no longer tied to a bipolar, Cold War-style world, or even national states. Instead, they contemplate the problem of weak or failing states, and so-called rogue states (meaning states typically seeking WMDs in order to assert themselves on a regional basis, often in violation of international law and in any case commonly in aggrandizement of individual leadership) which may harbor or encourage terrorism for their own purposes. The NSS aggressively mandates confronting states tied to terrorism, asserting a right of self-defense in legal terms allowing preemptive, unilateral action.

Afghanistan was invaded post-9/11 relatively quickly in October 2001 in the name of suppressing al Qaeda via the Taliban. The initial U.S. military action was justified in terms of self-defense, but the UN Security Council eventually embraced the use of armed force in Afghanistan under Chapter VII resolutions. Iraq was invaded in March 2003 expressly without the legal support of a Chapter VII Security Council Resolution. To date, there is no Chapter VII resolution post–Gulf War convincingly justifying the use of armed force in Iraq.

DEVELOPMENT OF LEGAL PRINCIPLES CONCERNING THE USE OF ARMED FORCE

We now set forth an abbreviated history of the development of public international law's restraints on the use of armed force. We also sketch conceptual differences within this area. Beyond history, our examination is cast largely in terms of the UN collective security structure and the proper reading of UN Charter Articles 2(4) and 51 (including legal concepts of self-defense with aspects of necessity and aggression). The focus is also largely on traditional *jus ad bellum* concerns, leaving the details of current *jus in bello* to parallel chapters. A short summary then follows how related legal positions are reflected in the Afghanistan and Iraq situations.

All these issues can be understood only against the backdrop of the intended supranational peacekeeping role of the Security Council under the UN Charter (and distant echoes of the predecessor League of Nations' failure). The Security Council's long-term Cold War institutional paralysis led to a situation in which the unilateral self-defense concept achieved predominance, conflict was often waged by proxy in insurgencies (thus not always international at first glance[2]), and states' cooperation was limited. Political changes in the former Soviet Union and then the first Bush administration's successful pursuit of a Security Council mandate to use armed force to dislodge Iraq from Kuwait revived hopes that regional conflicts could be managed under the multinational Security Council system (as contemplated in the immediate aftermath of World War II). The revival did not entirely live up to expectations, however, since the end of the Cold War did not herald a general peace so much as a changed international environment, including nonstate sponsored terrorism and similar threats in part coinciding with concerns about access to WMD.

For clarity's sake, we employ in the material that follows a certain conceptual shorthand in referring to different national views of international law in turn as the "American view," the "Socialist law view," the "Continental legal science view," and the "Developing Nations view." Three caveats are in order. First, as might be guessed from the names, these views have been influenced traditionally both by political and legal factors. Second, views of the law have always differed within these broad categories (so monolithic characterization is overly simplistic). In particular, political changes in Eastern Europe make reference to Socialist law views seem dated. However, the views arguably live on in still formally Socialist states such as in Asia the People's Republic of China or Vietnam, or under national views of the newer Eastern European states. Finally, time permits only a summary overview of the true legal complexity in this area since national views are influenced in a technical sense by domestic law, but any detailed comparative law exploration of differences lies beyond this chapter. Beyond the caveats, however, it is necessary to understand that non-American legal evaluations of the legality of military operations in Iraq and Afghanistan underpin the legitimacy question outside the United States.

Nascent Regulation of the Use of Force and Outlawing Aggression

The development of modern principles limiting armed force is best understood against the backdrop of nineteenth century views concerning legality of its use and the formal, legal concept of war. In opposition to older natural law views requiring "just cause" for a "just" or legal war (reviewed in parallel chapters of religion scholars), the positivistic nineteenth century international law concept of war adhered to the view that each state as an element of its sovereignty retained the right to go to war against another state at any time for any reason, or for no reason at all (under *jus belli ac pacis*). At the same time, the use of force in international relations was distinguishable from war per se if only arbitrarily under doctrines concerning the state of war (incorporating a subjective, intent-based test of *animo beligerendi* that required one or sometimes both parties intend or believe that a state of war exist before the use of force would be viewed as a hostile act in the course of a war). In spite of propagandistic attempts to justify the use of force in asserting another state's prior affront (real or imagined), it was generally acknowledged under nineteenth century views of international law that armed force could be used to protect a state's economic and other interests during peacetime as well as wartime (distinguished under traditional legal categories as involving the "law of peace" versus the "law of war").

Determining the legality of armed force had little meaning in the context of a system where the right to make war was legally unlimited. However, collateral views about rationales for recognizing the use of force retain some relevance for modern international law principles. For these purposes, one can distinguish between older views recognizing self-help or self-preservation as the justification for the use of force. The self-help rationale focused on the lack of an adjudicatory and enforcement mechanism under then-contemporary international law (providing a state with no effective recourse if an obligation owed by another state were violated). On the other hand, the self-preservation rationale responded to the perception that a state must have some right to resist attacks on its interests (and ultimately on its very existence).

The development of modern international law views concerning war and the use of force dates back to the end of the nineteenth century.[3] It incorporates two distinct areas of legal attention. Within the traditional coverage of the law of war, from the time of the First Hague Peace conference (resulting in the various 1899 *Hague Conventions and Declarations* largely limiting armaments, followed by the Second Peace Conference resulting in the 1907 *Hague Conventions,* and through modern day arms control agreements and the various *Geneva Protocols*), one legal strand has accepted the idea of armed conflict but sought essentially on humanitarian grounds to limit the fashion in which hostilities would be conducted. This has now become the international humanitarian law and the basic source of much of modern *jus in bello*, treated in subsequent chapters. We turn our attention instead to the second legal strand, namely the limitation of the use of force itself under international law. Development of the second legal strand dates back effectively to the founding of the League of Nations in the aftermath of World War I and through the applicable UN Charter interpretation ultimately affects all modern uses of armed force.

The League's founding is acknowledged as a watershed, reflecting the general political consensus in the aftermath of World War I that the traditional law *jus belli ac pacis* was grossly unsuitable as a method of resolving international disputes. Without addressing the League's eventual failure to maintain international peace, we focus here on three narrow legal points involving the treaty character of the 1919 League Covenant. First, the apparent renunciation of war as a method of settling international disputes was recognized at the time of the League's founding as a departure from existing customary law. This creation of new international law by treaty was thus effective only among League member states and did not immediately accede to the status of new and universally binding customary law. Most but not all of the major powers were members (e.g., the United States was not). Second, the operative Covenant provisions largely referred to a rejection of "war," with the result that at least initially older, intent-based state of war doctrines arguably permitted a state to use armed force in the conduct of international affairs (but then to deny that war was involved). To the extent Article 10 of the Covenant apparently required mutual assistance against "aggression" or its threat against the "territorial integrity and existing political independence" of League members, this undertaking was characterized as a moral rather than legal obligation by some states. Each member state was left individually to decide what its assistance should consist of in a specific instance. Third, while outlawing a "resort to war," in opposition to the current UN Charter the Covenant's language was literally silent on "self-defense." Covenant Article 16 stipulated that a member state's violation of its obligations in resorting to war would be deemed an act of war against all other members, and it contemplated that those states could then wage a defensive war against the transgressor (not avoiding the previously discussed problems inherent in keying the response to war). Mention is made of self-defense only indirectly or by inference as in the problematic mutual assistance undertaking of Covenant Article 10.

The Covenant's shortcomings were recognized already in the 1920s, and a combination of general antiwar sentiment and demands for structural improvement in the means for peaceful resolution of disputes (chiefly arbitration and conciliation) led to further conferences and treaties. By the time of the 1925 *Locarno Treaties* (providing for the peaceful arbitration of disputes among World War I's European protagonists), Article 2 of the centerpiece guaranty treaty distinguishes between "attack," "invasion," or "resort to war," and expressly recognizes that these do not include the use of armed force in the exercise of "legitimate defense" or pursuant to actions taken under the League's aegis or various Covenant provisions.

The 1928 *General Treaty for the Renunciation of War* (*"Kellogg–Briand Pact"*) represents the effective culmination of efforts between the World Wars to address perceived problems in the Covenant and League system. The fact that the United States was a signatory and the *Kellogg–Briand Pact*'s ambition to go beyond the Covenant substantively (and eventually to form the basis of new general international law excluding aggressive war) make it particularly important. By its terms, the *Kellogg–Briand Pact* condemned "recourse to war" to resolve disputes and "renounce[d] it as an instrument of national policy." The Covenant's unfortunate employment of "war" was repeated, raising questions whether the *Kellogg–Briand Pact* was subject to the same infirmities of whether it was intended generally to establish that, subject to limited exceptions, the use of armed-force to resolve disputes was unlawful. However, the better view is that signatory states' use of armed force without sufficient legal cause itself already was rendered generally unlawful. Customary law incorporated this view in any case during the 1930s (as confirmed by war crimes tribunals in the aftermath of World War II). Effectively, at this point "war" ceases to have much meaning as a term of art in public international law, for which purposes its employment correspondingly in the current language of "war on terrorism" largely represents rhetoric rather than possessing legal significance in a technical sense.[4]

The *Kellogg–Briand Pact* contained on its face no reference to self-defense, however, in the preparatory work and by exchange of diplomatic notes the parties variously reserved rights of "self-defense," "legitimate defense," or "legitimate self-defense." The United States itself expressly stated by note that nothing therein "restrict[ed] or impair [ed] in any way the right of self-defense" which is "inherent in every sovereign state and implicit in every treaty." The United States' note went on to characterize self-defense as an "inalienable" and "natural right," which "[e]very nation is free at all times and regardless of treaty provisions" to exercise and apparently laid claim to the ability of each state to decide for itself at least initially when its own right of self-defense applied.

During the 1930s, legal developments began to diverge. One branch eventually followed by Socialist law and Developing Nation views (predominantly under the Continental legal science view) focused on the legal concept of aggression chiefly in territorial, first-strike terms (harkening back to League Covenant Article 10, conceived of originally in response to Germany's World War I invasion of Belgium). Another branch incorporating the American view concentrated on the legal concept of self-defense (rooted in customary law ideas of self-preservation). Legal analysis under both viewed large-scale military invasion by an aggressor state as unlawful. However, opinions differed concerning the legality of low-level intervention in asserting traditional diplomatic protection (military operations carried out on foreign territory in protection of the lives or property of a state's nationals) and the assertion of "self-defense" in the protection of vital interests of a political or economic nature. Carrying such technical differences forward, nonstate actors like al Qaeda now split this problematic divide.

Collective Security, Self-defense, and Interpretation of the UN Charter

The most important difference between the League of Nations and United Nations arguably lies in enforcement mechanisms rather than fine substantive distinctions concerning views of armed force's legality. Given international law's inherent lack of coercive enforcement mechanisms (because there is no supranational "sovereign" to levy penalties in the Austinian sense), enforcement mechanisms and substantive law standards enjoy equal significance. The UN Charter incorporates both modern substantive law norms governing the use of armed force as well as a new organizational structure to enforce international peace in the form of the Security Council system.[5] The League structure permitted only coordination of individual states' voluntary responses to aggression, while the Security Council system permits designation of an aggressor state to be coupled with a mandatory coercive regime as discussed in a parallel chapter (requiring member states to oppose the disturbance of international peace, using force if necessary). At an extreme, traditional law's categories of belligerent and neutral states have been displaced by aggressor states and all other states (arrayed against them under Security Council direction).

The final treaty terms of the UN Charter were negotiated at the 1945 San Francisco Conference on International Organization (open to all interested states except the defeated Axis Powers). Under the circumstances, the UN collective security system was devised in a conscious effort to revive many of the League of Nations' aspirations in a more effective enforcement structure. Beyond the danger of general conflagration (World War II had just ended), the drafters of the Charter had before their eyes the example of the League's ultimate failure in its 1930s dealings with regional conflicts: Japan's 1931 invasion of Manchuria, the 1934–35 Italo-Abyssinian War, the 1939 Soviet-Finnish War, and Germany's progressive occupations of the Rhineland (1936), Austria (1938), and Czechoslovakia (1939).

The San Francisco Conference saw a variety of proposals by small states addressed to reconciliation of nonintervention principles with collective response to aggression along League lines (and an attempt to make collective response mandatory, a goal sought by weak states and resisted by strong states ever since the failure of League Covenant Article 10). The Security Council system agreed upon addressed perceived flaws in the League Covenant system by providing that a unified Security Council could compel all UN member states to respond to threats against international peace (under UN Charter Chapter VII). In matters concerning international peace, however, by virtue of special veto provisions, no action could be forced against the will of any Permanent Member of the Security Council (World War II's chief Allied Powers, France, Britain, China, the Soviet Union, and the United States). When united, however, the Security Council could (1) withdraw matters concerning international peace from UN General Assembly consideration as well as (2) preclude unilateral self-defense from interfering with Security Council measures. On a substantive law level, a fair reading of the San Francisco proceedings illuminates the conceptual interrelationship of current UN Charter Article 2(1) (sovereign equality of all states, the basis of the new general UN system), Article 2(3) (calling for the peaceful resolution of all disputes), Article 2(4) (apparently absolute prohibition of the use of armed force against the "territorial integrity or political independence of any State" recalling the language of League Covenant Article 10), and Article 51 (specifically recognizing the exercise of collective or individual self-defense pending Security Council action against threats to international peace).

On an institutional level, the opposing vetoes of the United States and the Soviet Union largely foreclosed Security Council-mandated coercive peacekeeping activity during the entire Cold War period. Korea was the sole significant exception prior to the First Gulf War Kuwait situation (minor exceptions include Zimbabwe, then Southern Rhodesia). As an organizational matter, a general form of collective security response evolved during the Korea situation in the form of voluntary action by member states acting through the UN General Assembly (so-called "Uniting for Peace Resolutions," controversial and, due to the voluntary nature of any state's assistance, subject to many of the League Covenant system's infirmities). For the most part, however, the legal basis for any state's collective security response revolved around divergent interpretations under the UN Charter of competing views of self-defense and aggression developing since the 1930s. As a technical matter, the substantive law issues revolve around concerns whether drafters of the UN Charter intended to depart from progressive legal developments concerning the use of armed force dating back to the creation of the League (as opposed to merely incorporating applicable customary law as understood on the eve of World War II). Different readings of the relevant treaty provisions are the literal source of widely divergent interpretations of modern self-defense rights: the proper interpretation and interplay between Articles 2(4) and 51 of the UN Charter. Departing from the Covenant's and *Kellogg–Briand Pact*'s problematic usage of the term "war," Article 2(4) is expressly directed against the "use of force":

> "All [member states] shall refrain in their international relations from the threat or use of force against the territorial integrity or political independence of any state, or in any other manner inconsistent with the Purposes of the United Nations."

Departing from prior treaties' literal silence, Article 51 expressly addresses "self-defense":

> "Nothing in the present Charter shall impair the inherent right of individual or collective self-defense if an armed attack occurs against a Member of the United Nations, until the Security Council has taken measures necessary to maintain international peace and security. Measures taken by Members...shall not in any way affect the authority and responsibility of the Security Council...to take at any time such action as it deems necessary in order to maintain or restore international peace and security."

Based upon technical principles of treaty interpretation, the correct reading of the UN Charter is that Article 2(4) is more than a general statement of principles and directly covers the use of armed force in international relations (as augmented by Article 2(1)'s sovereign equality concept). It largely incorporates the customary law in this area developed particularly in the wake of the *Kellogg–Briand Pact* (subject to a recognition that certain United Nations organs have a final power of determination in such matters). Article 51's specific mention of self-defense should not be understood as an independent locus of textual interpretation. Instead, Article 51 simply states a rule of preliminary disposition pending Security Council action (which preliminary disposition may remain permanently in place insofar as the Security Council is paralyzed by veto or chooses not to act). However, this statement of the law (essentially in terms of the American view) is probably a minority view in the international community of states.

On a structural basis, modern views of self-defense may be separated into two polar groups. The American view focuses on Article 51's "inherent right" language viewing

Article 51 largely as a general savings clause for the customary law (viewing Article 2(4) as a rather abstract general statement of principle rather than an operative treaty provision). Socialist law views (seemingly with Continental legal science and Developing Nation views) see Article 51 as the proper focus for examination of the modern concept of permissible self-defense (viewing Article 2(4) by its terms as permitting the use of armed force only under Article 51 self-defense or the authority of UN organ). Their interpretation of permissible self-defense under the UN Charter involves literal interpretation of Article 51's first clause (transforming "armed attack" into a term of art alternatively precluding self-defense claims in response to *de minimis* disturbances of international peace and anticipatory self-defense as recognized by traditional law). By this chain of reasoning, Article 51's armed attack terminology prescribing the boundaries of permissible self-defense is read into Article 2(4) as the source of the aggression prohibition. This is linked in the case of the Continental legal science view to a variety of doctrinal interpretations of the self-defense concept (apparently influenced in varying degrees by domestic law concepts of self-defense and necessity). In the case of Socialist law and certain Developing Nations views, they are joined more directly to aggression in a pairing of Articles 2(4) and 51.

Thus, the self-defense and aggression concepts are linked in uneasy fashion under modern international law. For our purposes, we distinguish here between the two basic approaches to self-defense noted above. On a technical level, the two differ on whether self-defense under the UN Charter should be treated as a definitional construct delimited by views of aggression itself or whether the content of the self-defense concept should be derived from a restrictive view of the older customary law embodying a self-preservation rationale. Both approaches nominally treat self-defense and aggression as independent concepts, but the definitional construct approach treats self-defense as aggression's mirror image while the customary law view itself is severed from the aggression concept. The aggression concept (and indirectly the true scope of UN Charter Article 2(4)'s textually absolute prohibition on violations of territorial integrity) over time has evaded any generally accepted definition in various UN-related proceedings.[6] Beyond the easy case of a large-scale military invasion (as with Iraq's 1990–91 attempted annexation of Kuwait), there continues to be substantial disagreement about the scope of aggression viewed as a legal concept. Beyond intellectual disputation, however, the determination of what constitutes aggression is vitally important under this approach when it is allowed negatively to define self-defense.

Major differences have revolved around issues such as "indirect aggression" (crucial during the Cold War). The American view maintains that sponsored insurgencies normally constitute grounds for collective self-defense measures against the sponsoring state. Meanwhile, Socialist law and Developing Nations views claim special rights to undisturbed external support of national liberation fronts and anticolonial movements under self-determination or similar principles (in the Middle East context, Arab states' support for the Palestine Liberation Organization). For technical reasons, the Continental legal science view characterizes such foreign sponsorship in most circumstances as "mere intervention" (not justifying collective self-defense measures against the sponsoring state or the use of force on a foreign state's territory against insurgents operating from cross-border sanctuaries under specific interpretations of UN Charter Article 2(4)). As a result, leading self-defense precedents supporting the American view have been rejected or recharacterized beyond recognition (e.g., *The Caroline*,[7] providing that self-defense requires the "necessity of self-defence is instant, overwhelming, and leaving no choice of means, and no moment for deliberation"). The American view itself has departed from traditional law principles from time to time in postulating a right for states to use armed force in a foreign State in support of its citizens' fundamental human rights (impinged on by totalitarian governments) in terms of humanitarian intervention.[8] Differing views are also apparent in connection with the use of armed force abroad in situations such as hostage rescues and antiterrorism measures.

Here is where we find one issue concerning terrorism or threats more generally involving nonstate actors. The issue may be stated in terms of the self-defense formulation that, if only an "armed attack" is valid grounds for self-defense, does a nonstate actor's terrorist bombing rise to the level of an "armed attack"? There is not much question that such activity could be criminalized under domestic law, so the real issue is whether states under international law may use armed force on the territory of another state to ward off the threat. In legal terms, it largely looks like a replay of "indirect aggression" analysis,[9] subject to a variety of claims that various treaty approaches to terrorism permit the use of armed force (except for the fact that the states harboring alleged terrorists are often not signatories to such treaties with the result that we are thrown back on customary law self-defense analysis). On the one hand, non-U.S. views of self-defense probably would characterize an individual bombing to be de minimus and so lacking as a justification for the use of force. On the other hand, the nonstate actor character itself may be used under non-U.S. views to deny that self-defense as such is involved, instead claiming mere necessity which is then deemed an insufficient ground for the use of armed force (because only a state and its representatives may commit aggression, understood as conversely defining self-defense).

As the converse of aggression, the definitional construct view of self-defense also has not usually been considered to incorporate restrictive elements accompanying the traditional customary law concept of self-defense (most notably the necessity and proportionality requirements under the *Caroline* test, as required under the American view). Instead, as a military matter, a state considered to be the victim of aggression might equally well restrict its military operations to driving out invaders (without its own troops crossing its borders), or might carry the war to the enemy by its troops' invasion of enemy territory. To the extent proportionality is required, however, there is precedent reaching back into the League period (the 1924 *Greco-Bulgarian Frontier Incident*) to the effect that excessive force initiated in putative self-defense itself is a violation (and may be characterized as aggression under some views).

The U.S. self-defense claims premised on the *Caroline* face one final legal issue, namely that of immediacy which normally translates into claims about whether anticipatory self-defense is permissible or whether a potential state victim of aggression must wait for the invader to strike first. The traditional U.S. view is no, there is no requirement to take the first blow, but the *Caroline* position is hedged in terms of immediacy and the lack of other choices. This is the hidden legal issue in the concept of "preemptive war," understood as the use of armed force against an eventual enemy rather than a current threat.

To appearances, the *Caroline* and traditional U.S. approaches focused on threat analysis rather than an enemy per se.[10] Recalling legal analysis of first strike discussions around the time of the 1962 Cuban Missile Crisis, however, it would appear that the traditional U.S. position on WMD and anticipatory self-defense still incorporates immediacy in the analysis even of preemptive nuclear strikes. This is also why it remains difficult legally to justify the use of force in Iraq based upon claims that, even if Iraqi WMDs had been destroyed by 2003, Saddam Hussein would in the future have developed new WMDs.

Thus the puzzling element in the Iraq situation, that the use of force argument seems to be made in terms of preemptive war beyond the bounds of the *Caroline* even while, at least at the time armed force was initially used, it was still possible in good faith to articulate an anticipatory self-defense position consistent with traditional U.S. views of self-defense doctrine (regardless of the fact that other countries might analyze self-defense under UN Charter Article 51 textually in terms of requiring a prior "armed attack" as condition precedent).

Postwar International Court of Justice cases addressing the use of armed force in any substantial way are only two in number. The 1949 *Corfu Channel Case* (*"Corfu Channel Case"*) involved the alleged State responsibility of Albania for foreign warships' mine-inflicted losses suffered in its territorial waters during peacetime.[11] As a substantive matter, the case's peculiar posture presented substantial issues both in the area of the law of straits and territorial waters as well as the threat or use of force within another State's jurisdiction, together with the basic issue of Albanian responsibility for the mine damage. For our purposes, it suffices to note that the decision in the *Corfu Channel Case* is inconsistent in important ways with the restrictive reading of UN Charter Article 2(4) customarily associated with the definitional construct approach to self-defense.

The 1984 *Case Concerning Military and Para-military Activities In and Against Nicaragua* (*"Contra Case"*)[12] is the Court's most recent pronouncement on the self-defense concept. On a very basic level, if for no other reason, the opinion is noteworthy as an implicit confirmation by the International Court of Justice of the post–World War II war crimes tribunals' rejection of the American view expressed in connection with its reservation to the *Kellogg–Briand Pact* (the position that a state is the sole judge of its own activities asserted to be in the exercise of self-defense rights). However, it attracted comparatively more attention among American jurists to compulsory jurisdiction issues and the International Court of Justice's general role than to its substantive pronouncements on self-defense (U.S. disagreement with jurisdictional findings led to withdrawal from the case between the preliminary and merits phases). Further, the Court's peculiar approach to limitations on its jurisdiction resulted in the application of what it referred to as a variety of customary law (despite liberal references to the UN and OAS Charters), rendering interpretation of the precedent problematic. However, read closely it appears that the Court effectively adopted the definitional construct approach to self-defense, essentially tying it to the related interpretation of UN Charter Articles 2(4) and 51 (that UN Charter Article 2(4) restrictions on the use of armed force permit its use only under the direction of a UN organ or under a restrictive idea of self-defense keyed to Article 51's "armed attack" language), largely divorcing it from traditional customary law views of self-defense.

A full discussion of the eventually settled and withdrawn case entitled *Aerial Incident of 3 July 1988 (Islamic Republic of Iran v. United States of America)* (*"Flight 655 Case,"* involving the 1988 downing of an Iranian civil airliner over the Persian Gulf by the U.S.S. *Vincennes*) is beyond the scope of this chapter.[13] However, it is important under the circumstances precisely because it presents the problem of mistake under use of force law including issues of self-defense, necessity and related matters under UN Charter Articles 2(4) and 51. On its face, the substance of the *Flight 655 Case* is directed at international civil aviation treaty law. The United States' position was that, while the downing of Flight 655 was a tragic mistake, it was incidental to the *Vincennes'* lawful use of force in self-defense and so no legal responsibility attached to the act. Given views of civil aviation treaty law expressed following the 1983 Soviet downing of Korean

Airlines Flight KE 007, it appeared that the civil aviation treaty undertakings are subject to the reservation of rights under the UN Charter (here in particular Articles 2(4) and 51). Thus, the issue was theoretically joined over the legality of the *Vincennes'* use of armed force against the aircraft. If it were lawful under the Charter, no violation of civil aviation law should have been recognized. The case was effectively settled and dropped from the ICJ list, however, scholarly analysis was that liability existed despite a good faith mistake.[14]

This result is reinforced by the use of force precedents from the League of Nations period before World War II. The Greco-Bulgarian Border Incident of 1924 is still recalled as a leading customary law precedent pre-UN Charter Article 51, concerning the line between lower grade "border incidents" involving small-scale border police or military hostilities versus "armed attack" justifying full scale self-defense measures, which has continuing relevance for textualist self-defense views now focused on the key "armed attack" concept. On its facts, the Greco-Bulgarian Frontier Incident involved a good faith mistake concerning the scope of the initial frontier incident, and whether in short order foreign troops were crossing the border in strength (the factual situation was that only a minor border incident involving apparent misunderstandings has taken place, but the misunderstanding occurred largely due to poor communications). If there were a viable mistake doctrine in traditional use of force law, it should have covered the mistaken, good faith overreaction which vitiated a claim of proportional self-defense. On that basis, we say there is no "oops" or good faith mistake doctrine absolving a state from responsibility for the unlawful but good faith use of armed force. This is the hidden danger of self-judging self-defense; "you break it, you buy it," paralleling Colin Powell's sentiments about Iraq generally, speaking as former Secretary of State and Chairman of the Joint Chiefs of Staff.

USE OF FORCE IN AFGHANISTAN AND IRAQ IN CONTEXT

We now return in summary fashion to the issue of legal doctrine as applied to the use of armed force in Afghanistan and Iraq presently. Discourse concerning use of force in Iraq and Afghanistan commonly employs a mixture of legal and nonlegal concepts. The largely nonlegal ones include preemptive war, WMDs, terrorism, the war on terror and rogue states. But, on the legal side, the traditional law of armed force is reasonably narrowly prescribed, and its parameters are set by collective security ideas under UN Charter Chapter VII and related ideas about self-defense law mostly under Articles 2(4) and 51. There are at times substantial differences between United States and some other countries' views of permissible self-defense, but beyond the differences it would appear that even a good faith mistake about the presence of self-defense law's requirements is not an excuse, legally speaking, for the unjustified use of armed force.

The differences between United States and some other countries' views are technical in nature, but have surfaced traditionally in discussions of indirect aggression (sponsored insurgencies) and now terrorism involving nonstate actors. The issues at stake involve ideas about territorial integrity and whether states may intervene on the territory of another to alleviate an imminent threat. Implicit in this formulation are concerns both about whether self-defense is necessary, and whether it can be carried out on the territory of another state without its consent. However, in the interest of maintaining international peace, the UN Security Council can act under a Chapter VII resolution beyond the technical bounds of self-defense and intervention laws' restraints.

While some states might differ, the United States followed its traditional views of self-defense in the use of force against Afghanistan and eventually the international community authorized the use of armed force under UN Charter Chapter VII. Thus, the United States' use of armed force in Afghanistan is largely unproblematic from a legal standpoint. However, Iraq is a different matter to the extent the United States early on abandoned from seeking a Chapter VII use of force resolution for military operations in Iraq post-9/11. By pursuing the so-called preemptive war doctrine, which exceeded even traditional United States self-defense views based on the *Caroline* precedent, the United States use of armed force in Iraq in the absence of WMDs arguably goes too far. The afterthought of trying to justify military intervention based on humanitarian intervention (the idea that Saddam Hussein was a bad man, and the United States was liberating the Iraqi people) seems weak at best. So a weak legal position has undermined the legitimacy of the U.S. actions in foreign eyes, now recognized at least as presenting serious public diplomacy problems, presumably with longer term consequences beyond Iraq and Afghanistan.

In closing, we hearken back to the idea that, from the lawyer's technical perspective, the most puzzling aspect of the preemptive war claim was that it was arguably unnecessary because initially it appeared as though U.S. military actions could have been covered by broadly accepted views about preemptive self-defense following the *Caroline* precedent. Perhaps the lawyer's answer is to be found in broad views of sovereignty, because essentially the U.S. government asserted an almost nineteenth century view in giving preeminence to something that looks more like international relations realism (preemptive war, which is not a legal term of art, but rather a political position) rather than even traditional U.S. views concerning permissible legal boundaries of early use of force (anticipatory self-defense, in doctrinal terms).

NOTES

1. See Michael N. Schmitt, "*Bellum Americanum* Revisited: U.S. Security Strategy and the *Jus ad Bellum*," *Military Law Review* 176 (2003) 364 (Sixteenth Waldemar A. Solf Lecture in International Law at the Judge Advocate General's School, Charlottesville).

2. The Cold War paradigm of proxy civil wars carried with it intervention law concerns (e.g., was the War in Vietnam of the 1960s–1970s an international war between North and South Vietnam, or merely the continuation of a civil and independence war in the 1950s of the former French colony, with resulting legal consequences). The traditional law of intervention itself has been in disarray ever since its rules were openly flouted in the Spanish Civil War, but there is significance at the *jus in bello* level whether an armed conflict is international or noninternational in terms of treatment of combatants (visible in domestic legal discourse in terms of arguments about the applicability of the Geneva Conventions to prisoners).

3. To a certain degree, dating the modern "humanitarian" arms limitation movement in the law of war to the First Hague Peace Conference is somewhat arbitrary. The Hague Conferences themselves were spawned in part by broader pacifist movements in late nineteenth century Europe. On the sea warfare side, it might be argued that the abolition of privateering and regulation of neutral shipping rights in the 1856 *Declaration of Paris* dating back to the Crimean War is a precursor if not part of this movement, while the 1864 *Geneva Agreement* covers treatment of the wounded and the 1868 *St. Petersburg Declaration Renouncing the Use, in Time of War, of Explosive Projectiles Under 400 Grams Weight* clearly concerns the limitation of specific weapons (explosive bullets) due to the special dangers and carnage they would wreak on troops. Despite these early agreements, it seems more reasonable to date the "movement" aspect from the First Hague Peace Conference.

4. This is true on the international law side, although there is a visible concern in recent Supreme Court cases that executive claims concerning detention of persons for the duration of the war on

terror raises difficult issues concerning when and how to determine that it is over (the indefinite detention problem).

5. Acknowledgment is due a continuing debate concerning the nature of constituent agreements creating IOs (international organizations) (as is the UN Charter, although our interest lies chiefly in its Articles 2(4) and 51). See generally Shabtai Rosenne, *Developments in the Law of Treaties 1945–1986* (Cambridge: Cambridge University Press, 1989), 181–258. Passing over long-standing academic distinctions, the debate is characterized by parties' attitudes towards IOs themselves and their political role. On the one hand, a constituent agreement may be viewed as a constitutional document, the interpretation of which may be given legitimately to its political or judicial organs. By analogy to a separation of powers analysis, it is possible that both organs have interpretive competencies. It is not clear, however, that a judicial interpretation generally would take precedence (and in the case of the International Court of Justice's interpretations of the UN Charter it may not). *Id.* at 225–26, citing 12 U.N.C.I.O. 709 (declaration prepared by Committee II/2 subsequently adopted by the entire conference at San Francisco). On the other hand, a constituent agreement may be viewed as an international law agreement like any other, the provisions of which are subject to the standard interpretive approach. While Articles 2(4) and 51 on their face relate to substantive norms, it might be argued that they are so bound up in the politically oriented Security Council peace-keeping system that their proper interpretation must be consigned to it and not the International Court of Justice (the Security Council would remain free to request an advisory opinion or call upon the parties under Article 33(2) to settle their dispute before the International Court of Justice). The issue is moot here to the extent a decision was made at a certain point to abandon the Security Council system itself in dealing with Iraq.

6. In the immediate aftermath of postwar war crimes trials, the United Nations undertook to define the aggression concept in the context of formulating a restatement of the so-called Nuremberg principles and the *Draft Code of Offenses Against Mankind* as substantive law to guide a proposed international criminal tribunal as a permanent replacement for the international military tribunals criticized in some quarters as drumhead courts of the victorious Allies. In various venues, these efforts continued sporadically from the late 1940s through the early 1980s. The General Assembly has promulgated certain generalized statements of principles and compromise definitions in this area (purporting to be statements of existing law), most notably the *Declaration on Principles of Internal Law Concerning Friendly Relations and Co-operation Among States in Accordance with the Charter of the United Nations,* G.A. Resolution 2625 (XXXV 1970), and the *Definition of Aggression Resolution,* G.A. Resolution 3314 Annex (XXIX 1974). However, their drafting history, text and generalized nature permit the judgment that they provide better evidence of diplomatic compromise than the law. Different States' views of applicable law are incorporated in different and often conflicting individual provisions. As a result, by stressing different provisions within the same document, different States may advance their own views. By trying to be all things to all States, these documents fail to provide guidance to applicable law in individual circumstances.

7. John Bassett Moore, *Digest of International Law* 2 (1906) 412 (Washington: Government Printing Office, 1906).

8. Advocates of humanitarian intervention typically parse the language of UN Charter Article 2(4) in arguing that said intervention is *consistent* with the purposes of the United Nations. As a general matter, however, unilateral humanitarian intervention outside the UN Security Council context has not found broad support outside the human rights community. The explanation is simple, that states generally fear humanitarian intervention would be employed by strong states as an excuse for armed intervention into weaker states' affairs. This is the background of challenges to selective use of humanitarian intervention theories, ranging from rightwing activists' claims that Tibet is suffering under China rule and leftwing activists' claims that Israel is oppressing Palestinians in the Occupied Territories, in both cases with activists claiming that consistency demands humanitarian intervention there too.

9. Compare Schmitt, "*Bellum Americanum* Revisited," 364, 375–92. Schmitt effectively reprises the *Caroline* analysis in reviewing responses immediately post-9/11, then notes seemingly puzzled,

id. at 387 n. 76, the armed attack analysis challenging the application of self-defense. The problem on a political level is that immediately post-9/11 and in conjunction more generally with the use of armed force in Afghanistan, the international community largely accepted the self-defense claims, which were not accepted by many states in the use of armed force against Iraq.

10. This reorientation arguably can be traced all the way back to the NSS and predecessor white papers' recharacterization in the post–Cold War world of moving the focus of threat analysis.

11. 1949 I.C.J. 3 (merits). For a detailed analysis of the case see David K. Linnan, "Self-defense, Necessity and U.N. Collective Security Under International Law: American and Other Views," *Duke Journal of Comparative and International Law* 57 (1991).

12. 1984 I.C.J. 4 (merits). For a detailed analysis of self-defense aspects of the case see David K. Linnan, "Self-defense, Necessity and U.N. Collective Security Under International Law: American and Other Views," *Duke Journal of Comparative and International Law* 57 (1991). Curiously and perhaps understandably given the *Contra Case's* politically inflammatory nature, the opinion studiously avoided examination or even significant mention of the legal concept of aggression as such (indirect or otherwise, whether on the part of the United States or Nicaragua). A similar effect is visible in current discussions of the Iraq situation.

13. 28 I.L.M. 843 (1989) (International Court of Justice 1989 General List No. 79).

14. David K. Linnan, "Iran Air Flight 655 and Beyond: Free Passage, Mistaken Self-Defense, and State Responsibility," *Yale Journal of International Law* 16 (1991) 245.

CHAPTER 14

The Concept of Superior Responsibility under International Law as Applied in Indonesia

HIKMAHANTO JUWANA

The concept of *superior* responsibility, as understood in international law, appears frequently in Indonesian legal discourse in the aftermath of the separation of East Timor (now Timor Leste) from the Republic of Indonesia. It appears as part of the debates and definitions in conjunction with the question who was legally responsible for the violence that accompanied Timor Leste's independence.[1] Superior responsibility is a technical term that is mostly widely used in the context of establishing individual responsibility for alleged commissions of international crimes. This concept has now been incorporated into, and applied in the Indonesian legal system. In the Indonesian context, it has become part of the specialized legal terminology related to the prosecution of grave breaches of human rights.[2] The concept of superior responsibility as used encompasses two intimately related notions, which are command responsibility and superior responsibility. The distinction between these two figures lies in the position of the alleged perpetrator(s), in the sense that command responsibility applies to individual commanders within a military organization, whereas superior responsibility would apply to civilian organizations, including the police.

How has superior responsibility been applied in the Indonesian context? What is the prevailing doctrinal view of the concept, and do such views have implications in practice? This notion is perplexing to most Indonesian legal practitioners. This confusion is responsible for officers and practitioners' practical mistakes. Moreover, these mistakes contribute to make it even more difficult to apply the doctrine with a uniform understanding. The reason is that such errors are translated into case-law and doctrinal positions, then the mistaken approaches end up perpetuating themselves with new references that other practitioners might use in future proceedings. Moreover, such mistakes then have an impact on how the Indonesian discussion of criminal responsibility is understood by other observers, both domestic and international, such as policymakers or NGOs (nongovernmental organizations), which develop strategies and responses to institutional practices based on the doctrine in question.

With these issues in mind, in the first part of this chapter, I seek to provide a succinct referential framework concerning how superior responsibility is commonly understood in international criminal law. Here, I will briefly discuss the origin of the concept of superior responsibility; provide a preliminary definition of this figure; give an overview of the different angles that justify the development of the doctrine; show how it has been conceived in international and domestic instruments, and to conclude I distinguish it from *administrative responsibility,* a notion with which international criminal law's *superior responsibility* tends to be confused.

Once superior responsibility has been analyzed in a doctrinal sense, I proceed to analyze its implementation in the Indonesian context. I focus on a simple case study, to illustrate the problems that arise out of a mistaken understanding of the said doctrine. Specifically, this chapter will analyze how superior responsibility was applied in the indictment, trial, and final decision in the *Jose Abilio Osorio Soares* case. Osorio Soares is an East-Timorese civilian, who held the position of Governor of former East Timor from 1992 through 1999. He was accused on the basis of his alleged superior responsibility for crimes against humanity committed in the midst of the violence that overtook East Timor in 1999. Such crimes were allegedly committed by governmental officials under his control.[3] However, his trial was not free from controversy, since to many critics he was merely a scapegoat for crimes for which military officers were responsible.[4] His trial is an excellent example of how the common wrongful assumptions referred above can end up having practical implications in determining individual responsibility. Our concerns should not only be doctrinal but, more importantly, practical.

Analyses of superior responsibility, and a proper understanding of their premises and limits, are more important today than ever. In the international arena, events like Abu Ghraib, and the subsequent debates concerning the responsibility of the officers involved in such deplorable situations—from those who carry out alleged torture activities all the way to the top officers in charge of designing and authorizing such policies—make it clear that the debate is timely and important. Quite possibly, the discussions that are taking place in a different setting, like Indonesia, can be useful to understanding the figures in question.

HUMAN RIGHTS CRIMES IN THE INTERNATIONAL AND DOMESTIC ARENAS

Prior to further analysis of the doctrine, we need to understand certain criteria about criminal responsibility in the international and domestic legal realms. In fact, criminal responsibility often involves an interrelationship between these two spheres. In this respect, legal scholarship generally distinguishes between *national* (also referred to as domestic) and *international* crimes. *National* crimes are conceptualized as those deemed by the community of any country as criminal acts, usually committed within the jurisdiction of that particular state, and judged by the state's judicial institutions. The moral dimension of a national crime, its legal connotation and subsequent application is determined by the people and institutions of that state, in the ways determined by the law and local judicial officers.

In contrast, an international crime is defined in the international community realm, crossing across boundaries. They are usually based on a common understanding shared by the nations and corroborated by international practice (international customs). They can also be defined by the express recognition of a number of governments that, as we just mentioned above, enter into covenants, or grant power to international organizations to define what these crimes are, and what organizations will be in charge of applying such laws in practice.

In fact, the process of formation and definition of these crimes mirrors other developments that have taken place in international law. For instance, the determination of which crimes qualify as international crimes is mainly derived from, and based on the customary practices of states. Therefore, across time, the customary practices of these states evolve into accepted customary international law. Once an international crime is well established in customary international law, it is usually codified and incorporated into international treaties. Once defined in international treaties, these international crimes can be incorporated into domestic laws, either via recognition of these international sources, or via domestic legislation creating or formally incorporating such crimes in the domestic arena. There are many practical examples of international crimes that have been gradually recognized through a process of this kind, including piracy and the four types of crime stated in the Rome Statute of the ICC (International Criminal Court). In this regard, crimes codified in the Rome Statute are classified into four broad categories: genocide, crimes against humanity, war crimes, and the crime of aggression.[5]

On the other hand, in Indonesian law, the types of international crimes that have been recognized and adopted pursuant to the provisions of Law No. 26/2000 on the Human Rights Tribunal (hereinafter Law 26/2000), are only crimes against humanity and genocide, excluding war crimes and the crime of aggression, as mentioned earlier.[6] Although this narrower definition might be open to disapproval, those who criticized this law in other instances agree that, by mirroring the Rome Statute, the Law 26/2000 made an important contribution to ensure that the standards used to judge crimes against humanity in the Indonesian context were up to the level required in the international arena. The doctrinal referential framework includes, therefore, theoretical and practical developments that take place in other settings. This contributes to develop a sophisticated and comprehensive platform to apply the new legislation, without having to build institutions from scratch. This has received praise from organizations beyond the Indonesian boundaries. For instance, Amnesty International expressed that "the use of the Rome Statute as the basis for the definitions is welcome since, together with other international instruments and treaties, it provides definitive standards for the investigation and prosecution of gross violations of Human Rights."[7]

This preliminary discussion has made clear that criminal responsibility should be understood both in the international and domestic domains. The substantive and procedural criteria upon which responsibility is defined should be analyzed in both respects. What follows now is a discussion about the notion of superior responsibility as applicable in Indonesia, with specific grounds on the international and national pertinent legal instruments.

SUPERIOR RESPONSIBILITY IN INTERNATIONAL CRIMINAL LAW

The *superior responsibility* doctrine is widely known in international law, particularly in international criminal law. The emergence of this doctrine should be analyzed from the perspective of the relatively recent trend of recognizing individuals as limited passive subjects of international law. Essentially, an individual was traditionally conceived of as a limited subject of international law, but it is a widely known fact that several recent developments, especially the internationalization of human rights, have changed this trend and allow a more prominent role to individuals in the international legal realm.

To discuss what is meant by superior responsibility, it is necessary to analyze which individuals may be liable for grave breaches of human rights. Essentially, these individuals are grouped into two categories. The first category includes those who plan, advocate, order, commit, help or support the planning, preparation, or execution of the grave breach of human rights. The second category includes those who hold a superior level position and did not participate in a grave breach of human rights, but whose subordinates under the superior's authority committed the alleged breach.

Notice that these two different categories focus on different individuals held responsible for the grave breach. The first category targets the main author; that is, the individual who allegedly committed a grave breach of human rights violations (therefore, the category focuses on the crime's *commission*). Meanwhile, in the second category, the individual is not charged with having committed the breach personally. Their subordinates have committed the breach, but since the individual assumes the post as the superior, he or she is deemed to having committed the offence (by *omission*). Hence, *omission* simply means that the individual did not personally commit the alleged crime, but in fact remains criminally liable for the acts of his or her respective subordinates. This is the most common category to hold individuals responsible for omission—even if it is not the only one.[8]

In this respect, *superior responsibility* initially evolved as a doctrine after World War I and consolidated in the aftermath of World War II. Ilias Bantekas, a leading author in the study of superior responsibility, mentions that the first instance of application of the doctrine was by the allies after World War I, in order "to assess responsibility of German officers, rightly (assuming) that a combination of power to intervene, knowledge of crimes and subsequent failure to act should render those concerned liable for the crimes of their subordinates."[9]

Bantekas states that superior responsibility under international criminal law can be defined as: *"People who fail to prevent or punish their subordinates' illegal acts."*[10] On the other hand, Kriangsak stated that: *"...a Superior is criminally responsible for the act committed by his subordinates if he knew or had reason to know that the subordinate was about to commit such acts or had done so and the superior failed to take the necessary and reasonable measures to prevent such act or to punish the perpetrators thereof."*[11] From these two conceptualizations, it can be simply stated that superior responsibility under international criminal law can be understood as the liability of individuals in superior positions for grave breaches of human rights committed by their subordinates. It must be noted that liability for grave breaches of human rights cannot be borne by a superior in those cases where the subordinates of that superior have not committed any crime, or where the alleged perpetrators are not the subordinates of the accused superior—in these cases, the link between superior and subordinates or perpetrators is absent.

The concept of superior responsibility is not a recent phenomenon or development in legal theory. It has expanded beyond its traditional context within military law into other areas of law. In military law, a commander assumes responsibility for any breach of prevailing laws and regulations by his or her subordinates, including breaches of discipline. The rationale for superior responsibility is simply to punish the commander for his or her negligence in preventing the breach, or for not punishing the subordinates who committed the offence. This means that the commander cannot avoid responsibility for the acts of his or her subordinates, provided that the commander was in fact in a position to control their acts, and hence was in a position to prevent the commission of the offence. The superior responsibility doctrine is featured in military law in several countries. It has been adopted into international instruments, particularly with respect to humanitarian law.

Historically, superior responsibility fell within the confines of international criminal law, so that an individual could be convicted for their involvement in the commission of an international crime. After World War II, people who committed a crime against humanity or a war crime were subject to international law. They were treated as having committed an international crime. Therefore, international jurisdiction was applicable. This meant that the accused could be brought to trial and prosecuted by any court, in any jurisdiction, and at any time.

The key objective of adopting the superior responsibility doctrine in international criminal law is to broaden the scope of individuals that may be subject to that law, so that it is not only the individual who is accused of committing the crime that falls within the provisions of the law, but also individuals who hold positions of authority over the perpetrators of international crimes yet fail to exercise that control to prevent the crime from being committed.[12]

The superior responsibility doctrine was first recognized at the multilateral level in the Hague Convention Respecting the Laws and Customs of War on Land (*Hague IV,* October 18, 1907), and the Hague Convention Adaptation to Maritime War of the Principles of the Geneva Convention (October 18, 1907), in the sense of the existence of duties on superiors 'in relation to the conduct of their subordinates.' [13] However, the superior responsibility doctrine in the sense defined above was not included in the international agreement that established the IMT (International Military Tribunal) or the IMTFE (International Military Tribunal for the Far East).[14] Individuals charged under the concept of superior responsibility were charged on the basis of national laws, such as those in the People's Republic of China, France, and Luxemburg.[15]

The concept of superior responsibility was incorporated in the United Nations Security Council Resolutions that established the ICTY (International Criminal Tribunal for the Former Yugoslavia) and the ICTR (International Criminal Tribunal for Rwanda). This concept was then incorporated into the Statute for the establishment of the ICC. The provisions that regulate superior responsibility are to be found in Article 6(3) of the ICTR Statute and Article 7(3) of the ICTY Statute. The two articles are formulated as follows:

> "The fact that any of the acts refered to in article 2 to 4 of the present Statute was committed by a subordinate does not relieve his or her superior of criminal responsibility if he or she knew or had reason to know that the subordinate was about to commit such acts or had done so and the superior failed to take the necessary and reasonable measures to prevent such acts or to punish the perpetrator thereof."

Meanwhile, in the Statute of the ICC, the concept of *command responsibility* is regulated in Article 28. Command responsibility is formulated as follows:

> In addition to other grounds of criminal responsibility under this Statute for crimes within the jurisdiction of the Court:
>
> (a) A military commander or person effectively acting as a military commander shall be criminally responsible for crimes within the jurisdiction of the Court committed by forces under his or her effective command and control, or effective authority and control as the case may be, as a result of his or her failure to exercise control properly over such forces, where:

(i) That military commander or person either knew or, owing to the circumstances at the time, should have known that the forces were committing or about to commit such crimes; and

(ii) That military commander or person failed to take all necessary and reasonable measures within his or her power to prevent or repress their commission or to submit the matter to the competent authorities for investigation and prosecution.

(b) With respect to superior and subordinate relationships not described in paragraph (a), a superior shall be criminally responsible for crimes within the jurisdiction of the Court committed by subordinates under his or her effective authority and control, as a result of his or her failure to exercise control properly over such subordinates, where:

(i) The superior either knew, or consciously disregarded information which clearly indicated, that the subordinates were committing or about to commit such crimes;

(ii) The crimes concerned activities that were within the effective responsibility and control of the superior; and

(iii) The superior failed to take all necessary and reasonable measures within his or her power to prevent or repress their commission or to submit the matter to the competent authorities for investigation and prosecution.

In Indonesia, the concept of command responsibility is taken from the Statute of the ICC, and was incorporated in Law No. 26/2000 on the Human Rights Court (Law No. 26/2000). The concept is specifically regulated in Article 42(1) and (2). The superior responsibility provisions contained in Law No. 26/2000 is essentially a translation of Article 28(2) of the ICC Statute. Hence, it is reasonable to state that the implementation of the superior responsibility doctrine in Indonesia should refer to standard practices under international criminal law with respect to this doctrine.

ADMINISTRATIVE AND SUPERIOR RESPONSIBILITY: SIMILARITIES AND DIFFERENCES

Any discussion of superior responsibility must contrast the disparate understandings of the term in the international criminal and administrative law realms. In Indonesia, the general impression is that these notions are in fact interchangeable. A good example of arguments based on this assumption is found on the Indonesian Public Prosecutor's indictments in the East Timor and Tanjung Priok cases,[16] grounded in arguments which evidenced an understanding of superior responsibility in the *administrative* sense, therefore misunderstanding the concept, and disregarding the doctrine that has evolved around superior responsibility in the international law field.

In order to determine who holds superior responsibility in the administrative sense, it must be established in the first place which individual holds the necessary mandate from the state to assume that position—the competency to exercise public authority in a specific issue. A key assumption is that, as a precondition of such prerogative, the superior must have subordinates placed under their direct control. The successful completion of the mandate by the superior may lead to promotion or some other reward. On the other hand, if the superior fails to fulfill the mandate successfully, then the superior can be charged with administrative responsibility. The administrative sanctions that may be levied as a consequence of this failure include various reprimands, demotion in position or rank, or even dismissal. This depends on how the law defines them and how administrative and judicial practice implements them.

Although they appear to be similar notions—both concepts attempt to hold superiors accountable for the way they exercise their powers, and for the consequences of their actions and omissions—administrative responsibility is very different from the notion of superior responsibility under international criminal law.

In order to file charges based on the notion of superior responsibility as it has been discussed in this chapter, it first must be evidenced that there is, at least initially, a grave breach of human rights, defined as a crime in a prior specific legal instrument. Then, it must be determined who the perpetrators of these crimes are, a preliminary finding that investigators should arrive at, based on the facts, the evidence at hand, and after conducting a procedure adjusted to due process of law and framed under the applicable legislation. Lastly, it must be determined whether these perpetrators have a superior who supervises or commands them. If the answer to this question is yes, then superiors can be held responsible for the grave breaches of human rights committed by their subordinates.

Therefore, in superior responsibility, the sanction imposed on the superior is inextricably linked to the criminal responsibility found in, and punishment imposed on the subordinates. Moreover, superior responsibility under international criminal law does not require any specific, express order to be issued or given by the superior. Usually, the subordinates commit the acts classified as grave breaches of human rights *on their own initiative,* or at least on the initiative of someone different from the hierarchical superior.

Instead, administrative responsibility requires an order from the superior to the subordinate in relation to the performance of their duties. This type of responsibility is related to the specific actions, plans, and instructions that the hierarchical superiors impart. If the subordinate fails to perform these duties, or carry them on in a wrongful way, the superior is considered *administratively* responsible for this failure.

Therefore, the contrast between the two forms of responsibility cannot be more startling. One is targeted at lack of diligence with respect to monitoring and punishing the wrongful actions committed by the hierarchical subordinates. The other is focused on the responsibility associated with giving specific orders to subordinates to carry out actions.

Thus, hierarchical superiors, in terms of the superior responsibility doctrine, are held accountable for the actions of his or her subordinates for grave breaches of human rights, because it is expected that the superior will take action to prevent or punish the subordinates for the acts of which he or she is aware. Hence, superior responsibility depends on the actual existence of effective control over the relevant subordinates. In the event that the superior does not take any action against the subordinates, this is equivalent to the legitimization of the acts that have been committed by their subordinates.

As a result of this conception, with respect to evidence—quite often the most difficult question to determine superior responsibility—for a superior to be held responsible under the doctrine of superior responsibility, three elements must be proven, which are: (a) effective control between the subordinate and the superior; (b) the superior either knew or should have known that the subordinates were committing or about to commit a grave breach of human rights; and (c) the commander or superior failed to take any action necessary to prevent or punish the subordinates who were committing or about to commit a grave breach of human rights. Let us analyze these three elements briefly.

Effective Control

In order to accuse an individual as a superior of subordinates who have allegedly committed a grave breach of human rights, the first element that must be proved is the existence of a relationship between the parties that gives rise to a presumption of *effective* control of the superior over the subordinates.

There are two important factors here. First, there must be some indication that a grave breach of human rights has been committed by the subordinates—it is not necessary to prove this prior to asserting superior responsibility, but the allegations should have at least reasonable credibility. Second, the term *effective*—as in 'effective control'—is an important factor in determining who the superiors are and the responsibility they assume. In this sense, *effective* must be translated as *control* that the superior has in the form of an immediate relationship with the relevant subordinates, in a way that it is reasonable to expect a well informed superior to take some action to prevent or stop the misdeeds.

For example, suppose a number of soldiers of a particular company commit a grave breach of human rights. Here, we can safely assume that superior responsibility falls upon the commander of that company. However, this superior responsibility cannot be passed endlessly up the chain of command to the highest point of the hierarchical order, without proving the *effective control* link. The superior of the company commander cannot be held responsible under the superior responsibility doctrine, unless he or she has an immediate relationship with the subordinates and their actions. This means that responsibility must end at the level where there is effective control over the actions of the subordinates.

Consequently, in order to charge a president or chief executive with superior responsibility in cases of breach of human rights, it first must be proved that the subordinates of the president, under his or her effective control—such as ministers or equivalent officials—have committed a grave breach of human rights. It is with respect to these subordinates that the president or chief executive, as *top commander,* has effective control. It just cannot be assumed that any action carried on by lower-rank officials will be under such effective control. This concept can be seen in the indictment against former President Slobodan Milosevic—although in his case, the indictment based on individual responsibility took preeminence over aspects of superior or joint responsibility.

Finally, to determine whether there is in fact effective control, two additional issues are critical. First, effective control can be established based on some form of legislation or regulation. This type of effective control is known as *de jure* control. Second, where effective control is not based on any regulation, then it must be proved that there is in real terms some type of effective control. This type of effective control is known as *de facto* control. Whether *de jure* or *de facto,* it is important to comply with any of these two paradigms.

Knowledge of the Superior

The second element that must be proved is that the superior knew or should have known that the subordinates would commit, or had already committed, a grave breach of human rights. The term *should have known* means that, even in those situations where the superior argues, to the contrary, that he or she did not know any reasonable and objective measurement of "should have known." It would mean that the superior was aware of the acts.

The *knowledge* element is important. If the superior did not know about the grave breach of human rights committed by the subordinates, the superior cannot be held responsible for the commission of these acts. The critical issue becomes, then, whether the superior is duly informed of the situation in question. The evidence provided should focus on this point to pass this leg of the test.

Legitimation by the Superior

The third element that must be proved is whether superiors allow the grave breaches of human rights to occur, or legitimize the act(s) committed by their subordinates. This takes place whenever a superior takes no action against the relevant subordinates. With respect to the grave breaches of human rights committed by the superior's subordinates, a superior with effective control *can* take action to prevent (prior to the act being committed) or punish (after the act has been committed) the subordinates' actions. In the event that the superior takes no action against the subordinates, then it is reasonable to consider this an endorsement of the grave breaches of human rights committed by the subordinates on behalf of the superior. The superior is in fact tolerating the breaches being committed by his or her subordinates. Hence, the point of prevention of punishment is subsequent to knowledge.

The three elements exposed here are essential to determine superior responsibility. Moreover, when applying the doctrine, it is important to keep the discussion in perspective and remember that, in any case, the superior responsibility doctrine should always be applied in a logical way, without unnecessary conceptual stretch and with a view to ensuring that the fundamental theoretic assumptions are followed. As Bantekas says, *"neither the normal use of the doctrine of superior responsibility nor the 'duty to control' theory unnecessarily widen the ambit of the liability of military or civilian superiors. They follow general principles of the criminal law of the vast majority of States, as well as the dictates of logic. They express what is expected of all those persons who, in a position of authority, must take every measure in their power to prevent or punish that which they would expect others to repress if they themselves were the victims."*[17]

THEORY VERSUS PRACTICE: SUPERIOR RESPONSIBILITY BEYOND THEORY

In practice, the legal principles of superior responsibility are frequently employed in two different fashions. First, as a subsidiary charge, as an accessory to the main indictment against the accused that holds the superior office. In case the principal cannot be considered personally responsible for the human rights crimes in question, at least he can be deemed guilty through superior responsibility. This is made in order to ensure that the accused does not escape punishment easily. Thus, the Public Prosecutor's primary charge will be that the superior is considered directly guilty of a grave breach of human rights. On the other hand, a second possibility is to employ superior responsibility together with the idea of his or her control over a number of subordinates. In this case, the subsidiary charge will be employed to reinforce the notion that the accused is a superior with actual hierarchical command over individuals who carry out the questionable misdeeds.

Notice that both indictments address the issue of superior responsibility. They embody charges against superiors who may have failed to commit any act to prevent the malfeasance. However, in the first case, the charge goes one step beyond and actually charges direct involvement in the crimes. In the latter indictment, superiors are charged based on the effective control that they had over the subordinates. The broader picture is that superiors must exercise this control in a way that would prevent or legitimize the grave breach of human rights as committed by their subordinates.

In Indonesia, the superior responsibility doctrine has been used to judge individuals who held superior positions concerning events which transpired in East Timor and Tanjung Priok. Nearly all of the indictments handed down by Indonesia's Public Prosecutor were based on Article 42 of Law No. 26/2000. As a matter of fact, these indictments are perfectly legal and feasible. However, the question that must be asked is whether the prosecutor employed the definition of superior responsibility as it is is commonly understood in the International Criminal Law realm, in the terms explained above, or whether his usage of this term is closer to administrative responsibility, or different in any other substantial respect.

After thoroughly analyzing the Public Prosecutor's line of action in the said cases, our impression is that the Public Prosecutor's understanding of superior responsibility is not totally accurate, or at least does not reflect the predominant consensus on the debate. To unravel this misguided interpretation of superior responsibility, we proceed to analyze the Prosecutor's arguments in the *Abilio Jose Osorio Soares* case, at both the indictment and decision phases, before the Indonesian ad hoc Human Rights Court.

In the *Abilio Jose Osorio Soares case (Abilio)*, the Public Prosecutor's indictment was based on Article 42(2)(a) of Law 26/2000, which regulates whether a crime against humanity has been committed by his subordinates. The Public Prosecutor indicted Abilio as a consequence of his formal position as Governor of East Timor. He was charged with two counts of grave breaches of human rights supposedly committed by his subordinates. The first charge stated that Abilio, as the individual that held superior office, legitimated the actions of his subordinates through his failure to take any action to prevent or punish the alleged grave breaches of human rights perpetrated by his subordinates, such as the murder of civilians. There were three districts where these murders were alleged to have occurred: Liquisa, Dilli and Covalima (Suai).

On the other hand, the second charge focuses on Abilio's alleged superior responsibility for the claimed torture committed by his subordinates in the three districts above. Therefore, the difference in the charges relates only to the alleged offences committed by his subordinates in these three districts. One was about homicides, whereas the other was about torture. However, both charges were theoretically linked to the notion of superior responsibility, as understood in the realm of international criminal law.

To analyze this case, following the outline established above, the first issue that must be decided is whether Abilio had *effective* control over his subordinates. This requires, first of all, establishing who the subordinates of Abilio are, and also requires a clear understanding of how these officers were related to Abilio. Then, the second issue is whether Abilio was in fact *aware* of the activities that these subordinates were undertaking (the 'accurate information' element, as explained above). Finally, it should be determined whether Abilio legitimated the offenses somehow, particularly by taking no action or clearly unsuitable measures to stop the violations in question. These three aspects are critical to determining whether the grave breaches of human rights which allegedly occurred were committed by subordinates over whom Abilio had effective control, that he was duly informed of the events, and that nevertheless these misdeeds were legitimated by him.

However, an alternative interpretation of the Public Prosecutor's indictment is viable. For example, it is possible that the subordinates of Abilio who allegedly committed the grave breaches of human rights, do not fall within the category of perpetrators of grave breaches of human rights, but are instead *superiors* themselves who have at their disposal subordinates who are, in turn, the perpetrators of the alleged acts. For instance, in the first and second indictment, the prosecutor considers the Regent of Liquisa, the Regent of

Covalima, and Deputy Commander of the Integration Forces PPI (Pasukan Pejuang Integrasi) as Abilio's subordinates.[18] Consequently, according to this interpretation, these officers are not the perpetrators who committed the alleged grave breaches of human rights. Instead, their respective subordinates are considered the perpetrators of the acts charged in the three districts noted above. In Liquisa, for example, the accused who were presumed to have committed the grave breaches of human rights are: Jose Matheus, Tome Diogo, Abilio Alves of the Indonesian Army, and Alfonso and Chico of the Police Department of Liquisa.

If we follow this line of reasoning, this means that Abilio cannot be charged based on the acts of his subordinates, because the subordinates were in fact the superiors of the individuals who committed the offences so charged. The indictment handed down by the Public Prosecutor is clearly inconsistent with the superior responsibility doctrine as understood in international criminal law, because it seeks to hold two different ranks of superiors responsible for the same crimes, disregarding both causal links and levels of hierarchy.

In this sense, superior responsibility requires the superior's effective control of the subordinates who allegedly committed the grave breaches of human rights. Abilio cannot be considered to have had effective control over the perpetrators of the grave breaches of human rights, because at all relevant times, the perpetrators of these acts were under the effective control of the Regent of Liquisa, the Regent of Covalima, and the Deputy Commander of the Integration Forces. Therefore, it is the subordinates under Abilio's authority who were in fact the superiors of the alleged perpetrators of the grave breaches, and therefore they should be charged in terms of *superior responsibility*.

Instead, following the logic of the Public Prosecutor, any superior could be charged and held criminally accountable under the doctrine of superior responsibility. In the Public Prosecutor's view, there is no possible end to the causal link that provides grounds to establish responsibility for a given crime. That is, the first requirement of the doctrine is unreasonably extended, without the accompanying theoretical or evidentiary justification that could provide grounds for this argument.

Moreover, the crucial error in the Public Prosecutor's arguments regarding the concept of superior responsibility is that the aforementioned officers were not positioned as *perpetrators* of grave breaches of human rights. How can we determine superior responsibility vis-à-vis a subordinate's action, where the said subordinate officer is not the perpetrator of the crime? This is a critical factor, because if the Regents and Deputy Commander do not constitute perpetrators, and consequently this is not proved, then it is not possible for Abilio to be found guilty based on the superior responsibility doctrine in accordance with prevailing views in international criminal law.

If the Public Prosecutor wanted to indict and prosecute Abilio based on the superior responsibility doctrine under international criminal law, then the Public Prosecutor should have argued that the Regents and the Deputy Commander of the Integration Forces were the individuals who committed the alleged crimes. This could be achieved by proving that the Regents and the Deputy Commander were responsible for the planning, order and commission of the grave breaches of human rights that are alleged in the indictment.

Therefore, the application of the theory of superior responsibility seems problematic in this case. The main argument of the Public Prosecutor was very weak, as a result of the inaccurate definition of superior responsibility. The Public Prosecutor argued that there was effective control between Abilio and his subordinates who were alleged to have committed the grave breaches of human rights. However, the major problem that the

Public Prosecutor encountered here is that Abilio's subordinates did not commit the grave breaches of human rights charged in the indictment. On the contrary, their respective positions were as the *superiors* of the perpetrators who committed the crimes. Abilio's subordinates, in turn, could only be held responsible based on the doctrine of superior responsibility. For that reason, it is reasonable to ask whether Abilio in fact had *effective control* of the actual perpetrators of the grave breaches of human rights or not.

The second requirement, as argued by the Public Prosecutor, was that Abilio was not only aware of the crimes through information provided to him, but also the information that he was aware of clearly indicated that his subordinates and other mass organizations— including the militia— were committing, and had recently committed a number of grave breaches of human rights. This included the murder of a number of pro-independence civilians at church in Liquisa, the Ave Maria church, and at a number of locations throughout East Timor. Here, the question then is which of the subordinates' acts should or could Abilio reasonably have been aware of. If the answer is that he was aware of the actions undertaken by the Regents and the Deputy Commander of the PPI, then the problem lies in resolving the issue whether they committed the alleged grave breaches. On the other hand, in case we believe that they can be conceived of as the actual perpetrators who committed the grave breaches of human rights, then the question is whether Abilio knew or should have known of these grave breaches of human rights—given that it is not clear whether he had any effective control over them.

Finally, it is clear then that the third element for determining superior responsibility as explained above—legitimation by the superior—was not formally satisfied. The arguments stating that Abilio did not undertake any reasonable or necessary action to prevent the grave breaches from occurring within the areas under his authority are difficult to sustain. Abilio was charged for not preventing or taking the necessary measures, such as issuing orders to the security forces to prevent the clashes between pro-integration and pro-independence groups, as well as not giving up the perpetrators to the relevant authorities for investigation and prosecution. These arguments were neither sustained nor proved.

However, if we analyze the process from the standpoint of the doctrine of administrative responsibility—as explained earlier—it becomes clear that the arguments made in court by the prosecution have a more appropriate framework to hold Abilio responsible, a framework that could have different consequences for Abilio. This relates to Abilio's failure to take the requisite administrative action in his capacity as Governor of East Timor. This possibility has not been analyzed so far, but it might provide a more appropriate form of sanction. But it would be administrative, rather than criminal in nature.

Unfortunately, both the Ad Hoc Human Rights Court, and the Supreme Court during the cassation phase of this case accepted the inaccurate interpretation of superior responsibility doctrine asserted by the Public Prosecutor. This meant that Abilio was found guilty by the Ad Hoc Human Rights Court, and this decision was affirmed later at the Supreme Court level. This interpretation of superior responsibility by Indonesian judicial bodies is clearly at odds with the accepted interpretation of the doctrine in international law, and does not comply with the rigorous theoretical framework that I have presented in this chapter. An analysis of Alibio's conduct from the perspective of administrative responsibility involves a completely different analysis, with potential radically diverse consequences. It could possibly have given Alibio more suitable legal treatment to hold him responsible for the misdeeds in question.

CONCLUSIONS

The concept of command responsibility in international criminal law has a well-defined, specific meaning. Despite the sophisticated discussions that have been elaborated in this regard, in Indonesia, this concept is still deeply misunderstood by many actors, including law enforcement agencies. With a view to making a contribution to our own understanding of the concept, and thus provide further basis for the proper construction of the rule of law in Indonesia and East Timor, this chapter has summed up the basic conceptual framework required to apply the superior responsibility concept to determine who should be liable for the alleged crimes against humankind committed in the process of independence of East Timor.

Nevertheless, when we turn from the scholar to the practical scene, we realize that there still is a long way to go concerning proven application of such notions. The *Abilio* case highlights the basic mistake relating to how the prosecution and other officers have understood command responsibility in Indonesia: *The fact that command responsibility in the military sense in international criminal law is assumed as similar and undistinguishable from administrative responsibility, which is a completely different legal concept.* Confusing one with the other can lead to unjust outcomes, as was probably the case with Alibio.

This misperception is also linked to how we understand in what sense subordinates are under effective control of a superior. In the *Abilio* case, the subordinates under the effective control of Abilio were not in fact the individuals who committed the alleged grave breaches of human rights, but rather officials who were, in turn, superiors of other individuals who might have had a clearer role in these alleged misdeeds. Hence, Alibio's subordinates should have been considered superiors with effective control over the actual perpetrators of the alleged grave breaches of human rights. In short, superior responsibility, if applicable at all, did not apply to Alibio, but rather only to his subordinates.

NOTES

1. The events that led to Timor Leste's independence unfolded mainly during the late 1990s. For a summary of East Timor history prior to the struggle for independence, see John G. Taylor, *East Timor: The Price of Freedom* (London: Zed Books, 1999), 2000. For a comprehensive account of Timor Leste's independence, especially the direct consultation process, see Ian Martin, *Self-Determination in East Timor: The United States, the Ballot and International Intervention* (Colorado: Lynne Rienner Publishers, 2001).

2. International Crimes as defined in the Rome Statute of the ICC and grave breaches of human rights as defined in Indonesia under Law No. 26/2000 on the Human Rights Court in this article are used interchangeably. Nevertheless, it must be pointed out that in Article 5 of the Rome Statute if the ICC, International Crimes includes (a) *crime of genocide,* (b) *crimes against humanity,* (c) *war crimes,* and (d) *the crime of aggression;* whereas according to Article 7 of Law No. 26/2000, grave breaches of human rights only include (a) crime of genocide, and (b) crimes against humanity. Therefore, the scope of the latter Indonesian legal text is more reduced than the ICC text. However, the present article shall set aside these controversies.

3. The news of the final judgment against Abilio Soares was publicized around the world. See, for example, the CNN news bit, Atika Shubert, "Governor Jailed for East Timor Violence," *CNN.com,* August 14, 2002, http://archives.cnn.com/2002/WORLD/asiapcf/southeast/08/14/timor.soares.trial/index.html.

4. See "Timor Governor's Sentence Upheld," *BBC News,* April 12, 2004, http://news.bbc.co.uk/2/hi/asia-pacific/3619487.stm.

5. Article 5 of the "Rome Statute of the International Criminal Court," available at http://www.un.org/law/icc/statute/romefra.htm.

6. This law was adopted by the Indonesian Peoples Representative Assembly (DPR) on November 6, 2000.

7. "Amnesty International's Comments on the Law on Human Rights Courts (Law No.26/2000)." *Amnesty International's Library,* February 9, 2001, http://web.amnesty.org/library/Index/engASA210052001?OpenDocument&of=COUNTRIES%5CINDONESIA?OpenDocument&of=COUNTRIES%5CINDONESIA.

8. For a thorough discussion of responsibility for 'commission by omission,' see Michael Duttwiler, "Liability for Omission in International Criminal Law," *International Criminal Law Review* 6 (2006): 1–61. Duttwiler believes that "there is a general principle of law, which for the purposes of criminal law equates the human conduct of omission with action, if a legal duty to act exists." Ibid, 1.

9. Ilias Bantekas, "The Contemporary Law of Superior Responsibility," *American Journal of International Law* 93 (1999): 573 (hereinafter cited as Bantekas, 1999).

10. Ibid.

11. Kittichaissaree Krinagsak, *International Criminal Law* (Oxford: Oxford University Press, 2001), 251.

12. According to Emily Langston, there are four key perspectives to appreciate the role of superior responsibility doctrine, particularly with respect to the East Timor context: "Firstly, the doctrine can be understood as the embodiment of the two 'value-laden principles' of military necessity and humanity. In this sense, the doctrine is located within the broader project of international law in humanizing conflict. Secondly, the superior responsibility doctrine can be conceptualized as a form of risk management. Thus, liability under the doctrine is imposed on the basis that the omission of the superior (to supervise) creates an unacceptable risk of a violation occurring.... Thirdly, the superior responsibility doctrine can be understood as an example of definitional selectivity, which arises from safe and unsafe tribunal practice...; The final approach locates the evolution of legal doctrine within the broader process of the proliferation of international courts and tribunals." Emily Langston, "The Superior Responsibility Doctrine in International Law: Historical Continuities, Innovation and Criminality: Can East Timor's Special Panels Bring Militia Leaders to Justice?" *International Criminal Law Review* 2 (2004): 141, 141–42.

13. Andrew D. Mitchell, "Failure to Halt, Prevent or Punish: The Doctrine of Command Responsibility for War Crimes," *Sydney Law Review* 22 (2000): 381, 383–84.

14. These two courts were the precursor to the establishment of the International Tribunal for the Former Yugoslavia and the International Criminal Tribunal for Rwanda. The ICTY and the ICTR then became the model for the creation and establishment of a permanent international criminal court, the ICC. The IMT was established to try German war criminals at Nuremberg and IMTFE was established to try Japanese war criminals in Tokyo.

15. Bantekas, 1999.

16. On September 12, 1984, Indonesian armed forces opened fire on Muslim protestors gathered in North Jakarta's Tanjung Priok harbour. Scores of protestors were shot. Numerous others were detained, and allegedly tortured, in connection with the demonstration. On July 6, 2000, Indonesia's National Human Rights Commission (*Komisi Nasional Hak Asasi Manusia,* usually shortened to KOMNAS HAM) presented President Abdurrahman Wahid with the final report of its special investigation into Tanjung Priok—one of the worst tragedies during the Suharto presidency. Although the KOMNAS HAM's report on Tanjung Priok was not made public, the Commission did issue an official statement summarizing its conclusions.

17. Ilias Bantekas, "The Interests of States Versus the Doctrine of Superior Responsibility," *International Review of the Red Cross,* no. 838 (2000): 391–402, http://www.icrc.org/Web/eng/siteeng0.nsf/html/57JQHP.

18. Indictment Letter, Reg. Number: 02/HAM/TIM-TIM/02/2002.

CHAPTER 15

The 2006 Conflict in Lebanon, or What Are the Armed Conflict Rules When Legal Principles Collide?

GEORGE K. WALKER

The law governing armed conflict is traditionally understood as having two branches. The first is *jus ad bellum,* which includes the law of going to war, but which can include circumstances when no war results, for example, a self-defense response to an attack where no ongoing conflict results. Today the *jus ad bellum* includes the law of the UN Charter (particularly Articles 2(4) and 51), general international law related to self-defense, and the like. The second is *jus in bello,* which includes the LOAC (law of armed conflict), i.e., principles which seek to prevent unnecessary destruction by controlling and mitigating harmful effects of hostilities, but which also includes rules applying to neutrality, ending hostilities (cease-fires and armistices), and the like. The traditional categories are now changed or supplemented in practice by disparate sources such as the UN Charter or human rights law. Such bodies of law may be aimed chiefly outside the armed conflict setting, but the generally articulated standards may also affect armed conflict situations.

There is disagreement concerning the hierarchy and applicability of multiple sources of LOAC. Furthermore, the boundaries between them are imprecise and subject to disparate and conflicting interpretations, particularly as regards international versus noninternational armed conflicts and increasingly prevalent nonstate actors within them (as witnessed by the reception of the International Committee of the Red Cross' 2005 study espousing the view that convergence has already occurred).[1] Beyond the theoretical discussion, the resulting lack of certainty hampers the ability to determine whether a specific action is lawful or not in practical terms. If there is no agreement on what the right conduct is, we cannot expect military officers and civilian leaders to follow the law successfully. This is a general modern problem which we shall illustrate in the context of the 2006 Lebanese conflict as representative of the typical modern armed conflict involving both state and nonstate actors.

The Israel–Hezbollah conflict involved Lebanon and, at least indirectly, other nearby states (Syria and Iran). It began in July 2006 and was the subject of an August 2006 UN Security Council cease-fire resolution,[2] and illustrates the colliding legal principles problem. Hezbollah, considered by some to be a terrorist organization operating in southern

Lebanon, launched rocket attacks, raided Israeli territory, and kidnapped two Israeli soldiers while killing others. Israel responded, claiming self-defense, with air and artillery attacks on Hezbollah sites in southern Lebanon, and an air and naval "blockade" of Lebanon, citing support of Iran and Syria for Hezbollah. Hezbollah fired rockets into Israel. Israel then began a ground campaign into southern Lebanon against Hezbollah.

States called for UN intervention or similar North Atlantic Treaty Organization action to calm the situation. Innocent civilians, civilians who may have sheltered combatants, and military personnel in Lebanon and Israel died or were seriously injured. Israeli reservists were recalled to active duty, and civilians on both sides lived for weeks in basements or bunkers. Damage to property was heavy. Israeli air strikes resulted in environmental damage to Lebanon's coast from petroleum leakage as well as forest fires in Lebanon, while Hezbollah rockets ignited forests in Israel. A Hezbollah rocket hit an Israeli warship 10 miles off Lebanon, and another struck a Cambodian-flagged merchantman 35 miles off the coast.

Beyond calling for a cease-fire, UN Security Council Resolution 1701 called for augmentation of the UNIFIL (United Nations Force in Lebanon) already in Lebanon when the raid and Israeli response occurred. As the cease-fire took hold, Israel eased its grip on Lebanon, and assistance was marshaled. Over 1000 Lebanese civilians had died and over 4000 were injured. Most of the 975,000 displaced persons returned home, although 250,000 remained homeless. Perhaps 95 percent of Lebanese farmers lost their crops. Power rationing due to bombed lines continued. Schools in southern Lebanon were damaged. Health issues remained as water, food, and necessities were pledged and shipped by neutrals, including those attending a Stockholm, Sweden donor conference, and by NGOs (nongovernmental organizations) and UN agencies. Thirty-nine Israeli civilians and 117 Israeli soldiers, many of them reservists, were reported killed through August 13, 2006. Early reports declared rocket attacks had injured up to 1200 Israeli civilians. Reports varied on the number of Hezbollah fighters killed, and there is no report of the number of Hezbollah fighters wounded or Lebanese armed forces casualties. The oil spill resulting from Israeli attacks on Lebanese oil tank farms covered 105 miles of Lebanon's coast, and it could take 10 years for the coast to recover.

The conflict's war damage has been placed at $9.4 billion for Lebanon and $3 billion for Israel. Six weeks after the Hezbollah raid and the start of the conflict, its leader, Sheikh Sayyed Hassan Nasrallah, said Hezbollah did not think its raid would have led to a war at that time and a response of that magnitude. According to Nasrallah, if it knew the operation would have led to such a war, it would not have been mounted. On the Israeli side, political echoes continue to the extent criticism of how the war was waged may yet cost current Israeli Prime Minister Ehud Olmert his job.

Several bodies of law arguably were involved: (1) Israel's claim of self-defense under the UN Charter and general international law, (2) the law of international armed conflict and the law of noninternational armed conflict, (3) human rights law, and (4) the law of the Charter, exemplified by Resolution 1701. This chapter analyzes these issues preliminarily, based largely on media reporting of events and without waiting for the certainty of historical facts. To resolve controversies among these bodies of law, I propose a flexible approach inspired by the due regard principle found in the LOS (law of the sea) and the law of naval warfare for its interface with the LOS.[3] The broader rationale is that whenever two or more bodies of law conflict, a decision-maker must give prominence to the controlling body or bodies of law that regulate the juridical situation in question, but he or she must have due regard for other possibly applicable bodies of law. To provide guidance with respect to what law applies to a specific situation, I suggest several criteria to inform such a due regard principle, and discuss its practical implications with examples largely drawn from the 2006 Lebanese conflict.

CHANGES IN WAR, CONFLICTS, AND INTERNATIONAL LAW SINCE 1945

Recent decades have witnessed significant changes in the nature of war and the kinds of conflicts the world faces. They are different, at least in degree, from nineteenth and twentieth century warfare. In the post-1945 world, there has been a pronounced tendency toward smaller international wars, and a growth in noninternational conflicts. Terrorism, always present (recalling anarchists of the late nineteenth and early twentieth centuries), has increased in scope and ferocity. Increasing prevalence of terrorism and noninternational conflicts have both contributed to the growing importance of nonstate actors in armed conflict (e.g., al Qaeda). Technically speaking, conflicts are designated as international versus noninternational typically on the basis of whether parties to the conflict are states, not simply based upon a conflict's transboundary reach. Big armies are largely, but not entirely, a phenomenon of the past, although there remain exceptions such as the armed forces of Iraq, the People's Republic of China, Russia, and North Korea. Instead, today's forces are more professional and yet rely often on citizen reservists or their equivalent to augment full time professional forces. Weapons have also changed—for example, the thermonuclear weapon, present since the mid-twentieth century, now has a dirty bomb cousin. There are smaller, although equally lethal, weapons (handheld surface to air missiles, plus drone or hijacked aircraft like the civil airliners involved in 9/11).

Not only have the characteristics of warfare changed, but the legal framework governing it has also changed. The LOAC is evolving into an intricate set of rules provided by different systems of law that interface and conflict within the larger body of international law. The law that applies to *jus ad bellum* and *jus in bello* circumstances has been impacted since 1945 by at least six relevant developments:

1. UN Charter supremacy over inconsistent treaties, established in its Article 103;

2. Inherent right of individual and collective self-defense under Charter Article 51, a traditional customary right of states, but now given, through Article 103, supremacy over treaties, and which involves a right of anticipatory self-defense, often debated but now probably admissible in the Charter era;[4]

3. Authority, under the Charter, for the UN Security Council as a political organ to issue "decisions" in resolutions binding states under Articles 25, 48, and 94(2), much as the Charter through Article 103 trumps all treaties;[5]

4. New standards for humanitarian law supplementing or superseding the 1899 and 1907 Hague Conventions and other rules, for example, in the 1949 Geneva Conventions[6] and the 1977 Protocols I and II to them,[7] but also the Hague Convention and its Protocols protecting cultural property,[8] and a greater emphasis, through Common Article 3 of the Geneva Conventions and Protocol II, on the law of noninternational armed conflicts. Another factor is the treaties' Martens clauses, following the Hague Conventions of 1899 and 1907, which require respect for principles of the law of nations, resulting from "usages established among civilized peoples, from the laws of humanity, and the dictates of the public conscience." Custom and general principles can flow from these treaties. In areas that treaties do not cover, for example, the law of naval warfare and neutrality encompassed by the 1995 *San Remo Manual,* expert bodies have offered compilations

of the law. New national military manuals (e.g., the 1999 American *Commander's Handbook on the Law of Naval Operations*[9]) also articulate current state views;

5. Human rights treaties and their derogation clauses; some treaties are global, for example, the ICCPR (International Covenant on Civil and Political Rights), and some are regional in scope, for example, the European Convention for Protection of Human Rights and Fundamental Freedoms. These agreements may also give rise to customary rules and general principles of law; and

6. Development of *jus cogens,* meaning fundamental rules that trump traditional sources of international law such as those restated in the Statute of the International Court of Justice— custom (practice accepted as law by states), treaties, and general principles of law.

In this chapter, the problem I address, cutting across *jus ad bellum* and *jus in bello,* is how to deal with the collision between the Charter and its Article 103, Security Council resolutions and *jus cogens*—which might include, for example, self-defense[10] as well as humanitarian law and human rights norms within its parameters,[11] in the context of IHL (international humanitarian law) applying to international and noninternational armed conflicts (civil wars), and human rights law. Several issues arise as the different bodies of law may apply to the same facts, so it is necessary to analyze each of these possibilities separately. I address six different types of "legal collisions," and suggest solutions based on the due regard paradigm.

ADOPTING A DUE REGARD PRINCIPLE

The due regard standard was initially adopted by the *San Remo* group as an experts' forum for neutral and belligerent relationships under the law of naval warfare. The underlying concern involved how rights based on the LOS, such as a neutral's rights in its EEZ (exclusive economic zone), interface with the law of naval warfare including belligerent rights to use the high seas (which is the status of the water column and surface of the sea within and outside the 200 mile EEZ seaward of the 12 mile territorial sea).[12] The due regard principle, taken from the 1958 and 1982 LOS conventions, says that belligerents must pay due regard to rights of a neutral in that neutral's EEZ, for example, to operate its fishing fleets. Similarly, under the LOS, states operating on the high seas must have due regard for others' use of the high seas (1982 LOS Convention Article 87), for example, a ship exercising freedom of navigation must have due regard for a fishing vessel engaged in fishing, also a high seas freedom.[13] Thus, although the LOS in the applicable 1958 and 1982 LOS conventions declares that the LOS is subject to the LOAC in armed conflict situations, belligerents must pay due regard to neutrals' rights under the LOS.

What does this tell us? The due regard principle is based on the assumption that whenever two states are lawfully entitled to act in a determined way on the grounds of disparate and even *competing* legal bases (i.e., when two rights collide), the legitimate exercise of one state's rights should not be considered as a reason to deny the lack of recognition of the other's rights, or of at least part of them. Given that either rights or sets of rights are based on valid legal sources, in the absence of a previously established solution to solve the conflict, the sphere of each right should be left intact to the greatest possible extent. Even the recognition of the hierarchical superiority of one of the legal sources (e.g., *jus cogens* principles) should not be interpreted as though other individuals cannot also have other rights based on other valid sources (i.e., other *jus cogens* principles, IHL, etc.). One law can have prominence over the others; however, this should not imply that the other laws should not be taken into account.

Hence, the due regard principle calls for a more flexible approach when assessing the boundaries of each normative domain. The correct interpretation when competing bodies of law (e.g., LOAC and LOS) apply to a given situation should not offer a zero-sum conclusion, but rather should reflect a decision-maker's respect for each applicable body of law. The dilemmas of what law to apply and how, as stated above, might be resolved through a theoretical framework, based on due regard and analysis of the Restatement (Third) of Foreign Relations Law of the United States §§ 401–03. Here we examine six different situations. The first three involve international armed conflicts where the UN Charter-based rights of individual and collective self-defense and parallel customary norms of individual and collective self-defense, mandatory implementation of UN Security Council "decisions" under Articles 25, 48, and 94(2), and *jus cogens* principles are involved (Principles I, II, III). The second three involve circumstances where competing humanitarian and human rights law norms clash either in international armed conflict situations, or in noninternational armed conflict situations, and where competing humanitarian law norms applying in international or noninternational armed conflicts and human rights norms clash (Principles IV, V, VI). The following six stated "principles" do not exhaust the multiple possibilities that can arise when the different legal sources interact, but offer insight into the question of how to determine each source's role.

Principle I: Self-Defense, Security Council Decisions, and Humanitarian or Human Rights Law Interfaces

This first general principle addresses the interface between the domain of individual and collective self-defense based on UN Charter law or UN Security Council decisions, and treaty obligations imposed on states, including humanitarian law or human rights treaties. This principle might be adopted:

> UN Charter law, meaning the law of the inherent right of individual or collective self-defense under Article 51 or the law of a UN Security Council decision taken pursuant to Council authority and mandatory on states under the Charter in Articles 25, 48 or 94(2), prevails under Article 103 of the Charter over any applicable treaty obligations of affected states, including obligations under humanitarian law or human rights treaties. If a Council decision authorizes self-defense but conditions use of self-defense measures, those conditions apply in states' exercise of individual or collective self-defense. However, actions taken pursuant to Article 51 or pursuant to Council decisions under Articles 25, 48 and 94(2) shall have due regard for humanitarian law or human rights standards, whether stated in international agreements, customary international law or general principles of law, the presumption being that these standards shall usually apply in any self-defense or Council decision-governed situation.[14]

An illustration of this principle is found in the enforcement of humanitarian law treaty rules protecting cultural property, so long as it is not used for military purposes.[15] Under the LOAC, those rules are mandatory among treaty partners during armed conflict and, to the extent they restate customary law or general principles are mandatory for all states, so long as the objects are not employed for military purposes.[16]

Israel's 2006 operations against Hezbollah in Lebanon supply other examples. Israel justified its actions, which included a naval "blockade" and aerial or rocket attacks in Lebanon as self-defense responses. Human rights groups, UN and Lebanon officials decried some attacks as LOAC violations or war crimes. Human rights groups condemned Israeli use of cluster bombs and Hezbollah attacks on civilians including use of ball bearings in projectiles. Israel accused Hezbollah of preventing civilians from leaving southern Lebanon villages, thereby making these people human shields, behind which Hezbollah could operate. Lebanese mariners were unable to fish in Mediterranean waters during their prime season because of Israel's "blockade," which continued due to Israeli concerns over arms smuggling into Lebanon.

Meanwhile, unlike other NGOs, the ICRC (International Committee of the Red Cross) followed its standard policy of confidentiality, although the ICRC reminded all parties to respect the principles of proportionality and distinction between civilians and civilian objects and military objectives, the most worrying aspect being the situation of civilians. Other concerns were access to those who needed assistance, medical evacuations, displaced persons fleeing the conflict, destruction, or damage to infrastructure, and the sea/air blockade. By early September 2006, Israel had lifted the air/sea "blockade" as part of its Resolution 1701 compliance and as a multinational naval force arrived in offshore Mediterranean waters to assume weapons policing duties. Israel saw policing Lebanese land borders with Syria as the "wild card and the real test of the arms embargo." Meanwhile, the new UN Human Rights Council also came under NGO criticism for putting politics above lives.

Under Principle I analysis, Israel, if acting in self-defense under the Charter, was not strictly bound by human rights or LOAC rules when conducting its bombing and rocket attacks (excepting necessity and proportionality). However, there is a very strong presumption that Israel should have so acted. The "blockade" of fishermen supplies another example for applying Principle I. Israel and Lebanon are subject to a 1949 armistice and later accords.[17] If there is a serious breach of an armistice, the target state may resume war, under the traditional view. Thus, if Lebanon's failure to contain Hezbollah was a serious breach, Israel was justified in acting. If Israel claimed to act in self-defense, long-standing treaty, and custom-based rules against keeping innocent coastal fishermen from their occupation were subject to self-defense principles. If these fishermen engaged in arms smuggling to aid Israel's enemy or were reasonably perceived to be doing so during war, they would lose their LOAC protections and most assuredly would lose them in a self-defense situation. Nevertheless, in acting in self-defense, Israel was required to give due regard to these LOAC rules. And as with Israeli air and missile attacks, the facts are too enveloped in the fog of war to venture a definitive view on whether the "blockade" of fishermen violated international law or whether it was legitimate under exceptions to the rule.

Israel claimed actions against Hezbollah fighters after the Resolution 1701 cease-fire were in self-defense. To local people near the shooting, it was provocation and a "flagrant breach of the cease-fire...." From the Israeli point of view, the right of self-defense continued unabated. As long as necessity and proportionality standards, which included presumptive observance of LOAC rules under Principle I, were met, a case can be made for lawfulness of the attacks if the facts, now so shrouded in the fog of war, are as originally reported. Moreover, if the Hezbollah actions were a serious breach of the cease-fire, under traditional law, Israel was entitled to resume the conflict, but only enough to quell Hezbollah actions.

In a UN Charter Article 51 self-defense situation, because of Article 103, these rules would be mandatory. Article 103 establishes the primacy of one source of law (UN Charter law) over other treaties. However, this hierarchical primacy does not mean that the treaties' obligations should not also be taken into consideration. Those ordering or executing a self-defense response must have due regard for these rules in planning and executing such action, a presumption being that the same standards shall usually, but not always, apply.

Similarly, states acting pursuant to a Security Council decision binding under Articles 25, 48, or 94(2), and the Council itself if it issues, for instance, a target-specific decision, must have due regard for treaty standards governing humanitarian law or human rights law. The presumption again is that usually, but not always, the same standards shall apply. The Security Council decision under Chapter VII should not be interpreted as the only applicable law. Instead, it should be assumed that a decision presumptively follows the ordinary armed conflict rules. As the multinational force assembled and entered Lebanon under Resolution 1701, this part of Principle I should govern its actions. Due regard must be paid to LOAC and human rights standards even if a Council decision is in force.

By extension of analysis, if a customary right of self-defense or customary right of action following Articles 25, 48, or 94(2) is claimed, or if humanitarian law norms reflect custom or general principles, the same kind of due regard analysis should be employed, with the presumption that the humanitarian law standards shall usually, but not always, prevail in self-defense or Charter decision situations. If a human rights norm is involved, due regard should be observed in either a self-defense response or action pursuant to a Council decision, with the same presumption that the humanitarian law or human rights law standards shall usually, but not always, prevail.

Therefore, following this rationale, although humanitarian or human rights law rules cannot trump the law of self-defense or Council-decided actions under the Charter, decision-makers do not have license to shoot up the countryside without regard for LOAC or human rights principles. Due regard must be given to humanitarian law or human rights law standards. These standards usually, but not always, should prevail.

What behavior should we expect from those in charge of military operations? As suggested elsewhere, a decision-maker faced with a self-defense situation should be held to what he or she knows, or reasonably should know, of applicable protections under humanitarian law or human rights law. The same standards should also apply in Security Council decision-supported actions. These knowledge standards are taken from LOAC principles. Declarations of understanding by countries party to Protocol I to the 1949 Geneva Conventions state that, for civilians' protection in Articles 51,[18] civilian objects protection in Article 52,[19] and precautions to be taken in attacks in Article 57,[20] a commander should be liable based on that commander's assessment of information available at the relevant time, meaning when a decision to attack is made. Two 1980 Conventional Weapons Convention protocols show similar terms, i.e., a commander is bound by information available when a decision to attack is made.[21] The Cultural Property Convention Second Protocol, art. 1(f), referring to Cultural Property Convention, also recites the principle. Geneva Protocol I of 1977, with its understandings, and the Conventional Weapons Convention Protocols are on their way to general acceptance among states, despite the fact that the United States has not ratified Protocol I. Hence, these treaties' common statements, in text or declarations, that commanders are accountable based on information they have at the time for determining whether attacks are necessary and proportional, has become a nearly universal norm. The *San Remo Manual* recognizes it as the naval warfare standard. Thus, it can be said with fair confidence that this is the *jus in bello* customary standard.

It should also be the standard for *jus ad bellum,* meaning for self-defense responses and for Security Council decision-directed operations. A national leader or military commander directing a self-defense response, or a response pursuant to a Council decision, whether reactive or anticipatory, should be held to the same standard as a commander in the field deciding on attacks. This means being held accountable for what he or she, or those reporting to the leader, knew or reasonably should have known, when a decision is made to respond in self-defense. As in the difference between necessity and proportionality standards for LOAC and self-defense situations, what is sufficient knowledge depends on each circumstance. What might be sufficient knowledge in a LOAC situation might not be sufficient knowledge in a self-defense situation, and vice versa.

The standards will not be the same in every self-defense or Security Council decision-based situation, any more than knowledge standards for self-defense situations will be the same as those for the LOAC. Once again, this depends on the circumstances. For example, a higher knowledge standard might apply in a LOAC-governed campaign where supersonic missiles have been fired from a protected structure on an enemy coast than in a situation where the same missiles fired from the same structure against a military aircraft lawfully flying over the high seas, to which the aircraft responds proportionally in self-defense. Similarly, a higher standard of knowledge might apply in a self-defense situation where there is time to consider options than in the 'attacked military aircraft' circumstance.

For further consideration, two examples of these principles are the 2001 response in Afghanistan to the 9/11 attacks and the 2003 Coalition's action against Iraq. States responding in Afghanistan were presumptively required to give due regard to humanitarian law standards, including treatment of detainees. The Security Council had denounced terrorist attacks and had authorized response in self-defense.[22] In the case of the 2003 invasion and occupation, although authorized under Council resolutions going back to 1990 and the LOAC applying to armistices,[23] Coalition forces were presumptively required to give due regard to humanitarian law standards, including treatment of detainees, i.e., were obliged to take into account all the different humanitarian law and human rights standards, as they were applicable. These principles applied to all sides in the 2006 Lebanon crisis.

What should inform the due regard criterion? How do we know what rules from the different applicable bodies should be taken into account? A factorial approach, like that developed in the Restatement (Third), suggests a way to refine the due regard principle.[24] The Restatement approach to prescriptive jurisdiction, i.e., a state's authority to apply its law to persons or activities outside its territory,[25] seems appropriate (see Restatement (Third), §§ 402–03). Analogous reasonableness factors are the heart of the proposed analysis.[26]

Initial General Factors

General factors for applying Principle I might be:

> A state responding pursuant to its inherent right of individual self-defense, or states responding pursuant to their inherent right of collective self-defense, must respond under principles of necessity and proportionality, and in the case of anticipatory self-defense under the principle that the situation admits of no other alternative. Such a State or States must also respond reasonably so as to take into account applicable rules of humanitarian law and human rights law. The UN Security Council, when it decides on action mandatory on states pursuant to UN Charter Articles 25, 48 or 94(2) must consider applicable rules of humanitarian law and human rights law. A state or states acting pursuant to a Council decision mandatory under Articles 25, 48 or 94(2) must respond reasonably so as to take into account applicable rules of humanitarian law and human rights law.

This proposed general reasonableness factor would not derogate from a state's responsibility, when responding in individual or collective self-defense, to do so in accordance with long-standing rules qualifying the right of individual and collective self-defense. These are the rules concerning necessity and proportionality and, in anticipatory self-defense situations, the additional requirement of no other alternative. This initial general factor would not require deferring or denying these rights when humanitarian law and human rights norms are considered. These norms must be taken into account. In many cases, the norms will inform the traditional qualifications on the right of self-defense, for example, a method of response under proportionality standards might fully meet the reasonableness principle. Similarly, this due regard principle also applies to Security Council decisions on action and a state or states' action pursuant to Council decisions. They must take into account applicable humanitarian law and human rights norms.

The Relevant Factors

Whether actions in self-defense, or actions to be directed or directed by a Security Council decision, are reasonable is determined by evaluating all relevant factors, which usually include the following:

Territory:

Link of the action, or proposed action, to territory of an affected state or states and humanitarian law or human rights law which would otherwise govern that state or those states upon whose territory the action is to be taken.

Although humanitarian law and human rights law may protect individuals and not states in some situations, the concept of territory remains relevant. It remains important where people or objects are located that may be subject to protection.[27] The law of treaties declares that unless a different intention appears from a treaty or is otherwise established, a treaty binds parties for all of their territories.[28] On the other hand, if customary law or general principles are involved, there is no such territorial limitation, except insofar as an affected state is a persistent objector,[29] or is not subject to a regional or local custom.[30] A state or states acting in self-defense, the Council deliberating action on a decision, or a state or states acting pursuant to that decision must consider humanitarian law or human rights norms applicable to an affected state through treaty law territorial application, customary law, or general principles of law. In the 2006 Israeli action against Lebanon, Israel was bound to take into account the LOAC and human rights law governing in the area of southern Lebanon. The same was true regarding Hezbollah attacks on Israeli territory. Lebanon, despite its seemingly weak control of its southern territory, had an obligation to consider the result of these attacks. Hezbollah also bore responsibility for its actions insofar as they violated international law.

Relevant Connections Supporting a Right to Military Action:

Such as national registry of vessels, aircraft, or other platforms; nationality, citizenship, or residence of persons or entities involved; with the cultural property in question; or economic activity, between the state or states asserting a right of individual or collective self-defense, between the asserting state or states and the affected state, or between the asserting state or states and those whom the action in self-defense is designed to protect. In the case of UN Security Council decisions mandatory on states pursuant to UN Charter Articles 25, 48, or 94(2), the connections, such as national registry of vessels, aircraft, or other platforms; nationality, citizenship, or residence of persons or entities involved; connections with the cultural property in question; or economic activity, between the decision and the affected state, or between the decision and those whom Council action is designed to protect.

An example of a connection supporting a right of self-defense is a situation where a state asserts such a right to intervene in another state's territory to protect the asserting state's citizens' lives or property.[31] If a state intervenes to succor indigenous peoples' human rights or rights under humanitarian law or its own nationals, the issue is even closer.[32] A state may not use force to recover contract debts,[33] an example of prohibited action that would otherwise affect a state's economic activity. Customary and treaty law require a blockading force to allow passage of food and other supplies essential for civilian population survival and medical supplies for that population or wounded and sick armed forces members,[34] an example of permitted economic activity. In its air/sea "blockade" of Lebanon, there is no evidence that Israel did not allow essential foodstuffs or civilian supplies to enter the country, although there may be a question of whether Israel could have done more to allow essential supplies to reach civilians in attacked areas of Lebanon. Loss of bridges throughout Lebanon through Israeli air strikes did not help the situation. Similarly, there the was responsibility of Lebanon, as territorial sovereign over its southern territory, for actions Hezbollah undertook that violated rights of civilians and other noncombatants involved, including the Hezbollah rockets that hit the Cambodian-flagged vessel on the high seas of the Mediterranean. Hezbollah also bore responsibility for its actions insofar as they violated international law.

Character of the Action:

Character of the action, importance of the action to the acting state or states or to the UN Security Council, the extent to which other states have acted or the Council has acted in the past, and the degree to which the desirability of the action is generally accepted by states.

The importance of the inherent right of individual or collective self-defense including anticipatory self-defense, a Security Council decision, or action pursuant to a decision, cannot be understated or minimized. There is no concept of precedent in international law; nevertheless, decision-makers should consider prior state practice and actions pursuant to Council decisions. The necessity doctrine, recently elucidated by the International Law Commission, should also be considered.[35] The nature, i.e., the character, of the proposed action should be considered.[36] Lastly, countries' statements of the relative desirability of the action should be taken into account. Examples are the issues of humanitarian intervention or intervention to protect an intervening state's citizens and nationals, for which there has been sharp disagreement within the world community. On the other hand, there appeared to be no disagreement about states' efforts to embark their nationals, and nationals of other states, from Lebanese ports during the 2006 conflict. In Israel's 2006 action against Hezbollah in southern Lebanon, Israel characterized the Hezbollah raid as an act of war necessitating a severe response. Lebanon and others decried the response as disproportionate. Other countries sided with Israel or Lebanon.

Expectations:

Existence of justified expectations that might be protected or hurt by a state or states acting in self-defense, or by a UN Security Council decision or a state or states' action pursuant to that decision.

Given the virtually universal acceptance of the 1949 Geneva Conventions, certain other humanitarian law norms and the same status for many principles that would protect cultural property, and many human rights treaties and other human rights norms, it is axiomatic that a state or states acting in self-defense or acting pursuant to a Security Council decision, or those drafting such a decision resolution, must take into account what may be states' and peoples' strong expectations that the actions or decision will take into account humanitarian and human rights law norms. There were these kinds of expectations in the 2006 Israeli incursion into Lebanon.

Importance of the Action:

The importance at the time of a state's or states' acting in self-defense, a UN Security Council decision, or action pursuant to that decision to the international political, legal, or economic systems.

As noted above, the importance of the inherent right of individual or collective self-defense including anticipatory self-defense, a Security Council decision or action pursuant to a decision, cannot be understated or minimized. Although the initial Hezbollah raid involved relatively few fighters, Israel perceived it as "an act of war," a serious matter. The Hezbollah leadership later said it never dreamed that Israel would respond so strongly. Quite clearly the Security Council saw the conflict as serious and decided, through its Resolution 1701, to augment the UN force already in Lebanon to oversee the cease-fire.

Traditions:

The extent to which a state's or states' acting in self-defense, a UN Security Council decision, or action pursuant to that decision, is consistent with the traditions of the international system.

Again, the importance of the inherent right of individual or collective self-defense including anticipatory self-defense, a Security Council decision or action pursuant to a decision, cannot be understated or minimized. Given Charter Article 103, which trumps all treaties, actions involving self-defense or Council decisions represent very strong traditions within the international system. Moreover, Article 51 recites preserving the "inherent" right of individual and collective self-defense, signifying that these rights of action reach back in time before the 1945 Charter.

Interests of Other State(s):

The extent to which another state or other states might have an interest or interests in asserting claims with respect to action in individual or collective self-defense, a UN Security Council decision, or action taken pursuant to a Council decision.

An obvious interest of another state is its interest in its territorial integrity or political independence under UN Charter Article 2(4). Another might be protecting its citizens' or nationals' interests or of those who would benefit from preservation of cultural property under humanitarian or human rights law. This was apparent when other countries marshaled air flights and shipping to evacuate their and other states' nationals during the 2006 Lebanon crisis. There were no reported Lebanese or Israeli objections.

Potential Conflicts with the Claims of Another State or of Other States:

The likelihood of conflict of assertions of the right of individual or collective self-defense, a UN Security Council decision, or action taken pursuant to a Council decision, with rights under international law claimed by an affected state.

UN Charter supremacy factors (Articles 25, 48, 51, 94[2], 103) will also be under consideration. There were many assertions of rights under international law by Lebanon and Israel as well as by third states and NGOs regarding individuals' human rights and rights under humanitarian law during the 2006 Israeli incursion into Lebanon, Lebanon's international responsibility for the attacks and the responsibility of Hezbollah.

The Final Consideration:

A final consideration, with regard to deference to rights of the other states is:

Where a prescription of individual or collective self-defense, a UN Security Council decision or action under a Council decision conflicts with interests that an affected state or states might claim or has or have claimed, each decision-maker (i.e., claimant[s] of a right of individual or collective self-defense or under a Council decision) must evaluate its or their own as well as the affected state or states' interests, in light of all relevant factors, including those set out as factors above; however, there should be deference to the claimant(s) of a right of individual or collective self-defense, a Council decision or action under a Council decision, regardless of whether an affected state or states' interest(s) is or are greater.

This formulation differs substantially from the Restatement (Third) rubric of state deference to the "clearly greater" interest. The reason for the difference is the Charter's supremacy. This consideration would almost always result in applying Charter-based principles, subject to the foregoing nonexclusive factors. This final consideration should lead to the affected state's or states' compliance with the Charter.

Summary

The foregoing is a suggested analysis and, as such, is open to refinements. This factorial approach will not be appropriate in nearly all anticipatory self-defense situations, where the response must be necessary and proportional (a response that is instant, overwhelming and leaves no reasonable peaceful alternative). No one expects a military aircraft commander or a warship captain to parse the foregoing principles when threatened with, or under imminent, missile attack, for example. Nor does anyone expect a state threatened with, or under imminent, annihilation within minutes from missile attack to analyze its anticipatory self-defense response. On the other hand, for example, if it is a situation that is moving from crisis to hostile intent (and thereby triggering the anticipatory self-defense option) through a long enough time, where legal and other resources can be maturely considered, the foregoing principles should be relevant. Thus, the use of the approach suggested thereby must be weighed against practical considerations of timing.

The same kind of caution applies in reactive self-defense situations, where a unit or a state has been attacked. No one expects a military aircraft commander or a warship captain to parse these principles if the platform has been hit and response must be rapid, for example. Nor does anyone expect a state hit by missiles, with threat of more on the way that could result in annihilation, to analyze its reactive self-defense response under these principles. But if it is a situation of an initial nonlethal strike on a state or a state's military unit(s) and the response time is long enough, where legal and other resources can be maturely considered, the foregoing principles may be useful.

The same considerations, for and against the proposed analysis, should apply to action under Security Council decisions. In some cases, there may be time where legal and other resources can be maturely considered; in other cases, the analysis may not be useful. In nearly all instances of Council discussions and debate on decision resolutions, however, the analysis may be helpful.

Principle II: *Jus Cogens* Norms

A second general principle might be:

> If the inherent right of individual or collective self-defense is a *jus cogens* norm, and would thereby prevail over any applicable humanitarian law or human rights obligations of affected states, including obligations pursuant to treaties, customary law or general principles of law, states acting in individual or collective self-defense shall have due regard for humanitarian law or human rights standards, whether stated in international agreements, customary international law or general principles of law, the presumption being that these standards shall usually apply in any self-defense situation. The same principles should apply if a UN Security Council decision mandatory under UN Charter Articles 25, 48 and 94(2) restates a *jus cogens* norm, or application of the decision would involve applying standards from *jus cogens*-based law.

The analyses and examples submitted for Principle I would apply here, i.e., action against cultural property, if it is assumed that the right of self-defense is a *jus cogens* norm. The same examples taken from the 2006 Israeli incursion into Lebanon would apply, although the historical facts may not be clear yet. The same factors would apply if it is a Council decision, or action pursuant to a decision, girded with *jus cogens*.[37] Due regard factors for Principle II would be similar, except that instead of Article 103, the principle of *jus cogens'* supremacy over treaties, customary law, and general principles would be invoked. Caveats on the use of factors that might be applied to Principle I, also apply under Principle II.

Suppose the reverse is true, meaning that individual or collective self-defense action, a Council decision or action under a Council decision is not supported by *jus cogens* principles and would run afoul of a humanitarian law or human rights norm supported by *jus cogens*. Under these circumstances, there is a reverse analysis, meaning a *jus cogens*-supported norm would trump action in self-defense, a Council decision, or action under a decision that is not *jus cogens*-supported, for example, where *jus cogens* norms protect cultural property and those persons involved with the property. Furthermore, in applying due regard principles, so would the caveats on applying the principles in many scenarios, so that in most anticipatory self-defense and probably many reactive self-defense situations, there would be no time to consider conditioning factors.

Principle III: Opposing *Jus Cogens* Norms

Principle III follows from Principle II for other *jus cogens* situations, whether they would be circumstances of conflicting *jus cogens* norms, for example, if the inherent right of self-defense and the Charter Article 2(4)-based territorial integrity principle are opposed or a humanitarian law norm with *jus cogens* character conflicts with a human rights customary, treaty, or general principles-based norm that also has *jus cogens* status. In those circumstances, due regard should be paid to the other norm (Principle III):

> If there are opposing *jus cogens* norms, e.g., if the right of individual or collective self-defense is a *jus cogens* norm and it conflicts with a humanitarian law or human rights norm with *jus cogens* status, or if a Security Council decision's terms or action under a Security Council decision involves a *jus cogens* norm and there is a conflict with a humanitarian law or human rights norm with *jus cogens* status, due regard must be paid to the humanitarian law or human rights norm in the exercise of individual or collective self-defense, approval of the Council decision, or action under the Council decision.

The due regard principle counsels consideration of and respect for what the other norms with *jus cogens* status provide. In this case, the equal validity and rank of each source of law makes it unfeasible to prefer one norm over the other without full consideration of all the particular details of the situation in question. How should the balance be struck between competing *jus cogens* norms? A Restatement (Third)-based approach, as in the two previous situations considered, suggests possible answers.

General Conditioning Factor

The difference between the following formulation and proposals under Principles I and II is that the balance has shifted. Instead of Charter supremacy or supremacy of self-defense under Article 103, a Security Council decision under *jus cogens* or action under a Council decision supported by *jus cogens* principles, these would be opposed by a humanitarian law or human rights law norm also supported by *jus cogens* principles. A general conditioning factor where there is a conflict between the right of self-defense as a *jus cogens* norm and a humanitarian law or human rights norm that has *jus cogens* status is:

> If a right of individual or collective self-defense is a *jus cogens* norm, a UN Security Council decision articulates a command grounded in *jus cogens* or action under a Council decision would be grounded in a *jus cogens* norm, and there is a conflict with a rule of humanitarian law or human rights law that also has *jus cogens* status, those deciding on acting in individual or collective self-defense, on wording of such a Council decision or action pursuant to a Council decision, must consider whether such action, the decision or action pursuant to a decision is reasonable under the circumstances.

This general reasonableness factor would not derogate from a state's responsibility, when responding in individual or collective self-defense, to recognize long-standing rules qualifying the inherent right of self-defense such as necessity, proportionality and, in anticipatory self-defense situations, where a situation is instant, overwhelming and admitting of no peaceful alternative. Principle III would not require deferring or denying these rights when humanitarian law and human rights norms are considered. These norms must be taken into account. Often the norms will inform qualifications on the right of self-defense, for example, a method of response under proportionality standards might fully meet the reasonableness principle. In a similar fashion, the Security Council, when it decides on action, must take into account applicable humanitarian law and human rights norms under Principle III. This would not require deferring or denying the Council's right to make a decision when humanitarian law and human rights norms are at stake. These norms must be taken into account. The same kind of analysis should follow for a state's or states' action pursuant to Council decisions.

The same kind of analysis would apply where there are conflicting *jus cogens*-supported humanitarian law and human rights law standards. The traditional view has been that these are discrete bodies of law, but recent attempts have been made at blending the two bodies of law.[38] Principle III offers a nonbinding method of analysis for this situation as well if competing humanitarian law and human rights norms are grounded in *jus cogens*.

Relevant Factors

Whether actions in self-defense or actions to be directed or directed by a Council decision are reasonable is determined, where appropriate, by balancing all relevant factors, as in the discussion regarding Principle I. Elements that should be taken into consideration to strike the most adequate balance include: territory,[39] relevant connections supporting a right to military action, specific characteristics of the action[40] and its importance, expectations by other states, general importance of the action to the international community, traditions, the interests of third state(s), and potential conflicts with other states' claims.

The Final Consideration

A final consideration is:

> Where a prescription of individual or collective self-defense, a UN Security Council decision or action under a Council decision conflicts with interests that an affected state or states might claim or has or have claimed, each decision-maker (i.e., claimant[s] of a right of individual or collective self-defense or under a Council decision) must evaluate its or their own as well as the affected state or states' interests, in light of all relevant factors, including those set out above; however, there should be deference to the claimant(s) of a right of individual or collective self-defense, a Council decision or action under a Council decision, regardless of whether an affected state or states' interest(s) is or are greater.

This formulation differs from the *Restatement* rubric of state deference to the "clearly greater" interest.[41] As in the principles above, the reason for the difference is UN Charter supremacy.[42] This consideration would usually result in applying Charter-based principles, subject to the nonexclusive balance of the previously mentioned factors. This final consideration will usually lead to a requirement for the affected state's compliance with the Charter and its rules, or rules, e.g., self-defense, with roots in the Charter. Although the final consideration is identical with the same consideration under Principle I, the cases for self-defense, a Charter decision or action under a Charter decision are weaker because of an opposing *jus cogens* principle and the general principle of States' acting within the law.

Summary

The foregoing is a suggested analysis, essentially the same as that for Principle I to which reference is made, except that a case for applying self-defense, a Security Council decision or action pursuant to a decision, is weaker because of a competing humanitarian law or human rights norm with *jus cogens* status.

Principle IV: Conflicts between Humanitarian Law and Human Rights Norms

There are other situations involving clashing and conflicting values if Charter norms and *jus cogens* norms are not involved. For instance, conflicts between humanitarian law and human rights norms, where different standards of humanitarian law might apply, or between norms applying to international armed conflicts and noninternational armed conflicts.[43] Similarly, conflicts may exist if human rights law and different standards of humanitarian law might apply, as among human rights rules, norms for international armed conflicts and norms for noninternational armed conflicts.[44] In these cases, the following discussion shows how due regard principles can also be helpful.

Where humanitarian law and human rights law conflict, Principle IV might be:

> In a situation of international armed conflict or non-international armed conflict, where there are humanitarian law principles conflicting with human rights principles, those bound by humanitarian law principles must pay due regard to human rights principles otherwise applicable to the situation, and those bound by human rights principles must pay due regard to humanitarian law principles applicable to the situation.

If the standards of humanitarian law and humanitarian law both apply, there should be no requirement that usually one will prevail over the other. The approach is more akin to comity analysis, meaning respect for a parallel legal system.[45] For example, to the extent that an occupying power can meet its humanitarian law and LOAC obligations while allowing otherwise applicable human rights, the occupying power should do so. Due regard should be given competing norms.

What should inform the content of due regard for this situation? Following the same rationale as in the previous criteria, a factorial approach, like that developed in the Restatement (Third), suggests a method of refining the due regard principle.

1. General Conditioning Factor

A general conditioning factor if there is a conflict between humanitarian law and human rights law might be stated:

> A state or states bound by the law of international or non-international armed conflict and applicable humanitarian law rules must act reasonably so as to take into account rules of human rights law otherwise also in force for a particular situation.

This general reasonableness factor would not derogate from a state's or states' responsibility, when operating under the law of international or noninternational armed conflict, and would not require deferring or denying that state's or those states' rights or obligations to act under the LOAC and humanitarian law when human rights norms are considered. These human rights norms must be taken into account. Derogation clauses in human rights treaties (such as in ICCPR Article 4), and perhaps customary law flowing from such clauses,[46] may limit application of human rights norms. Law of treaties principles, such as impossibility of performance, fundamental change of circumstances,[47] or armed conflict's effect on treaties[48] may also limit applying treaty-based human rights norms. Treaties, like those governing the LOS with their other rules clauses, for example, the LOS is subject to the LOAC, may also limit applying human rights norms by their terms.

2. Relevant Factors

Whether a state's actions under humanitarian law, or actions to be directed or directed by a Security Council decision involving humanitarian law, are reasonable when compared with human rights standards is determined, where appropriate, by evaluating all relevant factors, including territory; relevant connections supporting a right to military action, specific characteristics of the action and its importance, expectations by other states, general importance of the action to the international community,[49] traditions, interests of other state(s), positions,[50] and potential conflicts with other state's claims.

3. The Final Consideration

A final consideration is:

> When it would not be unreasonable for a claimant under humanitarian law and a claimant under human rights law to assert that humanitarian law or human rights law applies to a given situation, each claimant has an obligation to evaluate its own as well as the other claimant's interest in applying an asserted standard of humanitarian law or human rights law, in light of all relevant factors, including those set out above; a claimant should defer to the other claimant if that claimant's interest is clearly greater.

The final consideration is a tiebreaker. It applies when applying different standards is not unreasonable, but there are differences. When possible the opponents should consult with each other, a situation clearly not usually possible in armed conflict situations, but it might be feasible through mediation of third parties, for example, the UN Secretary-General when the United Nations is not involved through a governing resolution.

The consideration does not apply if there can be compliance with both sets of rules, i.e., humanitarian law and human rights law.

Principle V: Different Standards of Humanitarian Law: International Armed Conflict and Noninternational Armed Conflict

If different humanitarian law standards might apply, Principle V might be:

> In a situation of international armed conflict as between some states party to a conflict where other states party to the conflict are also engaged in non-international armed conflict, states engaged in international armed conflict must pay due regard to the law of non-international armed conflict as it applies to states and groups engaged in non-international armed conflict, and states and groups engaged in non-international armed conflict must pay due regard to the law of armed conflict as it applies to states engaged in international armed conflict.

The problem is illustrated by the different LOAC standards that may apply where opposing states are subject to, for example, the 1949 Geneva Convention rules and 1977 Protocol I, while standards governing a noninternational conflict between insurgents and a government also engaged in the same international armed conflict are found in the Conventions' Common Article 3 and 1977 Protocol II. Examples might be detainee treatment during the Afghanistan (2001–07) and Iraq (2003–07) operations, where international armed conflict and noninternational armed conflict standards may differ. The same was true for Kosovo operations. It may also be true for the augmented UNIFIL in peacekeeping operations in Lebanon after the 2006 crisis. Although the conflict may have involved interaction between Lebanon and Israel, it may also have invoked the law of noninternational armed conflict where Hezbollah, a force within Lebanon's borders, is concerned. The broader point is that Hezbollah as a nonstate actor, much as al Qaeda in Afghanistan, may be subject to noninternational armed conflict rules because it is not a state (which matters more broadly, because what is referred to as the war on terrorism typically involves nonstate actors in civil wars or at best mixed international and noninternational armed conflicts). In this case, due regard should be given to the competing norms. In this case, a factorial approach, like that developed in the *Restatement (Third)* and suggested for Principle IV above, where different humanitarian law and human rights law standards may apply, suggests a way to refine the due regard principle if norms for international armed conflict and noninternational armed conflict differ.

Principle VI: Conflicts among Standards for Human Rights Law, the Law of International Armed Conflict, and the Law of Noninternational Armed Conflict

If different humanitarian law and human rights law standards might apply, Principle VI might be:

> In an international armed conflict situation between some states party to a conflict where other states party to the conflict are also engaged in non-international armed conflict and human rights principles are at issue, states engaged in international armed conflict must pay due regard to the law of non-international armed conflict as it applies to states and groups engaged in non-international armed conflict and to the law of human rights; states and groups engaged in non-international armed conflict must pay due regard to the law of armed conflict as it applies to states engaged in international armed conflict and to the law of human rights.

This kind of trilateral due regard-comity formula is complex, and the foregoing may be a less than satisfactory solution. However, logic requires this kind of result. Even as states engaged in international armed conflict and thereby subject to humanitarian law governing that kind of war must have due regard for humanitarian law principles applying to the war's noninternational armed conflict aspects, they must also have due regard for applicable human rights norms. Similarly, groups engaged in noninternational armed conflict, and state forces opposing them, must have due regard for applicable international armed conflict norms and human rights norms besides observing rules applying to non-international armed conflict. Examples might be detainee treatment during the Kosovo, Afghanistan (2001–07), Iraq (2003–07), and Lebanon (2006) operations, where human rights law principles, standards for international armed conflict, and noninternational armed conflict standards may conflict. The due regard approach, rather than advocating a rigid solution, provides good theoretical grounds to solve the conflict of rules in a flexible way, respecting the rights of the different parties involved. Lastly, in this case, the comments made with respect to how to determine the best due regard approach based on the interpretation of a nonexclusive list of factors also apply.

APPLYING THE DUE REGARD PRINCIPLE: PRACTICAL CONSIDERATIONS

States' military operations begin with planning; the U.S. military planning process, developed over a century of analysis, is typical and described in an accompanying chapter.[51] Today, as always, the input of law is as crucial as logistics, communications, health, morale, weather, etc. Similarly, ROE (rules of engagement) rely on law as well as policy and other considerations to give commanders ranges of options from which to choose in planning and executing operations.[52] In multinational operations, ROE drafting and execution can be quite complex, for example, where some countries seconding forces adhere to a reactive self-defense policy, while others follow the view that anticipatory self-defense is permitted. Even if all participating states have the same general view, there may be differences of opinion on the same law. Recent examples of multinational operations that may raise these kinds of issues include Kosovo, Afghanistan, and UNIFIL operations in Lebanon. UN forces operate with their own ROE. These processes are necessary for successful, lawful military operations. A third component is education and training, not only in the profession of arms, but also in the applicable law. The 1949 Geneva Conventions, for example, require dissemination of and education and training in humanitarian law, as do other international agreements.[53] Lack of training is one likely reason for the Abu Ghraib guards' behavior.[54] A fourth factor is military operations' relatively high speed today, particularly in self-defense situations. A fifth factor is modern weapons' lethality. A first shot may be the last needed to achieve desired results. This tends to promote relatively rapid responses, perhaps to anticipate in self-defense the first shot. This can cut planning time to near zero. ROE underscore a hierarchical rule, enshrined in Charter Article 51 and customary law, of unit, force and national self-defense. ROE can create their own kinds of issues, such as differences among national ROEs, or differences in interpretation for multinational ROEs. Another problem is how states apply international law standards, since many countries invoke a dualist theory of application, meaning international law must be implemented under national law which may accordingly shape application of international law.[55]

We must also address the issue of nonstate actors, specifically terrorist groups, insurgents, and NGOs involved in civil wars and similar noninternational armed conflicts. How should these participants be educated and trained? Unlike states, governments of states, and military commands under them, there may be, and likely is, no education and training system within these groups.[56] A solution for these situations is a warning by affected states and the international community (e.g., through U.N. or other organizations') resolutions or similar proclamations of the law and consequences for its breach (i.e., education by proclamation),[57] and prosecution after the events. This was the practice before Nuremberg[58] and should be followed today.

CONCLUSIONS

The 60 years after World War II have been a watershed in warfare and in international law. Nuclear weapons helped end the war. Their legacy of proliferation and risk of use by rogue states and groups such as terrorists plagues us to this day. The United Nations was also an agent for decolonization and human rights, with its Charter that approved the inherent right of individual and collective self-defense, while affirming states' territorial integrity and political independence, and outlawing war as an instrument of national policy.

As the Charter era began, the time of mass armies and navies confronting each other, perhaps in coalitions or civil wars, changed to operations usually involving smaller forces and more professional cadres (with exceptions like the 1980–88 Iran–Iraq war). Conscription is seemingly becoming obsolete. However, states' retention of systems of part-time militaries, such as militias or the National Guard and reserves in the United States, held out a potential for larger forces on call but created problems of training and equipping them. Abu Ghraib and similar atrocities are as much a result of poor training and leadership as Lieutenant Calley's unlawful My Lai actions during Vietnam as the last American use of mass armies peopled with draftees. At the same time, the decolonization movement has promoted growth of new nations which all too often experienced civil wars that dragged on longer than in earlier times. The phenomenon of great power engagement in these conflicts before and after the Cold War's end resulted in multilateral confrontations where international armed conflicts often merged with noninternational conflicts.

The Charter era has been a time of change in international law. To be sure, the Cold War deformed development of the law to a certain extent, but self-defense claims, coupled with the Charter's Article 103 in the nature of a supremacy clause, have raised an issue of the relationship between Charter law and the existing and developing law of international and noninternational armed conflict and human rights. Alliance and coalition systems, with possible differing interpretations of law within them, further complicate the issue. A similar problem is the relationship between UN Security Council decisions, requiring UN member state action and which through Article 103 trump other treaty law.

Development of *jus cogens,* norms superior to traditional sources (custom, treaties, general principles) and ill-defined in scope, also creates uncertainty as to the law applying to a situation. Worldwide and regional human rights treaties, with their derogation clauses exempting coverage except core rights during war, and customary law and general principles paralleling these agreements, are in force alongside a developing and changing body of LOAC. Old law of treaties principles—the effect of armed conflict on treaties, impossibility of performance, and fundamental change of circumstances—remain. In LOS-related situations, the post-1945 conventions (1958, 1982) recite that the LOS is subject to other rules of law, meaning the LOAC. To further complicate analysis, prolonged civil wars with other states' involvement have created triangular issues of applicability of the law of international armed conflict, the law of noninternational armed conflict, and human rights law.[59]

Use of a due regard principle, taken from analysis targeting LOS and law of naval warfare interfaces, and the factorial model of the Restatement (Third), are advanced as a possible solution for these problems, e.g., a state responding in self-defense, although supported by Article 103 primacy in action under Article 51 of the Charter, must have due regard for humanitarian law and human rights norms and should presumptively apply them. Similarly, states engaged in international armed conflict must apply humanitarian law applicable to that aspect of a war but must also have due regard for rights protected by the law of noninternational armed conflict and human rights norms.

In these situations, discussed under Principles I–VI, careful factorial analysis is necessary. It is also necessary to consider whether a situation truly involves an Article 103 issue (Principle I) or an issue of *jus cogens* (Principle II), both of which under contemporary theory trump custom, treaties, or general principles. There must also be careful analysis to determine if there are competing *jus cogens*-backed standards (Principle III). The wish list for *jus cogens* may be long, but the reality may be that most situations do not involve any *jus cogens* claims. The result, more often than not, will involve competing human rights and humanitarian law norms (Principle IV), competing rules from the law of international armed conflict, and the law of noninternational armed conflict (Principle V), or the messiest situation, where human rights, the law of international armed conflict and the law of noninternational armed conflict (Principle VI) are all involved. Although the 2005 ICRC Study takes the position that most customary rules for international armed conflict and noninternational armed conflict are the same, that seems more aspiration in terms of progressive development than the unanimous view of states. Some countries have rejected Protocol I to the 1949 Geneva Conventions, notably the United States, and would undoubtedly be a persistent objector to some customary rules Protocol I purports to codify.

The due regard factorial approach is only one part of the analysis. Besides this law-oriented approach, other value systems must be considered: ethnic, moral and religious sensitivities, financial aspects, historical traditions, cultural sensitivities, etc.[60] Achieving this goal begins with comprehensive, systematic planning, which is a hallmark of modern military operations. Commanders receive orders and their options, in part, through operational plans and ROE. Personnel must be educated and trained in all aspects of an operation; humanitarian law requires it. This requirement, along with a failure of leadership, apparently was not fully accomplished for Abu Ghraib. The result was violations of international law, national law like the Uniform Code of Military Justice, and common standards of humanity and decency. There are lessons here for military commands and nations concerning what happens if they do not disseminate LOAC principles, then educate and train their forces adequately. If the commands and nations did so train those accused, the responsibility lies with the individuals who committed the offenses for which they were charged.

One education and training problem remains, namely the situation with respect to the nonstate actor terrorists or ethnic groups, who populate insurgencies and civil wars that bedevil our time. How should these groups be educated and trained? Unlike states and military commands under them, there likely is no training system for these groups. It would seem that one solution for these situations is warning by affected states and the international community (e.g., through UN resolutions) of the law and consequences for its breach (i.e., education by national and international proclamation), and prosecution after the events.

Undoubtedly, there are other problems with respect to proper application of the law for which Principles I–VI offer quite tentative analyses and possible solutions. As Charter law, the LOAC, human rights law and the concept of *jus cogens* move into this century, some questions may be resolved. For example, convergence may be hoped for between the law of international and noninternational armed conflict. States and scholars differ on whether anticipatory self-defense is lawful in the Charter era, although the trend seems to allow it. The Restatement (Third) analysis, upon which much of this chapter is based, without doubt will not be a final authority.[61] However, it is hoped that this chapter offers ideas and tentative solutions for applying the proper law, for which there are many sources in armed conflict situations.

NOTES

1. J.M. Henckaerts and L. Doswald-Beck, eds., *Customary International Humanitarian Law* (Cambridge: Cambridge University Press, 2005) ("ICRC Study").

2. UN Security Council Resolution 1701, S/RES/1701, 2006.

3. The "other rules" clauses of the 1958 LOS Conventions and "United Nations Convention on the Law of the Sea," December 10, 1982 (1982 LOS), e.g., in Article 87 of the 1982 LOS, mean that the LOS is subject to the LOAC in situations involving armed conflict at sea. Under UN Charter Article 103, the LOS is also subject to Charter law.

4. "Anticipatory" self-defense requires a necessary and proportional response that is instant, overwhelming, and admits of no reasonable peaceful alternative, whereas "reactive" self-defense allows an attacking state's first strike before a target state mounts a necessary and proportional response. Recently, the trend seems to recognize anticipatory self-defense as a lawful response. United Nations, *A More Secure World: Our Shared Responsibility: Report of the Secretary-General's High-Level Panel on Threats, Challenges and Change* (New York: United Nations, 2004) (citing Wolfgang Friedmann, *The Changing Structure of International Law* (New York: Columbia University Press, 1964); Louis Henkin, *How Nations Behave: Law and Foreign Policy,* 2nd ed. (New York: Columbia University Press, 1979)). Schachter says UN Charter art. 51 allows a threatened state, "according to long-established international law," to take military action as long as the threatened attack is "imminent, no other means would deflect it and the action is proportionate." Oscar Schachter, "The Rights of States to Use Armed Force," *Michigan Law Review* 82 (1984): 1620, 1633–34; see also International Law Commission, Fifty-Fifth Session, Official Records, Supplement 10, *Report on the Work of Its Fifty-Third Session, A/56/10,* 2001).

5. Article VI of the U.S. Constitution (The Supremacy Clause) was a source for Article 103. See also "Covenant of the League of Nations," art. 20, Restatement (Third) of Foreign Relations Law of the United States §102 comment h (1987) ("Restatement (Third)").

6. "Convention (I) for Amelioration of the Condition of the Wounded & Sick in Armed Forces in the Field," 1949 ("Wounded Convention"); "Convention for Amelioration of the Condition of the Sick, Wounded, & Shipwrecked Members of Armed Forces at Sea," 1949 ("Wounded Convention Sea"); "Convention Relative to Treatment of Prisoners of War," 1949 ("POW Convention"); "Convention Relative to Protection of Civilian Persons in Time of War," 1949 ("Civilian Convention").

7. "Protocol Additional to Geneva Conventions of 12 August 1949, & Relating to Protection of Victims of International Armed Conflicts," June 8, 1977 ("Protocol I"); "Protocol Additional to Geneva Conventions of 12 August 1949, & Relating to Protection of Victims of Non-International Armed Conflicts (Protocol II)," June 8, 1977 ("Protocol II").

8. "Convention for Protection of Cultural Property in Event of Armed Conflict & Regulations," May 14, 1954; "Second Protocol to Hague Convention of 1954 for Protection of Cultural Property in Event of Armed Conflict," March 26, 1999.

9. A.R. Thomas and James C. Duncan, eds., *Annotated Supplement to the Commander's Handbook on the Law of Naval Operations* (Newport, RI: Naval War College Press, 1999) ("NWP 1-14M Annotated"). This is the naval judge advocate's guide to the law; a text version is distributed to operational commands (Richard J. Grunawalt, "Introductory Note" in NWP 1-14M Annotated, at

iii). Its influence goes beyond American commands, and many other states use it. See Michael N. Schmitt, ed., *The Law of Military Operations: Liber Amicorum Professor Jack Grunawalt* (Newport, RI: Naval War College Press, 1998) ("Liber Amicorum"); Dieter Fleck, *The Handbook of Humanitarian Law in Armed Conflicts* (Oxford: Oxford University Press, 2000), 555 ("Fleck").

10. Carin Kaghan, "Jus Cogens and the Inherent Right of Self-Defense," *ILSA Journal of International and Comparative Law* 3 (1997): 767, 823–27.

11. For example, *Prosecutor v. Furundzija,* 121 *International Law Reports* 213, 254–57, 260–62 (1998); *Prosecutor v. Furundzija,* 121 *International Law Reports* 303, 318 (2000); Yoram Dinstein, *The Conduct of Hostilities Under the Law of International Armed Conflict* (Cambridge: Cambridge University Press: 2004) ("Dinstein"); Sandoz et al., eds., *Commentary on the Additional Protocols of 8 June 1977 to the Geneva Conventions of 12 August 1949* (London: Kluwer Law International, 1987), 1340–41 ("Sandoz et al."); and the Supreme Court of the United States' cases, e.g., *Hamdan v. Rumsfeld,* 126 Supreme Court 2749, 2786–98 (2006) (humanitarian law) and *Sosa v. Alvarez-Machain,* 542 U.S. 692, 724–38 (2004) (rejecting applying human rights law in that case).

12. See Louise Doswald-Beck, ed., *San Remo Manual on International Law Applicable to Armed Conflicts at Sea: International Institute of Humanitarian Law* (Cambridge: Cambridge Press University: 1995), ¶¶ 12, 34, 36, 88, 106(c) ("San Remo Manual"): ibid, ¶ 37, ("take care" to avoid damaging cables, pipelines not exclusively serving belligerent). See also Horace B. Robertson, "The 'New' Law of the Sea and the Law of Armed Conflict at Sea," in *Readings on International Law from the Naval War College Review 1978–1994,* eds. John Norton Moore and Robert F. Turner (Newport, RI: Naval War College Press, 1995), 263, 302.

13. This clause, sometimes stated slightly differently, appears throughout the 1982 LOS. It also appears in the "Convention on the High Seas," April 29, 1958, art. 2; and in the Convention on the Territorial Sea & Contiguous Zone, April 29, 1958, arts. 1(2), 14(4), 15.

14. "Affected state" in Principle I and hereafter refers to that state or those states against which action is to be taken under a UN Security Council decision, self-defense, etc.

15. See generally "Convention on Prohibitions or Restrictions on Use of Certain Conventional Weapons Which May Be Deemed to Be Excessively Injurious or to Have Indiscriminate Effects," October 10, 1980 ("Conventional Weapons Convention"), "Protocol II," art. 6(1)(b)(ix); amended May 3, 1996, art. 7(1)(i), in Dietrich Schindler and Jiri Toman, eds., *Law of Armed Conflicts: A Collection of Conventions, Resolutions & Other Documents* (Boston: Brill Academic Publishers, 2004) ("Law of Armed Conflicts"); "Protocol I," art. 53; "Protocol II," art. 16; "Cultural Property Convention and Protocol"; "Second Protocol to Cultural Property Convention"; "Convention Respecting the Laws & Customs of War on Land, with Annex of Regulations," October 18, 1907, art. 23(g) ("1907 Hague IV"); "Convention with Respect to the Laws & Customs of War on Land, with Annex of Regulations," July 29, 1899, art. 23(g), ("1899 Hague II"); and "Treaty on Protection of Artistic & Scientific Institutions & Historic Monuments," April 15, 1935. See also Michael Bothe et al., *New Rules for Victims of Armed Conflicts* (London: Kluwer Law International, 1982), 329–34, 686–89 ("New Rules"); Commission of Jurists, *Rules Concerning the Control of Wireless Telegraphy in Time of War and Air Warfare,* art. 25 in Schindler and Toman, *Law of Armed Conflicts,* 315, 319; Dinstein, 152–66; ICRC Study, R. 38–41; International Committee of the Red Cross, *Guidelines for Military Manuals and Instructions on the Protection of the Environment in Times of Armed Conflict* (Geneva: ICRC, 1994), ¶ 15, in Schindler and Toman, *Law of Armed Conflicts,* 303, 305 ("ICRC, Guidelines"); Sandoz et al., 640–49, 1466–70; Jiri Toman, *The Protection of Cultural Property in the Event of Armed Conflict: Commentary on the Hague Convention 14 May 1954* (Dartmouth: Unesco Publishing, 1996) ("Toman"); Karl Josef Partsch, "Protection of Cultural Property," in Fleck, chap. 9.

16. Protocol I, arts. 48, 52(2); *New Rules,* 282–86, 320–27; Dinstein, chap. 4; Leslie Green, *The Contemporary Law of Armed Conflict* (Huntington, NY: Juris Publishing, 2000), 155–56 ("Green"); ICRC Study, chap. 3; NWP 1-14M Annotated, ¶ 8.1.2; *San Remo Manual,* ¶¶ 39–40; Sandoz et al., 598–600, 635–37; Stefan Oeter, "Methods and Means of Combat," in Fleck, 441–47; 10. Horace B. Robertson, "The Principles of the Military Objective in the Law of Armed Conflict," in *Liber Amicorum.*

17. See Security Council Res. 1701, ¶¶ 3, 5, 8, 10, referring to General Armistice Agreement, Israel and Lebanon, March 23, 1949, *United Nations Treaty Series* 42, 287; "Taif Accords," October 22, 1989, Lebanon and Syria, in *The Arab Collection: Annual Reports,* vol. 1, eds. Yonah Lieberman and Willem-Jan van der Wolf (1995), 340; see also Adir Waldman, "Clashing Behavior, Converging Interests: A Legal Configuration Regulating a Military Conflict," *Yale Journal of International Law* 27 (2002): 249, 255 n. 13.

18. Protocol I, art. 51. See also *New Rules,* 299, n. 3; *San Remo Manual,* ¶ 39; NWP 1-14M Annotated, ¶¶ 6.2.3.2, 11.2 n. 3, 11.3; 4. Jean S. Pictet, ed., *The Geneva Conventions of 12 August 1949: Commentary: IV Geneva Convention Relative to the Protection of Civilian Persons in Time of War* (Geneva: International Committee of the Red Cross, 1958), 224–29 (Pictet); Sandoz et al., 618, 623–26; Julius Stone, *Legal Controls of International Conflict: A Treatise on the Dynamics of Disputes-and-War Law,* rev. (Holmes Beach, FL: W.W. Gaunt, 1959); U.S. Department of the Air Force, *International Law—the Conduct of Armed Conflict and Air Operations,* ch. 14, 1976; Michael J. Matheson, "Remarks in Session One: The United States Position on the Relation of Customary International Law to the 1977 Protocols Additional to the 1949 Geneva Conventions," *American University of International Law Review and Policy* 2 (1987) ("Matheson"): 419, 425 ; W.G. Schmidt, "The Protection of Victims of International Armed Conflict: Protocol I Additional to the Geneva Conventions," *Air Force Law Review* 24 (1984): 189 ("Schmidt"); Waldemar A. Solf, "Protection of Civilians Against the Effects of Hostilities Under Customary International Law and Under Protocol I," *American University Journal of International Law and Politics* 1 (1986): 117, 130–31 ("Solf"). Civilians may not be used as human shields, nor may they be subject of attacks intended to terrorize them; although otherwise legitimate attacks that happen to terrorize them are permissible. Specific intent to terrorize civilians is unlawful. NWP 1-14M Annotated, ¶¶ 11.2, 11.3; Pictet, 208–9, 224–29; Commission of Jurists to Consider and Report Upon Revision of Rules of Air Warfare, *Rules for Aerial Warfare,* art. 22 in Schindler and Toman, *Law of Armed Conflicts;* Matheson, 426; Schmidt, 227.

19. Protocol I, art. 52. See generally *New Rules,* 320–27; C. John Colombos, *The International Law of the Sea,* 6th rev. ed. (New York: David McKay & Co., 1967), §§ 510–11, 524–25, 528–29 ("Colombos"); Dinstein, chap. 4; NWP 1-14M Annotated, ¶¶ 6.2.3 & n. 36, 6.2.3.2, 8.1.1 & n. 9, 8.1.2 & n. 12; D.P. O'Connell, *The International Law of the Sea,* vol. 2 (New York: Oxford University Press, 1984) (hereinafter cited as O'Connell), 1105–6; Pictet, 131; Sandoz et al., 630–38; Matheson, 426; Robertson (which one?); Solf, 130–31.

20. Protocol I, art. 57; see also *New Rules,* 359–69; NWP 1-14M Annotated, ¶¶ 8.1–8.1.2.1; Sandoz et al., 678–89.

21. "Conventional Weapons Convention, Protocol II," art. 2(4), as amended, May 3, 1996, art. 2 (6); "Protocol on Prohibitions or Restrictions on Use of Incendiary Weapons (Protocol III)," October 10, 1980, art. 1(3). "Protocol I on Non-Detectable Fragments (Protocol I)," October 10, 1980, and "Protocol IV on Blinding Laser Weapons," May 3, 1995, do not have these provisions.

22. Security Counsel Res. 1368, 2001; Security Council Res. 1373, 2001; see also "High-Level Panel," ¶¶ 14, 18; "The 9/11 Commission Report," 2004; George K. Walker, "Principles for Collective Humanitarian Intervention to Succor Other Countries' Imperiled Indigenous Nationals," *American University International Law Review* 18 (2003): 35, n. 2.

23. Commentators debate whether prior Council resolutions supported the 2003 action. See generally, e.g., Lucy Martinez, "September 11th, Iraq and the Doctrine of Anticipatory Self-Defense," *University of Missouri—Kansas City Law Review* 72 (2003): 123; Ben Saul, "The Legality of the Use of Force Against Iraq in 2003: Did the Coalition Defend or Defy the United Nations?" *UCLA Journal of International Law and Foreign Affairs* 8 (2003): 267; and Joseph C. Sweeney, "The Just War Ethic in International Law," *Fordham International Law Journal* 27 (2004): 1865. Most commentators say serious breach of an armistice entitles a victor to resume hostilities; Lassa Oppenheim, *International Law,* vol. 2 (London: Green & Co., 1952): §239, citing "1907 Hague IV," Regs., art. 40, 36 Stat., 2305; "1899 Hague II," Regs., art. 40, 32 ibid., at 1821; see also "The Oxford Manual of Naval War," art. 97; Brussels Conference, Project of an International Declaration Concerning the Laws and Customs of War, art. 51 (August 27, 1894), 21, 28; Green, 86; C. Greenwood, "Historical Development and Legal Basis," in Fleck, §235 ("Greenwood").

24. George K. Walker, "The Tanker War 1980–88: Law and Policy," *Naval War College International Law Studies* 74 (2000): 544–52; George K. Walker, "The Lawfulness of Operations Enduring Freedom's Self-Defense Responses," *Valparaiso Law Review* 37 (2003): 489; advocate this kind of analysis.

25. Other categories of jurisdiction the Restatement (Third) recognizes are jurisdiction to adjudicate, defined as a state's authority to subject particular persons or things to its judicial process, and jurisdiction to enforce, or a state's authority to use governmental resources to induce or compel compliance with that state's law. *Id.* §401 & "Introductory Note" to Part IV, 231. Restatement (Second) of Conflict of Laws §6 (1971) ("Restatement (Second)") supplies an analogous approach to prescriptive jurisdiction for conflict of laws, i.e., private international law, among the fifty states of the United States.

26. Restatement (Third) §403(3) (1987) adds that when it would not be unreasonable for each of two states to exercise prescriptive jurisdiction, but the prescriptions are in conflict, "each state has an obligation to evaluate its own as well as the other state's interest in exercising jurisdiction, in light of all the relevant factors, including those set out in Subsection (2); a state should defer to the other state if that state's interest is clearly greater." This deference principle has partial utility in the ensuing analysis.

27. For example, "The International Covenant on Civil and Political Rights," art. 2, *U.N.T.S.* 999, 173, applies to those in a state's territories and those subject to that state's jurisdiction. Humanitarian conventions may apply to enemy or occupied territory. See, e.g., Geneva Civilian Convention; 1907 Hague IV, Regs., arts. 42–56; 1899 Hague II, Regs., arts. 42–56. See also ICRC Study, 305–6.

28. "Vienna Convention on the Law of Treaties," May 23, 1969, art. 29, ("Vienna Convention"); see also Anthony Aust, *Modern Treaty Law and Practice* (Cambridge: Cambridge University Press, 2000), chap. 11 ("Aust"); Robert Jennings and Arthur Watts, *Oppenheim's International Law* (Boston: Addison Wesley, 1996), §631 ("Jennings & Watts"); Restatement, § 322(2); Ian Sinclair, *The Vienna Convention on the Law of Treaties,* 2nd ed. (Manchester and Dover, NH: Manchester University Press, 1984) ("Sinclair").

29. See Ian Brownlie, *Principles of Public International Law,* 6th ed. (Boston: Oxford University Press, 2003) ("Brownlie"); Jennings & Watts, §10, at 29; NWP 1-14M Annotated, ¶ 5.4.1; Restatement (Third) §102, comments b, d (1987); Michael B. Akehurst, *A Modern Introduction to International Law,* ed. Brian Chapman (London: George Allen and Unwin, 1977), 23–27; Humpfrey Waldock, "General Course on Public International Law," *Recueil des Cours* 106 (1962): 1–251; Henckaerts and Doswald-Beck, "Introduction," in "ICRC Study," at xxxi–xlii. J. Ashley Roach and Robert W. Smith, United States Responses to Excessive Maritime Claims, 2nd ed. (The Hague: Martinus Nijhoff, 1996), an exhaustive study of the LOS (law of the sea) claims protests shows that the persistent objector rule is alive for LOS issues.

30. *Right of Passage Over Indian Territory (Portugal v. India),* 1960 I.C.J. 6, 39–40 (April 1960); *Right of Nationals of the United States in Morocco (France v. U.S.),* 1952 I.C.J. 176, 200 (August 1952); *Asylum (Colombia v. Peru),* 1950 I.C.J. 266, 277 (November 1950); Brownlie, 10–11; Jennings & Watts, §10, at 30; Restatement (Third) §102 comment e (1987).

31. NWP 1-14M Annotated, ¶ 4.3.2 n. 27, at 261.

32. George K. Walker, "Principles for Collective Humanitarian Intervention to Succor Other Countries' Imperiled Indigenous Nationals," *American University International Law Review* 18 (2002): 35.

33. "Hague Convention (II) Respecting Limitation of Employment of Force for Recovery of Contract Debts," October 18, 1907.

34. Wounded Convention Sea, art. 38; POW Convention, arts. 72–75 & "Annex III;" Civilian Convention, arts. 23, 59, 61; "Helsinki Principles on the Law of Maritime Neutrality," May 30, 1998, Principle 5.3 (in Schindler and Toman, 2004 at 1425, 1430); NWP 1-14M Annotated, ¶¶ 7.4.1.2, 7.7.3; Sandoz et al., ¶¶ 2095–96; *San Remo Manual,* ¶¶ 102(a), 103–4; George K. Walker, "The Tanker War 1980–88: Law and Policy," *Naval War College International Law Studies* 74 (2000): 391; see also Protocol I, art. 70.

35. "International Law Commission 2001 Report," at 194–206, reprinted in James Crawford, *The International Law Commission's Articles on State Responsibility: Introduction, Text and Commentaries* (Cambridge: Cambridge University Press, 2002), 178–86.

36. An example of the nature of the action to be taken was NATO's decision in 1999 to mount a largely air–sea interdiction campaign to protect the Kosovars. George K. Walker, "Principles for Collective Humanitarian Intervention to Succor Other Countries' Imperiled Indigenous Nationals," *American University International Law Review* 18 (2003): 58.

37. Compare Sandoz et al., 51 (reporting one delegation's view at the International Committee of the Red Cross (ICRC) conference).

38. The preamble of 1977 Protocol II links it within international human rights instruments: "[I]nternational instruments relating to human rights offer a basic protection to the human person," is the only international agreement like this. Why? Commentators have argued that humanitarian law and human rights law "are two distinct legal systems, each with its foundations and mechanisms, and IHL applies to situations of armed conflict. Human rights continue to apply concurrently in time of armed conflict." Sandoz et al., 1340; see also Dinstein, 20–25; Green, 46–49; 1. J.M. Henckaerts and L. Doswald-Beck, in *1 ICRC Study,* at xxxi; 299–305 (UN Human Rights Committee and international courts' opinions, 'extensive' state practice); Greenwood, §102(2). There is no other primary source (treaty, custom, general principles) defining the relationship of human rights law and humanitarian law. However, see General Assembly Resolution 2444, *UN General Assembly Office Record (GAOR),* 23d Sess., Supp. No. 18, at 50–51, UN Doc. A/7218 (1969), noted "International Conference on Human Rights," *Resolution XIII,* May 12, 1968, which denounced erosion of human rights and was "[c]onvinced that even during...armed conflict, humanitarian principles must prevail;" and "General Assembly Resolution 2675," *UN GAOR,* 25th Sess., Supp. No. 28, at 76, UN Doc. A/8028 (1971), declared, "[f]undamental human rights, as accepted in international law and laid down in international instruments, continue to apply fully in...armed conflict." Walker's "Principles for Collective Humanitarian Intervention" offer another, equally nonbinding analysis.

39. Although humanitarian law or human rights law usually protects individuals and not states, territory remains important. The law of treaties with respect to territorial application would not apply in a *jus cogens* situation, but because a human rights or humanitarian law *jus cogens*-supported norm is encased in a treaty term would give *a fortiori* strength to it. The same is true if general, regional or local custom applying to a state restates a *jus cogens* norm. A state or states acting in self-defense, the Council deliberating action on a decision, or a state or states acting pursuant to that decision must particularly consider humanitarian law or human rights norms otherwise applicable to an affected state through *jus cogens* principles if the same principle applies through treaty law territorial application, or general, local or regional custom.

40. There is no concept of precedent in international law; nevertheless, decision-makers should consider prior state practice and actions pursuant to Council decisions. They should consider the nature, i.e., the character, of the proposed action. An example of the nature of the action to be taken was NATO's decision in 1999 to mount a largely air and sea interdiction campaign to protect the Kosovars. Countries' statements of the relative desirability of the action should be considered. Examples are issues of humanitarian intervention or intervention to protect an intervening state's citizens and nationals, for which there has been sharp disagreement within the world community.

41. Compare Restatement (Third) § 403(3) (1987).

42. UN Charter art. 103.

43. "[D]rawing the line...between inter-State and intra-State armed conflicts may be a complicated task" if there is an horizontal mix between interstate and intrastate hostilities, as in Enduring Freedom Afghanistan operations after 9/11, or a "vertical" mix, if an intrastate conflict evolves into an interstate conflict, e.g., in Kosovo. See Dinstein, 14–15. The ICRC Study sees this as largely a "non-problem," i.e., the international and noninternational humanitarian law norms are the same, based on state practice analysis for the 161 Rules published. See ibid., R. 1–61, 64–81, 84–113, 115–44, 146–61; sometimes the Rules recite separate standards for international and noninternational armed conflicts with the same Rules. In a given situation states or groups involved in a conflict may

not concur with this view or may construe the norm(s) differently. Other customary rules may not be included in the Study; new ones may emerge. The ICRC Study did not include law of naval warfare analysis, except insofar as its rules, "restate[d] in the San Remo Manual...might be 'useful.'"

44. Here too there can be a horizontal mix between interstate and intrastate rules, with human rights norms thrown into analysis; Afghanistan and Kosovo are examples of each.

45. Hilton v. Guyot, 159 U.S. 113, 163–64 (1895); see also JP Morgan Chase Bank v. Altos Hornos de Mexico, S.A., 412 F.3d 418, 423–24 (2d Cir. 2005) (origins of comity).

46. Restatement (Third), §102(3) & comment f, r.n. 5.

47. Compare International Law Commission 2001 Report, arts. 23, 24, 25(2)(b) with Vienna Convention, arts. 61–62; see also Aust, 239–42; Brownlie, 594–98; Arie E. David, *The Strategy of Treaty Termination* (New Haven and London: Yale University Press, 1975), chap. 1; T.O. Elias, *The Modern Law of Treaties* (Dobbs Ferry, NY: Oceana Publications, 1974); "Harvard Draft Convention on the Law of Treaties," art. 28, 29 ("Harvard Draft Convention"); Jennings and Watts §§650–51; Restatement (Third), §336; "International Law Commission," 1966; György Haraszti, "Treaties and the Fundamental Change of Circumstances," *Recueil des Cours* 146 (1975): 1; R.D. Kearney and R.E. Dalton, "The Treaty on Treaties," *American Journal of International Law* 64 (1970): 535; O.J. Lissitzyn, "Treaties and Changed Circumstances," *American Journal of International Law* 61 (1967): 895.

48. Vienna Convention, art. 60(5), declaring that treaties of a humanitarian nature remain in force despite material breach is a cardinal exception to treaty breach principles. In other respects the Vienna Convention does not recite rules for armed conflict's effect on treaties. See also International Law Commission 2001 Report, art. 50 comment 8, at 336, reprinted in Crawford 2002, at 290; Aust, 238; Brownlie, 593–94; Hackworth, *Digest of International Law* 5 §513, at 383–84; Harvard Draft Convention, art. 35(a), at 664; "Institut de Droit International," 1985, arts. 3–4 (in Annuaire, 1986, at 278, 280); Jennings & Watts, §649, at 1302; Lassa Oppenheim, *International Law,* vol. 2 (London: Green & Co., 1952), §§99(2), 99(5); *Restatement (Third),* §335, comment c; Sinclair, 190; Louise Doswald-Beck and Sylvain Vite, "International Humanitarian Law and Human Rights Law," *International Review of the Red Cross,* no. 293 (1993): 94; Crawford, *Introduction,* at 41 (state cannot disregard human rights obligations because of another state's breach); G.G. Fitzmaurice, "The Judicial Clauses of the Peace Treaties," *Recueil des Cours* 73 (1948): 255; C.J.B. Hurst, "The Effect of War on Treaties," *British Yearbook for the Limitations Law* 1921, at 42; David Weissbrodt and Peggy L. Hicks, "Implementation of Human Rights and Humanitarian Law in Situations of Armed Conflict," *International Review of the Red Cross,* 33 (1993). Aust may be the only commentator applying Article 60(5) to human rights treaties; but see also Crawford. Preparatory works discussing other sources and the Article text ("treaties of a humanitarian character"), as distinguished from "treaties of a human rights character," suggest a possible misstatement of the law.

49. Humanitarian law and human rights law are equally important in world order. However, in a given situation where there is a claim that both may apply, a particular humanitarian law or human rights standard may be more appropriate as being more or less inclusive, higher or lower.

50. Nearly all states have adopted the major humanitarian law treaties, e.g., the 1949 Geneva Conventions and other humanitarian law norms and the principal human rights conventions. However, e.g., in a given state of affairs there may only be regional treaties or custom applying to a situation with respect to humanitarian law or human rights law, against which there may be nearly universal, but different, norms applying to the other corpus of law. Under these circumstances it may be more appropriate to choose the universal standard. On the other hand, the more particular humanitarian law or human rights law, embodied in regional treaties or custom, may outweigh a universal standard.

51. See generally Frank M. Snyder, "Introduction" to *Sound Military Decision* (Annapolis: Naval Institute Press, 1992); Walker, 1979.

52. See generally Dinstein, 4; Bradd C. Hayes, *Naval Rules of Engagement: Management Tools for Crisis* (Santa Monica, CA: Rand, 1989); "Preface" to NWP 1–14 Annotated, at 2, ¶¶ 3.11.5.1, 4.3.2.2, 5.5; Christopher Craig, "Fighting by the Rules," *Naval War College Review* 37, no. 3

(May/June 1984) (U.K. ROE during Falklands/Malvinas War); Richard J. Grunawalt, "JCS Standing Rules of Engagement: A Judge Advocate's Primer," *Air Force Law Review* 42 (1997) (particularly helpful analysis); O'Donnell and Kraska, "International Law of Armed Conflict and Computer Network Attack: Developing the Rules of Engagement," in *Computer Network Attack and International Law,* eds. Michael Schmitt and Brian O'Donnell (Newport, RI: Naval War College, 2002) (ROE History); Ashley Roach, "Rules of Engagement," *Naval War College Review* 36, no. 1 (1983): and 1998; Ivan Shearer, "Rules of Engagement and the Implementation of the Law of Naval Warfare," *Syracuse Journal of International Law and Commerce* 14 (1988): 767; 20. Terry in Computer *Network Attack and International Law,* eds. Schmitt and O'Donnell (Newport, RI: Naval War College, 2002); 11. Rose, "Crafting the Rules of Engagement for Haiti," in *Liber Amicorum.*

53. Dissemination, education and training requirements vary among treaties now in force, the more recent usually being more stringent. "Convention on Safety of United Nations & Associated Personnel," December 9, 1994, art. 19; "Convention on Rights of the Child," November 20, 1989, art. 42; "Convention Against Torture & Other Cruel, Inhuman or Degrading Treatment or Punishment," December 10, 1984, art. 10; Conventional Weapons Convention, art. 6; Protocol I, arts. 83, 87; Protocol II, art. 19; Cultural Property Convention, arts. 7, 25, 249 and its "Second Protocol," art. 30; Wounded Convention, art. 47; Wounded Convention Sea, art. 48; POW Convention, art. 127; Civilian Convention, art. 144; see also "Diplomatic Conference on the Reaffirmation and Development of International Humanitarian Law Applicable in Armed Conflicts," Resolution 21 1977; ICRC, *Guidelines,* ¶ 17; "International Conference for Protection of Victims of War, Declaration," Part II, ¶¶ 1–3, September 1, 1993; "International Institute of Humanitarian Law, Declaration on the Rules of International Humanitarian Law Governing the Conduct of Hostilities in Non-international Armed Conflicts," April 7, 1990; "International Committee of the Red Cross," *Fundamental Rules of International Humanitarian Law Applicable in Armed Conflicts* 1978; "International Committee of the Red Cross, Draft Rules for the Limitation of the Dangers Incurred by the Civilian Populations in Time of War," art. 20, 1957; *New Rules,* 502–4, 699–701; Green, 32–33, 69, 331; ICRC Study, 142–43; Pictet, 1 at 347–49; ibid., 2, at 257–59 (1960); ibid., 3, "Commentary," 613–15 (1960); ibid., 4, at 580–82; Sandoz et al., 93–95, 99, 312, 828, 948, 960–68, 1009, 1020–21, 1484–85, 1488–89; Toman, 91–93, 273–76; Rüdiger Wolfrum, "Enforcement of International Humanitarian Law," in Fleck, §1223.

54. As proceedings against the general (demoted to colonel) in charge of Abu Ghraib and others in the prison chain of command suggest, another major cause of the atrocities was failed leadership.

55. Brownlie, 31–32; Jennings and Watts, §§18–19. There are examples in U.S. law. Although treaties are part of the supreme law of the land under U.S. Constitution article VI, the later in time construction rule may result in applying federal legislation instead of a treaty. *Breard v. Greene,* 523 U.S. 371, 376 (1998) (per curiam); *Whitney v. Robertson,* 124 U.S. 190, 194 (1888). A treaty cannot contravene the Constitution. *Reid v. Covert,* 354 U.S. 1, 16–17 (1957). Custom, a primary international law source, compare. I.C.J. Stat. art. 38(1) and Restatement (Third), §102 (1987), applies if there is no contrary treaty, federal statute, executive action, or precedent. *Sosa v. Alvarez-Machain,* 542 U.S. at 729–30; *The Paquete Habana,* 175 U.S. 677, 700, 708 (1900). If a treaty is non-self-executing, i.e., the international agreement needs implementing statutes, U.S. courts are powerless to enforce it until Congress acts. *Foster v. Neilson,* 27 U.S. (2 Pet.) 253, 314 (1829); see also *Sei Fujii v. State,* 242 P.2d 617, 620–22 (Cal. 1952) (UN Charter non-self-executing, citing *Foster*). There are countervailing principles, e.g., federal legislation should not be construed to violate international law if any other possible construction remains. *Murray v. Schooner Charming Betsy,* 6 U.S. (2 Cranch) 64, 118 (1804).

56. As Green said: "The only statement (in 1977 Protocol II to the 1949 Geneva Conventions) with regard to educating the public of its rights or the government forces of their duties in the event of a non-international conflict is the single provision that it shall be disseminated 'as widely as possible.' In many cases, this may be little more than a pious hope, for countries prone to revolution are not likely to educate their civilian populations as to the rights they enjoy when seeking to overthrow the government." (at 331, quoting in part and citing Protocol II). Furthermore, ibid. at 69

admonishes that government forces engaged in noninternational armed conflict must be educated in the rules applying to their forces and those applying to "dissidents." In rare instances dissident groups have received training through neutral organizations, e.g., the ICRC. See Lloyd Roberts, "Remarks," in panel, "Law of Armed Conflict Dissemination," *Colloquium, the Law of War in the 21st Century: Weaponry and the Use of Force* (Newport, RI: Naval War College, 2005).

57. For example, the UN Security Council warned against breaches of international law during Gulf War I, 1990–91. George K. Walker, "The Crisis over Kuwait, August 1990–February 1991," *Duke Journal of Comparative and International Law* 1 (1991): 36–37.

58. "Inter-Allied Declaration," January 13, 1942; "Joint Four-Nation Declaration," October 1943, declared the Allies would prosecute those accused of war crimes after World War II ended. There were also individual national leaders' proclamations; see Erickson, "United States Navy War Crimes Trials (1945–1949)," *Washburn Law Journal* 5 (1965): 89.

59. The 2005 ICRC Study advocates the similarity between the LOAC applied to international armed conflicts and the law governing noninternational armed conflicts. Whether that approach, or whether the view human rights and humanitarian law should have the same standards during armed conflict as some advocate, will gain traction is also less than clear today.

60. See McDougal et al., "Theories About International Law: Prologue to a Configurative Jurisprudence," *Virginia Journal of International Law* 8 (1980): 188; J.N. Moore, "Prolegomenon to the Jurisprudence of Myres S. McDougal and Harold Lasswell," *Virginia Law Review* 54 (1968): 662; E. Suzuki, "The New Haven School of International Law: An Invitation to a Policy-Oriented Jurisprudence," *Yale Studies in World Public Order* 1 (1974): 1.

61. For example, Restatement (Second) preceded Restatement, see "UN Security Council Resolution 1701," S/RES/1701, 2006; Restatement, Conflict of Laws (1934) preceded Restatement (Second), see Protocol I, art. 52. See generally *New Rules,* 320–27; Colombos, §§510–11, 524–25, 528–29; Dinstein, chap. 4; NWP 1-14M Annotated, ¶¶ 6.2.3 & n. 36, 6.2.3.2, 8.1.1 & n. 9, 8.1.2 & n. 12; O'Connell, 1105–6; 4 Pictet, 131; Sandoz et al., at 630–38; Matheson, 426; Robertson; Solf, 130–31, which was supplemented in 1988.

CHAPTER 16

The Legal Way Ahead Between War and Peace

KEVIN H. GOVERN

> We know that we're going to have fewer "wars" but a lot more conflicts. There's a real blurring between the definitions of "war" and "peace," "domestic" and "nondomestic," "economic," and "military." All of this means that we need to be able to thrive in uncertainty. Our role is to support U.S. foreign policy. Increasingly, that means trying to keep large conflicts from breaking out—while also maintaining the ability to transition quickly to combat operations and, if necessary, to spearhead a decisive victory.
>
> General Peter J. Schoomaker, former U.S. Army Chief of Staff, speaking in 1999[1]

Military professionals have discovered that the post–Cold War world is rife with persistent, low-level violence, much like its predecessor. Many regions are experiencing a rise in the amount of conflict in the absence of restraints previously imposed by the superpowers. Frustration in many developing or "Third World" nations is increasing for economic or political reasons, and insurgency—the use of low-level, protracted violence to overthrow a political system or force fundamental change in the political and economic status quo—looks to be an enduring security problem. This generic description fits current conditions in Iraq and Afghanistan too, but can be applied far more broadly.[2]

This chapter is written from the perspective of the military operational lawyer in an attempt to explain where he fits in this world, from both the top-down and bottom-up perspectives in linking military operations to U.S. foreign policy. There are three issues hidden in this perspective. The first is tied to ideas about the changing nature of armed conflict. The operational lawyer currently functions most of the time in low-intensity armed conflicts like insurgencies or peacekeeping, precisely because that is the business his battlefield commander "clients" now do most of the time. So his professional world may be focused more often on civil affairs than traditional targeting law as such. The second is that his legal capacity is an advisory one (e.g., is not often devoted to running courts-martial or military commissions). And most of this advisory capacity is dedicated to planning military operations rather than their execution as such. Finally, combining advisory capacity with the point that "small wars" predominate, this version of armed conflict law is an amalgam of domestic and international law focusing currently on nontraditional questions like protection of NGO (nongovernmental organization) personnel providing humanitarian assistance, or how best to support civil authorities trying to reconstitute local courts and government in the face of targeted assassinations in the course of an insurgency. So the border seems porous between traditional military operations and something akin to law enforcement, and in any case involves a high degree of contact and often cooperation with nonmilitary bodies (i.e., foreign governments, the U.S. government interagency process, and NGOs).

For the balance of this chapter, I look first at the current taxonomy of armed conflict and the concept that it may be an uneasy fit with traditional ideas about "war." Thereafter, we examine how this affects military doctrine in supporting U.S. foreign policy generally, with consequent effects on the military operational lawyer. Finally, we look at the activities of military operational lawyers at the practical level in terms of planning operations. The hope is to provide some insight into what and how military operational lawyers actually make decisions touching upon the LOAC (law of armed conflict) in their workaday world.

DEFINING WHAT LIES BETWEEN WAR AND PEACE

In the sixty-plus years since the end of World War II, the world saw sixty major armed conflicts. Some twenty million people were killed, fifty million people were injured, 17.5 million people became war refugees, and twenty-four million became internally displaced persons. Some 85 percent of these conflicts were intrastate, and 95 percent of these conflicts were outside Europe (to include thirty-five in Africa alone).[3] By 2003–2004, the number of ongoing conflicts had escalated to forty-one.[4]

During those sixty-plus years of strife, a multitude of new terms have emerged to describe such armed conflicts, including but not limited to those in Table 16.1.

Table 16.1   Range of Military Operations (JP 3-0, 2006)[5]

Brush fire wars	Complex emergencies	Complex humanitarian operations
Complex contingency operations	Contingency operations	Crises
Dirty little wars	Disaster operations	Guerilla war
Humanitarian operations	Insurgencies and counterinsurgencies	Internal war/armed conflict
Irregular warfare	LIC (low intensity conflict)	LRC (localized regional conflicts);
MOOTW (military operations other than war)	OMO (other military operations)	OO (other operations)
OOTW (operations other than war)	Partisan war	Peace operations
Peace support operations	People's war	Revolutionary warfare
Rebellion	SASO/SOSO (stability and support operations) and small wars	SSTR (stability, support, transition, and reconstruction)
UW (Unconventional warfare)	Wars of national liberation	...and many other terms!

Not all of these terms/acronyms will be discussed, given overlap of some, or the favor in which others may be held in the international legal community. But this begs the most important question for any military professional: just exactly what is war? Elements of what traditionally constitutes a war may include: (1) contention, (2) between at least two nation states, (3) wherein armed force is employed, (4) with an intent to overwhelm.[6] But even this ignores the idea that many modern armed conflict situations may involve nonstate actors (e.g., al Qaeda). Political, economic, social welfare, military, and cultural institutions must plan for, or proscriptively cope with the consequences of such conflicts' first, second, and third-order effects. For instance:

- Unrest in Haiti leading to refugees fleeing to Florida;
- The *Zapatista* insurgency having economic effects on Mexico's industry and trade with other North American Free Trade Agreement nations;
- Serb repression of Kosovar Albanian nationalists leading to international peace enforcement presence with an unintended consequence of fostering regional crime syndicates; and
- Coalition-led combat operations in Afghanistan and Iraq, with follow-on stabilization and reconstruction efforts attacked by armed insurgents.

There are a variety of internationally recognized legal bases for use of force in relations between states, found in both customary and treaty law. Generally speaking, however, modern *jus ad bellum* (the law of resort to war) is reflected in the UN Charter. The Charter provides two bases for the resort to force in international relations: Chapter VII enforcement actions under the auspices of the Security Council, and self defense pursuant to Article 51 (governing acts of both individual and collective self defense). Insurgencies or similar intrastate armed conflicts typically involve nonstate actors, but may involve foreign military contingents deployed in support of a local government, as in Iraq and Afghanistan currently. International law concepts like intervention may lurk in the background, but technically foreign armed forces are typically present with the consent of the local government. Under those circumstances, *jus ad bellum* principles limiting the use of armed force between states are hardly applicable as a practical matter. Meanwhile, the consent concept raises its own tensions as witnessed by issues as currently in Iraq and Afghanistan concerning who commands joint foreign and local military operations, the effectiveness of local troops and collateral civilian casualties producing local political reaction (which feeds on itself in potentially narrowing consent's scope). Some form of *jus in bello* applies, which issues are discussed more fully in accompanying chapters, but for the moment, I turn to the broader hierarchy of applicable U.S. military principles in terms of the higher civilian level of command in terms of national security strategy, before reaching into the current taxonomy of military operations.

CIVILIAN–MILITARY PLANNING INTERFACE, OR THE TOP-DOWN VIEW

Joint Publication (JP) 3-0, *Joint Operations,* notes that the U.S. approach to national strategic guidance and responsibilities starts with the President and SecDef (Secretary of Defense). They, through the CJCS (Chairman of the Joint Chiefs of Staff), direct the national effort that supports combatant (regional theater) and subordinate commanders to ensure: (1) national strategic objectives and joint operation termination criteria are clearly defined, understood, and achievable; (2) forces are ready for combat or mobilization; (3) intelligence assets are focused on the operational environment; (4) the strategic direction is current and timely; (5) the DOD (Department of Defense), allies, coalition partners, and/or OGAs (other government agencies) are fully integrated for planning and operations; (6) all required support assets are ready; and (7) forces and associated sustaining capabilities deploy ready to support the concept of operations. The products of such planning are the NSS (National Security Strategy), NDS (National Defense Strategy), NSHS (National Strategy for Homeland Security), and NMS (National Military

Strategy), shaped by and oriented on national security policies, to provide strategic direction for U.S. combatant commanders (CCDRs) focused on regions and theaters of potential operations. In the words of JP 3-0, these strategies "integrate national and military objectives (ends), national policies and military plans (ways), and national resources and military forces and supplies (means)."[7]

JP 3-0 also highlights how U.S. military planning consists of joint strategic planning with its three subsets: (1) security cooperation planning, (2) force planning, and (3) joint operation planning. Specific to this chapter and the studied operations "between war and peace," the President and SecDef "direct joint operation planning to prepare and employ American military power in response to actual and potential contingencies," that is, emergencies "involving military forces caused by natural disasters, terrorists, subversives, or by required military operations."[8] Joint operation planning "is directed toward the employment of military power within the context of a military strategy to attain objectives by shaping events, meeting foreseen contingencies, and responding to unforeseen crises," whether planning for prospective and theoretical threats in the context of "contingency planning," or the reaction to developing or ongoing events through "crisis action planning."[9] While service-peculiar variants exist in conducting the planning process (e.g., the U.S. army service variant to be discussed later), the "joint" (multiservice) approach to the "joint operation planning process" consists of: (1) initiation; (2) mission analysis; (3) COA (course of action) development; (4) COA analysis and "wargaming" (predictive, simulation of a military operation); (5) COA comparison; (6) COA approval; and (7) plan or order development.

TAXONOMY OF MODERN ARMED CONFLICTS, OR THE BOTTOM-UP VIEW

Far below the NSS level, the military operational lawyer works typically in military operations formally occupying the legal space between war and peace. His operational categories are his commander's, which themselves come from civilian political leadership in the U.S. government insofar as the military operations in question invariably are in support of American foreign policy. The point to register here is that the operational character of armed conflicts is the framework for his advisory role.

It's A Small War After All

> The term "Small War" is often a vague name for any one of a great variety of military operations. As applied to the United States, small wars are operations undertaken under executive authority, wherein military force is combined with diplomatic pressure in the internal or external affairs of another state whose government is unstable, inadequate, or unsatisfactory for the preservation of life and of such interests are determined by the foreign policy of our Nation...The essence of a small war is its purpose and the circumstances surrounding its inception and conduct, the character of either one or all of the opposing forces, and the nature of the operations themselves.
>
> United States Marine Corps, Small Wars Manual (1940)

To the military professional, there is a certain déjà vu quality about post–Cold War armed conflict situations. They are increasingly compared in professional circles to the so-called "Banana Wars" which engaged the USMC (United States Marine Corps) before World War II. Thus, the USMC long ago wrestled with the practical as well as theoretical ramifications of these armed conflicts "between war and peace." Its role in Small Wars has a long and complex history. During the early years of the twentieth century, the USMC was widely viewed as the nation's overseas police and initial response force. Moreover, the actual execution of these de facto roles were a natural adjunct of the USMC's officially directed mission of "sea-based power projection" (military force from the sea) in turn buttressed by its fundamental "expeditionary operational character;" i.e., the availability for "sudden and immediate call." As a result of this "natural fit" and the experience of a series of guerilla wars and military interventions, the Marine Corps began systematically to analyze the character and requirements of operations short of war proper, or "Small Wars" in familiar terminology.

As a result, the USMC developed and published as part of its doctrine the 1940 SWM (Small Wars Manual, a "how to" manual in effect). Still cited as valid military doctrine today, the USMC CETO (Center for Emerging Threats and Opportunities) initiated an effort to rewrite the SWM in 2001–2004, but retained the original's wisdom while adding contemporary vignettes. The SWM defined the core of such operations with unusual prescience:

> [S]mall wars are operations undertaken under executive authority, wherein military force is combined with diplomatic pressure in the internal or external affairs of another state whose government is unstable, inadequate, or unsatisfactory for the preservation of life and of such interests as are determined by the foreign policy of our Nation.[10]

The SWM further noted that such operations are defined by their purpose, and not by their scope and scale. Purposes range from "assistance in governmental operations on one hand to full assumption of governmental responsibilities supported by an active combat force on the other: [b]etween these extremes may be found an infinite number of forms of friendly assistance or intervention which it is almost impossible to classify under a limited number of individual types of operations".[11]

Colored by the perspective of a military force organized and equipped to carry out the military aspects of America's foreign policy, the SWM noted that "according to international law, as recognized by the leading nations of the world, a nation may protect, or demand protection for, its citizens and their property wherever situated."[12] As for whether such intervention constituted "war," the SWM further noted that:

> The use of the forces of the United States in foreign countries to protect the lives and property of American citizens resident in those countries does not necessarily constitute an act of war, and is, therefore, not equivalent to a declaration of war. The President, as chief executive of the nation, charged with the responsibility of the lives and property of the United States citizens abroad, has the authority to use the forces of the United States to secure such protection in foreign countries.[13]

As equal parts historical review, and prescient prediction of future policy, the SWM also stated that:

> The history of the United States shows that in spite of the varying trend of the foreign policy of succeeding administrations, this Government has interposed or intervened in the affairs of other states with remarkable regularity, and it may be anticipated that the same general procedure will be followed in the future. It is well that the United States may be prepared for any emergency which may occur whether it is the result of either financial or physical disaster, or social revolution at home or abroad. Insofar as these conditions can be predicted, and as these plans and preparations can be undertaken, the United States should be ready for either

of these emergencies with strategical [sic] and tactical plans, preliminary preparations, organization, equipment, education, and training.[14]

In summarizing their broad character, the ongoing revised draft of the SWM notes that:

Small Wars demand the highest type of leadership directed by intelligence, resourcefulness, and ingenuity. Small Wars are conceived in uncertainty, are conducted often with precarious responsibility and doubtful authority, under indeterminate orders lacking specific instructions. Additionally, the key actors involved in these types of operations are highly eclectic, embracing the UN, the local village leader, and many intervening governmental, nongovernmental organization (NGO), military, and ad hoc organizations. Thus, cooperation, collaboration, and communication are absolutely essential for success.[15]

Military Operations Other Than War (MOOTW)

MOOTW as concept finds its origins in the 1950s–1960s.[16] The U.S. policy of COIN (Counterinsurgency), IDAD (Internal Defense and Development), low-intensity conflict (LIC) in the 1970s–1980s, and OOTW of the 1980s–1990s had helped shape MOOTW. That definition includes:

Operations that encompass the use of military capabilities across the range of military operations short of war. These military actions can be applied to complement any combination of the other instruments of national power and occur before, during, and after war.[17]

Generally, the role of military forces in MOOTW can or will be in support of other agencies. Military forces may be constrained by more restrictive ROE (rules of engagement) than in other deployments (e.g., small-scale contingencies and MTWs [major theater wars]—both discussed later). MOOTW will likely involve joint, combined, and interagency coordination and/or task organization, and likely include NGOs. Finally, MOOTW are generally conducted outside a military force provider's sovereign territory. MOOTW operations may include those in Table 16.2.

Table 16.2   Military Operations Other Than War (MOOTW) Categories (JP 3-07, 1995)

Arms control	Nation assistance/support to counterinsurgency
Combating terrorism	NEO (noncombatant evacuation operations)
Counterdrug operations	Peace operations
Sanctions enforcement	Protection of shipping
Enforcing exclusion zones	Recovery operations
Ensuring freedom of navigation	Show of force operations
Humanitarian assistance	Strikes and raids
Military support to civilian authorities	Support to insurgency/counterinsurgency

Political objectives drive MOOTW at every level, from strategic to tactical. A distinguishing characteristic of MOOTW is the degree to which political objectives influence operations and tactics. Two important factors about political primacy stand out. First, actions at the "lowest" level can potentially have national or international impact (e.g., in peacekeeping and dealing with feuding ethnic factions). Second, those studying or looking to influence events should remain aware of changes not only in the state of affairs in the nation(s) in question, but also in political objectives of the nation(s) intending to effect status quo or change.[18]

The concept of MOOTW lends itself to contrasting the differences between "peace-time" and "conflict." Peacetime is a state in which diplomatic, economic, informational, and military powers of the nation are employed to achieve national objectives. Since peacetime is the preferred state of affairs (as opposed to conflict or war), how well a government promotes and preserves peace will be vital to its own interests as well as other nations.[19] So-called "conflict" is a unique environment in which governmental and non-governmental leaders may work closely to control hostilities, with the goal of returning to peacetime conditions. In conflict, the military, as an element of national power, takes on a more prominent role than in peacetime. Military and police forces may participate in conflict as a component of a combined (multinational), joint (one nation, multiforce), or interagency (one nation, military and nonmilitary) organization that is usually an element of a multinational structure. Other government agencies, NGOs, PVOs (private volunteer organizations), and IOs (international organizations) often participate.[20]

Insurgencies and Counterinsurgencies

The much-heralded U.S. Army FM (Field Manual) 3-24, COIN (December 2006), the first doctrinal publication by the U.S. Army or Marine Corps in 20 years dedicated to counterinsurgency, expressed in its introduction the truism that "all insurgencies are different; however, broad historical trends underlie the factors motivating insurgents. Most insurgencies follow a similar course of development."[21] Insurgencies are organized movements aimed at the overthrow of a constituted government through use of subversion and armed conflict.[22] They may include protracted, organized violence which threatens security and requires a government response, whether revolutionary or nonrevolutionary, political or nonpolitical, and open or clandestine.[23] An example of support to an insur-gency would be the U.S. support to the *Mujahadeen*[24] during the Soviet Union's invasion and occupation of Afghanistan. In contrast, counterinsurgency is support provided to a government in the military, paramilitary, political, economic, psychological, and civic actions it undertakes to defeat insurgency. An example of counterinsurgency (as well as FID [foreign internal defense] and nation assistance at various junctures) would be the invited U.S. support to the Endara government to unseat the Noriega regime during Operation JUST CAUSE and PROMOTE LIBERTY in 1989–90.[25]

Closely related to that concept is the notion of FID: participation by civilian and military agencies of a government in any of the action programs taken by another government to free and protect its society from subversion, lawlessness, and insurgency.[26] Terrorism, in con-trast, is defined by 22 U.S.C. § 2656f(d)(2) as "premeditated, politically motivated violence perpetrated against noncombatant targets by subnational groups or clandestine agents."[27] The DOD definition is similar, but does not limit attacks to noncombatant targets and notes that the goals of terrorists are usually political, religious, or ideological in nature.[28]

Small-Scale Conflicts or SSCs

Yet another concept closely allied, but not synonymous with these conflicts other than war had been "small-scale contingencies" or "small-scale conflicts." Also known as "SSCs," these include a wide range of combined and joint operations beyond peacetime engagement and short of war.[29] These SSCs may, in light of national or coalition strategic objectives, give rise to protecting designated citizens abroad, the support of political initiatives, the facilitation of diplomacy, promotion of fundamental ideals, or disruption of specified illegal activities.[30] Operations related to SSCs may vary in size and duration (e.g., 100 to 30,000 personnel and from a few weeks engagement to several years), and are often coalition operations that involve "core states" and other foreign forces as well as governmental organizations and NGOs.[31]

The United States Department of Defense's QDR (Quadrennial Defense Review) report[32] no longer explicitly identifies SSCs as a mission for military operational requirements or a major consideration in deciding on force structure. In general, though, the United States, along with others in the international community, will seek to prevent and contain localized conflicts and crises before they require a military response. If, however, such efforts do not succeed, swift intervention by military forces may be the best way to contain, resolve, or mitigate the consequences of a conflict that could otherwise become far more costly and deadly. The National Defense University has noted that governments must maintain military forces prepared to conduct successfully multiple concurrent smaller-scale contingency operations worldwide, and it must be able to do so in any environment, including one in which an adversary uses "asymmetric means," such as nuclear, biological, or chemical weapons. Importantly, military forces must also be able to withdraw from smaller-scale contingency operations, reconstitute, and then deploy to a MTW in accordance with required timelines.[33]

The frequency of SSCs and their demands on military forces within the past decade have led to rethinking national security strategies, and, consequently, military doctrine, force structure, and training. In the view of the United States, SSC plans have helped to shape the international security environment, as well as the U.S. response to crises. Military activity, combined with political and diplomatic activity, can yield positive results, whereas alone, all activities are liable to fail. Failure allows a crisis to continue, risking the danger of expansion, and may damage the United States' ability to influence those countries directly concerned.[34]

As a general rule, participation in SSCs by other countries is seen as a distinct benefit, improving common military capabilities and engendering closer military-to-military relations with the United States. In operations supporting large-scale civilian efforts, international and NGO relief organizations (e.g., UNHCR [UN High Commission for Refugees], WFP [World Food Program], ICRC [International Committee of the Red Cross], CARE, Doctors without Borders, Oxfam, and IRC [International Rescue Committee]) were present before, during, and after military intervention. Considerable liaison and coordination are required. Much coordination is ad hoc, since there are evolving requirements for conducting combined military–civilian operations, but few internationally codified procedures. The American public has often voiced strong opinion in favor of multinational rather than unilateral efforts. The numerous exercises and training programs that the U.S. conducts with European, Asian, Latin American, African, and other military establishments to prepare for such contingencies (e.g., peace or humanitarian operations) are examples of positive effects on the international security environment.[35]

PLANNING AND APPROACHES TO CONFLICT

To varying degrees along the continuum "between war and peace," conflict and conflict resolution, various degrees of economic, political, and military influences can lead to de-escalation from disputes, political accommodations, and achievement of desired end states of unilateral or multilateral benefit. In spite of post–Cold War employment and deployment of troops for missions such as disaster relief and SASO (stability and security operations), with few exceptions such as dedicated peacekeeping forces, military forces still organize, train, and equip to fight and win their nations' wars in accordance with doctrine and national law and policy. The prescriptions and proscriptions of customary international law, and those based upon treaties and agreements, vary with the stage(s) of conflict and conflict resolution, and will be explored subsequently.

METT-T-C (And Other Military Approaches)

Military forces are particularly adept at anticipating and planning for operations. Functions performed by military commanders and staff members include providing information, making estimates, making recommendations, preparing plans and orders, and supervising the execution of decisions. Mission analysis is critical to the overall planning process and to the preparation of a military legal support plan. For instance, U.S. commanders and staff consider METT-T-C (mission, enemy, troops, terrain (and weather), time available, and civilian considerations) with respect to their operational planning as part of the overall MDMP (military decision-making process).[36] The MDMP's seven-step process includes: (1) receipt of mission; (2) mission analysis; (3) COA development; (4) COA analysis; (5) COA comparison; (6) COA approval; and (7) operational orders production.[37]

U.S. armed forces judge advocates, uniformed military staff attorneys serving in all the branches of the armed forces (Army, Navy Air Force, Marine Corps and Coast Guard), employ essentially the same six MDMP factors. Even though the legal issues confronted by a judge advocate in operations are varied, they are, to a great extent, predictable. One method of predicting legal issues is to read after action reports and lessons learned materials gathered by service "schoolhouses" and agencies with expertize in international and "operational law."[38] Another, proactive method of predicting legal issues is to conduct LPB (Legal Preparation of the Battlefield). LPB is a methodology, or a planning tool, derived from the Intelligence community's IPB (Intelligence Preparation of the Battlefield), to chart commonly encountered legal issues during operations.[39]

"POISED"—A Multidisciplinary Approach

While METT-T-C and IPB/LPB have proved themselves highly useful during U.S. and coalition military operations of the past 20+ years, an alternative approach at the military operational lawyer's level may help define preconflict, conflict, and postconflict states by embracing sociological, economic, political, as well as military factors. I propose the "POISED" method of analysis. It stands for:

- *Power structures* will include the *de jure* and *de facto* social, political, and cultural hierarchical entities which will have influence to stabilize or destabilize a region or a nation.

- *Others—Direct Parties to the Conflict, Actors, and Affected Third Parties* will include natural (human) persons, as well as other "legal" but also "artificial" persons such as corporate entities that have a stake in the outcome of stability or instability.

- *Issues and Causes of the Crisis or Conflict* will include behavioral influences as well as the other economic, political, and military influences which come into play (e.g., international involvement, inequitable distribution of resources, political exclusion, human rights abuses, and identity).

- *Stage in the Cycle of Crisis or Conflict* will include the aforementioned four crisis stages: dispute situations of submerged tensions, prehostility situations of rising tensions, hostile eruption phases of open confrontation and violent conflict, and posthostility and fragile transitional dispute settlement situations.

- *External factors and Influences* which are important but not key "triggering event" issues and causes of the crisis or conflict, (e.g., climactic changes, the discovery, exploitation, pollution, or exhaustion of natural resources).
- *Dynamics of the Crisis or Conflict Over Time* will include observable trends or anomalous events which chronicle the history of the crisis or conflict and help predict future developments.

Why should this analysis matter? Mastery of events, and the legal principles which should shape and guide individuals, organizations, and societies, will depend upon recognizing the genesis and evolution of conflict and conflict resolution, and the implementation, enhancement, amelioration, minimization, or avoidance of certain key factors and influences. The next section will discuss how the military employs a decision-making cycle towards those ends.

Origins and Applications of "OODA" or Observe, Orient, Decide and Act

Although roots of the concept go back over 2500 years, the idea of operating at a faster decision cycle than one's opponent was first codified in the 1980s. The theory is that "operating inside your opponent's OODA (observe, orient decide, and act) loop, you can cause uncertainty, doubt, mistrust, confusion, disorder, fear, panic, and chaos "within that opponent's thoughts and actions." An adversary so "shaped" would be easy to defeat, should physical combat still be necessary.[40]

How, then, might this four-phase decision cycle known as the OODA loop be applied to the law of armed conflict, international humanitarian law, or the other international and municipal (national) laws applying to armed conflict? The strategist, scholar, statesman, or aid provider, amongst others, who employs such a methodology to anticipate threats and challenges more quickly than the threats and challenges arise, will have a major influence on shaping perception as well as the reality of desired outcomes. Figure 16.1 is an example of how the "OODA" loop could be so employed.

The legal application of the "OODA" loop requires a prioritization of effort and focus. Saying that "everything is equally important," compounded by a failure to provide implicit guidance, necessary feedback, and coordinating control will result in unfocused efforts that spread time, effort, and resources woefully thin. Acting in an advisory role to a decision-maker, the military operational lawyer's role in the "OODA" process may be integrated in a synergistic manner with other subject matter experts (e.g., "fusion cell" with intelligence analysts, logisticians, comptrollers/budget analysts, etc.). In the "observe" and "orient" phases, advice would be given to commanders, strategists, directors, supervisors, or other leaders to make informed decisions that are legal, moral, ethical, and operationally sound in the "decide" phase. As the cycle continues, the attorney's role (along with other experts) will be to seek and provide feedback towards the refinement and issuance of implicit guidance and control.

Law and Policy Applied Between War and Peace

Here I discuss a methodology from the military operational lawyer's perspective of applying the law to all cases of declared war or any other armed conflicts that arise between and within nations, states, and regions, even if the "state of war" is not recognized by one of them. The military approach to operational legal issues could be rearranged into any number of other acronyms, but my *"FAIR ROSE"* method proposed here includes examination of: *F–Fiscal Law; A– Acquisition and Support; I–International Law; R–Rules of*

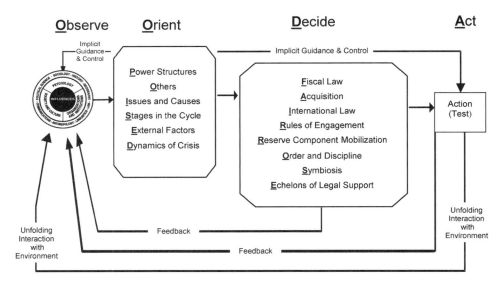

Figure 16.1 "POISED" and "FAIR ROSE" Methodology under the "OODA" Loop

Engagement and other Use of Force Considerations; R–Reserve Component Mobilization; O–Order and Discipline; S–Symbiosis of Operational and Interagency Elements, and E–Echelons of Legal Support to Operations.

F—Fiscal Law

The counselor considering the impact of fiscal law on operations "between war and peace" will make a threshold realization that money is the root cause of, or contributing factor to, crisis avoidance, precipitation, length, and remediation. The admonition to "follow the money" may be beyond the time or abilities of those in immediate positions of responsibility and decision-making. But counselors designated to "find the money" will be well-advised to proactively plan for and advise on the basic principles of fiscal law. Such operations and initiatives may span the spectrum of military operations discussed earlier, and involve military and developmental assistance, cooperative programs, (re) building and (re)construction, and transfer of articles or services to another nation or IO. That is one of the hidden challenges currently in Iraq and Afghanistan, what the military views traditionally as civil affairs and other U.S. government agencies (chiefly the State Department and USAID [United States Agency for International Development]) see normally as development work. These are not part of the LOAC as such, but represent the building blocks of medium term policy implementation for the military operational lawyer in the current operational environment of an Iraq or an Afghanistan, regardless whether he or she is serving in a civil affairs capacity, or is simply advising a unit commander with responsibility for a geographic area.

In the instance of government-funded operations, national legislatures or parliaments often provide "appropriations" or "allocations" for military, social welfare, diplomatic, and other initiatives. Such apportioned moneys then are reapportioned downwards to executive departments (e.g., Department of State, Department of Defense, etc.), with further apportionment and limitation. The NGOs and IOs may similarly apportion budgets, regardless of the sources of their money (e.g., donations, fundraising, government grants, loans, etc.).

Typically encountered fiscal law issues may include, but are not limited to the following:

- Developing judge advocate/attorney expertize in fiscal law and contract law;
- Determining, deconflicting, and accessing multiple sources of funding during operations;
- Conducting operations with already purchased supplies, equipment and services;
- Special authorities (e.g., Presidential Drawdown Authority—22 U.S.C. § 2318(a)(2);
- Donation of excess nonlethal supplies—10 U.S.C. § 2547;
- Conflict of laws and changing of laws and policies with phases of the operation;
- Space available transportation of relief supplies (Denton Amendment)—10 U.S.C. § 402);
- Use of cash for local purchasing;
- Unauthorized commitments;
- Contracting issues (e.g., the contracting process; use of the simplified acquisition threshold, etc.);
- Use of funds for gifts, awards, and morale, welfare, and recreation activities;
- Requests for support to non-DOD/foreign organizations, non-governmental organizations/receiving state or host nation military;
- Construction and improvements; and,
- Support to receiving state/host nation populace[41]

The repercussions of ignoring fiscal limitations (and spending money that does not exist or should not be so spent) can be severe: organizational sanction, violation of national law (e.g., federal statutes), and the jeopardizing of valuable ongoing and future operations and cooperative effort. Those studying the ramifications of fiscal law should consider the applicable sources that define fund obligation and expenditure authority, and apply those sources' prescriptions and proscriptions scrupulously, or finding that expenditure which would be "necessary and incident" to an existing authority.[42] Subsequent "FAIR ROSE" element discussions will delve into greater detail as to fiscal considerations and limitations which may be applicable.

A—Acquisition and Support

Under U.S. contract and fiscal law, forces are guided and authorized to expend congressionally appropriated funds under the Armed Services Procurement Act of 1947 (as amended in 10 U.S.C. §§ 2301–31), FAR (Federal Acquisition Regulation) and Agency/Command Supplements, Directives and Regulations (e.g., SOFAR (Special Operations Forces FAR), and Title 31, U.S. Code, and Executive Orders and Declarations. Congressional declarations of war or national emergency, and similar resolutions may result in subsequent legislation authorizing the President and heads of military departments to expend appropriated funds to prosecute the war or other operation. Some of these authorities have become quite broad. For instance, the Congress has authorized the President and his delegees to initiate contracts that facilitate national defense notwithstanding any other provision of law. Although these are broad powers, Congress still must provide the money to pay for obligations incurred under this authority.

The need to build new structures upon one's own national territory, in a receiving state, or elsewhere, may well require special authority, and consideration of international and receiving state/coalition laws which may apply, and careful supervision and control of contract administration during the "life" of the contract. So-called "policing the contract battlefield"; in other words, fiscal stewardship, in this and other areas of contracting has recently surfaced in the public's consciousness of Iraq.

Along with the necessity for purchasing items, military operations usually give rise to necessity to compensate or fix what has been broken, borrowed, used, or otherwise altered from its original state and ownership. Less often, claims arise for death or injury of individuals and animals. Claims for damages to real and personal property, both public and private, almost always follow deployments of United States and other coalition forces. Unless there is an agreement to the contrary (or a "combat claims" exclusion), the United States and other nations under international and municipal (national) law *will* be obligated to pay for damages caused by its forces. To avoid wholesale liability, state parties may agree under SOFAs (Status of Forces Agreements) or other arrangements to waive claims against each other, or for a receiving state to indemnify third party claims caused by visiting forces in the performance of official duty and release soldiers from any form of civil liability resulting from such acts. Claims will also arise "amongst the ranks" of service members and "civilians accompanying the force" serving on military operations for acts within and outside the scope of their duties. Establishing who will investigate and adjudicate, and settle (pay) claims at what locations is equally important to the calculus of claims.[43]

I–International Law

Customary international law, binding upon all nations, is derived from repetition and is generalized. Once a principle attains customary international law status, it basically binds all nations, not just states actively involved as with treaty signatories. The lawyer's task is to discern what is a valid customary law rule, which has gained force over time. On the other hand, treaty or conventional international law is only binding upon those nations that have ratified/signed a treaty (unless the treaty provisions become customary law). This category of international law refers to codified rules binding on nations based on express consent, whether by treaty, convention, protocol, annexed regulations, or other instrument. With respect to "international armed conflict," this threshold is codified in common article 2 of the Geneva Conventions of 1949. These conventions include:

- The Geneva Convention for the Amelioration of the Condition of the Wounded and Sick in Armed Forces in the Field, Aug 12, 1949 (Wounded Convention);
- The Geneva Convention for the Amelioration of the Condition of Wounded, Sick, and Shipwrecked; Members at Sea, Aug 12, 1949 (Wounded Convention Sea);
- The Geneva Convention Relative to the Treatment of Prisoners of War, Aug 12, 1949 (POW Convention); and
- The Geneva Convention Relative to the Treatment of Civilian Persons in Time of War, Aug 12, 1949 T.I.A.S. 3365. (Civilians Convention) (collectively Geneva Conventions, 1949, or GC).

The key is the term "international armed conflict" set forth in common Article 2 of the Conventions. Common Article 2 states: "[T]he present Convention shall apply to all cases of declared war or of any other armed conflict which may arise between two or more of the High Contracting Parties, even if the state of war is not recognized by one of them." This is a true *de facto* standard, where the subjective intent of the belligerents is not relevant. Armed conflicts such as the 1982 Malvinas (Argentina)/Falklands (UK) War, the Iran–Iraq War of the 1980s, and the first (1991) and second (2003–04) United States-led Coalition wars against Iraq could be considered "international armed conflicts" to which the law of war applied.[44] The 1977 Protocol I Additional to the 1949 Geneva Conventions (not accepted by the United States, but regarded in the interim as customary law by most other states) has expanded this scope of application to include certain wars of "national liberation" for states parties to that convention. According to a leading commentator, the law of war applies to: "any difference arising between two States and leading to the intervention of armed forces."[45]

Article 2 effectively requires that the law be applied broadly and automatically from the inception of the conflict. The following two facts result in application of the entire body of the law of war: (1) a dispute between states and (2) armed conflict.[46] An exception to the "dispute between states" requirement arises where there is a conflict between a state and a rebel movement recognized as belligerency. This concept arose as the result of the need to apply the laws of war to situations in which rebel forces had the de facto ability to wage war. The law of war ceases to apply under Article 5, Wounded Convention, and POW Convention; Article 6, GC upon: (1) final repatriation (Wounded Convention, POW Convention); (2) general close of military operations (GC); or (3) occupation (GC)—applies for 1 year after the general close of military operations. In situations where the occupying power still exercises governmental functions, however, that Power is bound to apply for the duration of the occupation certain key provisions of the GC.[47] For military operations under circumstances other than armed conflict (e.g., peacekeeping and peace enforcement in Somalia, Haiti, and Bosnia), the law of war, in general, will also apply, but the applicability of particular treaties is open to interpretation.

Conflicts which are not of an international character "occurring in the territory of one of the High Contracting Parties" will fall under Common Article 3, and make up the majority of the ongoing conflicts. International regulation over such conflicts is more attenuated than under international armed conflicts, and domestic law may control the application and use of force or other economic, political, or military applications of state authority.

"Internal armed conflict" presents its own challenges. A leading commentator listed several suggested criteria for distinguishing events like a simple civil disturbance from an insurgency: (1) the rebel group has an organized military force under responsible command, operates within a determinate territory, and has the means to respect the Geneva Conventions; and (2) the legal government is obliged to have recourse to the regular military forces against the rebels, who are organized and in control of a portion of the national territory.[48] Protocol II of The 1977 Protocols Additional to the Geneva Conventions, December 12, 1977 (not accepted by the United States, but regarded in the interim as customary law by most other states), was intended to supplement the substantive provisions of Common Article 3. It formalized the criteria for the application of that convention to a noninternational armed conflict that rebel groups are: (1) under responsible command and (2) exercise control over a part of a nation so as to enable them to carry out sustained and concerted military operations and to implement the requirements of Protocol II.

The legal justification for intervention into another state's affairs, or intervention against internal insurgencies/belligerencies/armed opposition groups, how such operations are authorized, how they should it be conducted, and how to mobilize sufficient political will have all been extensively analyzed under the rubric of intervention. This is an area of the law marked by controversy since traditional legal rules were flouted in the Spanish Civil War in the 1930s and further strained by proxy wars of the Cold War period. The legal justifications for such operations will lead to first- and subsequent-order effects including but not limited to: populations' rights to assistance and protection; whether an operation remains within its authorized limits or exceeds them; the right of affected populations and nations to call for intervention or protection; and the right of national and supranational bodies to shape, influence, and direct such operations and their follow-on requirements.[49]

The UN Charter, specifically Chapter VI, Pacific Settlement of Disputes (Articles 33–38), and Chapter VII, Action with Respect to Threats to the Peace, Breaches of the Peace, and Acts of Aggression (Articles 39–51), envisioned a Security Council role in assisting parties to "any dispute likely to endanger the maintenance of international peace and security" as they strive to resolve conflicts through "peaceful means of their own choice" (UN Charter, 1945). Chapter VI does not specifically envision or authorize the deployment of military forces under UN authority to interpose themselves between hostile parties. The frequent use of military forces as peacekeepers, however, evolved as an extension of the UN desire to facilitate the "adjustment or settlement of international disputes or situations which might lead to a breach of the peace." Peacekeeping is an internationally accepted mode of managing conflicts, giving states a buffer to seek long term, peaceful resolutions, and has become an inherent part of the UN strategy for resolving international disputes in the absence of more comprehensive and lethal collective security operations. UN Charter Chapter VII gives the Security Council authority to maintain international peace and security by taking "such action by air, sea, or land forces as may be necessary;" UN member states are obligated to "accept and carry" out decisions of the Security Council as reviewed in a parallel essay.

The IHRL (International Human Rights Law) obligates states to recognize and respect basic rights of the individual generally. The IHL (International Humanitarian Law) obligates states to recognize and respect certain rights in times of armed conflict. Precepts of IHRL should be respected in all circumstances but may be abrogated in emergencies, whereas IHL precepts may not be abrogated under any circumstances. In application:

- IHRL is applied to all persons in all circumstances;
- IHRL covers rights that are outside the scope of IHL (e.g. political rights);
- IHL is a specialized body of law for times of armed conflict; and,
- IHL rules may not have equivalencies in IHRL (e.g., rules for conduct of hostilities/use of weapons)

Table 16.3   Recent UN Authorizations for Peacekeeping

Country	Chapter VII authorization and UN mission	Chapter VII authorization delegated	No initial security council authorization
Liberia 1990–1997			ECOMOG
Northern Iraq 1991–		Coalition	Coalition
Former Yugoslavia 1992–	UNPROFOR	IFOR and SFOR	
Somalia 1992–1993	UNOSOM II	UNITAF	
Rwanda 1994–1996	UNAMIR II	Opération Turquoise	
Haiti 1994–1997	UNMH	MNF	
Sierra Leone 1997–	UNAMSIL		ECOMOG
Kosovo 1999–		KFOR	NATO
East Timor 1999–	UNAMET	INTERFET	

The U.S. military employs an additional generic category for humanitarian law, that being "Civilian Protection Law" (CPL). Useful as a model for comparison or contrast to other national or supranational legal perspectives, this "analytical template" describes the process for establishing protection for civilians across the operational spectrum, based on four "tiers" of legal authority:

- Tier 1: Fundamental Human Rights Recognized as Binding International Law by the United States;
- Tier 2: HN (Host Nation) Law Providing Specific Rights to an Indigenous Population;
- Tier 3: Conventional Law ("Hard Law"—imposed by treaties or functional equivalents); and,
- Tier 4: US Domestic Law and Policy (Including Law by Analogy/Extension)[50]

Humanitarian law refers to those conventions from the law of war that protect the victims of war (primarily the Geneva Conventions). Human rights law refers to a small core of basic individual rights embraced by the international community during the past forty years as reflected in various declarations, treaties, and other international provisions beginning with the UN Charter and Universal Declaration of Human Rights. The IHL regulates the conduct of state vis-à-vis state, whereas human rights law regulates the conduct of state vis-à-vis individual. The right to protection under humanitarian law is vested not in the individual, but in the state. Under human rights law, the protection flows to the individual directly, and theoretically protects individuals from their own state, which was a radical transition of international law.

R—Rules of Engagement and Other Use of Force Considerations

ROE are directives issued by competent superior authority that delineate the circumstances and limitations under which military forces will initiate and continue engagement with other forces.[51] ROE are drafted in consideration of the law of war, national policy, public opinion, and military operational constraints. ROE are often more restrictive than what the law of war would allow. ROE will normally determine the legally justified uses of force during international military operations; domestic operations may employ rules termed otherwise (e.g., RUF (Rules for Use of Force). During other peace operations, for example, UN peacekeeping operations, the UN position is that its forces will comply with the "principles and spirit" of IHL. This is reflected in the model UN Status of Mission Agreement (SOMA), which essentially utilizes this same law by analogy approach to regulating the conduct of the military forces executing UN missions.

ROE help ensures that national policy and objectives are reflected in the action of commanders in the field, particularly under circumstances in which communication with higher authority is not possible (e.g., the influence of international public opinion, particularly how it is affected by media coverage of a specific operation, the effect of host country law, and the SOFAs with the United States). ROE also provide parameters within which the commander must operate in order to accomplish his assigned mission; e.g., a "ceiling" (and potentially a "floor") on how far operations can and should go and ensure that military actions do not trigger undesired escalation, like forcing a potential opponent into a "self defense" response. ROE may regulate a commander's capability to influence a military action by granting or withholding the authority to use particular weapons systems by vesting or restricting authority to use certain types of weapons or tactics.

ROE may also reemphasize the scope of a mission. Units deployed overseas for training exercises may be limited to use of force only in self defense, reinforcing the training rather than combat nature of the mission. Finally, ROE provide restraints on a commander's action consistent with both domestic and international law and may, under certain circumstances, impose greater restrictions on action than those required by the law. For many contemporary missions, particularly peace operations, the mission is stated in a document such as a UN Security Council Resolution (e.g., UNSCR 940 in Haiti or UNSCR 1031 in Bosnia). These Security Council Resolutions also detail the scope of force authorized to accomplish the purpose stated therein. Commanders must therefore be intimately familiar with the legal bases for their mission. The commander may issue ROE to reinforce principles of the law of war, such as prohibitions on the destruction of religious or cultural property, and minimization of injury to civilians and civilian property.

An effective intervention force should have the authority to do what it needs to do, and be perceived as being credible in the nation or region where it operates. The credibility of operations, in turn, has depended on the belligerents' assessment of a force's capability to accomplish the mission. Military missions are prone to being hamstrung or condemned to failure where there are contradictory instructions for intervening forces dealing with belligerents, confusion regarding coalition command and control at the operational and tactical levels, and lack of consistent commitment within the coalition fully to employ war-fighting capacities. On the operational level, ROE determine authority and so shape perceptions.

Table 16.4   U.S. Reserve Component Mobilization/Deployment/Employment

10 U.S.C. 12301(a) Full mobilization	Require a Congressional declaration of war or national emergency	All reservists including members in an inactive statute and retired members
	Require a Congress in Session	No number limitation stated
		Duration of war or emergency + 6 months
10 U.S.C. 12302 Partial Mobilization	Requires declaration of national emergency by President	Ready Reserve
	Report to Congress every 6 months	Not more than 1,000,000
		2-year duration
10 U.S.C. 12304 presidential selected reserve call-up	Requires presidential notification of Congress	Selected reserve, with up to 30,000 IRR
	No Declaration of National emergency	Not more than 200,000
		270 days
		Now includes WMD incidents
10 U.S.C. 12301(b) 15-day statute	Service Secretaries may call Ready Reserve up to 15 days/year	Annual training
		Operational missions
		Involuntary
10 U.S.C. 12301(d) RC volunteers	Requires consent of reservist	All reservists
	Governors must consent to guard activation	No number limitation stated
		No duration stated
	. . .and consider unique Military Justice, civilian employment, and benefit considerations, amongst other matters	

R—Reserve Mobilization and Draw of Secondary Support

Mobilization is the process by which the armed forces or a part thereof are expanded and brought to a state of readiness for war or other national emergency.[52] These forces provide critical skills and assets to wartime missions as well as those lying "between war and peace," especially in supply, logistics, transportation, civil–military operations, military police, and a variety of other military specialties and capabilities. Mobilization includes calling all or part of the reserve components to active duty and assembling and organizing personnel supplies and material. While reserve component service members will likely share the same status under international law and receive state law while deployed, their status under municipal (domestic) law may vary. The call-up of reserve component units to active duty may include a number of different types of mobilization that effect the length of their active duty, how many forces may be mobilized, how they may be employed, and potential legal assistance problems. Operational demands placed on the U.S. military by Iraq and Afghanistan mean that the mobilization and deployment authority above for the reserve component of the armed forces is no longer just a theoretical matter. There are now a significant number of National Guard or reserve units which have been deployed to Iraq or Afghanistan more than once, and the reality of conducting operations between war and peace puts a premium on certain skills now concentrated in the reserve component, such as civil affairs and military police units.

The legal support required by reserve soldiers leaving families, businesses, and other commitments on short notice for an indeterminate period will give rise to substantial need for legal assistance (e.g., family law) support, especially since many reserve units are mobilizing at home station and going directly to a POE (Port of Embarcation), without going to a MS (Mobilization Station). Legal concerns common to both military and civilian agencies will be the requirements to, and consequences of, drawing other secondary support: contracting for or otherwise directing the deployment of key and essential civilians accompanying the force; determining their status under municipal (national), receiving state, and international law; their protection; pay; health care; order and discipline; redeployment; and veteran's/disability/reemployment rights and benefits.

O—Order and Discipline

The maintenance of order and discipline, not just among service members, but also in the area of military operations, is a fundamental aspect of successful military operations. In contemporary military operations, where restraint and legitimacy are often important to mission success, the misconduct and misdirected efforts of untrained or undisciplined forces will lead to adverse world opinion and, more seriously, friendly forces sustaining heavy casualties rather than inflicting them upon hostile opposing forces. How military forces fight marks them for what they are and what they stand for. The laws of war are only effective in reducing casualties and enhancing fair treatment of combatants and noncombatants alike as long as trained leaders ensure that those laws are obeyed. Commanders and civilian leaders must ensure the proper treatment of prisoners, noncombatants, and civilians by building good training programs and issuing orders that reinforce the practice of respecting those laws.

Such considerations include, but are not limited to the following:

- Predeployment/mobilization concerns (in addition to mobilization matters discussed above, criminal jurisdiction over offenses committed by deploying forces, new joint, combined, and interagency forces, and "rear detachment" forces).

- Deployment-unique considerations (e.g., "General Order #1" prescriptive policies with respect to conduct, contraband, etc.) and "time of war" unique considerations regarding offenses.
- Redeployment/demobilization considerations.
- Force protection and detention of civilians committing offenses against other civilians in assistance to/ the absence of civilian law enforcement authorities.
- Detention of PIFWCs (persons indicted for war crimes);
- Criminal jurisdiction over U.S. citizen civilians abroad and deploying with the force under the "Military Extraterritorial Jurisdiction Act of 2000" and domestically the USA "Providing Appropriate Tools Required to Intercept and Obstruct Terrorism (PATRIOT) Act of 2001."
- Military Tribunals and the Military Commissions Act of 2006, Pub. L. No. 109–366, 120 Stat. 2600 (Oct. 17, 2006).
- Impact of the International Criminal Court and jurisdiction over U.S. and coalition/interagency forces.

For instance, proactive efforts to resolve Uniform Code of Military Justice jurisdictions immediately (predeployment) will prove beneficial in the long run. This must be accomplished early in the process through meetings amongst decision makers and advisors (e.g., commanding general and staff, interagency heads, etc.), to explain options and to choose courses of action. Thorough research into the history of past similar operations will help in anticipating future issues which will arise with regard to order and discipline or military justice, and careful drafting, dissemination, training, and enforcement of pertinent documents (e.g., "General Order #1") will help with respect to prescriptive or preventative law. Forces remaining in the rear may decrease as others deploy forwards; the relative workload of "front" and "rear" may well increase inversely to size of force remaining due to a smaller workforce to resolve problems or execute missions, etc. Commanders should ensure that the right mix of personnel, equipment, and transportation are available and used for "front" and "rear," to include skilled personnel (e.g., criminal prosecution ["trial counsel"] and defense ["trial defense"]), information technology systems, and mission-capable vehicles), and that those who should or must deploy are trained and "deployable."

S—Symbiosis of Operational and Interagency Elements

United States, coalition, and interagency forces will continue to accomplish missions "between war and peace" in the future as "specified" (named) and "implied" (inherent) missions, and may have to stretch assets to cover essential, "specified" missions. Extensive force deployment, overall force drawdown, and slowed modernization/new systems acquisition will be countered, in part, with better knowledge (and ample funding) about how to do such missions. Commanders and troops have many "lessons learned" from recent combat and noncombat missions. Those "lessons learned" are finding their way into doctrine. Continued peace operations training at the United States National Training Center (NTC), Ft. Irwin, California, and the CMTC (Combat Maneuver Training Center) in Hohenfels, Germany, and during joint, combined and interagency training exercises will keep troops ready for those operations yet to come.

In addition to national governmental agencies, and nongovernmental business or private sector entities, missions "between war and peace" will require close coordination with other organizations as well, such as the UN and other IOs to include NGOs and PVOs. The UN, various other governmental organizations and NGOs will not contribute direct monetary support to United States or coalition humanitarian and civil assistance or other missions; however, they may be funding recipients or partnered with military forces through international policy, planning, or simply the circumstances of necessity. This odd-couple relationship finds expression in the idea that military presence is often necessary to provide sufficient security for (civilian) NGOs to carry out humanitarian relief operations.

The UN itself created a number of supranational organizations, including, but not limited to, the UNHCR, the WFP, and UNICEF. The UN Charter mentions the term NGO in Article 71; when the Charter was written, though, such organizations were, relatively few and far between and not the major players they are today. They include a wide range of primarily nonprofit organizations motivated by humanitarian and religious values, usually independent of government, UN and commercial sectors. Within the U.S. military, the terms PVO and VOLAG (voluntary agency) are sometimes used to describe the same spectrum of organizations. NGOs are legally different from UN agencies, the ICRC, and national Red Cross/Crescent Societies. NGOs form themselves and write their own charter and mission; the UN and Red Cross agencies formed and operate under international or national government mandates, conventions, and legislation. International/governmental aid agencies can be "multilateral," like the UN or the World Bank, or "bilateral" like the USAID (or Great Britain's Department for International Development). Funded by taxpayers to the tune of billions of dollars per year, these agencies are major players for aid, assistance, and relief worldwide, and have seen a dramatic upsurge in demands for their talents and challenges to their capabilities during the latter half of the twentieth century.[53]

Worldwide there are now over 1500 international NGOs registered as "observers" with the UN. Nonetheless, of the hundreds in existence there remains a first order of NGOs through which perhaps 75 percent of all emergency aid flows. Commentators have noted that the most effective NGOs have principled, knowledgeable, committed, and diverse organizations. Nevertheless, like any organization, they are dependent upon several key factors. They require sufficient resources, generally private donations as well as governmental grants and collections. Their organizational hierarchy, from top to bottom, must remain "mission focused," and not lose sight of the reason why they are constituted and funded. They must effectively deal with "the competition," as well, minimizing rivalry with other NGOs, and working towards a symbiosis with, rather than competition against, military forces. Finally, NGOs must cope with tangible "hostile forces," to include armed threats to security, disease, adverse terrain and weather, and limited time in which to accomplish missions. NGOs are a powerful force in the world, in many cases, providing the dynamics for positive change where despair and hopelessness might otherwise reign supreme. The revolution in communications technology, in networking and collaboration, and successful fund-raising appeals, has strengthened NGOs further, especially in the last 10 years.[54]

Some countries pursue humanitarian activities overseas through government-created agencies. Examples of these are the British Overseas Development Administration (ODA), the CIDA (Canadian International Development Agency), the SRB (Swedish Rescue Board), or the SDR (Swiss Disaster Relief) (akin to the United States Office for Foreign Disaster Assistance [OFDA]). Other countries offer assistance in times of emergencies through their Ministries of Foreign Affairs, according to their own priorities. Most of this kind of assistance will be offered on an ad hoc basis, as few governments have established agencies of the kind described above with standing mandates for foreign humanitarian emergency assistance. These governmental organizations operate with, and sometimes in lieu of, a wide range of governmental and international aid and relief agencies.

E—Echelons of Legal Support to Operations

So where do the military operational lawyers fit? National, coalition, and interagency forces will require trained, versatile legal assets where the missions are planned and executed. Legal staffs supporting military operations will succeed in their role not just because they have good lawyers, but also because the staff is competent in military skills and understands the military unit and the mission they are supporting. They will need "the training and experience to be first-class soldiers, outstanding lawyers, and polished diplomats."[55] Given the desirability of joint, combined and interagency interoperability, training proficiency and flexible capability, the following four basic tenets will be key to training and deploying/locating personnel and equipment to provide legal support to operations.

Train as You Fight—or Keep the Peace—and Locate Personnel Where
They Will Be Needed

It is critical to have assigned legal staffs at as many locations as possible where senior leaders/commanders, and planning/coordinating staffs make critical decisions, while preserving appropriate access to legal support for other personnel. This arrangement ensures that legal assets will be available where needed and when needed. These staffs should be adequately staffed with those skilled lawyers, office/legal administrators, and paralegals/legal specialists (by whatever title of office) to provide specialized and general legal support to operations. Those staffs should provide a continuous presence throughout the operations at each location for the variety of issues which may arise, to include but not limited to: targeting, ROE, claims, fiscal, contract law, and other issues within the traditional concept of legal support to operations. Those staffs will also be relied upon for common/shared expertize, and consistent, coordinated advice on operational planning and execution matters (e.g., where such staffs have played an integral role in the decision-making process like MDMP discussed earlier).

Train and Use Multiechelon Techniques—and Exploit Knowledge Management
Systems and Practices

Forward deployments in the military often occur in underdeveloped areas or conflict zones which present significant infrastructure challenges unknown to most civilian attorneys. Legal staffs should understand, have access to, and use wherever possible the best and most reliable means of Internet and (where available/accessible) SIPRNET (secret intranet protocol router network) web-based applications to consolidate information coming from various sources and levels of command, and disseminate information out as operationally required. In so doing, legal, and other staff members can foster what the U.S. military calls a COP (common operational picture). Still, where electronically based applications fail, the "analog" methods of pen and paper, typed documents and forms, acetate sheets, and oral briefings must be created as back-up to those matters retained or disseminated electronically. No matter what, information technology (IT)-based KM technologies and databases are no substitute for the professional judgment and expertize.

Train to (Build and) Sustain Proficiency—Make a Self-Fulfilling Prophecy

Success in any operation, whether giving a briefing or conducting a campaign in a conflict, cannot be based upon serendipity, coincidence, and fortuitous accidents. Lessons experienced during preparation for successful operations must be captured in writing, taught to those who will apply those lessons, and then implemented with adjustment to changing conditions (for instance, applying the "OODA" methodology). To memorialize observations and lessons learned from exercises and operations, staffs should create an AAR (after-action report) shell before the start of operations, and collect AAR comments from all echelons of legal staffs throughout train-up and conduct of operations. Throughout all operations, AAR comments should be collected and posted, then discussed to lead to necessary changes to operating procedures and future training events. Formalized self-criticism of the AAR variety would seem to be a rarity in the (nonmilitary) legal world.

Use Performance-oriented Training—and Review and Rehearse Support Requirements Before Deployment

Legal staffs can successfully plan and execute the large and small details of getting people, equipment, and work product where and when needed, when they prepare in identifying where they will be needed as well as where their needs are met—such as what "life support" will be provided by parent units, attached units, agencies, or organizations, and what the legal staffs will be responsible themselves to supply. Legal staffs must actively integrate themselves into operations, plan, and demonstrate what they would "pack outs" for their missions, and conduct performance-oriented training to help set and maintain common standards, anticipate the operational environment, prevent problems before they arise, and to take what will be needed where it will be needed to get the job done. If not otherwise provided for by leaders outside legal staffs, the legal staffs themselves should create and conduct themselves consistent with an overall "vision," such that standards of training and operations will help the staffs anticipate and fulfill requirements with the highest levels of professional competence, personal integrity, and dedication to duty.

Legal staffs can use such structured, guided efforts to prepare for and conduct their operations to develop future sustainment training, combining theoretical/classroom instruction with practical application and first-hand observation. The ultimate value of such training and guided operations lies in enhanced deployment readiness and peak performance during future missions.[56]

CONCLUSIONS

This chapter has examined policy, principles, and law which apply to declared and undeclared international and internal armed conflicts from the perspective of the military operational lawyer. His or her professional competencies now extend far beyond the traditional law of war. An orderly approach using multidisciplinary methodologies, supported by applicable law, policy, and operational principles, can help bring a confusingly divergent flow of information and ideas to a manageable confluence actionable "between war and peace." What is distinctive about the world of the military operational lawyer, however, is twofold. Since current U.S. military operations in a technical sense typically involve operations other than "war" in support of U.S. foreign policy, the military operational lawyer now tends to work in the gray area between war and peace. In practical terms, he or she is heavily involved in planning and advisory work, only portions of which involve the law of war in a classical sense. To the extent legal training may also have a role in military areas like civil affairs, the military operational lawyer may also interface in particular with the local government, foreign, and U.S. government agencies as well as the NGO community involved in reconstruction or humanitarian relief taking place in the geographic area of military operations. This is the workaday world of the military operational lawyer.

NOTES

1. Eli Cohen and Noel Tichy, "Operation—Leadership," *Fast Company,* no. 27 (September 1999): 278, http://www.fastcompany.com/magazine/27/operation.html).

2. Unfortunately, much of existing doctrine and strategy for dealing with insurgency is based on old forms of the phenomenon, especially rural, protracted, "peoples' wars," or is not "synchronized" between joint, combined, or interagency capabilities and efforts. As some forms of insurgency become obsolete, new forms of insurgencies will emerge, leaving strategists to speculate on these future forms, as they assist in the evolution of support to insurgency and COIN (counterinsurgency) strategy and doctrine. Ronald S. Mangum, "Linking Conventional and Special Operations Forces," *Joint Force Quarterly* 35 (Summer 2003): 58.

3. See, e.g., M. Adams and M. Bradbury, *SIPRI Theme Paper* (Birmingham NGO Workshop on Conflict, November 1994). Rudolf Rummel calculated that during the twentieth century, such wars, conflicts, and tyrannical regimes caused some 170 million deaths, as compared to 33 million persons killed in international military conflicts. See Rudolph J. Rummel, *Death by Government* (Birmingham NGO Workshop on Conflict, November 1994), 9. Another report estimated that from World War II through 1996, at least 220 noninternational conflicts involving civil war or oppressive regimes had caused some 86 million deaths. See Jennifer Balint, "An Empirical Study of Conflict, Conflict Victimization, and Legal Redress," in Reigning in Impunity for International Crimes and Serious Violations of Human Rights: Proceedings of the Siracusa Conference 17–21 September 1997 (Christopher C. Joyner. Special Editor), Nouvelles Etudes Pénales (Pau, FR: Association Internationale De Droit Pénal, 1998), at 107.

4. Data obtained from Arbeitsgemeinschaft Kriegsursachenforschung/Universität Hamburg (AKUF), http://www.sozialwiss.uni-hamburg.de/publish/Ipw/Akuf/index.htm, cited in G. Dometeit and K. Heidebreck, "Kriegsgebiete—Über die Jahreswende kämpfen und sterben Menschen in 41 Konflikten" [War Zones—over the years people have fought and died in 41 conflicts], *Focus,* no. 52 (December 20, 2003): 174–75 (available at www.focus.de). For a current list of active UN peacekeeping missions with personnel, budget, and fatality statistics see United Nations, "United Nations Peacekeeping," http://www.un.org/Depts/dpko/dpko/home.shtml. For a contemporary work on the 100-plus "small wars," "low intensity conflicts," and "military operations other than war" that involved the United States from 1801 through 2002, see Max Boot, *The Savage Wars of Peace: Small Wars and the Rise of American Power* (New York: Basic Books, 2002).

5. Joint Chiefs of Staff, *Joint Publication (JP) 3-0, Joint Operations* (Joint Electronic Library, September 17, 2006), I-13, http://www.dtic.mil/doctrine/jel/new_pubs/jp3_0.pdf (hereinafter cited as "JP 3-0").

6. See, e.g., Brian J. Bill, *Law of War Workshop Deskbook* (Charlottesville, VA: International and Operational Law Dept., The Judge Advocate General's School, U.S. Army, June 2000), 1 (hereinafter cited as *Law of War*).

7. JP 3-0, I-3.

8. Ibid., IV-1.

9. Ibid.

10. *Small Wars Manual, US Marine Corps* (Washington, DC: U.S. Government Printing Office, 1940), 1 (note: this reference was reprinted as *FMFRP 12-15, Small Wars Manual*—April 1, 1987, and is available as NAVMC 2890) (hereinafter cited as *Small Wars Manual*).

11. *Small Wars Manual,* 1–2.

12. Ibid., 2.

13. Ibid., 3.

14. Ibid., 1–2.

15. Ibid.

16. This term appeared in the *JP 1-02, Department of Defense Dictionary of Military and Associated Terms* (June 1998), 334, but by the 2001 iteration, it was incorporated by reference in two definitions but no longer defined. See, e.g., Joint Chiefs of Staff, *JP 1-02, Department of*

Defense Dictionary of Military and Associated Terms (Washington, DC: Office of the Joint Chiefs of Staff, April 12, 2001, as amended through March 22, 2007), 96, 100, http://www.dtic.mil/doctrine/jel/new_pubs/jp1_02.pdf (hereinafter cited as "JP 1-02").

17. JP 1-02, 334.

18. Ibid, 334.

19. See, e.g., Joint Chiefs of Staff, *JP 3-07, Joint Doctrine for Military Operations Other Than War* (Washington, DC: Office of Joint Chiefs of Staff, June 1995, http://www.dtic.mil/doctrine/jel/new_pubs/jp3_07.pdf (hereinafter cited as "JP 3-07").

20. JP 3-07.

21. *US Army Field Manual (FM) 3-24, Counterinsurgency* (Washington, DC: Headquarters, Department of the Army, December 15, 2006), ix, http://www.usgcoin.org/library/doctrine/COIN-FM3-24.pdf.

22. Steven Metz and Raymond Millen, "Insurgency and Counterinsurgency in the 21st Century Reconceptualizing Threat and Response," *Special Warfare* 17 (February 2005): 6

23. See, e.g., Steven Metz, *Counterinsurgency: Strategy and the Phoenix of American Capability* (US Army Strategic Studies Institute, February 18, 1995), http://carlisle-www.army.mil/usassi/ssipubs/pubs95/cntrinsr/cntrinsr.pdf.

24. The term "mujahadeen," also sometimes spelled "mujahideen," "mujahedeen," "mujahedin," "mujahidin," and "mujaheddin," refers to a military force of Muslim guerilla fighters engaged in a "holy war" or "jihad."

25. John E. Parkerson, Jr., "United States Compliance with Humanitarian Law Respecting Civilians During Operation JUST CAUSE," *Military Law Review* 111 (1991): 31, at 33. The State Department also cited article I, III, and IV(2) of the "Panama Canal Treaty" in support of U.S. actions, regarding U.S. rights to regulate transit of ships through the Panama Canal, and primary responsibility to protect and defend the Canal (September 7, 1977).

26. JP 1-02, 212.

27. 22 U.S.C. § 2656f(d)(2) (2000), http://www.law.cornell.edu/uscode/22/usc_sec_22_00002656—f000-.html.

28. JP 1-02, 540.

29. This term first appeared in the Department of Defense QDR (Quadrennial Defense Review Report) (May 6, 1997). (Department of Defense, "QDR," http://www.fas.org/man/docs/qdr/) (hereinafter cited as "QDR"). By 2006 the term was no longer to be found in the QDR, with focus instead upon "the long war" (which term by 2007 also fell into disfavor with the Combatant Commander of U.S. Central Command (USCENTCOM)—see Simon Jenkins, "They See It Here, They See It There, They See Al-Qaeda Everywhere," *The Sunday Times Online,* April 29, 2007, http://www.foxnews.com/story/0,2933,270098,00.html.

30. QDR. SSCs may include: strikes and other limited interventions; NEOs (noncombatant evacuation operations); counterdrug operations; shows of force; maritime sanctions and "no fly" enforcement; peace accord implementation and other forms of peacekeeping, and; support for humanitarian operations and disaster relief (e.g., preventative deployment of forces or aid assets).

31. QDR.

32. Department of Defense, "Quadrennial Defense Review Report (QDR)" (February 6, 2006), http://www.g8.army.mil/g8sitenewmj/Organization/QDR/docs/qdr_2006.pdf.

33. David C. Gompert et al., *Strategic Assessment 1998: Engaging Power for Peace* (Washington, DC: Institute for National Strategic Studies (INSS), National Defense University 1998), http://www.ndu.edu/inss/Strategic%20Assessments/sa98/sa98cont.html (hereinafter cited as Gompert et al.).

34. Gompert et al.

35. Ibid.

36. Department of Army, *Field Manual (FM) 101-5, Staff Organization and Operations* (Washington, DC: Headquarters, Department of the Army, May 31, 1997), 5–1, http://www.au.af.mil/au/awc/awcgate/army/fm101-5_mdmp.pdf (hereinafter cited as "FM 101-5").

37. FM 101-5, 5-2.

38. See, generally, Lieutenant Colonel Marc L. Warren, "Operational Law: A Concept Matures," *Military Law Review* 152 (1996): 33. While different nations' armed forces vary in their approach to legal support to military operations, the U.S. Army's *JA 422, Operational Law Handbook* (Charlottesville, VA: International and Operational Law Dept., The Judge Advocate General's School, 2006), 504, http://www.au.af.mil/au/awc/awcgate/law/oplaw_hdbk.pdf (hereinafter cited as "JA 422"), states "[t]he Operational Law Attorney must be capable of delivering legal support in the six traditional *core legal disciplines:* administrative and civil law; claims; contract and fiscal law; international law; legal assistance; and military justice. He or she must also be proficient in command and control functions to include interpreting, drafting, disseminating and training commanders, staffs and soldiers on ROE; participating in targeting cells; participating in the MDMP; participating in information operations; and dealing with the Law of Armed Conflict."

39. International and Operational Law Note, "A Problem Solving Model for Developing Operational Law Proficiency: An Analytical Tool for Managing the Complex," *Army Lawyer,* September 1998: 36.

40. See, e.g., Defense and the National Interest, "The OODA Loop," http://www.d-n-i.net/.

41. JA 422, 243 et seq.

42. Ibid., 245.

43. Ibid., 151 et seq.

44. Ibid., 14.

45. Jean Pictet, *Geneva Convention Relative to the Protection of Civilian Persons in Time of War, (The Geneva Conventions of 12 August; Commentary),* (Geneva: International Committee of the Red Cross, 1958), 20; see also Emanuela-Chiara Gillard, *Humanitarian Law, Human Rights and Refugee Law—Three Pillars* (Geneva: International Committee of the Red Cross, 2005), http://www.icrc.org/Web/eng/siteeng0.nsf/html/6T7G86.

46. See, e.g., Howard S. Levie, *The Code of International Armed Conflict* (London, New York: Oceana Publications, 1986), 11. See also Richard R. Baxter, "The Duties of Combatants and the Conduct of Hostilities (Law of the Hague)," in *International Dimensions of Humanitarian Law* (Geneva: Henry Dunant Institute, 1988), 97; *Law of War,* 29 et seq. According to Pictet, this article was intended to be broadly defined in order to expand the reach of the Conventions to as many conflicts as possible.

47. *Law of War,* 31.

48. Ibid.

49. At the United Nations (UN) Millennium Assembly in September 2000, Canadian Prime Minister Jean Chrétien announced that an independent International Commission on Intervention and State Sovereignty (ICISS) would be established as a response to Secretary-General Kofi Annan's challenge to the international community to endeavor to build a new international consensus on how to respond in the face of massive violations of human rights and humanitarian law. See, e.g., "International Commission on Intervention and State Sovereignty Turns to The CUNY Graduate Center to Orchestrate Research," November 6, 2000, http://www.gc.cuny.edu/press_information/archived_releases/nov_6_international.htm.

50. JA 422, 72.

51. JP 1-02, 72.

52. Ibid., 352

53. See, e.g., David Rieff, *A Bed for the Night. Humanitarianism in Crisis* (New York: Simon & Schuster, 2002), at 21.

54. Ibid.

55. Colonel Frederic L. Borch, *Judge Advocates in Combat: Army Lawyers in Military Operations from Vietnam to Haiti* (Charlottesville, VA: Office of the Judge Advocate General and Center of Military History, 2001), 327.

56. See, e.g., Kevin Govern, "Paving the Road to the Warfighter, Preparing to Provide Legal Support on the Battlefield," *The Army Lawyer,* March 2002, DA PAM 27-50-350.

PART VI

Legal Responsibility, Justice, and Reconciliation

CHAPTER 17

Discerning Justice in the Trial and Execution of Saddam Hussein

JOHN D. CARLSON

How should we think about justice for a country ruled by one of the most vicious dictators of the twentieth century? Even if one disputes this superlative, pointing to more horrid tyrants such as Hitler and Stalin, who can dispute Saddam Hussein's brutality? He was responsible for the deaths of hundreds of thousands of his own citizens; for numerous massacres and incidents of mass murder; for countless acts of torture and repression; for the invasion of two countries and the attendant deaths of millions in Iraq's wars against Kuwait and Iran; for the displacement and relocation of one million Iraqis; and for the destruction of critical natural resources and the withholding of basic necessities that resulted in the suffering of countless Iraqis who depended upon them.[1]

Following the United States-led invasion of Iraq in Spring 2003, Saddam Hussein was captured in December by American forces. He was brought to trial by an Iraqi judicial body formed in 2003 by the Iraqi Governing Council with the support of the United States. The tribunal that tried Saddam Hussein and other senior government officials has been known at different stages as the IST (Iraqi Special Tribunal), the IHT (Iraqi High Tribunal), or as of 2005, the Iraqi High Criminal Court. A national Iraqi court, it has applied both Iraqi and international law. The tribunal has operated with limited outside support, principally from the United States, and has been criticized by many people outside Iraq because it was not an international tribunal. Saddam Hussein was convicted by a chamber of five Iraqi judges in November 2006 and executed by the Iraq government (under the administration of President Nuri al-Maliki) on December 30, 2006.

The facts of Saddam's brutality are not in dispute, but judging from the range of editorials and commentaries that appeared immediately following the execution, the justice of his inglorious end certainly is. Headlines by critics in the United States decried "The Vengeance of the Victors" and "The Rush to Hang Saddam" and labeled the execution an "Act of Revenge." Others, though, declared "Justice Executed" and extolled the retribution that is "Thus All Too Seldom to Tyrants; Saddam's punishment was a rare instance of just deserts."[2] Similar disparity was seen in international reactions. The range of perspectives could lead one to conclude that justice is nothing more than what any particular individual or media outlet opines. But such disagreement is ensconced within a much broader and, at times, quite confused discourse over what justice, in the most general sense, involves or demands. This chapter argues that the lack of justice achieved by the trial and execution of Saddam Hussein flows not from the tribunal's various procedural failures that most critics frequently cite, but from ill-suited conceptions of justice that have been applied to Iraq. Demonstrating this claim entails, first, laying out two classical notions of justice: *justice as rights* and *justice as right order*. I then consider how an overemphasis on justice as rights has skewed our expectations and interpretations of the Saddam Hussein trial. I seek to amend this approach by arguing for a more comprehensive vision of justice as right order that equips us with sturdier resources for conceiving transitional justice. Within such a framework, one can better evaluate the successes and limits of war crimes trials for political leaders such as Saddam Hussein.

TWO CONCEPTS OF JUSTICE

Going back to the ancients, justice often has been described in shorthand as rendering to one what is due. Distributive justice, rectificatory justice, and retributive justice—respectively, the parsing of just deserts, just compensation, and just punishments—have been central features of justice. Distributive justice pertains primarily to fair economic, political, and social allocations in society (e.g., wages, honors, etc.). Rectificatory justice focuses on requiting rightful claims that have been violated by another (e.g., returning something wrongfully taken).[3] Retributive justice, in addition to rectifying the victim's claim to his or her own or something due to him or her, assesses the offender an additional "tribute," often payable to the state or community, as a form of punishment.[4] Over time, the modern West adopted the vernacular of rights as the surest way to defend individuals' claims to what is their own or what is due to them and, therefore, what others have an obligation to protect—an idea commonly recognizable today in an account we might call *justice as rights*.

The modern West also came to understand that the excessive and unchecked power of governments could result in unfair political treatment of individuals. Thus, modern retributive justice gradually incorporated legal protections and rights for the accused; after all, a system that compensates for the fallibility of government with due process rights stands the best chance of vindicating an innocent person who may be wrongly accused. By the mid to late twentieth century, the Western legacy that combines respect for rights with suspicion of government had developed such that individual heads of state and political leaders could be brought to trial for violating the human rights of their own citizens. The accused, in turn, would be accorded in international juridical venues those legal rights customarily afforded to defendants in domestic courts, at least the courts of Western countries.

Individuals and groups who are part of the growing international human rights movement generally embrace this rights-centered account of justice. They are staunch defenders of a model of modern retributive justice that is procedurally strict, individually centered, and rights based. Trials are carefully circumscribed to vindicate those whose human rights have been violated, but always with due regard to protect the rights of those accused of perpetrating genocide, war crimes, and "crimes against humanity" (such as ethnic cleansing, mass murder, torture, and other heinous misdeeds). Recent war crimes tribunals, such as the trial of Saddam Hussein, have largely followed this modern retributive model, which conceives justice through rights. Human rights advocates, however, have critiqued the trial for its failure to conform to certain aspects of this international retributive model.

This is one approach to fathoming justice. There are others, though. For justice transcends the mere defense of rights or the rectification of, and retribution for, violated rights. Returning again to the ancients, justice also has been understood as a comprehensive virtue and moral pursuit, both individually and collectively. Plato understood justice to be that virtue which orders and regulates the various parts of the human soul, allowing each to perform its role, the result of which is a certain inner harmony by which one can know that a person is just. Extended to the polity, this view of justice entails the proper ordering of citizens and relations in a society, again resulting in unity and harmony among distinct parts, groups, or individuals within a society.[5] St. Augustine assimilated this neo-Platonic conception into his own belief that justice pertains to order—for him, the proper ordering of human relations and their loves, the fruit of which is earthly peace: "the peace of the whole universe is the tranquility of order—and order is the arrangement of things equal and unequal in a pattern which assigns to each its proper position."[6] For Augustine and Plato alike, the justice of earthly political arrangements is discerned with respect to a cosmic moral order with a transcendent reference point. The two thinkers disagreed on the level of earthly order that could be achieved politically. For Augustine, sin made politics a more irreparably imperfect affair than it was for Plato. Yet, they both conceived injustice as a deviation from a moral pattern and transcendent order of reality that hovers above the laws or policies prescribed by a particular government. Augustine construed a rupture in the fabric of moral and civic life as evil, foremost because it violated divine norms of justice. Injustice severs the love that holds God, self, and neighbor together in a rightly ordered relationship of *justitia* or righteousness. Restoring justice in a polis is the process of aligning human pursuits and ordering human relations with respect to the moral order of reality. Human beings are linked to this transcendent order, in part, through their social and political relations.

Within this broader, relational view of politics that Plato and, to a greater extent, Augustine articulated—call it *justice as right order*—retributive justice plays an important, though by no means all-encompassing, role. Following a period of intense national crisis, this view of justice encompasses individual and collective efforts to restore the moral order that has been disturbed or violated and to set aright relationships disordered by political injustice. Coming to terms with the past, punishing political crimes, and vindicating or paying tribute to those moral principles that have been violated, all contribute to restoring proper relations—among citizens and between them and their governments—harmed by grievous human malevolence and political wrongdoing. In many cases, honoring rights is an important dimension of restoring the moral order of human relations. As such, affirming rights can be a means to justice as right order, though they are not the end or justice in itself.[7]

Some political societies that have experienced crimes against humanity and radical disordering of human relations that occur from such gross injustices have determined that retributive justice—a legal weighing of charges against the accused and rendering of due punishment—may jeopardize a broader vision of a just society and, thus, impair the process of righting disordered relations among aggrieved citizens. For this reason, these societies sometimes have opted to pursue truth and reconciliation bodies instead of individual trials (see the parallel chapters). On one level, the decision to pursue trials or reconciliation commissions could be viewed as a choice between two different versions of justice: justice as rights and justice as right order. More often, though, the decision has been couched as a choice between justice, on the one hand, and reconciliation, peace, or truth, on the other.[8] When no political accountability is required or punishment assigned, this may, in fact, be a correct way to distinguish them. But it also may be that this more comprehensive vision of justice as right order has been stunted in modern moral discourse and political practice and that, as a result, trials seeking retributive justice rarely are seen in the light of this broader, relational view of justice. Similarly, efforts to restore or reconcile disordered human relations (whether through retributive criminal trials or truth commissions) are rarely understood to involve justice in the more comprehensive moral and political sense I wish to lift up here.[9]

Transitional societies seeking to recover from gross human rights abuses and crimes against humanity are in particular need of this broader vision of justice. Retributive justice plays an imperative role within this framework of right order, but remains a quite deficient model when subsumed entirely within a justice as rights framework. The trial of Saddam Hussein is an apt case study in how a proceduralist preoccupation with justice as rights, common to modern legal forms of retributive justice and as espoused by international human rights groups, can both overwhelm and undercut a more substantive, relational account of justice as right order in society. It is this latter approach that should be of primary concern for troubled societies, such as Iraq, seeking a new order of stability and harmony following (or amidst) political periods of gross injustice.[10] We begin by assessing the inadequacies of a justice as rights interpretation of the trial and punishment of Saddam Hussein.

JUSTICE, RIGHTS, AND THE PREEMINENCE OF LEGALISM

International justice and human rights organizations are often strong proponents of the justice as rights approach. They are deeply committed to identifying human rights abuses and gross injustices worldwide—in most cases, when national governments are the ones committing them or ignoring them. These groups serve as legal watchdogs and, by extension, ethical watchdogs given a certain view that human rights preserve fundamental moral norms. Justice as rights thereby takes form through a legal and moral vision of retributive justice. The protection of human rights depends, first, upon prosecuting those who would violate such rights in committing genocide, crimes against humanity, war crimes, or other violations of international humanitarian law; and, second, upon safeguarding the legal rights of defendants who are brought before a tribunal to face such charges. Despite their commitment to justice as rights, human rights organizations also at times have been eloquent articulators of justice as right order. We will come to see, though, that this broader political vision easily can become eclipsed by a commitment to justice as rights, including a proceduralist fixation on the rule of law, fair trial principles, rights of the accused, and a legalistic interpretation of human rights.

A view of justice as right order is evident in the way that certain human rights groups rearticulated Iraqis' hopes and expectations for transitional justice following the overthrow of the Saddam Hussein regime. A May 2004 report, *"Iraqi Voices: Attitudes Toward Transitional Justice and Societal Reconstruction,"* admirably lives up to its charge of providing a "comprehensive and coordinated approach to social repair and transitional justice" in post-Saddam Iraq.[11] The report is keenly sensitive to illustrate the views of Iraqis, their widespread experience of human rights violations perpetrated by the Hussein regime, and how these experiences harmed individuals and sowed broader disorder in relations among citizens and between them and their government. The report observes, "The nearly universal exposure to human rights abuses and persecution under Saddam Hussein's regime may have fostered a kind of common national experience of suffering, a sense of unity in the injustice inflicted in the name of a readily identifiable individual figure."[12] The sweeping impact of Iraq's political injustices on civic relations and society writ large is documented at length: "Respondents blamed Saddam for degrading the social and cultural life of Iraqi society, and reducing it to a point where the moral fabric was in tatters, causing citizens to behave in ways that brought shame upon themselves."[13] One Iraqi comment summarized well the plight of the country: "The whole of Iraq was in jail."[14]

As Iraqi citizens reflected on their future, juxtaposed against the routine political abuses of their past, most of them intuitively and experientially "viewed the concept of justice as the inverse of the previous regime and a just society as everything that the old system was not." *Iraqi Voices* discusses Iraqis' desires to hold Saddam Hussein and other top officials accountable for their crimes through public trials. It goes on further to recount Iraqis' "broad support for an official truth-seeking and historical memory-preservation process, largely springing from desires to reveal to the rest of the world the truth about what happened in Iraq; prevent repetition of the past; process personal experiences through a larger national narrative; and obtain information from perpetrators on those missing."[15] The report includes a retributive dimension and attention to human and civil rights are situated within a broader, more holistic account of justice as right order. By airing the voices of Iraqis and their desire to restore moral order to their lives, *Iraqi Voices* provides a comprehensive vision of what transitional justice in Iraq might entail: fostering reconciliation, trust, unity, and social reconstruction; undertaking personal and political efforts to repudiate the past; generating national narratives and education reforms that can gesture towards a new beginning; and healing the damage performed by the previous regime to individual and collective identities. This is no tepid, minimalist view of justice. Rather, it is a robust moral idea of justice as a holistic project that seeks to restore hope and moral order to people whose humanity has been violated and to polities whose civic relations have been destroyed by severe oppression.

Iraqi Voices is a commendable document that ought to be read in its entirety. It is particularly praiseworthy for the extensive interviews with Iraqi citizens (of various religions and ethnicities) on which it relies and the heart-wrenching evidence it provides. Perhaps only Saddam Hussein himself would be unmoved by the testimony chronicling the many injustices and horrors that constituted daily life under his regime. *Iraqi Voices* displays Iraqis' views on a vast range of topics including infamous human rights abuses such as torture, rape, political abduction, ethnic cleansing, forced deportations, the use of chemical weapons, and genocide. But it also describes a host of iniquitous, lesser-known crimes that Iraqis found particularly odious: (1) a widespread culture of terror, (2) political favoritism in educational opportunities and the appointment of jobs, (3) propaganda and the regulation of political beliefs enforced under penalty of law, (4) internal sanctions or the withholding of food that was to be made available through the UN oil-for-food program, (5) regulation of religious ideas and practices that were seen to undermine the authority of the regime, and (6) other wide-scale arbitrary and oppressive misuse of Iraqi state agencies. The victims' voices are too many to recount here, and all of them deserve to be heard. I cull out a few that display the deep and direct social and political harm that Saddam Hussein's regime caused his people:

Our life was full of lies and fear. Our life was a big lie...

Lying has become a habit for us, out of fear.

Saddam didn't let anyone trust even themselves, let alone their brother or mother.

We need a moral revolution. Saddam has been in power for 35 years and he has

destroyed all social values.[16]

There is much common ground between the report's findings and Iraqis' call for trials for high-ranking members of the former regime. Integral to the effort to repair the moral fabric of Iraqi life that the prior regime violently sundered, the trial and punishment of Saddam Hussein is construed as part of the broad political vision of justice outlined in the report. Such trials would serve to clear the decks, so to speak, by laying out for the historical record the regime's worst abuses. Trials for top officials would hold offenders accountable through judicial punishment and would put into place a sorely lacking rule of law that would help define a new, post-Saddam Iraq. Trials also would be part of a "moral revolution" to reclaim, reaffirm, and pay tribute to values such as truth, trust, and human dignity, which were decimated under Saddam. The words of one Sunni man encapsulate well the hopes of many for developing a broad and desperately needed new order of justice: "We wish that justice would be achieved now, because during the Saddam period there was no justice."[17] The establishment of legal rights is a crucial piece of that project. Worrisome, however, is the way in which Iraqis' perspectives in this on-the-ground survey would become displaced by a legalist emphasis on rights when, 3 years later, international human rights groups (including one of the coauthors of *Iraqi Voices*) set about analyzing the work of the IHT.

The New York-based HRW (Human Rights Watch) and the ICTJ (International Center for Transitional Justice) were the only two NGOs (nongovernmental organizations) whose representatives observed the Saddam Hussein trial. They issued troubling reports in the wake of the Dujail trial, the first of several IHT trials in which Saddam Hussein and other high-level defendants were found guilty, sentenced, and executed.[18] In these reports, one finds little interest in the lives and concerns of Iraqi citizens and victims that had received such stirring attention in *Iraqi Voices*. In evaluating the trial, a concern for Iraqi justice on the ground is voiced over by an imperiously legalist conception of justice as rights held by international human rights observers who seem more concerned with due process for the defendants and procedural rule of law than for the transgressed rights of Iraqi victims, the trial's contribution to restoring moral order to society, or efforts to achieve social reconciliation and political unity.

The ICTJ report *Dujail: Trial and Error?* is replete with complaints over the trial's procedural fairness. ICTJ singled out the IHT for being "insufficiently specific" in its charges for crimes against humanity and also for violating the right of the accused to examine (or have examined) witnesses against him. Even though cross-examination was permitted in over half the cases, ICTJ complained that many witnesses whose statements had been provided as evidence were unavailable. Another critique was that the prosecution and defense were not given opportunity to present evidence under equal conditions (i.e., "equality of arms"). ICTJ faulted the judges for failing to find and disclose exculpatory evidence. The court was deemed unresponsive to defense motions. The chain of custody of documents was not clear. A lack of even-handedness in procedural matters gave unfair advantage to the prosecutors ("trial by ambush"), and finally, "witness statements were read into the record without reservation."[19]

No Western legal system would or should accept such shortcomings, and establishing judicial rule of law and procedural norms is certainly an eventual requisite for societies rejuvenating defunct legal systems in the wake of repressive regimes. But given the substantive moral vision of justice laid out in *Iraqi Voices,* one might have hoped that ICTJ would have dwelled less on legalistic and technical concerns in its post-trial report. Surely this is not the most instructive way to begin thinking about transitional justice in Iraq. There was no inclusion of *Iraqi voices* as had been the case in the earlier report. Nor was there a sustained discussion of the trial's ability to restore the dignity of victims (in spite of the report's brief admission that "the importance to the victims of recounting their experiences in a courtroom in front of the Iraqi leadership cannot be overstated").[20]

One very troubling concern the post-tribunal report did raise was the IHT's lack of outreach and its failure to extend justice from the courtroom into the political community through a vigorous public outreach and education process. Such a concern recaptures intimations of the broad justice as right order vision set out in *Iraqi Voices* and points to the need to translate the retribution achieved at the trial into terms that would help restore moral order in the wider political community. But the lack of Iraqi perspectives in the report makes it hard to appreciate just how Iraqis themselves interpreted and evaluated the reported lack of outreach.[21]

HRW's report *Judging Dujail: The First Trial before the Iraqi High Tribunal* reveals a striking inability to grasp the importance of substantive, nontechnical concerns of justice such as whether the trial would contribute to political reconciliation, whether it engendered a judgment among Iraqi citizens that their leaders were called to a proper accounting for their crimes, and whether Iraqi judges, acting as the people's representatives, had helped to establish an adequate historical record that the country could now commit to leaving behind. These concerns were more consistent with the kinds that Iraqis had expressed, more so than preoccupations with high rates of judicial turnover and lapses in presiding judges' demeanor, improper conduct of the defense counsel, or violations of defendants' rights to confront their witnesses. Not all legal observers agree with the legal assessments of ICTJ and HRW, it also should be said.[22]

Suffice it to say that the legal shortcomings that ICTJ and HRW identified demonstrate the imperfections of the trial and the need for improvements that will be required for a fully functioning and fair Iraqi judicial system to emerge one day. But in a country amidst great transition, where most citizens had personal knowledge and direct experience of Saddam's misdeeds, these objections hardly rise to the level of the most important considerations of the IHT's effort to secure justice for its citizens. HRW devoted thirty-three pages (over a third of its report) to technical "procedural concerns." By comparison, it took five pages to address other "substantive concerns" that consisted primarily of disputations over the tribunal's inability to provide "linkage evidence" that would establish proof that Saddam Hussein had full knowledge of, and prior intent to carry out, the regime's atrocities.[23]

Presumably, concerns about linkage evidence are deemed "substantive" because they refer to the definitions and requirements for prosecuting crimes against humanity. But one wonders, are these the "substantive concerns" of justice for Iraq's victims and citizens? Or only to those committed to a legalist conception of crimes against humanity, which exacts technical precision to prove and prosecute crimes for which ordinary Iraqi victims and citizens need no such proof? The lives of Iraqis were mercilessly crushed by Saddam Hussein's machinery of oppression and death. Contrary to what human rights groups seem to suggest, in order for proof of guilt to be determined, ordinary Iraqis did not seem to require a "systems engineer" to demonstrate how the various gears and mechanisms of the state machine operated against them. [24]

One might dub the justice as rights approach I have been describing as "procedural legalism," which seems the prevailing approach among international human rights groups, transitional justice communities, certain UN agencies, and other offices peopled by human rights lawyers. My concern about legalism's emphasis on rights, procedure, and rule of law in this discussion is how it limits the ways of morally conceiving justice. Squeezing the justice of a trial through the narrow opening of rights diminishes our ability to consider the broader societal import of justice for Iraq's victims and citizens. To be clear, legal rights and due process should never be overlooked or underappreciated. Supporters of legalism rightly believe that fair trials are always preferable to show trials.[25] They are also right to point out the need for continual improvement. But, the rush to condemn the IHT— at the expense of those on whose behalf the IHT operates—betrays a certain legalist preoccupation with justice as rights and due process that tends to displace conceptual alternatives, including earlier and quite commendable efforts to discern a more complex, comprehensive, and relational view of justice. That approach, as exemplified in *Iraqi Voices,* prioritizes the citizens and victims of Hussein's regime, the moral order and values it violated, and the efforts to realign human relations within Iraqi society towards a vision of a new political order. One begins to worry, though, that certain human rights advocates and international observers may be too content with a stinted legalist view of justice in Iraq, under which the voices of victims of human rights abuses, who have far more immediate experiences of injustice, begin to recede. When this attitude takes hold, Iraqis' experiences of injustice, their own sense of the measures needed to rectify these wrongs and their stakes in the project to restore moral order in their society—all of these concerns fall steadily out of view.

CRIMES AGAINST HUMANITY (AND HUMAN BEINGS)

The legalist vision of justice prevalent among human rights organizations also is problematic in the way it subsumes crimes against humanity entirely within an international legal framework of rights. Such rights are two-pronged and inextricable: they include, on the one hand, the protections afforded by universal human rights (which crimes against humanity violate) and, on the other, the procedural rights that defendants (i.e., accused perpetrators of crimes against humanity) are to be accorded in international courts of law. The legal principle tying procedural, due process rights to human rights is described in a HRW document: "Crimes such as genocide and crimes against humanity achieved recognition as crimes through international law; the legitimacy of trying them is thus inextricably linked to whether the trial meets international fair trial standards and correctly applies substantive international criminal law."[26] This overtly legal (and overly legalistic) emphasis on crimes against humanity and on the international requirements for prosecuting them tends to siphon off other vital forms of moral and political reflection, including how such crimes impact their victims and violate the moral order of those societies.

Before offering this critique, let me be quite clear: nations are to be commended for the tremendous strides they have made since the Nuremberg trials and Universal Declaration of Human Rights to outlaw collectively the most egregious crimes that human beings can commit against another. We should never have to wonder again whether political leaders can or will be held to account for their grossest misdeeds, abuses of power and failures to protect their own citizens, as proscribed by international law. Human rights organizations, moreover, often have been on the leading edge of identifying crimes against humanity and urging states and international political bodies to take action against them.

Having said that, let me suggest another way of morally deliberating on the matter of crimes against humanity. Crimes against humanity are so named not simply because they violate widely accepted legal norms, but because they violate a view of human dignity that extends—or should extend—to all people regardless of nationality, race, religion, ethnicity, gender, or tribe. They are universal *moral* crimes, wherein the "universal" status accrues because such atrocities violate standards that have their source in a moral order that transcends the polity—indeed that transcends all polities. Most people intuitively perceive this moral order. They universally understand when this order is violated at their expense and, in response, exhibit shared human attributes: pain, terror, sorrow, anxiety, horror, and death. For this reason, crimes against humanity are not (and should not) be permitted by or within any nation. They are sins of the worst order—the most immoral acts known to human history—because they fail to honor or pay tribute to a moral order in which humanity is, if not sacred, deeply respected.

But when such universal crimes and sins do occur, the victim is always a human being, never just an idea of humanity itself. Crimes against humanity always take place against *particular* people in *specific* political communities, where such traits as nationality, race, religion, ethnicity, or tribe are essential. Where atrocities occur, identity is not abstracted from some noumenal notion of human dignity but, rather, is concrete, involving individuals with unique names, bodies, personalities and families; and communities with particular histories, traditions, cultures, and beliefs. Viewed through this kind of moral framework, crimes against humanity are not principally violations of international law protecting some disembodied ideality of humanity, for which human rights groups— surrogates or representatives for all humanity—possess a special claim.[27] Rather, crimes against humanity rip apart the fabric of human relations that holds social communities together much as they rip apart these bodies and those souls that constitute a particular community. The individuals and communities experiencing such crimes are shaped irrevocably by them; victims, therefore, accrue special claims—needs, obligations, responsibilities, and prerogatives—to restore the order of justice ruptured in their community and to repair the human relations that are damaged as a consequence.

This account of justice as rightly ordered human relations was blurred and obscured by human rights groups that weighed in on the Saddam Hussein trial and argued for Western-style international tribunals over a local (national) tribunal. These groups seemed more concerned with scrupulously protecting certain legal rights and processes and preserving international legal prerogatives than they were with supporting Iraqis' efforts to restore justly ordered relations within their own society. For human rights groups, the failure to meet international legal standards demarcates a failure to uphold the universal element of crimes against humanity. This way of conceiving justice through rights, however, does not permit us to maintain an important distinction: between a *universal moral order* that crimes against humanity violate and an *international legal order* that a legalist approach to crimes against humanity presupposes. Distinguishing moral universalism from legal universalism enables us to prioritize the vindication of transcendent moral principles over procedural consistency. This is imperative in cases where moral culpability and political responsibility are not in doubt, as in the case of Saddam Hussein.

Conceiving crimes against humanity as a universal moral category, not simply a legal one, allows us to appreciate that, even if the IHT failed to meet certain legal and procedural tests required to prosecute crimes against humanity as determined by international law, it does not follow that the IHT failed a higher moral test: the principle of *equity*, which allows that universal moral norms may be preserved (and universal crimes punished) in ways consistent with national particularities and social contexts.[28] In weighing the claims of justice, equity permits the scales to be fashioned from many different metals; the various scales of justice may not all function exactly the same or equally well, but in order to function at all in local contexts, they must make use of materials readily available and recognizable in those milieus.

A tribunal's ability to restore moral order and to right disordered relations within a political community is a more complex and comprehensive concern than simply embracing the rules of an international tribunal as human rights organizations seek. Iraqis unanimously articulated that the trial of Saddam Hussein must not go the way of other international tribunals, administered by foreign bodies, drawn out, and often far removed from the victims and citizens most deeply in need of justice.[29] Legitimacy among Iraqis required an Iraqi trial: administered by Iraqis, held in Iraq, governed by Iraqi laws to prosecute Iraqi crimes against fellow Iraqis. The *Iraqi Voices* report recounted many Iraqis' suspicions of "outsider" interference in the trials—whether UN representatives or American occupiers—and noted that "a commonly articulated reason for the emphasis on an *Iraqi* process [was] that Iraqis understand best what they have suffered over the past 35 years, and so Iraqis should sit in judgment." In the words of one Turkoman woman of Kirkuk, "People living outside Iraq have never suffered from our problems." A Sunni man similarly averred, "International organizations did not interfere when Saddam was killing us, and they will not interfere in Saddam's trial."[30]

Finally, the violation of Iraqi laws was a particular point of concern raised by many Iraqis in the *Iraqi Voices* report. While Iraqis understood that the violations they suffered fell under the international legal umbrella of "crimes against humanity," they regarded many of these crimes as distinctly Iraqi abuses of Iraq's law and government. Iraq's citizens were deeply outraged by the ways Saddam Hussein had perverted the nation's government and exploited Iraqis. For these reasons, Article 14 of the Statute of the IST was crafted to punish those whose corruption of Iraq's judicial system and exploitation of its natural resources had ruined the country. While there may be international provisions that also pertain to such crimes, proud Iraqis clearly saw this as a violation of *their* laws. Thus did the IHT statute lay out the following:

> The Tribunal shall have the power to prosecute persons who have committed the following crimes under Iraqi law:
>
>   a) For those outside the judiciary, the attempt to manipulate the judiciary or involvement in the functions of the judiciary, in violation, *inter alia,* of the Iraqi interim constitution of 1970, as amended;
>
>   b) The wastage of national resources and the squandering of public assets and funds, pursuant to, *inter alia,* Article 2(g) of Law Number 7 of 1958, as amended; and
>
>   c) The abuse of position and the pursuit of policies that may lead to the threat of war or the use of the armed forces of Iraq against an Arab country, in accordance with Article 1 of Law Number 7 of 1958, as amended.[31]

In short, these were Iraqi crimes, which made them particularly egregious. Therefore, the tribunal featured "hybrid" dimensions that allowed for prosecution of both international war crimes and national crimes specific to Iraq.

Yet the legalist focus on international conceptions and standards of justice—including the assumption that crimes against humanity should be tried in international venues— had the effect of marginalizing real people and the ways that Iraqis' particular culture, nation, and history were not only a crucial part of their past but essential to a new future as well. All of this is to say that a more capacious, less rigid account of justice is needed than international forms of legalism can provide. Ironically, international human rights groups, who at one time were the strongest advocates for the justice that Iraqis hoped for, eventually collapsed Iraqis' concern for justice with an abstract legalist approach that vitiated the force, character, and context of Iraqi justice. One worries that some human rights organizations may be more committed to preserving their own legal conceptions of justice and their own rarefied notion of "humanity" than they are with real Iraqi human beings. It was on Iraqis' behalf that the trial succeeded or failed to achieve justice by confronting the horrors of the nation's past; by reaffirming the moral order so violently disturbed under Saddam Hussein; and by setting a course for a new Iraq in which civic relations among citizens might be held together by mutual trust and respect, rather than fear, loathing, and shame. It would seem that these substantive moral matters, rather than certain legal technicalities, would have been the preferred basis for evaluating the justice of Saddam Hussein's trial.

INTERNATIONAL JUSTICE AND POLITICS

A final example reveals how the legalist commitment to justice as rights marginalizes the potency of Iraqi claims to conceive justice for themselves and to decide how best to restore moral order to their own political community. Capital punishment is the case in point. For international human rights NGOs such as HRW and ICTJ, the resort to capital punishment violates the fundamental right to life.[32] For this reason, it is deemed unjust and out of bounds under any circumstance regardless of the severity of crime. International governmental organizations such as the United Nations also oppose the death penalty, even though some of its member nations have not outlawed it.

Let me stipulate at the outset that there are, in my view, compelling arguments for opposing the death penalty in most circumstances. There are quite understandable reasons for the growing international wave of opposition to it, particularly among Western nations.[33] What is striking, though, about the opposition to the death penalty among human rights groups and their supporters is the rigidity with which it was applied to the Iraqi tribunal such that support for Iraqis in the trial of their former leaders would stand or fall on their decision to pursue capital punishment. One might think that even groups that oppose capital punishment in principle would recognize that the moral and political stakes of the Iraqi tribunal outsized any particular sentence it might impose. But here we see the commitment to justice as rights moves beyond upholding international law to protect human rights and creeps into an effort to shape national policy that lies outside the scope of international law.[34] Such an approach interweaves human rights law, moral beliefs, and political activism together into a wooly rubric one might call *international justice,* a position that militates against local forms of justice where justice is most needed.

Iraqis rejected the idea of an United Nations-sponsored tribunal in part because they were worried that the United Nations would impose a certain model that would eliminate capital punishment from consideration, a penalty most Iraqis viewed as a legitimate sentencing option. Iraqis were right to worry, though they may not have anticipated that their decision would cost them the assistance they requested for their trial. According to

Kingsley Chiedu Moghalu, legal advisor for the International Criminal Tribunal for Rwanda, "For the United Nations, Kofi Annan pronounced the world body's position in a number of media encounters that the UN would not sponsor or actively participate in a trial of Saddam that could hand down capital punishment."[35]

The presumption that capital punishment is an indefensible violation of human or civil rights and, therefore, a priori unjust strikes an overly pious chord. Such a view—issuing from legal observers, international officials, and citizens from highly developed nations far removed from the kind of suffering experienced by Iraqi citizens—must seem quite patronizing to many Iraqis and would explain their skepticism expressed towards IOs (international organizations).[36] Consider one of the recommendations in the *Iraqi Voices* report which argues for the need to educate "the Iraqi people about how other countries view the death penalty and its place in retributive punishment."[37] One can imagine being a fly on the wall as a human rights advocate explains to an Iraqi victim of Saddam Hussein's rule that, even for the most bloody acts carried out by Saddam, it would be unjust to hang him because "the death penalty is the ultimate cruel, inhuman, and degrading punishment and a violation of the right to life." [38] How exactly execution is more ultimate than shredding human bodies alive, subjecting women to rape rooms, and torturing people while their family members are forced to watch may be difficult to grasp for citizens and victims of the former regime. Here, the ICTJ report seems to be doing more speaking than listening to voices of Iraqis.

International justice may be the best way to describe what turns out to be a comprehensive legal–moral–political theory of justice to which many human rights groups seem to subscribe, which seeks to expand the influence of rights vernacular into an international regime of universal legal–moral–political expectations. Such a position seems uncontroversial in the case of treaties and conventions outlawing, say, genocide or crimes against humanity; only a rogue nation would refuse to sign. But what about capital punishment? Human rights groups presuppose that the practice of capital punishment by any country is beyond the pale. The stated argument is that capital punishment entails violating inviolable human rights. (I suspect it may also offend the sensibilities of "humanity" or at least a certain cross-section of the "international community" that speaks for humanity.) As with crimes against humanity and other human rights violations, it follows, there are no occasions or contexts anywhere in the world in which the death penalty is acceptable, not even in the case of punishing those who commit crimes against humanity.

Now one might counter that, in fact, most forms of punishment entail the violation of human rights. Whether a particular sentence abridges life, liberty, or some other protection set out in the Universal Declaration of Human Rights, punishment quite deliberately deprives those judged to be guilty of some basic right to which other human beings, *qua* human beings, are entitled. That is precisely in what punishment consists. Political societies do not (at least, they should not) differ over the question of whether human rights *ever* may be curtailed as forms of punishment (and life imprisonment is certainly a violation of one's human rights). But we should anticipate that, as polities deliberate about punishment appropriate for their societies, they may reach different determinations over which rights may be abridged and under what circumstances.

When, as part of a commitment to international justice, human rights organizations condemn abuses such as crimes against humanity, every nation should lend its support. But when calls for the abolition of the death penalty are lumped together on the same plate, one should recognize that the *legal* enforcement of human rights has crossed a *political* threshold. The political dimension of international justice, that is, does not stop with efforts to safeguard human rights protected under existing international law to which countries are already bound, but also aspires to create new laws and shape national policies that are not in violation of international law. The language of rights that is invoked casts a legal sheen and provides a moral imprimatur to such political activism.

Finally, international justice includes an ethical dimension, establishing a bar of moral intolerance—for crimes against humanity and capital punishment alike—that can brook no challenge. Those who believe that the death penalty is "the ultimate cruel, inhuman and degrading punishment," which violates the human right to life, place capital punishment beyond the *moral* pale, whether or not the practice is legal and accepted widely in a given country. International justice becomes the supreme arbiter of morality that *de facto* trumps other forms of moral discernment. For example, the world's religions, which have long served as crucial sources of moral instruction, particularly on matters of life and death, would not be deemed relevant if they took stances contradictory to international justice. Yet, Islam, a source of ethical guidance and inspiration for most Iraqis, allows for capital punishment (particularly if one looks to debates within the juristic tradition associated with classical Islamic law). Of course, it also must be noted that Islam allows for clemency.[39] In either case, Iraqi citizens would need to weigh these decisions for themselves. But it would unduly limit the place of religious or other forms of ethical reflection if citizens' moral reasoning and political judgment about achieving justice in the community must be bound by absolutist standards of international justice.

One need not be an enthusiastic supporter of capital punishment (I, for one, am not) to value the freedom of other peoples to discern and shape the order of justice for their own communities. Following the ouster of Saddam Hussein, the reality was that, for many Iraqis, the only way they envisioned justice in Iraq, given the consummate barbarity their government inflicted upon them, was for the architect, executor, and chief symbol of that regime to hang. One wonders if it is appropriate for certain Western and international observers to use the trial of the most brutal dictator in the Middle East to promote their moral and political cause to abolish the death penalty.

There were, of course, Iraqis who opposed executing Saddam for various reasons. Had they persuaded enough of their fellow countrymen and women of their position, it would have been equally inappropriate for outsiders to insist that execution was necessary. *Iraqi Voices* mentions an intriguing idea put forth by one Iraqi who thought that the death penalty should be applied to senior figures but abolished immediately after, presumably as a sign of a new era in Iraq.[40] But the point remains that if the Iraqi people were seeking to take back their society and government from their oppressors and to hold them accountable, then it is legitimate and appropriate for a nation's citizens to come together and make their own decisions about trials and sentencing, consistent with national laws, religious mores, and civil practices of their own country. Iraqis distrustful of many in the international community, for its inaction while they suffered under Saddam Hussein and UN sanctions, would be justifiably resentful of sanctimonious attestations about his right to life being violated once he was removed from power and placed in the dock.

International justice, I have tried to show, is about law, morality, and politics, and that admixture may put international justice at odds with local justice in those countries that are actually reeling from atrocities and gross human rights abuses. Supporters of IOs such as the United Nations called into question their own commitment to Iraqi justice when they withheld from the Iraqi tribunal badly needed legal support and advisory assistance because, in the United Nations' view, the Iraqi people did not heed certain international standards of sentencing or punishment. The cold shoulder of international justice that Iraqis received was not limited to the United Nations. Human rights groups also withheld materials and assistance that could have aided the prosecution team (which they later criticized in post-trial reports). It seems difficult *not* to conclude that the political motivations at work in international justice are at odds with its moral and legal commitments to prosecute crimes against humanity. Again, to cite Moghalu,

> Western human rights organizations have declined to support the tribunal. Most notably, organizations such as Human Rights Watch refused to turn over to the Iraqi tribunal witness statements it obtained from victims of Saddam Hussein's oppression while preparing for the trial of the ousted leader—no doubt because they had hoped he would be tried by an international court, or at least by a court that would not have the death penalty.
>
> This decision on noncooperation with the Iraqi tribunal was made without consulting the Iraqi victims who gave their testimony to human rights investigators in the hope that they were playing a concrete role in bringing Saddam to justice and establishing the rule of law in Iraq. This position can be interpreted as a political one, for it is doubtful the Iraqis who gave these statements would have objected to their testimony being transmitted with or without the death penalty. [41]

Moghalu also recalls that there were deep reservations within the United Nations that its involvement could be perceived to legitimate the United States-led invasion of Iraq, which had failed to achieve a final Security Council resolution specifically calling for military force. [42]

Iraqis' distrust of outsiders perhaps is explained by the inconsistency (some have called it hypocrisy[43]) exhibited by those who claim to be most concerned with justice in Iraq, and yet who decline to help when help is most needed. International justice takes shape through a strenuous legal–moral–political view of justice grounded in rights that would seek to trump Iraqi notions of justice as right order. For justice as right order, as I am articulating the position, could permit executing high-ranking criminals of the old regime as one element of a more comprehensive vision of justice that punishes and holds accountable those guilty of committing wide-scale atrocities against their own citizens; that restores moral order to a nation by vindicating the values that citizens cherish and that have been tarnished by such crimes; and that publicly recognizes the injuries of citizens whose lives have been torn asunder by criminals of humanity. This process of retribution, or rendering tribute to moral values by reestablishing political accountability, may be a decisive element of a much broader process of rightly ordering human relations within a society— of repairing and renewing those relations that have been damaged among citizens and between them and their government. An international view of justice, grounded exclusively in rights, provides too little room for a relational view of transitional justice in which retribution is related to moral reconstruction, social reconciliation, and political repair. A more holistic approach resounds more with Iraqis' beliefs as laid out in *Iraqi Voices*. In short, the trial of Saddam Hussein should have been part of a broader process of conceiving justice as the establishment of right order in Iraqi society.

EXECUTING JUSTICE AND SADDAM

This chapter has considered how an overemphasis on *justice as rights* and a related comprehensive philosophy of international justice can hinder a broader moral and political outlook that is needed for nations seeking transitional justice in the wake of crimes against humanity and other gross violations of human dignity. By concentrating exclusively on the Iraqi tribunal's failure to adopt certain legal standards of procedural fairness and to adhere to certain moral–political interpretations of human rights (particularly regarding the death penalty), those committed to international justice neglected to reflect upon Iraqi justice, that is, how Iraqi citizens and victims of Sadam Hussein's regime discerned the justice afforded by the trial and execution of their former leader. I also have tried to show that an alternative conception—*justice as right order*—offers a more promising mode for thinking through issues of transitional justice because it locates war crimes trials within a more comprehensive, relational account of justice that recognizes the multiform challenges and goals of conflict-ridden societies as they strive to overcome their past and to restore justice to human relations within their polity. And while protecting rights and ensuring procedural fairness are certainly important elements for establishing a tribunal's legitimacy or a nation's rule of law—and central for establishing moral order in society—there are broader conceptions of justice that also must be pondered. Let me close, then, by signaling how justice as right order provides a standard by which we can begin to assess Saddam's final sentence.

At the outset, I conceived justice as right order as an effort to order citizens' relations among one another and vis-à-vis their government with respect to a transcendent or objective moral order. Crimes against humanity often entail the most egregious transgression of that order and, therefore, call for vigorous efforts to repair the human lives and social relations damaged by such evils. A political community's efforts to reclaim or affirm this moral order can take multiple forms: (1) rendering judgment by providing an accounting of the past and issuing an historical record for posterity through which present and future generations can identify injustice by its proper name; (2) cohering diverse elements of society around a shared set of moral values and political aspirations; (3) vindicating—paying tribute to—those values and aspirations such as human dignity that have been denigrated; (4) punishing and holding accountable a society's greatest enemies of justice; (5) creating new laws and institutions that will prevent such crimes and injustice from occurring again (including the codification and protection of basic human rights as well as rights of the accused); and (6) establishing the possibility of hope and political renewal that provides conditions for citizens to leave behind their ugly past and to create a new future that reflects a shared vision of a moral order that is just and humane. Justice as right order seeks to assign all of these parts and pursuits their proper due as part of a broad, comprehensive vision of moral reconstruction and social reconciliation that restores trust among citizens and improves relations between them and their government. The fruits of such a vision are improved levels of unity and social harmony.

The pursuit of retribution through war crimes tribunals can further this view of justice as right order and some of the elements on which it depends. A tribunal serves as a means towards, not the end of, justice as right order. Within this framework, the trial and punishment of Saddam Hussein and other high-ranking Baathists established a prominent foothold on justice that leaves behind the injustices of Iraq's authoritarian past, that affirms a moral order that Saddam's hideous crimes violated, and that points towards possibilities of a new beginning for Iraq. By holding accountable and punishing Iraq's criminals of humanity, the trial of Saddam Hussein rendered a tribute to the universal (human) and particular (Iraqi) moral–political values that his regime trampled underfoot. The tribunal established precedent in Iraq: it implemented an imperfect rule of law and regime of rights that made it possible to prosecute Iraq's worst crimes and deter future political leaders from committing such crimes.

The notion of justice as right order also helps us to appreciate the many shortcomings of the Saddam Hussein trial and execution. For reasons mostly having to do with the very transitional, conflict-ridden state of post-Saddam Iraq—involving deep ethnic divisions, power struggles, interreligious and intertribal strife, military occupation, violent militias and insurgencies resorting to acts of terror, and wide-scale lack of political order—the trial and execution of Saddam Hussein did not live up to its potential to restore moral order to Iraq or to fulfill Iraqis' hopes for justice. For a broken society such as Iraq in the wake of its fallen tyranny, transitional justice would entail a thorough-going reordering of human lives and relations within the political order. The trial and execution of Saddam Hussein may be seen as a successful effort to render retributive justice to a political criminal, but the broader notion of justice that such a judgment should betoken was not achieved. This would have involved the restoration of a moral and political order that unites citizens in their common esteem of human dignity and the sanctity of human life, values Saddam Hussein held in contempt. The fruit of such rightly ordered relations is—or should be—civic harmony, peace and a sense of renewal that puts the nation on a new moral footing, renouncing the injustice of its tyrannical past. But in the "new" Iraq, the moral disorder of tyrannical injustice simply has been replaced by anarchic injustice and political disorder in which—as hundreds of Iraqis die each month in sectarian violence—the sanctity of human life is even more threatened than before.

Within a justice as right order conceptual framework, the trial of criminals of humanity represents—or should represent—citizens' yearnings for the rebirth of a new moral and political order of justice. The hunger for renewal was encapsulated well in one man's reactions to Saddam's execution: "I felt like my mother delivered me for the first time. It's my birthday."[44] But Saddam's final sentence became anything but a new beginning for the country writ large, however fulfilling it was to some Iraqis and however promising such a prospect at one time may have been for the nation as a whole.

Justice, I have tried to show, involves more than the simple application of law, protection of rights and assignment of just deserts. Justice is more than a fair trial or a sentence properly carried out. Rather, it entails restoring right order in human relations in the wake of gross atrocities and cohering a community around a common view of the moral order. So while I have argued that Iraqis possessed a strong moral claim and right to execute Saddam Hussein (he certainly *deserved* to hang for what he did), there also may have been good reasons for Iraqis *not* to execute him, or at least to postpone his sentence indefinitely. For at the time of the execution, there was intense sectarian violence, which, one reasonably could have anticipated, the execution would inflame. While, at one time, the symbol of Saddam at the gallows might have united Iraq's Arab Sunni, Shia, and Kurdish populations in their effort to forge a common vision of justice that rejected the injustice that Saddam personified, that day had well passed by the time his noose was being prepared.

The macabre execution, it turned out, possessed the trappings of "a revenge killing"[45] and, as predicted, exacerbated Iraq's ethnic and religious divisions, furthered sectarian violence, and raised grave doubts that Iraqis, as a whole, could perceive the trial as part of a process of moving forward. A civic rite that should have—and, at one time, would have—united Sunni, Shiite, and Kurdish Iraqis only fractured them further in the end. Sunnis who once loathed Saddam generally saw his execution as an act of Shia retribution. Any final hopes that the trial could reunite Iraq's Muslims of different sects around their rejections of a shared past and their common hopes for a peaceful future was eroded when Saddam was delivered to his death on Id-al-Adha, a sacred holiday commemorating Abraham's faith and willingness to sacrifice his son Ishmael.[46] The symbolic effect, for some Sunnis, was to turn a tyrant into a sacrificial lamb.[47] The shedding of his blood became a bastardized form of ritualistic justice that prefigured the acts of those who later slaughtered sheep in honor of their former leader turned "martyr."[48] The perversity of all of this is compounded when one recalls that, even during Saddam's rule, executions on religious holidays were prohibited.[49]

The Iraqi tribunal ultimately was undercut by its own commitment to a form of Iraqi legalism. Because the IHT statute forbid commutation of sentences for any reason, Saddam's sentence could not be postponed or commuted for mitigating circumstances (such as the propensity that it would heighten sectarian violence and cause even more disorder and injustice). Furthermore, because the IHT statute required sentencing defendants within 30 days of conviction, many of Saddam's worst atrocities were never brought before the court, never entered into its historical record, and never formally judged and decried. Consequently, many Kurds resented the execution, which foreclosed the trial on behalf of Kurdish victims of the Anfal campaign and provided no vindication for the tens of thousands it killed.[50] Nor were Shia able to see Saddam tried in court for the worst crimes he had committed against them. In the end, there was neither a full judgment of past injustices, nor a full tribute to those values that might lead Iraq towards a new beginning. The moral of the story is clear: a hasty execution did not hasten the arrival of justice in Iraq. Justice itself was foreclosed—prematurely executed alongside Saddam Hussein. This unfortunate narrative can be explained by an unyielding commitment to rule of law, which undermined broader efforts to restore a social–political order of justice. This is irony of the worst kind: Iraq's strict commitment to a legalist view of procedural justice undermined the achievement of a more robust vision of justice that would have extended the impact to the broader society, shaped civic relations more directly, and left more room for the political reconciliation that Iraqi justice in a post-Saddam era required.

The effort to render a tyrant his due offered, at best, a partial and limited glimpse of justice. The measure of retribution that was achieved through Saddam's trial and sentence was outweighed by the just reordering of human relations that was not achieved. In order to appreciate both the successes and failures of trials such as Saddam Hussein's, a more expansive notion of justice is needed than what legalist theories of justice can muster. For a more comprehensive vision of transitional justice to take hold, modern war crimes tribunals must construe justice as the proper ordering of human relations as citizens from diverse groups struggle to become a nation, united and at peace. Such a relational account of justice encourages citizens to acknowledge and mend the ruptured moral fabric of their past; to seek reconciliation by stitching together social relations and civic institutions out of the tatters of their current state of affairs; and to cut, from the cloth of common aspirations, moral patterns for a new political order that can guide their future.

NOTES

1. See the remarks of former U.S. Ambassador-at-Large for War Crimes Issues, David Scheffer, "The Case for Justice in Iraq" (Washington, DC: The Middle East Institute and the Iraq Foundation National Press Club, September 18, 2000), http://www.fas.org/news/iraq/2000/09/iraq-000918.htm; the report by the Foreign and Commonwealth Office of London, "Saddam Hussein: Crimes and Human Rights Abuses," November, 2002, http://www.iraqfoundation.org/hr/2002/cdec/irdp.pdf; the White House statement "Life Under Saddam Hussein," http://www.whitehouse.gov/news/releases/2003/04/20030404-1.html; and numerous documents available on the Web sites of Amnesty International, Human Rights Watch, and International Center for Transitional Justice.

2. Fareed Zakaria, "The Vengeance of the Victors," *Newsweek,* January 8, 2007, 25; Editorial, "The Rush to Hang Saddam Hussein," *New York Times,* December 29, 2006; Editorial, "Act of Revenge," *The Nation,* December 31, 2006; Editorial, "Justice Executed," *National Review Online,* December 30, 2006; David Gelertner, "Thus All to Seldom to Tyrants; Saddam's Punishment Was a Rare Instance of Just Deserts," *Weekly Standard,* January 15, 2007.

3. See, for example, Aristotle, Hachett, (Indianapolis, 1985) translated by Torence Irwin *Ethics,* Book 5.

4. See Harold Berman, *Law and Revolution: The Formation of the Western Legal Tradition* (Cambridge, MA: Harvard University Press, 1983), 183.

5. See, for example, Plato, *The Republic,* 2nd ed. (rev. ed.), translated and introduced by Desmond Lee, (New York: Penguin Press), 1987, Book 4.

6. Augustine, *City of God,* trans. Henry Bettenson (New York: Penguin Classics, 1972), 19.13, 870.

7. John Witte, in his discussion of subjective and objective right, provides a complementary way to consider the distinction I seek to make here. After all, the term right (*jus*) shares a common root with justice (*justitia*). A subjective right is so named, Witte explains, because it "is vested in a subject (whether an individual, group, or entity), and the subject usually can have that right vindicated before an appropriate authority when the right is threatened or violated. The subjective sense of right is quite different from right in an 'objective sense.' 'Objective right' (or 'rightness') means that something is the objectively right thing or action in the circumstances. Objective right obtains when something is rightly ordered, is just or proper, is considered to be right when judged against some objective or external standard. 'Right' is here being used as an adjective, not as a noun: it is what is correct or proper—'due and meet,' as the Victorians used to put it." John Witte, *God's Joust, God's Justice: Law and Religion in the Western Tradition* (Grand Rapids, MI: Eerdmans, 2006), 32.

8. See Robert I. Rotberg and Dennis Thompson, eds., *Truth v. Justice* (Princeton, NJ: Princeton University Press, 2000); Nigel Biggar, ed., *Burying the Past: Making Peace and Doing Justice after Civil Conflict* (Washington, DC: Georgetown University Press, 2003); Daniel Philpott, ed., *The Politics of Past Evil: Religion, Reconciliation, and the Dilemmas of Transitional Justice* (Notre Dame: University of Notre Dame Press, 2006). For a brief look at the issue of justice versus reconciliation in Iraq, see Daniel Philpott, "Along with trials, Iraq needs truth," *Boston Globe,* December 8, 2005.

9. "Restorative justice" and "retributive justice" are often defined in contradistinction to one another, a dichotomy that I reject. The position of "justice as right order," which I describe here, might be seen as incorporating elements of both concepts, though it is reducible to neither.

10. To foreclose any potential misunderstanding, the position I am putting forth does not equate simply to achieving a particular outcome in a trial—process be damned. But it is also distinct from "procedural justice" which reduces justice to fairness and due process. Justice as right order pertains to the broad, societal ways in which citizens confront the abuses of their morally disordered past and restore proper order to relations among citizens within society and between them and their government. Such a vision must be attentive to process and how that process is structured and limited, but those structures and limits constitute neither the moral totality of the process nor the totality of justice itself.

11. The International Center for Transitional Justice (ICTJ) and the Human Rights Center at the University of California Berkeley, *Iraqi Voices: Attitudes Toward Transitional Justice and Societal Reconstruction* (New York: ICTJ, 2004), i, http://www.ictj.org/images/content/1/0/108.pdf (accessed June 29, 2007) (hereafter cited as *Iraqi Voices*).

12. Ibid., 15.

13. Ibid., 19.

14. Ibid., 13.

15. Ibid., ii.

16. Ibid., 21–22.

17. Ibid., 25. Other comments include: "They should be tried by an open, public trial and their punishment should be defined according to law," one Shia cleric pronounced. A Sunni cleric similarly advised, "The trials should be public, in front of the people, so that they feel that they have

truly been liberated and that their rights have been returned to them by those who stole them." An Assyrian woman similarly avers, "At least we want to give them the right to a trial, even though the former regime did not extend this right," *Iraqi Voices,* 25–26.

18. See especially International Center for Transitional Justice, "Dujail: Trial and Error?" (New York: ICTJ, 2006), http://www.ictj.org/static/MENA/Iraq/ICTJDujailBrief.eng.pdf (hereafter cited as *Dujail: Trial and Error?*); and Human Rights Watch, *Judging Dujail: The First Trial Before the Iraqi High Tribunal* (New York: Seven Stories Press, 2006), 18, no. 9 (E). http://hrw.org/reports/2006/iraq1106/iraq1106web.pdf (hereafter cited as *Judging Dujail*).

19. *"Dujail: Trial and Error?"* 12–13. One notes that, in the case of this complaint, recording the testimony of witnesses can be an important part of the process of seeking justice by establishing an historical record of political wrongdoing and abuse.

20. Ibid., 13.

21. Perhaps the instability and violence of post-Saddam Iraq limited the ability to garner Iraqi reflections.

22. See, for example, Kingsley Chiedu Moghalu, "Saddam Hussein's Trial Meets the 'Fairness' Test," *Ethics and International Affairs* 20, no. 4 (Winter 2006): 517–25. In a stinging rebuke Moghalu charges, "There is surely something incomplete about international war crimes trials in which the rights of the defendant appear to be far more important than those of hundreds of thousands of victims and survivors and become the sole yardstick for assessments of such trials," 521–2. See also works by Michael A. Newton, former Senior Adviser to the US Ambassador-at-Large for War Crimes Issues, who helped train IHT judges: "The Iraqi High Criminal Court: Controversy and Contributions," *International Review of the Red Cross* 88, no. 862 (June 2006): 399–425; "The Iraqi Special Tribunal: A Human Rights Perspective," *Cornell International Law Journal* 38 (2005): 863–97.

23. "...Saddam Hussein signed an order ratifying the death sentences [carried out in Dujail]. The death sentences appear to have been implemented in March 1985. The haste with which the accused persons were tried and convicted, and with which the death sentences were ratified, clearly raises suspicions that the process was no more than part of a de facto plan to carry out extrajudicial executions. However, no evidence was presented [in the trial] from which the intent and state of knowledge of Saddam Hussein could be discerned or inferred in relation to these actions," *Judging Dujail,* 79. See also *"Dujail: Trial and Error?"* 10.

24. To investigate system crimes, the ICTJ report propounds, one ought to approach the matter like an engineer: "If an investigation were to demonstrate the responsibility of members of a criminal regime, the task would [be] to expose clearly how the various parts of the 'machinery' functioned to culminate in crimes such as murder on a massive scale," *Dujail: Trial and Error?* 9.

25. For a cogent and comprehensive history of war crimes tribunals and how legalism has surpassed extra-legal ways of punishing war criminals, see Gary Jonathan Bass, *Stay the Hand of Vengeance: The Politics of War Crimes Tribunals* (Princeton, NJ: Princeton University Press, 2000).

26. *Judging Dujail,* 6. See also *"Dujail: Trial and Error?"* 2.

27. I discuss these themes, including the grounding of human dignity, at greater length in my "Trials, Tribunals, and Tribulations of Sovereignty: Crimes against Humanity and the *imago Dei,*" in *The Sacred and the Sovereign: Religion and International Politics,* eds. John D. Carlson and Erik C. Owens (Washington, DC: Georgetown University Press, 2003), 196–232 (hereinafter cited as "Trials, Tribunals, and Tribulations").

28. See "Trials, Tribunals, and Tribulations," 220–7.

29. It should be noted that even though Iraqis objected to an international, Hague-styled UN tribunal, they welcomed international assistance from the United States, United Nations, and other organizations; Iraqis' prudently recognized that the dilapidated and corrupt Iraq criminal justice system was in no position to undertake the judicial process alone (*Iraqi Voices,* 31–3). This is an important issue to which I return later.

30. *Iraqi Voices,* 32.

31. Available at http://www.cpa-iraq.org/human_rights/Statute.htm (accessed June 29, 2007).

32. *Iraqi Voices,* 55.

33. For a broad range of religious perspectives both for and against capital punishment, see Erik C. Owens, John D. Carlson, and Eric P. Elshtain, eds., *Religion and the Death Penalty: A Call for Reckoning* (Grand Rapids, MI: Eerdmans, 2004) (hereafter cited as *Religion and the Death Penalty*). My own views on the matter are discussed at length in my chapter "Human Nature, Limited Justice, and the Irony of Capital Punishment," in *Religion and the Death Penalty*, 158–94.

34. For one legal discussion of the death penalty in international and U.S. law, see Laurence E. Rothenberg, "International Law, U.S. Sovereignty, and the Death Penalty," *Georgetown Journal of International Law* 35 (2004): 547–95.

35. Kingsley Chiedu Moghalu, *Global Justice: The Politics of War Crimes Tribunals* (Westport, CT: Praeger Security International, 2006), 160–61 (hereafter cited as *Global Justice*). According to one news report, Kofi Anan barred the participation of UN lawyers and judges in the IHT. The story went on to say, "A letter from Mr. Annan's office expressed 'serious doubts' that the IST could meet 'relevant international standards.' It reiterated his view that the United Nations should not assist national courts that can order the death penalty and said that the organization [UN] had no legal mandate to assist the tribunal." Marlise Simons, "Iraq Not Ready for Trials; UN to Withhold Training," *New York Times,* October 22, 2004.

36. *Iraqi Voices,* 32.

37. Ibid., 55.

38. Ibid., 55.

39. See the excellent essay by Khaled Abou El Fadl, "The Death Penalty, Mercy, and Islam: A Call for Retrospection," in *Religion and the Death Penalty,* 73–105.

40. *Iraqi Voices,* 35.

41. Moghalu, *Global Justice,* 165.

42. Ibid., 160.

43. Michael A. Newton, "Iraq's New Court Finds Itself on Trial," *New York Times,* November 24, 2004.

44. Sabrina Tavernise, "The Struggle for Iraq: Dividing Iraq, Even in Death," *New York Times,* December 31, 2006.

45. President George W. Bush, interview by Jim Lehrer, *MacNeil/Lehrer NewsHour,* PBS, January 16, 2007, http://www.pbs.org/newshour/bb/white_house/jan-june07/bush_01-16.html (accessed June 29, 2007).

46. "'We wanted him to be executed on a special day,' [Iraqi] National Security adviser Mouwafak al-Rubale told state-run Iraqiyah," *Al Bawaba,* "Shiites in Baghdad Celebrate Saddam Hussein Execution," http://www.albawaba.com/en/news/207992 (accessed June 29, 2007).

47. Hassan M. Fattah, "For Arab Critics, Hussein's Execution Symbolizes the Victory of Vengeance Over Justice," *New York Times,* December 31, 2006.

48. Associated Press, "Angry Protests in Iraq Suggest Sunni Arab Shift to Militants," *New York Times,* January 2, 2007.

49. John F. Burns, "In Days Before Hanging, a Push for Revenge and a Push Back from the U.S.," *New York Times,* January 7, 2007.

50. Here Human Rights Watch was entirely right to condemn this aspect of the IHT statute, *Judging Dujail,* 87.

CHAPTER 18

Individual Responsibility, Tribunals, and Truth and Reconciliation Commissions: Are We Asking the Wrong Questions?

DAVID K. LINNAN

We examine domestic versus international tribunals, and truth and reconciliation commissions addressing crimes against humanity and similar grave human rights violations in a post-conflict setting under transitional justice. The hidden issue is that arguments about international tribunals and truth and reconciliation commissions were largely shaped by events starting with the overthrow of authoritarian military regimes in 1970s Latin America, carried forward through the 1990s in post–Cold War Eastern Europe under the rubric of transitional justice. The problem is how well such institutions forged in the West operate in the non-Western world's noninternational armed conflicts projected for the next 20+ years to predominate.

We aspire to understanding what is actually happening, hence the idea that the international legal community's strong focus on internationalized tribunals since the 1990s (ICC or International Criminal Court,[1] ICTY or International Criminal Tribunal for the former Yugoslavia,[2] and ICTR or International Criminal Tribunal for Rwanda[3]) may be misplaced since, judging by state practice, local tribunals, and truth and reconciliation commissions predominate. Traditional approaches to transitional justice decried "impunity," pushing norm creation under international criminal law, while argument has now descended to both oddly instrumentalist views of "justice" and more technical arguments about the nature of international law (e.g., arguments about amnesties covering *jus cogens* offenses, or the so-called peremptory norms typically violated in atrocities). There is also a notable omission from the transitional justice paradigm, namely any attention to the constitutional or internal political process that typically accompanies the ferment of a society in transition. So what is going on?

TRANSITIONAL JUSTICE: HISTORY AND APPROACHES

Transitional justice refers to the concept of accountability for past mass atrocity or human rights abuses in countries emerging from repressive rule or armed conflict, whether in the form of emergence from authoritarian government, or a real or feared insurgency or civil war. The concept of international versus noninternational armed conflict is a distinction rooted more in the law of armed conflict[4] than human rights, but serves as useful reminder that we are concerned with problems within a single state and society, which are reachable via human rights discourse only in positing a broader international community.[5] Mass atrocities and human rights abuses may also occur in international armed conflict (e.g., crimes against humanity in World War II or ethnic cleansing in the former Yugoslavia), but typically fall outside the scope of transitional justice, which aims to address the troubles of a single country. Accountability is itself a flexible concept, since it can encompass, beyond legal responsibility, also political or historical responsibility, which may in turn address both questions of "justice" for victims looking backward and "peace" for society looking forward.

There are at least four institutional approaches theoretically available for accountability, namely: (a) an international tribunal applying international law (such as the ICC ; "mixed" tribunals such as the SCSL or Special Court for Sierra Leone tend seemingly to become distant international courts, as with the SCSL transfer of the Charles Taylor proceedings to the ICC in the Hague[6]), (b) a domestic tribunal applying international or domestic law (such as Saddam Hussein's trial, described in another chapter), (c) a nonjudicial truth and reconciliation commission (which could be local, international, or mixed, although local seemingly is the predominant form[7]), and (d) via universal jurisdiction civil suits in other countries (such as under the Belgian statute, or the U.S. Alien Tort Claims Act, as with the antiapartheid cases). The approaches are not entirely mutually exclusive and serve different purposes, but after circa 25 years of practical experience are accompanied by considerable intellectual baggage reflecting different currents under the general rubrics of democracy, human rights, and rule of law. We shall concentrate mostly on the juxtaposition of international tribunals versus truth and reconciliation commissions.

International tribunals customarily invoke the Nuremburg proceedings post–World War II as lineage, but reflect in fact the growth of the concept of international criminal law reaching not much further back than the 1980s. The ICC was established in 2002 under the Rome Treaty as standing international tribunal in large part in opposition to the temporary character of the Nuremburg Tribunal. However, its way was paved substantially by the ICTY established in 1993 to address war crimes and similar offenses associated with the armed conflicts that accompanied the breakup of Yugoslavia as multiethnic state, and the ICTR established in 1994 following the Rwandan genocide. The ICTY and ICTR were constituted under UN Security Council Chapter VII resolutions, while the ICC was created by the Rome Treaty which, however, ultimately met United States opposition.

The Yugoslavian conflict was technically an international war, but grew out of still ongoing ethnic secessions,[8] so to that extent looked more like a long-running series of civil wars entailing both war crimes and crimes against humanity in the context of ethnic cleansing. Rwanda involved instead a genocide as crime against humanity, tied to differing tribal and ethnic groups, and reflected traditional tensions triggered by events. Both implicitly reflected perceived failures of the international community to undertake operations in the nature of humanitarian intervention, however, itself a sometimes disputed concept under jus ad bellum. To the extent it is possible to assign provenance, the ICC, ICTY, and ICTR are post-conflict creatures arising largely on the armed conflict law side (international humanitarian law).

The truth and reconciliation commission concept, on the other hand, is anchored traditionally more in democracy and human rights concerns associated with authoritarian regime change. The traditional model involves mastering the transition from military to civilian rule where there is a history of violent repression and a weak rule of law (e.g., forced "disappearing" of social or political activists opposed to authoritarian rule). Low-grade insurgencies may be involved, but they tended initially to be ideologically motivated (and to reflect Cold War politics of the left and right in Latin America, but in Africa more often ethnic tensions including South Africa's racially based experience). The truth and reconciliation commission model arguably exists in opposition to domestic criminal trials under domestic law. The crimes involved might also constitute gross human rights violations, but are typically criminalized domestically under ordinary criminal law since extrajudicial executions almost invariably constitute garden variety murder under local criminal law, and torture is covered similarly.

What is missing from normal discussions of transitional justice, as opposed to discussions of states or governments in transition (democratization), is a focus on the formal remaking of such a society's governing principles in constitutional terms. There is an immense literature on democratization and constitutionalism, particularly in the Eastern European context, but the procedural literature on how best to create or revise a constitution in the midst of social turmoil is mostly remarkable by its absence in conceptualizing transitional justice. This oddity may be explained in at least three ways. First, in the original Latin American setting,

> "[A] common quandary defined most Latin American countries' democratic transitions and framed the central dilemma of transitional justice two decades ago: Although military juntas had formally ceded political power to democratically elected governments, armed forces continued to occupy an autonomous realm of power with the potential for imperiling their countries' fragile transition if the new government breached their citadel of impunity."[9]

Seemingly, the assumption was that power relationships controlled over formal democracy (at least in the sense of a veto), so that presumably the domestic legal situation or institutions were ignored as unimportant because of the perceived impunity. Beyond ignoring any budding constitutional process, this approach assumed that local judicial institutions were simply inadequate to the task, so that the available choices in terms of policy responses were either an international tribunal, or nonjudicial truth and reconciliation commission as second best choice (because it was perceived commonly as a social but not legal measure, leaving the armed services' citadel intact).

Second, to the extent the focus ex ante was on (internationalized) tribunals and judicial process rather than political process, disregarding the implied impunity veto, the goal was to create a rights-based, judicialized approach formally separated from the local or even international political process. One collateral issue was the extent to which the (international) judicial process itself was desirable as a way of anchoring, otherwise theoretical human rights norms in recognizable "practice" (an interest of activists at the level of the international human rights community, as opposed to individual victims seeking specific recourse within the society in transition).

Truth and reconciliation commissions, as nonjudicial institutions and inheritors of the international law tradition of factually based commissions of inquiry, simply looked more political and provided few opportunities to push the envelope in creating new "norms." Even the successful conclusion of their task generally left open what, beyond the arguably cathartic exercise of acknowledging past bad acts, should be done with the newly (re) gained specific knowledge of a nation's dark history. It was often acknowledged in the early stages that a truth and reconciliation commission's activities did not formally exclude prosecutions for misdeeds uncovered by its investigations, but in practice, follow-up prosecutions were exceedingly rare (categorized as de facto versus de jure amnesties).[10] So again, any political process would be conceived of as undercutting a "rights analysis," with the result that it was presumably disfavored where it might interfere with the rights-based analysis in its traditional sense at the core of human rights theory of allowing individuals to challenge their own government also under international law.

Third, development and democracy practitioners working in post-conflict states have stressed "rule of law"[11] as the philosopher's stone, even while in practice, they stress localized measures to achieve it like courts and truth and reconciliation commissions both as tools rather than ends in themselves.[12] At one level, the presumed conflict is submerged by the ad hoc language of unique, country-specific models and tool bags. On another level, the problem in stressing democracy and politics is indeed, what to do if the political process yielded an unimpeachable good-faith decision (as arguably was the case in South Africa in introducing amnesty proceedings into the truth and reconciliation commission process) on the local level in which a decision is made to remove all future legal responsibility from perpetrators of grave human rights abuses? The original presumption of transitional justice theory quoted above was based on the concept of impunity, that local legal and political institutions simply continued to be at the mercy of hulking human rights violators (who might theoretically unleash havoc if their interests were threatened). But if amnesties or pardons came on an uncoerced basis out of a truly democratic local political process, that undercut the whole idea that truth and reconciliation commissions were just a second best option. The unanswered question was why the parties might opt for the nonjudicial approach other than arguments about the local judiciary's inadequacy; meanwhile, South Africa was recognized as possessing a strong judiciary.

This quandary is what has led over time to seemingly technical arguments covering the effectiveness of amnesties of *jus cogens* offenses in the transitional justice setting. There was an early, doubtful practice in Latin America of governments effectively amnestying themselves. However, the ultimate issue is whether the well-considered amnesty by legitimate political authorities not acting under any undue influence, but simply as part of a global political settlement, should be allowed to extinguish perpetrators' legal responsibility, or whether international criminal law means that the international legal community can still prosecute these matters, regardless of the local political settlement (under an erga omnes or similar approach).[13]

The precise treatment of amnesties was sufficiently controversial so that it was expressly omitted from the Rome Treaty creating the ICC (because of differences of opinion among the state parties). This is particularly significant to the extent that the Rome Treaty goes beyond creation of the tribunal to treat the substance of the criminal law to be applied, and at the same time renders arguments about customary law recognizing a duty not to amnesty *jus cogens* offenses as doubtful. The dispute has grown technically beyond the original impunity claims within local society, to the extent there are now inconsistent judicial decisions on the validity of amnesties under international law by the ICT as international court, the SCSL as mixed tribunal, and the Supreme Court of South Africa.[14] This leaves open the comparison to the traditional question of subsidiarity and the proper relationship between states making law and the UN Security Council and International Court of Justice in interpreting international law in resolving threats to international peace. To that extent, rather than technical issues like the nature of *jus cogens* offenses (with collateral effects on purported amnesties), the real concerns involve judicialization of international law and the primacy of judicial versus political institutions for purposes of maintaining international peace.

INSTRUMENTALIST JUSTICE AND THE GOALS OF (INTERNATIONAL) CRIMINAL LAW

The underlying problem in opposing international tribunals to truth and reconciliation commissions in transitional justice may be a disagreement about the concept of justice itself, a topic addressed analogously in a parallel chapter concerning Saddam Hussein's trial and execution. At a very basic level, the international tribunals approach is rooted in ideas about retributive justice tied to the human rights concept itself, while the nonjudicial truth and reconciliation commission approach largely embraces restorative justice. Translating that into the language of the criminal law and sanctions, the international tribunals retributive strain is focused on punishment as a matter of morals and justice (just desserts), while the truth and reconciliation commission approach is focused on utilitarian concerns in restoring society to its preoffense state (via publicity if not formal sanctions, specific and general deterrence, rehabilitation, and social incapacitation).

Hidden behind the concepts of justice as individual right versus right order, already explored in conjunction with Saddam Hussein's trial, are ideas about a new state or social order to be, the goals of criminal law or sanctions, plus a standing question in terms of whether the correct party in interest in the analysis of the transitional justice situation is the individual victim, or whether it is society at large trying to make a successful transition. It could be recast in terms of collective versus individual rights claims, but is subject to clearer analysis in examining criminal law and sanction goals overlaid over the judicial tribunal versus the nonjudicial truth and reconciliation commission. The material difference between retributive and restorative justice in this context is the extent to which the former looks backward, while the later looks forward. Here there is a hidden link also to issues of the ongoing constitutional or internal political process running in parallel in a society or state in transition, which we already noted was curiously absent from the transitional justice concept as formal matter. The efforts on the constitutional level are perhaps best understood as efforts in the direction of the "right order" concept itself as formal legal matter. So where do criminal law concepts like individual responsibility fit, as the focus shifts between interests of individual victims, society's interest in transition, and retributive versus restorative justice?

Argumentation within transitional justice circles has tended to muddy the distinctions between backward versus forward-looking retributive and restorative justice. Human rights proponents of international tribunals have tried to make the case that prosecution of grave human rights violations serves forward looking purposes such as deterrence and creating the rule of law,[15] under the general rubric of "no peace without justice" (meaning leaving grave human rights violators unpunished in the midst of society would preclude any real social peace). They also have rarely pressed beyond rhetoric for comprehensive prosecutions of all offenders, instead focusing on leadership prosecutions in the image of the Nuremburg proceedings (e.g., in the current SCSL proceedings).

This in itself would be inconsistent with a pure retributive justice approach, to the extent just desserts as moral justice would seemingly require broad prosecutions. On the other hand, focusing on relatively few, high-level prosecutions may be the most effective approach to undergirding human rights norms in practice, theoretically distinguishing between general and special deterrence. Questions aside about deterrence as empirical proposition, the difficulty is that selective, symbolic prosecutions themselves are hard to reconcile with criminal law claims about individual responsibility, not to mention problems with the principle of legality mandating prosecutions where possible.[16] To that extent, the human rights community's pressure for the ICC itself in opposition to impunity has hardly registered the differences between Anglo-American criminal law's structural aspects like prosecutorial discretion and international criminal law's drawing more upon Continental legal science, as visible in the Rome Treaty itself.

Standard criminal law theory stresses the separate interests of both the victim and the state in any prosecution. Analogous argumentation is followed typically also in analyzing how an amnesty issued by a state itself should only be valid for domestic law purposes, because the international community is considered a party whose interests are implicated in the parallel international law offense based upon a grave human rights or similar *jus cogens* violation. The problem is that amnesty or pardon powers in domestic law are equally dismissive of victim interests, while arguments seemingly paralleling double jeopardy sovereignty analysis seem overly formalistic. So the real question is who are the true parties in interest, and which should take precedence.

Recast in terms of the purposes of criminal law or sanctions, the complex issue is that retributive and utilitarian or restorative ideals themselves may be focused on different parties in interest, moving between the individual victim and society (or the international community, for purposes of human rights). Traditionally, retributive justice is conceptualized as a violation leading to a social imbalance, whether specifically a loss on the victim's part, or more broadly a disturbance in the social fabric, which is offset by punishment as a matter of morality or justice. But it seems chiefly to be viewed in terms of impact of the offense on the victim, and punishment should be in proportion to the loss inflicted. In that sense, the grave human rights violation will presumably be judged in terms of impact on the victim, since in classic liberal terms, it is ultimately the violation of the victim's autonomy which constitutes the social loss. Even if there is a corresponding social loss, it seems relatively less because the loss would be measured in terms of effect on the victim.

On the other hand, utilitarian theories of criminal law and sanctions offer a more mixed perspective. We separate them in the classic categories of specific and general deterrence, rehabilitation, and incapacitation. Insofar as general deterrence aims to deter other potential violators, the benefit seems strong at the social level, but fairly weak at the victim level. Theoretically, the victim might avoid being revictimized by a different perpetrator as member of society generally, but if the violations are so widespread that lightning effectively strikes the same victim twice, then general deterrence seems a failure anyway. Specific deterrence of the individual perpetrator seems also to be more of general benefit to society than the victim, unless the potential repeated violation was perceived as likely directed against the victim individually. However, that seems unlikely insofar as the typical gross human rights violation is understood in practice as a violation directed against a stranger (e.g., violence against persons from other ethnic groups or tribes, on the example of genocide).

Incapacitation would work similarly, to the extent it simply removes the violator from society, rather than leaving the violator in society but hoping him sufficiently deterred that the offense is not repeated. Rehabilitation is really aimed at the perpetrator anyway, so that society in general again benefits the most presumably in the general safety that the grave human rights violation is not repeated. The general outlook for utilitarian uses of the criminal sanction is that they target benefits to society much more than the individual victim, so that presumably any approach following utilitarian lines would almost invariably find greater interests in society rather than in the victim.

Restorative justice can be understood also in procedural terms (e.g., victim and perpetrator meeting to attempt a reconciliation of sorts). It differs from analysis of the criminal sanction, if for no other reason than the idea that victim-oriented, restorative justice is typically understood as alternative to sanctioning the offender in the domestic criminal law setting. So, rather than paying a fine to the state, the thief may make restitution to his victim. The problem in the domestic criminal law setting is that restorative justice approaches paying special attention to the victim in restoring the social fabric seem much commoner for minor crimes (e.g., property crimes like theft) than major crimes of violence approximating gross human rights violations (e.g., murder or torture). So, in some cases, restorative justice may also be more oriented towards individual victim than societal interests. But is there a difference to justify potentially differing views of the relative importance of the community's versus individual victim interests in approaching grave human rights violations as offenses under international law?

The answer may lie in the idea that the individual offense in domestic criminal law assumes a different, and intact, society in which the crime is viewed by all as aberration. On the other hand, the grave human rights violation in the transitional justice context may be wrong, but it typically reflects a widespread pattern of behavior (e.g., genocide will distinguish itself from a single murder in being widespread and systematic). Were there no widespread pattern of behavior, there would be an individual case as opposed to a society-wide transitional justice issue. To stop the widespread behavior is not exactly deterrence, but it arguably is utilitarian, whence the argument that peace may be more important than punishment (which we would associate with retributive justice).

If we look back now upon the distinction between international tribunals versus truth and reconciliation commissions, we see that the ideas of justice itself differ between the two. International tribunals serve retributive justice, while truth and reconciliation commissions look more suitable for utilitarian ideals or restorative justice. The problem is that the interests of individual victims arguably are given priority under retributive justice, hence might favor international tribunals. On the other hand, the interests of society are seemingly paramount under restorative or utilitarian approaches to justice. For better or worse, whose interests take precedence when a choice is necessary? A victim may prefer retributive to restorative justice based upon what they consider a personal wrong, but does society's interest or their individual claim control? In theory, the criminal law recognizes no private punishments, so the more weight that is placed upon victims' demands for "justice" implying retribution to be a claim of right, the less the entire process resembles criminal law serving public rather than private interests.[17]

There is a tendency to conceive of the individual victim's claims in terms of (human) rights, whereas the social good is presumably a peaceful and successful transition. Arguments based solely on the international community's interest in the assertion of human rights violations seem misplaced, to the extent they implicitly assume that the international community has no serious counterbalancing interest in the peaceful and successful transition (easily translatable into traditional ideas of international peace and security). To the extent proponents of international tribunals over truth and reconciliation commissions reach for arguments beyond retributive justice (deterrence, etc.), they seemingly arrive where social interests in fact predominate over victim interests, which pushes the balance in favor of truth and reconciliation commissions.

To the extent they argue that there is room for both international tribunals and truth and reconciliation commissions, they need to more clearly confront the issue that they may be based upon differing ideas of justice, and address the implicit question whether they may interfere with each other as a result.[18] Just pushing for the primacy of international tribunals may be problematic in the post-conflict setting, so the disproportionate level of attention and investment of resources since the 1990s in international tribunals may be a distraction if the actual desired outcome is international peace. We now pick up the theme, employing the case of South Africa, of how constitutional and similar concerns fit with transitional justice.

SOUTH AFRICA AND THE BROADER FRAMEWORK

South Africa is recognized as one of the leading examples of truth and reconciliation commissions, of particular interest to us for three reasons. First, South Africa contains all the elements of a broader transitional setting, including selective amnesty of gross human rights violations commonly considered *jus cogens* offenses (starting with apartheid itself, argued to be a crime against humanity) as well as a parallel constitutional process culminating in its 1996 constitution.[19] Second, a political settlement was achieved ending a de facto insurgency cum dirty war, which opted for a well-resourced truth and reconciliation commission to document gross human rights violations committed by all sides for all reasons in the period 1960–94. The TRCSA (Truth and Reconciliation Commission of South Africa) Report[20] documented all sides of the conflict, from the individual victims' and from the institutional and social points of view, interviewed in excess of 20,000 witnesses in public proceedings all over South Africa, made reparations recommendations, and issued a significant number of amnesties for full disclosure in public hearings. Third, the new South African government has, as a matter of policy, rejected all attempts outside South Africa by any party to pursue any claim of legal responsibility for any of these acts.

The transformational process, lasting from the January–February 1990 talks between then President de Klerk and Nelson Mandela to the April–May 1994 democratic election and inauguration of President Mandela as leader of a national unity government, provides the political background for the TRCSA on three levels. First, in contemporary eyes, the negotiated transition in government avoided a very real possibility of civil war. Second, the November–December 1993 Interim Constitution provided in principle for amnesties as well as a truth and reconciliation commission, which political settlement was thought necessary to avoid the civil war.[21] Third, the transition process itself was conceived of as constitutional exercise in which the South African state was to be remade in a fully democratic, multiracial image, but as practical matter, the formal constitutional process to create the new South Africa and the truth and reconciliation process had to run in parallel. The final constitution was not finished until December 1996, while the TRCSA was created by Parliament in July 1995, but its constituent amnesty provisions actually predate the April–May 1994 democratic election that led to South Africa's formal shift in power. The overlapping processes are visible in the chronology itself, while the idea that amnesty was also a subject of (interim) constitutional attention infers the underlying conflict that pressing on judicial proceedings had the potential to derail the constitutional process itself. Thus, most would view the new democratic South Africa to be created as part of the constitutional process as important enough at the social level to justify detriment to individuals (balancing concerns about the relative interests of the society or international community, versus potential detriment to individual victims).

The TRCSA was created under the Promotion of National Unity and Reconciliation Act No. 34 of 1995,[22] and incorporated a Committee on Human Rights Violations, a Committee on Amnesty, and a Committee on Reparations. There were again at least three interlocking concepts as visible in its constituent committees. The Committee on Human

Rights Violations grew out of the conviction that truth-telling was necessary to achieve national unity and morally acceptable reconciliation (in the words of then Justice Minister Dullah Omar). The Committee on Amnesty was interlinked to the extent it was felt that the truth would be substantially furthered by a selective amnesty process covering only fully disclosed actions (paralleling the concern that criminal trials would not be an effective means of uncovering factual events). The amnesty possibility itself was sharply criticized, then challenged in court by victim's representatives such as those of murdered activist Steve Biko, but the 1995 Act's amnesty provisions were upheld by the South African Constitutional Court.[23]

To the extent the Committee on Amnesty was viewed as benefiting perpetrators, the Committee on Reparations was considered to benefit victims, many of whom were relatively impoverished and had pending civil cases seeking damages against the former government security forces (for support, evidencing local views that domestic South African courts were actually strong and suitable for "justice" actions). As witnessed by the Constitutional Court challenge, the amnesty possibility itself was not uncontroversial.[24] The amnesty proceedings themselves were commonly considered to have taken on a religious tone in terms of reconciliation[25] (remembering that Archbishop Desmond Tutu was the leading public figure in the Committee on Amnesty), even though opinions on ultimate reconciliation of victims and survivors were mixed.[26] It is not entirely accurate to say that victims had no recourse, to the extent some monetary compensation was available for victim losses (a measure of restorative justice, although the TRCSA recommended a financial grant of approximately $375 million be awarded to 22,000 victims identified through the TRCSA process, yet the South African government funded only a single payment of approximately $74 million). The financial compensation paid amounted to less than 20 percent of the recommended amount, even while victims might have felt themselves denied retributive justice in the inability to pursue criminal prosecution following amnesties.

Finally, we return to our initial mapping of four institutional approaches theoretically available for accountability (international tribunal, domestic tribunal, truth and reconciliation commission, and universal jurisdiction civil suits in third party countries) as relevant to the South African experience. Reaching back to the 1979 leading case of *Filartiga v Pena-Irala,*[27] in which a former Paraguayan government torturer was successfully sued for damages by a deceased victim's relatives under the ATCA (Alien Tort Claims Act), U.S. federal courts have on occasion provided a forum for transitional justice cases under universal jurisdiction in the form of ATCA lawsuits based on violations of public international law, typically charging grave human rights violations.

In the 2002 consolidated multidistrict apartheid litigation, ATCA claims were brought against multinational banks and corporations doing business in South Africa on the basis of their claimed complicity in apartheid (e.g., a computer company providing IT services used to administer apartheid's pass laws), and the South African government opposed such law suits on the basis that:

> "[W]e consider it completely unacceptable that matters that are central to the future of our country should be adjudicated in foreign courts which bear no responsibility for the well-being of our country and the observance of the perspective contained in our Constitution on the promotion of national reconciliation."[28]

The U.S. government through the Office of the Legal Adviser at the Department of State joined in South Africa's request that the litigation be dismissed.[29] The district court dismissed the ATCA apartheid lawsuit,[30] and, while the case is still on appeal in the Second Circuit, the U.S. Supreme Court heard its first modern ATCA case *Sosa v. Alvarez-Machain* in 2004.[31] The ATCA apartheid litigation was argued by amici to the Supreme Court in *Sosa,* and the Court seemingly indicated approval of the dismissal since South Africa had elected for the forward-looking truth and reconciliation commission approach over victor's justice style premised on Nuremburg,[32] particularly where the Executive Branch took a position on the foreign policy matters in question.[33] The appeal is still pending in the Second Circuit perhaps because, in opposition to the ANC-led South African government, which opposed with Executive Branch support the ATCA lawsuit, former members of the TRCSA have now filed a brief in support of the ATCA plaintiffs, basically arguing that since multinational businesses largely did not participate in the TRCSA process, they should not be entitled to claim the equivalent of an amnesty without having made full disclosure. Meanwhile, the substance of the apartheid ATCA case is now wrapped up in larger symbolic and legal questions of a broader business "complicity" human rights argument that multinational corporations doing business in countries with repressive regimes should be responsible via something beyond traditional aider and abettor liability (e.g., multinational oil companies drilling for oil in Sudan's Darfur region in the midst of an argued genocide). So the former TRCSA representatives of South African civil society on behalf of apartheid victims are now at odds with the new ANC-led South African government effectively on who should control the process of dealing with the legacy of apartheid, and in this particular case, whether the proper mechanism even lies outside South Africa.[34]

The entire South African constitutional process was extremely open, and it incorporated in principle the concepts of amnesty and the truth and reconciliation approach. Further, South Africa enjoyed a high-quality judiciary with a relatively high reputation still across the population in the 1990s, so that it would be inaccurate to describe the selection of the truth and reconciliation commission approach over tribunals as a conscious second best option. The new South African government in the form of the ANC was itself a victim of apartheid, so that we are not looking at the traditional suspect circumstances of a (Latin American) government amnestying itself in opting for a truth and reconciliation commission approach. Instead, a democratically elected government as part of a general constitutional transition process has asserted its overwhelming social interest in controlling alone prospectively the development of a new South Africa. And it made a choice, embedded in the very constitutional process that led to the creation of a new South Africa, for the truth and reconciliation approach and against what the South African government terms a Nuremburg-style tribunal. Some prosecutions have been carried out against apartheid era security personnel (when the TRCSA was active in processing amnesty applications, many of them were submitted from prison by such middle and lower level security personnel), but in the specific area of business responsibility, the new South African government articulated a clear policy decision for de facto amnesty in the interests of future economic development.

The TRCSA process itself was exemplary, so that to a great extent, the current disputes visible in areas like the ATCA apartheid litigation concern who controls and what should be done after the truth and reconciliation commission process has yielded up its work product. To that extent, the new South African government's view is all forward looking and utilitarian at the social level, while the former TRCSA itself and leaders of South African civil society disagree with their own government in asserting victims' interests in receiving more compensation. The visible differences of opinion seemingly represent a classic case of a government making hard (political) choices, which decisions victims and human rights activists seek to avoid in an international forum. Either the former TRCSA members and civil society groups believe that there is an entitlement to individual compensation taking precedence over social interests, or they believe that they more truly represent South Africa than their own government.

The agency problem is palpable, as human rights and civil society activists on behalf of the victims have set themselves up in opposition to the new South African government's considered political decisions concerning the direction and control of the new South Africa. Beyond the agency issue seemingly lie differing ideas about justice itself (retributive versus restorative or utilitarian approaches), and how properly to balance the retrospective views of victims against society's prospective interests.

Looking specifically at the issue of non-Western application of the (international) tribunal versus truth and reconciliation approaches, what may be visible in South Africa and relatively more pronounced in parts of Africa, Asia, and the Islamic world is a much stronger sense of nationalism, regionalism, or ideas like religious communities than in the West. So there is a natural tendency towards cultural relativism on the human rights doctrinal level, and corresponding suspicion of motivations behind Western activism, also in transitional justice, premised on universalism. To that extent, there is a significant question whether the non-Western states would accept the premise of a single international community in areas like human rights, while the Asians look to their Asian peers, and the Africans look to their African peers.

Cultural arguments aside, while there is relatively widespread accession to the ICC's Rome Treaty in sub-Saharan Africa, there are relatively few accessions to the Rome Treaty, and almost none among major states, in the Islamic world or Asia. So if predictions are realized that armed conflicts will be typically noninternational and mostly centered in the non-Western world over the next 25+ years, it seems unlikely that international tribunals will have the same prominence enjoyed since the 1990s in the post-conflict setting. Instead, it would seem that the likelier outcome will be increased use of the truth and reconciliation commission approach, or domestic tribunals, focused more on reconstituting local societies politically rather than affirming the international community's international judicialization of post-conflict solutions. But this may also be viewed as a positive development, to the extent South Africa demonstrates that the truth and reconciliation commission option is not necessarily a second best choice. In the interim, the problem is the extent to which the rhetoric and focus on international tribunals since the 1990s may concentrate on the wrong processes looking forward.

NOTES

1. ICC, http://www.icc-cpi.int/ (accessed July 29, 2007).
2. ICTY, http://www.un.org/icty/ (accessed July 29, 2007).
3. ICTR, http://69.94.11.53/ (accessed July 29, 2007).
4. Such issues are addressed more technically in parallel chapters, but international armed conflict law is well established largely in treaty form (Geneva Conventions, etc.), while noninternational armed conflict law is more reliant on customary law. Some international humanitarian law experts take the basic position that the international armed conflict law treaty rules have become now customary law for noninternational armed conflict law, see Jean-Marie Henckaerts and Louise Doswald-Beck, eds., *Customary International Humanitarian Law* (Cambridge: Cambridge University, 2005) (ICRC report). However, the United States would not subscribe to that theory as witnessed by disagreements about combatant status and similar issues. As a technical matter,

nonstate actors such as al Qaeda participating in noninternational armed conflict are largely not covered by treaty rules aimed at international armed conflict, which is why the characterization of Afghanistan and Iraq as international or noninternational armed conflicts as terms of art matter.

5. The UN Security Council has in the last decade expanded its jurisdiction under Chapter VII in seeing threats to international peace and security also in civil wars that would have traditionally been regarded as purely internal matters. This raises issues at a certain level about the United Nations' growing involvement in intrastate affairs, but we simply note the relevance of this changed view for noninternational wars without exploring the broader issues presented by this interpretation.

6. See Katy Glassborow, "Turf War Over Charles Taylor Case," Global Policy Forum (Institute for Peace and War Reporting, March 23, 2007), http://www.globalpolicy.org/intljustice/tribunals/sierra/2007/0323turfwar.htm (accessed July 29, 2007).

7. See generally Priscilla B. Hayner, *Unspeakable Truths: Confronting State Terror and Atrocity* (New York: Routledge, 2001), 32–71, 219–20; Office of the UN High Commissioner for Human Rights, *Rule-of-Law Tools for Post-Conflict States: Truth Commissions* (New York: UN, 2006), http://www.ohchr.org/english/about/publications/docs/ruleoflaw-TruthCommissions_en.pdf (accessed July 29, 2007).

8. Following the Dayton Accords the continuing status of Kosovo as part of Serbia was left open, but the general consensus is that it will eventually achieve independence following the wishes of its ethnic Albanian majority.

9. Diane F. Orentlicher, "Settling Accounts Revisited: Reconciling Global Norms with Local Agency," *International Journal of Transitional Justice* (Oxford Journals) 1 (2007): 10, 11.

10. This changed with the South African Truth and Reconciliation Commission, to the extent its proceedings incorporated a formal amnesty for admission procedure.

11. The question of what is the rule of law is more open than most scholars would admit, since it is a veritable Rohrsach test for some, typically within groups pushing democracy, who think it implies liberal politics in the Western sense, as opposed to many modernizing developing countries who see in it a better set of rules to coordinate economic policy, but who would reject Western liberal politics. See Randall Peerenboom, "Human Rights and Rule of Law: What's the Relationship," *Georgetown Journal of International Law* 36 (2005): 809, for examples. The same problem replays itself on the human rights front, since much of the universalism vs. cultural relativism debate tended in that direction. As simple thought experiment, consider on-going "creeping Islamization" in many significant developing countries and debates about the introduction or influence of sharia law (without getting into precisely what "sharia law" means). Introduction of rule of (sharia) law would not commonly be accepted as "rule of law" by most non-Islamic scholars who talk about the rule of law. Similarly, within Asia, China and Vietnam as formal socialist states recognize the primacy of the party, even while they develop courts and attempt legal reforms on the commercial side following WTO entry. It is a commonplace admission in Asian law circles that the ultimate question in countries like China and Vietnam is whether they can successfully develop commercial law and courts in the name of economic development, even while they are not eager, for example, to develop an independent constitutional court (with halfway houses including approaches modeled on the French Conseil de l'Etat as executive body deemed to be also a court). Hong Kong people have discovered the difference in the form of the view that the People's Congress in Beijing is the ultimate authorized interpreter of the Basic Law, as opposed to the judiciary.

12. See Office of the UN High Commissioner for Human Rights, *Rule-of-Law Tools for Post-Conflict States: Truth Commissions* (New York: UN, 2006), 5–6, http://www.ohchr.org/english/about/publications/docs/ruleoflaw-TruthCommissions_en.pdf (accessed July 29, 2007).

13. Positions seem to be changing, since the second generation of transitional justice scholars reject the effectiveness of a jus cogens offense amnesty on international tribunals, see Leila Nadya Sadat, "Exile, Amnesty and International Law," *Notre Dame Law Review* 81 (2006): 955, while the first generation now appear willing to accept it, see Orentlicher, "'Settling Accounts' Revisited," 10, 13–22 (treatment of Lord's Resistance Army leadership in ending its long-running Nigerian insurrection).

14. See Leila Nadya Sadat, "Exile, Amnesty and International Law," *Notre Dame Law Review* 81 (2006): 955.

15. Ruth Teitel, "From Dictatorship to Democracy: The Role of Transitional Justice" in *Deliberative Democracy & Human Rights,* eds. Harold Hongju Koh and Ronald C. Slye (New Haven, CT: Yale University, 1999), 272–73.

16. Compare George P. Fletcher, *Basic Concepts of Criminal Law* (Oxford: Oxford University, 1998), 206–11. Fletcher has separately criticized human rights oriented scholarship proposing criminalization of customary law violations for international tribunals as paying insufficient attention to criminal law principles generally. See George P. Fletcher and Jens David Ohlin, "Reclaiming Fundamental Principles of Criminal Law in the Dafur Case," *Journal of International Criminal Justice* 3 (2005): 539.

17. More of the pressure has been associated with argumentation that a duty exists to prosecute human rights violators, see Dianne F. Orentlicher, "Settling Accounts: The Duty to Prosecute Human Rights Violations of a Prior Regime," *Yale Law Journal* 100 (1991): 2537, with the case for a truth and reconciliation approach made in return, see Carlos Nino, "The Duty to Punish Past Abuses of Human Rights Put into Context: The Case of Argentina," *Yale Law Journal* 100 (1991): 2619. But in fact the mandatory prosecution argument is normally made in opposition to the truth and reconciliation commission approach, rather than doing nothing as option.

18. Martha Minow, *Between Vengeance and Forgiveness: Facing History after Genocide and Mass Violence* (Boston: Beacon Press, 1998), 89.

19. Concerning the broader framework of South African developments see T.R.H. Davenport, *The Birth of a New South Africa: The 1995 Joanne Goodman Lectures* (Toronto: University of Toronto, 1998).

20. *Truth and Reconciliation Commission of South Africa Report* (Basingstoke: Macmillan Reference, 1998) (five volumes, see especially volume 2 for the commission of gross human rights violations on the part of all parties to the conflict, volume 3 for the victims' perspective, and volume 4 for the nature of the society in which the gross violations of human rights took place).

21. Kenneth Christie, *The South African Truth Commission* (New York: St. Martin's, 2000), 120–41.

22. Republic of South Africa, *Government Gazette,* vol. 361, no. 16579 (Capetown), July 26, 1995.

23. *Azanian People's Organization v. President of the Republic of South Africa,* Case Constitutional Court 17.96, Constitutional Court of South Africa, July 25, 1996; Casenote, *American Journal of International Law* 91 (1997): 360.

24. Kenneth Christie, *The South African Truth Commission* (New York: St. Martin's, 2000), 120–41.

25. Andre du Toit speaking for The Human Rights Program Harvard Law School and World Peace Foundation, *Truth Commissions: A Comparative Assessment* (Boston: Harvard Law School Human Rights Program, 1997), 20 (Andre du Toit).

26. Christie, *South African Truth Commission,* 142–72.

27. 630 F.2d 876 (2d Cir.1980).

28. Letter of South African Minister of Foreign Affairs Nkosozana Dlamini Zuma to US Secretary of State Colin Powell, May 22, 2002, quoting South African President's statement to Parliament on the tabling of the Truth and Reconciliation Commission of South Africa Report, http://www.nftc.org/default/ussabc/DAE8515.pdf (accessed July 29, 2007); Letter and Declaration of South African Minister of Justice PM Maduna, July 11, 2003, sent to the presiding District Court Judge, affirming the South African President's statement as the position of the South African government, http://www.nftc.org/default/ussabc/Maduna%20Declaration.pdf (accessed July 29, 2007).

29. See Letter of William H. Taft, IV, Legal Adviser, Department of State, October 27, 2003, Appendix A & Declaration of the Government of South Africa, July 11, 2003, Appendix B, Amicus Curiae Brief of the Governments of Australia, Switzerland and the United Kingdom,

Sosa v. Alvarez-Machain (January 23, 2004, Supreme Court Docket 03-339), http://www.sdshh.com /Alvarez/Sosa%20Brief%20Final.pdf (accessed July 29, 2007).

30. *In re South African Apartheid Litigation,* 346 F. Supp.2d 538 (SDNY 2004).

31. 542 U.S. 692 (2004).

32. Ibid. at 733, fn 21.

33. While dismissing an ATCA claim is played out in terms of deference to the executive branch in the area of foreign affairs, the judicialization issues associated with ATCA are in many ways analogous to the choice between (judicial) tribunal and (nonjudicial) truth and reconciliation commission insofar as it represents a choice for the legal as opposed to political approaches in the international law and affairs setting. Much of the pending Second Circuit argument tries to avoid the embarrassing Supreme Court language in claiming an insufficient basis for the dismissal at the joint request of the South African and U.S. governments. See Brief of Amici Curiae Professors of International and Constitutional Law in Support of Plaintiffs and Seeking Reversal of the Decision Below, 05-2141 and 05-2326 in the US Court of Appeals for the Second Circuit, August 29, 2005, http://www.sdshh.com/Apartheid/pdfs/Brief_Professors_of_Const.pdf (accessed July 29, 2007).

34. See Christelle Terreblanche, "TRC Joins Fight as Apartheid Victims and State Clash," *The Sunday Independent,* January 22, 2006, http://www.sundayindependent.co.za/index.php? fSectionId=1042&fArticleId=3076415 (accessed July 29, 2007).

APPENDIX

"Religion, Ethics, and Armed Conflict Law: Afghanistan, Iraq, and the War on Terror"

AUTHOR PANEL AND ROUNDTABLE DISCUSSION TRANSCRIPTS
FROM THE RUDOLPH C. BARNES SR. SYMPOSIUM (APRIL 8, 2005)
RELIGION, ETHICS & LAW PANEL
[PART IV]

PARTICIPANTS:

Professor A. Kevin Reinhart, Dartmouth Dept of Religion
Dr. Michael Skerker, DePaul Dept of Religion
Rabbi Jonathan Crane, University of Toronto Dept for the Study of Religion, Canada
Dean Marsudi Triatmodjo, Gadjah Mada University Faculty of Law, Indonesia

KEVIN REINHART: It was clear to me from the presentations of my colleagues that one of the interesting domains for discussion in this symposium is defining the scope and significance of the doctrine of double effect. That is, to what extent and how you can rationalize collateral damage, it seems to me is one of the crucial issues here. Certainly the reading that I have done—most of which is not in the paper that I have done on what are called self-sacrificing operations. That is to say, concerning so-called suicide bombings make the case that when genuine civilians are killed, that is no different from when genuine civilians are killed in the case of bombings from a jet, or shootings from a rocket, or something like that. So it seems that the three of us who are presenting today, it seems to me that we have three slightly different, and three interestingly different, doctrines of double effect.

The other thing that is striking to me and the presentation of my colleagues in Indonesia and my two colleagues here—it is striking to me that at least in contemporary rhetoric, there is no longer the possibility of an argument for an offensive war. That in the premodern period or even arguably during the colonial period, you have arguments that say simply the world is a better place if we control this other domain. It seems to me that what is striking to me in these presentations now is that, in the post–World War II era defense is the only acceptable rhetoric. I think this was quite clear in the American discussion of Iraq. That we have now shifted to a sort of premodern argument, while we have now brought democracy so on and so forth. But the initial rhetoric was one of defense, as if that is the really persuasive stance and to argue otherwise. To argue that somehow the world was better if we control, it is not an acceptable argument, and I think that is an important change in ethical thinking concerning war in the postmodern period, and one perhaps that ought not to be so easily given up.

MICHAEL SKERKER: I just want to draw our attention to the distinction between natural law and religious particularity. The idea being that natural law is the conception that normative principles stems from human rationality and not from a particular revelation, and so for instance, you can have Catholic tradition, the idea that the just war principles are articulated, are those that any rational person could arrive at, and therefore that one could expect conformity to abide by anyone including enemies. I wonder if there does seem to be some difference between the three traditions on that issue, whether or not one could expect one's enemies to endorse these just war principles or not?

JONATHAN CRANE: I too am also struck by the conversation about double effect about being able to differentiate between legitimate targets for armed attack versus nonlegitimate targets. I think that it is increasingly difficult—particularly as weapons become increasingly more sophisticated and gruesome, and have greater penetration. I think that our conversation today will, I hope, be the beginning of a fruitful conversation by understanding the moral difficulties greater technological sophistication can pose for us, as we address how to meaningfully negotiate conflict mediation.

ROBERT TURNER: (FROM U.S. AUDIENCE) I was wondering how the different religious speakers here would talk about if we had gone—if the United States had gone before the United Nations and said that we wanted to invade Iraq because we were convinced from a military intelligence that Saddam Hussein had been committing genocide against his own people, the Kurds? And I was also wondering if we had gone before the United Nations about the same situation in Somalia how the religious leaders would feel about that?

JONATHAN CRANE: On the topic of genocide, there are strong condemnations within the Judaic legal and ethical traditions saying that it is a crime against humanity, essentially although it does not use that rhetoric, and that those people who can intervene to stop a potential genocide, but do not speak up about stopping that genocide, have transgressed certain Biblical commandments on protecting the weak and the vulnerable. So the Judaic tradition largely would support a state going to the United Nations asking for just international backing to intervene in another state, so as to prevent a genocide from actually coming to full force.

MICHAEL SKERKER: Nonpacifist Christian thinkers would agree with that statement since the basic justification for force is to uphold justice and protect the innocent. A humanitarian intervention is a paradigm example and paradigm justification. The only caveat is that there are some historic peace churches, like the Quakers, Mennonites, and Amish, who are pacifists in all regards.

KEVIN REINHART: There is no doubt, as far as I know every significant Islamic scholar was an enemy essentially of Saddam Hussein. He persecuted particularly the religious. Everyone was aware of the activities of the Iraqi state and saw that as an evil. As for the specific mode of intervention, the only caveat would have been the question of dominance by non-Muslims over Muslims. This a complicated and fraught issue, and symbolically Muslim expect superintendency over themselves. So it might be argued that an international force comprised in part of Muslims would have satisfied that problem or that concern. But the disregarding of the deliberative body and then the wholly national character of the invading army is what various people like Musawi or Qardawi and so on have cited as grounds of justifying the Iraq resistance against the Americans.

The question is, does the lapse of time between the acts against the Kurds and the actual invasion make us appear to be disingenuous, does not seem like a religious question to me. But certainly as an American citizen, and I hope an observer, yes, I think that was pretty clear to everybody that it was only after the invasion of Kuwait and the series of events through the 1990s and early parts of the century that we suddenly found ourselves concerned about things that were being done to the Kurds.

INDONESIAN AUDIENCE, VIA VIDEOCONFERENCING: From Gadjah Mada University, Yogyakarta. My question I give to Professor Skerker and Rabbi Crane. Do you think that religion can resolve the conflict over war, or do you think that religion is one of the reasons of the conflict of the war?

MICHAEL SKERKER: Yes sir, that is a huge question. On a level of generality, it cannot be answered in specific ways religion works to limit the scope of military damage. It often historically has been a way of limiting destruction and, of course, historically also its been a motive for awful carnage often times worse carnage than what we would expect without religious motivation. So I think it is something that is wedded to human nature, and so just as human nature has good and evil in it there will constantly be sources of hope that religion will provide in terms of armed conflict and sources of discord.

JONATHAN CRANE: I agree that is a very important question, but my answer is going to be in the negative. This is why. Religions cannot solve conflicts. It is people who solve conflicts. And the rhetoric that we invoke, the rationales that we rely upon to justify, explain, permit, or prohibit certain behaviors that we are about to engage in. That is our choice and that is our responsibility, it is to think very critically about why we are doing what we are doing. Religions themselves are inert. We are the people who bring them to earth and make them alive, make them important and meaningful. So no religions do not cause conflict, and they cannot solve conflicts. It is human beings who do both.

ROBERT TURNER (FROM U.S. AUDIENCE): I would like to follow up on the earlier line of questioning about Operation Iraqi Freedom, I was actually asked to write a book chapter explaining the legal basis of it before it happened. I spent about a third of it talking about what today is often called humanitarian intervention and pointing out that—for example, you and human rights experts said that the human rights situation in Iraq during the 1990s and into this century found few parallels in terms of its horror since World War II. Amnesty International, supported by figures released by the UN, concluded that more than half a million children under the age of five in Iraq died from starvation, disease, malnutrition, and so forth because Saddam Hussein would not allow the food and medicine being imported under the Oil for Food program to reach them. He was basically playing chicken with the world, knowing we cared more about the lives of his women and children than he did. Now if we accepted that as fact, and I am not asking you to do that, but as a hypothetical, if you accept it as fact that Saddam Hussein's regime not only is brutal against the Kurds, but the UN report said that virtually everyone in Iraq was a victim of his terror, that not only were large numbers of people being killed, not only did he have a long history of massive international aggression against his neighbors, but that more specifically he was starving to death hundreds of thousands of small children, defenseless small children, would your religious views authorize international intervention in that setting?

KEVIN REINHART: Well, to respond to that, I guess the first thing to say is that it is important to recognize that unlike my colleagues that I am reporting on the Muslim tradition rather than representing it. I think that is an important distinction. But I think that it is perfectly fair to say that the question that many friends of mine in the Muslim world ask is, why the selective attention of Iraq as opposed to some place else, without getting into the questions of the actual cause of the starvation of the children and so on? I think it is fair to say that the United States' attention in particular has been selective, that we were not concerned nor were we reactive in preventing Saddam Hussein's actions in the 1980s, it was only when for whatever reason we sort of changed our policy that we became concerned. And the question is why then are we not moving to eliminate other regimes in which there is mass murder, so on and so forth, and I could list them, but I think it would be pernicious to do so. But I think you are aware that there are many states in the world that are morally deplorable, and yet there seems to be no particular interest at this point in invading and correcting those states. So I guess the question that Muslims have asked, quite reasonably, is why is it that Muslim states get a disproportionate amount of American attention, and that calls into question the general issue of the legitimacy of the rhetoric that used to justify those activities.

MICHAEL SKERKER: In the tradition, there is a difference between a war being justifiable and justified, so that in principle there would be many potential conflicts that would have just causes and so humanitarian intervention in Iraq for the last two decades might have been a just cause. There are some differences of opinion amongst Christian thinkers, but many would say that, until you trigger the last resort option, a given war is not justified so that just as the last speaker said there are many places where there is reason to go and there are many evil dictators out there, and the question is why this war and do we absolutely have to do this war now is the damage done worth the good achieved in this particular instance? For example, Pope John Paul, II felt that both Iraq conflicts were unjust, were unjustified. So I should be more careful, were unjustified in that they did not meet that last resort criterion. So both Desert Storm and Iraqi Freedom.

INDONESIAN AUDIENCE, VIA VIDEOCONFERENCING : I would like to ask Mr. Crane a question regarding the Jewish tactics and everything. You mentioned earlier that the military, if I am not mistaken, should not be involved in religious matters. In a way I agree, and in a way I do not agree with that statement. The reason is that in some countries, sometimes military enforcement is necessary at an early stage to stop the chaos, and in another country maybe it is not necessary (because of the different stages of the people's development and everything else). So could you please explain it more clearly to us on this level, how you could define that military should not be interpose itself in religion matters?

INDONESIAN AUDIENCE, VIA VIDEOCONFERENCING: From Military Law School, Jakarta. I would like to make a comment, first concerning the issue of the use of torture against suspected terrorists, the use of suicide bombing and hostage-taking. In my view, suicide bombing could not be applied as a method of war even in the war against terrorism. Suicide bombing as a method of war is not fully addressed by Islamic law. However, suicide itself is prohibited according to Islamic law. The second point that I would like to address is a question for Jonathan Crane concerning the conflict in Palestine between Israeli forces and the Palestinian armed forces. We already know that the practice of violence in Palestine indicated that the military force of the Israelis killing some of the Palestinian leaders by attacking them through surrogate people or surrogate leaders of the Palestinians. I think that this practice is similar to the terrorists' actions against civilian people. On the other hand, if you look at the incident a few years before we saw that the Israeli forces conducted an [1982] attack on the refugee camps in Sabra and Shatila. As we noted, the Sabra and Shatila camps are mostly inhabited by the civilian population. What do you think, are these actions taken by the Israeli forces justified according to the Jewish legal tradition, or whether this action is consistent with reprisal concepts, but even if this action is called in this context reprisal, it is still questionable because reprisal is prohibited against the civilian population?

Another point I would like to make is a comment on the concept of jihad. I am a Muslim, but actually I am not expert in Islamic law. I think that jihad is not directed to make an aggressive war on infidels. It is a concept that directs us to make an ultimate defense, not just as a basis to make a war on the infidels or as a basis to make a just cause in Islamic tradition. In other words, I would like to say that the jihad is not directed to any subjugation of the infidel. Islamic practices in past times, especially during the life of the Prophet Muhammad, indicated that the Prophet Muhammad gave freedom and independence for various ethnic peoples to practice their religion. This shows that the Islamic traditions or Islamic legal systems can live in peaceful coexistence between the Muslim and the non-Muslim people around the world.

JONATHAN CRANE: Thank you very much for those questions. That the military ought not to be involved in religious matters is one that might be my own personal opinion. On the other hand, a military operation or a police operation has as its ultimate purpose to protect the public, its citizens, and the interest of the public body. Its defense maneuvers can be shaped by religious sensibilities. I think that is possible, and I think all of our scholars here could agree that religious sensibilities can infuse defense maneuvers. However, the practicality of an emergency situation may preclude a thorough-going religious deliberation prior to actually enacting a defensive maneuver or a police maneuver. Therefore, at least in the Judaic tradition, we have a principle called pikuach nefesh, which I have mentioned briefly, which means to save life, and you must save life by going to almost any extreme possible, so as to preserve the most quality of life for human beings as possible, even of enemy combatants. So, while I personally would want any military personnel, be it of Indonesia, the United States, Israel, Canada, France, or wherever you are, while I would want them to be guided by the principle of pikuach nefesh, it may be that even when pushed against the wall an emergency situation, defensive maneuvers may not be able to maintain human dignity at all times. In regard to the Israeli–Palestinian conflict, I would have to say that the Sabra–Shatila massacres in 1982 were not justified by Jewish law. Again, I must reiterate that Israel is not bound to halakhah, to Jewish law. And there were and are continuing deliberations going on in Israel about whether that attack was justified or justifiable within the Judaic tradition. And there are people who are holding the people involved morally accountable for those actions. As for targeted assassinations, again invoking the principle of pikuach nefesh may be one mechanism, one rhetorical mechanism to justify targeting particular leaders who have made it their life's goal to invoke suffering upon another population, and that other population may happen to be Jews. But I am not saying that targeted assassinations are on the whole, across the board without any exceptions, justified by the halakhah or ethical tradition at all. I am just saying that it is possible that one could justify it by invoking that principle.

KEVIN REINHART: I would like to begin by observing that my colleague in Indonesia's question is very much a demonstration of the point that I made in the course of my talk, which is that he identifies himself as not an expert in Islamic law, and goes on to provide I think a soundly reasoned argument of what it is that in his understanding Islam requires, and this is, I think, a very important development in the history of Islamic thought. That in the eighteenth century for example, it would have been very unlikely that someone would have ventured to offer an opinion. But in an age of heightened literacy and scholarship, and public scholarship and so on, Muslims do not feel necessarily that they need to have gone to the Al Azhar University or to have been trained in sharia to be able to respond to the Islamic summons, and I think that is an important development.

On the question of suicide bombing, I think it is important to in some ways again validate my colleague's question. That is, if we were to pose the question as a hypothetical in the nineteenth century, I believe that the tradition would fairly soundly have rejected the suicide bombing technique. There is considerable sunnah support for the idea that seeking martyrdom, then—as opposed to accepting it when it is thrust upon you—is unacceptable, and certainly the ban on iftar, which is deliberately inflicted self-killing is a very strong Islamic one. But I would note that the contemporary justification for it is also sophisticated, and I think not without a kind of rationale, that is that to die in war is something you often recognize as the not merely likely, but almost certain outcome, and that distinctions between civilians and noncivilians on the one hand are less justified in an environment where everyone is a soldier, whether a reservist or active, and then the old people, the children, and so on who were killed that comes under the doctrine of double effect. Now myself, I would say, and here I step out of my persona as an Islamicist and would pretend to be an aesthetic for a moment. I think that the important question is whether a civilian who is killed by a suicide bomber is in some way killed more wrongly than a civilian who is killed by a rocket, or by weapons fired by someone who is wearing a uniform. I think that the ethical position has to be the death of civilians is reprehensible no matter what the agency. But it is important to recognize that within the Islamic tradition, there has been a change over time, although many people, and again if you read the Islamic nets and so on as I do, would agree with my colleague in Indonesia that in fact suicide bombing is not an acceptable tactic.

CONSTITUTIONAL AND DOMESTIC LAW: INDIVIDUAL RIGHTS PANEL
[PART III]

Participants:

Kenneth Hurwitz, Senior Associate, US Law and Security Program, Human Rights First
Geremy Kamens, Assistant Federal Public Defender Eastern District of Virginia, lawyer for Yasir Esam Hamdi

Dr. H. Wayne Elliott, Col. USA JAG (retired), former Head of the International Law Department, Judge Advocate General's School, Charlottesville
Dr. Michael Skerker, DePaul Dept of Religion

GEREMY KAMENS: (directing a question to Wayne Elliott) Couple of questions for Wayne here on military commissions. I happened to go to the *Hamdan* argument at the D.C. Circuit yesterday before I hopped on a plane here. One of the arguments made by Mr. Hamdan's lawyer, Commander Swift, was that the military commission that is contemplated here is entirely different from the military commission that we have had in the past in that one fundamental principle as you were talking about in the past has been the presence of the defendant at the commission. For example, the military commissions against the German saboteurs involved some very highly sensitive secret information that the government did not at all want the German government to learn about. Specifically, what Commander Swift said, is that the reason those individuals were found was not because of their own incompetence, because many of the saboteurs that actually come into the United States were here for quite a period of time. But in fact one of them had defected and had then gone to the FBI, and if the German government had learned that then they would have realized that it was not because of our real strong protections against this type of sabotage effort that these individuals were found out, and that would have encouraged the German government to continue to do that in the future. Now this was considered the highest of most secret information that they did not want to get out, nonetheless the German saboteurs were allowed to stay in at the tribunal. Now the public was excluded, and he used this as an example to say this is a fundamental principle that has always been used in military commissions that is not being used now, and the procedures now can be changed on the fly, in the middle of the proceedings, the rules are being changed, and seemed to be making a significant argument that this is not the military commissions that we know and love from the past.

WAYNE ELLIOTT: That is a valid point. I think Commander Swift has made a good point. But on the other hand, this is a different kind of war than the one we had in World War II, but I did not get to this, but since you now give me the opportunity. About the necessities of the case, if we take Nuremburg as setting the standard for military commissions and what is required for a fair trial by military commissions, we look at Article 12 of the Nuremburg rules, and it permitted the exclusion of the defendant. It said that the tribunals have the right to take proceedings against a person charged with a crime in his absence, if the tribunal for any reason finds it necessary in the interest of justice to conduct the hearing in his absence. Now it is interesting that these rules from the Nuremburg trials were written in August 1945, four months after pretty much the end of any combat in the European theater of operations. But still, the people writing the rules said it is permissible to exclude the defendant. There are some rules that some people look at in the Geneva Prisoner of War Convention. I will not get into that, but the judge, Judge Robertson, talked about the International Covenant on Civil and Political Rights. Article 14, sure enough it does say what he said it says, that the accused has the right to be tried in his presence, but there is another article there which says that states can derogate from their obligations under the covenant in time of public emergency, which threatens the life of the nation and the existence of which is officially proclaimed. President Bush proclaimed a national emergency on September 14, 2001. Now, the International Covenant on Civil and Political

Rights has a list of provisions from which you cannot derogate, you have to comply with them. This requirement that the accused be present in his own trial is not one of those. Therefore, you could stay within that International Covenant on Civil and Political Rights and exclude the defendant. I do think there is a problem in excluding the defendant. I hope they will figure out a way not to have to do that, but you also have to realize it is not the substance of that information that is all that important at this point, it is the sources and methods by which it was gathered. You have electronic surveillance, you have bugs. The defendant is already going to know what the substance of it is, maybe because he would have been there, but now he will know how it was gathered and that will affect the ongoing war effort. This is a problem, and I do not know what the solution is. I do not think the solution is to stop the military commission process right now. Let us go on and let it play out, and see if the defendant can claim some true prejudice rather than potential prejudice.

GEREMY KAMENS: The second question I had was that there are a number of detainees who were not picked up in the war in Afghanistan. This goes to your point about how we are in a different type of conflict, perhaps a global insurgency against an Islamic extremist set of individuals. So there are individuals that we have detained in Guantanamo, who were picked up in Bosnia. I think there was one individual who was picked up in Italy perhaps, and you mentioned that military commissions are limited to those who were associated with an armed conflict. That is why Timothy McVeigh, for example, would not be subject to a military commission. Would these individuals who have been picked up outside of Afghanistan, in your mind, also be immune from military commissions?

WAYNE ELLIOTT: No, I do not think they would if they were involved in the overall criminal activity that is being prosecuted. The Geneva Convention says it is territorial to a certain extent, but here we are looking for criminal activity that might cross borders. I am trying to think if there was any case in World War II that involved that, and I know that we had Germans that were held here that had been turned over to us by neutral countries or nonparticipant countries.

ROBERT TURNER (FROM U.S. AUDIENCE): What about the concept of criminal enterprise?

WAYNE ELLIOTT: That I thought about too, because there the Nuremburg tribunal, you know, there were certain German organizations which were simply designated as a criminal enterprise in theory for the follow-up military commissions. The only thing the prosecution would have to show was that this person was a member of this organization. In reality, it did not work that way. They required that you proved somehow real involvement in the major decisions. The end result was that it really did not mean as much. But al Qaeda could certainly be considered a criminal organization, and we might use the Nuremburg precedent and say well, if you are involved with al Qaeda, then at least you have made your first cut toward being properly tried for a crime.

U.S. AUDIENCE: Can you differentiate this from the young man from the Bay area who was incarcerated?

GEREMY KAMENS: Well, John Walker Lindh is the person that you are talking about, and he was prosecuted criminally so assume he was given all the rights that a normal criminal defendant is afforded. He had an appearance before a magistrate judge. His father, as you mentioned, retained counsel, James Brosnahan, from a firm out in California. He had as local counsel the former U.S. Attorney in Alexandria, Virginia. He was prosecuted in the normal way that we prosecute any other criminal defendant. Yasir Hamdi was brought to the United States in approximately early April of 2002. He did not see an attorney, me, and my boss Frank Dome, until February 2004. John Walker Lindh was held at the Alexandria detention center. He could see his family. He could see his lawyers. They have visiting hours there. I go there on a regular basis, but there was a consistent way by which he could meet with the people who were trying to represent his interests. Yasir Hamdi was held in solitary confinement at a naval brig incommunicado. We had no idea for a long time whether he had any idea that there was anybody who was trying to represent his interests. We did learn that the Red Cross went to visit him several times before we went in to see him. He was able to send some censored letters to his family.

U.S. AUDIENCE: Hamdi and Lindh, how can we treat one one way, and one another?

GEREMY KAMENS: That is a good point. You know that was a part of the argument. But there is a fundamental principle that is that the government, the executive branch, has the power and discretion to decide whom they are going to prosecute, and they decided to prosecute John Walker Lindh. Perhaps, partly because John Walker Lindh had spoken to the media. There were statements that were inculpatory that he had made, and there is an assortment of criminal statutes that could easily apply to his conduct. Yasir Hamdi made virtually no statements to the press. There was no way that the Government could use any of the statement that he had made in an interrogation, and there was a much more difficult hurdle the government would have had to overcome if they wanted to prosecute him criminally. After the government decided at the end of the case, after the Supreme Court had come down with their ruling and the case was remanded to the district court for an actual hearing, and then we started to negotiate release terms. One of the issues was whether the government would give up its ability to prosecute criminally Yasir Hamdi. At the end of the day, the things that they wanted were too high and we felt that he would have had the mother of all speed trial defenses, if they did try to bring a criminal case. If you ever looked at the settlement agreement, there is nothing in there that prevents the government from trying to prosecute him criminally. The most kind of "devious" way to look at this is that the government had the evidence to prosecute John Walker Lindh, and they did not have the evidence to prosecute Yasir Hamdi. But it was basically the decision by the government, and they did what they did.

U.S. AUDIENCE: Equal protection has not caught that at all?

GEREMY KAMENS: Well, I mean the government has the discretion about who to prosecute. There is not an equal protection argument necessarily there. I think there is a Supreme Court case from 1990 where the litigant argued that the government was exercising that discretion in a way that violated equal protection by prosecuting poor black kids in the intercity and not prosecuting relatively wealthy Caucasian users or sellers of narcotics. The standard to establish such a violation is incredibly high. In our case, the simple question was did the government have an independent power to detain Yasir Hamdi as an enemy combatant?

U.S. AUDIENCE: My question is actually very similar. Is there a principled way to distinguish between who should be treated as a criminal defendant, and who is an enemy combatant?

GEREMY KAMENS: I think that the government has not made any distinction. They have, for example, asserted the authority to prosecute individuals found overseas as criminal defendants, like John Walker Lindh, and prosecute individuals, or detain individuals they have found in the United States like Jose Padilla, as an enemy combatant. There is not really a distinction in the government's mind because, according to the government's position, the executive branch has inherent power by virtue of Article 2 of the Constitution to do what it wants. The Court, I think, has made somewhat of a distinction, and that distinction from the Court's view is that the executive branch has been authorized, in limited circumstances, to detain American citizens as enemy combatants, individuals who are found overseas in an area of armed conflict who are accused of bearing arms against the United States, and that accusation can be the basis for authority to detain an individual as an enemy combatant. I think it is very difficult for the government now to say that they have that authority to detain individuals found in the United States as enemy combatants. That is an issue that was before the district court down here in South Carolina that is going before the Fourth Circuit Court of Appeals. But I think it is likely that the Supreme Court will say that the executive branch, and the military in particular, has very limited authority to detain American citizens in the United States not found in an area of armed conflict.

WAYNE ELLIOTT: Well, I agree, but there would be one exception and that is if they are prisoners of war. Unfortunately, the Administration has tried in a way have it both ways, declaring these people be enemy combatants, but not prisoners of war. But we hold prisoners of war, or we held prisoners of war, who were American citizens and there is at least one case *In re* Torito, an Italian captured with the Italian army in World War II brought here and immediately sues saying worst case of mistaken identity I have ever seen, I am an American. And the court says it does not matter, you are a prisoner of war. Nationality is irrelevant for that purpose. In the first Gulf War, we captured a lot of Iraqis who were American citizens. The war had started in the summer. These were Americans visiting relatives in Iraq who got drafted into the Iraqi army, captured, and held as a prisoner of war. Now, we pretty quickly let all of those people go. Those who wanted to go back to Iraq, they went back. The ones who wanted to come home to the United States, they came home. But there is that difference.

GEREMY KAMENS: Let me just say that Wayne is absolutely right about Mr. Torito. I would say that Mr. Torito was released on bond, actually got a girlfriend and was outside in California when he was trying to assert his citizenship as a reason why he should be allowed to stay in the United States. But it is true that the Ninth Circuit Court of Appeals ultimately found that if he is determined in a hearing to be a prisoner of war, then he can be detained as such.

KEN HURWITZ: The language that Geremy just referred to in the decision, Justice O'Connor's decision in *Hamdi,* in this case we are talking about someone who was affiliated with forces or supporting forces that were taking up arms in Afghanistan during the conflict against the United States and its coalition. That language, if you look at it in the opinion, is very striking and very significant in what it does not say. It does not say that we are talking about enemies in a global war on terrorism. It does not say that anywhere in the whole world is the battlefield for this war, as the Administration has repeatedly said. It does not say that we are at war with al Qaeda. It says we are talking about an armed conflict in the territory of Afghanistan, and I think that is one of the very significant points in about that case, and one of the points that we are making, or one of the points that I am making, is that the discretion to decide who is an enemy combatant is part of the new system, and that is exactly why they have kept it so vague. Alberto Gonzales, when he spoke to the ABA last February, was very clear. He said they do not have any rights to challenge a determination. We do not owe them any due process, any process at all. It is part of our repertoire of possibilities that we can choose to make them enemy combatants or not. They do not have rights, and that is exactly what I think it should be focused on. O'Connor focused on the fact that we are talking about a territorial conflict in Afghanistan, is a very useful and important starting point for being able to do that.

U.S. AUDIENCE: How did the public defenders of Eastern Virginia even come to know the presence of Hamdi in your jurisdiction? What procedural assurances do we have that there are not American citizens being held in Afghanistan?

GEREMY KAMENS: That's a good point. We learned from an article in the Virginian-Pilot and Ledger-Star on April 6, 2002, and your point, I think, is that if the reporter from the Ledger-Star or some other paper does not get wind of an American citizen being detained as an enemy combatant, then it is very difficult for that individual to get representation. I did hear, I think a week and half ago, that the military has announced that they detained another individual in Baghdad who is a naturalized American citizen, and he has been detained since December of 2004. But you know the point I think is a good one, and that is that if we do not learn by other means that an individual is being detained, it is very hard for the rights that Justice O'Connor talked about to be effectuated.

CONSTITUTIONAL AND DOMESTIC LAW: STRUCTURAL AND INSTITUTIONAL PANEL
[PART II]

PARTICIPANTS:
Professor John Mansfield, Harvard Law School
Professor Robert Turner, Associate Director, University of Virginia Center for National Security Law and former counsel, President's Intelligence Oversight Board
Professor Norman Bay, University of New Mexico Law School and former U.S. Attorney
Michael Hurley, 9/11 Commission and 9/11 Public Disclosure Project senior staff and retired career CIA officer
Professor A. Kevin Reinhart, Dartmouth Dept of Religion

U.S. AUDIENCE: Quickly from Professor Bay, I want to know about your thoughts about the man who worked, the engineer who worked at the nuclear facility who was arrested, and I guess finally prosecuted for taking the computer information home. And then after that, I want to ask, not press, Mr. Hurley and Professor Turner, because they do not seem like they need to be pressed about, if you feel that the fact that our military intelligence community is not part, I am assuming I am correct, is not part of the fifteen agencies. If they cannot communicate with each other, what problems are we going to have that the military intelligence is not included in this, and also whether or not you think the American public has been affected by perhaps less than popular CIA operatives who now we have find out later have been people we have been trying to depose such as Saddam Hussein, Manuel Norriega, some of these other people who in the past have been paid as CIA operatives.

NORMAN BAY: I really do not have much to say about the case. I am assuming you are referring to the Wen Ho Lee case. He was prosecuted in Federal court in Albuquerque, New Mexico. And I do not have much to say about it. All that happened pre-9/11. Even the judge in that case, Judge Parker, acknowledged at the sentencing hearing that Dr. Lee had taken information and downloaded it, that he wasn't supposed to, and there had been ample testimony by scientists at Los Alamos that these materials included some of the most sensitive nuclear secrets that the United States possessed. So I do not really have a lot to comment on that particular case.

ROBERT TURNER: Unless things have changed a lot since I was in the intelligence oversight business 20 some odd years ago, the military intelligence elements are part of the intelligence community. Certainly DIA, and you know there are a whole bunch of acronyms, some of which in fact used to be classified. The NRO (National Reconnaissance Office) used to be, the term itself was classified, but now there is a problem, obviously the Secretary of Defense has had operational control over a number of agencies and that has been thought out, I guess. I am not even sure how that came out. Seems to me when we are involved in a war, you know unity of command is an important principle, and you ought to be using your intelligence resources in an intelligent manner as part of the grand chess game, if you will. I am not sure how responsive that is, but I do not think, there is, it is not my impression that the military intelligence operations are somehow not part of the intelligence community. At least they were. Executive Order 12333 includes them in the definition of the community.

U.S. AUDIENCE: Can they all still be under this umbrella?

MICHAEL HURLEY: Well, the answer to that is, that is a little bit different because each of the services has as you rightly point out has their own. There is army intelligence, air force intelligence, naval intelligence, etc. They are still going to report through their chains of command, but it is more of the national collectors.

ROBERT TURNER: I was thinking like DIA for example.

MICHAEL HURLEY: DIA.

U.S. AUDIENCE: If each of the individual military branches do not share among themselves, and do not share under the umbrella, how will this be successful?

MICHAEL HURLEY: They will share. The question really is, I think, in part who is in command of them, and did the command arrangements change? There is sharing going on all the time. There were glitches in it before 9/11, and I think our Commission pointed to many of those. But I think that can be overstated. But there is, I think you rightly point to a problem, and that is this is all rather new. We believe that the creation of a Director of National Intelligence will sort of impose this unity of effort that was rather lacking before 9/11. Just to cite you one thing that we talk about in our book (9/11 Commission Report). In December 1998, the Director of Central Intelligence, George Tenant sent a memo to the, let us call it, the interagency to the intelligence community. In that memo he declared war on al Qaeda. Now, obviously the Director of Central Intelligence does not declare war, so I am not saying he usurped the powers of the President. What that really meant was, he said, for the intelligence community, this is going to be our highest priority. And yet it kind of showed how, and I do not mean this as a criticism of Mr. Tenant, but it kind of showed how lacking in authority the Director of Central Intelligence really was because none of the agencies within the intelligence community did much. It did not lead, for example, to a doubling of money or resources being spent on the al Qaeda target. There was no sort of significant change in how they were going about doing their business. So our view was that we had to make a proposal for a leader, a manager of all of this that could really make those shifts and shift priorities among the agencies. So we hope that is what this proposal does.

ROBERT TURNER: Let me pick up at your second question which is, as I understand it, what we call the unsavory sources problem. Henry Simpson as Secretary of State back in the late 1920s shut down the code breaking section of the State Department on the theory that "gentlemen don't read other people's mail." John Foster Dulles said "gentlemen do read each other's mail if they have the opportunity and when the national security is at stake." Over the years, it is not just the intelligence community, the FBI has had the problem. You are trying to investigate organized crime. Are you allowed to give money to people that could not be choir boys or boy scouts? If all you are allowed to do is give money to boy scouts, you are either not going to get any information on al Qaeda, or you are going to be getting pieces of boy scouts coming back in bags, because they are not going to infiltrate. You are going to have to get people who live in that community, that work, who are credible in that community. You use the word operative. There are a lot of words used. One of the telltales, if you ever go into a bar and you meet somebody who speaks English fluently and looks American and says they were a CIA agent, you can pretty much be sure you have got yourself a liar because CIA officers, CIA case officers do not refer to themselves as agents. Agents are the people they run, the foreign nationals they control, or run, or direct, and in that you know we have officers in the Directorate of Operations, officers who work with a variety of foreign nationals trying to infiltrate and get information. Sometimes these people are volunteers, more often they are compensated in some way. Sometimes it is in our interest to work with someone like Norriega or someone like Saddam Hussein, we know they are not nice, sometimes we do not know how bad they are. Sometimes we do not know a lot about them, but in some cases, we also know we would not want to have them at our house to dinner, but we know that they are in a position to either influence something, or get information on something, that may be critical to our security. And you have to make that decision. I did not get to the pressure that was put on the CIA during the post–Cold War period. Congress did a lot of harm to the intelligence community. Jim Woolsey has been a friend of mine for 30 some years now, and he basically was chased out of the CIA because he fought so hard against especially the Chairman of the House Committee who wanted to cut back on CIA programs, thinking "hey, the Cold War is over, we do not really need intelligence". Pat Monihan, whom

I had a lot of respect for and had a fairly decent relationship with, he introduced a bill in 1995 to terminate the CIA. The idea was the State Department should get us any intelligence we needed. There are a lot of problems. Bob Torricelli was a House member before he was elected to the Senate. One of his former Hill staff members had gone to the State Department, and he leaked some fairly sensitive intelligence information that Torricelli immediately made public. And he accused the CIA of paying money to a Guatemalan colonel whom he said had been involved in the torture and death of a Marxist terrorist group leader in Guatemala, who happened to be married to a revolutionary-minded American lawyer. Torricelli basically told the CIA if you do not agree to put constraints, to basically set a policy that, except under exceptional circumstances, you won't pay money to people that have serious human rights problems, I am going to push through a law or an amendment that will make you do that. I am told the CIA agreed that they would toughen up their policy in dealing with these unsavory people. Well, if you have that policy you do not get much on al Qaeda, because again you do not send choir boys into al Qaeda meetings. I do not know answer to it. There is a moral issue there. Do we want to be giving money to bad people around the world? My own sense is the single most important reason we won World War II was intelligence. There are a lot of people who can quarrel with that. We had a good navy, good air force, and so forth, but I think the decisive factors were our intelligence breakthroughs, breaking codes, and so forth both in the Atlantic and the Pacific. Intelligence is tremendously important, and the idea that we cannot break any china, we cannot do anything, that we cannot deal with anybody we would not want dating our daughters, or what have you. I think we are going to lose a lot of lives either not knowing when we get hit, or having to play catch up ball once we do get hit. (looking at MICHAEL HURLEY) You have got a hundred times more experience in this, and I will defer if you see it differently, or especially if I have got the facts wrong.

MICHAEL HURLEY: I will just make a quick comment. I agree with Professor Turner's analysis. I think perhaps maybe the best and most recent example of this actually has to do with Afghanistan itself in which during the anti-Soviet jihad there, of course CIA with other countries actually financed the Afghan Mujahideen that were trying to expel the Soviets. And a lot of Arabs, foreign fighters, were involved in fighting against the Soviets, and the remnants were left there after the United States walked away from Afghanistan in 1990. Some of them actually formed into al Qaeda. So that we were supporting them at one time, and then later on they became a big problem for us. But yes, it is actually rather an unsavory business at times. So I agree with Professor Turner's analysis. I do disagree with a statement you made in your presentation, though. I will try to get it right. I think you said that the Pike and Church Committees, and I think by extension some of the strict constraints and handcuffs that were placed on the intelligence community, hurt us in terms of 9/11, being able to anticipate it. I think what really hurt us on that is that we just, it was that was a tough nut to crack. Bin Laden and the people around him are clannish and tribal, and to get a source in there that close or even close to Saddam Hussein in Iraq is extremely hard to do, and we failed at it. But I doubt, or I would challenge you to find, any Director of Central Intelligence who turned down a good source because of those handcuffs or constraints that were placed on them.

ROBERT TURNER: I do not disagree with your comment there. I guess what I was really saying is a lot of things that came out of that made it harder to get information, decreased human assets, and so forth. But it may well be in that particular case that, had we had ten times the human capability, we still would not have cracked that nut. I do not disagree with that. One just tidbit of history, Jimmy Carter gets a lot of criticism for his national security performance, much of the time I am right up there chirping with the critics, but one of the not well-known aspects of the support for the Mujahidheen was initially a Carter policy. Actually Carter in his final months, Carter was an interesting fellow, very moral and decent man, but he, very much like FDR, he did not understand Leninism, and when the Soviets invaded Afghanistan , which was an obvious target of opportunity, we had no airlift capability, there was nothing we could do about it, besides the nukes around, to them, you know, you take it. Carter took that as a personal affront, his buddy had betrayed him, and in his final weeks in office he cut aid to the Sandinistas in Nicaragua, started military aid to the Salvadorians, which he had cut on human rights grounds, and began to support the Mujihadheen, which in the Reagan administration was increased further, but I think he does deserve some credit for, at least at the end, recognizing that maybe Leninism was a bigger problem than it had first appeared to be. Maybe you remember that he went to Notre Dame early on in his administration and said Americans have an inordinate fear of communism, and I was one of many people who felt we could have lost the Cold War, if he would have been reelected. That has not changed, but that is another lecture. But I certainly do not, I did not mean to be saying that specifically with respect to al Qaeda, but rather the general intelligence community I think was degraded for a variety of reasons, I think, the culture, we talked about the risk avoidance culture, I think that was the direct product of a variety of Congressional operations where they went after individuals in the intelligence community and also did it in the military after the Beirut bombing, which I think Congress bears a great deal of responsibility for, if you follow that, that is another debate, but if you are interested, contact me, because I wrote a book on it, and I coauthored an article with the Commandant of the Marine Corps at that time on it. But their idea was, we want the head of the Marine to blame this on after 241 Marines have been already killed. I thought that was outrageous.

MICHAEL HURLEY: Just a preliminary comment on that, this whole question of kind of dealing with unsavory people in order to get intelligence, and actually use them perhaps in covert action. I would urge you to read a book called "GhostWars" by Steve Call, with the editor of the *Washington Post,* and that book just won the Pulitzer Prize for nonfiction. It is a fantastic book, and I think that might address your question in part. This is a fascinating read. Professor Mansfield, you cited, I think a federal case concerning the violation of the Establishment Cause because of U.S. government money that was provided to the overseas religious school. I think that is very interesting, because this is the problem we definitely are going to have to be dealing with in the future, because the U.S. government in its strategy against terrorism has offensive elements, defensive, etc. But also it is trying to deal with the root causes of terrorism. And sort of lack of education in terrorist sanctuaries, and potential terrorist sanctuaries, and in many of these parts of the world, the basic education is provided via religious schools. I guess we generically call them madrasahs. And then so the question really is as the U.S. government addresses this, to what extent can the U.S. government get involved in funding madrasahs perhaps, or some version of madrasahs, where there is a religious curriculum but also a secular curriculum, which we would obviously like to promote.

JOHN MANSFIELD: The case I was referring to was a pre-9/11 case. So that was not in an intense emergency context. And as I said, I would not be surprised if the interpretation of the Religion Clause, including the Establishment Clause, that was affected by what is going on in other areas. As to the funding of religious schools, it may be, I drew this distinction which seems to me important between cases in which a foreign government has its policy to maintain certain preference for religion or particular religion, and the United States comes in and indirectly in some way facilitates that, or assists in that, compared to the situation in which we do it on our own, it is our decision, and whether the foreign government permits us to act in the country that way, or we actually go ahead and act in violation of the laws of this other country. It seems to me that is a crucial distinction that in terms of the Establishment Clause values we are on much weaker ground where we go on our own. On the other hand, as I say, that earlier case was a pre-9/11 case, and who knows, some understanding of the war power, the emergency powers, the power over foreign relations might come in there now to alter the result.

KEVIN REINHART: If I could just add one remark, I think that the discomfort you feel ought not to be affected necessarily by the 9/11 concerns, that the way to proceed is to help the, in this case, Afghan Department of Education develop the system of state schools, rather than funding madrasahs, which always will be dependent on outside money of one sort or another. And therefore, kind of be a channel for external influence. So what is really in our interest is, I think, to develop a centralized state curriculum within Afghanistan. And that goes for Pakistan as well, of course, because you know Pakistan has the same problems.

CONSTITUTIONAL LAW ROUNDTABLE
[PARTS II AND III]

PARTICIPANTS:

Kenneth Hurwitz, Senior Associate, US Law and Security Program, Human Rights First
Dr. H. Wayne Elliott, Col USA JAGC (retired), former Head of the International Law Department, Judge Advocate General's School, Charlottesville
Professor John Mansfield, Harvard Law School
Professor Robert Turner, Associate Director, University of Virginia Center for National Security Law and former counsel, President's Intelligence Oversight Board
Professor Norman Bay, University of New Mexico Law School and former U.S. Attorney
Michael Hurley, 9/11 Commission and 9/11 Public Disclosure Project senior staff and retired career CIA officer

DAVID LINNAN (MODERATOR): The essential question, I think, stated in legal terms is if you looked at last summer's cases, the discussion of the executive power and a lack of, let us say, statutory authority for detentions. Well, there are a variety of drafts that are floating around in Congress that might establish a sort of national security detention statute. But there are considerable questions about its constitutionality, so we would like to hear the opinions of the constitutional lawyers on that issue as well as from the religion scholars.

ROBERT TURNER: I think there is a very important distinction, although I agree there are an awful lot of cases where you cannot draw a line, there are a lot of close cases, but

I think there is a distinction between external and internal issues, that is to say I think Congress has a great role to play when we are talking about individual rights of U.S. persons. I think that when you are talking about gathering intelligence in foreign countries and foreign negotiations and so forth, the President has a great deal of power that is not supposed to be checked by Congress. So I would personally like to see Congress make some policy working closely with the President, set down in law some rules consistent with international law providing, making it clear that the President does have authority to do whatever Congress thinks is proper in terms of trying detainees and so forth. I think it is a very important role. I think it would also help improve acceptance within this country and around the world to have that done through the legal process, and I think Congress certainly has the power to do so as long as they do not violate a provision of the Constitution. In the statute, they have the power to make not only rules for the government of the military, but also to define and punish crimes against the law of nations and so forth.

U.S. AUDIENCE: The concept of the unlimited detention, what about it? Of course there was always concept of parole, from Guantanamo on parole and next week they are in battle, so it is a change in the mentality of what soldiers do?

ROBERT TURNER: Well, actually it never did work that well, and that is why they came to the current system. One thing that is very important and misunderstood, in the law of armed conflict a prisoner of war is not considered to be a wrongdoer. The history of war was, centuries ago, when you overcame your enemy, you slaughtered all of the soldiers. Then somebody said "hey, you know we do not have to kill them. We can sell them as slaves, or we can keep them as slaves for ourselves". And it kept moving up, they played with parole but some of them came back, and so the modern theory is they are not wrongdoers, they are just soldiers who have the misfortune of falling into the hands of the enemy, and in return for reciprocal treatment they are warehoused for the duration of the conflict. Under international law, they have no right to a lawyer, they have no right to be tried in federal district court, indeed almost nobody mentions it but under the Third Geneva Convention, if we were to take a real prisoner of war and send him into federal district court, we would be violating international law because the Third Geneva Convention provides that prisoners of war may be punished either for crimes committed as detainees (let us say he knifes a guard or another prisoner) or for war crimes committed during the war. But the trial must be by military tribunal, it cannot be by domestic court, just as you cannot keep them in a domestic prison or a jail because they are covered by military law, the law of armed conflict. The idea that when an American is picked up, you either have to try him or let him go, you cannot detain him. But that misses the theory of the law of armed conflict, that they are military detainees, and the argument for giving terrorists greater rights than we would give our own soldiers or lawful enemy combatants, strikes me as being a stretch. You are not punishing them, you are warehousing them for the duration of the conflict as agreed by the entire world community, and I am not sure there is a single treaty out that has more parties than the Geneva Conventions. They are accepted by virtually every state. The question is when you hold them, are you punishing them, or are you simply detaining them as the law of armed conflict normally would prescribe?

WAYNE ELLIOTT: One of the complaints about all of this has been how do you determine when the war against terrorism is over. That issue has been around a while.

Maybe 20 or 25 years ago, we had a problem with Puerto Rican terrorists. There was a law review article written then by Professor Alfred Rubin, in which he suggested that, well, maybe the solution to this problem is we try them, but continue to hold them after they are tried, and hold them until somehow or another there is no more problem with Puerto Rican terrorism, and we will just hold them indefinitely. That was 25 years ago. I guess now of course it is more of a real world problem for us. Just as a follow-up to the whole panel this morning, one thing that has always kind of bothered me about all these debates, about where we are going or what to do about terrorism. Put yourself back just after September 11, 2001. You go in the airport, and you find a 17-year old national guardsman standing there with an M-16, and people might kind of worry a little bit, but they were not too concerned about it. I do not understand why we would accept that, but be concerned about the possibility of having a 45-year old professional soldier, a full colonel, sit in judgment of the people that started the whole process in the first place. There just seems to be an inconsistency there. I think we ought to trust the people in the military to do what they are trained to do, and that is fight the war and sit on these commissions and try people as we have done it for the last couple of hundred years for war crimes.

ROBERT TURNER: I have to add on that, because it is such an important point. I served in the military, but I have been out for 30 some odd years and was never professional. But I do work with them a lot. Our law school is right next door to the United States Army's JAG School. I taught at the Naval War College, and I am on their International Law Advisory Committee, and a lot of the senior JAG officers in fact are former students, a number of them are. Jane Dalton, a former legal counsel to the Chairman of the Joint Chiefs, was one of my best students. These are outstanding people, they are conscientious people, and just as military doctors think of themselves as doctors and then officers, look at the way those assigned to defend the Guantanamo people are acting sending in amicus briefs in a very vigorous defense. I would trust them to defend me. The idea that they are good enough to defend American troops accused of heinous crimes, but not good enough to defend terrorists, strikes me as an insult to our military because one of the things that really surprised me as I started dealing with JAG officers, it is very easy to say "hey, a lawyer should make a lot of money in the private sector". These guys who settle for military wages could not find a job somewhere else. Some of the smartest and most able international lawyers that I have found are wearing military uniforms or are retired from having worn military uniforms for, how many years were you in [directing to WAYNE ELLIOTT]?—22 years. They are very good, and they are not going to allow anything to be whitewashed, nor is Griffin Bell, and that review panel, remember we have got a review panel, the Chief Justice of Rhode Island, the former Attorney General of Pennsylvania, Griffin Bell, a former Circuit Court of Appeals Judge, and U.S. Attorney General. They have an absolute right to toss out a case, to remand under any grounds they want, or to affirm it. They cannot increase the punishment, but this is not a kangaroo court situation. Nobody would have put Griffin Bell on that review panel if they were expecting this to be a kangaroo court, and most of the officers that have been involved in the GITMO process have been friends of mine in one capacity or another, and they are the cream of the crop of the military. These people are going to do a hell of a good job.

JOHN MANSFIELD: I would like to make two comments. One of the disturbing aspects of the whole story here is the lack of clarity that the Administration has put forward with regard to whether people are being detained because they have done something wrong, criminal, violation of the law of war, or some other part of the law of crime, ordinary crimes, or they are being detained for some other reason? Among those other reasons could be that they are enemy combatants whom we do not want to let go back to the battlefield and carry on the struggle. There is no implication of wrongfulness in that respect, or other examples of detention with no implication of wrongfulness. Say like somebody with an infectious disease, or somebody who is insane and a danger to himself and others. So in our law, there has been a very clear distinction, and the distinction is which path you are going to go down, and this is very clear, and it has to be made soon, and it has to be made promptly. So that the policeman who arrests somebody or detains somebody has to bring that person before a magistrate for this matter to be decided, which path you are going to go down. In the case of not only the people in Guantanamo, people being detained in Iraq, or people being detained in the United States here 2 or 3 years after 9/11, in many of these cases, we still do not know the answer to that. So refusal to take a position about that matter which is so crucial in our constitutional law, whether the ordinary criminal process is to go into operation or some other reason for detention is put forward, they have managed to avoid that. The other point that I want to make is this. I do not believe under the Constitution, taking into account the Fourth Amendment and the Fifth Amendment, though it is somehow suggested often in the media, that there is any constitutional basis for detaining somebody in order to get information. There is simply no opening for that there, and that is where the arrest of many people under the material witness statute shortly after 9/11 was an abuse of power there, because the material witness statutes authorize you to detain a witness not to get information, but in order so that the witness would be available for the trial. The purpose of the detention is to make sure that he is there, he is around for the trial, not to put him under circumstances in which his will be affected, and he will then provide information that he would not otherwise provide. But I find it very widespread this idea, well of course you can detain people for the purpose of getting information. Now I do not know that much about the law of war or the Geneva Conventions, but I understand that even prisoners of war are not supposed to be detained in order to get information out of them. They need to be detained to prevent them from going back to the armed forces of the enemy. So anyway, those are two thoughts that I wait for further light on from other members of the panel.

NORMAN BAY: I do not know if I can cast light on that question, but I wanted to return to David's initial question, which I think is a great one. He asked, what about the constitutionality at some sort of national security detention act? I would say generally that there are going to be two questions that a court will have to answer. The first question is because we have a constitution that provides for limited powers. The government can only act if there is some enumerated power that it is relying upon. The first question is going to be does Congress have the constitutional power to pass this law? Most of the powers are found in Article 1 Section 8. The second question is going to be, even if Congress has that power, does that law violate some other constitutional right generally found in the Bill of Rights, right? Is there some right that the individual has that is being violated if this law is applied to the individual? So that is going to be the general constitutional framework when examining that kind of law. But let me share with you possible legislation in this area and get your views on it. Let us say that Congress considers a law in which if there is an invasion of the United States, or an insurrection, or a declaration of war by Congress, and the President makes a finding that one of those three conditions has occurred where the law would then give the President the power to detain any citizen, a U.S. citizen in the United

States, if there is "reasonable grounds to believe that such person probably will engage, in or probably will conspire with others to engage in, acts of sabotage." What do you think of that law? A law that would give the President that kind of power if those conditions were met, and the President makes the requisite findings? I think most of us would be very, very concerned. The thought is why should the President have the power to detain an individual based on the fear, the reasonable belief that this person probably will do something in the future? Indeed, it violates a precept in a criminal law that you do not punish people for thoughts. Why? Well, among other reasons, that individual might repent and relent. You have no way of knowing whether thoughts will translate into action. And yet the question I asked you is really an unfair one. Because as it turns out that was a law passed by Congress. That was a law passed by Congress in 1950. It was called the Internal Security Detention Act, and it was passed by Congress during the height of the Cold War. Twenty years later Congress saw fit to repeal that law in the Non-Detention Act of 1970. But that does give you some historical perspective on the kinds of measures that have been considered in the past, even measures which now in a time where we do not have that particular fear relating to the Cold War. We might be hesitant to want such a law on the books, or to give the President that kind of power. Now that law was never challenged, because it was never put into effect, no one was ever detained under it. There is however, as David pointed out, an attempt now to pass laws that would allow for national security-type detentions. I see that on March 3, a law was introduced in the House called the Detention of Enemy Combatants Act. This Act would directly apply in a case like Padilla, and would, if the President made the appropriate findings, allow Padilla to be detained.

ROBERT TURNER: Let me pick up the two things, one on this. There is a great deal of misunderstanding, I think, about the Steel Seizure case. In *Goldwater v. Carter,* the Taiwan Treaty case, a plurality of the Court, including the current Chief Justice and Burger, the past Chief Justice, drew a big distinction between internal and external cases. Steel Seizure was a Fifth Amendment case. It was the taking of property, private property without due process of law, and for that the President needed approval of Congress. The Taiwan Treaty case was an external case involving meaning of a foreign treaty, and what I was talking about in my talk was foreign intelligence. What I would like to see Congress do is through its very clear power to make rules for the government of the Armed Forces, which includes, that is where the Articles of War, the Uniform Code of Military Justice came from. They could set up a process, consistent with international law, by which the President could detain enemy combatants for the duration of the war. Under international law that is a right, it presumably is a right implicit in the President's power, as Commander in Chief. That power has some content that comes from international law, and that includes the right to detain combatants without charging them and hold them for the duration of the war, or to decide in the case of this 15-year-old drummer boy who is really no threat, send him home to his Mom. In other words, discretion is allowed, and further you can hold him for 2 years and then decide "hey, we have got good enough evidence now, he committed a war crime". You know, 6 years ago, there was no statute of limitations on war crimes, so then you put him into your judicial process, but Congress would set up the process with the procedural protections and so forth, just as they did in the Uniform Code of Military Justice, and I do not see that as being a problem. But if we are talking about laws authorizing the President to act against U.S. persons, U.S. citizens, permanent residents, aliens and the like, it is going to have to, I think, comply with the Constitution and Bill of Rights. I do not think that Congress can even during time of war deprive

Americans of their rights. Now what constitutes a reasonable search certainly can vary when there is a threat to the nation's security or something like that. Making that judgment of whether given a threat of terrorism a certain search is reasonable or not, it is certainly a valid factor, but I do not think again we should sacrifice the Bill of Rights on the war on terrorism. I think that is important.

KENNETH HURWITZ: A couple of quick comments, and one of them I am sorry that to have to repeat, but I think is very important to really stress this point about what the Supreme Court has understood this war to be, and because a lot of the issue is that this metaphor of the war on terror, the question is coming up. Well, how do we know when it's over? It is obviously never going to be over. And that is the thing the Administration and many supporters simply do not have the courage to tell people, because they are saying, they cannot bring themselves to say we have got a problem, and we cannot solve the problem, we can control the problem but we cannot solve the problem. The other point I wanted to stress is that, just to draw that out, the point is if you use the understanding of the war as being the war within the territory that was fought in Afghanistan or in the case of Iraq, then you have a much clearer understanding of who is who, what is what, when is, when the war is over, when the war is not over, what regime applies. This was a very important part of O'Connor's opinion, and she goes out of her way to say so far, as far as we can tell, the traditional understanding of the war on this is something that works. If we find in a future occasion that it is no longer viable, then we can address it there. But she makes it very clear that for the time being the war is not a war on terror, it was a war on Afghanistan in the *Hamdi* case, and presumably it would be a war in Iraq if it were dealing with the Iraqi situation. Professor Mansfield mentioned the point about detaining somebody for the purpose of interrogation. Another thing, the *Hamdi* opinion is turning out to be really my favorite. She makes it very clear. You simply cannot detain somebody solely for the purpose of interrogation. The Administration has set up, for example in Guantanamo, these combatant status review tribunals in which they have said well, because we did not give them the Geneva hearings at the time and because the *Hamdi* decision says we should have given them some kind of hearing on the battlefield, we will give them one 3 years later and allow them to try to persuade us that they are not really enemy combatants. Of course, we won't give them any of the evidence that we used to conclude that they are. But the standards, even in their rules that they say we will then use, and they have another form called the administrative review boards which is largely similar. If someone is no longer a danger, or put it the other way, if someone continues to be a danger, we will decide he can continue to be held, or and it is an or, if he has continuing intelligence value, we will continue to hold him. That is a violation of international law, and although the *Hamdi* decision really dealt with the U.S. citizen and so it is not on 100 percent all fours with that, it seems very clearly a violation of the principle that Justice O'Connor was putting in that position about interrogation.

ROBERT TURNER: I think that is a key point. I think you are wrong, you may be right, but I think you are wrong. I think the legal basis for holding them is they are enemy combatants. I think there is discretion to decide, as I said earlier, you can send the little 14-year old drummer boy home and decide to keep somebody else. Once you have a legal right to hold him it is perfectly reasonable to say, in making the decision on whether or not to hold him, the fact that he may have intelligence value, you did not have arrest him because he has intelligence value. You warehoused him, or you apprehended him, or are keeping him because he is an enemy combatant, and that is all you need. But after that, you also have a right to send him home or send him back to his country, and in the decision of whether to let him go or not things like does he have intelligence value, you are then at a discretionary situation, you have a legal right to hold him, you also have the option of letting him go.

LAW OF ARMED CONFLICT AND INTERNATIONAL LAW: OPERATIONAL LAW PANEL
[PART V]

Participants:
Dean Hikmahanto Juwana, University of Indonesia Faculty of Law
Dr. Dino Kritsiotis, University of Michigan Law School & University of Nottingham, Faculty of Law, UK
Professor George Walker, Wake Forest Law School
Professor Kevin Govern, Lt Col USA JAGC (retired), Former USMA at West Point Dept of Law
Rabbi Jonathan Crane, University of Toronto Dept for the Study of Religion, Canada

U.S. AUDIENCE: In terms of psychology, they call it an external locus of control, which means that you feel like you do not have any internal control, which is how most terrorists or terrorist sympathizers feel, meaning they do not have any way to express their grievances. And the forum that they are getting, they feel is inadequate. In reference to policy, law, or intelligence, how can we give them that meaningful forum and at the same time combat the hijacking of the sharia or fiqh, which is their law or jurisprudence, by extremists who always evoke Allah in the name of their cause for their people?

DINO KRITSIOTIS: Well, it seems to me that the debate that we seem to be having can be characterized in two levels. The one level is the technical level, which most of us have been talking about today in terms of what is the law. How do we form the law; what are rules of engagement; how do the bodies of law relate to one another? I think your question is addressed at a much higher level, and probably a more important level, which is that this is all quite meaningless if we are not actually communicating in the same language, and my view is that these conventions, the Geneva Conventions, have a proud ownership. They are the most recognized treaties in all of international law, and they actually happen to be the oldest branch of international law. It has always struck me as quite ironic that one of the first eras where nations came together was in a treaty forum to decide how they would kill and not kill each other's nationals. How do you kill kindly? And that is what these conventions are, they are a testament to the natural reality of warfare. They take warfare as a starting point, and it seems to me that the reason why they are there is precisely because they accept the psychology of warfare. They accept that in the heat of the battlefield people are going to tend to take certain decisions that they otherwise would not have taken, and, in a way, what these conventions try and do, to my mind, is they try and take away a lot of that temptation. They allow certain acts in the name of military necessity, but they also disallow certain acts categorically, and while you may read these conventions, in fact my students at Michigan have thought that the conventions are trying to choreograph warfare, every step and movement is neatly depicted in the script of the conventions, and I won't give you there is a certain quaintness about them, particularly the language that is used. But I think that the idea is to effectively preempt moral wrongs on the battlefield, and I am not sure that that message would be lost on al Qaeda or Taliban. They will certainly turn around one day and say, "wait a minute, they are not torturing individuals as the opposing side". Now maybe this an element of my naiveté, but I think we cannot even get to that debate if we are still arguing whether or not the conventions apply, when they should be applied.

GEORGE WALKER: Well let me just comment that one of the things as I have worked on this model, and is incomplete, is the idea as I mention in my paper. First of all, we are talking about law, it is a much more complicated process than that. That is one of the functions really of this day, we have here because it has to do with, it mentions money, it has to do with law, and it also has to do with faith; that is the Islamic faith and so forth. I think Myers McDougall, and some of his followers at Yale, have worked out a complicated model on that, that I am trying to figure out how to plug into this. That is one aspect of it. Another aspect of it, is the factoral approach that I would put as a subset under my analysis for these six principles. That is the idea that national law, I mean looking at the sharia not as a law of faith but as a national law, would also be inputted as much as in a since our system of law or systems of law in the United States. Now that is not a complete answer, but that is something I am working on right now.

KEVIN GOVERN: When I was looking at violent conflict and instability trying to figure out some of these factors, there was a good quote by a fellow by the name of Steven Metz. Some of you may have read some of what he has written. He said that conflict is chaotic, confusing, and messy. Internal and expansionistic conflicts have to do with the selection and control over the leverage points of the social contact, and the dependency structure and the priority of the target is dependent upon its value to the other side. So as we anticipate that there are emerging threats or emerging instabilities, we have to use whether it is that OODA loop I talked about, or some other process, to get ahead of the power curve. To get ahead of where the crisis is, to use economic, political military aspects in order to be able to either keep stability, build stability, or counter a threat when we have figured out that it is a problem too late to solve it otherwise. So part of this is anticipating far off in advance and not reacting to crises around the world.

U.S. AUDIENCE: I think it is a danger to use this kind of thing. It becomes a way we memorize something to try to plan every action. When I looked at your graph this way, this way, this way. It is that kind of thing that gives us the lack of preparation in which we dropped a type of food that no one in Afghanistan would eat, and also written in a language that no one could read. I think that if we try to follow these steps without trying to imagine ourselves as being somewhat other than American is what gets us into a lot of problems. I think if perhaps America could quit thinking of ourselves as the sun and trying to pretend that we are just a planet revolving around it, that would help us a lot. I went to a talk we had here the other day with international law professors, and we were talking about the fact that still most of our dealings with the UN General Assembly, other countries. The fact that we tried to go forward in the United Nations without agreement amongst other groups when we have the temerity to not pay our dues. We talked Britain into going in with us, and then do not allow them to participate in the rebuilding contracts until after we are forced to by the outcry of other countries. I think that is the problem we are having ahead of time, and we need to think more about how do I try to avoid these.

Sometimes I am afraid it feels like we are parsing so many things of how to try to deal with it after the fact, rather than trying to avoid getting into it to begin with.

KEVIN GOVERN: I fear that I may have oversimplified things, or perhaps made them too complex by putting these various diagrams up there. Let me give you a quick story of ground truth. In the aftermath of the first Gulf War I personally, along with a number of other individuals, was planning logistic supplies in order to be able to feed over a million Kurds in Northern Iraq and Southern Turkey. And it was critical that we got the information as quickly as possible in order to get the right supplies, the right things to the right destinations with a limited number of assets because over 400 people a day were dying of dysentery or other forms of disease. So, that even back in that example of some 14 years ago, is an example of where military forces can and do the right thing. Now we cannot do this without having a lot of assistance. We had a lot of great nongovernmental organizations, private volunteer organizations from around the world, the support. Your cautionary note is very important we cannot think of ourselves in a law-centered universe, that everything is about the law. Nor for that matter does the sun, the moon, the stars, revolve around the United States. However, there are ways in which we can prevent things from falling through the cracks by having established methodologies. And there are times when an established military methodology may be foreign. It may be alien to a nongovernmental organization or another bureaucracy in the government that does not have military expertise. Which is why it is important you have dialog between those different agencies and aspects and to come to a common approach, or at least understand the differences such that you are not working at odds with each other.

MODERATOR: Do we sometimes have so many charts and structures that when we are faced with something totally different, in our country have a tough time adjusting and applying maybe not necessarily doctrine but, wait a minute, this situation is different, and we need to adjust and maybe not go by what we have established as "this is our doctrine"? The rules of engagement, for example, as you know, say in the Balkans comes from European Command, and then you follow those things, but then you see things that you must adjust if you can, but you cannot within certain military doctrine. Do you all feel sometimes, not only in our country but other countries, when you set too many doctrines down it is hard when these changing things happen to adjust to them?

GEORGE WALKER: Well, I speak primarily from a naval perspective. I am a former naval officer. And I think that I go back, to what I recall in giving a lecture like this a number of years ago that we talked about rules of engagement but when it got down to it; the primary rule in the Navy at least, and I think everywhere, is first defend your force; defend your ship; defend your unit. And I think that an intelligent commander is going to take a look at these rules and know where, if you will, the fences really are and exercise initiative. At least that has been the training, I think, of naval officers and I think marines. I am a sea service person so I cannot speak for the Army or the Air Force, but I think that that is true. But I do think we get caught up in our own webs of complexity. And that may be a failing of this type of analysis that I am thinking about.

DINO KRITSIOTIS: I speak as a noncombatant, and my view is that a large part of this is persuasion. It is not so much what the military get up to. It is more the tone that is set by political leaderships. Particularly those who are keen on initiating a prolonged set of hostilities. And I think that one of the most telling validations of international law occurred on September 11th. After the towers came down the Security Council, in a way that it had never been galvanized before, was moved into action, and I have very rarely seen a dissent free United Nations. And that to my mind said something really important, it said that international law needs to be taken seriously by governments, because it is precisely that language that is used to persuade others about the rights and wrongs of what we do, whether or not it occurs on the battlefield or off it.

KEVIN REINHART: I just wanted to sort of confirm what our last speaker just said, and take off from a remark by Professor Walker. It turns out that, in fact, it is not as if the terrorists are uninterested in these issues. They have their own Alberto Gonzaleses and their own views, who as part of the training at al Qaeda that explain why, despite the intuition, the moral intuition, that most people have that you should not kill noncombatants and so on, that does not apply. And so, just as we have had justifications for things that have happened in Iraq and that have happened afterwards, or happened in Afghanistan, happened at Guantanamo and so on, that explain why our moral intuitions do not apply. It is exactly that, that the terrorists did in the training camps in Afghanistan and continue to circulate. There is an extensive body, that means hundreds and hundreds and hundreds of pages, in captured documents and in hard drives and so on that are precisely about thinking through the rules of engagement. And questions, of course, Osama declared that it is okay to kill Americans, and distinctions between American civilians and noncivilians do not matter and so on. But that actually then had be backed up by argument and then discussions about, for example, can you kill Muslims in the process? The car bomb, there has been considerable discussion about the car bombs in Iraq that are done by this kind of franchise operation of al Qaeda which everyone knows are going to kill only Iraqi civilians, the majority of whom are Muslims. This is discussed. So it seems to me that there are moral intuitions or there are instantiated beliefs that are a result of this international law that have to be countered, and if we say international law does not matter, and the terrorists say international law does not matter, then it seems to me we are sort of in a formal swear off. It is particularly important for us, it seems to me, to defend international law and that gives us, that plays into the intuition that most people have, even those who are opposed to our policies. So I would second Professor Kritsiotis and Professor Walker's presentations, but suggest that that extends even to those that are, that we see as, ignoring international law.

DINO KRITSIOTIS: I mean I may be wrong in this, but if the Geneva Conventions did not apply on September 11th, it was a legal impossibility for al Qaeda to have committed a war crime. You can only commit a crime if you have a war or an armed conflict going on. So I think the Bush administration needs to make its calculations quite clear, but it has to take the rough with the smooth in the game of Russian Roulette it is playing with the conventions. The other point I want to make is to actually look at some of the statements that have been put out by al Qaeda in connection with events after September 11th. And it is interesting to me that some of the logic and legal argument that is put forward by governments, or has been put forward by governments, is actually repeated and replayed in some of what al Qaeda is saying. I was interested to note what Professor Walker said about the Gas Protocol of 1925 where Western governments, including the United States, upon signing basically said that they will consider themselves bound by the Gas Protocol, until or unless another state uses gas against them, then they will use gas against others. And in a newspaper interview with a Pakistani newspaper actually, with Dawn, in November 2001, Osama bin Laden actually, when asked the question about nuclear weapons, did he have them, his response was well if we do have them, do not worry, we are only going to use them if they are used against us. So the rationales that have accompanied legal argument in international humanitarian law for decades are now being played back to governments, and I think that that is decidedly troubling.

GEORGE WALKER: Two points, number one I was referring to Roosevelt's statement during World War II. The United States did not ratify the Gas Protocol until 1972, but it was basically that sort of, if you will, maybe a customary rule that he was referring to. Number two, is that assuming no, I would assume that maybe no war existed. If we assume that, does not so-called universal criminality apply? For example, genocide, as one, would it be a stretch, to say that bin Laden's point, his statements were genocidal in nature? But if terrorism itself is the new universal crime, as I think most would agree to today, can you not then apprehend those folks on that basis the same as piracy?

DINO KRITSIOTIS: Crimes against humanity.

GEORGE WALKER: Yes.Crimes against humanity as opposed to war crimes, which can occur only during armed conflict.

U.S. AUDIENCE: Lieutenant Colonel Govern, the My Lai incident created the so-called Law of War Program in the military, primarily the Army, participated in for years. Since the last, this present conflict in Iraq, and going back to what Mr. Hurwitz said about the present Administration sort of using a cafeteria approach toward picking and choosing what part of the Geneva Conventions will be applicable, instead of taking it as a lump sum approach as taught in the Law of War program. Where is that program now, and what do you teach at West Point?

KEVIN GOVERN: Just as all my comments are caveated by the principle that I do not necessarily represent the principles, or the thoughts, or the policies of the United States Department of Defense, West Point, or, for that matter, the United States Army. I can comment on things from personal experience and personal observation. Law of armed conflict training had gone on quite some time prior to Lieutenant Calley having been involved in the abuses at Vietnam. It was incredible that he had never received any training. But it has been revitalized and reinvigorated after that time frame. It is an integral part of what we do at West Point, for those who go through officer candidate school, at Fort Bragg or elsewhere in career services, as well as the reserve officer training corps programs at USC, or any other school across the nation. Every soldier, sailor, airmen, or marine, before they ever graduate boot camp of whatever variety, always, always receives law of armed conflict training. If they say something to the contrary, it simply is not the case. The state of training is high, and it is particularly good when a unit is activated, or is alerted that it is going to go off on a deployment. Very careful training, not just to have a lawyer get up and talk for 10–15 minutes about generalized principles, but to go through situational training exercises. As the Judge's, our moderator's, unit had gone to Bosnia, or rather to Kosovo, very elaborate training was orchestrated to make sure that the threats that they would encounter would be put into that training, and then the appropriate response would be back briefed to them, if they had inadvertently or intentionally violated the law of armed conflict in that training scenario. Investigations are careful and thorough, but the key is really to not make everybody scared of the law, or fearful that they are going to get whacked upside the head because they have done something wrong. It is to be confident that the law will protect the rights of humanity and the rights of citizens. I cannot really comment on U.S. policy with regards to Geneva Conventions.

U.S. AUDIENCE: The law of armed conflict at West Point or in these other places as you say. It appears now that the application has led to symposia like this talking about torture and similar matters. I mean the application of the law of war as we knew it prior to 9/11, now seems to be somewhat different.

KEVIN GOVERN: The abuses at Abu Gharib and elsewhere, sir, have been universally condemned by the U.S. Government, the U.S. administration and by others. I can say that the training for troops, factors in the things that they need to do, they need to know. For instance, this summer I am going to be doing situational training with cadets so that they understand how to deal with civilians on the battlefield. How can you create that training in part of what they do in the course of them going along. I cannot comment on ongoing investigations of which there are a number to still look at the Abu Gharib and other incidents. When the dust settles from that, I think we will all know a little better on how we might need to adjust, not just national policy, but also the training to ensure that future abuses do not take place.

U.S. AUDIENCE: One thing that has run through this discussion so far, if Rabbi Crane would comment on this, is the asymmetric nature of this conflict. We are talking about something very close to holy war here. We have spent a lot of time discussing our law and how we are trying to adopt and adapt our law to this unique situation. And I hope I am not misunderstanding the law, if there is a law, that our opponents, and I am not talking about Muslims generally, I know that they do adhere to a moral law, but the al Qaeda apparently does not. They seem to be motivated by practicality or expediency. And the history of holy war beginning biblically, at least as I understand, with Joshua and Jericho implementing the ban, is one that you define your enemy in battle as those who believe differently than you do, not by whether they wear a uniform, not by any other criteria that we use, but what they believe. And that is the difficulty I think we have today is dealing with that. The last time I think we dealt with it was when we attacked Okinawa, and we had the kamikazi pilots. They had the same problem we have with suicide bombers today. We are dealing with an enemy that thinks fundamentally differently than we do. I do not think that, unfortunately, our adherence to the law is going to change their way of seeing things. I am afraid the real enemy that we are dealing with can only be dealt with force, unfortunately.

JONATHAN CRANE: I think that it is really important to pay attention to the rhetoric coming from terrorist groups, whether they are framing it as a holy war or as a different kind of struggle. Their perspective of whatever pursuits they are pursuing. It is really important for us to be able to assess what our response ought to be, because we are all concerned about certain levels of proportionality. The discussion today has been around how extraordinary the war, the so-called war on terror, is and how it is pushing the legal, military, and ethical envelopes for us. And because of its extraordinary nature, we find ourselves creating exceptions for ourselves, bending the rules of war, bending our normal understanding of what is moral behavior in conflict situations. And this is extraordinarily troubling for us, because the longer this endures, and the longer we exist and sustain a culture of exceptionality, what we normally understand to be moral grounding and moral behavior and law abiding behavior becomes blurred. Because we want our soldiers and our leaders and our religions to justify and behave in superogatory ways. Above the letter of the law, so as to protect ourselves to protect our securities and our civil liberties. But this is morally untenable in the long run, because it will fundamentally shift our moral foundations of what we understand to be law abiding behavior or moral behavior. And I think that is why this conversation is so important. It is because we are beginning to feel ourselves, just in the last 4 years, to feel out the ground, the moral ground beneath ourselves beginning to shake. And we are scared, I think legitimately so, of turning into our enemies. And we have seen glimpses of that in certain operations around the world, not so far from here even. So, your question is very important, and I think that we need to continue to revisit it, particularly as this so-called war on terror, as we have all acknowledged today, does not have a definite clearly defined end point. We do not know what success means. And until we can define what success means, I think we are going to be in difficult times.

GEORGE WALKER: I am going to respond as a lawyer. I am going to respond by saying that I think that first of all, there are certain concepts in the law such as necessity, proportionality, the doctrine, the separate doctrine of necessity and so forth. All of those may have different standards, different meanings depending on whether one is dealing with a self-defense situation, with a law of war situation, or maybe a defense against terrorists. Remember, at one time, the idea of self-defense was invoked against pirates. Do we not have a sort of universal type of folks similar to pirates? I think another thing is we are relearning in the sense of revisiting old concepts in the law. At one time, as you know, pirates were strung out along the coasts of this area where we are now all the way to Latin America. The Royal Navy and to a certain extent the United States Navy cleaned them out. The same thing is true about slavery. Which still, unfortunately, exists in the world today. And some of those concepts that have been long since gone, may be coming back. For example, there is law, much of it, but there is law that has approved the idea of intervening in certain areas. Cleaning out nests of pirates. They do not levitate and they have to go home to a home base somewhere. Well, can you go in and clean them out when the sovereign power, in this case Colonial Spain and Cuba, could not do so? The few cases I found say the answer is yes. Could you not then, perhaps, go in and clean out terrorists in a similar situation? Well, law by analogy might suggest the answer is yes to that too. And I just simply say there are new ideas and the use of old concepts, I think, I am a little more confident, I guess, as a lawyer.

DINO KRITSIOTIS: My understanding is that the Geneva Conventions are not "a la carte". They specify certain obligations, which have to be followed. There are some parts of the Geneva Conventions that entitle or empower states to act in certain ways. And we have seen that with regard to the occupation of Iraq where the United States followed the essential structure of the Fourth Geneva Convention and the 1907 Hague Regulations. But I think, technically speaking, you have to come up with some kind of overwhelming argument to say you are no longer bound by the compulsory law that is there. I think, try as it has, the Bush administration has not been as successful as it might have, at least with me. Number two, I think it does actually matter, compliance, for another reason.

Not so much in terms of the technical position of these Conventions, but the proof that compliance matters, to me, is demonstrated in the fact that the world outcry has now moved from what happened on September 11th, to what is happening in Guantanamo and what has been happening at Abu Gharib. It seems to me that, if one reads international law and reads these conventions, one can actually decipher/understand/basically comprehend why that outcry is the way it is.

HIKMAHANTO JUWANA: Well, one thing from the, this is from the Indonesian perspective. After 9/11, probably, some Indonesians felt that they could relate to, what you call here, the Islamic extremists. Now, of course this picture has changed in recent years. Why has it changed? Because firstly, Indonesia itself is a victim of terrorist attacks. Secondly, terrorist means have been used by an insurgent movement within Indonesia. One of the questions that we are confronted with, is, for example, like in the U.S. military, our military, would want to assert their force. But the question is, many people because of the awareness of human rights, they tend to say that this may contravene human rights. So the problem of the military applying full force like the previous "authoritarian" government does not exist anymore. So this is the problem that also confronts Indonesia, whether you want to use force to eradicate terrorists or, of course, comply with the laws and then the question, of course, if you preserve human rights, whether this thing kind of makes the use of force not sufficient. So this is the problem that I think we are facing, and again as mentioned by previous speakers, this is something that I think our community, the international community has to face on the new challenges of these terrorist issues

U.S. AUDIENCE: The way it has appeared to me over the past however many decades is that we seem in the United States to be moving away from a true freedom of religion background in terms of having lawsuits about prayer in schools, the Ten Commandments being put in a governmental building. We seem to have moved to a belief that it is Christianity or Atheism, and we Christians do not seem to recognize that there are other religions. We seem to discount those, and I am afraid that around the world that lack of respect for the religions of other countries, our ueber-consumerism, the fact that we do not want to become global citizens, join the Kyoto Protocol. All these types of things, I am afraid, that have made us targets. And I think that people who say after 9/11, why do they hate us? It is a very naïve viewpoint without looking in the mirror to see that, perhaps in some ways, we are causing some of the enmity around the world to be directed toward us, and perhaps if we could consider that maybe there are some things we could change about our own behavior, perhaps that would, maybe change the view other countries toward us.

KEVIN GOVERN: One of the things that has transpired since 9/11 is more high school students and college students than ever before are studying about Islam, because they are wondering why is it that a religion purportedly would support actions that Osama bin Laden claims. They will find out that he has no authority to issue a fatwa. He has no authority under Islam. They find out that is a peaceable religion. It is a religion that is founded on peace and submission to Allah. So, sometimes the media will present an image such that it is Christianity or Atheism. But perhaps we, in fact, have moved, if we talk to our kids, talk to teenagers, talk to other individuals that really there is an underlying but unspoken movement, to try and come to a greater understanding. Maybe to find that there are more similarities than differences. It is one man's viewpoint, but I try to be part of the solution and part of what I teach is talking about world events, talking world religions, specifically talking about the world of Islam and how that law and religion are intertwined in much of the world, in one-sixth of the world.

GEORGE WALKER: I just was saying the CNN effect. That one of the problems we have got out there is instantaneous worldwide communications via two media. Number one is television, exactly as we had linkups between here and Indonesia today, and number two is the internet. And I think that, unfortunately, there is some stuff on the internet that I send away on my spam catcher that, you know, is not very flattering if it is perceived as coming from the United States. I do not know where it comes from, but you know. And I think that that is another factor.

LEGAL RESPONSIBILITY AND NATIONAL VIEWS PANEL
[PART VI]

Participants:

Miriam J. Aukerman, Western Michigan Legal Services, former consultant to the Open Society Institute
Professor David Linnan, University of South Carolina School of Law
Professor Carl Evans, University of South Carolina Dept of Religion

MODERATOR: I will ask an initial question/comment that draws, I think, on the remarks made by all three of our panelists. But I think you will share my view that this final panel has provoked a lot of questions, hopefully for all of us, so I then will open the floor for questions or comments from the audience. I would like to start by asking a some what rhetorical question that relates really more to the remarks that David and Miriam made, and then make a broader comment/question that relates more to something that everyone talked about. The first question that I would ask, which is framed in the form of a question, as Alex Trebeck would say, but it is more a comment. With regard to the distinction between truth and reconciliation commissions and criminal prosecutions, whether the crimes that we are talking about, particularly when we are thinking about mass atrocities, are in the domain of the domestic law of the state were they occurred, or whether they are more part of a broader domain in international law, whether as violation of a jus cogens norm, or for some other reason for violations of customary international law? This was a question that occurred to me during the course of Miriam's remarks initially, but particularly David's remarks, when he began talking about the Sosa case. The question there really gets to the extent to which transitional states have the right to exercise sole authority over crimes committed in their countries, or the extent to which those crimes raise larger concerns that the international community has the right, or indeed in some cases, a responsibility to become involved in. That leads me directly into the second thought that I have, and it ties directly into the remarks Carl was just making. It began for me when Miriam was talking about the relationship of the goals of crime to mass atrocities, and I initially wondered whether the goals of those, of a domestic criminal system, are similar to or different from the goals in a mass atrocities situation. Presuming, and I would have asked that question, presuming that the answer would be no, and then ask what can we learn from that? It then led directly into what David was talking about, when he was talking about truth and reconciliation commissions, and talking about their purpose, that perhaps they may come about largely because the states in question simply cannot prosecute, or lack the judicial resources. But I think that there is one thing that may have been missing in David's remarks, but that came up a little bit later but not explicitly, which is that, at least in the rhetoric of some of those states, it is also about being able to move forward, that has certainly been in the rhetoric of South Africa, a state which did have the judicial resources, though had other problems that led to a truth and reconciliation commission there or other concerns. But to the extent that it is about moving forward, and to the extent that, and now I tie in Carl's remarks, that it comes from a notion of collective or societal good over individual responsibility. The comparativist in me, wonders what lessons we can import into domestic law from, and I pose this to the panel, what lessons we could import into domestic law from the truth and reconciliation commission process, to the extent that we see it as something that is different from what we have in our domestic legal systems. Perhaps there is something that it responds to that we do not have. Now we typically do not take lessons, for better or worse, from the developing world, particularly from transitional societies. But maybe there is something here, I wonder, that we might be able to import? Not, and I do not need to bring us at the end of our day into domestic criminal law, but rather to think more broadly, both as a society bringing in our religious mores, societal mores, and legal mores into sort of unitary framework, whether there is a lesson that we might draw from this transitional justice and transitional truth and reconciliation commission process? Whether prosecution is always the right answer, or whether there are other solutions to be found? So, I pose that set of questions to you all for your thoughts.

MIRIAM AUKERMAN: I think in domestic systems we think about crimes as being both crimes against victims and crimes against the public. And in the international context, I think we can to the same things. These are crimes against a particular society but they are also crimes against the international community, they are both. How you prioritize that, we know, where you are going to do the prosecution, or whether you are going to do truth and reconciliation commission, how are you going to respond to those things. I think it ultimately comes down to what the goals are. I mean, I think that international prosecutions have a great condemnatory function of sort of saying, we as an international community will not put up with this. On the other hand, if we are talking about, as David has said, sort of moving a society forward, maybe a truth and reconciliation commission in the country in question, is preferable because, you know, it is not like everybody in the former Yugoslavia is watching what is going on. It is much easier to do that if it is within your own context. The South African Truth and Reconciliation Commission got a tremendous amount of attention there, partly because it was local, partly because of the way it was structured. And then, in response to your second, sort of, point or last point, about what we can learn from the international context. I think one of the things that truth and reconciliation commissions do, is they really look at a restorative justice framework. They really sort of say, how do we bring, how do we repair relationships in societies that are deeply brutalized, deeply fractured, where there is just tremendous pain? And in the domestic context, there have been some efforts to look at restorative justice as well. I mean, it is very different because restorative justice efforts in domestic context are typically low level offenders where you have got the shoplifter and the shopkeeper. You know, you are not having rapist sitting down with rape victims, generally in the domestic context. And in the international context, you are talking about really the most horrific crimes and moving on from those. And what we have done in the restorative justice context in the United States and domestic law has really been about minor violations of law, but I think it is an interesting approach to think about how we can move more into restorative justice framework within our own criminal justice system, as well.

MODERATOR: I just want to point something out for those who are not particularly familiar with truth and reconciliation commissions. They generally do not provide amnesties for violations of criminal law, that is for criminal violations that occurred during the period. That is, ordinary crime violations that occurred during the period for which amnesties are being granted. So, it is not that these truth and reconciliation commissions are about resolving all the crimes during that period. But rather those crimes that are at the heart of the transition of the society.

DAVID LINNAN: I would give a couple of different comments to the extent that you ask the question, what can we learn for domestic consumption. I am not sure whether you are asking what you might call a legal culture question. You could say, if what the truth and reconciliation kind of process is, it is a sort of nonindividualized justice process, if it is not political, let us say at least it does not aim to resolve something in the traditional sense with the judge, or you could say that is what ADR is. If you are to talk about it in the criminal law context, you sometimes hear about privatized justice. You know this is the idea that you have instead of prosecutions via the solicitor, or something like that, in conjunction with shoplifting or the like, you may have some sort of financial or other penalty via the stores. So, people actually talk about this stuff in the criminal law area, but what is distinctive about it, is that it basically removes the state. So, you take things out of the formalized criminal justice system. Now, that is one comment. I would, however, reflect that one of the reasons why I was careful not to get too deep into this other than time, is I have a strong suspicion that Ken Hurwitz's skin may have been crawling while I was talking about this for the following reason that, you brought up, specifically, the idea of jus cogens and mandatory rules. And one of the implicit questions is, if in fact they are not applying the rules because they are not doing the prosecutions. Yes, jus cogens is nice in the books, but if state practice means we are really not following those rules that we say are immutable, what about it? Well, you know you would eventually have to say, are they really immutable or what does it mean? So, if you look further, I think the other kind of problem for people in the human rights community is, as soon as you go the cultural route and you say, well, we have a strong view of individual responsibility and, therefore, we favor the prosecution model; and, on the other hand, you talk about, in different societies, there is the reference to more belief in some sort of collective social welfare or the like, where that tends to head you, over time, is towards questions about whether you have universal views of human rights, which is a much bigger argument. So the whole issue is when you start going down the road and you say, people are not behaving the way that, let us say, the international human rights community or, let us say, the academic world may want them to behave in terms of favoring individual responsibility, favoring the ICC, and you look at behavior, and then you begin trying to interpret it. Well, I think what is more interesting in that sense is not necessarily how you feel about transitional justice or how you feel about international tribunal versus truth and reconciliation commission, but what it really tells you, about what people believe in fact are the substantive rules based upon state practice in the international law area.

U.S. AUDIENCE: Miriam, it kind of ties into your restorative justice. If the remedy we want to provide is the restoration of the individual dignity, it seems to me that the truth and reconciliation process works, but it is not what David is describing as let bygones be bygones, and move to the future. What is critical is, you are pinning individual responsibility on the wrongdoer, and by doing so in public forum you are elevating the people whose human rights are being destroyed or damaged. And by, and it seems to me, maybe the truth and reconciliation process, you know, meets the sort of individual issues that David was raising and it also, if we are trying to restore the dignity of the violated folks, it is an explanation for the goal of the criminal process within this context.

MIRIAM AUKERMAN: I would just say that I think that in a lot of traumatized societies often what, you know say surviving family members want, what they really want, is they want to know what happened. They want to know, where the bodies are buried literally, and how their loved ones disappeared, and those sorts of things. And prosecutions are not really very effective for getting at that. Because, you know, your defendants are going to deny, or they are going to do the equivalent of pleading the Fifth Amendment, or whatever it is. Whereas a truth and reconciliation commission, where people come forward, I mean essentially, if you tie, if you require perpetrators to tell the stories and tie that with amnesty, you can get at a lot of the facts that do not come out in prosecutions. You cannot give people retribution because you are giving the amnesty, and so you are not giving them punishment. But you can give them the information, that for some of them may be more important which is, what actually happened to my child? How did my child die? Where is my child's body? That can be more important.

U.S. AUDIENCE: I think that is true, but also the public humiliation of the perpetrator, the fact that now all society knows what a horrible thing you have done. That by bringing the wrongdoer down, you elevate the victim up, and the victim feels some satisfaction from that. I mean, I do not know for sure that is true, but there is some anecdotal evidence I have seen that it is, and some very neat little social psychology experiments that added a lot of credibility in my mind to it.

MODERATOR: It does though raise some concerns, I think, on Carl's point about valuing individual responsibility there over the collective societal good because there we are weighting the victim's rights perhaps above the long term societal rights.

U.S. AUDIENCE: I think it is probably good for the society. I mean, I think if you heal a large group of people who have been damaged by human rights violations. Through the process, I mean this sounds sort of a panacea, but it seems to me it sanctions the criminals, it elevates the victims, and it reunites the society.

U.S. AUDIENCE: We have something of precedent for truth and reconciliation, and I had not thought about it until David made his presentation here. But within the last month, I read an article in the United Methodist magazine about how the United Methodist church is now promoting truth and reconciliation as a means of resolving what would otherwise be criminal matters. A typical case is where the church treasurer embezzles money, and rather than having that person tried for a criminal offense. We actually have people, I did not know about this until I read it, who are being trained to conduct this process within the church, to conduct this healing. My lawyerly instincts says, oh that is a bad thing; we ought to hold that person responsible for their actions. But frankly, I think I am seeing it in a little different light now, and I think the church may well be onto something good. And that is within our culture of, you know, individual responsibility, so perhaps the church may have something, and I do not think the United Methodist church is the only one doing this. But the shifting of the remedy from one of enforcement of the law and individual responsibility, to one of truth and reconciliation, is happening now in our country.

U.S. AUDIENCE: Is the whole congregation involved in the process?

U.S. AUDIENCE: That's right.

U.S. AUDIENCE: See, that would be very consistent.

U.S. AUDIENCE: And there is, the focus is on healing. And both ways the congregation and the person and, I need to know more about it, I will have to admit that I am not that familiar with the process, but I am going to become so.

U.S. AUDIENCE: I would like to just kind of throw out, you talked about perhaps tribunals being like a first tier, and truth and reconciliation being a second tier. I wonder if perhaps that it might not be best to look at them as like different tools used in a tool box in different situations. And take into consideration all the contexts in the situations, i.e., what are the cultures involved? How much, you know, are the parties that are involved, is one party going to be able to leave and go away from the other party or they going to have to continue to live together under all, for all times? Is there a rule of law, a strong rule of law, or is it a society that does not really have a background or setup for rule of law? And if all of those things are taken into consideration, sometimes it is not a matter of something being better or worse, it is some times one tool works better in certain situations.

KEN HURWITZ: I find a lot of the discussion has been very helpful, and the analysis is very useful, and the considerations to different alternative approaches to things are very enlightening. But I am very troubled by the notions that these things are dichotomies, I really think that it is a false dichotomy to think that it is justice verses truth, or that it is accountability versus social reparation and social improvement. I think nobody who is a strong advocate of accountability measures, I think, would have any disagreement with the points about other forms of prevention, of reparations, of reconciliation, of community, community communications and so forth. All of those things are crucial and nobody, I think, really seriously would say that you could dispense with them all simply to have trials. Nor would anybody really seriously suggest that a process either requires, or it is a failure if it does not succeed in prosecuting everybody who commits a serious crime. The analogy, I think Miriam made it with epidemics, I think is helpful but risky. These kinds of crimes are epidemics in the way that they spread. But I think the empirical research generally shows that they do not just arise out of themselves. They arise because there are people who are leaders in them, and they get stirred up and the leadership is a crucial factor in these kinds of crimes. The accountability issue really is about the admission. Part of the point of accountability is to show that not everyone in the other ethnic group or in the other political tribe, is equally responsible, or is fundamentally and essentially responsible even if thousands or tens of thousands of people have committed serious crimes. The other thing that I think should be supplemented, is David's invocation of state practice for two reasons. One of which is, the jury really should still be considered out on this. This is a very new area of activity. Countries are really finding their way on their own. There has not been great precedence, but I think that there has been great progress and lessons learned. You point to the brief in *Sosa,* and okay that is fine. But you do not mention that South Africa also was one of the very early advocates of the International Criminal Court, and one of the very first states to pass a very comprehensive implementation statute for domestic requirements under the Rome Statute, which includes a universal jurisdiction provision. One of the points that has been made recently in the debates regarding the Security Council referral of Darfur to the International Criminal Court, that was made last week, was the United States is saying, was putting forward a position, well this should really be a African court that does it. And dozens of countries basically said listen, this is an African court. There are twenty some countries that have either signed or signed in ratified the Rome Statute in Africa. And it is no coincidence that several of these have been self-referrals, such as Uganda, Democratic Republic of Congo, Cote d'Ivoire. The other thing is that I think that nobody argues that these are alternatives to national justice. The International Criminal Court obviously could not possibly pretend to be substituting for the world's justice system, and it does not see itself that way. The prosecutor pointed out, perhaps a little glibly, he said we would really be succeeding if I do not have anything to do. And the whole point is the principle complimentary, the International Criminal Court is intended to be an anchor, to handle the heaviest lifting so that other judicial systems are able to handle still very important, but less overwhelming tasks of accountability. I also think it is important to keep in mind some of the implications. Chile, for example, even the unsuccessful attempt to extradite Pinochet from England to Spain for prosecution, triggered a major opening up of the political system and a opening up of the sense of transparency there. And, of course, it resulted in criminal action against Pinochet there. A freezing of the system that was only able to be opened up perhaps from the push that it got from abroad. El Salvador, which is one of the countries, if I am not mistaken, I think it is actually the first situation, where there was a truth commission. The truth commission there was a very successful document. It was a very successful investigation of what happened. It did not focus on naming names, but it definitely did indicate serious major figures who are responsible for many of the crimes. And it definitely allocated a relative responsibility among the different forces. That truth commission very explicitly called in its recommendations that there be prosecutions. It saw itself as a front-runner, front leader to prosecutions. The fact that the El Salvador government never did engage in prosecutions resulted in a serious price. It was a seamless transition from people who were leaders of death squads to now people who were godfathers of criminal mafias. And it is not a successful example of where truth rather than prosecution made for a comfortable transition to anything. People walked around in El Salvador and see the people who tortured them or their fathers. That is not a situation in which the rule of law has advanced very significantly at all. Just two other quick examples, I am sorry for taking so much time. Liberia, Charles Taylor, one of the things about this Taylor situation is that he has been reportedly, very blatantly and very constantly, violating the terms of his asylum agreement with Nigeria. He has been intervening in many different ways in internal politics and in economic actions, and in criminal actions in Liberia and elsewhere. And, in fact, there is real concern, from what I have been hearing, that in the coming elections in October, that his party may well be reelected. And that is an example of how there is a shadow that comes from allowing these major leaders to continue to be seen as impervious and powerful. The last example is Afghanistan, when the major fighting, excuse the term, stopped in Afghanistan, there were lots of international human rights groups that were saying we must have accountability for crimes, and that does not just mean the Taliban. It also means the warlords and those in the Northern Alliance and the drug gangs. And, of course, the United States and the other realists were saying, well that is ridiculous, I mean, how can we do that? There is no stability in the country otherwise. And, of course, the United States was largely dependent on paying warlords to carry out as proxy fighters. Well, what happened? Well, now we have situation, where the present government is continually threatened by the power of the warlords. Where Afghanistan has returned to the position of the overwhelmingly major drug producer in the world. Where constant income was coming in. Where basically, continuing four years later, that the official government in Afghanistan largely is a de facto mayor of Kabul. So I think there are prices, yes, to having accountability, but there are prices that are very serious in social reconciliation in not having accountability.

INTERNATIONAL LAW ROUNDTABLE
[PARTS V AND VI]

PARTICIPANTS:

Dean Hikmahanto Juwana, University of Indonesia Faculty of Law
Dr. Dino Kritsiotis, University of Michigan Law School and University of Nottingham, Faculty of Law, UK
Professor George Walker, Wake Forest Law School
Professor Kevin Govern, Lt Col, USA JAGC (retired), Former USMA at West Point Dept of Law
Miriam J. Aukerman, Western Michigan Legal Studies and former consultant to the Open Society Institute
Professor David Linnan, University of South Carolina School of Law
Professor Carl Evans, University of South Carolina Dept of Religion

U.S. AUDIENCE: Are we to the point that say, this panel, this time, this place that we can have a Islamic leader, someone who is familiar with Islamic law stand up in front of us and unabashedly and unashamed say, he thinks law should be this way because God told him? Because the Koran says it is that way, or Mohamed said it has to be that way. Are we comfortable with that yet? Because that is what they are doing, and if we are not comfortable with it yet, what are we here for?

DAVID LINNAN: Speaking in purely practical terms, you would invite him in by video-conferencing, because you would be worried about whether you could get a visa for him to enter the US. And it is possible to do that, and one of the reasons why we imported the Indonesians via videoconferencing was I thought it was good to hear something from the other person's point of view. I guess if you ask me though the interesting question is that what I think we're going to try to do prospectively is actually, we had in mind bringing in three women who are in the area of Islam, human rights, and women's rights. And then, adding people on for what you might call non-Western views of human rights. And, I do not know, Ken's skin is probably crawling again. But what happens in that case, is the interesting question, is actually if you work in the Islamic world but you are not a full time Islamicist like Kevin, what happens is these people you know, well, yes they may be sort of leading human right scholars and they believe in their religion but, of course, as women they have something of a problem with their treatment. So that the funny thing is if you wanted to get the man to stand up and say, well all you people are oppressing the living daylights out of us. It would be perfectly possible to produce that person, and it would be relatively easy except he might have to be videoconferenced in. But I think it is actually more interesting from the point of view of bringing people in so you see a little bit more how it is not even a unitary view, because of what happens, meaning that if you bring in the person who is the human rights and women's rights activist, well she has her own domestic problems, on the religion side. So that, yes, it is possible but in some ways, I think you would learn more if you look at it more as the question about, well how do these people really think about this? It is not particularly useful to my way of thinking if we just bring somebody in to say, all you people just do not understand us.

U.S. AUDIENCE: We talked about inviting the world in to a greater discussion, but the world is not on the same page we are on, or they view the page we are on as sacrilege, not all of them, but a good majority of them. My question is, are we going to be comfortable with that person sitting here and having nothing, no discourse anymore heated than we had today, but just be confident in the fact that the reason he believes what he believes, is because God told him?

DINO KRITSIOTIS: I think the bigger problem for al Qaeda is not so much its fundamentalist beliefs in terms of religion, it is the fact it is a nonstate actor. So, as an international lawyer, we do not have to take any account of what they say. They simply do not have any authority, any platform, to change the laws or give a rival interpretation. And I think I would have found it much more troublesome, as an international lawyer, if Islamic states had closed ranks behind al Qaeda's interpretations at the Geneva Conventions by saying that the twin towers were legitimate targets. To my knowledge, no state, with the exception of Afghanistan, came out and supported al Qaeda's position. So religious fundamentalism does not amend the rules in any way. I think I have a deeper concern with your President, actually, because I remember just after 9/11, it was President Bush, he used religious language in terms of talking about crusades and, in fact, originally Operation Enjoying Freedom was designated as Operation Infinite Justice, which quite ironically is a phrase from the Quran, I am not quite sure he was aware he was doing that.

U.S. AUDIENCE: One thing, when we were talking about before about truth and reconciliation, I started thinking about comparative negligence for some reason. Because it seems like, within the countries, I do not know about everybody else, but there never really seems to be a right and a wrong. It seems like that there are war crimes being committed on all sides.

MIRIAM AUKERMAN: Yes, I mean think this goes to the points that were made earlier. It seems to me that, whether or not that is true, really depends on the society in question. I mean there are going to be cases like Nazi Germany, where you have really horrific leadership and where you really have to have that individual accountability, and really go after that leadership. There are also going to be times when you are dealing much more with comparative fault, where there is fault on all sides, and I think it is not a binary choice between prosecution and truth and reconciliation. It is a question of looking at what we are trying to achieve. What is it that we want to get? And in the context of the particular society and particular atrocity in question, are we going to get that through prosecutions, are we going to get that through reconciliation commissions, or are we going to get that through a combination? How are we going to get to where we want to be? And sometimes it is a combination, sometimes you really need that individual responsibility piece, sometimes you want something else, and sometimes you want both.

U.S. AUDIENCE: Sometimes it may end up entering into a cycle of violence. Sometimes it is a place like Chiapas that was fairly early in a cycle of violence. It might lend itself more truth and reconciliation commissions than some place like Rwanda, where a hundred thousand people are killed in eight days. By that time it is massive genocide, and that may not lend itself.

KEVIN GOVERN: It is an interesting point on Rwanda. My colleagues probably know about this better than I, but I learned fairly recently that Rwanda has what are called gachacha courts, community courts. So-called "courts on the grass," where you do have so many culpable actors that, I do not know if I necessarily would go with a comparative negligence argument, but to call out the ones that are least culpable, the ones that could be handled with a restorative justice in the community. Over twenty-five thousand judges, in the course of really a few months, were trained at a grass-roots level, pun intended, to do these grass courts by the few lawyers that were in Rwanda in order to do that. Is it the best form of justice? Is it a perfect form of justice? Would we call it tier 1 or tier 2? No, but it is at least a step, and it was home grown. It was from the people for the people; so interesting notion on Rwanda that you probably did not get from Hotel Rwanda.

JOHN MANSFIELD: It should be recognized some of the philosophies talked about are in a direct conflict with the Anglo-American legal traditions. This is not to focus on individual responsibility, as is the focus of criminal law, but individual harm, the rights of the individual who has been harmed to have a remedy. To take a very garden variety example, supposing your land has been trespassed upon or your property has been seized. This is a basic late eighteenth century situation. You bring an action for compensation for the trespass. It is not an answer in the Anglo-American tradition that, yes, do not cause us trouble, we are dealing with larger issues, the larger issues of social reconciliations, of the future, of the harmony of the society. No, no my land has been trespassed upon. Now I was very struck by the reference to the Alien Tort Claims Act, where the South Africans said apparently, according to David, please do not cause us trouble in South Africa by providing a tort remedy under the Alien Tort Claims Act in the United States by somebody who has been tortured in South Africa and then ends up in the United States, and manages to serve process upon the torturer in the United States. The Alien Tort Claims Act represents, no, this person has been injured and wronged. These are individual rights, and we are not going to sacrifice this individual to some larger good. So, I am just trying to point out that it seems to me, you are fighting a very strong current of individual rights and remedies for the violation of rights that is represented embodied in the Anglo-American tradition.

DAVID LINNAN: The one thing I would say is actually, if you look at most of the developing world, they are more from the non-Anglo-American legal side. If you look in Asia, for example, those are with very few exceptions Civil Law jurisdictions, much of Africa is Civil Law, South American is basically Civil Law, so that I think what is unusual is that, in some ways, we do not want to talk about some differing views of human rights and how people in Civil Law jurisdictions approach them, as opposed to, how you might in Anglo-American jurisdictions. But I think it is fair to say that, at least in the international sphere, there is sort of an assumption that that kind of thing follows our model, but one of the issues is actually, if you were to go around and count noses, I think it is fair to say that most of the developing world, for example, is not a Common Law jurisdiction. So you have India, yes, you have Singapore, you have Malaysia, you have got Nigeria. But pretty soon you start finding out the Chinese, the Japanese, the Vietnamese, the Indonesians, the Thais, all of those folks are Civil Law jurisdictions traditionally. Since Latin America was colonized by the Portuguese or the Spanish, those countries are all ex-colonial Civil Law jurisdictions. And it is, I think, about a 1/3–2/3 split in Africa, in terms of the French versus the English-speaking ex-colonies. So actually part of the question that is hidden, when we say Anglo-American human rights law and the like. I admit that, indeed, it is, let us say, a provocative opinion. But I approach this from the point of view of asking the question not what people say, but what they do. And if you look at, for example, the number of countries in which you, staying with the example of transitional justice, you see that instead of going with the international tribunal, or even the domestic tribunal. I would fully admit that it is an uncomfortable trade, but the question is, do you pay attention to what they say, or do you pay attention to what they do? And then you recognize that the people in these situations are probably largely not from our legal family, if you want to put it in those terms.

JOHN MANSFIELD: I agree with you entirely in your description, it only brings out more starkly that there is a conflict here to now focus upon, individual rights and individual damage. With another conception, where the individual is more subordinated to a larger vision of the good. With all my work in India, I am very familiar with what you are describing to me, and the introduction of the British torts and ideas of individual rights produced a stark contrast between these. But I am just trying to point out that it is fairly recent, this idea that, well maybe that was a mistake and the British would not have introduced into India these kinds of institutions to vindicate these individual rights and damage to individuals, you know, because that maybe a better way to handle it was the indigenous way for these other people.

DINO KRITSIOTIS: I think that it is worth while bearing in mind that in the Pinochet case amnesties were actually reached in Chile. And while we may want to respect the validity of those amnesties amongst the Chilean people, as we would with the amnesties in South Africa, it is not all clear to me why an amnesty reached in one country would bind the courts of another country. If amnesties are effectively contractual relationships established among citizens of one country, I'm not sure that they would bind the court of a third country. And what I find very interesting is that the question of amnesties actually has been left silent in the Rome Statute. Now there are silences and there are silences. It may well be the silence on the amnesties on the Rome Statute was deliberate, or was just meant to leave the door open for another day. Speaking on my own behalf, I had a look at some of these amnesties and I think we need to qualify, we need to make qualifications between the different types of amnesties. I can see the amnesties as part of a prolonged process in South Africa, but when I saw the amnesties deals being reached in Sierra Leone in 1999 against the background of limbs being torn from 2-year old kids, I think that that is much more terrifying prospect. And I think the African continent, whether you are looking at Nigeria or Sierra Leone or South Africa, it is experiencing something of an amnesty epidemic. And I am not sure that sits well with an order that wants to commit itself with the rule of law.

DAVID LINNAN: The one thing that I would say is that this is not new. I speak from the point of view as someone who moves in what you would call "Asian law" circles. Because the question that you are asking is both an old and a new one when you ask, is this is a new development? If you ask yourself why did the Japanese adopt largely German law of the nineteenth century, and then the Koreans German law in the early twentieth century, and now, frankly, the Chinese are doing it? The interesting thing is if you pay attention and talk to people from there, the answer is, that it is a political matter. The feeling was it was more congenial in those states in the nineteenth century with the emperors, in Korea as a social matter in the early twentieth century, and in China now, there is a sense from those in power that, yes, they want to have better rules. But in fact they are more comfortable with a less individual rights-centered, heavily expertized, state-centered system. And so, putting aside history, instead of trying to imitate the House of Lords or the U.S. Congress, the Chinese in the public law area, for example, basically the People's Congress has procured all their legal reform consultants not from USAID but from the Germans, because they have decided they like the Continental public law view of how you regulate the state, which tends to be, let us say, less open to democracy, a more expertized system, and arguably allows for more community interest. But this is something where the Japanese made that decision 150 years ago, the Koreans made that decision 100 years ago, the Chinese had made that decision in the last 10 years, and there still, the Germans in the form of consultants, or Chinese academics returned from writing dissertations in Germany, are still giving advice on writing the statutes.

Further Reading

PART I. MEDIA, POLITICS, AND RELIGION

Baylis, John, and Steve Smith. *The Globalization of World Politics: An Introduction to International Relations.* New York, NY: Oxford University Press, 2001.

Brown, L. Carl. *The International Relations of the Middle East.* Princeton, NJ: Princeton University Press, 1984.

Eichenberg, Richard C., Richard J. Stoll, and Matthew Lebo. "War President: The Approval Ratings of George W. Bush." *Journal of Conflict Resolution* 50, no. 6 (2006): 783–808.

Elshtain, Jean Bethke. *Just War Against Terror.* New York, NY: Basic Books, 2003.

Fullerton, Jami A., and Alice Kendrick. *Advertising's War on Terrorism: The Story of the U.S. State Department's Shared Values Initiative.* Spokane, WA: Marquette Books, 2006.

Gelpi, Christopher, Peter D. Feaver, and Jason Reifler. "Success Matters: Casualty Sensitivity and the War in Iraq." *International Security* 30, no. 3 (Winter 2005–2006): 7–46.

Kaplan, Robert. *The Coming Anarchy: Shattering the Dreams of the Post Cold War.* New York, NY: Random House, 2000.

Nye, Joseph. *The Paradox of American Power: Why the World's Only Superpower Can't Go It Alone.* New York, NY: Oxford University Press, 2002.

Peters, Rudolph. *Islam and Colonialism: The Doctrine of Jihad in Islamic History.* The Hague: Mouton, 1979.

Sobel, Richard. *The Impact of Public Opinion on U.S. Foreign Policy.* New York, NY: Oxford University Press, 2001.

United States Department of Defense, Office of the Undersecretary of Defense for Acquisition, Technology and Logistics. Defense Science Board. *Report of the Defense Science Board Task Force on Strategic Communication.* Washington, DC, 2004.

Voeten, Erik, and Paul R. Brewer. "Public Opinion, the War in Iraq, and Presidential Accountability." *Journal of Conflict Resolution* 50, no. 5 (2006): 809–32.

Wald, Kenneth D. *Religion and Politics in the United States.* Washington, DC: Congressional Quarterly Press, 1997.

PART II. CONSTITUTIONAL AND DOMESTIC LAW: STRUCTURAL AND INSTITUTIONAL EMPHASIS

Ackerman, Bruce. "The Emergency Constitution." *Yale Law Journal* 113, no. 5 (2004): 1029–91.

Chemerinsky, Erwin. "Enemy Combatants and Separation of Powers." *Journal of National Security Law and Policy* 1 (2005): 72–87.

Coll, Steve. *Ghost Wars: The Secret History of the CIA, Afghanistan, and Bin Ladin from the Soviet Invasion to September 10, 2001.* New York, NY: The Penguin Press, 2004.

Feldman, Noah. "From Liberty to Equality: The Transformation of the Establishment Clause." *California Law Review* 90, no. 3 (2002): 673–732.

Goldsmith, Jack. *The Terror Presidency: Law and Judgment Inside the Bush Administration.* New York, NY: W.W. Norton, 2007.

Greenawalt, Kent. "Common Sense About Original and Subsequent Understandings of the Religion Clauses." *University of Pennsylvania Journal of Constitutional Law* 8, no. 3 (2006): 479–512.

Hayden, Jessica Powley. "Mullahs on a Bus: The Establishment Clause and U.S. Foreign Aid." *Georgetown Law Journal* 95, no. 1 (2006): 171–206.

Kohn, Richard H. "Using the Military at Home: Yesterday, Today, and Tomorrow." *Chicago Journal of International Law* 4, no. 1 (Spring 2003): 165–92.

Levy, Leonard W. *The Establishment Clause: Religion and the First Amendment.* Chapel Hill, NC: University of North Carolina Press, 1994.

Mansfield, John H. "The Religion Clauses of the First Amendment and Foreign Relations." *DePaul Law Review* 36, no. 1 (Fall 1986): 1–40.

National Commission on Terrorist Attacks Upon the United States. *The 9/11 Commission Report.* New York, NY: W.W. Norton, 2004.

Posner, Richard A. *Not a Suicide Pact: The Constitution in a Time of National Emergency.* Oxford and New York: Oxford University Press, 2006.

Posner, Richard A. *Preventing Surprise Attacks: Intelligence Reform in the Wake of 9/11.* Lanham, MD: Rowman & Littlefield, 2005.

Sievert, Ronald J. "War on Terror or Global Law Enforcement Operation?" *Notre Dame Law Review* 78, no. 2 (2003): 307–53.

PART III. CONSTITUTIONAL AND DOMESTIC LAW: INDIVIDUAL RIGHTS EMPHASIS

Ackerman, Bruce A. *Before the Next Attack: Preserving Civil Liberties in the Age of Terrorism.* New Haven, CT: Yale University Press, 2006.

Baker, Thomas E., and John F. Stack, Jr., eds. *At War with Civil Rights and Civil Liberties.* Lanham, MD: Rowman & Littlefield Publishers, 2006.

Berkowitz, Peter, ed. *Terrorism, the Laws of War, and the Constitution: Debating the Enemy Combatant Cases.* Stanford, CA: Hoover Institution, 2005.

Berman, Nathaniel. "Privileging Combat? Contemporary Conflict and the Legal Construction of War." *Columbia Journal of Transnational Law* 43, no. 1 (Fall 2004): 1–71.

Bradley, Curtis A. "AGORA: Military Commissions Act of 2006: The Military Commissions Act, Habeas Corpus, and the Geneva Conventions." *American Journal of International Law* 101, no. 2 (2007): 322–45.

Brooks, Rosa Ehrenreich. "War Everywhere: Rights, National Security Law, and the Law of Armed Conflict in the Age of Terror." *University of Pennsylvania Law Review* 153, no. 2 (2004): 675–762.

Cole, David. *Enemy Aliens: Double Standards and Constitutional Freedoms in the War on Terrorism.* New York: New Press, 2003.

Jinks, Derek. "The Declining Significance of POW Status." *Harvard International Law Journal* 45, no. 2 (Summer 2004): 367–442.

Kutz, Christopher. "The Difference Uniforms Make: Collective Violence in Criminal Law and War." *Philosophy & Public Affairs* 33, no. 2 (Spring 2005): 148–80.

Margulies, Joseph. *Guantanamo and the Abuse of Presidential Power.* New York: Simon & Schuster, 2006.

Posner, Eric A., and Adrian Vermeule. *Terror in the Balance: Security, Liberty, and the Courts.* Oxford and New York, NY: Oxford University Press, 2007.

Rotunda, Ronald D. "The Detainee Cases of 2004 and 2006 and Their Aftermath." *Syracuse Law Review* 57, no. 1 (2006): 1–62.

Spark, Thomas M., and Glenn M. Sulmasy, eds. *International Law Challenges: Homeland Security and Combating Terrorism.* Newport, RI: Naval War College, 2006.

PART IV. LAW OF ARMED CONFLICT: RELIGION AND ARMED CONFLICT

Augustine. *Reply to Faustus the Manichean* 22. *The Nicene and Post-Nicene Fathers* (1st series). Translated by R. Stothert. Edited by Philip Schaff. Grand Rapids, MI: W. R. Eerdmans Pub. Co., 1956.

Asad, Talal. *Formations of the Secular: Christianity, Islam, Modernity.* Stanford, CA: Stanford University Press, 2003.

Baron, Salo W., and George S. Wise, eds. *Violence and Defense in the Jewish Experience.* Philadelphia, PA: Jewish Publication Society of America, 1977.

Eickelman, Dale F., and Jon W. Anderson. *New Media in the Muslim World: The Emerging Public Sphere.* 2nd ed. Indiana Series in Middle East Studies. Bloomington, IN: Indiana University Press, 2003.

Freamon, Bernard K. "Martyrdom, Suicide, and the Islamic Law of War: A Short Legal History." *Fordham International Law Journal* 27, no. 1 (2003): 299–369.

Hashmi, Sohail H., ed. *Islamic Political Ethics: Civil Society, Pluralism, and Conflict. The Ethikon Series in Comparative Ethics.* Princeton, NJ: Princeton University Press, 2002.

Johnson, James Turner. "Historical Roots and Sources of the Just War Tradition in Western Culture." In *Just War and Jihad,* edited by J. Kelsay and James Turner Johnson, 4–30. New York, NY: Greenwood, 1991.

Kelsay, John. *Islam and War: A Study in Comparative Ethics.* Louisville, KY: Westminster/John Knox Press, 1993.

Levinson, Sanford, ed. *Torture: A Collection.* New York, NY: Oxford University Press, 2004.

Luther, Martin. "Whether Soldiers, Too, Can Be Saved." In *Luther's Works,* vol. 46 *The Christian in Society III,* translated by C.M. Jacobs and revised by Robert C. Schultz, edited by Helmut T. Lehman, 87–139. Philadelphia, PA: Fortress Press, 1967.

Miller, Richard B., ed. *War in the Twentieth Century: Sources in Theological Ethics.* Louisville, KY: Westminster/John Knox Press, 1992.

Novak, David. *Covenantal Rights: A Study in Jewish Political Theory.* Princeton, NJ: Princeton University Press, 2000.

Pape, Robert Anthony. *Dying to Win: The Strategic Logic of Suicide Terrorism.* New York, NY: Random House, 2005.

Wright, Lawrence. *The Looming Tower: Al-Qaeda and the Road to 9/11.* New York, NY: Knopf, 2006.

PART V. LAW OF ARMED CONFLICT AND INTERNATIONAL LAW: OPERATIONAL LAW

Bantekas, Ilias. "The Contemporary Law of Superior Responsibility," *American Journal of International Law* 93, no. 3 (1999): 573–595.

Boot, Max. *The Savage Wars of Peace: Small Wars and the Rise of American Power.* New York, NY: Basic Books, 2002.

Brownlie, Ian. *Principles of Public International Law.* 6th ed. New York, NY: Oxford University Press, 2003.

Dinstein, Yoram. *The Conduct of Hostilities Under the Law of International Armed Conflict.* New York, NY: Cambridge University Press, 2004.

Doswald-Beck, Louise, and Jean-Marie Henckaerts, eds., *Customary International Humanitarian Law*. Cambridge: Cambridge University Press, 2005.

Fleck, Dieter, ed. *The Handbook of Humanitarian Law in Armed Conflicts*. New York, NY: Oxford University Press, 1995.

Langston, Emily. "The Superior Responsibility Doctrine in International Law: Historical Continuities, Innovation and Criminality: Can East Timor's Special Panels Bring Militia Leaders to Justice?" *International Criminal Law Review* 2 (2004): 141–183.

Linnan, David K. "Self Defense, Necessity and UN Collective Security: United States and Other Views." *Duke Journal of Comparative and International Law* 1991, no. 1 (1991): 57–123.

Metz, Steven, and Raymond Millen. "Insurgency and Counterinsurgency in the 21st Century: Reconceptualizing Threat and Response." Carlisle Barracks, Strategic Studies Institute, Army War College, November 2004. http://www.carlisle.army.mil/pdffiles/PUB586.pdf.

National Security Strategy of the United States of America. Washington, DC: US Government Printing Office, March 2006. http://www.whitehouse.gov/nsc/nss/2006/nss2006.pdf.

Schindler, Dietrich, and Jiri Toman, eds. *The Laws of Armed Conflicts*. 4th ed. Leiden: Martinus Nijhoff Publishers, 2004.

Small Wars Manual, US Marine Corps. Washington, DC: U.S. Government Printing Office, 1940.

Taylor, John G. *East Timor: The Price of Freedom*. London: Zed Books, 2000.

Warren, Lieutenant Colonel Marc L. "Operational Law: A Concept Matures." *Military Law Review*, no. 152 (1996): 33–74.

PART VI. LEGAL RESPONSIBILITY, JUSTICE, AND RECONCILIATION

Bass, Gary Jonathan. *Stay the Hand of Vengeance: The Politics of War Crimes Tribunals*. Princeton, NJ: Princeton University, 2000.

Christie, Kenneth. *The South African Truth Commission*. Basingstoke: Macmillan Press, 2000.

Hayner, Priscilla B. *Unspeakable Truths: Confronting State Terror and Atrocities*. New York, NY and London: Routledge, 2001.

Human Rights Program, Harvard Law School and World Peace Foundation. *Truth Commissions: A Comparative Assessment*. Cambridge, MA: Harvard Law School Human Rights Program, 1997.

Kittichaisaree, Kriangsak. *International Criminal Law*. Oxford: Oxford University Press, 2001.

Koh, Harold Hongju, and Ronald C. Slye. *Deliberative Democracy and Human Rights*. New Haven, CT and London: Yale University, 1999.

Kritz, Neil, ed. *Transitional Justice: How Emerging Democracies Reckon with Former Regimes*. (3 Volumes) Washington, DC: United States Institute of Peace Press, 1995.

Malleson, Kate, and Peter Russell, eds. *Appointing Judges in an Age of Judicial Power*. Toronto: University of Toronto Press, 2006.

Mayer-Rieckh, Alexander, and Pablo de Greiff, eds. *Justice as Prevention: Vetting Public Employees in Transitional Societies*. New York, NY: Social Science Research Council, 2007.

Moghalu, Kingsley Chiedu. *Global Justice: The Politics of War Crimes Tribunals*. Westport, CT: Praeger Security International, 2006.

Moghalu, Kingsley Chiedu. "Saddam Hussein's Trial Meets the 'Fairness' Test," *Ethics and International Affairs* 20, no. 4 (Winter 2006): 517–25.

Newton, Michael A. "The Iraqi High Criminal Court: Controversy and Contributions." *International Review of the Red Cross* 88, no. 862 (2006): 399–425.

Philpott, Daniel, ed. *The Politics of Past Evil: Religion, Reconciliation, and the Dilemmas of Transitional Justice*. Notre Dame, IN: University of Notre Dame, 2006.

Index

AAR (after-action report), 301
Abilio Jose Osorio Soares case, 247–9
Abu Ghraib, 16, 109, 239, 269, 270, 271, 278
  n.54
Action with Respect to Threats to the Peace,
  Breaches of the Peace, and Acts of
  Aggression, 294*t,* 328, 338 n.5
additional protocols (1977), 138 n.8
advertising campaign, War on Terrorism, 28,
  35 n.36
Advisory Group on Public Diplomacy, 28–29,
  35 n.37
Aerial Incident of July 3, 1988, 233
Afghanistan, 269; detainees seized from, 70,
  71, 107–8, 109, 110, 111, 112–18, 115, 121,
  151; legality of U.S. invasion, 47–48, 234–
  35; legitimacy of use of force, 234–35
aggression: concept of, 231, 236 n.6; indirect,
  231, 232, 234
Aikens and Seevers, 123–24,
Algeria, army coup in, 41
Al-Hakim, Muhammad Baqir, 48
Al-Marri, Ali Saleh Kahlah, 110
Al-Marri v. Hanft, 72, 73
al Qaeda, 42, 148–50, 152, 153–4, 155, 159;
  training camps, 139 n.28
al-Qaradāwī, Yūsuf, 47, 50 n.12, 178–81
al-Sistani, Ali, 43, 48
Amir, Yigal, 198–99
amnesty, 336; selective, 334, 335; in South
  Africa, 330, 334, 335; in South America,
  330, 332
Amnesty International, 240

Anand, Sowmya, 9–10, 31 n.3
Anglo-American Committee of Inquiry, 41
Animo beligerendi, 226
Annan, Kofi, 304 n.49, 318
anticipatory defense, classification of, 199
  n.5–200 n.5
anticipatory self-defense, 224, 231, 232–33,
  235, 254, 259–60, 261, 262, 263, 264, 265,
  269, 272 n.4
apartheid, 328, 334, 335–6
Appropriations Committee, 94, 100
Aquinas, Thomas (saint), 211, 213
Arab Americans, 27, 168
armed conflict: changing nature of, 281*t*–2;
  insurgencies and counterinsurgencies, 286;
  military operations other than war, 285*t*–6;
  small-scale conflicts, 286–87, 303 n.30;
  small war, 283–5; taxonomy of modern,
  283–7
armed conflict law. *See* LOAC
Armed Services Committee, 94, 95, 100, 291
Armstrong, Karen, 56
Army FM (Field Manual), 286
article 2, League of Nations, 228, 229
article 2, UCMJ (court martial), 123, 125, 126,
  127, 128, 132, 293
article 2(4), UN Charter (self-defense), 229,
  230–31, 233, 262, 264
article 21, of UCMJ (court martial), 128, 129
article 25, UN Charter (mandatory
  implementation of decisions), 256, 258,
  259, 260, 262–63, 264
article 48, UN Charter (mandatory

implementation of decisions), 256, 258, 259, 260, 262–63, 264
article 51, UN Charter (self-defense), 231, 254, 256, 257, 262–63, 271, 282
article 94(2), UN Charter (mandatory implementation of decisions), 256, 258, 259, 260, 262–63
article 102, Geneva Conventions (POWs), 126, 127–8, 140 n.44
article 103, UN Charter (self-defense), 254, 257, 262–63, 264, 270, 271
ATCA (Alien Tort Claims Act) apartheid lawsuit, 328, 335–6, 340 n.33
Augustine (saint), 208–10, 213, 214
AUMF (Authorization for Use of Military Force), 70–71, 72, 73, 113, 116, 117–8

Baker, James, 28, 42
Baker, Stuart, 73
Baker v. Carr, 68–69
Banana Wars, 283–4
Bantekas, Ilias, 241
Ba'thist regime, 46, 218, 321; and Iraqi Kurds, 42; and WMDs, 41
Beers, Charlotte, 28
Bentham, Jeremy, 156
Bin Laden, Osama, 29, 42, 47–48, 93, 151
Bissonette v. Haig, 76
Bosnia, 59, 293, 296
Bremer, Paul, 48
Brewer, Paul R., 25–26
British Mandate, 41
Brown, Carl, 43
Browning, Edmond, 56
Brown v. United States, 114,
Bush, George W., approval ratings: autoregressive nature of approval ratings, 24; combat casualties of Iraq War effect on, 23, 24, 25, 26; domestic economic performance effect on, 23; on handling situation in Iraq, 20, 21*f,* 26; on handling terrorism, 20–21*f;* honeymoon effect, 24; intensity and length of media coverage effect on, 24; Iraq war support and success, and casualties, current trends, 26*f;* 9/11, Iraq war, Saddam capture rallies, 24–25*f;* overall, 21–22*f,* 25, 26; volume of media coverage effect on, 23
Bush, George W., public opinion on war on terrorism policy, 11
Bush administration, justification for Iraq invasion, 42
Bybee, Jay S., 109

Calvin, Jean, 214
Canadian International Development Administration (CIDA), 299
Caroline analysis, 231–3, 235, 236 n.9–237 n.9
Case Concerning Military and Para-military Activities In and Against Nicaragua (Contra Case, 1949), 233, 237 n.12
Catholics. *See* Just war tradition, Christian
Chapter VI, Pacific Settlement of Dispute, 294
Chapter VII, Action with Respect to Threats to the Peace, Breaches of the Peace, and Acts of Aggression, 258, 282, 294*t,* 328, 338 n.5
Cheney, Richard, 42
China, 226, 229, 236 n.8, 242, 254; and commercial law, 338 n.11; open door policy, 53–54
CIA (Central Intelligence Agency), 73, 75, 77
civilian convention, 121, 143 n.94, 154
civil liberties, 1, 2, 3, 16, 96, 97, 168, 191
Civil Liberties Oversight Board, 93, 97, 100
civil war, U.S., 107, 125
Colepaugh v. Looney, 133
combatant's privilege, 146–47
comedy TV show, as candidate news source, 12, 13*t,*
comity analysis, 267
Commander in Chief Clause, 111, 112
commercial law, 338 n.11
Commission on the Intelligence Capabilities of the United States Regarding WMDs, 74
Committee on Amnesty, 334, 335
Committee on Human Rights Violations, 334–35
Committee on Reparations, 334, 335
common article 2, Geneva Conventions, 121, 135, 163 n.8, 292, 293
common article 3, Geneva Conventions, 117, 121, 135, 254 n.4, 268, 293
conflict prosecution, 188, 193
congress, U.S., job approval ratings, 22
congressional committee reform, 95–96
constitutional law, 1, 87, 224
constitutional law roundtable, 356–62
contested morality, in U.S. foreign policy: benevolent domination *vs.* imperialism, 53–54, 62 n.14; christian perspectives on war, 57–58; church responses to 2003 invasion of Iraq, 58–60; crusade tradition, 58; evangelicals, 2, 4, 56; hard *vs.* soft power, 51, 52, 61 n.5; humanitarian intervention ethics, 59–60; just war tradition, 51, 57–59; nonsocial policy initiatives, 2; pacifist

perspective, 57; televangelists, 2, 4, 51, 56, 58–59, 61; U.S. Christian leader perspectives, 54–57; Vietnam War effect on church leader perspectives, 55–56
continental legal science, 226, 228, 231–2, 332
Contra Case (1949), 233, 237 n.12
Conventional Weapons Convention Protocols, 258
COP (common operational picture), 300
core legal disciplines, 304 n.38
Corfu Channel Case (1949), 233
counterinsurgency, 285, 286
CPL (Civilian Protection Law), 295
crescent societies, 299
crimes against humanity (and human being), 314–17
criminal sanctions, 332–33
crusade tradition, 58
Cuban missile crisis, 232
Cultural Property Second Protocol, 258

Darfur, 336
DCI (Director of Central Intelligence), 73
Declaration of Paris, 1856, 235 n.3
De Klerk, William, 334
Denton Amendment, 291
Detainee Treatment Act (2005), 109–10, 118
detaining enemy combatants, international legal limits on: Abu Ghraib detainees, 16, 109, 239, 269, 270, 271, 278 n.54; article II and, 111–12; Geneva conventions obligations, 108–10; Guantanamo Bay detainees, 109–10, 111, 115; *Hamdi v. Rumsfeld,* 110, 111; *Hamdi v. Rumsfeld,* background to, 112–14; *Hamdi v. Rumsfeld,* implications for citizens, 114–15; *Hamdi v. Rumsfeld,* noncitizens detained by U.S., 115–8; source of authority to detain, 111–18; Supreme Court decisions, 110–18
detaining power, 127, 135, 136, 139 nn.32 and 37, 140 n.44, 143 n.88, 153, 164 n.17
deterrence, 137, 156, 159–60, 331–2, 332, 333
DHS (Department of Homeland Security), oversight of, 95–96
discretionary war, 185, 199 n.5–200 n.5, 204 n.64
distributive justice, 308
Djerejian, Ed, 28
DNI (Director of National Intelligence), 67, 74, 75, 77, 78, 94, 96–97, 98
Dominion Theology, 56
double effect doctrine, 190, 211, 217–8, 220 n.25

double jeopardy, 332
double jeopardy clause, 78
draft code of offenses against mankind, 236 n.6
due process, 71, 113, 118, 145, 160, 244, 308, 314; and dragnet arrests, 216; Hussein trial and, 312; and military, 76; and noncitizens, 72, 77, 91 n.22; and past criminal acts, 158; and POW Convention, 154; and terrorists, 160, 161
due process clause, 72, 87, 88, 90
due regard principle, 259, 269–70

East Timor case, 238, 243, 247–9, 251 n.12
Edsall, Thomas B., 31 n.11–32 n.11
Eichenberg, Richard C., 23–26, 34 nn.24 and 26
Elser, Janet, 11
Elshtain, Jean Bethke, 59
embedded journalists program, 33 n.14
enduring Freedom Afghanistan, 276 n.43
enemy combatant, defining, 114–15
equity principle, 316
erastianism, 85
establishment clause, 85–87, 88, 89–90
ethics: humanitarian intervention ethics, 59–60; and international justice, 319; religion, ethics, and law panel, 341–6. *See also* Judaic ethics, on power in extraordinary warfare.
European Convention for Protection of Human Rights and Fundamental Freedoms, 255
evangelicals, 2, 4, 56
Everts, Philip, 27
Executive power, and War on Terror: centralization *vs.* decentralization, 76–77; citizen captured in U.S., 71–72; citizen captured overseas, 70–71; director of national intelligence, 73–74; noncitizen captured in U.S., 72–73; noncitizen captured overseas, 72; paradigm shift, criminal justice to military response, 70; paradigm shift, impact of, 77–78; paradigm shift, military response to terrorism, 70; Patriot Act and foreign intelligence, 74–78; pure law enforcement; rise during Cold War, 76; role of courts, 67–69
exit strategies, 2, 37, 49
Ex parte Milligan, 69, 111
Ex Parte Quirin, 125–6

FAA (Federal Aviation Administration), 94
FAIR ROSE method: F—fiscal law, 290–91;

A—acquisition and support, 291–2; I—
international law, 292–94; R—rules of
engagement and other use of force
considerations, 295–6; R—reserve
mobilization and draw of secondary
support, 297; O—order and discipline, 297–
8; overview, 290*f;* S—symbiosis of
operational and interagency elements, 298–
99; E—echelons of legal support to
operations, 300–301.
Falangist Maronites, 41
FBI (Federal Bureau of Investigation),
authority over, 74, 75, 77
Feaver, Peter D., 22–23, 25–26
Feith, Douglas, 42
Fifth Amendment, 72, 76, 77, 87, 88, 89, 91
n.17, 129
Filartiga v. Pena-Irala, 335
First Amendment, 2, 33 n.14, 85. *See also*
establishment clause
First Hague Peace Conference, 235 n.3
FISA (Foreign Intelligence Surveillance Act),
74, 75, 77, 82 n.90
Fleming v. Page, 111
Flight 655 Case, 233–4
Foreign Affairs Committee, 95, 100
foreign environmental pollution, public
opinion on, 11
foreign policy leadership, U.S. public opinion
on, 11
fourth amendment, 77, 82 n.90, 88, 89–90
Fourth Geneva Convention (Protection of
Civilian Persons in Time of War), 121
Fox News Cable Channel, 15, 32 n.13–33 n.13
Free Exercise Clause, 86, 88, 89, 90
Friedman, Thomas, 53

Gelpi, Christopher, 22–23, 25–26
*General Treaty for the Renunciation of War
(Kellogg–Briand Pact),* 228, 230, 233
Geneva Agreement, 1864, 235 n.3
Geneva Civilian Convention, 121, 143 n.94,
154
Geneva Convention (1929), 113
Geneva Convention Relative to the Treatment
of Prisoners of War (1949), 122, 134; and al
Qaeda and Taliban detainees, 109; common
article 2, 121, 135, 163 n.8, 292, 293;
common article 3, 117, 121, 135, 254 n.4,
268, 293; on defendant right to appear at
own trial, 130–31; on detainee status, 115–
6, 127–8, 163 n.14, 163 n.17–164 n.17; on
humanitarian law, 254; on lawful/unlawful
combatants, 153–4, 155; on length of
detention, 113; on precapture offenses, 126;
Protocol I Additional, 293
Geneva POW Convention. *See* Geneva
Convention Relative to the Treatment of
Prisoners of War.
Geneva Protocols, 227
genocide, 153, 240, 250 n.2, 308, 310, 314,
318, 332, 333; in Darfur, 336; in Iraq, 311;
in Rwanda, 328;
German prisoners, WW II, 114
German saboteur case, 125–6, 139 n.28, 140
n.46–141 n.46
Glassman, James, 28–29
global warming, 9
Goldstein, Baruch, 198
Goldwater v. Carter, 360
Gonzales, Alberto, 109
government-funded operations, 290
Greco-Bulgarian Border Incident (1924):
legitimacy, legal issues in, 232, 234
Grotius, Hugo, 212
Guantanamo Bay detainees, 109–10, 111, 115;
status of, 154, 155, 162 n.2
Gulf War, first. *See* Kuwait

Hague Convention Adaptation to Maritime
War of the Principles of the Geneva
Convention (1907), 242
Hague Convention Respecting the Laws and
Customs of War on Land (*Hague IV,* 1907),
117, 227, 242, 254
Hague Conventions and Declarations, 1899,
227
Hague Peace Conference, first, 235 n.3
Haiti, 293, 296
Hamdam, Salim Ahmed. *See Hamdam v.
Rumsfeld*
Hamdam v. Rumsfeld, 107–8, 121, 122, 126–
27, 128, 129, 132, 135, 151
Hamdeen, Salim, 151
Hamdi, Yaser Esam. *See Hamdi v. Rumsfeld*
Hamdi v. Rumsfeld, 70, 71, 107–8, 110, 111,
121, 151; background to, 112–14;
implications for citizens, 114–15; and
noncitizens detained by U.S., 115–8
hard *vs.* soft power, 51, 52, 61 nn.3 and 5
Hassan (King of Morocco), 41
Henry J. Kaiser family Foundation/*Public
Perspective* Polling and Democracy
Survey, 31 n.11–32 n.11
high contracting parties, 150, 154, 163 n.8,
292

Hourani, Albert Habib, 171
HRW (Human Rights Watch), 312, 313, 317
Hughes, Karen, 28, 35 n.37
humanitarian intervention, legitimacy of, 224, 227, 232, 235, 236 n.8
humanitarian law: *vs.* human rights law, 276 n.38, 295; *vs.* human rights norms, 266–68. *See also* Israel–Hezbollah conflict
Human Rights Council (UN), 257
human rights crimes, in international and domestic arenas, 239–40. *See also* superior responsibility concept
human shields, 274 n.18
Huntington, Samuel, 53
Hussein, Saddam, discerning justice in trial and execution of: critical reactions to justice of, 307–8; executing justice and Saddam, 320–23; international justice and politics, 317–20; international war crimes and national crime context of, 316, 319–20; *Iraqi Voices* report on, 310–12, 313, 314, 316, 318; justice, rights, and preeminence of legalism, 310–14; and justice as right order, 310–14, 321–2; and justice as rights, 315, 321; Kurds and, 323; legalist focus of, 317; nontechnical justice concerns, 313; procedural concerns, 312–13; rejection of UN-sponsored tribunal, 317–8; and retributive justice, 311; substantive concerns, 313–4; symbolic effect of execution, 322–23; and transitional justice, 328
Hussein (King of Jordan), 41

ICC (International Criminal Court), 240, 242–43, 250 n.2, 251 n.14, 327, 328, 330, 331–2, 337
ICCPR (International Covenant on Civil and Political Rights), 131, 255, 267
ICISS (International Commission on Intervention and State Sovereignty), 304 n.49
ICRC (International Committee of the Red Cross), 257, 271, 276 n.43–277 n.43, 279 n.59, 287, 299
ICTJ (International Center for Transitional Justice), 312, 313, 317, 318, 325 n.24, 330
ICTR (International Criminal Tribunal for Rwanda), 242, 251 n.14, 327, 328
ICTY (International Tribunal for the Former Yugoslavia), 242, 251 n.14, 327, 328
IDF (Israel Defense Forces), 187, 200 n.13
IHL (international humanitarian law), 255, 276 n.38, 294, 295

IHRL (international human rights law), 294
IHT (Iraqi High Tribunal), 307, 312, 313, 314, 316, 323, 326 n.35
illegal combatant status, 162 n.2
impunity concept, in transitional justice, 330
IMTFE (International Military Tribunal for the Far East), 242
IMT (International Military Tribunal), 242
incapacitation, as prevention, 156–59, 160, 331, 332
Indian Civil Rights Act (1968), 90
indirect aggression, 231, 232, 234
Individual Rights Panel, 346–51
Indonesia: muslims view toward U.S., 28; U.S. promotion of liberal Islam in, 85–86. *See also* superior responsibility concept, in Indonesia.
In re Sealed Case, 82 n.90
instrumentalist justice, 331–4
The Insular Cases, 88
insurgencies, 231, 232, 234, 286
Intelligence and Terrorism Prevention Act (2005), 67
internal armed conflict, 293
International Committee of the Red Cross, 257
international crime, 239–40
international justice, 318–20; ethical dimension of, 319; political dimension of, 318–19
International Law Roundtable, 376–80
International Monetary Fund, 54
International Red Cross, 136, 252
Internet, as news source, 12, 13*t,* 15, 32 n.12
interrogation, permissible bounds of, 1
IO (international organization), 236 n.5, 290
Iran–Iraq War (1980–1988), poison gas use, 41–42
Iraq, 34 n.21, 269; death sentence in, 325 n.23; government-funded operations, 290; legitimacy of use of force in, 234–35; U.S. military deaths in, 34 n.21. *See also* public opinion, since 9/11
Iraqi Voices: Attitudes Toward Transitional Justice and Societal Reconstruction, 310–12
Iraq war: civilian casualties, 48; "Major Combat" stage of, 23; military casualties, 48–49; "Occupation" stage of, 23; "Sovereignty" stage of, 23; as top priority issue for government, 12
Irish Republic Army, 149
IRTPA (Intelligence Reform and Terrorism Prevention Act), 73, 74, 75, 76–77, 92, 96

Isernia, Pierangelo, 27
Islam: capital-punishment in, 319; *jihad* in,
    38; law in, 37–38; morality in, 38. *See also*
    martyrdom acts/suicide bombings, legiti-
    macy/authority in Islamic discussions of
Islam, U.S. promotion of liberal, 85–91; and
    Due Process Clause, 87, 88, 90; and
    erastianism, 85; and establishment clause,
    85–87, 88, 89–90; and Free Exercise
    Clause, 87, 88, 89; in Indonesia, 85–86;
    islamic school funding, 86–88
Islamic Republic of Iran v. United States of
    America, 233
Israel–Hezbollah conflict: character of action,
    261; civilian–military planning interface,
    282–83; and claims of other states, 262–63;
    due regard principle, 255–69, 259, 269–70;
    expectations of states and peoples, 261–62;
    humanitarian law *vs.* human rights norms,
    266–68; importance of action, 262;
    individual/collective self-defense, 256–63;
    interests of other states, 262; and
    international armed conflict law, 268–69;
    jus cogens norms, 264; *jus cogens* norms,
    opposition to, 264–66; and LOAC, 254–55,
    256–59, 260, 267; and noninternational
    armed conflict law, 268–69; overview of,
    252–54; right to military action, 260; state
    citizen rights, 261; territorial issues, 260,
    276 n.39; and traditions, 262
IST (Iraqi Special Tribunal), 307, 316
IT (Information technology), 300

Japan, 53, 54, 124, 139 n.30, 229
Japanese–Americans, internment of, 69, 70,
    114
Jihad, 38, 50 n.12, 175, 176, 177
John Paul II (pope), 215–6
Johnson v. Eisentrager, 114, 115, 131
John XXIII (pope), 216
Joint Publication (JP) 3-0, *Joint Operations,*
    282–83
Jordan, 29, 41, 46
Judaic ethics, on power in extraordinary
    warfare: abuse of textual tradition, 198–99;
    categories of war, 185, 199 n.5–200 n.5;
    collective punishment, 192–94;
    extraordinary warfare concept, 188–89;
    general geopolitical context of, 186–87;
    halakhah, 4, 187–8, 194, 200 n.13, 203
    n.51; *halakhah,* external extension of, 188;
    halakhah, internal extension of, 187, 200
    n.16; individual punishment, 194–97;

individual *vs.* collective responsibility,
    192–93; interrogation, 194–95, 206 n.90;
    means of livelihood destruction, 194;
    methodological issues, 186–88; modern
    Jewish thought on violence and war, 185;
    mosrim, 194–95, 205 n.86, 205 nn.74–75;
    preemptive defensive war, 190; preemptive
    intervention, 195–6; prevention, 198;
    preventive detention, 197; privacy
    principle, 191; privileged spaces principle,
    190–91; property destruction, 193–4;
    proportionality principle, 190, 196; reactive
    defense, 190; retribution/vengeance, 190,
    201 n.29–202 n.29; self-defense, 201 n.23;
    sovereignty concept, 186–87; strategic
    principles, 189–91; terrorism concept, tra-
    ditional, 185–6; timing issues, 197–8; tor-
    ture, 195–6; torture, worth of intelligence
    from, 196–97; traditional categories of war,
    185
Judicial review, 67, 71, 107, 109–10, 113, 114,
    118
Judiciary Committee, 95, 100
jus ad bellum, 57, 188, 207, 210, 211, 219
    n.15, 223, 224, 225, 252, 282
jus belli ac pacis, 226, 227
jus cogens, 255, 264–65, 266, 270, 271, 272,
    330
jus in bello, 57, 149, 188, 207, 212, 219 n.15,
    223–4, 227, 252, 282
just desserts, 331
justice: in ancient world, 308, 309;
    distributive, 308; procedural, 324 n.10;
    rectificatory, 308, 309; restorative, 5–6, 324
    n.9, 331, 332–33, 335, 337; retributive,
    308–9, 310, 321, 322, 324 n.9, 331, 337; as
    right order, 309, 310, 324 n.9; as rights,
    308, 310, 331. *See also* Hussein, Saddam,
    discerning justice in trial and execution of
justiciability, 67–68
just war tradition, 51, 57–59. *See also* just war
    tradition, Christian
just war tradition, Christian: agricultural
    destruction hypothetical, 217; aim of peace
    criterion, 209; aquinas on, 211, 213;
    Augustine on, 208–10, 213, 214; Calvin on,
    214; civilian suffering hypothetical, 217–8;
    Doctrine of Double Effect, 190, 211, 217–8,
    220 n.25; dragnet arrest hypothetical, 216;
    early Christianity, 207–8; Erasmus on, 211–
    2; Grotius on, 212; holy places as storage
    hypothetical, 217; interrogatory torture
    hypothetical, 218; just cause criterion, 209;

last resort criterion, 209; Luther on, 213–4; modern Catholic views, 215–6; natural law perspective, 211, 213; protestant reformer views, 213–5; right authority criterion, 209; right intention standard, 210; Suarez on, 212; suicide bomber as combatant hypothetical, 216–17; Vitoria on, 212; "War on Terror" hypothetical, 216–18
Juwana, Hikmahanto, 4–5, 362, 369

Kaplan, Robert, 53
Kellogg–Briand Pact, 228, 230, 233
Kelsey, John, 169
Kimball, Charles, 56
Kissinger, Henry, 42
Kittichaisaree, Kriangsak, 241
Knowledge standard, 258, 259
Korea, 230, 233–4
Korematsu v. United States, 69
Kosovo, 269, 276 n.40
Kritsiotis, Dino, 362, 366
Krosnick, Jon A., 9–10, 31 n.3
Kurdish Iraqis, 39, 40, 42, 43, 46, 322, 323
Kurdish Turks, 46, 49
Kuwait, 42, 45, 226, 230, 231

Lamont v. Woods, 89
Langston, Emily, 251 n.12
Latin America, 329, 336
law in Islam, 37–38
law of treaties, 260
League of Nations, 227
Lebanese Civil War of 1975–1991, 41
Lebanon, 269. *See also* Israel–Hezbollah conflict
Lebo, Matthew, 23–26, 34 nn.24 and 26
legal disciplines, core, 304 n.38
legal Responsibility and National Views Panel, 370–76
legal *vs.* illegal combatants, 189
legal *vs.* moral universalism, 315–6
legitimacy. *See* legitimacy, legal issues in; martyrdom acts/suicide bombings, legitimacy/authority in islamic discussions of
legitimacy, legal issues in: *Aerial Incident of July 3, 1988,* 233; aggression, indirect, 231, 232, 234; aggression concept, 231, 236 n.6; aggression, outlawing, 227–9; American view, 4, 226, 228–29, 230–32, 233; armed force legal principle development, 225–34; article 2(4), UN Charter, 230, 231, 233, 234; article 10, of 1919 League Covenant,

227, 228, 229; article 16, of 1919 League Covenant, 227–8; article 51, UN Charter, 230–31, 233, 234; *Caroline* analysis, 231–3, 235, 236 n.9–237 n.9; Chapter VII, UN Charter, 234, 235; collective security, under UN, 229–30, 234; continental legal science view, 226, 228, 231, 332; *Contra Case* (1949), 233, 237 n.12; *Corfu Channel Case* (1949), 233; Developing Nation view, 228, 231; Greco-Bulgarian Border Incident (1924), 232, 234; humanitarian intervention, 224, 227, 232, 235, 236 n.8; interpretation of UN charter, 229–34; *Kellogg–Briand Pact,* 228, 230, 233; League of Nations and, 227; *Locarno Treaties,* 228; modern use of force law, 223–4; post-9/11 factual and policy background, 225; San Francisco Conference, 229–30; self-defense rationale, 227–9, 230–31, 232, 233, 234, 235; self-help rationale, 227; self-preservation rationale, 227; socialist law view, 228, 231; use of force, context in Afghanistan and Iraq, 234–35; use of force, regulation of, 226–27
Lieber Code, 107
LOAC (law of armed conflict), 116, 118, 252, 254, 268, 270, 271–2, 279 n.59, 281, 290; and Israel–Hezbollah conflict, 256–59, 260, 267; knowledge standard, 258; and law of the sea, 255, 272 n.3; necessity standard, 259; proportionality standard, 259
LOS (law of the sea), 254, 255, 256, 267, 270–71
LPB (Legal Preparation of the Battlefield), 288

Madsen v. Kinsella, 142 n.78
maimonides, 195–6, 200 n.17, 202 n.42–203 n.42, 203 n.53–204 n.53, 205 nn.74–75
Mandela, Nelson, 334
Mansfield, John, 2, 90 n.4, 355, 358, 378–79
Marbury v. Madison, 67–68
Martens clauses, 254
Martone, James, 44
martyrdom acts/suicide bombings, legitimacy/authority in islamic discussions of: hypotheticals/response to, 167–9; independent magisterium, 178–81; islam as field of discourse, 170–72; martyrdom acts, 178–81; muslim academy, 172, 177; new developments in Muslim moral discourse, 172–81; noncombatant protection, 169; preventative detention, 168; property

destruction, 168–69; proportionality of force problems, 169; Protestantization of Islam, 172–78; suicide attacks, 169; torture, 168; tradition, 169–70; using mosque as fighting position, 168
Maryland v. Craig, 130
Mathews v. Eldridge, 71
MCA (Military Commissions Act), 108, 110, 118, 121, 122, 125, 128, 129, 130, 133, 298
McVeigh, Timothy, 160–61
MDMP (military decision-making process), 288
media: divergence areas between public/press, 31 n.11–32 n.12; journalist/support worker deaths in Iraq, 34 n.21; public/policymaker resentment of, 31 n.11; supposed bias against international news, 11; watch dog role of, 15–16. *See also* public opinion, since 9/11
METT-T-C (mission, enemy, troops, terrain [and weather], time available, and civilian considerations), 288
Mexican War (1847), 124–25
Mexico, violations of U.S. law in, 88, 89
military commissions: background to, 122; civilians, 132–33; confrontation concern, 129–32; death sentences, 143 n.92; executions, 143 n.94; general courts-martial, 121, 122–24; history of, 124–26; impact of 1949 Geneva Conventions, 134–35; last military commission trial, 133–4; and prisoners of war, 126–28; procedural issues, 128–29; trial safeguards in international law, 135–7; U.S. citizens, 133; valid sentences, 140 n.44; war crimes trial fora, 122–35
military operational lawyer: advisory capacity of, 280; changing nature of armed conflict, 281*t*–282; and civilian–military planning interface, 282–83; decision-making cycle, 289, 300; decision-making process, 288; FAIR ROSE method, 290–301, 291–2; multidisciplinary approach to analysis, 288–89, 290*f;* multiechelon techniques, 300; performance-oriented training, 301; planning and approaches to conflict, 287–301; proficiency training, 300–301; range of military operations, 281*t;* Small Wars, 283–5; and taxonomy of modern armed conflicts, 283–7; training/personnel, 300
Milosevic, Slobodan, 245
missionaries, protestant, 55
mission creep, 76

Missouri v. Holland, 84 n.130
mixed tribunal, 328, 330
Moghalu, Kinglsey Chiedu, 318, 320, 325 n.22
morality: in Islam, 38. *See also* contested morality, in U.S. foreign policy
moral *vs.* legal universalism, 315–6
Mosrim (informers), 194–95, 205 n.86, 205 nn.74–75
Mubarak, Husni, 45
Murray v. The Schooner Charming Betsy, 117–8
Musaddiq, Muhammad, 41
muslim Americans, attitudes toward Islam, 27
muslim perspectives, on invasion of Iraq, 38–48; changes from 2004 to 2005, 44*t;* four Arab states, 2202/2004, 44*t;* informed publics, 39–45; jurist perspectives, 46–48; regime perspectives, 45–46
My Lai incident, 143 n.83, 270

Nahmanides, 200 n.17
Nasrallah, Sayyed Hassan, 253
national crime, 239
national guard, 270
nationalism, 171
National Security Act (1947), 73, 75, 102 n.5
National Security Agency (NSA), 13, 74
NCCCUSA (National Council of Churches of Christ in the USA), 58, 59–60, 62 n.27
New Christian Right (NCR), 56, 59
Niebuhr, R., 215
9/11 Commission: and DNI, 74, 94, 96–97, 98; and NCTC, 96; Privacy and Civil Liberties Oversight Board, 97, 100; report and public discourse project, 92–103. *See also* 9/11 Commission, Public Discourse Project
9/11 Commission, Public Discourse Project (PDP), 92–103; budget control, 100; committee jurisdiction, 100; congress, structural changes in, 93, 96–97, 98; congressional committee reform, 95–96; congressional oversight, 94–95, 97; congressional shortcomings in preventing terrorist attacks, 93–94, 99, 101–2; foreign policy/public diplomacy/nonproliferation, 92; homeland security/emergency preparedness/response, 92; intelligence reform, 98; intelligence shortcomings in preventing terrorist attacks, 93–94; oversight reform, 98; Privacy and Civil Liberties Oversight Board, 93, 100; public monitoring, 99–101

1951 Manual for Courts-Martial, 123
1969 Manual for Courts-Martial, 123, 132
1984 Manual for Courts-Martial, 123
Non-Detention Act, 71, 72, 73
nongovernmental organizations (NGOs):
   government-funded operations, 290, 291;
   and humanitarian relief, 299
Nonintercourse Act, 117
nonjudicial truth and reconciliation
   commission, 328–30, 331, 333
nonstatutory review, 118
Noriega regime, 386
North Atlantic Treaty Organization (NATO),
   253
Nuremberg, 162 n.5, 236 n.6, 328, 331, 336
Nye, Joseph, 52, 54, 61 n.5

objective right, 324 n.7
ODA (Overseas Development
   Administration), 299
Olmert, Ehud, 253
OODA (observe, orient, decide, and act), 289,
   300
open door policy, 53–54, 62 n.16
operational law panel, 362–70
ordinary least squares (OLS) regression, 34
   nn.24 and 26
Osorio Soares, Jose Abilio, 239

Pacific Settlement of Dispute, 294
pacifist, 57, 62
Padilla, Jose, 71–72
Padilla v. Bush, 164 n.22
Padilla v. Rumsfeld, 164 n.22
Palestine, 41
Palestinian suicide bombers, 149
Panagopoulos, Costas, 27
Pape, Robert, 171
Paraguay, 335
Paris Club, 54
Patriot Act, 29, 67, 73, 74–78, 298
Pax Americana, 54
Pax Romana, 208
PDP (Public Discourse Project), of 9/11
   Commission, 92–103
Pius XII (pope), 215
pluralists, on power, 52
POISED multidisciplinary approach to
   analysis, 288–89, 290f
Posner, Richard, 77
POW Convention. *See* Geneva Convention
   Relative to the Treatment of Prisoners of
   War (1949)

power: capability/influence distinction, 52; 51,
   soft *vs.* hard, 52, 61nn.3 and 5
predeployment, 297, 298
preemptive attack, 11, 42, 225
preemptive defense *vs.* preventive defense,
   194
preemptive detention, 207
preemptive intervention, 195–6
preemptive war, 190, 232–33, 234, 235
Presidential Drawdown Authority, 291
presidential election, and public opinion, 9–10
press. *See* public opinion, since 9/11
preventive *vs.* preemptive defense, 194
Prince Abdallah (Saudi Arabia), 45
Privacy and Civil Liberties Oversight Board,
   93, 97, 100
protecting power, 131, 135–6, 143 nn.88 and
   94
protestants. *See* Just war tradition, Christian
protocol II, to 1949 Geneva Conventions, 254
   n.4, 268, 276 n.38, 278 n.56–279 n.56, 293
proxy civil war, 235 n.2
public diplomacy, U.S., international opinion
   on, 26–29, 35 n.37
public opinion, since 9/11: data change over
   time, 16–22; factors affecting presidential
   approval ratings, 22–26; on foreign
   affairs/national security issues relevance for
   domestic politics, 9–12; on foreign policy
   goals, 10t; international, on U.S. foreign
   policy, 26–29; international news followers,
   13; interpretation issues, 34 n.20; on
   keeping forces in Iraq, 19; on likelihood of
   further terrorists acts in U.S., 16f–17; on
   media, 15–16; on military effort in Iraq,
   18f; 19; news sources, demographic
   differences in choice of, 12, 14t–15t; news
   sources, domestic and international
   preferences, 12–16; news sources, 2004
   presidential campaign, 12, 13t; on personal
   importance of foreign policy issues, 10t; on
   presidential election, 9–10; on use of
   military force in Iraq, 19–20f; on winning
   War on Terrorism, 17f; on worth of fighting
   war in Iraq, 17–19, 18f
pure law enforcement, 2
PVO (private volunteer organization), 286,
   298, 299

Qatar, 29, 110
QDR (Quadrennial Defense Review), 287

Rabin, Yitzhak, 198

radio, as news source, 12, 15, 32 n.12
Rasul v. Bush, 72, 110
READ ID Act (2005), 83 n.130–84 n.130
realists, on power, 52
reasonableness factor, 259–60
Reconstruction Theology, 56
rectificatory justice, 308
red cross, 299
red cross commentary, 143 n.96–144 n.96, 154
rehabilitation, as prevention, 156, 159, 331, 332
Reifler, Jason, 22–23, 25–26
relief organizations, 287
religion, ethics, and law panel, 341–6
reparations, 209, 284–85, 334, 335
reserve, U.S., mobilization/deployment/employment, 296*t*
Restatement (Second) of Foreign Relations Law of the United States, 275 n.25
Restatement (Third) of Foreign Relations Law of the United States, 256, 259, 263, 265, 266, 267, 268, 271, 272, 275 nn.25–26
restorative justice, 5–6, 324 n.9, 331, 332–33, 335, 337
retributive justice, 308–9, 310, 321, 322, 324 n.9, 331, 337
revictimization, 332
revolutionary war, 138 n.23
Rice, Condoleezza, 42
Rodef (one person pursuing another), 193, 196, 198, 204 n.60, 206 nn.87–88
ROE (rules of engagement), 146, 147, 269, 271, 295–6
Roman Catholics. *See* Just war tradition, Christian
Rome Statute of ICC, 240, 242–43, 250 n.2
Rome Treaty, 121, 138 n.8, 328, 330, 332, 337
Roosevelt, Franklin, 129
Rudolph C. Barnes Sr. Symposium, 341–80; constitutional law roundtable, 356–62; individual rights panel, 346–51; international law roundtable, 376–80; legal responsibility and national views panel, 370–76; operational law panel, 362–70; religion, ethics, and law panel, 341–6; structural and institutional panel, 351–6
RUF (Rules for Use of Force), 295
rule of law, defining, 338 n.11
Rumsfeld, Donald, 42
Rumsfeld v. Padilla, 110
Rwanda, 318, 328

San Francisco Conference on International Organization, 229–30
San Remo Manual (1995), 254–55, 258
SASO (stability and security operation), 287
Saudi Arabia, 29, 41, 43, 45, 70, 101, 171
Scott, Winfield, 124–25
SCSL (Special Court for Sierra Leone), 328, 330, 331
SDR (Swedish Disaster Relief), 299
self-defense: anticipatory, 224, 231, 232–33, 235, 254, 259–60, 261, 262, 263, 264, 265, 269, 272 n.4; and legitimacy, 227–9, 230–31, 232, 233, 234, 235
self-help rationale, and legitimacy, 227
separation of powers, 67–69, 71, 72, 75, 76, 78, 113, 114, 119 n.5, 236 n.5
shared values initiative, 28
Sharia law, 338 n.11
Shi'i Iraqis, 39, 40, 49, 322, 323
Shi'i Islam, 37
Shi'i law, 37, 46, 47, 48
significant purpose test, of FISA, 75, 77
SIPRNET (secret intranet protocol router network), 300
sixth amendment, 129, 130
small wars, 283–5
Sobel, Richard, 11
socialist law view, 228, 231
SOFA (status of force agreement), 292
soft *vs.* hard power, 51, 52, 61 nn.3 and 5
Somalia, 293
SOMA (Status of Mission Agreements), 295
Sosa v. Alvarez-Machain, 336
South Africa, 329, 330, 334–37
Spain, 29
Spanish Civil War, 235 n.2, 293
SRB (Swedish Rescue Board), 299
SSC (small-scale conflict), 286–87, 303 n.30
state sovereignty, 84 n.130
steel seizure case, 118
Stoll, Richard J., 23–26, 34 nn.24 and 26
structural and institutional panel, 351–6
Suarez, Francisco, 212
subjective right, 324 n.7
Sunni Iraqis, 39, 43, 316, 322, 323
Sunni Islam, 37, 170
Sunni law, 38, 46, 47
superior responsibility concept: administrative *vs.* superior responsibility, 243–6; command responsibility, 242–43; commission of crime, 241; commitment of offense by omission, 241; defining, 238, 241; domestic/international human rights

crimes, 239–40; effective control evidence, 245, 247–8, 249; evidence elements, 244; in international criminal law, 240–43; key perspectives of, 251 n.12; knowledge of superior evidence, 245–6, 249; legitimation by superior evidence, 246, 247; in military law, 241. *See also* superior responsibility concept, in Indonesia

superior responsibility concept, in Indonesia, 251 n.12; *Abilio Jose Osorio Soares case,* 247–9; East Timor case, 238, 243, 247–9, 251 n.12; Law 26/2000, 240, 243, 247; Tanjung Priok case, 238, 243, 247, 251 n.16

supremacy factors, 254, 256, 257, 258, 259, 260, 262–63, 264, 270, 271, 282

SWM (small wars manual), 284

system crimes, 325 n.24

Tanjung Priok case, 238, 243, 247, 251 n.16

Taylor, Charles, 328

televangelists, 2, 4, 51, 56, 58–59, 61

television, as news source, 12, 13, 15, 32 n.12, 32 n.13–33 n.13

terrorism: congressional shortcomings in preventing attacks, 93–94, 99, 101–2; public opinion on likelihood of further acts in U.S., 16*f*–17. *See also* terrorism, as war *vs.* crime

terrorism, as war *vs.* crime: and al Qaeda, 148–50, 152, 153–4, 155, 159; combatant's privilege, 146–47; communication as prevention, 160–61; deterrence as prevention, 137, 156, 159–60, 331–2, 332, 333; illegitimate *vs.* legitimate violence, 146–48; immunity from liability under war paradigm, 150–51; incapacitation as prevention, 156–59, 160, 331, 332; lawful *vs.* unlawful combatants, 152–55; legitimacy of violence under war paradigm, 148–50; post-hostility release of prisoners under war paradigm, 151–52; prevention measures, 156–61; rehabilitation as prevention, 156, 159, 331, 332; retribution, 155–6; and Taliban, 150, 153

Third Geneva Convention. *See* Geneva Convention Relative to the Treatment of Prisoners of War (1949)

time-series regression, 23, 24, 34 nn.24 and 27

Timor Leste, 238, 243, 247–9, 251 n.12

title III, 75, 77, 82 n.90

title 18 U.S. Code section 2441, 117

Toner, Robin, 11

transitional justice, 327–30; amnesties and, 330; civil suits, 328; defining, 327–8; domestic tribunals, 328; impunity concept in, 330; and instrumentalist justice, 331–4; international tribunals, 328, 331, 333–4; and nonjudicial truth and reconciliation commission, 328–30, 331, 333; and rule of law, 330; and South Africa, 334–37

TRCSA (Truth and Reconciliation Commission of South Africa) Report, 334–35, 336–37

Truman, Harry, 41, 118

Turkey, 28–29, 46, 49

Turner, Stansfield, 77

Tutwiler, Margaret, 28

2002 Manual for Courts-Martial, 123, 124

UCMJ (Uniform Code of Military Justice), 122, 123, 125, 126, 127–8, 129–30, 132, 134, 298

Ulama, 37, 170, 178

UN Charter: article 25, 256, 258, 259, 260, 262–63, 264; article 48, 256, 258, 259, 260, 262–63, 264; article 51, 254, 256, 257, 262–63, 271, 282; article 94(2), 256, 258, 259, 260, 262–63; article 103, 254, 257, 262–63, 264, 270, 271; Chapter VI, Pacific Settlement of Dispute, 294; Chapter VII, Action with Respect to Threats to the Peace, Breaches of the Peace, and Acts of Aggression, 294*t*, 328, 338 n.5

Undersecretary of State for Public Diplomacy and Public Affairs, 27–28

UN Human Rights Council, 257

UNIFIL (United Nations Force in Lebanon), 253, 268, 269

United Kingdom, 29, 49, 140 n.43

United States v. Flick, 137,

United States v. Klein, 119 n.5,

United States v. Tiede, 133–4,

United States v. Verdugo-Urquidez, 88, 89

Uniting for Peace Resolutions (UN), 230

UN Security Council Resolution 1546, 23

UN Security Council Resolution 1701, 253, 257, 258, 262

UN Security Council Resolutions, 296

U.S. Army FM (Field Manual), 286

USAID (United States Agency for International Development), 290, 299

USS *Cole,* 70, 94, 100, 149, 225

USS *Sullivans,* 94

USS *Vincennes,* 233–4

Utilitarian theory, 332, 333, 337

Valentine v. United States, 112
Vienna Convention, 277 n.48
Vietnam, 143 n.83, 226, 270; and commercial
    law, 338 n.11
Vietnam War, 30, 54, 55–56, 235 n.2; My Lai
    incident, 143 n.83, 270
Vitoria, Franciscus de, 212
Voeten, Erik, 25–26
VOLAG (voluntary agency), 299

Wahid, Abdurraham, 251 n.16
War of 1812, 112, 116
War on Terror. *See* Executive power, and War
    on Terror
War on Terrorism: public opinion on winning,
    17*f*

WCC (World Council of Churches), 58, 59
WMD (Weapons of Mass Destruction), 41, 76,
    102, 222, 226, 234, 235; intelligence
    concerning, 15, 23, 30, 32–33, 224, 225
WMD Commission Report, 74
Wolfowitz, Paul, 42
Woods v. Cloyd W. Miller Co., 69
World Bank, 54, 299
WTO (World Trade Organization), 338 n.11

Youngstown Sheet & Tube Co. v. Sawyer, 72,
    80 n.35, 122, 128–29
Yugoslavia, 142 n.82–143 n.82, 328

Zogby, J., 45

About the Editor and the Contributors

Shahrough Akhavi teaches comparative politics in the Department of Political Science at the University of South Carolina. He studied international relations at Brown University (BA 1962), Middle Eastern Regional Studies at Harvard University (MA 1964) and political science at Columbia University (PhD 1969). His current field of research is the dialectics of scripturalist and modernist discourses in contemporary Islamic thought.

Miriam J. Aukerman has pursued a domestic and international career in the area of civil rights and international justice, and currently directs the Reentry Law Project at Legal Aid of Western Michigan. She studied history at Cornell University (BA 1991), international relations at Balliol College, Oxford (MPhil 1993), and law at New York University (JD 2000). Her professional experience in societies in transition includes work at the Vera Institute of Justice on Eastern European police accountability programs 1998–99, for the Russia and Eastern Europe Program of the Ford Foundation in New York and Moscow 1994–97, as a Bosch Foundation Fellow in the German Federal Foreign Ministry and Brandenburg Office for Foreigner and Refugee Affairs 1993–94, and as U.S. Representative to the GULAG Museum in New York City and Perm, Russia 1997.

Norman C. Bay teaches criminal and international law at the University of New Mexico School of Law. He studied history at Dartmouth College (BA 1982) and law at Harvard University (JD 1986). He joined the Office of Legal Adviser at the U.S. Department of State in 1987, then in 1989 became an Assistant U.S. Attorney at the U.S. Attorney's Office in Washington, DC, where he worked in the criminal division. In 1995, he transferred to the U.S. Attorney's Office in Albuquerque, New Mexico, where in 2000 he was appointed U.S. Attorney for the District of New Mexico.

John O. Carlson is Assistant Professor of Religious Studies at Arizona State University, where he also serves as Associate Director of the Center for the Study of Religion and Conflict. He studied political science at Vanderbilt University (BA 1992) and religious ethics at The University of Chicago (MA 1999; PhD 2005), and held an Erasmus Fellowship at the University of Notre Dame (2004–05). His research focuses on how religious and ethical inquiry renews our understanding of political life.

Jonathan K. Crane, an ordained rabbi of the Reform Jewish Movement, has taught political science, Jewish ethics, and conflict resolution in higher education. He currently is writing his dissertation in modern Jewish ethics as a SSHRC PhD Fellow in the Department of Religion at the University of Toronto. Previous studies include Hebrew literature at Hebrew Union College (MA 2003), Gandhian thought at Gujarat Vidyapith University in India (MPhil 1998), international peace studies at the University of Notre Dame (MA 1997), and international relations at Wheaton College in Massachusetts (BA 1995).

H. Wayne Elliott is a Lieutenant Colonel USA, JAGC (retired) who currently teaches at the American Military University and was formerly Chief, International Law Division at the chief training school for all U.S. Army lawyers, The Judge Advocate General's School at Charlottesville, Virginia. He studied political science at The Citadel (BA 1968) and law at the University of South Carolina (JD 1971), The Judge Advocate General's School (LLM equivalent 1978), and the University of Virginia (LLM 1982; SJD 1997).

Kevin H. Govern is a visiting faculty member at Ave Maria Law School in Ann Arbor, Michigan and recently retired as Lieutenant Colonel, USA, JAGC while serving as a faculty member in the Department of Law at the U.S. Military Academy at West Point. He studied history and German at Marquette University (BA 1984) and law at Marquette University (JD 1987), The Judge Advocate General's School at Charlottesville, Virginia (LLM 1995), and University of Notre Dame (LLM 2004). During the period 1990–2003, he served in a legal advisory capacity for the 10th Special Forces Group in the United States and Turkey, for the 1st Armored Division/Task Force Eagle in Bosnia, the Command Operations Review Board of the U.S. Special Operations Command at MacDill Air Force Base-Tampa, for the XVIII Airborne Corps at Fort Bragg-North Carolina, and for the U.S. Army Special Operations Command at Fort Bragg.

Michael Hurley is currently the Special Advisor on Counterterrorism to the Nuclear Threat Initiative (NTI). He is a retired career CIA officer who was seconded to the 9/11 Commission's staff as a Senior Counsel and director of its counterterrorism policy investigation, then became Deputy and Senior Director of the 9/11 Public Discourse Project, the follow-on organization to the 9/11 Commission. He has also served in the Office of the Coordinator for Counterterrorism at the U.S. Department of State. He studied European history, political science and law at the University of Minnesota (BA 1977; JD 1980). On 9/11 he volunteered to work in CIA's Counterterrorism Center and to deploy to Afghanistan. He served three tours in Afghanistan post-9/11, leading Agency employees, and Special Forces in southeastern Afghanistan. He was one of the Agency's lead coordinators on the ground for Operation Anaconda, the largest battle against al Qaeda in the campaign in Afghanistan. From 1998–1999, and again in 2000, he was detailed to the National Security Council, where he was director for the Balkans, and advised the National Security Advisor and the President on Balkans policy. Over the past decade he has been a leader in U.S. interventions in troubled areas: Kosovo (1999–2000), Bosnia (1995–1996), and Haiti (during the U.S. intervention, 1994–1995).

Hikmahanto Juwana is Dean of the University of Indonesia Faculty of Law, and a scholar of, and advisor in, economic and public international law to the Indonesian government. He studied law at the University of Indonesia (SH 1987), Keio University-Japan (LLM 1992), and the University of Nottingham-UK (PhD 1997). While teaching fulltime at the University of Indonesia Faculty of Law, he has simultaneously served the Republic of Indonesia as Senior Legal Adviser to the Coordinating Minister for Economic Affairs, member of the Council of Experts at the Ministry of Justice and Human Rights, and adviser on specific matters to the Ministry of Foreign Affairs. In the specific area of armed conflict law, he was expert witness on command responsibility in the domestic war crimes trials relating to alleged human rights abuses arising out of East Timorese independence.

Geremy C. Kamens represented Yaser Esam Hamdi, one of the two American citizens imprisoned by the U.S. government without trial, as an Assistant Federal Public Defender in the Eastern District of Virginia through his appearance in the U.S. Supreme Court. He studied religion and government at the College of William and Mary (BA 1992) and law at the University of Virginia (JD 1997). He is a frequent public speaker on national-security related detentions and the judicial process including representation of alleged terror suspects since 9/11.

David K. Linnan teaches comparative, international and business law at the University of South Carolina School of Law. He studied humanities at Emory University (BA 1976) and law at the University of Chicago (JD 1979), and has held research or visiting appointments at the University of Washington-Seattle, the Australian National University (RSPAS and Faculty of Law), the University of Indonesia Faculty of Law and Graduate Law Program (separately), and the Max-Planck-Institut (Strafrecht), Freiburg i.Br., Germany. He is an associate of the Asian Law Centre, University of Melbourne, and program director of the Law & Finance Institutional Partnership (http://www.lfip.org).

Janice Love is Dean and Professor of Christianity and World Politics at Candler School of Theology, Emory University. A graduate of Eckerd College (BA 1975) and Ohio State University (MA 1977; PhD 1983), her teaching interests include world Christianity, religion and world politics, conflict transformation and international relations. She is the first woman to serve as dean of the Candler School of Theology. Prior to Emory, she was chief executive officer of the Women's Division of the United Methodist Church, the administrative arm of the approximately one million member strong United Methodist Women. For over 30 years, she represented the United Methodist Church in various positions of leadership in the World Council of Churches.

John H. Mansfield is the John H. Watson, Jr Professor of Law at Harvard Law School and a scholar of the first amendment. He studied history (BA 1952) and law (LLB 1956) at Harvard University. His research interests are in the areas of comparative and constitutional law, chiefly in the first amendment (religion/church and state), and comparative constitutional law.

A. Kevin Reinhart teaches Islamic religious studies in the Department of Religion, Dartmouth College. He was trained in the study of religion at Harvard (MA 1978; PhD 1986) and in Middle Eastern and Arabic Studies at the University of Texas, Austin (BA 1974). He has lived and traveled extensively in the Middle East, including spending the summer of 2003 in Karbala and Najaf, Iraq doing humanitarian work. His research focuses on Islamic religious and legal thought, primarily in the premodern period, and in late Ottoman religiosity and proto-fundamentalism.

Michael Skerker teaches religious ethics and political philosophy at DePaul University and the University of Chicago as a visiting faculty member. He was trained in the study of religion at the University of Chicago Divinity School (MA 1999; PhD 2004) and Brown University (BA 1997). His research interests include moral pluralism, religion and the political order, and professional ethics. Recent research has focused on the application of just war theory to asymmetrical conflicts and has included inquiries into detainees' rights and interrogation ethics.

Lowndes F. Stephens teaches in the School of Journalism and Mass Communications at the University of South Carolina. He studied economics (BA 1967) and communications (MA 1969) at the University of Kentucky and mass communications research at the University of Wisconsin-Madison (PhD 1975). Outside the academy his professional experience includes working as a research economist in the private sector and communications work in government planning, and in various public affairs capacities as U.S. Army reserve officer (Lieutenant Colonel, retired 1990).

George K. Walker teaches international, international litigation, conflicts and admiralty law at Wake Forest University School of Law with a special scholarly interest in the law of armed conflict. He studied history and classics at the University of Alabama (BA 1960) and diplomatic history at Duke University (AM 1968), and law at Vanderbilt University (LLB 1966) and the University of Virginia (LLM 1972). He was the Charles H. Stockton Professor of International Law at the U.S. Naval War College 1992–93, and has held research fellowships at Duke University and Yale University.